Lecture Notes in Computer Science 12202

More information about this series at http://www.springer.com/series/7409

Aaron Marcus · Elizabeth Rosenzweig (Eds.)

Design, User Experience, and Usability

Case Studies in Public and Personal Interactive Systems

9th International Conference, DUXU 2020
Held as Part of the 22nd HCI International Conference, HCII 2020
Copenhagen, Denmark, July 19–24, 2020
Proceedings, Part III

Springer

Editors
Aaron Marcus
Aaron Marcus and Associates
Berkeley, CA, USA

Elizabeth Rosenzweig
World Usability Day and Bentley User
Experience Center
Newton Center, MA, USA

ISSN 0302-9743   ISSN 1611-3349   (electronic)
Lecture Notes in Computer Science
ISBN 978-3-030-49756-9   ISBN 978-3-030-49757-6   (eBook)
https://doi.org/10.1007/978-3-030-49757-6

LNCS Sublibrary: SL3 – Information Systems and Applications, incl. Internet/Web, and HCI

This Springer imprint is published by the registered company Springer Nature Switzerland AG
The registered company address is: Gewerbestrasse 11, 6330 Cham, Switzerland

Foreword

The 22nd International Conference on Human-Computer Interaction, HCI International 2020 (HCII 2020), was planned to be held at the AC Bella Sky Hotel and Bella Center, Copenhagen, Denmark, during July 19–24, 2020. Due to the COVID-19 coronavirus pandemic and the resolution of the Danish government not to allow events larger than 500 people to be hosted until September 1, 2020, HCII 2020 had to be held virtually. It incorporated the 21 thematic areas and affiliated conferences listed on the following page.

A total of 6,326 individuals from academia, research institutes, industry, and governmental agencies from 97 countries submitted contributions, and 1,439 papers and 238 posters were included in the conference proceedings. These contributions address the latest research and development efforts and highlight the human aspects of design and use of computing systems. The contributions thoroughly cover the entire field of human-computer interaction, addressing major advances in knowledge and effective use of computers in a variety of application areas. The volumes constituting the full set of the conference proceedings are listed in the following pages.

The HCI International (HCII) conference also offers the option of "late-breaking work" which applies both for papers and posters and the corresponding volume(s) of the proceedings will be published just after the conference. Full papers will be included in the "HCII 2020 - Late Breaking Papers" volume of the proceedings to be published in the Springer LNCS series, while poster extended abstracts will be included as short papers in the "HCII 2020 - Late Breaking Posters" volume to be published in the Springer CCIS series.

I would like to thank the program board chairs and the members of the program boards of all thematic areas and affiliated conferences for their contribution to the highest scientific quality and the overall success of the HCI International 2020 conference.

This conference would not have been possible without the continuous and unwavering support and advice of the founder, Conference General Chair Emeritus and Conference Scientific Advisor Prof. Gavriel Salvendy. For his outstanding efforts, I would like to express my appreciation to the communications chair and editor of HCI International News, Dr. Abbas Moallem.

July 2020   Constantine Stephanidis

HCI International 2020 Thematic Areas and Affiliated Conferences

Thematic areas:

- HCI 2020: Human-Computer Interaction
- HIMI 2020: Human Interface and the Management of Information

Affiliated conferences:

- EPCE: 17th International Conference on Engineering Psychology and Cognitive Ergonomics
- UAHCI: 14th International Conference on Universal Access in Human-Computer Interaction
- VAMR: 12th International Conference on Virtual, Augmented and Mixed Reality
- CCD: 12th International Conference on Cross-Cultural Design
- SCSM: 12th International Conference on Social Computing and Social Media
- AC: 14th International Conference on Augmented Cognition
- DHM: 11th International Conference on Digital Human Modeling and Applications in Health, Safety, Ergonomics and Risk Management
- DUXU: 9th International Conference on Design, User Experience and Usability
- DAPI: 8th International Conference on Distributed, Ambient and Pervasive Interactions
- HCIBGO: 7th International Conference on HCI in Business, Government and Organizations
- LCT: 7th International Conference on Learning and Collaboration Technologies
- ITAP: 6th International Conference on Human Aspects of IT for the Aged Population
- HCI-CPT: Second International Conference on HCI for Cybersecurity, Privacy and Trust
- HCI-Games: Second International Conference on HCI in Games
- MobiTAS: Second International Conference on HCI in Mobility, Transport and Automotive Systems
- AIS: Second International Conference on Adaptive Instructional Systems
- C&C: 8th International Conference on Culture and Computing
- MOBILE: First International Conference on Design, Operation and Evaluation of Mobile Communications
- AI-HCI: First International Conference on Artificial Intelligence in HCI

Conference Proceedings Volumes Full List

1. LNCS 12181, Human-Computer Interaction: Design and User Experience (Part I), edited by Masaaki Kurosu
2. LNCS 12182, Human-Computer Interaction: Multimodal and Natural Interaction (Part II), edited by Masaaki Kurosu
3. LNCS 12183, Human-Computer Interaction: Human Values and Quality of Life (Part III), edited by Masaaki Kurosu
4. LNCS 12184, Human Interface and the Management of Information: Designing Information (Part I), edited by Sakae Yamamoto and Hirohiko Mori
5. LNCS 12185, Human Interface and the Management of Information: Interacting with Information (Part II), edited by Sakae Yamamoto and Hirohiko Mori
6. LNAI 12186, Engineering Psychology and Cognitive Ergonomics: Mental Workload, Human Physiology, and Human Energy (Part I), edited by Don Harris and Wen-Chin Li
7. LNAI 12187, Engineering Psychology and Cognitive Ergonomics: Cognition and Design (Part II), edited by Don Harris and Wen-Chin Li
8. LNCS 12188, Universal Access in Human-Computer Interaction: Design Approaches and Supporting Technologies (Part I), edited by Margherita Antona and Constantine Stephanidis
9. LNCS 12189, Universal Access in Human-Computer Interaction: Applications and Practice (Part II), edited by Margherita Antona and Constantine Stephanidis
10. LNCS 12190, Virtual, Augmented and Mixed Reality: Design and Interaction (Part I), edited by Jessie Y. C. Chen and Gino Fragomeni
11. LNCS 12191, Virtual, Augmented and Mixed Reality: Industrial and Everyday Life Applications (Part II), edited by Jessie Y. C. Chen and Gino Fragomeni
12. LNCS 12192, Cross-Cultural Design: User Experience of Products, Services, and Intelligent Environments (Part I), edited by P. L. Patrick Rau
13. LNCS 12193, Cross-Cultural Design: Applications in Health, Learning, Communication, and Creativity (Part II), edited by P. L. Patrick Rau
14. LNCS 12194, Social Computing and Social Media: Design, Ethics, User Behavior, and Social Network Analysis (Part I), edited by Gabriele Meiselwitz
15. LNCS 12195, Social Computing and Social Media: Participation, User Experience, Consumer Experience, and Applications of Social Computing (Part II), edited by Gabriele Meiselwitz
16. LNAI 12196, Augmented Cognition: Theoretical and Technological Approaches (Part I), edited by Dylan D. Schmorrow and Cali M. Fidopiastis
17. LNAI 12197, Augmented Cognition: Human Cognition and Behaviour (Part II), edited by Dylan D. Schmorrow and Cali M. Fidopiastis

http://2020.hci.international/proceedings

9th International Conference on Design, User Experience, and Usability (DUXU 2020)

Program Board Chairs: Aaron Marcus, Aaron Marcus and Associates, USA, and Elizabeth Rosenzweig, World Usability Day and Bentley User Experience Center, USA

- Sisira Adikari, Australia
- Claire Ancient, UK
- Silvia de los Rios, Spain
- Marc Fabri, UK
- Juliana J. Ferreira, Brazil
- Josh Halstead, USA
- Chris Hass, USA
- Wei Liu, China
- Martin Maguire, UK
- Judith A. Moldenhauer, USA
- Kerem Rızvanoğlu, Turkey
- Francisco Rebelo, Portugal
- Christine Riedmann-Streitz, Germany
- Patricia Search, USA
- Marcelo M. Soares, China
- Carla G. Spinillo, Brazil
- Virgínia Tiradentes Souto, Brazil

The full list with the Program Board Chairs and the members of the Program Boards of all thematic areas and affiliated conferences is available online at:

http://www.hci.international/board-members-2020.php

HCI International 2021

The 23rd International Conference on Human-Computer Interaction, HCI International 2021 (HCII 2021), will be held jointly with the affiliated conferences in Washington DC, USA, at the Washington Hilton Hotel, July 24–29, 2021. It will cover a broad spectrum of themes related to Human-Computer Interaction (HCI), including theoretical issues, methods, tools, processes, and case studies in HCI design, as well as novel interaction techniques, interfaces, and applications. The proceedings will be published by Springer. More information will be available on the conference website: http://2021.hci.international/.

General Chair
Prof. Constantine Stephanidis
University of Crete and ICS-FORTH
Heraklion, Crete, Greece
Email: general_chair@hcii2021.org

http://2021.hci.international/

Contents – Part III

UX Design for Health and Well-Being

DUXU for Creativity, Learning and Collaboration

DUXU for Culture and Tourism

Interactions in Public, Urban and Rural Contexts

Applying a UCD Framework for ATM Interfaces on the Design of QR Withdrawal: A Case Study

Joel Aguirre[1]([✉]) [iD], Samira Benazar[2] [iD], and Arturo Moquillaza[1,2] [iD]

[1] Pontificia Universidad Católica del Perú, Lima 32, Lima, Peru
{aguirre.joel,amoquillaza}@pucp.pe
[2] Universidad San Ignacio de Loyola, Lima 12, Lima, Peru
{samira.benazar,miguel.moquillaza}@usil.pe

Abstract. The Automated Teller Machines or ATM carry out transactions through the use of physical magnetic smart cards and four-digit PINs. To this is added the fact that physical cards could be easily lost and the combinations for PINs are insufficient. By employing a QR-based withdrawal system in combination with mobile banking, the user is allowed to perform cardless withdrawals and avoid the risk of peeping attacks and save valuable time. The difficulty is that the user should be familiar with mobile phones and QR codes scanning processes. Although there is insufficient knowledge of usability in the ATM field, attempts to the application of a systematic user-centered approach have delivered encouraging results, improving the satisfaction of the users in withdrawal operations. In this study, we apply a user-centered design framework, proposed in previous works by the authors, for the design of the interfaces of the QR-based withdrawal transaction.

Keywords: Automated Teller Machine · Framework · User-centered design · User interface · Financial sector · Usability

1 Introduction

In the current competitive market, final users are more concerned about quality attributes than the functionality a product could have [1]. In the financial sector, it is critical to design usable banking software; for the user, final interfaces are the product and frustrating experiences could harm the institutional brand [2].

Self-Service Technologies (SST) and Automated Teller Machines (or ATM) are becoming ubiquitous [3]. Therefore, ATM transactions have become a common activity in everyone's daily life [4].

The existing ATM is based on a system that employs four-digit PINs and physical cards that are read to identify and authenticate a user [4]. However, studies and surveys confirmed that at least 52.8% cardholders share their bank cards and PIN with at least one friend or relative, introducing the risk of fraud and loss of privacy [5].

According to Maqua et al. [6], a criminal has several devices to skim or scam different areas on an ATM, such as fake card readers or an overlaid skimmer plate over the existing keypad. Added to this is the fact that when a cardholder loses a physical card, there is

© Springer Nature Switzerland AG 2020
A. Marcus and E. Rosenzweig (Eds.): HCII 2020, LNCS 12202, pp. 3–19, 2020.
https://doi.org/10.1007/978-3-030-49757-6_1

no quick way to use the ATM and get cash since a replacement card requires hours or even days to be emitted [5].

Several companies and studies had proposed different methods to not force the customer to make use of his card nor the ATM pin pad by using his smartphone in combination with QR codes to withdraw money [6]. For instance, NCR company developed back in 2012 a Smart ATM that reduced transaction time to ten seconds by using the smartphones cameras to scan a QR displayed at the ATM interface [7]. More recently, Bank of India implemented QR withdrawal within its Unified Payment Interface or UPI, which keeps the transaction secure by two-factor authentication; however, this cardless withdrawal has limitations on the withdrawable amount by now [8].

The interest in the use of QR visual tags is a natural consequence of the evolution of mobile phones, and it has been used also to enhanced baking authentication security [9]. Tandon et al. [10] considered that the QR code itself is advantageous for customers in terms of security, and for vendors in terms of efficiency.

Subpratatsavee and Kuacharoen [11] proposed a scheme where QR code is used as a transaction authentication that prevents online phishing attacks, eavesdropping, and message modification; however, it is scoped only for mobile and internet banking. According to Malathi et al. [12], a better approach to avoid internet banking's own problems is that the ATM contains a QR code and the smartphone decodes it with a mobile application.

Even though several proposals for cardless withdrawal are reported in the literature, the problem of the user experience and usability persists. Ruslan et al. [13] consider that QR on Mobile Banking is still not perfect and needs to be improved to be integrated with ATM. Besides, Alhothaily et al. [5] and Malathi et al. [12], left the usability for future works and investigations.

In that sense, BBVA Perú, a leading bank in Perú, summed up to the cardless operations trend and wanted to develop a cash withdrawal system based on mobile banking and QR scanning. This Case Study focuses on the design phase of this project, where the authors applied the user-centered design framework for ATM interfaces proposed by Aguirre et al. in previous works. This paper is structured as follows. In Sect. 2, we described the methods employed from the mentioned ATM design framework. In Sect. 3, the process conducted in the Case Study is carefully described. In Sect. 4, we show the ATM interfaces obtained from the application of the framework and its mobile complement that integrates with the whole cardless withdrawal system. Conclusions close the paper, where we expose principal learned lessons from the whole presented experience.

2 User-Centered Design Framework for ATM Interfaces

In the ATM domain, there is little evidence on how to apply design of usability guidelines to the ATM interfaces [14]. As a consequence, the low consideration for the needs of the final user in the design of these interfaces affected negatively the user experience when employing a self-service technology such as ATM [15].

In 2019, the authors proposed a user-centered design framework for the design of usable ATM interfaces based on methods reported in the literature and validated by ATM and usability experts [2]. This framework includes four processes that would fit in a determinate context of a team. Figure 1 shows the framework at a high level.

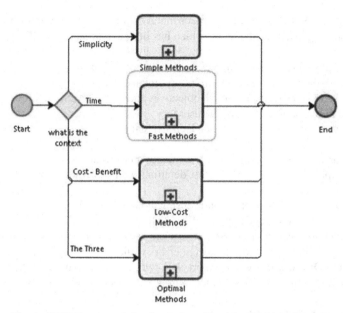

Fig. 1. UCD Framework for the design of usable ATM interfaces [2].

Each subprocess, the simple one, the fast one, the low-cost one, and the optimal one was diagrammed as a process, in order to define a real workflow [2]. The methods employed in each phase of the framework are described in Subsect. 2.1.

2.1 Methods Employed

In real-life projects, when a team decides to follow a user-centered approach, there are still fundamental questions about how to conduct the methods selected, how to manage them and even how long will they take [2].

The UCD Framework proposes three sub-processes, so the BBVA Perú ATM developer team could select the most suitable methods for its context. The team started the process with the fast methods that are described in Table 1.

Table 1. Fast methods for the design of ATM interfaces. Adapted from Aguirre et al. [2]

Phase	Method	Support technique	Est. time
Context	Identify stakeholders	User groups	0.5 d
	Field study/observation		2 d
Requirements	Competitor analysis	Free	1 d
	Scenario of use	–	3 d
	Persona	User profile	2 d
Design	Parallel design	Interactive prototyping	8 d
Evaluation	Controlled user testing	Cognitive walkthrough	3 d
	Satisfaction questionnaires	SUS questionnaire	2 d

Aguirre et al. also describes the approach that ATM developers would follow [2]. This serves as a starting point for the team, which has little experience in UCD approaches.

- **Identify Stakeholders:** List all users and stakeholders of the system. If possible, a meeting with the project manager and representative users.
- **Field Study/Observation:** Establish objectives and type of events. The observer must take notes of the performance of the user.
- **Competitor Analysis:** Compare through evaluations of the systems that own the competitors.
- **Scenario of Use:** Define scenarios with images and explanations.
- **Persona:** Specify typical user profiles, detailing their motivations and activities in a context.
- **Parallel Design:** Two or more groups design at the same time multiple ideas. After a meeting, a unique design is elaborated from all the ideas.
- **Controlled User Testing:** Representative users or experts in the process and workflow try the new design and try to find design errors while completing guided tasks.
- **Satisfaction Questionnaire:** An expert elaborates a questionnaire with representative questions. Between 8 and 10 is an ideal number to consider the sample representative.

3 Design of QR Withdrawal

The BBVA Perú, a leading bank in the country, proposed a challenge to its ATM department. The objective was to deliver a solution that simplifies and optimizes the cash withdrawal without the use or a physical card, without losing security.

To achieve the goal of the challenge, the ATM team had to find the pain points and problems that users present while performing other cardless withdrawal transactions that the bank already has. For this, the three phases UCD process shown in Fig. 2 were conducted.

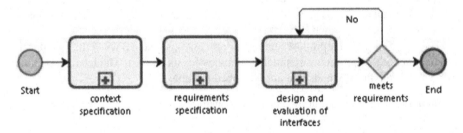

Fig. 2. The three phases of the UCD Framework proposed by Aguirre et al. [2].

3.1 Context

Identify Stakeholders. In this activity, developers met regularly with the stakeholders, so they could understand the problem from their point of view. In addition, it was the first attempt for them to think in the final user as the center of the project. We explained with detail each identified stakeholder in the following list.

- External User or Final Client. It is the actual user of an ATM who is hard to define with little information. It is because the ATM is widely used by different people with different profiles.
- Internal User o Developing Stakeholders. This user is responsible for the project and leads its development. It is a crucial member and aids with communication between the ATM developer team and other internal stakeholders.
- Internal-Support User. This internal user monitors the proper functioning of ATM in the whole country. It is the first one to notice or be informed about incidents occurred with the ATM or any impact on them.
- Architecture User. It is the one who provides the facilities for the infrastructure needed for the correct development and integration of the systems. Also, this user cooperates in the design of the back-end applications and services.
- Business User. This user is the one with knowledge about historical final client preference over the products offered by the bank. Also, is one of the most interested users, because its main function is to ensure the business goals.
- Owner of the mobile channel. This user is responsible for the mobile banking app and its participation is crucial to seek options for cardless authentication using this channel. Solutions that integrate mobile banking and SMS already exist; for instance, SMS withdrawal.

Field Study/Observation. For the observation and field study, the ATM team established to observe clients who performed withdrawals in a lapse of one hour at ATM of a centric office located at a business district of Lima, the capital of Perú.

A total of six people performed withdrawals in that lapse of time but using a physical card. Because of that, the team decided to complement the observation with a small survey. The survey focused on three main topics: the experiences with existing cardless withdrawals, the preference for cardless withdrawals and the security perception of this kind of withdrawal measured with a one-to-five Likert scale.

Two of them were women and all the participants were between twenty and forty years old. From the total, only 33% had performed cardless withdrawals for themselves, the other 67% had done these operations but not for themselves. However, all of them were interested or had a clear inclination for cardless withdrawals. The perception of security was 3.83 on average due to misinformation about the existing cardless withdrawal operations (the need for additional physical tags, SMS, or wait times).

In addition, this information was complemented with small semi-structured interviews performed with workers of the bank office and another seven representative final clients.

The office hostess indicated that frequently she helps from three to five people to complete their cardless operations that involved a secret password sent from a mobile banking app called "*efectivo móvil*" or mobile cash. The security guard claimed that over 20 of these transactions are withdrawn daily.

Finally, from the other seven representative final clients interviewed, three of them had never done cardless withdrawals. From the other four, half of them stop doing this kind of transaction due to fees charged when the withdrawal was for another person. The other half stated that it was a bother to wait ten minutes in order to withdraw their "*efectivo movil*". The three participants that have never used the existing cardless withdrawals claimed that it was because of unfriendly workflows and the loss of their withdraw passcode.

Conclusions from the Analysis of the Context of Use. From the analysis of the context of use, the team and the stakeholders agreed in developing a QR-based solution. This would improve the current cardless solutions that the ATM has and optimize the time a user spends in front of one by reducing the interaction with the aid of a smartphone app.

The bank provided the infrastructure and the technology for the development of back-end applications and services; however, the interfaces were an important question for everybody. Not only the ATM interfaces but how these would interact with and complement the smartphone app interfaces.

In that sense, the team continued with the next phases to design a possible solution.

3.2 Requirements Specification

Competitor Analysis. BBVA Perú is a leading bank in Perú, so its direct competitors are other leading banks in the country. For this activity, the team selected the other top three banks. The systems they own are diverse. For instance, they have solutions similar to "efectivo móvil", which uses their corresponding mobile banking app. Also, they promote cardless operations (such as money transfer and cardless payments) by using QR-code scanning but only in the mobile app. Figure 3 shows the products they own classified according to their functionality and if they are integrated with the ATM.

The first column refers to only mobile app QR payments and cashless transactions. These solutions are widely used because the final clients are more pressed for time and are seeking convenient channels such as self-service and mobile banking, which fits their needs very well [16]. However, the client couldn't get cash with these solutions due to the lack of integration with ATM. The other two columns refer to cardless withdrawal solutions that use a passcode or and special tag for authentication. As the interviewed participants said in the last phase, this passcode is easily lost, and the workflow seems unfriendly.

	QR Payment Visa	Cash withdrawal at ATM and payments with special tag	Only Cash withdrawal at ATM
BBVA	Lukita	Wallet	Efectivo móvil Cash withdrawal at ATM
Interbank	Tunki	Walli	
>BCP>	Yape		
Scotiabank			Efectivo móvil

Fig. 3. Analysis of the competitor's cardless solutions.

The team took the time to evaluate the workflow of the solutions that were integrated with ATM that need a passcode authentication. What they observed was that, despite the fact that the interaction with the ATM was reduced, the interfaces were unfriendly. Figure 4 shows the ATM interfaces of the last competitor and Fig. 5 shows the interfaces of BBVA current solutions.

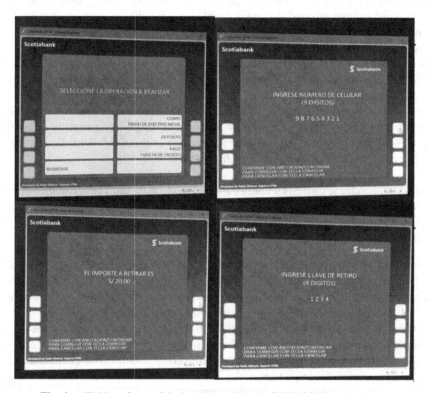

Fig. 4. ATM interfaces of the last competitor cardless withdrawal solution.

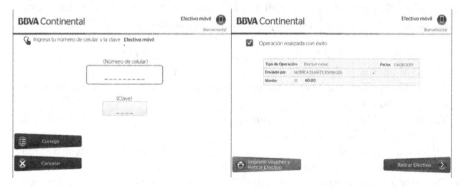

Fig. 5. ATM interfaces of the BBVA cardless withdrawal solution.

The competitor analysis was not limited to national competitors, the team expand the scope to foreign solutions and found some interesting solutions that are described in the following list.

- NCR proposed in 2012 a QR-based withdrawal system which allowed people to withdraw cash with only an android app. With this solution, they eliminated the need for a passcode and attested that users would soon be able to perform that kind of transaction [17]. They were not wrong.
- The Standard Chartered Bank in Hong Kong [18] presented a similar solution for cardless withdrawal. The promise of this solution was to get cash as fast as possible. This solution successfully integrates ATM and Mobile Banking app with just four steps to be done at the ATM.
- BMO Harris Bank reduced the ATM instructions to just two steps. Almost all the workflow is made in their mobile banking app and the user just need to select the cardless withdraw option and scan a QR-code store in the ATM. With this, the bank reduced the withdrawal operation time from 45 s to 15 s [19].

In addition to these cardless withdrawal options, the team found interesting cardless authentication systems based on NFC, virtual cards and Face Recognition. However, these solutions are not used for the withdrawal of cash. The workflow of the operation is still the same as using a physical card.

Persona and Scenario of Use. For this activity, the team defined three users "Persona" based on the observation conducted in the Analysis of the Context of Use phase. Two young people and one middle-aged adult. Their profiles were described in the activity, detailing their daily activities and their motivations to use cardless operations.

These Personas defined were associated with their respective scenarios of use where the whole activity of performing an "*efectivo móvil*" or other cardless withdrawal options was ideated. This exercise helped the team to empathize with the final client and know the limitations that different profiles could encounter; for example, not basic knowledge of how to operate mobile banking or QR scanning.

List of User Requirements. With all the information gathered and new knowledge acquired, the team specified the following user requirements for the ATM interfaces.

- The interfaces should be few enough to reduce time at the ATM.
- The ATM interfaces should not ask for authentication.
- The ATM interfaces must notify the user to previously authenticate themselves using the mobile banking app.
- The functionality name must coincide with the module presented to the user in the mobile app for a correct association.
- All the lettering and messages used in the ATM interfaces must be the same in meaning and style with the mobile module.
- The error messages must be displayed in a friendly way and must be associated with the error messages presented in the mobile app.

3.3 Design of Prototypes

Brainstorming. Despite the fact Brainstorming was not part of the fast methods selected for this Case of Study, the team decided to use it because of their lack of experience with design methods. According to Aguirre et al. [2], the framework allows the team to select any method that better fits the context of the project, so adding brainstorming is therefore allowed.

This activity was held with three members of the team who gathered in a meeting and proposed various ideas to initiate the next activity, Parallel Design. Figure 6 shows the board after the brainstorming with optimistic and pessimistic ideas.

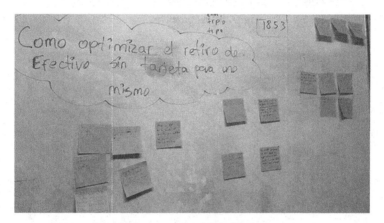

Fig. 6. Brainstorming held with the team.

Parallel Design. After putting on paper all the ideas, the team divided in three design groups. Each group made its best to deliver some prototypes design using paper prototyping. A meeting was held to show the different proposals and made a consensus about a definitive prototype that was prototyped in high fidelity after the Parallel Design.

Figure 7, Fig. 8, and Fig. 9 show the three different paper prototypes resultant of this activity.

Interactive Prototypes. For the ATM workflow, the interfaces were reduced to four including the main menu, were a button for the new functionality was added. This menu could be reached without inserting a physical card for authentication. Figure 10 shows how to access to the cardless options and how to select QR withdrawal, while Fig. 11 shows the actual QR withdrawal process.

Figure 12 shows the message that the ATM displays in case of any error during the QR withdrawal.

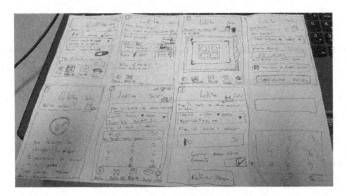

Fig. 7. Paper prototype 1.

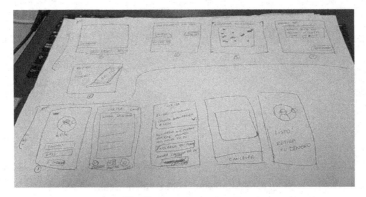

Fig. 8. Paper prototype 2.

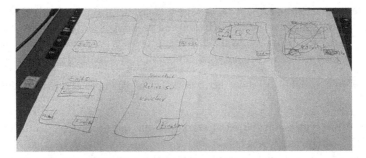

Fig. 9. Paper prototype 3.

3.4 Evaluation

The evaluation was held at the ATM laboratory of the BBVA Perú. Seven participants were recruited for the user testing evaluation. This test consisted in performing a QR withdrawal simulation using the prototypes of the mobile app in combination with the ATM prototypes designed in the previous phase.

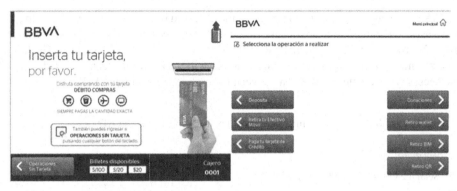

Fig. 10. Accessing the cardless transactions and QR withdrawal.

Fig. 11. Actual QR withdrawal workflow.

Fig. 12. Message showed by the ATM in case of error.

A survey was elaborated to complement the observed in the user testing. This helped to measure the perceptions about ease of use and security in a one-to-five Likert scale. Table 2 shows the punctuation given to each question by the seven participants. The last column shows the average punctuation given. From these results, the team could identify the necessity of a better integration between the mobile app and the ATM.

Table 2. Results of the user test held with seven users in the ATM lab.

Survey questions	Results							
Is "Scan the QR Code" understandable?	3	4	4	5	5	5	5	4.2
Do you think choosing bill denominations would be useful?	3	5	2	4	1	1	4	3.0
Do you think frequent withdrawals would improve the workflow?	5	3	5	5	3	5	5	4.2
Do you think that error messages should replicate in the mobile app?	5	5	5	5	1	5	5	4.2
Was the navigation easy?	4	4	4	4	4	5	5	4
The messages showed in the ATM and mobile app were clear?	4	5	5	4	4	4	3	4.4
The interfaces gave you a sense of security?	5	5	4	4	5	4	5	4.6
What is the probability that you use this transaction again?	5	5	5	4	5	3	5	4.8
What is the probability that you recommend the QR withdrawal?	5	5	5	4	5	4	5	4.8

After analyzing the results of the test, the team found doubts and improvements from the users that were taken into consideration in the following design iteration. Some of these findings were about the available bills and if it was possible for the user of the QR withdrawal to select the denominations from the mobile app, about the wait and expiration time, and instructions of how to scan the code.

There were also findings about the mobile app, this might be due to the fact that the workflow starts at the mobile app, where the clients authenticate themselves using their mobile banking accounts.

The new designs improved the first prototypes by adding the available bills in the mobile app interfaces, so the user could know if the ATM has the preferred denominations. A complete screen is dedicated to the QR in both, the ATM and the mobile app. At the ATM we tell the user to follow the instructions mentioned in the mobile app, while in the mobile app, the instructions are shown while the camera is ready to scan the code. The wait time that is present in "*efectivo móvil*" operations was removed, while the expiration time of this transaction was kept, so the withdrawal could have a pending status.

This approach also helped to reduce the interactions with the ATM and reduce time when using it, but the integration between the two technologies could still be improved.

4   Final Proposal

With the information obtained in the Evaluation phase, a new design iteration was conducted, but this time it was focused on resolving the conflicts found by the users. The redesigned interfaces were tested again to validate the correctness of them. In the next subsections, the final interfaces of the ATM are shown in Fig. 13 and Fig. 14, while Fig. 15 and Fig. 16 show the integration between ATM and Mobile App where the status must match.

4.1   ATM Interfaces

Fig. 13. Final QR withdrawal interfaces.

Fig. 14. QR withdrawal successful operation screen.

4.2   Mobile Interfaces

Fig. 15. Mobile app QR withdrawal proposed interfaces.

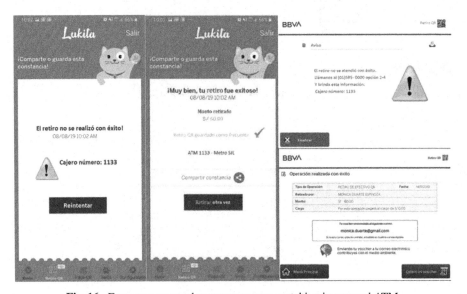

Fig. 16. Error message and success message matching in app and ATM.

5   Conclusions

From this Case Study, the team could design from scratch the interfaces for a QR withdrawal system at ATM. Performing a structured design process with established phases helped the team to understand the real context of the actual cardless solutions that are available on the market. In the first two phases, the analysis of the context and the requirements specification allowed the team to empathize with the final client and discover some pain points such as waiting times in the current cardless withdrawal authorizations and loss of the passcode for cardless authentications.

These new activities performed, and the information gathered after performing them helped to reach an agreement faster than before with all the stakeholders. A QR-based withdrawal system was the ideal solution to improve the current cardless withdrawal and satisfy (and relieve some points of pain) the final user requirements, which is the center of this process.

Through the evaluation phases, the team realized the importance of matching the status between the Mobile App and the ATM during the operation in order to improve the perception of security. Also, this phase allowed the team to find possible improvements in the initial designs.

The framework is specific for the design of ATM interfaces and not intended to be used in the design of mobile graphics interfaces; however, taking into consideration the Mobile App interfaces was mandatory due to the nature of the ideated system. The resultant mobile interfaces could be taken as an input for the mobile channel stakeholders in a future design that uses specific mobile design methods.

By the application of this framework, the development team could interact with stakeholders and final users, and could empathize with user needs and become aware of the importance of the user's needs and their satisfaction as the main objective of the design process.

In addition, the participation of the development team in design tasks allowed them to learn new skills and get involved with the end-to-end process, in addition to allowing them to prepare more and better test cases for the future implementation of the proposed.

According to the previous information presented, the feedback of final user, the feedback of stakeholders, and the proper feedback of the development team, we are able to conclude that the application of this framework let the team to reach the design objectives. In this sense, we recommend to the ATM team, keep using this framework for present and future projects.

Acknowledgments. We want to thank all participants from BBVA Perú, especially its ATM development team for their participation in this Case Study. Also, we thank to the "HCI, Design, User Experience, Accessibility & Innovation Technologies (HCIDUXAIT)" a research group from the *Pontificia Universidad Católica del Perú* (PUCP) whose previous studies served as a base to initiate this work.

References

1. Paz, F., Paz, F.A., Moquillaza, A., Falconi, F.: A teaching experience of the human-computer interaction course in a master program. In: Karwowski, W., Ahram, T., Nazir, S. (eds.) AHFE 2019. AISC, vol. 963, pp. 131–142. Springer, Cham (2020). https://doi.org/10.1007/978-3-030-20135-7_13

2. Aguirre, J., Moquillaza, A., Paz, F.: A user-centered framework for the design of usable ATM interfaces. In: Marcus, A., Wang, W. (eds.) HCII 2019. LNCS, vol. 11583, pp. 163–178. Springer, Cham (2019). https://doi.org/10.1007/978-3-030-23570-3_13

3. Kaptelinin, V., Rizzo, A., Robertson, P., Rosenbaum, S.: Crafting user experience of self-service technologies. In: Proceedings of the 2014 Companion Publication on Designing Interactive Systems - DIS Companion 2014, pp. 199–202 (2014). https://doi.org/10.1145/2598784.2598798

4. Jacob, M., Jose, R.M., Mathew, N., Siby, S.: QR based Card-less ATM Transactions. J. Res. **02**(02), 81–83 (2016)

5. Alhothaily, A., Alrawais, A., Song, T., Lin, B., Cheng, X.: Quickcash: secure transfer payment systems. Sens. (Switz.) **17**(6), 1–20 (2017). https://doi.org/10.3390/s17061376

6. Maqua, T., Neff, R., Wbbeling, M.: Improve ATM withdrawal security and usability with your smartphone (2016)

7. Flacy, M.: Smart ATM uses QR codes instead of cards to dispense cash (2012). https://www.digitaltrends.com/cool-tech/smart-atm-uses-qr-codes-instead-of-cards-to-dispense-cash/. Accessed 13 Jan 2020

8. BS Web Team: Tired of ATM frauds? Soon, you can withdraw money from ATMs using UPI (2019). https://www.business-standard.com/article/finance/tired-of-atm-frauds-soon-you-can-withdraw-money-from-atms-using-upi-119091100419_1.html. Accessed 13 Jan 2020

9. Adsul, A.P., Sinojia, J., Shukla, A., Sinkar, R., Jagtap, S.: Secure authentication for online banking using QR code. Int. J. Adv. Res. Comput. Sci. Manag. Stud. **3**(3), 378–385 (2015)

10. Tandon, A., Sharma, R., Sodhiya, S., Durai Raj Vincent, P.M.: QR code based secure OTP distribution scheme for authentication in net-banking. Int. J. Eng. Technol. **5**(3), 2502–2505 (2013)

11. Subpratatsavee, P., Kuacharoen, P.: Transaction authentication using HMAC-based one-time password and QR code. In: Lecture Notes in Electrical Engineering, vol. 330, pp. 93–98. Springer, Berlin (2015). https://doi.org/10.1007/978-3-662-45402-2_14

12. Malathi, V., Balamurugan, B., Eshwar, S.: Achieving privacy and security using QR code by means of encryption technique in ATM. In: Proceedings - 2017 2nd International Conference on Recent Trends and Challenges in Computational Models, ICRTCCM 2017, pp. 281–285 (2017). https://doi.org/10.1109/icrtccm.2017.36

13. Ruslan Karmawan, G.M., Suharjito Fernandoand, Y., Gui, A.: QR code payment in Indonesia and its application on mobile banking. In: KnE Social Sciences, 2019, pp. 551–568 (2019). https://doi.org/10.18502/kss.v3i22.5073

14. Aguirre, J., Moquillaza, A., Paz, F.: Methodologies for the design of ATM interfaces: a systematic review. In: Ahram, T., Karwowski, W., Taiar, R. (eds.) IHSED 2018. AISC, vol. 876, pp. 256–262. Springer, Cham (2019). https://doi.org/10.1007/978-3-030-02053-8_39

15. Moquillaza, A., et al.: Developing an ATM interface using user-centered design techniques. In: Marcus, A., Wang, W. (eds.) DUXU 2017. LNCS, vol. 10290, pp. 690–701. Springer, Cham (2017). https://doi.org/10.1007/978-3-319-58640-3_49

16. Thakur, R.: What keeps mobile banking customers loyal? Int. J. Bank Mark. **32**(7), 628–646 (2014). https://doi.org/10.1108/IJBM-07-2013-0062

17. Dumitru, A.: We will soon be able to make ATM withdrawals with just a smartphone and QR code (2012). https://www.android.gs/atm-withdraw-qr-code. Accessed 31 Dec 2019
18. Kwong, C.: SC QR cash cardless cash withdrawal (2018)
19. Tode, C.: QR Cash – Standard Chartered HK (2015). https://www.sc.com/hk/bank-with-us/app-sc-mobile/qrcash/?intcid=banner-1_Jun17-hk-qr-cash_qr_en. Accessed 31 Dec 2019

Research on the Service Design of Smart Campus Based on Sustainable Strategy – Taking Smart Canteen as an Example

Ruiqian An and Tao Xi[✉]

Shanghai Jiaotong University, Shanghai, China
`torchx@sjtu.edu.cn`

Abstract. With the rapid development of big data, Internet of things, artificial intelligence and 5G technology, the construction of smart campus has become the development trend of Chinese universities. Objective: through the combination of sustainable methods and service systems, to reconstruct the Chinese campus service system, optimize teaching, management and information systems, improve user experience, and promote the transformation, upgrading and sustainable development of smart campus. Methods: firstly, this paper analyzes the literature, summarizes the current situation of the construction of smart campus in China, and then from the point of view of problems, this paper constructs the service system framework of smart campus with the method of sustainable design. Finally, author choses a campus scene, canteen, and uses the method of service design to verify the theory.

Keywords: User experience · Service design · Sustainable · Smart campus

1 Smart Campus Research

1.1 Smart Campus Overview

The concept of smart campus originated from IBM's vision of "smart city". Due to the scale of the school, the user groups and various mixed activities are similar to small cities, so the smart campus is called the epitome of "smart city", which is an experimental platform for the construction of smart cities [1].

Smart campus is the further expansion and promotion of digital campus. It comprehensively applies the Internet of things, big data, cloud computing, AR/VR, 5G and other emerging information technologies, and can fully perceive the physical environment of campus, intelligently identify the learning, working situation and individual behavior characteristics of teachers and students, fully integrate teaching, scientific research management and campus life, and realize the smart campus Intelligent service and management, to establish an intelligent and open teaching environment and a comfortable and safe living environment for campus users [2]. At the same time, the development of smart campus also changes the user's interaction mode and improves the user's experience in the campus.

© Springer Nature Switzerland AG 2020
A. Marcus and E. Rosenzweig (Eds.): HCII 2020, LNCS 12202, pp. 20–30, 2020.
https://doi.org/10.1007/978-3-030-49757-6_2

1.2 China Smart Campus Construction

China's smart campus construction is in the development stage. Universities are in the stage of transformation from digital campus to smart campus. Among them, Zhejiang University first proposed the blueprint of "smart campus": ubiquitous network learning, innovative network research, transparent and efficient school administration, rich and colorful campus culture, convenient and thoughtful campus life [3]. At the same time, the Chinese government has issued relevant policies and regulations, and Chinese technology enterprises have launched a variety of related intelligent products and services.

However, there are still many difficulties and problems in the construction of smart campus in China [4]. After reading the relevant literature and on-the-spot investigation of the construction of smart campus in Chinese universities, the author summarizes the following three problems:

1. Lack of top-level design [5]
   Many colleges in China did not carry out a unified planning and design at the beginning of building smart campus. Each campus scene could not be connected with each other, and campus information could not be shared, which caused a lot of waste of resources.
2. Lack of information management
   With the introduction of intelligent equipment, the degree of informatization in Chinese universities is gradually deepened, but the information literacy is insufficient, and there is a lack of talents to manage information equipment, which often leads to the phenomenon of "separation of purchase and use" of intelligent equipment in the process of construction.
3. Lack of effective data management
   China's universities lack of data application, which is mainly reflected in two aspects: first, the data can not be shared; second, the lack of effective data analysis and integration [6]. This directly leads to the formation of data information island, which is not conducive to the analysis and mining of education big data and the construction of data services, and can not achieve a real "smart" campus.

2 Sustainable Design Strategy

2.1 Sustainable Design Overview

"Design For Sustainability (DFS)" originates from the concept of "sustainable development", which is the practice course of deep thinking and constant seeking for change of the relationship between human development and environmental issues in the design field. The evolution of its concept can be roughly divided into four aspects: "Green design", "Ecological design", "Product service system design" and "Design for social equity and harmony", which focus on social equity and harmony, as well as people's consumption concept and experience, is the most cutting-edge aspect of sustainable design research. Fundamentally speaking, sustainable development depends on the transformation of people's values and consumption views [7]. Therefore, from the perspective of users, exploring sustainable "lifestyle" and "development mode" is the core content of sustainable development.

According to the definition of smart city, the sustainable smart campus is an innovative campus. Based on the development of big data, Internet of things, artificial intelligence and 5g technology, it can share services and data, realize the mutual supplement and data association of all departments of the campus, reduce the waste of campus resources, and fundamentally realize "green campus" [1].

2.2 Sustainability Approach

At present, there are many methods and framework systems that can provide us with solutions to realize the sustainable development of products or services [7]. The author studies and analyzes some of the most influential and widely used methods here (see Table 1), hoping to extract useful information from them and explore sustainable methods suitable for building smart campus.

Table 1. Methods of sustainable design

Sustainability approach	Basic framework	Advantage	Disadvantage
Natural Capitalism	Rethinking the relationship between society and the value of natural resources in the context of business	(1) Simple and easy to use (2) Comprehensive (3) Good combination of design and business functions	Broad description
Cradle to Cradle	The Cradle to Cradle design concept distinguishes between the biological and the technological cycles for materials. Waste materials in an old product become the "food" for a new product [8]	(1) Simple and easy to use (2) Good combination of design and business functions	Incomplete
Total Beauty	Estimate the overall impact of products and services on the environment by quantitative analysis	(1) Simple and easy to use (2) Assessable product and service system	Subjective, incomplete
Life Cycle Analysis (LCA)	Evaluate system scheme design by quantitative analysis	(1) Comprehensive and objective (2) Easy to use	Difficult operation
Sustainability Helix	The system is used to assess the overall organizational commitment and process in Sustainability	(1) Practical (2) Comprehensive	Partial subjectivity

3   Construction of Smart Campus Service Design Framework

Service design is an overall analysis and design process integrating strategy, system, process and touchpoint design decision, which solves the problem of the whole system [9]. In the service system design of smart campus, we should explore the potential connection between the smart campus and the integrated service system, integrate all resources of the campus in a systematic perspective, and design the experience process as a whole. In the construction of the whole service system, we should not only pay attention to "things", but also pay more attention to "users". We should take users as participants in the construction of smart campus and build campus experience and service from "users".

Through the research on the current situation of smart campus, combined with the sustainable development strategy, this paper attempts to put forward a service solution for the overall construction of smart campus from the perspective of product service system design [10]. This plan includes four levels (see Fig. 1): the first level is a set of system, which can coordinate the development and construction of the whole smart campus; the second level is a data information management center, which can manage the campus data; the third level is the campus platform, which includes the teaching environment platform, teaching resources platform, campus management platform and campus service platform; the fourth level is N campus scenes. These four levels are not independent of each other. Each level will radiate upward or downward, influence and improve each other. For example, the second level will store and analyze all kinds of data in the third level, which can form a big database of campus. This big database of campus can provide support for the improvement of the first level and create conditions for the realization of sustainable campus.

Fig. 1. Smart campus service design framework

4   A Practical Case of Sustainable Smart Campus Service Design with Smart Canteen as an Example

Through the early theoretical research, the author from the smart campus service design framework of the campus scene design practice, to verify the theoretical research.

Selected scene: canteen of Shanghai Jiaotong University (six canteens in total).

4.1 User Analysis

User Role Model. Through the field observation of user behavior, online questionnaire survey and in-depth interview, the author divides users into three categories: reading students, teaching staff and tourists. The user role model is described as follows (see Fig. 2).

Reading students

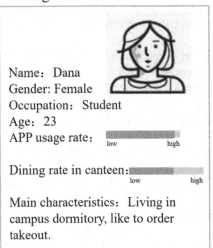

Name: Dana
Gender: Female
Occupation: Student
Age: 23
APP usage rate:
Dining rate in canteen:
Main characteristics: Living in campus dormitory, like to order takeout.

Teaching staff

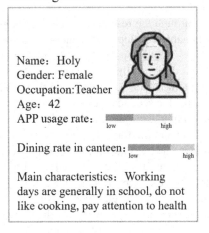

Name: Holy
Gender: Female
Occupation: Teacher
Age: 42
APP usage rate:
Dining rate in canteen:
Main characteristics: Working days are generally in school, do not like cooking, pay attention to health

Tourists

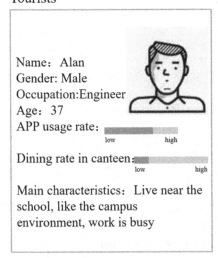

Name: Alan
Gender: Male
Occupation: Engineer
Age: 37
APP usage rate:
Dining rate in canteen:
Main characteristics: Live near the school, like the campus environment, work is busy

Fig. 2. User role model

User Demand Analysis. According to the user role model, there are many users in the canteen of Shanghai Jiaotong University. In order to meet the user's expectations in the whole service cycle of the canteen, it is necessary to fully consider the needs of different types of users and find out the pain points of users, so as to provide reference information for later design. See Table 2 for demand analysis.

Table 2. User demand analysis

User type	User demand	Pain spots	Design strategy
Student	The frequency of choosing canteen is high; when there is no class, the dining time is not fixed; when there is class, the dining time is tight, and they don't like to line up; sometimes they enjoy a person's dining time, like to pack or order takeout; some male and female students have demand for healthy meals	The number of students is large, and their dining time span is large; They have more needs, such as liking delicious food, liking healthy food, liking quiet eating, liking social interaction during eating, etc.	Users can use App to order meals, App can calculate calories; the number of people in each canteen is updated in real time, and users can select canteen as required
Teaching staff	In the morning and noon, they usually eat in the canteen; they usually have plenty of time to eat; they will choose the canteen according to their preference; sometimes they need to order working meals; most of them pay attention to healthy diet	They don't like to line up. They like good food and healthy meals	App introduces the daily special meals of canteen
Tourists	They seldom use the canteen; they will choose the canteen with special features or delicious meals; generally, they have plenty of time to eat and don't mind queuing up	They are not familiar with the campus canteen	App introduces the location of canteen and daily special meals

According to the analysis of users' needs, the main design points are as follows: (1) helping users to choose a satisfactory canteen; (2) evaluating healthy meals; (3) reducing food waste and reusing leftover food waste.

4.2 App Information Framework

Through the analysis and sorting of the research results, the author designed to reconstruct the canteen service system of Shanghai Jiaotong University through app application, using the sustainable method from cradle to cradle to reduce food waste at the root. At the same time, the author redefined the definition of meal waste to achieve "green canteen". The information framework of app is as follows (see Fig. 3).

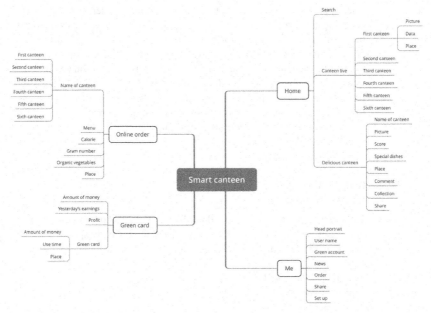

Fig. 3. App information framework

4.3 App Design

The design of APP takes users as the center and encourages users to eat scientifically and reduce food waste through green stimulation (see Fig. 4). Users can watch the flow of diners in six canteens of Shanghai Jiaotong University in real time through the "Canteen live" on the home page, and select the canteen reasonably. The home page also has the function of canteen specialty recommendation and canteen positioning, which can maximize the user's dining experience. In addition, the "Online order" can reduce the user's queuing time in the canteen, at the same time, it can let the user know the calories of the food to help users eat healthy and moderate, and reduce food waste. Users can get green cards by sharing photos of "Clean plate", and get a discount in the next purchase process.

Fig. 4. App interface design

4.4 Stakeholder Analysis

The relevant stakeholders of Shanghai Jiaotong University Canteen include Canteen manager, Logistics management department, Users, Farmers and Scientific research laboratory. In the smart canteen system, the relationship between stakeholders has changed (see Table 3).

Table 3. Stakeholder analysis

Stakeholders	Services provided	Benefits gained
Logistics management department	1. User information management and platform maintenance 2. Disposal of meal waste	1. Intelligent management to reduce costs 2. Can get real-time data information
Canteen manager	1. Providing online order and offline order taking service 2. Good dining environment and healthy meals	1. Reduced operating costs and food waste 2. Increased users and improved economic benefits
Users	Personal dining information	1. Healthy food 2. Good user experience
Farmers	Low cost organic vegetables	Free fertilizer for planting
Scientific research laboratory	1. Providing clean energy for Campus 2. Guiding the logistics department to deal with kitchen waste, such as making fertilizer	Free research materials

4.5 Smart Canteen Service System of Shanghai Jiaotong University

Through research and app design, the author has built the smart canteen service system of Shanghai Jiaotong University (see Fig. 5). The service system of the smart canteen has the following characteristics: (1) the combination of online and offline services. In the original offline services, mobile app provides online services for users to meet the needs of users collected in the research process. In addition, the user meal information collected through the app can help campus managers to make more reasonable management policies. (2) Smart canteen service system is connected with other levels. The dining system relies on the scientific research laboratory of Shanghai Jiaotong University to transform food waste into fertilizer and clean energy, so as to realize "from cradle to cradle".

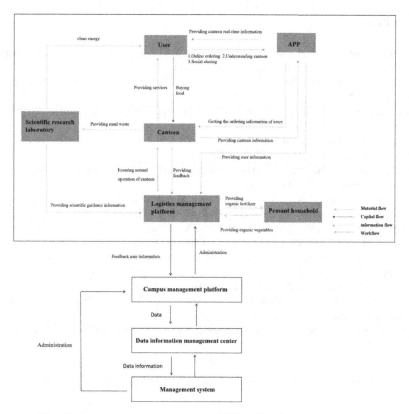

Fig. 5. Smart canteen service system of Shanghai Jiaotong University

5 Conclusion

Through literature analysis and design practice, this paper finds that: the construction of smart campus must be user-centered, so that users can participate in the campus construction to form an effective large database of campus, and the large database of campus can help the campus to be truly "intelligent", and help to realize the visualization, controllability, intelligence and sustainability of the whole system. In the process of building a smart campus, we should pay attention to the top-level design, reasonable planning of each link, clear division of labor, so as to avoid the waste of resources in the campus and promote the sustainable development of the smart campus.

In the future, there is still a lot of room for progress in the construction of China's smart campus. The author hopes that the analysis and research of this paper can play an enlightening role in the successful transformation of China's digital campus into a smart campus and the sustainable development of the smart campus.

References

1. Gleizes, M.-P., Boes, J., Lartigue, B., Thiébolt, F.: neOCampus: a demonstrator of connected, innovative, intelligent and sustainable campus. In: De Pietro, G., Gallo, L., Howlett, R.J., Jain, L.C. (eds.) KES-IIMSS 2017. SIST, vol. 76, pp. 482–491. Springer, Cham (2018). https://doi.org/10.1007/978-3-319-59480-4_48
2. Lei, G.L., Li, J.: Application and practice of intelligent campus based on Internet of Things. Logist. Technol. **13**(17), 414–416 (2012)
3. https://baike.baidu.com/item/%E6%99%BA%E6%85%A7%E6%A0%A1%E5%9B%AD/9845341?fr=aladdin. Accessed 21 Jan 2020
4. Yu, C.H., Wang, Y.W., Ma, W.: The current situation, problems and Countermeasures of smart campus construction **33**(06), 48–51(2015)
5. Xia, J.S., Hong, H.Q., Ning, Y.W., Zhang, B.H.: Research hotspot and typical case analysis of foreign smart campus. Modern Educ. Technol. **12**, 13–20 (2019)
6. Mayer-Schönberger, V., Cukier, K.: Big Data: A Revolution That Will Transform How We Live, Work, and Think. Zhejiang People's Publishing House, Hangzhou (2013)
7. Shedroff, N.: Design Reflection: Sustainable Design Strategy and Practice. Tsinghua Press, Beijing (2011)
8. https://epea-hamburg.com/cradle-to-cradle/. Accessed 08 Feb 2020
9. Lockwood, T.: Design Thinking-Integrating Innovation: Customer Experience and Brand Value. Electronic Industry Press, Beijing (2012)
10. Luo, S., Zhou, W.: Research status and development of service design. Pack. Eng. **39**(24), 45–53 (2018)

Applications of Real-Time Data to Reduce Air Emissions in Maritime Ports

Philip Cammin$^{(\boxtimes)}$ ⓘ, Malek Sarhani ⓘ, Leonard Heilig ⓘ, and Stefan Voß ⓘ

Institute of Information Systems, University of Hamburg,
Von-Melle-Park 5, 20146 Hamburg, Germany
philip.cammin@uni-hamburg.de

Abstract. Emission production in maritime ports has received a lot attention in the last few years. Under the current social and political trend, ports are likely to receive even more pressure in their endeavor to reduce emissions. Monitoring and reporting of emissions enable port authorities to formulate and track the progress of effective emission-reduction measures. As a means, emission inventories are created annually. In this paper, we explore how real-time data can be used to reduce emissions in the port. Applications utilize real-time data for improving the operational efficiency on the landside and seaside while reducing energy consumption and emissions. Hereby, we concentrate on the area of planning and optimization as one area of environmental sustainability in maritime ports. We present applications that deal with inter-terminal truck routing, berth allocation planning, and assistant systems for economic driving. These applications depend on optimization models, machine learning (ML), and gamification. Our research indicates the need for cooperation between the various port stakeholders to share the relevant data as well as proper visualization techniques.

Keywords: Air emissions · Real-time · Optimization · Predictive analytics · Gamification · Maritime ports

1 Introduction

Nowadays, ports rely mainly on static emission inventories (EIs) for monitoring air emissions. An EI can be defined as a quantification of emissions within a specified scope (geographic domain, emission sources) over a specified time frame [16], usually a year. Monitored emissions can be utilized in regard of the as-is analysis of the emission production, decision-making for emission reduction projects and to track the progress for such (see, e.g., [11,12]). In summary, it is used to support the emission reduction.

Methodologies for creating EIs can depend on auxiliary data to estimate emissions. These auxiliary data can be classified into activity data of concrete emission sources (e.g., a truck) such as energy by load and time duration, and

© Springer Nature Switzerland AG 2020
A. Marcus and E. Rosenzweig (Eds.): HCII 2020, LNCS 12202, pp. 31–48, 2020.
https://doi.org/10.1007/978-3-030-49757-6_3

emission factors. Annual EIs aggregate emission production on an annual basis, separated by emission source categories. Measured emission data using sensors can also be included (e.g., see [3]), but its usage is restricted as measured emissions can origin from different emission sources. Therefore, EIs are mainly based on emission source auxiliary data.

As it can take quite some time until an EI is released,[1] the question arises if the activity data or measured emissions can be utilized faster or in real time to ultimately reduce emissions. We consider real-time data as data that is utilized after a fixed time elapsed, after the associated event, contributing to the solution to a problem statement, which defines the fixed time constraint (with preference to a shorter time, e.g., seconds or minutes rather than days or months). In this regard, the interested reader is referred to the discussion of [31] on real time where it is concluded that the key characteristic of a real-time system is "its ability to guarantee a response after a fixed time has elapsed, where that fixed time is provided as a part of the problem statement."

According to [6], vessels emit the largest amount of pollutants at ports. For instance, in the Port of Long Beach and the Port of Los Angeles, ocean-going vessels' NO_x emissions are reported as 60.0% and 44.0%, respectively [10,11]. Thereby, emission reduction plans on ocean-going vessels could have a large impact on the total amount of emissions of the port. Regarding carbon dioxide equivalent units (CO_2e), the Port of Los Angeles reports that heavy-duty vehicles contribute the largest amount of emissions to the port (42.5%) followed by ocean-going vessels (22.0%). To achieve the largest impact for emission reduction, port authorities need to focus on the largest emitters of emissions.

A relevant question is if the activity data of emission sources is available in a higher sampling frequency (e.g., in equally spaced time series) so that real-time systems could continuously utilize this data. Also, it is not clear which stakeholders (e.g., owners, observers), have to be involved to realize real-time systems in a port. Such stakeholders are decision-makers with their own goals and motivations; as such, it is necessary to support their decision-making process as well as to increase their motivation to use supportive systems. Moreover, the question arises, how the interaction with these systems is organized to enable users to fully utilize real-time data, visualizations might be necessary which is in contrast with static tables and diagrams of EI documents. Applied research in this area shows potential in the application of real-time data. For example, the project dashPORT aims to reduce the energy consumption by visualizing and forecasting energy flows and formulating recommendations for action in real time based on data of both a port operator and a transshipment company [2,4].

The aim of this paper is to provide insights into how optimization models, ML and gamification can be applied in conjunction with real-time data generated at ports. In Sect. 2 we provide an overview about the presented applications and embed them into the scheme of environmental sustainability. Subsequently, we present each application. Finally, some conclusions are drawn.

---

[1] For instance, the 2018 Los Angeles port EI was released in September 2019.

2   Applications and Opportunities

Ports consist of several organizations such as a port authority and its tenants. Port authorities usually define green strategic objectives linked with their main functions: landlord function, regulatory function, operator function, and community manager function [13, 27]. For example, the regulatory function can comprise not only air emissions but also waste management and energy efficiency. In the context of air emissions, energy efficiency is also relevant as the consumption of energy can indirectly produce emissions in the port. In this domain, four major areas of environmental sustainability have been identified, namely, *policies and regulations, management practices, infrastructure and technologies,* and *planning and optimization* [27]. Within this scheme, we concentrate on the planning and optimization area that yields potential to increase the efficiency of maritime logistics, i.e. the ports' terminals' landside and seaside operations as well as the shipping companies' operations. Based on our research projects, in Sect. 2.1, we address the truck drayage operations on the landside. In Sect. 2.2, we present a model to predict the delay of vessels' arrivals using ML. The results can be used as input for the berth allocation problem (BAP) involving the terminal and the shipping company in the context of seaside operations. Finally, Sect. 2.3 shows how gamification can be applied to reduce emissions from truck operations in the port's vicinity. An overview about the presented applications is given in Table 1. Hereby, specified goals that result in a reduction of emissions are shown, along with the data and its source as well as the application users.

2.1   Optimization Models

Real-time data can be used as input data for optimization models for a plethora of problems. In this section, we present an application that addresses green vehicle routing to enable efficient landside operations. In the context of seaside operations, the BAP is a problem that is also solved with optimization models [35]. However, in this paper, we are interested in how ML could be used to support BAP optimization models using real-time data, which is shown in Sect. 2.2.

Vehicle Routing. On the landside, a considerable proportion of port-related transports and traffic is produced by truck drayage operations, such as inter-terminal transportation (ITT), which refers to any kind of land and sea transportation moving containers and cargo between organizationally separated areas within a seaport [26]. Those operations have a major environmental impact on ports, such as in terms of air pollution and noise [28]. In today's digital age, one promising way to influence organizational practices and processes towards both economic and environmental sustainability is an extensive exploitation of operational data and visualizations. In this section, we show how multi-objective optimization and visualization can be used to consider trade-offs between economic and environmental objectives. More specifically, we demonstrate how greenhouse gas emissions (GHG) can be integrated into a vehicle routing problem and how

Table 1. Overview of the presented applications.

Goal	Efficient use of trucks	Low waiting times at anchorage	Correct input parameters for BAP optimization	Truck drivers drive economically
Example application	Multi-objective inter-terminal truck routing	BAP optimization models with a rolling planning horizon	Prediction of delay of ship arrivals	Eco-driving assistance system
Method	Optimization models	Optimization models	Machine learning	Gamification
Data sources	Transport company, truckers	Terminal operator, vessel	Terminal operator, vessel	Port authority, sensor station network
Data	Truck data, emission factors	Actual vessel sailing data, current berth allocation plan, terminal conditions[a]	(Actual) Vessel sailing data[b]	Emissions concentration
Users	Truck dispatchers	Berth planner	Berth planner	Truck driver
Visualization form	Web GUI	Integrated into berth planning software	Integrated into berth planning software	Smartphone app

[a]Vessel data (e.g., updated ETA (estimated time of arrival), ETD (estimated time of departure), length, draft) and terminal condition data (e.g., number of vessels in port, suitable berth for vessel in regard of length and draft, delay in departure costs).
[b]Training data requires ETA and ATA (actual time of arrival) data, implementation requires continuous actual vessel sailing data (ETA).

the resulting solution dimensions can be transformed to a two-dimensional visualization to be human-readable, such as by dispatchers.

Use Case: Real-Time Green Vehicle Routing. As an example for solving the mentioned trade-offs in drayage operations, we use the multi-objective Green Inter-Terminal Truck Routing Problem (Green-ITTRP) presented in [24]. In the article, a multi-objective optimization method, a mobile cloud-based information system and a visualization technique is presented and applied in the Port of Hamburg (Germany). Using a fast and efficient metaheuristic, dispatching decisions can be made in real time based on the operational data retrieved from different port-related systems and the trucker app. For solving the multi-objective vehicle routing problem, the authors propose a greedy algorithm, an Archived Multi-Objective Simulated Annealing (AMOSA) approach with and without k-means clustering.

To estimate CO_2 (carbon dioxide) and GHG emissions, a state-of-the-art calculation method from the European standard EN 16258, published by the European Committee for Standardization (CEN), has been used. The standard contains methods for either a rough or detailed calculation of emissions. Gathering all necessary data from external and internal information systems and apps, it is already possible to apply a detailed analytical emission consumption model. It is even possible to integrate real-time sensor data, referred to as on-road measurements, to estimate emissions more accurately (see, e.g., [21]).

In the example, the objective function includes fixed and variable costs to cover the expenses and profit-demands of the trucker, penalties for late deliveries, and the estimated emissions.

$$minimize\ (costs_{fix} + costs_{var} + penalities + emissions) \qquad (1)$$

The calculated emissions are dependent on the truck and transport order, as the consumption model considers many related factors, such as cargo payload, empty trips, truck energy consumption, gross vehicle mass, fuel type, travel distance, etc.

The results of the experiments have shown that the approach helps to drastically improve the resource utilization with a high impact on overall costs and emissions. Trade-offs could be deeply analyzed. As an example, the decision makers have found out that empty trips play only a subordinate role when optimizing routes in the context of seaports. In fact, avoiding empty trips is not always viable due to the individual structure of the road network and related traffic situations. Accepting empty trips could even have a positive impact on both economic and environmental objectives. The results have also indicated that remarkable emission reductions could be achieved even though the decision makers selected the most profitable solutions. Overall, the approach has helped decision makers in adapting their way of making decisions, especially under the new regulatory and environmental requirements. However, it also became obvious that decision makers would have problems analyzing the trade-off solutions without proper visualizations.

Visualization. In a scenario with manual dispatching, practitioners need to select just one solution and apply it. Without a proper visualization, it is difficult to make the right decisions. In a case with automated dispatching, a visualization of the results can help to better configure the algorithm depending on the current requirements regarding the different objectives. However, for analyzing the different trade-off solutions, a three-dimensional representation is not sufficient as the differences between solutions are difficult to grasp.

For this purpose, a transformation of the three-dimensional representation into a ternary two-dimensional representation, as depicted in Fig. 1 (right), can be applied [24]. This representation allows decision-makers to compare the solutions in terms of all objectives and outcomes. Taking into account the current requirements and measurements, the decision makers are able to control the optimization in a way that it best fits the interests of the organization. Since the optimization can be performed frequently based on real-time operational data, adjustments can be applied immediately, allowing decision makers to respond to certain events or situations.

For generating a visualization given a Pareto front F, as described in [24], we first normalize the objective values of all points and we determine the solution

$s' \in F$ with the highest sum of normalized values, K. Later, we scale all normalized values according to K. Notice that in this case, the sum of all the resulting values of the point s' is 1. Moreover, to provide the ternary two-dimension and, hence, to ensure the equality to 1 of the remaining points required by this type of plots, to each solution $s \in F$ an additional value ϵ is added. The value of ϵ is calculated as depicted in Eq. (2).

$$1 - \sum_{i=1}^{|M|} (x_i^s) = \epsilon \tag{2}$$

where $|M|$ indicates the dimensions according to the objectives considered and x_i^s is the corresponding coordinate of solution $s \in F$ for the dimension $i \in M$. If $\epsilon > 0$, the contribution to each dimension ϵ_i^s is equal to $\frac{\epsilon}{|M|}$ and added as indicated in Eq. (3).

$$\sum_{i=1}^{|M|} (x_i^s + \epsilon_i^s) = 1 \tag{3}$$

This example shows that optimization models alone are not sufficient when it comes to real-time processing of data and decision-making; instead, we need research investigating means to properly visualize results as shown for the multi-objective optimization approach.

2.2 Machine Learning

The aim of this section is motivate the adoption of prediction models. For this, we first introduce the BAP, and then we show how prediction model-based ML could be used to manage real-time data.

Berth Allocation Planning. Berth allocation planning refers to the assignment of a "berthing position and a berthing time to every vessel projected to be served within a given planning horizon" [39]. A berth allocation plan can be disrupted by changes of the vessel arrival time due to, e.g., weather conditions or port congestion. Berth allocation plans that cannot be adhered to can create costs for ports and shipping lines for unused facilities and waiting times in the port area [17]. During the waiting times at anchorage, vessels use at least one of their auxiliary engines and auxiliary boilers to generate power [5] and thereby produce emissions. As opposed to stochastic optimization models, robust (recovery) optimization models with a rolling planning horizon can modify a berth allocation plan in real-time using continuous input of newly available real-time data, e.g., as shown by Umang et al. [35]. The authors use input data that is fixed vessel data such as the length and the draft as well as the expected and actual arrival and handling time, berthing positions and cargo tonnages. The used input data is generated based on a real data sample from a port. The sample covers data for "20 vessels for a time horizon of roughly 10 days" and

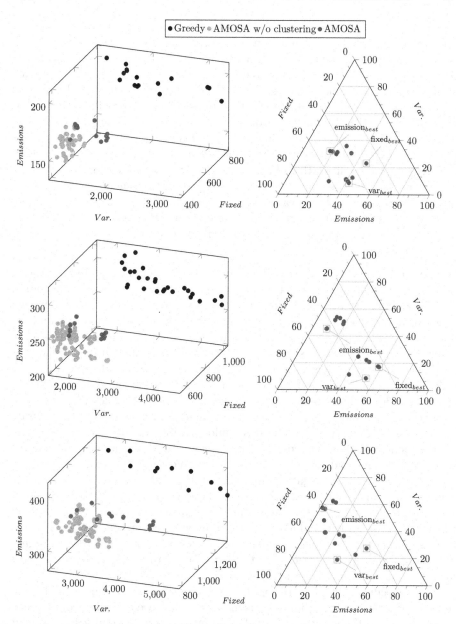

Fig. 1. Three-dimensional visualization of different approximated Pareto fronts (left) and two-dimensional visualization of archived solutions composing an approximated Pareto front (right) for scenarios with 35, 50, and 75 transport orders (from top to bottom) [24].

was used to estimate the range of values for the generation of input data. Our prior research in the area of emission inventories has revealed that this data can be confidential to the port and its tenants. However, real data covering a larger time horizon could be used to validate the results. The key user role of such optimization models and results is the berth planner. The results can be utilized by the relevant software applications that are used to, e.g., provide a time-space diagram to visualize berth allocation plans. To make use of such optimization models in the real world, real-time data of vessels' ETA have to be used as input. Incorrect ETA data can disturb the berth allocation planning. Therefore, researchers have applied ML to predict the deviation of ETA. However, some of these papers did not take into account some good practices likely to improve the prediction accuracy and the evaluation credibility [25]. Our aim in the remaining part of this section is to provide a ML approach that processes data in the most useful way in order to make these predictions more accurate.

Background. In this part, we will explore how ML could be adopted to process real-time data and its potential benefits for reducing emissions in maritime ports. In fact, in an era of increasing complexity and volume of data, it is well known that ML approaches may provide a competitive advantage in all areas and are nowadays among the techniques commonly used for prediction tasks as they are adapted to such data types. In particular, the field of maritime shipping has also been affected by the appearance of these techniques. Although there is a lack of adoption of such methods to improve this field as pointed out in [25], the referenced paper shows many opportunities and some examples of works that have tried to take advantage of the growing amount of data to provide accurate predictions. Indeed, these predictions could provide support for efficient port management, including the reduction of emissions. In particular, current research shows that delays and uncertainties regarding the time of arrival of ships are an important source of negative environmental impacts. Therefore, it is of the utmost importance to have an accurate prediction of the time of arrival in order to reduce the waiting time of ships and their carbon emissions. An example of this is that if we anticipate a delay or early arrival of a ship in advance, it could increase or decrease its speed (depending on each situation) in order to reduce its waiting time. At the same time, the respective terminal operator can adjust operations and resources to the new situation.

More specifically, to use ML for this problem, we need to build a model and test it. Then, after being validated, the model could be used for all upcoming real-time data of an estimated ship arrival in order to predict its real value. In what follows, we will mainly focus on the issue of how to build such a model by considering a well-known ML algorithm. In fact, we can notice that a certain number of these articles have just applied it while neglecting certain good practices likely to improve the performance of ML methods. The interested reader is referred to [25] for such examples of work that has used ML to predict arrival times of ships. In this paper, instead of re-iterating the survey, we will show through an example using the same data adopted in [38], some insights that are important to take into account when applying ML. With regard to [38], which was not included in [25] as it was published later, it applied three data-mining models to predict the arrival time of ships in the Ningbo Ganji (Yining) Container Terminal (GYCT) and compared their performances. Also, it was interested in detecting the relevant features using statistical analysis. This paper could be considered then as an extension and a contribution to the referenced paper. Therefore, we have a particular interest in the issues of data-processing, feature and model selection, and we investigate their impact while adopting support vector machines (SVM) [14], which is one of the most-known ML algorithms, and it was shown to be effective for this problem as in [32].

Data Pre-processing. Generally, data pre-processing, is a crucial step in the prediction process. Indeed, most real-world data are incomplete, and they could be either lacking some features values (also named attributes, input variables and predictors), or lacking certain features of interest or even aggregating them. In the data adopted in this paper, after transforming categorical features into numerical features (as they could be treated by ML algorithms), we expanded the information on *ETA*, which was aggregated in a single feature, into two different features which are: date and time. Also, we added a feature reflecting the corresponding weekday (from 1 to 7) as it could have an impact on the vessel arrival time (e.g. weekends) and then could provide a useful information to the ML algorithm. In fact, for the data adopted in this paper, more than half of the ships prefer to arrive on Friday, Saturday and Sunday [38]). The list of features is depicted in Table 2.

Table 2. Problem features.

Feature type	Ship features	ETA features
Feature name	Ship name, ship type, length	Date, time and weekday

However, while developing the time component adds additional information, it increases the number of features, which will introduce us to the feature selection (FS) problem that is described below. In addition, another pre-processing step that must be taken into account is the splitting of data. Indeed, in order to have a credible evaluation of the ML algorithm, it is necessary to split the dataset into a training and a test set. More precisely, the training set is used to build the model and the test set is considered to evaluate it on a new unseen data (by simulating the case of a new real-time). In this experiment, 80% of samples are used in training while the remaining 20% are used in testing.

Feature and Model Selection. On the one hand, FS could be defined as the process of selecting a subset of the most relevant features to be used in the model construction. FS may enhance the performance of the prediction by eliminating irrelevant inputs; it may also reach data reduction for accelerated training and increases computational efficiency. Also, the determination of the optimal feature subset may enhance the generalization capacity (performance on the test set). FS has shown to be effective while using ML approaches in many occasions (e.g. [29]). In this paper, we adopt FS by using a wrapper approach [23] included in the Scikit-learn library [33], which is nowadays one of the most known frameworks used to build ML prediction algorithms. The output of this step indicates that the following features could be considered as irrelevant for the learning process:

- Ship name
- Shipping line

We can see here that this result is consistent with the results shown in [38] (the authors adopted a statistical approach to achieve this).

On the other hand, another issue that has to be considered while building the ML model is model selection. In fact, to deal with real problems, ML models have to be adjusted to produce a more desirable outcome. In particular, the configuration of SVM parameters (model selection) plays an important role in the success of SVM: the purpose is to reach the bias/variance trade-off and to avoid both overfitting and underfitting by enhancing the robustness of the model. Nowadays, there is a tendency to orient research on feature and model selection in a unified framework as illustrated in [29]. In this paper, we adopt Scikit-learn which includes also an efficient approach for automatic model selection.

In addition, we should note here that since the output (arrival time) is continuous, we have adopted support vector regression (SVR), which is the regression version of SVM. Finally, we note that we have adopted the variant ϵ-SVR (the main difference between these variants concerns the mathematical formulation which has to be improved as pointed out in [15]). But in the sequel, we adopt the term SVM as it is the most adopted in the literature.

Experimental Results. In this part, to examine the effectiveness of our extension for the data considered, in Table 3, we compare its results to the native SVM without the transformation of time feature and without FS (named SVM_1) and with SVM with data transformation but without FS (named SVM_2); the measures adopted in this paper are: R^2 (coefficient of determination), Mean Absolute Error (MAE), Mean Squared Error (MSE) and Root Mean Squared Error (RMSE).

Table 3. Investigation of the importance of our extension.

Data sets	Our approach	SVM_2	SVM_1
R^2	**0.096**	0.056	0.053
Mean Absolute Error	**223.624**	238.604	238.997
Mean Squared Error	**68486.197**	74880.512	75885.526
Root Mean Squared Error	**261.699**	272.292	275.473

We can notice from the results of Table 3 that our contributions to [38] both have a positive impact on the performance of the learning algorithm in the test set. In fact, even though they were both taken into account in the discussion throughout the paper, it is important to add them as an input to the ML model to improve its performance. But, we can notice also, notably from the R^2 coefficient, that the predictions could be further improved. In fact, it is of utmost importance to add additional information (e.g., weather conditions) which have a great impact on the arrival of ships.

Also, by computing the difference between the predicted and the actual arrival of vessels, we show in Fig. 2 the actual delays compared to the predictions provided by different approaches highlighted above (a delay value is considered negative in the case of a ship arriving earlier than its estimated time).

Next, after showing through an example how to use ML to predict the arrival time of ships and how to make the data available in the most meaningful way for the learning process, a challenging issue for the relevant port actors (e.g., the berth planner) is how to leverage this information to reduce emissions by considering real-time data on vessel ETA and other features. Here, as indicated above, we recommend that it takes advantage of these predictions by updating the ETA of the ships and communicating this information to the ships so that they can change their speed and thus reduce their waiting time and emissions.

2.3 Gamification

In this section, we provide an overview about possible data sources and the problems in sharing confidential data based on the example of the San Pedro Bay Area ports. Subsequently, we introduce the impact of driving behavior on energy efficiency and related Eco-driving assistance systems (EDAS). Based on an existing EDAS gamification concept, we propose to include real-time emission concentration data.

Data Sources and Confidentiality. As most ports follow the landlord model and related port authorities operate only low emission sources (e.g., vehicle fleet, office buildings, yard lights) compared to the aforementioned emission sources, the share of the port authorities to the total port emissions is less compared to terminal operators, vessel owners or the industry within the port area. In the context of the mentioned organizational-overarching main functions (see Sect. 2), port authorities create port EIs (e.g., [11]), and monitor emissions (e.g., [8]) and energy flows [2] port-wide, and in real time.

Based on the experience from our current projects, the activity data of the tenants (e.g., a terminal operator's count of reach stackers), its operating hours and fuel consumption) is confidential to the tenants and not always shared with the port authority. Thereby, activity data can be assumed or proxy data (of similar ports) can be used along with scaling factors if appropriate for the problem statement. Sharing activity data in real time requires even more trust between the port authority and its tenants. A common way to share activity data are manually populated questionnaire spreadsheet files that are sent by email, which

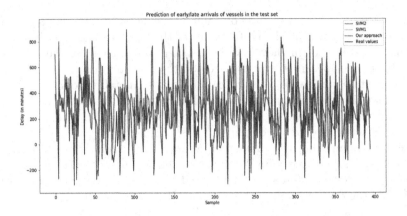

Fig. 2. ML-based SVM approaches for prediction delays of vessels.

would not be sufficient for data transfer within a real-time system. To ensure the real-time aspect of data, interfaces with an automatic data transfer have to be implemented. The feasibility of such implementation is linked with the willingness of the owners of the activity data.

Emission Monitoring Station-Network. From the perspective of the port authority, the problem of sharing confidential data is therefore avoided once the port authority itself employs data-generation systems. An example for this is the monitoring station network of the San Pedro Bay Area ports. The siting of the stations is in and at the border of the ports. The network of six stations measures pollutants such as sulfur dioxide and particulate matter as well as meteorological data such as wind speed and wind direction, and ambient temperature. Analysis of the data (e.g., trends) is presented in annual reports, which purpose is to compare the air quality data to, e.g., national standards and to "communicate the data to the communities surrounding the port." The continuously generated data is uploaded hourly to a publicly available website [1]. The generated time-series data allows detailed daily analysis to be conducted. For instance, it is observed that during morning and evening rush hours, emissions are increased [8], for which correlations are drawn. Because the time-series data does not include activity data of emission sources, the annual reports can only show correlations and assume causality between certain events and emission trends [8,9]. Inclusion of activity data of emission sources (e.g., traffic) near the stations is thereby recommended [7]. In conclusion, we see two implemented utilizations of the station networks' generated high frequency sampling time-series data. The first is to conduct in-depth analysis, annually. The second is to communicate the data near real-time to the public; hence, the latter is the only utilization of real-time data. However, a change in emission reduction policies through public pressure needs time.

Driving Behavior and EDAS. The question arises if and how the data can be further utilized to reduce emissions in real time in the port. In this regard, we think of the utilization of real-time data as an act that has an immediate effect on emission production. As heavy-duty vehicles contribute the largest amount of CO_2e emissions to the port of Los Angeles, we focus on this emission source. Apart from routing-optimization as presented in Sect. 2.1, consumed fuel, and thus emissions, can be reduced by altering the behavior of the drivers (e.g., speed adaptation, limited acceleration, anticipating driving), which can be influenced indirectly by measures [36]. Van Mierlo et al. [36] further specify these measures as traffic measures (e.g., phased traffic lights) and policy measures (e.g., driver education and training, periodical inspection). Experiments show a significant impact on fuel consumption by driving behavior of different drivers on all road types. The results for a single driver can also change between single runs without changing the parameters [34]. Dorrer [20] lists three impact factors for driving behavior towards economical driving: the knowledge, ability and the willingness of the driver. Drivers have to understand how to drive economically but also external (e.g., weather) and internal conditions (e.g., well-being) are important to enable economically driving. Independent of how strong a driver's knowledge and ability to drive economic presents itself, ultimately, a driver's willingness impacts how and if at all economic driving is realized (see Daun and Lienkamp [19]).

EDAS support drivers to drive economically, by intervening (e.g., enforce acceleration limit) or by providing information or recommend actions to the driver (e.g., a warning message to reduce acceleration) [18,19]. In [18], an experiment shows that without extending travel time, instructions without system support alone lead to a reduction (about 6.0%) in fuel consumption. The use of an EDAS results in additional (about 6.6%) fuel consumption reduction in all modes except highway driving. The used EDAS communicates advisory messages that comprise of a recommended action and an explanation. The action is communicated by a synthesized voice message and by text and pictograph (to enable a fast reaction of the driver), and the explanation is provided only by text and pictograph (to add comprehensibility, and thus, foster acceptance).

Gamification of EDAS. How can acceptance or the willingness to use an EDAS be increased? Daun and Lienkamp [19] propose to apply gamification to driving assistance systems. According to Werbach [37], gamification can be defined as "the process of making activities more game-like." The author argues that the application of game design elements (points, badges, etc.) does not necessarily result in gamification. Instead, gamification covers "coordinated practices that objectively manifest the intent to produce more of the kinds of experiences that typify games." Werbach refers to Mollick and Rothbard [30] who characterize a game as "purposefully created with reinforcing context, interactions, and mechanism that create a more immersive feeling of play." Thereby, gamification tries to create game-like experiences to motivate (influence) people. Daun and Lienkamp [19] promote a situation-dependent, activity-centric gamification concept that uses activity challenges. Here, the cognitive and motor performance is rated by the system which triggers a driver's motivation to perform well in these challenges. For instance, when a driver is approaching a village, a challenge is communicated such as, the driver should slow down to arrive at a speed limit sign with approximately the speed designated by the sign. The purpose is to create a game experience, that can be increased by game design elements or elements that "create a more immersive feeling of play" [30]; for instance, by playing a stimulating sound with increasing volume nearing the end of the time-window to economically slow down. In an activity-centric gamification concept, the gamified activity is not seen as effort by the user, and the real purpose of the system can be *masked* [19]. In contrast, a purpose-centric gamification concept emphasizes the benefits for the user in using the system. Thereby, the user carries out a trade-off analysis between the effort to use a system and the achievable benefits. An example is the gamification approach from Gatta et al. [22] in the area of urban logistics. Here, a fundamental element is the setup of a reward system (e.g., ranking, points, badges) that must consider the players' aims. The authors exemplify such aims as, e.g., discounts in city shops for citizens as players.

EDAS Gamification Using Emission Data. The aforementioned generic gamification concepts are applicable to the trucks used in the maritime ports domain. Now, the question is how real-time data of the port can be utilized to enhance the gamification process. Trucks move cargo between terminals of the port as well as in the hinterland. The mentioned monitoring station network covers the vicinity of the port. Independent of gamification, real-time emission production data can be utilized in the intervention system of EDAS to enforce an eco-driving style if an emission threshold level is reached, e.g., by turning on economic driving modes that limit the acceleration or speed. In the context of purpose-centric gamification concepts, we propose to modify the reward system so that the reward depends on the current real-time emission concentration. For instance, once rewards for eco-friendly driving actions are expressed as points, such points can correlate positively with the current overall emission concentration. The current location of a truck and the current spatial distribution of emissions can be utilized to further modify the points. For example, if a truck driver in a highly polluted area follows the recommended actions by the system, the associated points are increased. Once a truck driver can decide between different routes of which the length and the arrival time of the truck are acceptable, a problem can occur: The driver may prefer the route with a higher pollution to achieve more points. Thereby, this result will lead to an increase of emissions in this area which is in contrast to the goal of the system. To avoid this problem, a penalization mechanism can be integrated. Thereby, the yielded points can be constrained to the points yielded by the less polluted route or less. For this penalization system to work, the possible routes have to be calculated and thus, the start and end points of the route have to be known to the system. Such a system has different objectives compared to the multi-objective inter-terminal truck routing optimization model presented in Sect. 2.1 which can lead to a conflict. For instance, a route is proposed by the optimization model but once the truck follows this route, the truck driver is penalized by the gamified EDAS. Thereby, given that the optimization model's solutions are to be prioritized and drivers follow these solutions, one option is to omit the penalizing mechanism.

3   Conclusions

In this paper we have presented three different applications for real-time data to reducing emissions in maritime ports. The applications use three different methods (optimization models, ML, gamification) to reduce energy consumption, and thus, produced emissions. As one of the major areas of environmental sustainability in ports, we concentrate on the area of planning and optimization. Hereby, landside and seaside operations are optimized and their energy efficiency is increased.

In the area of landside operations, in some ports, heavy-duty vehicles such as trucks contribute the largest amount of CO_2e emissions. Here, we present a paper based on the Green-ITTRP that features a multi-objective optimization method, a mobile cloud-based information system and a visualization technique. The example shows the importance of a proper visualization of the results. A three-dimensional representation was transformed into a ternary two-dimensional representation to enable decision-makers to better identify the differences between solutions.

To further reduce trucks' emissions, gamification can be applied in the driver's cockpit. We utilize real-time emission concentration data from a sensor station network to enhance a gamification concept for EDAS, that motivates and supports drivers to drive economically. In the area of seaside operations, the alignment between terminal operators and shipping companies is critical to allow appropriate berth allocation. Ocean-going vessels are a major producer of emissions in ports. In case of a vessel's delay, a berth allocation plan is updated to avoid, e.g., the need for a vessel to wait for a free berth in the port area; hence, emissions can be avoided. In this context, accurate ETA need to be communicated from the shipping companies to the terminals. In this context, we present a prediction model using ML to predict the delay of vessels' arrival times. Experimental results show that the use of adding additional extracted features and the elimination of other irrelevant inputs could have a positive impact on the performance of ML algorithms.

The applications show that the cooperation between port stakeholders such as the port authority, transport firms and shipping companies is necessary to share the relevant real-time data. For example, the multi-objective optimization method could integrate real-time traffic sensor data. Once the port authority employs such sensors, the generated data must be provided to the terminal operator. Further to that, the enhanced gamification concept requires both the port authority, transport companies and terminal operators to share data of trucks such as the engine, the current location and route, and emission concentration in different areas of the port. Finally, it is shown that proper visualizations play an important role, i.e., to support and to motivate a user to use a system.

Future work will concentrate on real-time systems to exchange all kinds of activity and environmental data of port stakeholders relevant to individual applications. We hope that the presented applications, and future potential applications are perceived beneficial by the various port stakeholders to foster their cooperation. This could eventually support data sharing, and hence, the accuracy and availability of activity and environmental data, not only for real-time applications but also to create EIs. Though, a major lesson learned from our study is the comprehensive involvement of the user (e.g., decision maker, truck driver) as otherwise the intended impact cannot be achieved. While gamification is one option, we need to come up with and explore others.

References

1. Current data - San Pedro bay ports clean air action plan. https://monitoring. cleanairactionplan.org/current-data/. Accessed 24 Jan 2020
2. dashPORT. https://www.offis.de/en/offis/project/dashport.html. Accessed 15 Jan 2020
3. Environmental report 2018: Ports of Bremen/Bremerhaven. https://bremenports. de/greenports/wp-content/uploads/sites/3/2017/04/PERS-Rezertifizierung_ Report_2018_en.pdf. Accessed 15 Jan 2020
4. News 4.19. https://www.cml.fraunhofer.de/content/dam/cml/de/documents/ Newsletter/Newsletter. Accessed 15 Jan 2020
5. Emissions estimation methodology for ocean-going vessels (2008). https://ww3. arb.ca.gov/regact/2008/fuelogv08/appdfuel.pdf. Accessed 23 Jan 2020
6. Current methodologies in preparing mobile source port-related emission inventories: final report (2009). https://www.epa.gov/sites/production/files/2016-06/ documents/2009-port-inventory-guidance.pdf. Accessed 12 Jan 2020
7. The port of Los Angeles community-based air toxics exposure study (2009). https://monitoring.cleanairactionplan.org/wp-content/uploads/2019/07/ POLA_PAH_Final_Report_092309.pdf. Accessed 24 Jan 2020
8. Air quality monitoring program at the port of Los Angeles: year thirteen data summary May 2017–April 2018 (2018). https://monitoring.cleanairactionplan. org/wp-content/uploads/2019/07/POLA-13th-Annual-Monitoring-Report-May-2017-April-2018.pdf. Accessed 23 Jan 2020
9. Air quality monitoring program at the port of Long Beach: annual summary report calendar year 2018 (2019). https://monitoring.cleanairactionplan.org/wp-content/uploads/2019/07/POLB-Summary-Annual-Report-for-2018-PDF.pdf. Accessed 23 Jan 2020
10. Inventory of air emissions for calendar year 2018 [port of Los Angeles] (2019). https://kentico.portoflosangeles.org/getmedia/0e10199c-173e-4c70-9d1d-c87b9f3738b1/2018_Air_Emissions_Inventory. Accessed 18 Oct 2019
11. Port of Long Beach - 2018 air emissions inventory (2019). http://www.polb.com/ civica/filebank/blobdload.asp?BlobID=15271. Accessed 10 Oct 2019
12. San Pedro Bay ports emissions inventory methodology report - Version 1 (2019). http://www.polb.com/civica/filebank/blobdload.asp?BlobID=15032. Accessed 26 Aug 2019

13. Acciaro, M., et al.: Environmental sustainability in seaports: a framework for successful innovation. Marit. Policy Manag. **41**(5), 480–500 (2014). https://doi.org/10.1080/03088839.2014.932926
14. Boser, B.E., Guyon, I.M., Vapnik, V.N.: A training algorithm for optimal margin classifiers. In: Proceedings of the 5th Annual Workshop on Computational Learning Theory - COLT 1992, pp. 144–152. ACM Press (1992). https://doi.org/10.1145%2F130385.130401
15. Brandner, H., Lessmann, S., Voß, S.: A memetic approach to construct transductive discrete support vector machines. Eur. J. Oper. Res. **230**(3), 581–595 (2013). https://doi.org/10.1016/j.ejor.2013.05.010
16. Browning, L., Bailey, K.: Current methodologies and best practices for preparing port emission inventories. https://www3.epa.gov/ttnchie1/conference/ei15/session1/browning.pdf. Accessed 30 Dec 2019
17. Budipriyanto, A., Wirjodirdjo, B., Pujawan, N., Gurning, S.: Berth allocation problem under uncertainty: a conceptual model using collaborative approach. Procedia Manuf. **4**, 429–437 (2015). https://doi.org/10.1016/j.promfg.2015.11.059
18. Daun, T.J., Braun, D.G., Frank, C., Haug, S., Lienkamp, M.: Evaluation of driving behavior and the efficacy of a predictive eco-driving assistance system for heavy commercial vehicles in a driving simulator experiment. In: 16th International IEEE Conference on Intelligent Transportation Systems (ITSC 2013), pp. 2379–2386. IEEE (2013). https://doi.org/10.1109/ITSC.2013.6728583
19. Daun, T.J., Lienkamp, M.: Spielend Fahren: Gamification-Konzept für Fahrerassistenzsysteme (2012). https://nbn-resolving.org/urn/resolver.pl?urn:nbn:de:bvb:91-epub-20120000-1129558-0-3
20. Dorrer, C.: Effizienzbestimmung von Fahrweisen und Fahrerassistenz zur Reduzierung des Kraftstoffverbrauchs unter Nutzung telematischer Informationen: Stuttgart, Univ., Diss., 2003, Schriftenreihe des Instituts für Verbrennungsmotoren und Kraftfahrwesen der Universität Stuttgart, vol. 24. Expert-Verl., Renningen (2004)
21. Eglese, R., Bektas, T.: Green vehicle routing. In: Toth, P., Vigo, D. (eds.) Vehicle Routing: Problems, Methods, and Applications, 2nd edn., pp. 437–459. SIAM, Philadelphia (2014)
22. Gatta, V., Marcucci, E., Sorice, F., Tretola, G.: A gamification approach to promote positive behaviours in urban logistics (2015). https://www.researchgate.net/publication/282609851_A_Gamification_approach_to_promote_positive_behaviours_in_Urban_Logistics. Accessed 5 Jan 2020
23. Guyon, I., Nikravesh, M., Gunn, S., Zadeh, L.A. (eds.): Feature Extraction. Springer, Heidelberg (2006). https://doi.org/10.1007/978-3-540-35488-8
24. Heilig, L., Lalla-Ruiz, E., Voß, S.: Multi-objective inter-terminal truck routing. Transp. Res. Part E Logist. Transp. Rev. **106**, 178–202 (2017)
25. Heilig, L., Stahlbock, R., Voß, S.: From digitalization to data-driven decision making in container terminals. arXiv preprint arXiv:1904.13251
26. Heilig, L., Voß, S.: Inter-terminal transportation: an annotated bibliography and research agenda. Flex. Serv. Manuf. J. **29**(1), 35–63 (2016). https://doi.org/10.1007/s10696-016-9237-7
27. Lalla-Ruiz, E., Heilig, L., Voß, S.: Environmental sustainability in ports. In: Sustainable Transportation and Smart Logistics, pp. 65–89. Elsevier (2019). https://doi.org/10.1016/B978-0-12-814242-4.00003-X
28. Lam, J.S.L., Van de Voorde, E.: Green port strategy for sustainable growth and development. In: Proceedings of the International Forum on Shipping, Ports and Airports (IFSPA), pp. 27–30 (2012)

29. Lessmann, S., Voß, S.: Feature selection in marketing applications. In: Huang, R., Yang, Q., Pei, J., Gama, J., Meng, X., Li, X. (eds.) ADMA 2009. LNCS (LNAI), vol. 5678, pp. 200–208. Springer, Heidelberg (2009). https://doi.org/10.1007/978-3-642-03348-3_21

30. Mollick, E.R., Rothbard, N.: Mandatory fun: gamification and the impact of games at work. SSRN Electron. J. (2013). https://doi.org/10.2139/ssrn.2277103

31. O'Reilly, C.A., Cromarty, A.S.: Fast is not real-time: Designing effective real-time AI systems. In: Gilmore, J.F. (ed.) Applications of Artificial Intelligence II. SPIE Proceedings, pp. 249–257. SPIE (1985). https://doi.org/10.1117/12.948443

32. Parolas, I.: ETA predictions for container ships at the port of Rotterdam using machine learning techniques (2016). https://repository.tudelft.nl/islandora/object/uuid%3A9e95d11f-35ba-4a12-8b34-d137c0a4261d

33. Pedregosa, F., et al.: Scikit-learn: machine learning in Python. J. Mach. Learn. Res. **12**, 2825–2830 (2011)

34. Rommerskirchen, C.: Verbrauchsreduzierung durch Fahrerassistenz unter dem Einfluss von Langzeitnutzung und Situationskomplexität. Dissertation, Technische Universität München, München (2018)

35. Umang, N., Bierlaire, M., Erera, A.L.: Real-time management of berth allocation with stochastic arrival and handling times. J. Sched. **20**(1), 67–83 (2016). https://doi.org/10.1007/s10951-016-0480-2

36. van Mierlo, J., Maggetto, G., van de Burgwal, E., Gense, R.: Driving style and traffic measures-influence on vehicle emissions and fuel consumption. Proc. Inst. Mech. Eng. Part D J. Automob. Eng. **218**(1), 43–50 (2004). https://doi.org/10.1243/095440704322829155

37. Werbach, K.: (Re)defining gamification: a process approach. In: Spagnolli, A., Chittaro, L., Gamberini, L. (eds.) PERSUASIVE 2014. LNCS, vol. 8462, pp. 266–272. Springer, Cham (2014). https://doi.org/10.1007/978-3-319-07127-5_23

38. Yu, J., Tang, G., Song, X., Yu, X., Qi, Y., Li, D., Zhang, Y.: Ship arrival prediction and its value on daily container terminal operation. Ocean Eng. **157**, 73–86 (2018). https://doi.org/10.1016/j.oceaneng.2018.03.038

39. Zhen, L., Chang, D.F.: A bi-objective model for robust berth allocation scheduling. Comput. Ind. Eng. **63**(1), 262–273 (2012). https://doi.org/10.1016/j.cie.2012.03.003

Experience and Design of Rural Cultural Well-Being in the New Media Age: A Case Study of Shatan Village in China

Yuanyuan Chen[1,2]([✉]) and Li Wang[3]

[1] College of Design and Innovation, Tongji University, Shanghai, China
chenyy@tongji.edu.cn
[2] College of Media and Arts, NJUPT, Nanjing, China
[3] College of Arts and Media, Tongji University, Shanghai, China

Abstract. Generally speaking, the acquisition of cultural well-being by villagers is defined as follows. On the one hand, it refers to the identification with and self-confidence concerning the local culture of residents in a rural space for the local culture. On the other hand, it interconnects with the rural cultural ecology and spiritual ecology, with there being many possible methods for acquiring cultural well-being. However, the formation and maintenance of rural culture have suffered during the era of new media. In this paper, the data obtained while conducting empirical research on Shatan Village, Huangyan District, Taizhou City, and Zhejiang Province was utilized to conduct a social investigation and analysis for the villagers' experiences of acquiring cultural well-being. The goal of the research is to expand the current situation and influence mechanisms used by the villagers in obtaining cultural well-being. In addition, the design path of cultural well-being experience is classified and defined through case explanation.

Keywords: Rural cultural well-being · Experience and design · Rural development · Case study of village · New media age

1 Introduction

According to China's national "Wild China" and "Rural Revitalization" policies, the report of the 19th National Congress of the Communist Party of China of 2017 established the significant goals of building a beautiful China, realizing rural revitalization, and ensuring the sustainable development of the Chinese nation. The report also suggests the "implementation of the rural revitalization strategy," which included the improvement of the beautiful countryside strategy in China over the past 5 years. In addition to coordinating the development of urban and rural areas and the protection of traditional villages, the report established a new policy basis for matters concerning society, economy, culture, and ecology. China's 5,000 years of agricultural civilization has resulted in many (traditional) villages with differing histories and cultures. Therefore, we must protect these villages as they represent the foundation of the culture of the nation. Indeed, the restoration and preservation of traditional Chinese rural culture and the revitalization of

© Springer Nature Switzerland AG 2020
A. Marcus and E. Rosenzweig (Eds.): HCII 2020, LNCS 12202, pp. 49–61, 2020.
https://doi.org/10.1007/978-3-030-49757-6_4

traditional Chinese agricultural practices will benefit well-being in rural areas, as well as national rejuvenation and social reproduction. Currently, in business and industry, new cultures are emerging as a result of the popularity of the Internet, the penetration of sensor networks, the emergence of big data, the rise of the information community, and the cross integration and interaction of data and information in society, physical space, and information space. As a result, all of these factors influence the digital design applications and developing trends of contemporary rural culture, thus changing the structure of rural social life.

First, rural cultural well-being experience refers to rural residents' feelings for, identification with, and self-confidence concerning their own local culture. Second, this concept is also associated with rural cultural ecology and spiritual ecology. Indeed, this concept covers all aspects of the villagers' experiences and consciousness, including the integration of rural economic construction and development and industrial economic adjustment, the re-creation of the rural environment, rural social image and social function, rural space art, characteristics of village culture, and cultural ecological changes, etc.; Third, rural cultural well-being is constructed from macro to micro and from behavior to content. Moreover, this term describes the multiple methods through which residents can acquire new behaviors, such as local, rural resource information sharing, co-creation of local culture, active participation of villagers in culture and cultural interactions, and the desire of residents to develop local, rural culture synergistically.

2 Literature Review

2.1 Review of Research on Rural Cultural Connotation and Rural Cultural Construction

In *Nostalgia* (1971), Taiwanese poet Yu Kwang-chung spoke of the pure and deep homesickness that resides in a wanderer's heart. Modernization has brought about the disintegration of tradition. This loss has caused Chinese people to be confused and disoriented with regard to the value of Chinese agricultural practices in the face of industrial civilization. That is, although Chinese people attempt to retain national traditions, they simultaneously lack confidence in their own culture. Feng Jicai (2013) argues that traditional villages must not die out and that we must not only consider economic viability during the urbanization processes but also be attentive to the transition from an agricultural civilization to an urban civilization. Moreover, the diversity of Chinese civilization lies not in cities, but in villages, which are important vessels for preserving and perpetuating Chinese civilization. Wu Liangyong (2003) proposed a scientific theory of Chinese human settlement environment and established a planning and design method and practice for the construction of human settlement with environment at its core. Wu also emphasized that the development of agricultural areas should not be ignored during urbanization. In addition, Wu argues that a beautiful human settlement environment and a harmonious society cannot be created without the joint development of both urban and rural areas. *In The City: New Town or Home Town?* (1973), German sociologist Felizitas Lenz-Romeiss pointed out that "hometown" is a form of spiritual property. Accordingly, the hometown is like a god who guards the lives of villagers, with the village becoming a peaceful and beautiful ideal garden that can be felt on the skin [5].

This theory supported the revitalization of new rural construction in the original scenes of Japan in the 1980s. Furthermore, rural development policies in the European Union have also been actively promoted during the past 30 years. For example, Italian scholars, cultural associations, and related departments have researched and designed "ecological museums" in the Italian countryside (2000). This has resulted in the emergence of the "ecological museum." Without doors or walls, these museums are able to effectively protect and preserve cultural heritage, such as natural landscapes, history, and culture, folk customs, production method and life style of villages as a whole, thus making the whole Italian countryside show a style of rural space, and village lifestyles.

2.2 Regional Research on the Governance of Rural Culture and Experience Research from a Sociological Perspective

Utilizing the results of the surveys conducted in and research on Kaixiangong Village in Wujiang, Jiangsu Province, China, Fei Xiaotong (1939) described in detail the geographical environment, family structure of villagers, economic mode of production, and property distribution, and inheritance of Kaixiangong Village. Fei's anthropological description of the village reveals the deep structure and function of traditional rural society in China. In 1982, Fei summarized several regional economic developmental models and applied the concept of "cultural awareness," thus influencing the economic layout and development of many regions, including Pudong along the upper section of the Yellow River and the Southern Silk Road [2]. Chen Ye (2016) introduced the "cultural governance" perspective, which provided a theoretical perspective and practical method for "the governance of the urban village" and "the urbanization of people." Chen also conducted detailed interviews and research on individual villagers, as well as sorted out the text information (transcript of interview in more detail) [3]. Taking Zhejiang Anji's practice of creating "beautiful countryside in China" as an example, Shu Chuangen (2010) proved that cultural creativity can facilitate generational transmission and innovation of local cultural resources, enriching the spiritual lives of farmers [4]. Amartya Sen (1981 and 1982) argues that a person's sense of happiness includes the "functions" (the "existence" and "behavior" valued) that one realizes and one's enthusiasm and degree of freedom for choosing and realizing these functions. Based on Amartya Sen's two theories of capabilities, this paper asserts that there are many factors influencing villagers' acquisition of cultural well-being. Taking into account different social and economic environments and different life stages, Arianne M. Gaetan and Tamara Jacka (2004) used field surveys and analysis to investigate the impact of immigration on rural women in China and elucidated the factors influencing rural women's sense of happiness in Sichuan Province [6].

In summary, many scholars have researched the connotation, construction, and governance of rural culture and collected substantial field research data. However, there is a lack of relevant research that takes into account social background, data analysis research, and the investigation of design and practice in the context of the new media era. While conducting research for this paper, it was found that the well-being experience of rural culture faces certain challenges in the new media era.

First, the construction of rural culture has suffered from fast-paced societal changes and the introduction of new media technology. In the process of cultural planning and design, capital investment in the construction of rural public culture has been limited. Thus, the construction of public cultural facilities has been inadequate. Rural public cultural service systems are almost nonexistent, and both rural cultural activities and cultural exchange activities are seldom performed. Therefore, in many areas of China, the basic cultural rights, and interests of villagers are not guaranteed. For example, the majority of villagers in rural areas have relatively poor opportunities for leisure and entertainment. Although young village residents use new media devices in their lives, their sense of cultural well-being is derived from fast-food cultures, such as the smartphone applications "Kwai" and "Tik Tok", etc.

Second, most villages exhibit little interest in their local culture and heritage. For example, many villages have not yet started compiling local histories of their townships or villages, and most have little knowledge on the precious historical relics that are preserved in their villages or townships. Additionally, rural residents do not understand the need to protect tangible and intangible historical and cultural heritage for future generations. Residents are not aware of their local culture and history, nor do they identify with it; therefore, prospects for the development, and digitization of rural culture for future generations are poor. For instance, elderly villagers often have their own unique versions of stories about local legends and village history and culture, whereas young villagers are often completely ignorant of this knowledge. At present, despite people's material lives improving greatly, their spiritual and cultural lives lack experience and self-confidence, as well as a sense of cultural well-being.

3   Quantification and Analysis of Empirical Research: Research on Cultural Well-Being Experience in Shatan Village

In this research project, Shatan Village in Huangyan District, Taizhou City, and Zhejiang Province were studied as examples, and both empirical and quantitative research methods were used to conduct social surveys of the villagers and the subjective and objective of analysis. The following questions were analyzed through empirical research:

1. Has the villagers' sense of happiness in Shatan Village improved in the new media era?
2. What does cultural happiness mean to villagers?
3. What influence does rural public culture have on the villagers' sense of happiness in the new media era?

By analyzing answers to these questions, this paper attempts to elucidate the source of cultural happiness experience of the villagers in Shatan Village and other influencing factors.

The investigation of cultural well-being experience in Shatan Village was first conducted applying quantitative objective analysis. The research process included the selection of participating villagers, social surveys of and interviews with the villagers to assess their sense of happiness, the collation and verification of interview content, and subject and object analysis of the empirical investigation of the villagers, etc. Subsequently, the key semantics of the text were summarized in terms of the content of general and unstructured interviews on the basis of the fact statements and the collection of field interviews with the villagers. After that, the Matlab quantitative model was applied to analyze transcripts of villagers' interviewers, refine keywords, and, finally, apply data analysis methods (As the Fig. 1 shows).

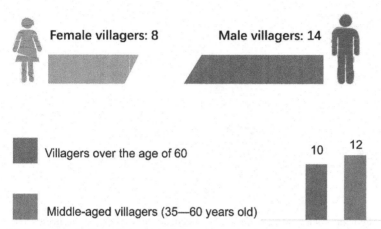

Fig. 1. According to the existing population size and age (generational) structure, distribution of the village area, villagers' surnames, villagers' occupations, villagers' genders, and other such factors, one representative was chosen for every 50 villagers, resulting in a total of 22 representatives.

The research results of our quantitative analysis determined whether the villagers' sense of happiness in Shatan Village had improved during the new media era and how the villagers understand the concept of cultural happiness.

3.1 Determining Whether the Villagers' Sense of Happiness in Shatan Village Improved During the New Media Era

Analyzing the plain and simple comments and expressions of the villagers, it is possible to grasp the villagers' straightforward aesthetic evaluation of their living environment. Furthermore, the empirical object analysis of the villagers in Shatan Village revealed that rural cultural construction has significantly affected and improved the villagers' sense of happiness.

A total of 22 interviews were collected in Shatan Village, with 63944 words spoken by the interviewees. Moreover, the analysis incorporated emotional considerations by applying such analytical methods as text assignment, keyword frequency analysis, keyword management analysis, and vocabulary distribution. The weight of each assignment value was based on the cultural happiness of the villagers in Shatan Village. According to the record of the interviews conducted during the social investigation of the villagers in Shatan Village, long-term village investigations, and individual research on rural communities, as well as all levels of government, both national and local, cultural happiness experience is classified into three levels: very happy, happy and moderately happy (and there are proposals for the construction of rural culture). The assignment values of which are 3, 2, 1 respectively and the proportions in the interview chapters are 59.1%, 22.7%, 18.2% respectively (As the Fig. 2 shows).

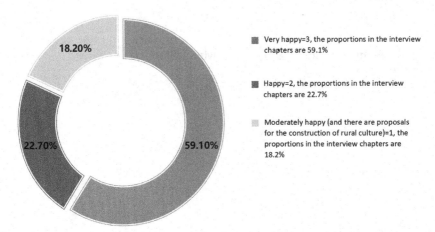

Fig. 2. The assignment values of which are 3, 2, 1 respectively and the proportions in the interview chapters are 59.1%, 22.7%, 18.2% respectively.

First, interviews were divided into three categories corresponding to the three levels of cultural happiness experience. Secondly, the value of happiness experience was used as classification and the word frequency analysis was applied to analyze the frequency of certain words as per each cultural happiness experience level. Furthermore, the filtered search word data was ranked according to frequency. Although the ranking of words may not accurately surround the theme of "cultural well-being," it demonstrates which words are mentioned most frequently by the villagers in interviews and their relation (or lack of relation) to cultural happiness experience. Third, according to the below filtered results, high-frequency words from each interview were integrated into the search word

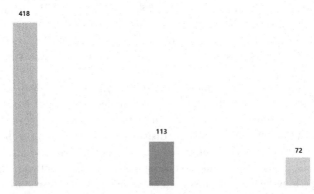

Fig. 3. Corresponding to 3, 2, 1 value of cultural happiness experience, the number of words in the search word library were 418, 113, 72 respectively.

Moderately happy (and there are proposals for the construction of rural culture)=1		Happy=2		Very happy=3	
Search word	Frequency	Search word	Frequency	Search word	Frequency
Good	120	Home	82	We	213
Ordinary people	62	Good	65	Good	187
None	50	Construction	53	Right now /At present	106
Money	43	Land	43	Steamed bread	78
Beauty / Beautiful	39	Programme /Plan	37	Many	65
How	36	Beautiful countryside	37	Jobs	54
Beautiful countryside	32	House	36	Book	53
Develop/Development	31	Ordinary people	33	Loquat	48
Problem	27	Develop/Developmen	32	At home	47
Sensation	27	Can	30	Compare	41
Reservoir	25	Temple	24	Business	40
Income	25	Revitalize	24	Liqueur	40
As far as possible do one's best	24	Rural revitalization	22	Before	39
Life	23	Tourism	19	Planting	39
Unable	22	Problem	19	Bee	36
Environment	22	Transform	16	Can	34
Enhance/Improve	20	Loquat	16	Later	33
Academy	20	Collection	14	Construction	31
Environmental protection	20	Life	13	Ordinary people	31
Indeed / Certainly	19	Old street	13	Women	29
…		…		…	

Fig. 4. The filtered search word data can be supervised through frequency ranking. According to the below filtered results, high-frequency words were integrated into the search word library according to the value of happiness experience in combination with the semantic environment of the interview.

library according to the value of happiness experience in combination with the semantic environment of the interview and then filtered and classified again. Corresponding to 3, 2, 1 value of cultural happiness experience, the number of words in the search word library were 418, 113, 72 respectively (As the Fig. 3, Fig. 4 show).

The analysis results are shown in the figure (As the Fig. 5, Fig. 6, Fig. 7 show).

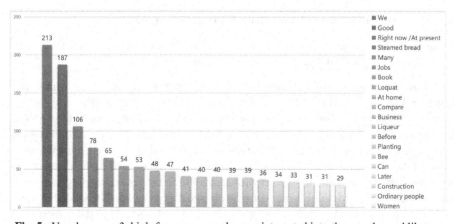

Fig. 5. Very happy = 3, high-frequency words were integrated into the search word library.

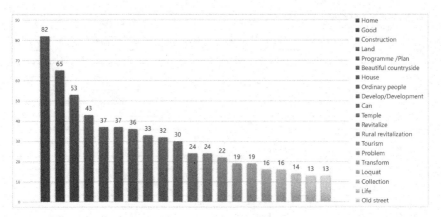

Fig. 6. Happy = 2, high-frequency words were integrated into the search word library.

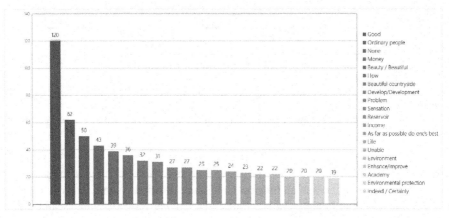

Fig. 7. Moderately happy (and there are proposals for the construction of rural culture) = 1, high-frequency words were integrated into the search word library.

3.2 What Do the Villagers Expect from Cultural Happiness?

According to the above analysis results, the villagers in Shatan Village have the following expectations of cultural happiness (As the Fig. 8 shows).

The Construction of Infrastructure and Distribution Mechanisms which can Improve Life Satisfaction. The first method for improving life satisfaction is implementing changes to infrastructure construction and life. Speaking about life in Shatan Village before the economic reform and open up in China, particularly before liberation, the villagers experienced endless suffering and often felt sad. In contrast, the implementation of the "beautiful countryside" policy has brought more value to their lives while allowing them to maintain the small environment of their homes and the larger environment of their village. In addition, the villagers can see the obvious and beneficial changes to their hometowns and have come to appreciate and look forward to the construction of village infrastructure. They are also attentive to the maintenance of environmental

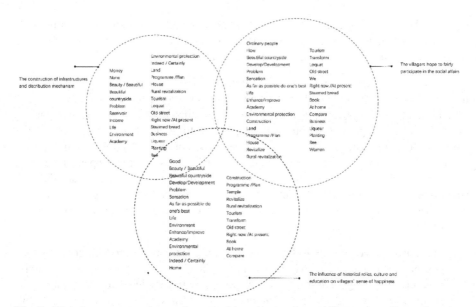

Fig. 8. High-frequency words were integrated into the search word library according to the value of happiness experience and then filtered and classified again.

sanitation, with their experience of the reconstruction of an old street in Shatan Village serving as a paradigmatic example. Such changes have improved their sense of cultural happiness concerning their hometown.

The second factor which can contribute to the improvement of life satisfaction is the tangible benefit resulting from the distribution mechanism for villagers. The land use and management rights of government lands have become perfect, resulting in a stable land contract relationship. Therefore, villagers have started to think more about how to use the land more reasonably and adjust what they plant according to market demand and how they plant to improve product quality. In particular, villagers not only can enjoy the right of independence but also have a deeper understanding of the transfer of land use rights. After continually striving to enhance the vitality of agricultural operations and strengthen agricultural infrastructure, villagers can enjoy the dividends resulting from redistribution, thus increasing their sense of social equity and life satisfaction.

The Desire of Villagers to Fairly Participate in Social Affairs. Taking Shatan Village as an example, there are a variety of rural festivals which occur throughout the year and correspond to particular agricultural events, such as the Loquat Festival, the Eighth Day Festival which originates from ancestor worship practices and local culture, and the H Tribal Assembly and Village Opera Festival in memory of Huang Xidan's birthday (Huang's ancestor, etc.). In fact, villagers have a strong desire to "share and co-build" various rural cultural practices, including participation in entertainment activities, folk festivals, and traditional festivals. Some villagers spontaneously arrange and organize their own programs and share and collaborate with others through various performances. Villagers still treasure there performances, which are written and performed by themselves, and they never get tired of seeing them.

Villagers hope to participate more in public cultural affairs during multiple infrastructure projects and public cultural policy implementations. On the one hand, many local agricultural and production practices in Shatan Village, such as beekeeping, honey making, winemaking, steamed bun baking, paper cutting, and bamboo weaving, etc., have been featured extensively during the reconstruction of the "Old Street" in Shatan Village. Such projects greatly stimulate the villagers' enthusiasm to take part in the cultural life of their hometown. On the other hand, the establishment of the Shatan Village Committee and Cultural Activity Center around "Old Street" and "Zhongying Temple" has provided villagers with a place for performance and enhanced their spiritual and cultural lives.

The Influence of Historical Relics, Culture, and Education on Villagers' Sense of Happiness. Villagers want to fully understand their village's history and relics, such as the precise meaning of inscriptions on "Zhongying Temple Stele." According to conversations with villagers and textual analysis of interviews, it can be deduced that education and reading are important factors influencing villagers' perceptions of cultural happiness experience. Indeed, the connection between prosperity and education originated in the Southern Song Dynasty. As the political and economic center of China moved south, the cultural center also moved from the Central Plains to the Southeast Coast, whereas the development of the culture of Taizhou City accelerated. Even today, the teaching of cultivation, farming, and reading still forms the foundation of local education and acts as the guiding principle running throughout all education practices and is diffused widely among villagers in Shatan Village. They often teach their children that they should study hard and not give up despite the difficulty.

4 Design Practice of Rural Cultural Well-Being in the New Media Era: Visualization Methods for Digital Media

How should villagers acquire and build cultural well-being and digital heritage? In this paper, we elaborate one of the design practices of rural cultural happiness in Shatan Village. This visual method uses digital media to incorporate the digital language of "nostalgia memory" into village life, thus promoting digital interaction among residents and the exchange of rural culture in Shatan Village.

First, it is the interpretation of the source of Shatan Village history and culture. To summarize our research findings, villagers desire to fully understand their village's history and relics because they are proud of their family names and the legacy of their ancestors, and therefore, they anticipate learning more about the history of their hometown. Project researchers visited local villagers, consulted relevant documents, and reinterpreted the inscription of "Zhongying Temple Stele" in Shatan Village. For example, researchers deciphered and interpreted important historical relics belonging to village ancestors. The inscription was created by Huang Chaoran, a great Confucian scholar of the Song Dynasty. The inscription records and praises the heroic deeds of the founder of the village, Huang Xidan. However, after thousands of years of being exposed to the elements, the inscription is worn and corroded, and the handwriting is no longer clear due to years of neglect. As a result, the villagers and tourists cannot easily read or understand the inscription. In order to preserve and protect these historical materials and relics, the researchers rerubbed, and protected the inscription together with the Huangyan District Administration of Culture, Radio, Film, Press, and Publication and Yutou Township Government. "Beautiful Yutou," the official WeChat account of the Yutou Township government, documented the research work being conducted on the inscription, namely, in a piece entitled "Re-rubbing the Zhongying Temple inscription and protecting historical relics" (As the Fig. 9 shows) Moreover, the reinterpreted transcript of the inscription was released using the official account, so as to help the villagers understand the cultural and historical heritage of their hometown.

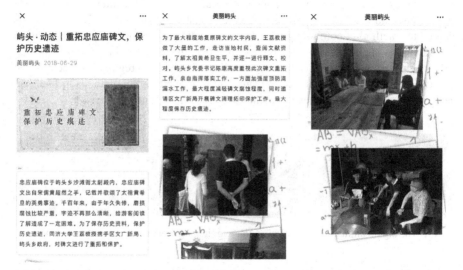

Fig. 9. "Beautiful Yutou," the official WeChat account of the Yutou Township government, documented the research work being conducted on the inscription, namely, in a piece entitled "Re-rubbing the Zhongying Temple inscription and protecting historical relics."

Second, it took more than 2 years to conduct the research and complete the documentary *Shatan Village*. The filming and narration of this documentary were dictated by culture. The film was oriented toward understanding and excavating the history and culture of Shatan Village and acted as a stepping stone for future research projects. In other words, by taking the inherent unity of the logic of history, practice, and theory as a basic requirement, a comprehensive investigation of the development history was conducted, changing and adjusting the trajectory and strategy of Shatan Village in the context of the social "big transformation" that has taken place since the reforms of 1978 (As the Fig. 10 shows).

Fig. 10. Part of this project research process.

Third, the researchers used digital animation to tell the legendary story of an Huang ancestor hero of Shatan Village fighting a fire in the documentary *Shatan Village*. We also depicted Huang ancestor Rou Chuan Shu Yuan in the form of an animation. The digital animation was based on the traditional regional aesthetics of Shatan Village, visits with the villagers, archival research of village history, and studies of the interactions between local culture and media art. In terms of narrating historical legends, digital animations adopted the method of combining tradition with digitization. In terms of overall design and drawing, it applied traditional drawing methods. In particular, in terms of choosing the story environment and visual language, it adopted traditional regional characteristics. In terms of postproduction effects, the animations applied digital methods to facilitate the digital transmission and development of culture (As the Fig. 11 shows).

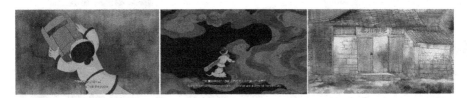

Fig. 11. The digital animation was based on the traditional regional aesthetics of Shatan Village.

In addition, images with regional aesthetics run through the documentary and animation production. The documentary adheres to the principle of creativity and cultural traditions of story structure, animation art design, drawing method, and post editing, allowing local cultural traditions to dictate aesthetic choices. Representations in the digital animations were based on the traditional regional aesthetic of Shatan Village, and inspiration was drawn from the villagers themselves, historical records, and interaction of characteristics of the local culture and media art from the local area. This media design adopted a combination of traditional and digital forms. The overall design and drawing combined traditional drawing methods, especially scene design and digital visual language, incorporating traditional regional features. For example, the narrative of the animation is informed by the interpretation of the Zhongying Temple inscription, establishing the origin of this legendary story. The Shatan Village has a beautiful local environment; the mountains are covered with bamboo forests. In traditional Chinese culture, the morphological characteristics of bamboo are said to symbolize the spirituality of the people, such as modesty, integrity, virtuousness, honesty, selflessness, and simplicity, etc. Therefore, "bamboo" is taken as a typical intention during the animation covering the story of "Rou Chuan Shu Yuan," which not only conforms to the local natural environment but also uses "bamboo" to symbolize family values and thought, such as cultivation, farming, studying, reading, and heritage. This also embodies the quiet and simple aesthetic image advocated by the village.

5 Conclusion

By combining field research with the data analysis of textual data, the cultural well-being of villagers in Shatan Village was analyzed, and the design of rural cultural well-being in the new media era was investigated through practice design. It was determined that villagers' acquisition of cultural well-being and its sustainable development are not targets which can be achieved in the short term. Moreover, villagers' self-confidence and awareness of cultural well-being are closely related to their level of happiness.

It can be said that the developmental trend of rural cultural construction has been heavily influenced by the involvement of external resources and digital technologies, especially when considering the large differences in the current situation of culture, economy, and construction of traditional Chinese villages. In the context of responding to rural revitalization, rural culture can be effectively combined with traditional rural cultural forms as a way for adjusting the social spirit to the new media era, thus achieving a sustainable state to help villagers achieve a better life and improve their experience of cultural well-being. Furthermore, the establishment of a sense of belonging through rural culture in the new media era, and even the establishment of a villager's own individual sense of cultural confidence, depends on their individual understanding of regional culture and history, their respect and consciousness of culture, and their experience of acquiring cultural well-being. In conclusion, villagers' experience, and design of cultural well-being in the new media era is a process that contains group wisdom, cultural experience, and cultural extension.

Acknowledgements. This paper represents a set of the research results drawn from the Zhejiang Sample Study of Contemporary Chinese Villages: Study of Shatan Village (17WH20016ZD-7Z). This paper also is supported by the grants of MOE (Ministry of Education in China) Project of Humanities and Social Sciences (15YJC760014).

References

1. Leong, Y.K., Tao, L.K.: Village and Town Life in China. The Commercial Press, Beijing (2015)
2. Fei, X.: Peasant Life in China. Peking University Press, Beijing (2012)
3. Ye, C.: Where is the Hometown: A Study of Luojiazhuang Village History and Urbanization Transformation. Zhejiang People's Publishing House, Hangzhou (2016)
4. Shu, C.: The organic combination of cultural creativity and the construction of new countryside—taking anji county to create "Beautiful Countryside in China" as an Example. Zhejiang Soc. Sci. **7**, 120–122 (2010)
5. Lenz-Romeiss, F., Küstner, E., Underwood, J.A.: The City: New Town or Home Town?. Pall Mall Press, London (1973)
6. Gaetano, A.M., Jacka, T.: On the move: women and rural-to-urban migration in contemporary China. Columbia University Press, New York (2004)

User Experience and Usability Design Centered Smart Application Design to Waste Sorting for Citizens Living in Smart City in China

Ziyuan Chi and Zhen Liu$^{(\boxtimes)}$ (iD)

School of Design, South China University of Technology, Guangzhou 510006, People's Republic of China
liuzjames@scut.edu.cn

Abstract. This paper discusses the usability of user experience in the field of waste treatment in smart city, where the waste sorting is an important part of the research on smart cities in China currently. At present, there are various waste sorting related smart applications in the Alipay, and WeChat applet. These applications are very complicated and less usability of user experience design for users, which they cannot perfectly solve the user problems and the user experience needs to be improved. As such, this paper is aiming to solve the problem with user research centered smart application design for users to sorting and deal with the waste accurately with improved user experience and usability living in smart city. This research firstly looks for the relevant research and technology of waste treatment and the process design of user experience through literature, and then carries out the user test and comparative analysis through the existing platform to find out the special points, common points and important points. User research helps to get the user needs and collect the data for the main function optimization design for waste sorting in smart city, and pass the user test about its availability. A smart application has been proposed to make the waste sorting more simple and accurate, and improve the user experience, usability, and satisfaction.

Keywords: User experience · Usability design · Waste sorting · Smart city

1 Introduction

1.1 Waste Treatment

Waste treatment has always been a hot issue in the world. At present, there have been many studies on the three steps of collection path, organic separation and value recovery. For the first step, Medvedev et al. proposed a decision support system (DSS) based on cloud technology to make waste collection efficient [1]. Anagnostopoulos et al. considered the balance between waste collection and cost [2], improved the waste collection path by randomly redistributing trucks to reduce the citizen health problems caused by the negative impact of waste on the environment [3]. In the step of organic separation and value recovery, Digiesi et al. proposed to configure an integrated waste management

© Springer Nature Switzerland AG 2020
A. Marcus and E. Rosenzweig (Eds.): HCII 2020, LNCS 12202, pp. 62–81, 2020.
https://doi.org/10.1007/978-3-030-49757-6_5

system (IWMS) that meets the environmental requirements. Marques et al. proposed a multi-level intelligent urban infrastructure management architecture based on IOT, which can manage 3902 waste bins at the same time and correctly separate organic and recyclable waste in indoor and outdoor environment, bringing high-quality experience for users [4]. Shah et al. emphasized the importance of recycling value from waste bins, and introduced a stochastic optimization model to improve the value recovery rate of collection [5].

China has issued a series of policies on domestic waste treatment, solid waste treatment, urban environmental protection, renewable resources and waste power generation. The implementation of these policies has indeed implemented classified recycling work, but at present, there are few cities involved, the recycling effect is still poor, and there are many problems. In 2017, the state issued the notice on the implementation scheme of domestic waste classification system, and major TV stations produced waste classification related programs and reports to publicize how to classify. However, the results are not particularly outstanding, and the understanding of the public is not in-depth. At present, waste sorting still needs a lot of manpower input, which not only causes the increase of labor cost, but also causes the problems of low sorting efficiency and backward technology.

Now, there are many online software such as app, Mini Programs, but not mature enough, which are improved with the increase of users' data. For example, there are more than one million and seven hundred thousand users in Alipay waste sorting process. Now, four hundred thousand kilograms of carbon emissions are reduced. From the data, the number looks very large and meaningful. Through the combination of online recycling platform and offline collection of resources, the waste sorting can be managed orderly [6].

1.2 User Experience and Usability

User experience is not the experience of each product user, but the experience of the product target user. User experience is not the experience of each product target user, but the experience of the product target user group. Because it is possible for each user's subjectivity to reach a completely opposite experience conclusion, the target user group can help solve this standard problem. Providing high-quality user experience can form important competitive advantages and corporate reputation for enterprises, form a good experience impression for customers, and increase the chance to visit again. Usability is an attribute to evaluate whether the user interface is easy to use, efficient and satisfactory.

User experience is a multi-dimensional structure with many experience points. Its importance to user experience depends on product type. It is classified according to the established user experience aspects [7] obtained from the user experience questionnaire. Through three experience senses: emotional experience, interactive experience and visual experience to understand user experience design, as shown in Fig. 1.

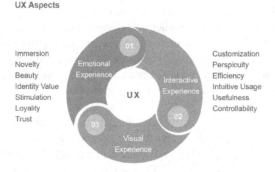

UX Aspects

Immersion
Novelty
Beauty
Identity Value
Stimulation
Loyality
Trust

Emotional Experience

Interactive Experience

UX

Visual Experience

Customization
Perspicuity
Efficiency
Intuitive Usage
Usefulness
Controllability

Content Quality, clarity, color, voice, picture

Fig. 1. User experience aspects (devised by the authors based on the literature).

Emotional experience: it gives users psychological experience and emphasizes psychological identity. It allows users to identify and express their inner feelings through the site, which shows that the user experience effect is deep. The sublimation of emotional experience is the spread of word-of-mouth, forming a highly emotional recognition effect, such as immersion, novelty, beauty, identity, value, stimulation, loyalty and trust.

Interactive experience: the interface gives users the experience of using and communicating process, emphasizing the characteristics of interaction. The process of interactive experience runs through the process of browsing, clicking, input and output, which provides customization, perspicuity, efficiency, intuitive usage, usefulness and capability of control.

Visual experience: the experience presented to users in audio-visual, emphasizing comfort in color, sound, image, text content and website layout, via means of content quality, clarity, color, voice and picture.

1.3 Waste and Experience

In order to achieve the goal of reduction, recycling and reuse of waste treatment, the accurate sorting of waste is the premise. Accurate sorting has little effect on the condition of relying on manpower completely, and the sorting is simple: recyclable and non-recyclable waste. In the notice of the implementation plan of the domestic waste sorting system in 2017, it was mentioned that the 'Internet +' mode should be adopted to promote waste sorting. In the past, the streets and communities could always hear the trumpet sound of 'recycling old mobile phones, old refrigerators, waste paper and old newspapers'. Now, with strict community management and mandatory waste treatment, residents are puzzled about how to deal with recyclable waste, and do not know how to deal with it. Therefore, how to improve the user's experience in the waste disposal process is very important. A good user experience can bring sustained feedback and attraction. The whole waste treatment process includes: waste generation - accurate waste sorting - collection and selection according to different delivery modes of each city and each community - regular collection by special recycling vehicles - inspection and treatment by special personnel - final end treatment, as shown in Fig. 2. In this general process, it can be divided into citizen participation and commissioner processing. This design focuses on the user experience of citizen participation. In this part of the experience, the closest thing to the public is the sorting of query waste.

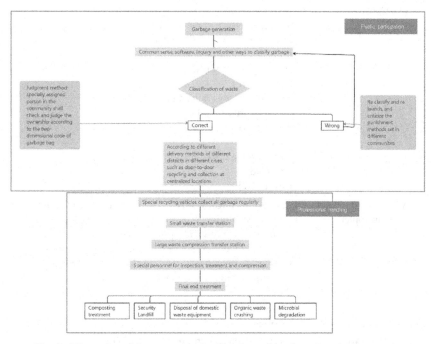

Fig. 2. Waste disposal process (devised by the authors based on the literature).

2 Evaluation

2.1 Test Comparison of Each Platform

Firstly, the platform with large number of users, high degree of online promotion and certain popularity (authority) is selected for testing and comparison. Through the observation and application of the current program, a necessary function of the program is found and the advantages and disadvantages of each program are found through user testing. The test platform has a waste sorting guide (WeChat applet), a waste sorting guide (Alipay applet), an E throw (WeChat applet) and what waste (IOS system software) as shown in Table 1.

The Table 1 lists the UI display and main function settings of each program interface. It can be found that the common point is the text query and recognition. The recognition function and sorting function are the key points. The special points of each program are different, including paying attention to whether the query is comprehensive, whether the interface is beautiful, and associating words to provide users with a better user experience. Through the user interviews later, this paper can determine whether some functions are necessary and which are special points that can bring better experience for users.

Table 1. Comparison of program advantages and disadvantages.

No.	Name	Advantage	Vacancies and Enhancements
1	Waste Sorting Guide (WeChat applet)	Support for China-UK Enquiries Simple interface, four categories are listed waste data for users to learn reference High accuracy of text recognition The word base is rich and the related words are refined There are popular sorting topics Self-Testable Classification Knowledge Cover 46 cities	No photos No voice
2	Waste Sorting Guide (Alipay applet)	Can take pictures, words, speech recognition Introduction to four categories Associated with recyclable services Location of cities throughout the country Reward for answering questions	Popular search features weak Low photo recognition accuracy Function jump more pages, ease of use needs to be strengthened
3	E Throw (WeChat applet)	Word, speech recognition Enquiry will give warm handling tips Voice response for illiterate people	No photos No associative lexicon Interface Design General
4	What Waste (IOS system software)	The interface is clear and simple and the UI design is beautiful Replaceable homepage icon, personalized highlight Mainly speech recognition Word recognition Cover 46 cities	Speech recognition accuracy needs to be improved Restrictions on Mobile User System No photos

2.2 User Interview

The participants for the interview include community residents, college students, enterprise employees, business travelers, outsiders, etc. Therefore, when choosing users, this paper selects five people of each of the above five types for interviews. The interview questions are listed in Table 2. According to the user interview, the obtained information is sorted out and screened, and the affinity graph model is made for analysis, as shown in Fig. 3

Table 2. The main questions mentioned in the interview.

No.	Questions
1	Have you ever responded to the national waste classification online or offline (have you taken the initiative to classify and throw waste, and have you used tools when classifying)?
2	What do you think about the release of waste sorting (how to view the current national trial waste sorting)?
3	What problems have you encountered in waste sorting (recall the whole process of waste disposal)?
4	Where do you base your sorting? (self-feelings, TV, articles, software)?
5	What do you think of the effect of learning through TV, articles, software, and so on?
6	Do you think it's meaningful to build a special waste sorting and recycling app? Will you download and use it?
7	Have you ever used any relevant software? Small programs or apps to view real-time things that are being classified but don't know how to classify them?
8	After using the programs, how will you experience them in the future?
9	Where do you think it is smooth and difficult to use?

Fig. 3. The affinity graph model.

Affinity maps are mainly divided into user experience in dealing with waste and using Alipay applet. Yellow and green are used respectively, as shown in Fig. 4.

Fig. 4. The affinity graph model. (Color figure online)

The information above is summarized in Fig. 5, which are:

- People respond to waste sorting and contribute to environmental protection from their perspectives;
- With the rapid development of the country, more and more waste is produced than ever before. If the waste is not treated according to the sorting, it will lead to more trouble, slower treatment and accelerated environmental degradation; if the waste is treated according to the standard, it will make the most of the resources and reduce the waste of resources; if the waste is classified correctly, it can improve people's quality of life and protect the ecological environment. Forming the habit of waste sorting can effectively reduce a lot of unnecessary work;
- The most common problem that people encountered in waste sorting are insufficient knowledge of waste sorting, lack of knowledge of sorting, open app applet to jump

Fig. 5. The affinity graph model.

through many steps, too troublesome to use, insufficient investment in waste sorting equipment, inconvenient to put waste and psychological discomfort due to wrong sorting;

- The ways of sorting are raised from the publicity of TV advertisements, the surrounding environment, the courses offered by schools or communities, the internet, the cognition of individuals, the inquiry of others, the signs on the waste cans and the community bulletin boards;

- The learning effects of these ways are general, but they are still useful in learning depending on their initiatives. There are too many ways to learn in a systematic and comprehensive way. It is better to make them into animated films to increase their interest and ease of learning;

- Whether the software is practical or not, the evaluation is mixed. The general reason for its utility is that it takes up memory and is not the software that is to be opened frequently. Obviously, it is a step to throw waste, and it will not be troublesome to use the software. The reason for its utility is that it is meaningful to know more about the types of sorting processing and sorting, which is conducive to improving the efficiency of waste sorting.

2.3 Personas

Through the above analysis, the main portrait of a character is established. She is a citizen of Shanghai, as shown in Fig. 6.

Mrs Wang

A 37-year-old resident in Shanghai, housewife, has work, feed one child

"It's hard to sort garbage sometimes, too many clas- sifications make me trouble"

status
1. Too busy very day
2. Want everything easy to deal
3. have trouble with garbage sorting

behavior
1. Trash every day
2. Sort garbage
3. Misclassification (fine)
4. Forget regular processing time

goal
1. Easy and correct sorting
2. Save time & fluently

motivation
1. Environmental protection
2. Respond to national policies
3. Reduce waste of resources

affect
1. Learning source
2. Initiative
3. Bonus system
4. Punishment
5. Knowledge

Fig. 6. The persona detail.

According to the user model, a process map is made to sort out the journey map of the typical user waste sorting, as shown in Fig. 7.

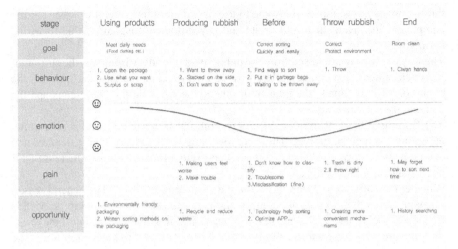

Fig. 7. The user journey map.

3 Problem Definition

3.1 User Requirements

According to the above analysis of touch points and user interviews, the user needs are listed in Table 3.

Table 3. The user needs.

Type	Needs
Emotional experience needs	Keep in mind that it is a convenient procedure for retrieving and classifying popular science wastes at any time
	It can be used by people at home and abroad (Chinese and English)
	Do not force the account to log in. It's useless and annoying
	Do not develop social functions
	What the psychology wants is to learn the correct sorting
	The procedure should be authoritative

(continued)

Table 3. (*continued*)

Type	Needs
Interactive experience requirements	Note that the interactive gestures are not complicated Note that the interaction range is within the easy operation range Interface jump is simple and direct, one step is in place, not two steps Voice assistant interaction, directly ask and directly give the answer
Visual experience needs	Simplify the interface content, less is more Clear and simple interface style to meet the trend of the times
Functional requirement	Improve ease of use The text recognition technology improves the search function, including default search, popular search, historical search and associative word search Take photos to identify and strengthen AI technology Strengthen speech recognition, like accent, add voice assistant Hope to have video teaching or illustration for dealing with more complex waste, so that people can deal with it more regularly Strengthen the connection with the actual situation, add the geographical location technology, and find the location of nearby waste cans List download function, used when offline Integrate platform data, reduce data overlap and save cost

3.2 Experience Objectives

According to the above analysis of user needs, and based on the functions of existing programs to optimize the design of a second program. "Go away, trash!" is for all the people who are confused and need help in waste sorting. Quickly start program does not occupy memory and is not attached to app. It can be started in second without extra steps. And it is associated with the mobile phone's own voice assistant to transmit waste sorting data, so that users can ask for sorting when they can't touch the mobile phone. It provides text, photo and voice recognition functions, and provides information related to waste sorting nearby, which is simple and easy to use, without any burden to users.

4 Solutions

4.1 Software Architecture

In order to solve the problems reflected by users and realize users' needs, this paper proposes the optimal solution, which is to realize the process of waste type identification and correct discarding by opening programs in seconds, and to make users get a better user experience of waste sorting in simple and easy-to-use programs, as shown in Fig. 8.

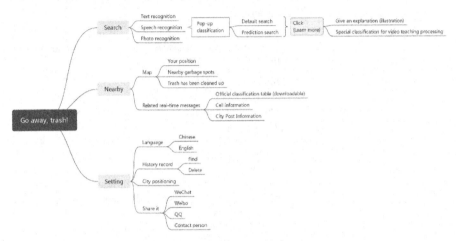

Fig. 8. The software architecture.

4.2 Task Flow

In order to understand the whole workflow more intuitively, this design shows through the flow chart. The purpose of the design is to quickly and simply search, classify and process, so a voice assistant independent of the application program is set up to facilitate fast query results, as shown in Fig. 9. For objects that cannot be accurately identified, it provides more accurate program queries, which provides users with different ways to query in different situations to improve efficiency and user experience. For example, when the object name is uncertain, the photo recognition will be used; if the hands are not easy to touch the mobile phone, the voice function will be implemented, where the text recognition function provides the most accurate results for the user.

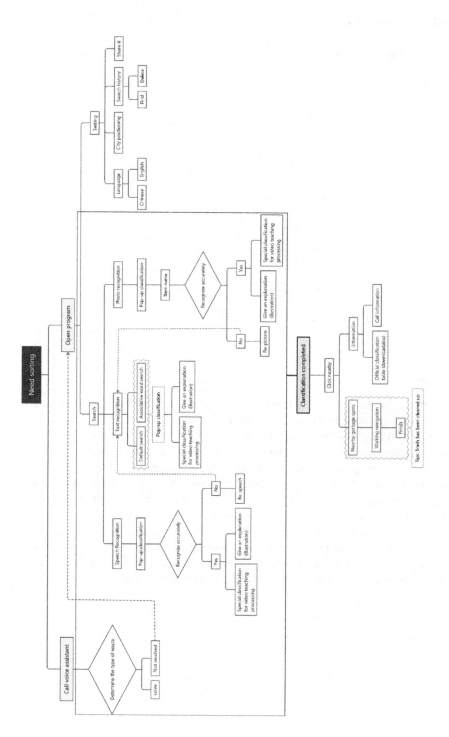

Fig. 9. The task flow.

5 Prototype Design

5.1 Low Fidelity Interface

The main pages of app are illustrated in Fig. 10.

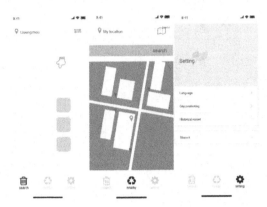

Fig. 10. Main pages of low fidelity prototype.

5.2 Usage Flow

The overall goal of the program is to reduce skip steps, keep the interface clear and improve usability and availability. It can be seen from the Fig. 11 that the basic operations of the three query methods are completed in two steps as far as possible. The most accurate character recognition is the lowest guarantee of the query program. And it provides support in the process of deep learning of voice and photo technology.

In order to facilitate the user in a strange environment to deal with waste, the program sets up a map mode, as shown in Fig. 12. In this interface, users can find the nearest waste disposal point and locate it by navigation. At the same time, in order to make users have a sense of mission to correctly classify waste, after the waste truck is cleaned, the interface will also display the prompt notice as 'waste has been processed'. The interface also provides real-time information to help the original residents and residents staying for a short time to understand the waste disposal situation in this area.

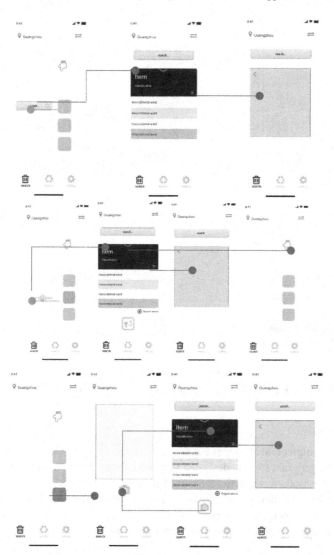

Fig. 11. Main function use process.

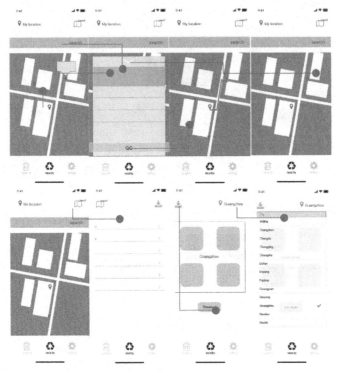

Fig. 12. Main function use process of map mode.

5.3 Design Style

Design style is implemented to make it easier for users to accept and use the program. First of all, the program logo is designed in a modern style with simple and generous, in line with the modern aesthetic. The overall color is blue tone, giving a clean and refreshing feeling. Secondly, the program opens quickly, functions are clear, skip is simple and easy to operate, as shown in Fig. 13. At last, every step of the design is to improve the user's preference value and attract more users.

Fig. 13. The APP logo design. (Color figure online)

5.4 High Fidelity Interface

Subsequently, a high fidelity interface of the APP as shown in Fig. 14 is designed based on the low fidelity version.

Fig. 14. Main interface display.

Fig. 14. (*continued*)

5.5 Usability Test

In user testing, four test scenarios are provided for 20 users, which results are showing in Table 4 and Table 5. Scenario 1: when you have just finished eating KFC family buckets and have oil on your hands, you want to clean up and throw into the waste bin, but you

Table 4. Scenario test results.

	User 1				User 2				User 3				User 4			
Scenario 1	1	2	3	4	1	2	3	4	1	2	3	4	1	2	3	4
Finish (time)	79	15	34	27	63	16	15	20	72	25	20	30	50	13	21	29
Skip (time)	9	3	5	6	6	3	2	5	7	5	3	7	5	3	3	7
Mistake	2	0	0	0	1	0	0	0	2	1	0	0	0	0	0	0
	User 5				User 6				User 7				User 8			
Scenario 2	1	2	3	4	1	2	3	4	1	2	3	4	1	2	3	4
Finish (time)	50	15	14	26	34	14	20	30	70	15	14	29	48	14	19	30
Skip (time)	6	4	2	6	4	3	3	7	9	3	2	7	6	3	3	7
Mistake	0	0	0	0	0	0	0	0	2	0	0	0	0	0	0	0
	User 9				User 10				User 11				User 12			
Scenario 3	1	2	3	4	1	2	3	4	1	2	3	4	1	2	3	4
Finish (time)	59	15	14	21	21	15	14	27	68	16	21	21	35	13	17	28
Skip (time)	6	3	2	5	2	3	2	6	7	3	3	5	4	3	2	7
Mistake	1	0	0	0	0	0	0	0	1	0	0	0	0	0	0	0
	User 13				User 14				User 15				User 16			
Scenario 4	1	2	3	4	1	2	3	4	1	2	3	4	1	2	3	4
Finish (time)	74	19	34	26	27	20	15	21	46	15	23	28	40	14	14	31
Skip (time)	8	5	4	6	2	5	2	5	7	4	3	7	6	3	2	7
Mistake	2	1	0	0	0	1	0	0	0	0	0	0	0	0	0	0
	User 17				User 18				User 19				User 20			
Scenario 5	1	2	3	4	1	2	3	4	1	2	3	4	1	2	3	4
Finish (time)	68	14	30	20	61	12	13	26	40	16	15	29	50	14	14	28
Skip (time)	7	3	4	5	7	3	2	6	5	4	2	7	6	3	2	7
Mistake	2	0	0	0	1	0	0	0	0	0	0	0	0	0	0	0

don't know how to accurately classify them, and how do you use the software? Scenario 2: how do you use the software when you can't tell the object's name clearly? Scenario 3: how do you classify and deal with old refrigerators? Scenario 4: you are on the street and there is no waste bin nearby you.

Table 5. User comments.

No.	Comments
1	I don't know much about waste sorting. The design of the topic is ingenious. It's easy to make mistakes in the first use
2	The voice interface can be improved and looks tight at the moment
3	I found that the recognized categories are all blue, resulting in a little visual fatigue, which can be changed
4	The interface is simple in general, and each page is easy to operate, and there is no redundant content interference
5	When searching in the refrigerator, I got help in jumping to how recyclable
6	There are many recognition methods to choose, but the voice assistant uses less, and I always forget this function. Users trust text recognition most
7	The accuracy of photographing and speech recognition needs to be enhanced

In the scenario 1, due to the complexity and bewilderment of KFC family buckets, there is no corresponding sorting at present, which cannot be found by direct search. Inertia thinking makes nine users making mistakes and causes the search time is prolonged. Others search just for uncertain object sorting separately, which takes a short time. In the scenario 2, all the users took photos for recognition, and three of them were not identified clearly. In the scenario 3, two users prefer voice assistant, seven of them choose voice and 11 users choose character recognition. In the scenario 4, 10 users choose character recognition, five of them choose voice recognition and the rest choose photo recognition. There is no obstacle to skip to the map interface. The further optimized APP interfaces are as shown in Fig. 15.

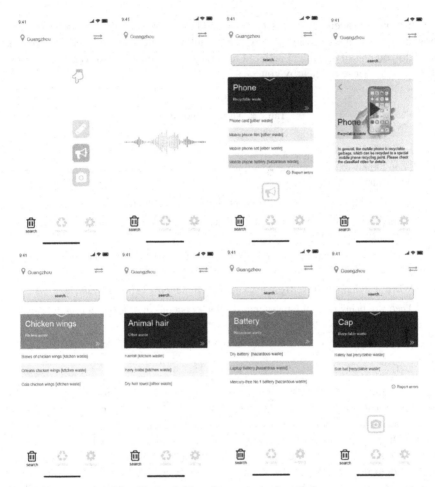

Fig. 15. Partial interface optimization display.

6   Conclusion

This paper discusses the usability of user experience in the field of waste treatment in smart city, where the waste sorting is an important part of the research on smart cities in China currently. At present, there are various waste sorting related smart applications in the Alipay, and WeChat applet. These applications are very complicated and less usability of user experience design for users, which they cannot perfectly solve the user problems and the user experience needs to be improved. As such, the purpose of this paper is to solve the problem with user research centered smart application design for users to sorting and deal with the waste accurately with improved user experience and usability living in smart city. Through literature review and user research to find the pain points of the users, this study proposes to design a quickly program to solve the problem, which uses authoritative data, simple style and crisp interaction to provide users with a quick, convenient and simple way to solve sorting problems. In addition, it provides a simple map for people who are not familiar with the area and cannot find a waste disposal place to dispose waste. Finally, the usability is used to test and iterate the program to form the final optimization program. The result of this design is to provide an application program for waste sorting to help user better to respond to national policies. And through improving the usability of the program, the user's experience in the waste disposal process is improved.

Acknowledgements. The authors wish to thank all the people who involved in this study. This research is supported by "South China University of Technology Central University Basic Scientific Research Operating Expenses Subsidy (project approval no. XYZD201928)".

References

1. Medvedev, A., Fedchenkov, P., Zaslavsky, A., Anagnostopoulos, T., Khoruzhnikov, S.: Waste management as an IoT-enabled service in smart cities. In: Balandin, S., Andreev, S., Koucheryavy, Y. (eds.) ruSMART 2015. LNCS, vol. 9247, pp. 104–115. Springer, Cham (2015). https://doi.org/10.1007/978-3-319-23126-6_10
2. Anagnostopoulos, T., Kolomvatsos, K., Anagnostopoulos, C., Zaslavsky, A., Hadjiefthymiades, S.: Assessing dynamic models for high priority waste collection in smart cities. J. Syst. Softw. **110**, 178–192 (2015)
3. Anagnostopoulos, T., et al.: A stochastic multi-agent system for Internet of Things-enabled waste management in smart cities. Waste Manage. Res. **36**(11), 1113–1121 (2018)
4. Marques, P., et al.: An IoT-based smart cities infrastructure architecture applied to a waste management scenario. Ad Hoc Netw. **87**, 200–208 (2019)
5. Shah, P.J., Anagnostopoulos, T., Zaslavsky, A., Behdad, S.: A stochastic optimization framework for planning of waste collection and value recovery operations in smart and sustainable cities. Waste Manag **78**, 104–114 (2018)
6. Tong, Y., Liu, J., Liu, S.: China is implementing "Garbage Classification" action. Environ. Pollut. **259**, 113707 (2020)
7. Santoso, H.B., Schrepp, M.: The impact of culture and product on the subjective importance of user experience aspects. Heliyon **5**(9), e02434 (2019)

Evolution of Public Transport in Rural Areas - New Technologies and Digitization

Joachim R. Daduna[✉]

Berlin School of Economics and Law, Berlin 14050, Germany
daduna@hwr-berlin.de

Abstract. Public transport in rural areas is currently often characterized by inadequate services, so that motorized private transport dominates these areas. This situation is considered to be unsatisfactory from an economic and social policy perspective, as it has considerable negative environmental effects. The main problems here are a decline in economic performance and an aging population as well as an increasing rural exodus. With the development of autonomously driving vehicles, it is now possible to achieve fundamental changes in the design of public transport services especially in terms of cost structures and attractiveness. However, this does not mean that the current structures of line-based service should be eliminated and completely replaced by new, quasi-individual forms of services. Rather, the objective is to extend the existing structures in order to significantly improve mobility provision through more flexibility and thus more attractiveness. The technical basics required for this exist or are already very advanced in the developments. In addition to the necessary vehicles, it is in particular the information and communication systems required for extensive interconnected network structures. However, to make the transformation successful, new organizational concepts and in particular a fundamental rethinking are required. It is not only the technical design of transport, but also to ensure the mobility needs of the population. The related developments and future tasks are outlined and discussed below.

Keywords: Public transport in rural areas · Autonomous vehicles · Quasi-individual mobility

1 Introduction

Public transport is on the way to a comprehensive redesign. The reasons for this far-reaching transition result from the changed requirements in mobility services, the necessary reduction of current individual motorized traffic and the simultaneous growth in public transport, especially from an ecological point of view. Within the (technical) framework in the last years, however, there have been substantial limits that, together with a strong focus on (private) individual mobility, have led to a situation that is not politically desirable for a number of reasons.

However, a structural differentiation must be made here. In urban areas, public transport has steadily increased in importance due to the existing settlement structures and

© Springer Nature Switzerland AG 2020
A. Marcus and E. Rosenzweig (Eds.): HCII 2020, LNCS 12202, pp. 82–99, 2020.
https://doi.org/10.1007/978-3-030-49757-6_6

the framework conditions of the existing traffic infrastructure. The focus here is on rail-based transport systems with high capacities as well as efficient *bus rapid transit* (BRT) *systems* both in connection with established busses (standard and articulated busses) with varying capacities for feeder and distribution services. The reason for using these types of vehicles are primarily the limitation of the available traffic area and the resulting inner-city traffic congestion problems. However (especially in urban areas) there is an increasing change in personal attitudes towards individual mobility as well as a greater awareness of traffic-related environmental pollution.

The current weaknesses in public transport, on the other hand, are evident in rural areas (see, e.g., Petersen 2016; Šipuš and Abramoviś 2017; Berg and Ihlström 2019). Individual mobility dominates here, primarily in developed countries. The reasons for this are the very low volume of demand in these regions (apart from commuter traffic) and the higher costs associated with a better service level. The revenue that can be achieved on the basis of socially justifiable fares cannot be cost-covering in anyway, that means, there is a high need for subsidies which, under realistic assumptions, cannot generally be met by the public budgets.

With the technological developments of the past few years, especially here due to autonomous driving, completely new possibilities to organize public transport arise. A necessary prerequisite for this, however, is comprehensive digitization, which is imperative to develop attractive service structures and to control the associated processes as well as to communicate the offered services to (potential) users. The last point is of considerable importance for the realization of new service structures, because a fundamental rule from marketing says that a customer will not buy a product he do not know.

In the following description, the current situation of public passenger transport in rural areas is outlined first. This is followed by a brief summary of the current developments in autonomous vehicle techniques for passenger transport in the field of road transport. Afterwards, the general conditions for an area-wide use of autonomously driving vehicles are discussed as well as the main advantages for their operational use. Based on this, quasi-individual forms of mobility are described, with the help of which public passenger transport in rural areas can be made more efficient and more attractive. Then the necessary technical and organizational requirements are explained, in particular with regard to the required information and communication structures. Finally, there are a short outlook and some comments on the further developments.

2   Public Transport in Rural Areas

Public transport in rural areas is a problem that has been repeatedly discussed for decades. Before the beginning of the expansion of wide-ranging individual mobility through the availability of private cars for a broad share of the population, regional rail and interurban bus transport in the (developed) countries was of considerable importance for ensuring mobility services. With the evolving changes in mobility behavior, the demand and with it the importance of these services decreased considerably, so that they currently only play an essential role in commuter traffic and local and regional school traffic.

In terms of transport volume in passenger transport, especially in developed countries, the demand in rural areas is often very low. This means that the existing mobility demand is largely covered by the use of private cars, with corresponding negative effects regarding to traffic-related environmental pollution. In the Federal Republic of Germany, the share of private car transport in rural area is up to 70%, with a public transport share of 5%, (see, Nobis and Kuhnimhof 2018, p. 40) which is to be regarded as completely unsatisfactory. Also with a view to the increasingly propagated climate policy objectives, it is necessary not only to make the appropriate changes in the long term, but as soon as possible.

In the developing and emerging countries, the available services in rural areas are often insufficient due to the framework conditions there. Even if regional rail and bus transport networks exist to a certain extent, in most cases the line network structure and the range of services offered are not suitable to meet existing demand (see, e.g., Sonderegger et al. 2019). Parallel to these there exist flexible and (partly) demand-dependent services with an often individual vehicle design, also known as *paratransit* (see, e.g., Cervero 1991; Cervero and Golub 2007; Phun and Yai 2016), but also in urban areas (see, the examples in Wicaksono et al. 2015). Examples from the rural area can be found around the world. These are usually less structured services operated normally by micro-entrepreneurs applying smaller vehicles (mainly mini and midi busses, but also different types of converted trucks), which run worldwide under different names, e.g., Camiones (Cuba), Camioneta (Guatemala), Dolmuş (Turkey) Marschrutka (in countries from the former Sowjet Union), Porpuesto (South American countries), Tanka tanka (Gambia) and Taxi pirata (Costa Rica) (see, e.g., the examples in Fig. 1).

Fig. 1. Paratransit vehicles operating in Cuba (l) and Colombia (r).

In recent years, however, new technical developments have emerged in many fields that can form an essential basis for disruptive changes. For public passenger transport in rural areas, two developments are in the foreground, the availability of autonomous vehicles for use in the public road network and the (almost complete) digitization of information management. In the medium and long term, these can offer the opportunity to develop and introduce new and more attractive public transport service structures.

3   Developments in Autonomous Driving

The estimations regarding future developments in the area of autonomously driving vehicles in road transport can be seen very clearly in the changes in market participants in the automotive sector. It is no longer just the traditional car manufacturers (e.g., BMW AG, Daimler AG, Toyota Motor Corporation and Volkswagen AG) and also new car manufacturers who enter the market (e.g., Tesla, Inc.), but also companies from the internet industry (e.g., Alphabet Inc.) and from the electronics industry (e.g., Sony Corporation). From this, however, it can be seen that this is a long-term important sales market, in which, however, it is still open who will ensure market leadership with which (technical) focus. In any case, the decisive development steps for the introduction of autonomously driving vehicles in road traffic have been successfully implemented in recent years (see, e.g., Fagnant and Kockelman 2015; Chan 2017; Haboucha et al. 2017; Meyer et al. 2017; Ainsalu et al. 2018; Martínez-Díaz and Soriguera 2018; Hulse et al. 2018; Schwarting et al. 2018; Martínez-Díaz et al. 2019; Soteropoulos et al. 2019; Doerr and Romstorfer 2020).

The technical basics for autonomous driving are largely in place. These are primarily the components that are already available or in the process of further development from the field of *Advanced Driver Assistance Systems* (ADAS) (see, e.g., Ainsalu et al. 2018; Kukkala et al. 2018; Arnold et al. 2019; Haas et al. 2020). Another field is a sufficient performance of location and environment recognition techniques, which is also available (see, e.g., Bresson et al. 2017; Chindhe 2018; Kuutti et al. 2018). This includes satellite-based positioning, for example based on the *Differential Global Positioning System* (DGPS) or the (European) navigation system *Galileo*, as well as a continuous and real-time environmental detection based on *Simultaneous Localization and Mapping* (SLAM) *technologies*, the components of which some are also integrated into the ADAS structures. But the information and communication structures for connected driving, such as *vehicle-to-vehicle* (V2V) *communication*, *vehicle-to-infrastructure* (V2I) *communication*, and *vehicle-to-everything* (V2X) *communication* have not yet been sufficiently developed (see, e.g., Arena and Pau 2019; Montanaro et al. 2019; Tiwari and Akhilesh 2020).

Associated with the discussions about the introduction of autonomous driving in the political environment is often the question of the form of drive of the vehicles, even if this does not play a role with regard to the conceptual design. The reason for this is the close connection of the vehicle development with ecological objectives, also with a view to the negative environmental influences of road traffic. This has led to that, despite of significant technical developments, the diesel drive is often considered to be an undesirable technique. As an alternative, other fuels with comparatively lower emissions were also tested for use but could not prevail. Biodiesel proved to be a very controversial solution due to the lack of sustainability in terms of production, especially with regard to the competition with the food sector. Also in the last decades the use of *Liquefied Natural Gas* (LNG) was ultimately unsuccessful for technical and economic reasons.

At present, therefore, electric traction is the preferred solution, although this technology is not uncontroversial (see, e.g., Piatkowski and Puszkiewicz 2018). At a first view, it seems to be an appropriate step in order to reduce emission loads. However, this effect only occurs locally in the affected urban areas. It is not taken into account that there exist negative environmental effects in the manufacturing processes, amongst other things, in connection with the procurement of raw materials for the production of the required batteries. Therefore, long-term sustainability of electro mobility will ultimately depend on longstanding ecological and economic benefits. In addition, it must be waited whether in the next years with the fuel cell a better alternative will be available (see, e.g., Alaswad et al. 2016; Miotti et al. 2017; Moriarty and Honnery 2019; Tang et al. 2019), especially in the commercial vehicle sector.

Regardless of the question of the drive technology used, which is currently still often based on diesel engines, the developments in autonomous vehicles show a clear market expansion. Worldwide, there are more and more applications in the field of public road transport networks that go beyond a test operation, both in freight and in passenger transport. Even if the "learning phase" of the vehicles, that means, the training of the software for autonomous control and monitoring of the vehicles, has not yet been completed, the transition to real operation begins in a number of cases.

A significant increase in the use of autonomous vehicles in passenger road transport is forecast for the coming years (see, e.g., Möller et al. 2019). It is assumed that the traffic volume (in passenger kilometers) will triple from 2018 to 2040, based on the situation in major cities worldwide. In 2040 the share that is generated by autonomously driving vehicles is assumed to 66%, with 83.3% being public transport services in different forms. At the same time the share of mobility volume with private cars will decrease from 90% to 39%. With a view to the (politically prescribed) climate policy objectives, it must be assumed, however, that these forecast developments will only be possible on the framework condition that emission-free drive techniques can prevail on the market in the long term (see, e.g., Martínez-Díaz et al. 2019).

The use of autonomously driving vehicles is also associated with an expansion of individual mobility (see, e.g., Kaplan et al. 2019). The present access restriction to defined groups of people (age, driving license, physical aptitude) can be dropped. In this way, under-aged, elder, and handicapped people in particular also have their own access, which will have very significant positive effects on the design of social structures (see, e.g., Milakis and van Wee 2020). This applies in particular to rural areas, where there are significant mobility restrictions due to the undersupply in public passenger transport, especially for the mentioned groups of people.

In the development of autonomous driving, a number of vehicles have also been developed in recent years which are intended for use in *public passenger transport*. These are essentially three basic types with different capacities (*passenger cars* and *vans*, *small*, *mid-sized* and *greater minibuses* as well as *standard* and *articulated busses*), which can be used in accordance with the existing spatial based demand structures (see, e.g., López-Lambas and Alonso 2019). This applies to urban areas (see, e.g. Ainsalu et al. 2018) but much more to rural areas (see Sect. 2).

4 Advantages and Framework Conditions for the Use of Autonomous Vehicles

The acceptance of vehicle systems does not only depend on the technical performance, but also to a considerable extent on economic and increasingly also on ecological advantages. Adequate market penetration and thus economic viability can only be achieved under these conditions (see, e.g., Acheampong and Cugurullo 2019).

Looking at the advantages of autonomous driving a focus is on personnel costs (see, e.g., Tirachini and Antoniou 2020), because these are reduced to a considerable extent, apart from the costs for service, maintenance and repair personnel. This has a particular impact on the transport of people in the area of road traffic, because here, in comparison with other modes of transport, there is the most unfavorable relation between personnel costs and transport capacity. In addition, there are no longer any restrictive labor law regulations (e.g., working time, driving time, mandatory breaks, minimum duration of rest periods, etc.), through which both the service and the operations design can take place in a completely new framework.

By eliminating the human factor when driving a vehicle, emotionally influenced behaviors are eliminated. This causes significant fuel savings between 15% and 30% and thereby also a reduction of traffic-related emissions. With an increasing of CO_2 pricing, this also results in additional savings in operational costs.

Further, also very considerable cost savings result from the reduction of road traffic accidents (see, e.g., Ilkova and Ilka 2017). On the one hand it is a *quantitative cost reduction*, relating to the number of accidents and on the other hand it is a *qualitative cost reduction* in terms of severity. Taking the number of accidents recorded by the police of the Federal Republic of Germany in 2018 as an example, it shows that 88.4% of all road traffic accidents (of 2,636,468) were caused by vehicle drivers (and 3.2% by pedestrians), that means, 91.6% of accidents are caused by human error (see, Destatis 2020, p. 49). This is not a specific German situation because the share for all countries of the European Union is about 90% (see, e.g., Martínez-Díaz et al. 2019). In the case of accidents with personal injuries (a total of 15% of all accidents), the causes lies in human errors when turning, turning around, reversing as well as entering and exiting (15.5%), disregarding the right of way and priority (13.8%), inadequate distance to other vehicles (13.4%), driving at inappropriate speed (11.0%), as well as when driving under the influence of alcohol (3.2%) (see, Destatis 2020, p. 50).

The data show the importance of the human factor in the occurrence of traffic accidents in road traffic (see, e.g., Ainsalu et al. 2018; Grunwald 2019; Martínez-Díaz et al. 2019) and thus in the direct accident-related costs as well as the long-term follow-up costs. However, autonomous driving will not make it possible to completely avoid accidents in the future, especially if the traffic infrastructure is shared with conventionally used vehicles (see, e.g., Grunwald 2019). In addition, there are accidents caused by pedestrians or cyclists, which cannot be prevented (or only to a limited extent) by a high level of performance in situational detection in autonomous vehicles. However, halving the number of accidents, not only in the Federal Republic of Germany, would lead to considerable (short-term) savings at the operational level and also to a reduction in (long-term) economic costs, particularly in the health care system and in accident-related (public) care services.

The elimination of the human factor not only has an impact on the cost structures, but there are completely new possibilities in the design of the operational service processes in both freight and passenger transport. Only technical restrictions can influence these processes, but for example, not labor law regulations. In addition to the advantage of greater flexibility with regard to serving customer requirements, there are also cost advantages that result from more efficient and more customer-oriented process design for the operational procedures.

However, not only economical and technical aspects are important at this point, but also the question of adapting the legal framework conditions (see, e.g., Gasser 2016; Schreurs and Steuwer 2015; Bartolini et al. 2017; Ainsalu et al. 2018; Stender-Vorwachs and Steege 2018). The main legal problem is the ban that the public traffic area is used simultaneously by manually operated and autonomous vehicles. The basis for this is the *European Agreement, Supplementing the 1968 Convention on Road Traffic*, in conjunction with the national traffic laws. The regulation for ADAS-supported operation that has been in force in the European Union since 2016 continues to require a driver who can or may have to intervene. This clearly clarifies the legal responsibility. Apart from a few examples, test projects can currently only be carried out with exceptional permits. Another question to be discussed is which legal regulations are necessary for the use of the data collected, especially by third parties (see, e.g., Stender-Vorwachs and Steege 2018).

For the future use of autonomous driving, a suitable legal basis must be created for damage cases. That means, the question of the culpability of machines must ultimately be clarified within the legal framework (see, e.g., Stender-Vorwachs and Steege 2018; Grunwald 2019; Lenk 2019; Martínez-Díaz et al. 2019). For example, the vehicle manufacturer, a software or component supplier, the owner or the respective user is liable or there is another form of claim settlement. The critical point here is the occurrence of dilemma situations in which serious consequences of an accident for individual road users depend on situational decisions made by machines (see, e.g., Stender-Vorwachs and Steege 2018; Grunwald 2019; Lenk 2019). In conventional driving, people decide, in autonomous operation the designer of the corresponding software systems makes the rules for the decision. Relating to this critical problem there are very controversial discussions regarding ethical acceptability, but these have not yet led to a satisfactory solution.

Another legal problem field is the question of responsibility for traffic offences (see, e.g., Gasser 2016), which must be examined. An important step here can be a complete recording of all processes via black box systems, which (but then for all vehicles in public road traffic) would have to be prescribed by law.

In addition, the question of public acceptance is of considerable importance for future market penetration (see, e.g., Fraedrich and Lenz 2016; Acheampong and Cugurullo 2019; López-Lambas and Alonso 2019; Avermann and Schlüter 2020; Bissell et al. 2020). The focus here is on the discussion of possible uses and any risks that may arise, but these must also be seen in a changing environment. With the decline in the importance of one's own private car as a social status symbol and an increasing spread of the sharing economy, some changes in the societal framework are associated. It follows, for example, that a renouncement of the individual mobility that has been propagated for decades as a symbol of individual freedom. This is accepted much more strongly in urban regions, depending on the offered public transport services. In contrast, due to insufficient services in rural areas, its use is low. For this purpose, the use of private cars is seen as necessary, and viewed less critically due to the greater availability of space and less traffic problems. Furthermore, the fundamental position towards questions on environmental protection also plays a role, as well as consistent rejections of technological developments, partly due to the uncertainty regarding unpredictable negative consequences.

5 Re-design of Public Transport in Rural Areas

The availability of autonomous vehicles for passenger transport in rural areas is of particular importance. This opens up completely new possibilities for the design of an efficient and attractive public transport system that has never been possible before (see, e.g., Sonderegger et al. 2019; Soteropoulos et al. 2019). The far-reaching elimination of the personnel cost as a substantial factor and the detachment of the service planning from labor law restrictions is the essential basis. In principle, individual customer demand can be the decisive basis for planning public transport services. The main objective must be to ensure a basic mobility, especially regarding to services of public interest. In the foreground is, for example, an extension of service periods, also with an orientation to seven days with a 24-h service.

In addition to the (regional) rail passenger transport systems as well as the regional bus and school bus systems, which must continue to form a basic network with timetable-based services, new forms can be included that enable *quasi-individual mobility* (see, e.g., Saeed and Kurauchi 2015) that lead to a transition from a technical oriented (traditional) passenger transport to connected mobility services (see, e.g., Jittrapirom et al. 2018; Mulley et al. 2018; Utriainen and Pöllänen 2018). The main forms of such *mobility as a service* (MaaS) *concepts* are innovative taxi services, modified carsharing concepts, ridesharing concepts and on-demand transport services based on autonomous vehicles (see. e.g., Kamargianni et al. 2016; Shaheen and Cohen 2020; Tyrinopoulos and Antoniou 2020).

Autonomous Taxis: This is a cost-effective extension of the classic range of individual transport services (see, e.g., Tussyadiah et al. 2017). The main aspects are the cost savings due to the elimination of the driver as well as the possibility of an unrestricted service time.

Modified Carsharing Concepts: The classical (station-based) carsharing services (see, e.g., Lenz and Fraedrich 2016; Namazu et al. 2018; Perboli et al. 2018; Webb et al. 2019; Shaheen et al. 2020), where vehicles have to be returned at defined locations, are only applied in urban areas usually. This is possible here due to the existing demand structures, but not in rural areas. However, if autonomously driving vehicles are available, an assignment to determined stations after finishing a trip is no longer necessary and a transition to free floating carsharing (see, e.g., Shaheen et al. 2020) is possible. Here, the vehicles can either be sent to the location of a next customer, or they can be made available at a specified location, close to expected customers. In a long-term view such a service may be a chance to reduce the high level of private car ownership (see, e.g. the current situation from the Federal Republic of Germany in Nobis and Kuhnimhof 2018, p. 40) and therefore the number car trips (see also, Kaplan et al. 2019 and Liao et al. 2018).

Ridesharing: This form, in which several customers use a vehicle together on different sections of a route, is not new from the basic approach (see, e.g., Najmi et al. 2017; Dong et al. 2018; Farhan and Chen 2018; Hyland and Mahmassani 2018; Richter et al. 2019; Shaheen et al. 2020). Such carpooling has been taking place for many years, mostly in rush hour transport, where a time and direction-related bundling of trips is possible, or within the framework of informal structures at the local level (see, e.g., Meyer 1982). However, there are also limitations due to various restrictive conditions that have previously prevented widespread applications. With the use of autonomously driving vehicles, ridesharing can be made much more flexible and integrated as an additional component in public passenger transport.

On-Demand Public Transport Services: These are primarily *dial-a-bus concepts* or *demand-responsive transport* (DRT) *concepts* mostly based on minibuses. Characteristic of these types of services is a demand-dependent transport, which is ordered by customers, either ad hoc in connection with an immediately intended departure, or in advance for a specific date or time slot. The aim here is to try to counteract existing supply deficits, whereby different organizational forms can occur. The services can be organized *line-based*, *corridor-based* and *area-based* (as the variant with the most flexibility). Such types of services have been discussed for several decades and have been operationally tested in various forms, including as group-specific services (for example handicapped persons or elder people) (see, e.g., Schiefelbusch 2016).

However, such concepts were implemented successfully in practice only in a few cases but then often discontinued. The main reasons for this were the high costs of conventionally operated vehicles (see, e.g., Meyer 1982; Ryley et al. 2014), the lack of suitable information and communication systems, an inadequately accurate description of the road network structures, and an unreasonable range of services, especially due to restrictive working time regulations. In addition, there were also politically desired restrictions to avoid competition with existing public transport services, as well as resistance from the trade unions regarding the reduction of jobs when volunteer drivers were deployed in locally oriented on demand services (see, e.g., Meyer 1982).

With the availability of autonomously driving minibuses and the technical developments in the context of digitization, new operating options have emerged worldwide in recent years. There are currently various applications, especially in urban areas (see, e.g., Ainsalu et al. 2018), which are still predominantly in test operation. Similar developments are also increasingly evident in rural areas such as in the Federal Republic of Germany, but not across the whole country and not very structured (see, e.g., Hänsch et al. 2019). In some cases, however, the transition to regular operation has already taken place, for example, in the Bad Birnbach area (see, e.g., Barillère-Scholz et al. 2020; Kolb et al. 2020). Such services will be an essential element in the redesign of public transport, especially in rural areas (see, e.g., von Mörner and Boltze 2018) due to the operational framework and the significant quality improvements.

The core problem of the design is the connection of these four outlined forms of quasi-individual mobility based on autonomous vehicles with the traditional public transport services. Due to the existing demand structures, these are still mandatory for the operation of commuter traffic in rural areas (see, e.g., Robson et al. 2018). A substitution with the new services is not possible, neither organizational nor traffic related (see, e.g., Metz

2018). A major restriction is that especially in the cities the availability of traffic space is limited, and this is also to be reduced more and more in connection with an inner-city redesign.

The convergence of transport systems in public passenger transport towards a dominance of quasi-individual mobility outlined by Ennoch (2015) seems to be unlikely under these framework conditions. A displacement of buses from the transport services in the cities (see also Hannon et al. 2019 and Sonderegger et al. 2019) is not realistic due to the existing demand structures. However, a substitution of underutilized standard buses in rural areas or in smaller cities (see, e.g., Winter et al. 2018) can be possible and also be useful. This applies to public transport access at local level and to a certain extent on regional level as well as feeder and distribution traffic (on the last mile) for the connection to higher-level traffic systems (see, e.g., Scheltes and de Almeida Correia 2017). Figure 2 shows a basic concept of such an interconnected service structure for public passenger transport in rural areas.

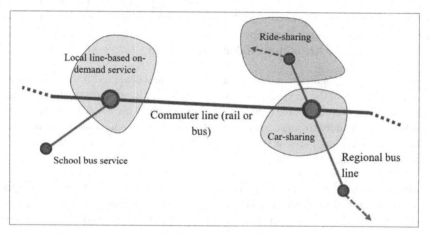

Fig. 2. Interconnected service structures for public passenger transport in rural areas.

A sufficiently qualified transport infrastructure, the availability of the required vehicle systems and (largely) comprehensive digitization of the transport sector are necessary for the operational implementation of novative transport services. Even if the technical developments mentioned have not yet been completed, it is still necessary to design the conceptual structures in a targeted manner so that corrections do not have to be made later. This applies in particular to road traffic infrastructure and an efficient digital infrastructure.

6 Planning and Control of Passenger Transport Processes

A mandatory prerequisite for the successful integration of quasi-individual mobility services in public transport in rural areas is their interconnection with the actual existing services, but not their substitution. However, this requires a profound change in the planning processes as well as in the control and monitoring of operations. In addition, continuous online communication between provider and customer must be guaranteed on the basis of planned data as well as on real-time data. Perhaps the most difficult part of the implementation is the development of a suitable tariff structure and the revenue sharing system among the service providers involved. With regard to the planning and control measures, the tasks outlined below result.

Network and Service Planning: There are no significant changes when planning the conventionally designed transport services (for train and standard busses), since the functional tasks remain the same. For this area, on a centralized level there will continue the planning of area-based line networks and timetables as well as the timetable synchronization. Afterwards, a coordinated vehicle and personnel requirements planning for the participating transport companies follows. With regard to the quasi-individual parts of the services, only transfer points to the higher-level network can be defined and an estimation of the vehicle requirement based on expected demand volumes, apart from the cases in which a line or corridor-based operating structure is intended. Applying line-based services the route and stops must be defined and in the case corridor-based services in addition the size of the corridors must be fixed.

Operative Planning: In this area, too, not any fundamental changes for the network and timetable-based part of the services is necessary. On the one hand, appropriate computer-aided planning tools are available here, with the help of which the needed vehicle blocks, duty schedules, and duty rosters can be calculated for the transport companies involved. For the quasi-individual parts of the services, on the other hand, only the number of required vehicles can be planned.

Operational Control and Monitoring: These tasks require new concepts, since all operations in a complex interconnected network structure must be monitored simultaneously in real time. This is imperative in order to be able to handle the on-demand customer requests even at short notice, especially when connecting to conventional transport services. The autonomous vehicles are scheduled dynamically at this level, where short-term changes in demand, for example, additional customer requests, have to be permanently included.

Passenger Information: The currently available passenger information systems based on *stationary* or *mobile devices* (smartphones, tablet computers, etc.) are only suitable to a limited extent for the integration of on-demand services within the framework of quasi-individual mobility structures. They are based on line network and timetable data that are known, partly including actual deviations that are recorded and made available with the help of *Intermodal Transport Control Systems* (ITCS) or, for example, real-time data based on information from *automated fare collection systems* (see, e.g., Jevinger and Persson (2019) as the basis for *dynamic passenger information* (see, e.g., Papangelis et al. 2016; Viergutz 2016; Corsar et al. 2017; Harmony and Gayah 2017). These are generally suitable to display multimodal connections based on classical transport modes, but not for including on-demand trips. Only information regarding the fixed transfer options to on-demand services can be integrated into the existing systems, which is not a sufficient solution to offer attractive information services from customer's point of view.

This means that new information systems with a significantly higher scope of performance are required (see, e.g., Lathia et al. 2012; Beutel et al. 2016; Szigeti et al. 2017), which are based on a communication platform through which a constant communication between the service provider and the customer is guaranteed. The provision of information must include, among others, two variants of queries. On the one hand, it is about querying information regarding an immediately intended (also multimodal) trip and then booking when a suitable offer is suggested. However, interactive communication processes may also be necessary until an offer is accepted. On the other hand, there must be the option of ordering a trip for a later date and, if desired, also reserving it, whereby a certain flexibility must remain possible for the on-demand trips involved, until a customer actually starts his trip.

In addition, a fundamental structural change to the information systems is necessary. These must be uniformly designed and operated systems in which all the transport providers involved are integrated. These must be connected to the higher-level communication platform mentioned above, regardless of the used communication devices. The underlying service areas should be large and overlap with neighboring areas in the peripheral zones to enable an attractive offer.

Tariff Structure and Revenue Allocation: The development of a suitable tariff structure is a very complex problem because it is a decisive factor for the acceptance of public passenger transport services. It must base on a clear and understandable concept and thereby the principle *"one trip - one price"* must be adhered to. In the case of multimodal trips with very different means of transport, however, the question then arises as to how the isolated trip segments of the different transport companies are to be valued in monetary terms and how a total price (which is acceptable for the customer) can be calculated from this. If the distance traveled is taken as a basis, the price is comparatively easy to calculate and also understandable for a customer. However, in this case another problem arises, the revenue allocation among the companies involved.

The development of a solution that is acceptable from the point of view of all those involved presents a complex problem, especially when public transport is seen as a service of public general interest or other political objectives are also included in the discussions (e.g., special tariffs for elder and handicapped people). For this reason, it can only be case-specific decisions that should not be considered here. Regardless of this problem, the determination of permissible payment systems, which can also have an impact on a tariff system, is independent of the fundamental questions to be solved.

In addition to these largely technical and process-related discussions, the question of organizational structures and responsibility for the design and implementation of services is a central point for a successful restructuring and further development of public passenger transport in the rural area. Since multimodal trips are usually provided by different operating companies, it is necessary to have a superordinate level for planning and implementation of central tasks. In connection with the discussions about the developments of service structures in the sense of MaaS, private sector solutions are proposed. However, if the mobility of people is seen as part of a service of public general interest and is also financed accordingly, as it is often the case, the primacy of politics applies.

Ultimately, this excludes a form of private business organization. However, the question must also be asked whether an integration of such organization into the public administration can make sense. A cooperative organizational form can therefore be a better solution, for example within the framework of a *Public Private Partnership* (PPP) *concept*. If public passenger transport is viewed as a private service, there are various organizational models that should not be discussed further here, as these are usually very strongly influenced by the respective national legal framework and the different interests of the involved parties.

7 Outlook and Further Developments

The need to improve and expand public transport in the rural area is uncontroversial. The main reasons for this are the reduction in traffic-related environmental pollution, the improvement of mobility, also with a view to under-aged as well as elderly and handicapped people (see, e.g., Milakis and van Wee 2020), as well as the reduction in rural exodus and thus the resulting increase in urbanization. In addition the demographic change has to be seen (see, e.g., Kaplan et al. 2019; Avermann and Schlüter 2020). The use of autonomously driving vehicles in public transport is seen as an essential approach to the implementation of these goals (see Sect. 4). Even if these developments are just beginning, the operational and financial advantages of autonomous driving are obvious. This is also evident worldwide through a large number of ongoing test projects and the first realizations in practice, as well as comprehensive political support, also with regard to the necessary adjustments in international and national traffic law.

However, some (partly supposed) negative effects that result from autonomous driving must also be seen. The focus is on the loss of jobs that will come (see, e.g. the forecasts of Frey and Osborne 2017 as well as Grunwald 2019 and Bissell et al. 2020). On the other hand, looking at the age structure of the current population development, a different valuation is possible. The again and again discussed lack of vehicle drivers, for example, may be compensated by such a technical solution. Moreover, there is of course a risk for autonomously driving vehicles to be attacked electronically, but the question arises as to how the comparison with manually operated vehicles currently looks. The problem of external interventions in vehicle electronics is not a system-inherent problem of autonomous driving, this also applies to manually operated vehicles with appropriate on-board electronics, for example when using ADAS components. In addition, it may be in the first few years a problematic situation applying driverless vehicles in public road networks. It is necessary to get used to the changing conditions in road traffic if there is a shared use of the traffic space by autonomous and manually controlled vehicles.

For the future it must be assumed that it is not a question of whether autonomous driving will prevail, but how quickly and with what market penetration. The essential factors are the progress of the qualification of the technical systems (vehicle technology, electronic components, information and communication technology) as well as the speed of the "learning" of the vehicles, whereby an extensive database can be generated by sufficient mileage (in kilometers driven). This is the crucial basis to ensure adequate security in daily operation.

Public passenger transport in rural areas can be an important field of application in order to demonstrate in a first step suitability for everyday of use autonomous vehicles, since the general traffic conditions are less critical here. In addition, the achievable improvements in the operating structures are clearly visible, not only on the technical level, but in particular also with regard to an improvement in living conditions in an area that was previously largely undersupplied with regard to public transport. This can significantly influence the choice of means of transport in rural areas, combined with a corresponding reduction in traffic-related environmental pollution as well as cost savings for customers by eliminating fixed costs (for owning a car) and replacing them with usage-dependent variable costs.

References

Acheampong, R.A., Cugurullo, F.: Capturing the behavioural determinants behind the adoption of autonomous vehicles - conceptual frameworks and measurement models to predict public transport, sharing and ownership trends of self-driving cars. Transp. Res. Part F **62**, 349–375 (2019)

Ainsal, J., et al.: State of the art of automated buses. Sustainablity **10**(9), 3118 (2018)

Alaswad, A., Baroutaji, A., Achour, H., Carton, J., Al Makky, A., Olabi, A.G.: Developments in fuel cell technologies in the transport sector. Int. J. Hydrogen Energy **41**(37), 16499–16508 (2016)

Arena, F., Pau, G.: An overview of vehicular communications. Future Internet **11**, 27 (2019)

Arnold, E., Al-Jarrah, O.Y., Dianati, M., Fallah, S., Oxtoby, D., Mouzakitis, A.: A survey on 3D object detection methods for autonomous driving applications. IEEE Trans. Intell. Transp. Syst. **20**(10), 3782–3795 (2019)

Avermann, N., Schlüter, J.: Determinants of customer satisfaction with a true door-to-door DRT service in rural Germany. Research in Transportation Business & Management (2020). https://doi.org/10.1016/j.rtbm.2019.100420. (in press)

Barillère-Scholz, M., Büttner, C., Becker, A.: Mobilität 4.0: Deutschlands erste autonome Buslinie in Bad Birnbach als Pionierleistung für neue Verkehrskonzepte. In: Riener, A., Appel, A., Dorner, W., Huber, T., Kolb, J.C., Wagner, H. (eds.) Autonome Shuttlebusse im ÖPNV, pp. 15–22. Springer, Heidelberg (2020). https://doi.org/10.1007/978-3-662-59406-3_2

Bartolini, C., Tettamanti, T., Varga, I.: Critical features of autonomous road transport from the perspective of technological regulation and law. Transp. Res. Procedia **27**, 791–798 (2017)

Berg, J., Ihlström, J.: The importance of public transport for mobility and everyday activities among rural residents. Soc. Sci. **8**, 58 (2019)

Beutel, M.C., et al.: Information integration for advanced travel information systems. J. Traffic Transp. Eng. **4**, 177–185 (2016)

Bissell, D., Birtchnell, T., Elliott, A., Hsu, E.L.: Autonomous automobilities -the social impacts of driverless vehicles. Curr. Sociol. **68**(1), 116–134 (2020)

Bresson, G., Alsayed, Z., Yu, L., Glaser, S.: Simultaneous localization and mapping - a survey of current trends in autonomous driving. IEEE Trans. Intell. Vehicles **2**(3), 194–220 (2017)

Cervero, R.: Paratransit in Southeast Asia - a market response to poor roads? Rev. Urban Regional Dev. Stud. **3**(1), 3–27 (1991)

Cervero, R., Golub, A.: Informal transport - A global perspective. Transp. Policy **14**, 445–457 (2007)

Chan, C.-Y.: Advancements, prospects, and impacts of automated driving systems. Int. J. Transp. Sci. Technol. **6**, 208–216 (2017)

Chindhe, G., Javali, A., Patil, P., Budhawant, P.: A survey on various location tracking systems. Int. Res. J. Eng. Technol. **5**(12), 671–675 (2018)

Corsar, D., Edwards, P., Nelson, J., Baillie, C., Papangelis, K., Velaga, N.: Linking open data and the crowd for real-time passenger information. J. Web Semant. **43**, 18–24 (2017)

Destatis/ Statistisches Bundesamt: Verkehr - Verkehrsunfälle (Fachserie 8/ Reihe 7) (2020). https://www.destatis.de/DE/Themen/Gesellschaft-Umwelt/Verkehrsunfaelle/Publikati onen/Downloads-Verkehrsunfaelle/verkehrsunfaelle-monat-2080700191104.html

Doerr, H., Romstorfer, A.: Implemetation of autonomous vehicle onto roadways. Internationales Verkehrswesen **72**(1), 66–70 (2020)

Dong, Y., Wanga, S., Lia, L., Zhang, Z.: An empirical study on travel patterns of internet based ride-sharing. Transportation Res. C **86**, 1–22 (2018)

Enoch, M.P.: How a rapid modal convergence into a universal automated taxi service could be the future for local passenger transport. Technol. Anal. Strateg. Manag. **27**, 910–924 (2015)

Farhan, J., Chen, T.D.: Impact of ridesharing on operational efficiency of shared autonomous electric vehicle fleet. Transp. Res. C **93**, 310–321 (2018)

Fagnant, D.J., Kockelman, K.: Preparing a nation for autonomous vehicles - opportunities, barriers and policy recommendations for capitalizing on self-driving vehicles. Transp. Res. A **77**, 167–181 (2015)

Fraedrich, E., Lenz, B.: Societal and individual acceptance of autonomous driving. In: Maurer, M., Gerdes, J.C., Lenz, B., Winner, H. (eds.) Autonomous Driving, pp. 621–640. Springer, Heidelberg (2016). https://doi.org/10.1007/978-3-662-48847-8_29

Frey, C.B., Osborne, M.A.: The future of employment - how susceptible are jobs to computerisation? Technol. Forecast. Soc. Change **114**, 254–280 (2017)

Gasser, T.M.: Fundamental and special legal questions for autonomous vehicles. In: Maurer, M., Gerdes, J.Christian, Lenz, B., Winner, H. (eds.) Autonomous Driving, pp. 523–551. Springer, Heidelberg (2016). https://doi.org/10.1007/978-3-662-48847-8_25

Grunwald, A.; Autonomes Fahren - Technikfolgen, Ethik und Risiken. Straßenverkehrsrecht 19(3), 81–86 (2019)

Haas, R.E., Bhattacharjee, S., Möller, D.P.F.: Advanced driver assistance systems. In: Akhilesh, K.B., Möller, D.P.F. (eds.) Smart Technologies, pp. 345–371. Springer, Singapore (2020). https://doi.org/10.1007/978-981-13-7139-4_27

Haboucha, C.J., Ishaq, R., Shiftan, Y.: User preferences regarding autonomous vehicles. Transp. Res. C **78**, 37–49 (2017)

Hänsch, R., Hoelzmann, J., Mielke, S.: Flächendeckend Rufbusse? Eine Untersuchung zur Verbreitung alternativer Mobilitätskonzepte. Der Nahverkehr 37(1+2), 39–43 (2019)

Hannon, E., Knupfer, S., Stern, S., Sumers, B., Nijssen, J.T.: An integrated perspective on the future of mobility - Part 3: Setting the direction towards seamless mobility. McKinsey Center for Future Mobility (2019)

Harmony, X.J., Gayah, V.V.: Evaluation of real-time transit information systems - an information demand and supply approach. Int. J. Transp. Sci. Technol. **6**, 86–98 (2017)

Hulse, L.M., Xie, H., Galea, E.R.: Perceptions of autonomous vehicles - relationships with road users, risk, gender and age. Saf. Sci. **102**, 1–13 (2018)

Hyland, M., Mahmassani, H.: Dynamic autonomous vehicle fleet operations - optimization-based strategies to assign AVs to immediate traveler demand requests. Transp. Res. C **92**, 278–297 (2018)

Ilkova, V., Ilka, A.: Legal aspects of autonomous vehicles - An overview. In: Proceedings 21st International Conference on Process Control (PC), pp. 427–433. IEEE, New York (2017)

Jevinger, Å., Persson, J.A.: Exploring the potential of using reatime traveler data in public transport disturbance management. Public Transp. **11**, 413–441 (2019)

Jittrapirom, P., Marchau, V., van der Heijden, R., Meurs, H.: Dynamic adaptive policymaking for implementing Mobility-as-a Service (MaaS). Res. Transp. Bus. Manage. **27**, 46–55 (2018)

Kamargianni, M., Li, W., Matyas, M., Schäfer, A.: A critical review of new mobility services for urban transport. Transp. Res. Procedia **14**, 3294–3303 (2016)

Kaplan, S., Gordon, B., El Zarwi, F., Walker, J.L., Zilberman, D.: The future of autonomous vehicles - lessons from the literature on technology adoption. Appl. Econ. Perspectives Policy **41**(4), 583–597 (2019)

Kolb, J.C., Wech, L., Schwabe, M., Ruzok, C., Trost, C.: Technische Aspekte des automatisierten Fahrens am Projekt des autonomen Shuttlebusses in Bad Birnbach. In: Riener, A., Appel, A., Dorner, W., Huber, T., Kolb, J.C., Wagner, H. (eds.) Autonome Shuttlebusse im ÖPNV, pp. 57–91. Springer, Heidelberg (2020). https://doi.org/10.1007/978-3-662-59406-3_5

Kukkala, V.K., Tunnell, J., Pasricha, S., Bradley, T.: Advanced driver-assistance systems - a path towards autonomous vehicles. IEEE Consum. Electron. Mag. **7**(5), 18–25 (2018)

Kuutti, S., Fallah, S., Katsaros, K., Dianati, M., Mccullough, F., Mouzakitis, A.: A survey of the state-of-the-art localisation techniques and their potentials for autonomous vehicle applications. IEEE Internet of Things J. **5**(2), 829–846 (2018)

Lathia, N., Capra, L., Magliocchetti, D., De Vigili, F., Conti, G., De Amicis, R., Arentze, T., Zhang, J., Cali, D., Alexa, V.: Personalizing mobile travel information services. Procedia – Soc. Behav. Sci. **48**, 1195–1204 (2012)

Lenk, M.: Der programmierte Tod? Autonomes Fahren und die strafrechtliche Behandlung dilemmatischer Situationen. Straßenverkehrsrecht **19**(5), 166–171 (2019)

Lenz, B., Fraedrich, E.: New mobility concepts and autonomous driving - the potential for change. In: Maurer, M., Gerdes, J.C., Lenz, B., Winner, H. (eds.) Autonomous Driving, pp. 173–191. Springer, Heidelberg (2016). https://doi.org/10.1007/978-3-662-48847-8_9

Liao, F., Molin, E., Timmermans, H., van Wee, B.: Carsharing - the impact of system characteristics on its potential to replace private car trips and reduce car ownership. Transportation (2018). https://doi.org/10.1007/s11116-018-9929-9

López-Lambas, M.E., Alonso, A.: The driverless bus - an analysis of public perceptions and acceptability. Sustainability **11**, 4986 (2019)

Martínez-Díaz, M., Soriguera, F.: Autonomous vehicles - theoretical and practical challenges. Transp. Res. Procedia **33**, 275–282 (2018)

Martínez-Díaz, M., Soriguera, F., Pérez, I.: Autonomous driving - a bird's eye view. IET Intel. Transp. Syst. **13**(4), 563–579 (2019)

Metz, D.: Developing policy for urban autonomous vehicles - impact on congestion. Urban Sci. **2**, 33 (2018)

Meyer, J., Becker, H., Bösch, P.M., Axhausen, K.W.: Autonomous vehicles - the next jump in accessibilities? Res. Transp. Econ. **62**, 80–91 (2017)

Meyer, M.: Bedarfsorientierte ÖPNV-Bedienung in der Fläche - Erfahrungen mit neuartigen Betriebsformen in der Bundesrepublik Deutschland und in den Niederlanden. Verkehr + Technik **41**(7), 280–289 (1982)

Milakis, D., van Wee, B.: Implications of vehicle automation for accessibility and social inclusion of people on low income, people with physical and sensory disabilities, and older people. In: Antoniou, C., Efthymiou, D., Chaniotakis, E. (eds.) Demand for emerging transportation systems, pp. 61–73. Elsevier, Amsterdam (2020)

Miotti, M., Hofer, J., Bauer, C.: Integrated environmental and economic assessment of current and future fuel cell vehicles. Int. J. Life Cycle Assess. **22**, 94–110 (2017)

Möller, T., Padhi, A., Pinner, D., Tschiesner, A.: The future of mobility is at our doorstep. McKinsey Center for Future Mobility (2019)

von Mörner, M., Boltze, M.: Sammelverkehr mit autonomen Fahrzeugen im ländlichen Raum. Der Nahverkehr **36**(11), 6–13 (2018)

Montanaro, U., et al.: Towards connected autonomous driving - review of use-cases. Veh. Syst. Dyn. **57**(6), 779–814 (2019)

Moriarty, P., Honnery, D.: Prospects for hydrogen as a transport fuel. Int. J. Hydrogen Energy **44**(31), 16029–16037 (2019)

Mulley, C., Nelson, J.D., Steve Wright, S.: Community transport meets mobility as a service - on the road to a new a flexible future. Res. Transp. Econ. **69**, 583–591 (2018)

Najmi, A., Rey, D., Rashidi, T.H.: Novel dynamic formulations for real-time ride-sharing systems. Transp. Res. E **108**, 122–140 (2017)

Namazu, M., MacKenzie, D., Zerriffi, H., Dowlatabadi, H.: Is carsharing for everyone? understanding the diffusion of carsharing services. Transp. Policy **63**, 189–199 (2018)

Nobis, C., Kuhnimhof, T.: Mobilität in Deutschland - MiD Ergebnisbericht, Studie von Infas, DLR, IVT und Infas 360 im Auftrag des Bundesministers für Verkehr und digitale Infrastruktur (FE-Nr. 70904/15) Bonn, Berlin (2018). https://www.mobilitaet-in-deutschland.de

Papangelis, K., Nelson, J.D., Sripada, S., Beecroft, M.: The effects of mobile real time information on rural passengers. Transp. Plann. Technol. **39**(1), 97–114 (2016)

Perboli, G., Ferrero, F., Musso, S., Vesco, A.: Business models and tariff simulation in car-sharing services. Transp. Res. A **115**, 32–48 (2018)

Petersen, T.: Watching the Swiss - a network approach to rural and exurban public transport. Transp. Policy **52**, 175–185 (2016)

Phun, V.K., Yai, T.: State of the art of paratransit in Asian developing countries. Asian Transp. Stud. **4**(1), 57–77 (2016)

Piatkowski, P., Puszkiewicz, W.: Electric vehicles - problems or solutions. J. Mech. Energy Eng. **2**(1), 59–66 (2018)

Richter, E., Friedrich, M., Migl, A., Hartleb, J.: Integrating ridesharing services with automated vehicles into macroscopic travel demand models. In: Proceedings IEEE 6th International Conference on Models and Technologies for Intelligent Transportation Systems (MT-ITS), pp. 1–8 (2019)

Robson, K., Gharehbaghi, K., Scott-Young, C.: Planning effective and efficient public transport systems. Int. J. Real Estate Land Plann. **1**, 385–392 (2018)

Ryley, T.J., Stanley, P.A., Enoch, M.P., Zanni, A.M., Quddus, M.A.: Investigating the contribution of demand responsive transport to a sustainable local public transport system. Res. Transp. Econ. **48**, 364–374 (2014)

Saeed, K., Kurauchi, F.: Enhancing the service quality of transit systems in rural areas by flexible transport services. Transp. Res. Procedia **10**, 514–523 (2015)

Scheltes, A., de Almeida Correia, G.H.: Exploring the use of automated vehicles as last mile connection of train trips through an agent-based simulation model - an application to Delft, Netherlands. Int. J. Transp. Sci. Technol. **6**, 28–41 (2017)

Schiefelbusch, M.: German experiences with volunteer-based paratransit and public transport. In: Mulley, C., Nelson, J.D. (eds.) Paratransit - Shaping the Flexible Transport Future, pp. 77–102. Bingley, Emerald Group (2016)

Schreurs, M.A., Steuwer, S.D.: Autonomous driving – political, legal, social, and sustainability dimensions. In: Maurer, M., Gerdes, J.C., Lenz, B., Winner, H. (eds.) Autonomes Fahren, pp. 151–173. Springer, Heidelberg (2015). https://doi.org/10.1007/978-3-662-45854-9_8

Schwarting, W., Alonso-Mora, J., Rus, D.: Planning and decision-making for autonomous vehicles. Ann. Rev. Control, Robot. Autonom. Syst. **1**, 187–210 (2018)

Shaheen, S., Cohen, A.: Mobility on demand (MOD) and mobility as a service (MaaS) - early understanding of shared mobility impacts and public transit partnerships. In: Antoniou, C., Efthymiou, D., Chaniotakis, E. (eds.) Demand for emerging transportation systems, pp. 37–60. Elsevier, Amsterdam (2020)

Shaheen, S., Cohen, A., Chan, N., Bansal, A.: Sharing strategies - carsharing, shared micromobility (bikesharing and scooter sharing), transportation network companies, microtransit, and other innovative mobility modes. In: Deakin, E. (ed.) Transportation, Land Use, and Environmental Planning, pp. 237–262. Elsevier, Amsterdam and Kidlington (2020)

Šipuš, D., Abramoviś, B.: The possibility of using public transport in rural area. Procedia Eng. **192**, 788–793 (2017)

Sonderegger, R., Imhof, S., von Arx, W., Frölicher, J.: Selbstfahrende Fahrzeuge im ländlichen Raum. Der Nahverkehr **37**(4), 57–61 (2019)

Soteropoulos, A., Berger, M., Ciari, F.: Impacts of automated vehicles on travel behaviour and land use - an international review of modelling studies. Transp. Rev. **39**(1), 29–49 (2019)

Stender-Vorwachs, J., Steege, H.: Legal aspects of autonomous driving. Internationales Verkehrswesen **70**(Special edition) 18–20 (2018)

Szigeti, S., Csiszár, C., Földes, D.: Information management of demand-responsive mobility service. Procedia Eng. **187**, 483–491 (2017)

Tang, B., Arat, H.T., Baltacıoğlu, E., Aydin, K.: Overview of the next quarter century vision of hydrogen fuel cell electric vehicles. Int. J. Hydrogen Energy **44**(20), 10120–10128 (2019)

Tirachini, A., Antoniou, C.: The economics of automated public transport - effects on operator cost, travel time, fare and subsidy. Econ. Transp. **21**, 100151 (2020)

Tiwari, A., Akhilesh, K.B.: Exploring connected cars. In: Akhilesh, K.B., Möller, D.P.F. (eds.) Smart Technologies, pp. 305–315. Springer, Singapore (2020). https://doi.org/10.1007/978-981-13-7139-4_23

Tussyadiah, I.P., Zach, F.J., Wang, J.: Attitudes toward autonomous on demand mobility system: the case of self-driving taxi. In: Schegg, R., Stangl, B. (eds.) Information and Communication Technologies in Tourism 2017, pp. 755–766. Springer, Cham (2017). https://doi.org/10.1007/978-3-319-51168-9_54

Tyrinopoulos, Y., Antoniou, C.: Review of factors affecting transportation systems adoption & satisfaction. In: Antoniou, C., Efthymiou, D., Chaniotakis, E. (eds.) Demand for Emerging Transportation Systems, pp. 11–36. Elsevier, Amsterdam and Kidlington (2020)

Utriainen, R., Pöllänen, M.: Review on mobility as a service in scientific publications. Res. Transp. Bus. Manage. **27**, 15–23 (2018)

Viergutz, K.: Echtzeitdaten im ÖPNV. Internationales Verkehrswesen **68**(4), 47–49 (2016)

Webb, J., Wilson, C., Kularatne, T.: Will people accept shared autonomous electric vehicles? a survey before and after receipt of the costs and benefits. Econ. Anal. Policy **61**, 118–135 (2019)

Wicaksono, A., et al.: Road-based urban public transport and paratransit in six Asian countries - Legal conditions and intermodal issues. J. Eastern Asia Society Transp. Stud. **11**, 227–242 (2015)

Winter, K., Cats, O., de Almeida Correia, G.H., van Arem, B.: Performance analysis and fleet requirements of automated demand-responsive transport systems as an urban public transport service. Int. J. Transp. Sci. Technol. **7**, 151–167 (2018)

A Systematic Literature Review About Quantitative Metrics to Evaluate Usability and Security of ATM Interfaces

Fiorella Falconi[✉] [iD], Claudia Zapata[iD], Arturo Moquillaza[iD], and Freddy Paz[iD]

Pontificia Universidad Católica del Perú, Lima 32, Lima, Peru
{ffalconit,zapata.cmp}@pucp.edu.pe, {amoquillaza,fpaz}@pucp.pe

Abstract. Automatic Telle Machine or ATM remains one of the most used banking channels and have been transformed into complex machines, where multiple operations can be carried out, not just cash withdrawals as was at the beginning. In this context, the usability and security of interfaces become essential aspects for users to interact with ATM interfaces efficiently. About usability, several studies support its important on the user experience, which also applies to the ATM domain. About security, previous works manifest its importance especially in the ATM domain. In this sense, it is intended to utilize usability and security metrics that allow establishing the degree of usability or security of ATM interfaces. In order to identify whether there are already metrics that may be valid for evaluating ATM interfaces, the authors present a systematic literature review they made about metrics that assess usability and security in banking software. After executing the review, five relevant documents were obtained. Of these, the most significant contribution is that of 160 metrics divided into 13 categories of metrics to assess the security and usability of an Internet Banking. Future research will be focused on evaluating the relevance of these proposals in the ATM domain.

Keywords: Systematic literature review · Automated Teller Machine · Software metrics · Usability evaluation · Security

1 Introduction

More than 50 years ago, John Shepherd-Barron invented the first ATM (Automatic Teller Machine) in London at the request of Barclays Bank [1]. Since then, ATMs have evolved. At the beginning, it was only aimed at withdrawing cash, over time they became more complex machines and were added another financial transactions of a very varied nature, such as mobile phone, balance inquiries, data updates, among others [2].

Considering that, the most used transaction in ATM is cash dispensing, we cannot ignore that when adopting new functions, ATM should be as friendly as possible [3]. An important aspect to improve the usability, and, in general, the user experience is to consider the emotional state, feelings, and emotions that the final user experiences before, during and after interacting with the ATM [4].

© Springer Nature Switzerland AG 2020
A. Marcus and E. Rosenzweig (Eds.): HCII 2020, LNCS 12202, pp. 100–113, 2020.
https://doi.org/10.1007/978-3-030-49757-6_7

In addition, when we are talking about ATMs, security and safety aspects should be considered since ATM are targets of different criminal acts, so that financial institutions add surveillance cameras, electronic devices and others, so that users can perform their operations in a safe way in ATM [5]. Additionally, several studies mentioned that security is an important aspect in the UX [6, 7], especially for users in the ATM domain [8, 9].

In this context, the industry needs to use techniques to obtain quantitative results over the ATM interfaces, to objectively measure aspects of usability and security of ATM applications.

In this paper, the authors present a systematic literature review about metrics that are reported in the literature to assess usability and security in banking software. The objective is to identify whether there are currently specific metrics for ATM interfaces and others that evaluate bank software that can be input to build the mentioned metrics. The works that were taken into account are those published from 2014 to 2019. The final intention of this work is to carry out as a future work a proposal of consolidated metrics for the ATM domain.

2 Background

2.1 Automatic Teller Machine

Automatic Teller Machine (ATM) is a computerized telecommunications device that provides, in real time, access to the clients of a financial institution to their bank accounts in a public space without intervention of the administration of the financial institution [10].

The customer is identified by inserting the card and entering a personal identification number (PIN). This process allows customers to access their bank accounts and perform the operations available according to the bank.

2.2 Metric

It is a measurement scale and method used for the measurement of attributes that influence one or more sub-quality characteristics [11].

2.3 Usability

There are many usability concepts proposed by different authors, but Jakob Nielsen provides a more complete definition, which covers most of the characteristics mentioned by other specialists [12].

Nielsen states that usability has multiple components and is associated with the following attributes: Learning, Efficiency, Memory, Mistakes and Satisfaction [13].

2.4 Usability Metrics

They quantitatively demonstrate whether the evaluated software can be understandable, learned, operated, attractive and compatible with the standards and usability guidelines [11].

An example of usability metrics can be the time that a user takes to perform a certain task, in order to find the ease that users have to perform a task. This time being closer to 0 will show that the user has managed to perform the task quickly and efficiently [14].

2.5 Security

Security will be interpreted as the perception of security that customers have when making a transaction from the beginning to the end of it. The lack of security perception causes the client not to use a certain channel to carry out their transactions. For this reason, perceived security is the extent to which a customer believes that a channel is safe to perform their bank transaction [15].

2.6 Security Metrics

Security metrics are designed to facilitate the decision-making process and improve results. They anticipate user needs to ensure compliance the security objectives [16].

3 Systematic Literature Review

This systematic literature review was conducted as a starting point to identify the current state of research related to usability and security metrics of ATM interfaces or other banking systems. This review was carried out following the methodology established by B. A. Kitchenham and S. Charters [17].

The definition of research questions was carried out based on the PICOC method, where the following criteria are considered: Population, Intervention, Comparison, Outcomes and Context. In this work, a comparison between variables will not be made, for this reason in Table 1 this criterion does not apply.

Table 1. Definition of concepts using PICOC

Criterion	Description
Population	Banking systems
Intervention	Usability and security metrics
Comparison	Not apply
Outcomes	Study cases which report quantitative metrics can be used for a usability and security for ATM
Context	Academic context and software industry

The research questions that were established for this Review Literature Systematic are the following:

- What metrics have been reported in the literature in the last five years for the evaluation of usability and safety that can be applied to ATM?

- What metrics have been reported in the literature in the last five years for the evaluation of usability and security of banking software?

According to the research questions, the terms used to compose the search strings were defined. To perform the search, synonyms and acronyms were taken into account to structure the search strings to avoid omitting any relevant results. The established search strings are the following:

- C1: (ATM OR automatic teller machine OR automated teller machine OR banking OR bank OR financial)
- C2: (metrics OR measurement)
- C3: (Security OR secure interface)
- C4: (Usability OR UX).

The string used for the search was formed as follows:

`C1 AND C2 AND C3 AND C4`

The search was carried out in the following relevant databases in the research area of this work:

- Scopus
- IEEEXplore
- ACM Digital Library
- SpringerLink.

The search strings of primary studies that will be used for each of the specified databases are detailed below:

- Scopus: `(TITLE-ABS-KEY (metrics OR measurement) AND TITLE-ABS-KEY (ux OR usability OR "secure interface") AND TITLE-ABS-KEY (banking OR bank OR financial OR atm)) AND PUBYEAR > 2013 AND (LIMIT-TO (SUBJAREA, "COMP") OR LIMIT-TO (SUB-JAREA, "ENGI") OR LIMIT-TO (SUBJAREA, "BUSI") OR LIMIT-TO (SUBJAREA, "DECI")) AND (LIMIT-TO (LANGUAGE, "English"))`
- IEEEXplore: `("Publication Title":metrics OR measurement) AND ("Abstract":usability OR "secure interface" OR UX) AND ("Abstract":bank OR financial OR banking OR ATM)`
- ACM Digital Library: `acmdlTitle:(metrics measurement) AND content.ftsec:(+interface bank financial ATM) AND recordAbstract:(usability security UX)`
- SpringerLink: `(metrics or measurement) AND banking AND (usability OR "secure interface") AND NOT(game AND health AND traffic)`
- Subdiscipline: User Interfaces and Human Computer Interaction
- Date published: 2014–2019.

To consider a primary study, it must have the following inclusion criteria:

- Information about usability or security metrics for ATM.
- Relevant information about usability or security metrics used in other channels and that could be used for ATM.
- Case studies on usability or security evaluations of financial channels.
- Aspects to be considered in the elaboration of usability and security metrics.

The following criteria were taken to exclude a primary study:

- Information and aspects that do not correspond to the banking or financial field.
- Information not found in the English or Spanish language.
- Articles published before 2014.

4 Search Results

After searching in the mentioned databases, 354 articles were found. In order to make the selection of the relevant articles, the title and the summary of all articles found in the search were reviewed. Table 2 shows the search results in each of the databases, duplicate articles and relevant articles.

Table 2. Number of papers founded

Data base	Results	Duplicates	Relevants
Scopus	31	0	4
ACM	101	0	0
IEEE Xplore	9	3	0
SpringerLink	203	0	1
Total	354	3	5

The relevant papers of the area of interest are the following:

- "Evaluating mobile banking application: Usability dimensions and measurements" [18].
- "Measurement on Usage of the Internet Banking in Colombia" [19].
- "Online Banking Security and Usability - Towards an Effective Evaluation Framework" [20].
- "A model for evaluating the security and usability of e-banking platforms" [21].
- "Development of Questionnaire to Measure User Acceptance Towards User Interface Design" [22].

Table 3 shows a summary of the content of each of the relevant papers:

Table 3. Summary of the relevant papers

Paper	Summary
1 [9]	The authors mention how evaluation models for mobile banking applications are general, and do not represent the complexity of the area and proposes a set of dimensions and usability measures
2 [10]	Evidence the lack of studies to measure the use of Internet Banking in Colombia. It also shows the factors that influence this use such as quality, familiarity and usability
3 [11]	Compilation of usability and security metrics from the literature to evaluate online banking, indicating the lack of metrics for this area
4 [12]	It searches for the most used frameworks to evaluate usability and security and proposes 160 metrics to evaluate aspects of usability and security to evaluate internet-banking platforms
5 [13]	It develops a questionnaire to measure the acceptance of the interface of explored the expectations of ASEAN users based on constructions in the Theory of Expectation-Confirmation (ECT)

Of these five articles, the most significant contribution is that of 160 metrics divided into 13 categories of metrics to evaluate security and usability of Internet Banking. The authors indicate the points that would be evaluated in each of these categories, which are divided into 6 categories to evaluate safety (Table 4) and 7 categories to evaluate usability (Table 5).

Table 4. Security metrics

Subcategory	Metric
Category: General online security and privacy information to the Internet banking customers	
1. Account aggregation or privacy and confidentiality	1.1. Complied with the national privacy principles and privacy law
2. Losses compensation guarantee	2.1. Liability for any claim where the user identification or password used by unauthorized persons 2.2. Compensate client when bank website get hacked/unauthorized access 2.3. Compensate client when client computer get hacked/unauthorized access 2.4. Responsibility for losses or damages or expense incurred by the customer as a result of his violation of the terms and conditions 2.5. Responsibility for all telecommunications expenses (internet services)

(*continued*)

Table 4. (*continued*)

Subcategory	Metric
3. Online/Internet banking security information that the banks provide	3.1. "Customer Protection Code" document by the country's responsible authority 3.2. Threats: Hoax email, scam, phishing, spyware, virus and Trojan 3.3. Fraud Awareness 3.4. Key logger 3.5. General online security guidelines 3.6. Security alert/up-to-date issue 3.7. Provides Password security tips
Category: IT assistance, monitoring and support	
1. Hotline/helpdesk service availability	1.1. 24/7 customer contact center by phone 1.2. Messaging system (similar to an email) 1.3. FAQ/online support form
Category: Bank site authentication technology	
1. Employed encryption and digital certificate technologies	1.1. SSL encryption 1.2. Extended validation SSL certificates 1.3. Signing CA
Category: User site authentication technology	
1. Two-factor authentication for logon and/or for transaction verification available	1.1. Tokens 1.2. SMS 1.3. Site key 1.4. Not in use
2. Logon requirements	2.1. Bank credit cards number 2.2. Bank register/customer ID 2.3. Email address 2.4. Password 2.5. Other (e.g. personal code or security number) 2.6. Two-factor authentication
3. Logon failure limitation	3.1. Max. (times) 3.2. In use but does not specific maximum number of failures allowed
4. Password restriction/requirement	4.1. Enforce good Password practice 4.2. Password length restriction (characters) 4.3. Combination of numbers and letters 4.4. Combination of upper and lower cases 4.5. Special characters 4.6. Different passwords as compared to any of previously used passwords 4.7. Automatically check password strength when creating or changing password

(*continued*)

Table 4. (*continued*)

Subcategory	Metric
5.5. Password recovery method (Using ATM card number and PIN/username)	5.1. User ID, Card Number and PIN Number 5.2. Users can reset password online 5.3. Restore via ATM 5.4. SMS code 5.5. Answer Security Question 5.6. Restore via Email 5.7. Call customer service to complete this action
6. Transaction verification	6.1. All transactions required token/SMS 6.2. All external transactions required token/SMS 6.3. Other method e.g. password
Category: Internet banking application security features	
1. Automatic timeout feature for inactivity	1.1. Expiration time limit (maximum minutes) 1.2. In use but does not specific maximum number of failures allowed
2. Session management	2.1. Session tokens 2.2. Page tokens 2.3. Clear session Cookie information after logoff or shut down the Internet browser
3. Limited default daily transfer amount to third party account/BPAY/international transactions	3.1. Less or up to 5,000 USD 3.2. More than 5,000 USD 3.3. The default maximum daily limit transfer is vary depending on the type of the Internet banking customer 3.4. The maximum daily limit transfer may be increased with the approval by the banks 3.5. International transfer limit is different from the national transfer limit
Category: Software and system requirements and settings information	
1. Compatibility best with the popular Internet browsers (based on the banks information provided)	1.1. Chrome 1.2. Firefox 1.3. Internet Explorer 1.4. Netscape 1.5. Opera 1.6. Safari
2. Internet banking user device system and browser setting requirement	2.1. Operating System 2.2. Type of browser 2.3. Browser setting 2.4. Screen resolution
3. Free/paid security software/tool available to the Internet banking customers	3.1. Antivirus/anti-spyware 3.2. Internet security suite 3.3. Browser setting 3.4. Provides Internet links to security software vendor(s)

Table 5. Usability metrics

Subcategory	Metric
Category: Interface	
1. Design principles	1.1. Home page is concise and clear 1.2. Effective use of white space 1.3. Effective and consistent use of color, color combination and backgrounds 1.4. Effective graphics 1.5. Aesthetics and minimalist design - apply appropriate visual representation of security elements and not provide irrelevant security information
2. Graphics and multimedia	2.1. Site is visually attractive 2.2. Graphics and multimedia help the navigation 2.3. Icons are easy to understand 2.4. Not excessively used 2.5. No negative impact on loading times
3. Style and text	3.1. Consistent use of pages style and format 3.2. Consistent use and easy to read fonts 3.3. Correct spelling and grammar 3.4. Text is concise and relevant 3.5. Purpose of site is made clear on home page 3.6. User language - the use of plain language that users can understand with regard to security
4. Flexibility and compatibility	4.1. Pages sized to fit in browser window 4.2. Printable versions of pages are available 4.3. Text-only version is available 4.4. Options of many available languages 4.5. Accommodation made for users with special needs 4.6. User suitability - provide options for users with diverse levels of skill and experience in security
Category: Navigation	
1. Logical structure	1.1. Intuitively progressing (proceeding) 1.2. Rational design of the content 1.3. Menus are understandable and straightforward 1.4. Sitemap is available 1.5. Consistent navigation throughout the site 1.6. Navigation bar is available

(*continued*)

Table 5. (*continued*)

Subcategory	Metric
2. Ease use of the site	2.1. Easy to find the site 2.2. Easy to learn and navigate the site 2.3. Easy to use the navigation bar 2.4. Easy to return to main page 2.5. Easy to modify users settings
3. Ease use of the online banking pages	3.1. Easy to access complete online banking range 3.2. Separation of online banking pages from the rest pages 3.3. Separation between individual and business customers, as well among various channels
4. Search feature	4.1. Easy to use search engine 4.2. Search engine provides accurate and useful results 4.3. Good description of search engine findings 4.4. No search engine errors
5. Navigational necessities	5.1. No broken links 5.2. No under-construction pages 5.3. Links are clearly discernible, well labeled and defined 5.4. Clear label of current position on the site 5.5. Effective use of frames, non-frames version is available
Category: Content	
1. Online banking information	1.1. Full information about the purpose of each service 1.2. Full information about the charges 1.3. Terms and conditions are easily accessed 1.4. Full information about Technical Requirements 1.5. Familiarity programs and demo are available
2. Bank information and communications	2.1. Full bank information is available 2.2. Different ways for communication with the banks employees are available 2.3. Telephone and fax numbers are available 2.4. Postal and physical addresses are available
3. Advertisement	3.1. Adequate advertisement of banks services 3.2. Controlled amount of advertisements by other companies 3.3. Careful advertisement use 3.4. Effective use of advertisement techniques

(*continued*)

Table 5. (*continued*)

Subcategory	Metric
4. Website users support	4.1. Feedback forms are available 4.2. Telephone and email numbers for providing help 4.3. Round the clock support 4.4. Free or toll free telephone assistance 4.5. Security help are relevant and apparent to users
5. Competency of the provided assistance	5.1. Detailed information about every step 5.2. Easily understandable assistance for amateur users 5.3. Assistance regarding settings is provided 5.4. Transaction guide is provided
Category: Services offered	
1. General services	1.1. Information about banks announcements 1.2. Profile/username/password management 1.3. Ease use of services 1.4. Revocability - allow users to revoke security actions where appropriate 1.5. Tools such as organizer and calculator are available 1.6. Extra services such as ticket booking, shop online, charity
2. Financial services	2.1. Account and loan information 2.2. Credit card and check information 2.3. Loan request
3. Provided transactions	3.1. Bill payments 3.2. Mobile phone bill or card recharge
Category: Reliability	
1. Registration	1.1. Easy to register 1.2. Easy to log on to the site 1.3. Adjustable customer profile is stored 1.4. Email request for receiving offers or information 1.5. Easy modification of users profile
2. Transaction procedure	2.1. Foreign language support is available 2.2. Disconnection management 2.3. Actions history is available
Category: Technical aspects	

(*continued*)

Table 5. (*continued*)

Subcategory	Metric
1. Loading speed	1.1. Fast loading speed of the home page as well the rest pages 1.2. Consideration of non-broadband users
Category: Multi-factor authentication methods	
1. Tokens	1.1. Hardware tokens 1.2. Software tokens 1.3. Easy to get the code from the device 1.4. Security and stability 1.5. User adoption 1.6. Total Cost of Ownership (TCO) 1.7. Replacement of the token in the event of defects
2. SMS	2.1. Multiple mobile numbers allowed (maximum)
3. Tokens	3.1. Effective use of site key

5 Discussion

After the Systematic Literature Review carried out, we were able to answer the two research questions mentioned at the beginning.

- What metrics have been reported in the literature in the last five years for the evaluation of usability and safety that can be applied to ATM?

   No documents were found with could be answered the first question, this evidences the absence of specific metrics to evaluate the usability of ATM interfaces or to evaluate the security of the interfaces from this same channel.

- What metrics have been reported in the literature in the last five years for the evaluation of usability and security of banking software?

   It is observed that by extending the scope of search to other financial systems, contributions are found since the issue has been addressed and deepened in the case of Internet Banking and mobile banking. The most important contribution was the list of metrics found for Internet Banking to assess usability and security.

6 Conclusions and Future Work

In the papers founded, it is expressed the importance of the evaluation of two aspects: Usability and Security, and the close relationship between them. It should be noted that several of the points evaluated for security are not related to the interface but to the communication issue of the banking channel and the banking entity, an aspect that is not relevant for the purposes of this investigation.

According to the above, we can conclude that there is an absence of specific metrics to evaluate the usability and security of ATM interfaces.

As future work, we will adapt the usability and interface security metrics obtained for other banking systems in the systematic literature review to identify a proposal that is valid and that applies to the ATM domain. To validate this proposal of metrics, the opinion of industry experts will be considered, who should be interviewed and conducted surveys in order to define the points that can be replicated in ATM and those that cannot.

References

1. Redacción, E.C.: El cajero automático cumple 50 años: ¿Cuándo llegó y cuántos hay en el Perú? Obtained from (2017). https://elcomercio.pe/economia/cajero-automatico-cumple-50-anos-llego-hay-peru-437983
2. Kamfiroozie, A., Ahmadzadeh, M.: Personalized ATMs: improve ATMs usability. In: Stephanidis, C. (ed.) HCI 2011. CCIS, vol. 173, pp. 161–166. Springer, Heidelberg (2011). https://doi.org/10.1007/978-3-642-22098-2_33
3. Hellmann, R.: In a mobile banking era, the ATM is more important than ever. Obtained from (2018). https://www.atmmarketplace.com/blogs/in-a-mobile-banking-era-the-atm-is-more-important-than-ever/
4. Van der Geest, T., Ramey, J., Rosenbaum, S., Van Velsen, L.: Introduction to the special section: designing a better user experience for self-service systems. IEEE Trans. Prof. Commun. 56(2), 92–96 (2013). https://doi.org/10.1109/tpc.2013.2258731
5. McGlasson, L.: ATM Security: Customers And Machines Are At Risk. Obtained from (2008). https://www.bankinfosecurity.com/atm-security-customers-machines-are-at-risk-a-686
6. Weir, C.S., Douglas, G., Richardson, T., Jack, M.: Usable security: user preferences for authentication methods in eBanking and the effects of experience. Interact. Comput. 22(3), 153–164 (2010). https://doi.org/10.1016/j.intcom.2009.10.001
7. Gutmann, P., Grigg, I.: Security usability. IEEE Secur. Priv. Mag. 3(4), 56–58 (2005). https://doi.org/10.1109/msp.2005.104
8. Chanco, C., Moquillaza, A., Paz, F.: Development and validation of usability heuristics for evaluation of interfaces in ATMs. In: Marcus, A., Wang, W. (eds.) HCII 2019. LNCS, vol. 11586, pp. 3–18. Springer, Cham (2019). https://doi.org/10.1007/978-3-030-23535-2_1
9. Aguirre, J., Moquillaza, A., Paz, F.: Methodologies for the design of ATM interfaces: a systematic review. In: Ahram, T., Karwowski, W., Taiar, R. (eds.) IHSED 2018. AISC, vol. 876, pp. 256–262. Springer, Cham (2019). https://doi.org/10.1007/978-3-030-02053-8_39
10. Khalifa, S.S.M., Saadan, K.: The formal design model of an Automatic Teller Machine (ATM). Lect. Notes Inf. Theory 1(1), 56–59 (2013). https://doi.org/10.12720/lnit.1.1.56-59
11. ISO: IEC 9126: Software Engineering-Product Quality. Geneva, Switzerland (2000)
12. Paz, F.: Método para la evaluación de usabilidad de sitios web transaccionales basado en el proceso de inspección heurística (Doctoral Thesis). Universidad Católica del Perú, Perú (2017)
13. Nielsen, J.: Usability Engineering, 1st edn. Academic Press, San Diego (1993)
14. Diaz, E., Arenas, J.J., Moquillaza, A., Paz, F.: A systematic literature review about quantitative metrics to evaluate the usability of e-commerce web sites. In: Karwowski, W., Ahram, T. (eds.) IHSI 2019. AISC, vol. 903, pp. 332–338. Springer, Cham (2019). https://doi.org/10.1007/978-3-030-11051-2_51

15. Chang, H.H., Chen, S.W.: Consumer perception of interface quality, security, and loyalty in electronic commerce. Inf. Manag. **46**(7), 411–417 (2009). https://doi.org/10.1016/j.im.2009.08.002
16. González, W., Almeida, G., Díaz, D.: Especificación de métricas para la evaluación de la seguridad en productos software. Iberoam. J. Proj. Manag. **5**(1), 35–45 (2014). https://doi.org/10.1016/j.im.2009.08.002
17. Kitchenham, B., Charters, S.: Guidelines for performing systematic literature reviews in software engineering version 2.3. Engineering **45**(4), 1051 (2007). https://doi.org/10.1145/1134285.1134500
18. Hussain, A., Abubakar, H.I., Hashim, N.B.: Evaluating mobile banking application: usability dimensions and measurements. In: Proceedings of the 6th International Conference on Information Technology and Multimedia (2014). https://doi.org/10.1109/icimu.2014.7066618
19. Torres, J.M.S., Fredy, E.: Measurement on usage of the Internet banking in Colombia. J. Internet Bank. Commer. **20**(2) (2015). https://doi.org/10.4172/1204-5357.1000105
20. Alsaleh, M., Alarifi, A., Alshaikh, Z., Zarour, M.: Online banking security and usability - towards an effective evaluation framework. In: Proceedings of the 11th International Conference on Web Information Systems and Technologies (2015). https://doi.org/10.5220/0005493901410149
21. Alarifi, A., Alsaleh, M., Alomar, N.: A model for evaluating the security and usability of e-banking platforms. Computing **99**(5), 519–535 (2017). https://doi.org/10.1007/s00607-017-0546-9
22. Baharum, A., Amirul, S.M., Yusop, N.M.M., Halamy, S., Fabeil, N.F., Ramli, R.Z.: Development of questionnaire to measure user acceptance towards user interface design. In: Advances in Visual Informatics, pp 531–543. Springer, Berlin (2017). https://doi.org/10.1007/978-3-319-70010-6_49

Appropriation, Design and User Experience in Public Spaces as a Part of the Language of the City

Pavel Farkas[✉]

Faculty of Humanities, Charles University in Prague, 162 00 Prague 6, Czech Republic
pf@pfarkas.com

Abstract. Semiotic thinking about cities, that is through the prism of their ways of representing various meanings, symbolic values and communication in this text is set into the framework of the User Experience (UX) Design. The primary aspect through which the city is perceived is the appropriation of public spaces by two different communities: Experts and Users – two groups engaged in daily communication situations within a city. Design and appropriation are viewed as a tool for modulation of a language of the city. While it is the inhabitants who use the city, and thus define it, experts exercise the power of setting communication norms and have the responsibility for the User-Centered Design approach in built environments. Elements of the "Language of the City" concept are explored and offered in a perspective of the User-Centered Design.

Keywords: Appropriation · Built environment · Communication · Design · Interaction · Philosophy of the city · Semiotics · Urban-centered design · Urban spaces · User experience

1 Living in the City – Researching the City

Let us begin to map our research interests with the following questions: how do we feel in a city we just arrived at for the very first time? What works the way we are used to, what is new and what in fact caused that we have gotten lost? In other words how do we understand the city we are in: do we feel welcome or frightened, engaged or lost, happy or angry? What is our *user experience* from the city? Aside from the basic function of inhabiting, cities are an indefinite source of inspiration for research. Historians, archaeologists, architects, transit engineers, artists, semioticians… as well as citizens: children, seniors, foreigners, people from all walks of life observe their environment every day and find answers to their questions in regards to function of the city they live in – or one that they are visiting. What they see, how they read, represent and comprehend the reality, understand the past and deal with the presence? How do they execute their intentions on moving around and reach their goals within a city? Communication situations that the inhabitants deal will constitute the framework of this text, described as the *Language of the City* (LOTC).

© Springer Nature Switzerland AG 2020
A. Marcus and E. Rosenzweig (Eds.): HCII 2020, LNCS 12202, pp. 114–129, 2020.
https://doi.org/10.1007/978-3-030-49757-6_8

1.1 Memory of the City

"[…] In fact memory is a sort of anti-museum: it is not localizable. Fragments of it come out in legends." Michel de Certeau's thought in one of the chapters of his book on the everyday behavior of city users summarizes the fact which these forms of living are inevitably encountering in the last centuries of its expansion. For a modern city observer, it may not be the most crucial (yet still is of interest) to remember that… "Here, there used to be a bakery." "That's where old lady Dupius used to live." (Certeau 1988) We are also surrounded with forgotten and hidden reminders of history, covered with a layer of dust and pigeon droppings… fragments of cities still present and "talking" to us, often taken for granted. Similarly, citizens are still influenced by paths and directions designed generations ago, they use names of streets or districts whose meaning may not be straightforward today. History is imprinted in them as well as the consequences of expansion, taking over – or physical *appropriation* – for example like during the Swedish expansion in Europe in the 17th century (Fig. 1).

Fig. 1. One of the reminders of the Swedish siege in the Czech Republic can be found on the facade on the Smetanova street No. 593/41 in Brno.

Fig. 2. Following historical patterns: information screens in the Copenhagen Subway system were modernized in 2019 in relation to the opening of the new "circle line". New screens provide more information, but their location was not reconsidered in order to provide the passengers information on the way to the trains.

Why should we actually consider history in relation to *user experience* (UX) in public spaces? The notion of following old patterns introduced by history might have interesting implications: how often is a space used the way it was *always* being used, ignoring the potential brought by a change, re-design? Certainly, in case of highways or other structural elements it is rather difficult to change the flow that was once initiated; an example may be the network of so called Emperor's highways built at the end of the 18th century in Bohemia, Moravia and parts of the Austrian-Hungarian Empire and which serves to this day, in practically unchanged directions (Holbová 2015). We could also think of historical connotations when riding the Stockholm subway – where escalators in most older stations are going up on the left side of the corridors, despite the norm is to walk on the right side of the corridor (unlike in London). It appears to be an imprint of an historical pattern, as the Stockholm subway was built before the country changed the car traffic direction in the streets[1]. Similarly, the subway trains exercise the left-hand traffic to this day (arriving from left to the platform).

When it comes to modern technologies in environments (Fig. 2), we could argue that instead of following the existing patterns, there should be more attention paid to the user experience and thus the need arises to adjust the information distribution accordingly to cover the needs of users of any given system. A redesign like the one which took place in Copenhagen subway in the second half of 2019, where information screens were replaced throughout the transit system, could justify reconsidering the UX. Instead, in the long corridor through which passengers rush from the airport terminals to the city-bound trains, provides information about the train departure only just when reaching the platform. There are large screens in those long corridors that could contain useful transport information to the user, but instead they mediate advertisement. Initially, somebody *appropriated* the space and decided what content these screens will broadcast.

1.2   Appropriation in Historical and Symbolical Context

Appropriation can be viewed from many directions and perspectives of different fields. Busse and Strang (2011) define it as *the act of making something one's own*; and while it may also be "part of the process of owning objects obtained through exchange or inheritance (in case of objects previously belonging to others), such acts are not confined to laying claims to things that are previously 'un-owned'". But is appropriation only limited to physical objects? Certainly not: "What did they do to *my* city?" I ask myself upon my return from a foreign stay when I notice new elements introduced into "*my*" cityscape. It is important to stress that appropriation is not limited to a physical dimension; there can be also appropriation of information, in extreme cases leading to hybrid war which may open the door to a physical annexation (see Hoffman 2007).

Appropriation in the city environment takes place on all hierarchical levels, as Klodnerová (2015) summarizes; through the politics, urban planning, financial subjects, interest groups as well as inhabitants alone. "In this light, the city appears as a dynamic and always changing space, in which political, economic and social interests co-exist and clash," Klodnerová closes. In this respect, appropriation takes place with mere *living* in the city, *inhabiting* its space, as well as symbolic acts such as installing (or removing) statues[2] or engaging in outdoor activities. But who in fact stands behind such acts of appropriation? In the following chapter, two main actors will be identified, at least those related to the interest of this paper.

---

[1] The decision to build the Metro was taken by the Stockholm City Council in 1941. The first part of the Stockholm Metro was opened in 1950 and most of the system was completed by 1960, although further parts were added until the middle of the 1970s. (Börjesson et al. 2014) The "Högertrafikomläggningen", or the day of change of the traffic direction in Sweden, took place on September 3rd, 1967. (Norén 2019).

[2] An activity recently discussed in Prague in a dramatic way, in relation to the politically controversial statue of Ivan Konev, the Soviet general on Vítězné náměstí; or to the reinstallation of the religiously controversial Marian Column on the Old Town Square (Staroměstské náměstí).

Appropriation in this text is viewed from the perspective of the information design, a crucial actor within communication situations in public spaces; in the anthropological sense where a human (*a user*) is in the fore of our consideration. Marcelli (2011), who considers the theoretical reflection of today's city processes even claims that "life has taken over the urban space and began to appropriate it". I see it as important to pay attention to patterns of appropriation seen in public spaces, identify them and learn to work with them, before the level of complexity rises too high to comprehend.

Architect Eliel Saarinen (1943) once said that "many achievements of humankind were ignored just because they took place in slow-growing communities. And such times were viewed with contempt in the periods of fast growth, when materialism was perceived as the only sign of vitality." The speed of development and the rhythm are in this case of relative magnitudes; we may perceive the 19th century as a slow one today. Significant urban-planning interventions into the city organism, like the Paris reconstruction in the second half of the 19th century by the architect Baron Haussmann, can be seen as the new normal in the course of a century. But a man who realizes the existence in the context of historical development will keep reminding these moments (new literature on Haussmann's massive modernization act is being published to this day[3]) and realize that rebuilding a city, too, in fact is a form of appropriation.

Even in an old city we can trace such *modulation* of communication with physical appropriation – when designing the paths, districts, nodes and other categories of urban semantics defined by Lynch (1960). The arrangement of the urban environment does indeed closely relate to my interest in communication within the city organism, but for the purpose of this text, it is only a backdrop to a scene in which we direct our attention to a more saddle demonstrations of symbolic power in modern cities. That is, an added information and interactive layer influencing the way we understand and *use* cities, instead of their hardware redisposition. The layer of interest in this text may be perceived as a kind of a *software of a city*. Acts of interaction between the public and the city are indeed fascinating from the semiotic, social and even physical point of view. The inhabitants are further viewed as users of a given system. The city organism in this view is a complex system of actions and reactions, physical and mental limitations, affordances, social conventions and even poetic possibilities. In this framework, the *usage* of the cityscape itself is a very rich source of inspiration and knowledge on anthropological interactions and functions of the whole generations. *Appropriation* then logically takes an important position in this perception.

1.3   Language of the City

I am considering two groups of inhabitants in the city: (1) *Experts*, as defined by Barthes (1995), who have the formal license and means for forming what I am going to call the *Language of the City*. And also (2) *Users* of a space formed this way, who are *inhabitants* of the city. Understanding of such a *city language* is crucial for their function within the city system and their satisfaction or frustration stemming from everyday communication situations. Or even better said, their *user experience*.

---

[3] For example see Gautrand 2016.

Roland Barthes also used the term *Language of the City* in an essay from 1967,[4] where he argues that indeed, the city speaks to its inhabitants and we speak to our city [...] simply by inhabiting it. "The real scientific leap will be achieved when we can speak of the language of the city without metaphor." (Barthes, 1995) His call for "multiplying the readings of the city" will rightly so employ professions he names as those one has to master (all at once) in order to sketch a semiotics of the city: "semiologist (a specialist in signs), a geographer, a historian, an urbanist, an architect, and probably a psychotherapist." I will humbly add another specialization, in my view very helpful in the 21st century: a UX designer.

The main question remains how to step out of metaphors in order to find a valid methodology for city research. Michel de Certeau (1988: 100) may give us a certain direction when saying that: "[...] the geometrical space of urbanists and architects seems to have the status of the 'proper meaning' constituted by grammarians and linguists in order to have a normal and normative level to which they can compare the drifting of 'figurative' language." Let us have this idea linger, despite the fact that De Certeau himself immediately claims that defining such 'proper meaning' is a fiction. We could say "of course!", having in mind Hall's words about the audiences who decode "offered meanings in relation to their own perspectives and wishes, even if often in some framework of shared experience" (McQuail, c1997: 101). First of all it is important to realize who decodes the offered 'text', being it a newspaper article or a city pedestrian signals – to give a simple example of a city user interface with its "language". Here, we are only a step away from HCI ideology, which Brejcha (2015) sees as a system of ideas and beliefs on which a user interface stands. In order to build a new user interface, Brejcha suggests deconstructing the present ones and uncover their design/intent. Interestingly, now we have to admit that ideology also stands behind the language of the city considered in this writing.

If I should now come up with a definition valid for the framework of this essay, I could say that: **The language of the city (LOTC) considers all sign systems present in the built environment, bearing information and communicating their purpose in order to allow the inhabitant a purposeful function in such an environment. LOTC reflects existing communication functions as well as generates new speech acts.** There are a number of units involved and I do not intend to provide an exhausting list in this short paper. Some of them are purely functional, others follow an aesthetic or educational function. This language also involves affordances, communicates values or shows persuasive connotations.

1.4 Flâneur as the City Researcher

The researcher recognizes processes and identifies behavior of city users may be perceived as the *flâneur*, "a term introduced by Baudelaire [and developed by Walter Benjamin] as a type of spectator and storyteller of modern life". (Jenks 1995: 146) Jenks further describes this figure that "moves through space and among the people with a viscosity that both enables and privileges vision." Jenks also argues why this type of person has its place in a city: "The flâneur, though grounded in everyday life, is an analytical

---

[4] His collection of essays from 1963–1973 was not published until 1995. See Barthes, 1995.

form, a narrative device, an attitude towards knowledge and its social context. It is an image of movement through the social space of modernity…". (Jenks 1995: 148) This perception goes along with the qualitative research techniques so essential for social sciences. Hendl (2016) approaches both, Barthes' list of necessary professions to sketch a semiotics of the city as well as the importance of flâneur for the research of cityscapes: "[…] the researcher seeks and analyzes any information contributing to shedding light on his questions and comes to both deductive and inductive conclusions…".

2 Appropriation in Public Spaces

Let us state that cities rely on experts who are educated, competent and chosen for designing the direction of development for a given community. De Certeau (1988: 7) reminds that thanks to achieving this authority, an *expert* can, even […] "on questions foreign to his technical competence […] pronounce with authority a discourse which is no longer a function of knowledge, but rather a function of the socio-economic order." This *expert* has means and formal license to the way appropriation of public spaces takes place. This happens with resolution and force unavailable to an inhabitant (user). Thus, I argue that the user appropriates public spaces with different means and in a different way. Within sign systems in focus of this text, it can be an artistic approach, expression or revolt, but even a meaningful appropriation in case that the user experience lacks something that the expert did not consider as important. In both cases, design is the means of expression and along with appropriation can be used for a *modulation of the city language*. The *expert* in fact becomes a *designer* with formal license to appropriate. Below, I will offer categories and examples to consider when talking about appropriation in public spaces.

2.1 Visual Appropriation

It is commonly accepted as a fact that vision provides the most information about our surroundings. It is inevitable that the perception in cities is disturbed by agents fighting for attention (e.g. advertisement); it is essential from my perspective, though, that information for orientation and circulation of users is kept on a higher level in the hierarchy. Symbolic content of cities visible to users provided by the significant elements (like the urban semantic, mentioned before) will not be further discussed; instead attention will be given to the urban information system.

Signs, symbols, pictograms and other smaller-scale means of communication spread throughout the city are providing latent form of urban communication. These elements are reinforcing given norms but also reflect the ideology of their creators (Fig. 3 (left) and (right)). In Copenhagen, Denmark, where gender-neutral signs are normally used, it is possible to come across with pedestrian crosswalks with both genders displayed (Fig. 4). Similarly, Stockholm, Sweden equips crosswalks with different genders on opposite sides of the streets (Fig. 5). Sometimes these may be single projects of social group engagements but they do exist and they participate in city communication. In other cases, gender-balanced signs are part of the usual city language.

Fig. 3. Different approach to displaying gender on the same traffic signs in Prague (left) and Riga (right).

Fig. 4. A pedestrian light in Copenhagen (H.C. Andersens Boulevard) using both figures for the stop signal.

Fig. 5. A sign with a female figure in Stockholm (Pålsundsgatan) denoting a crosswalk (there is a male figure on the other side of the street).

In Büdelsdorf, Germany, one can notice two sets of pedestrian walkway signs coexisting in the summer of 2019. The older signs were displaying a woman figure with a little girl. The new signs used a woman with half-boy/half-girl, which could be understood as a trans-gender reference. Similar situations seen in the cityscape bring questions on the interest group activities and the attitudes of city governments to portraying the content of information system through the prism of the post-modern society. Such symbols become a texture of every day, despite Norman's resolute approach saying that perfect detail in case of symbols is not necessary (Norman 2013). Yet, the snow-ball effect when many different communities demanded the inclusion of their religious or cultural customs into the icon sets of Apple products[5] could serve here as a warning before similar adjustments in public spaces due to possibly overwhelming consequences. There can be seen a typical square pattern encoding the national identity in Riga, Latvia. It is not only used on sweaters and tourist souvenirs, but also on curbs of sidewalks in some parts of the town (Fig. 6). The practical reason for this is not obvious, yet it is possible to consider that this is to express a symbolic value for the local culture.

---

[5] The situation was recently covered in the Czech press by Formánek 2019.

Fig. 6. The sidewalk curb in Riga reflects the pattern typical for local culture.

Fig. 7. The blue light illuminating a platform at Horley station near Gatwick Airport, U.K.

Another form of visual appropriation, which here means using the visible spectrum of the light rays, may be seen in Japan where sometimes the traveling public is disturbed by news of a collision of a train with the human body, which obviously is not an exceptional way to end one's life (see Rod et al. 2011). Only in recent years, attempts to manipulate the traveling public behavior with light rays was conducted. Richarz (2018) describes both visual and sonic means to change the intention of a person with suicide potential. Using the overhead source of blue light (also possible to see in Europe, Fig. 7) on the platforms is supposed to calm such a disturbed individual and change his intention. Matsubayahi et al. (2013) describes the success of this attempt: within ten years, there was 84% decrease in the number of suicides at 71 surveyed train stations in Japan.

Fig. 8. London, the bridge under the Finsbury Park station (January, 2019 – replaced with white lighting in March, 2019).

Fig. 9. Stockholm, the bridge over Långholmsgatan (March, 2019). Both places use the same principle of appropriation in public spaces, only with different color schemes.

London and Stockholm, shown on Figs. 8 and 9 are examples of yet another kind of visual appropriation and sub-conscious intervention in public spaces. The theory of defensible spaces was described by the beginning of the 1970's by Oskar Newman (1996), after observing the social problems in the neighborhood of the Pruitt-Igoe residential complex in St. Louis. The problems of defensible space were then heavily pronounced in general after the terrorist attack of September 11th, 2001 in New York.

Architect Michael Sorkin (2007) claims that it was "this one act which caused the erosion of self-confidence and growing paranoia, to which the elements in public space must react." The strict airport security checks, barricades in front of the synagogues, installing heavy permanent columns at the entrance to significant city squares or open spaces – all of this reacts once forever to our feeling of security and the view of a city in the 21st century. Lighting dark public spaces, possibly attracting illegal or non-desirable activity, is supposed to cause the change in perception of the public space and increasing its defensibility. The desired effect is then increasing the safety of the neighborhood. Perhaps artistic interventions with lights of different colors are an updated way to deal with the defensibility of particular problematic spaces.

Visual leads or "nudges" is yet another visible way with which experts appropriate the public spaces and mediate the norm, the preferred behavior of users. Throughout different cities, they are reminding the preferred side to walk on, the approach to recycling, the way to prevent congestion in frequented areas etc. (Figs. 10, 11 and 12). These are not always perceived as positive (I even encountered indignant reactions from people who "were brought up in a way where they would know how to behave, thus they do not need to be reminded of the correct behavior") and would deserve a separate research to uncover social attitudes amongst city users.

Fig. 10. Visual leads mediating the recommended norm of behavior. Waiting zones in Copenhagen subway (Frederiksberg st.).

Fig. 11. Escalators at St. Pancras station in London.

Fig. 12. Entrance to the Konzertsaal im Schloss in Kiel, Germany.

2.2 Invisible Appropriation

The visual channel may provide the most information to the city user, but other senses such as the rhythms are also an important part of our lives and our city experience. Similarly to the visual appropriation, an expert designs a lasting solution which is then being mediated. Take the clicking sound of the pedestrian lights in Prague. The frequency of their clicking, in 1992, when they began spreading throughout the city, was in fact set arbitrarily[6]. In other cities (Eger, Hungary) there is a stable tone used instead of clicking; in San Diego, California, a voice countdown is heard by users with visual impairment. The same problem is solved with a different approach and design solutions in different environments; based on the decision of an expert in charge, who is exercising his power – and subsequently appropriating the public space.

It was the composer Thomas Laub who in 1904 decided on ways to appropriate the Copenhagen central square area acoustically. Laub's brother-in-law Martin Nyrop, the architect of the Copenhagen Town Hall, wanted to achieve a similar symbolic effect as heard in London when Big Ben strikes. And so Laub, who was a great fan of Danish folk music, composed a tune which to this day brings together the citizens with a sound element of national identity (Rådhusklokkerne i København c2008). Every fifteen minutes, a part of this melody is played, letting the listener know which part of the hour came, without raising their eyes to the clock dial.

In a small medieval town of Artena, Italy, one can experience quite a different way of sound appropriation with the local tower clock: first the number of the whole hours is announced in one key, followed by the quarter/half/three quarters in another key. For a Central European user, this way of announcing time is in fact unusual and confusing. Again, the same situation in different locations called for different ways in which the expert designed a solution to a communication situation.

If a town hall clock can mediate a tune with a certain significance for the community, so can railroad station speakers. In Kolín, Czech Republic, a well-known folk tune "Kolíne, Kolíne" – written about this very city – is used to announce every train arrival. Similarly, Japanese subway stations also have their own audio identity.

Cities give opportunities to learn about many different ways of acoustic appropriations. A typical sound of a mechanical bell used in tramways in Prague or Lisbon is replaced by a *recording* of the bell in new tramway cars of Amsterdam, Strasbourg or Bordeaux – which is in fact an example of remediation[7]. When two ships pass each other in Kiel, Germany, they sound a humorous greeting; the life in any port city has its specifics and stable patterns to signal arrival or leaving of a ship from port. Soundscapes are now also enriched by the new phenomena in cities across the world: electric scooters of Bird, Frog, Lime or other companies disturb citizens with their typical noise with every movement of such vehicles without paying (meant to discourage unauthorized use). These sounds of cities did not just *appear* – they had to be once *designed*. And as such they appropriate the space which the citizens cohabit.

2.3 Appropriation with Other Senses

Physical footprint of the place shows certain idleness, as Vacek (2011) reminds us. Cities thus can be perceived as "mirrors reflecting multi-layered images of hidden cultural and spiritual meanings". Such idleness is present even in structural appropriations; let me

---

[6] As admitted by Viktor Dudr from SONS (Prague organization of people with visual impairment) in my 2012 personal interview. Dudr had to decide on the frequency during the telephone call with a technician making the setting on-site.

[7] A representation of one medium in another; Bolter and Grusin (2000) argue that remediation is a defining characteristic of the new digital media.

again mention Prague here as an example. The radius of the tramway tracks between the Main train station (Hlavní nádraží) and Husinecká stop underwent a slight correction during the 2009 reconstruction of the highway in the proximity of the station. As a result, to this day, all passengers feel a certain demonstration of accumulated kinetic energy during a fast ride of the tramway uphill. In the moment of reaching the connection of the new track to the old track, all passengers experience a short moment of instability. Maybe their memory does not hold the major long-lasting transportation inconvenience that this reconstruction caused in the area eleven years ago. But there is still a way to track down the act of an expert's appropriation of public space – and its consequences.

Practically all senses can be entertained in considering the environment of the city. Haptic leads as well as olfactory maps of our cities do already exist (imagine living next to a bakery or a brewery; also people who lived in Chicago in the mid-20th century during the operation of the famous Union Stock Yards tell me in interviews about their unforgettable memories of the city smell). Here it is a good moment to think again of Barthes (1995): If the city is like a text that we can read, then the user of the city is in fact *a reader* – and that is why it is important to "multiply the *readings* of the city" as that might be the right approach in search of a definition of the city language (as opposed to "multiplying the investigations or functional styles of the city").

2.4 Conveying Ideology, Conventions and Extra Information

There is an extra layer connected to the appropriations by experts (designers) mentioned above, a layer mediating the ideology in a similar direction as Brejcha (2015) suggests. The amount of seconds allowing pedestrians to cross the street implicitly gives us a message about how much a walker is welcome in a street. The language used in city information systems may hint peculiarities, specifics or a way of thinking in a given culture[8]. How much information, though, should the city interfaces actually provide? What kind of information? While the compacting trash bin in the Hartsfield–Jackson Atlanta International Airport indicates with LED whether it is ready for more waste or still compacting the load previously entered, a solar-powered compacting waste bin in the streets of Helsingør, Denmark *thanks you* for keeping the city clean, with an audio message… Where is in fact the border in what such interfaces *should* do? When may they already cause an irritation to the user? In other words, should they provide straight clean-cut information, or should they show "care" of the user, educate him or pamper him? See Fig. 13.

Appropriation also takes place when projecting a media content onto a city surface (typically a large building), which becomes a popular addition to summer festivals or New Year's celebrations (so called videomapping). But the city language may also contain *simulacrum*, an empty reference. In the case of Prague, this creates visual pollution with pointless signs. Individual transportation vehicles known as Segway were banned from most of the central district of Prague in July 2016 and despite the fact that there are court disputes in process still four years later, challenging this decision, Segways

---

[8] In the subway system in Stockholm, Sweden, the sign marking the escalator from the platform to the higher level, will read "*Upp*" (Up). The opposite side will not be marked with a word Down, but "*Ej upp*" (Not up). So, in fact the message is not signifying the direction of the escalator's motion, but the passenger's destination after taking the ride.

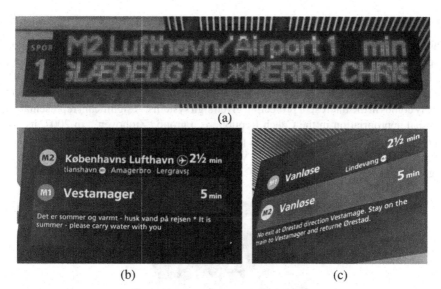

(a)

(b)   (c)

Fig. 13. The panels in Copenhagen subway wish you Happy Christmas orremind you that you should stay hydrated in the hot weather. Typos and misspellings in the text give the user of the system an impression that some recommendations were entered by a person with limited knowledge of English. Still, with the license to appropriate the public space.

are practically non-existent (they were readily replaced with the electric scooters). The result is that the only reminder of Segways in the historical center of Prague, is about 600 signs (Fig. 14) prohibiting Segways from their presence (Český rozhlas 2016)[9]. An example from Budapest (Fig. 15) conveys clearly the fact how the complexity of this problem may rise in the post-modern world.

Fig. 14. Simulacrum in public spaces: Segways practically disappeared from the center of Prague but there are hundreds of signs left behind, prohibiting these vehicles and creating visual pollution.

Fig. 15. Budapest is using similar large-sized signs to prohibit more than one transportation device at the same time.

---

[9] In February 2020, new signs prohibiting so called "Beer Bikes" began to appear in the streets of Prague.

2.5   Appropriation by the User

While users of the city execute a certain appropriation of public spaces like neighborhood happenings, markets, festivals, theater or music performances and so on, they do not have the license to appropriate the same sign systems (that means those in the focus of this text) and means of value as the experts do. When attempting doing so, a punishment usually comes in the interest of protecting given sign systems. A significant representative of visual appropriation in the Czech Republic is a group "Ztohoven". In 2007, its co-founder Roman Týc was charged with paying a fine and serving a 1-month sentence for exchanging the traffic light glasses with non-standardized stencils in the center of Prague (Fig. 16). (Česká televize 2012)

Fig. 16. Roman Týc replaced about 50 glass stencils on Prague traffic lights an attempt to express a criticism of the Czech society. A wave of support to the artist from the public, artists and even from the political representation followed his trial. Photo credit: Creative Commons – ŠJů, April the 10th 2007.

In this case, the syntagmatic function of the traffic lights was kept intact and all replaced stencils were only those signaling to pedestrians. Breaching a formal sign system of a city in a way that the user is confused or lost happens relatively seldom, we may see a slightly altered design with added connotations in some cultures, shooting into traffic signs is relatively common in order to satisfy artistic aspirations (Fig. 17) or to add a missing information (Fig. 17), but the primary function of traffic signs or other elements in the information system does not seem to be often the target of unauthorized manipulation.

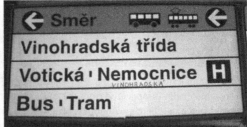

Fig. 17. Altered signs in London (left) and Prague (right). On the right example, the name of a hospital was added.

How can then users of the city react to the hegemony of experts (designers) who de facto create the language of the city? Their options are limited. One way is to express their civic attitude without giving up the right to use the public spaces[10]. Another way would be civic participation and co-creation of the language of the city. Using Denis McQuail's (c1997) approach, we may see the user of a city as a co-creator of the language of the city, thanks to his or her unique perception. But differences in reading or applying the End-User Programming[11] would likely create more discrepancies and decrease the effectivity of the system. In the interest of clarity and effectivity, it is desirable that the information system of the city is clear and does not allow for alternative reading or creating multiple mental models.

3   Discussion: Bridging the Gap Between the Designer and the User

From the semiotic perspective, there are interesting ways of expressing meanings related to the local culture, its history and values, as well as problems, solutions or regulations. These ways of appropriating the public space and communication with citizens (users) were perceived as a language of a kind. "A city is an object that we see, a model that is looked at by architects, engineers and urbanists, it is a construction, or even a machinery; from the beginning subject to technological flows and the will of state control...", says Olivier Mongin (2017). But first of all, it is defined by the way it is used by its inhabitants (De Certeau 1984). The purpose of this examining reflection was to bring an attention to the User-Experience and User-Centered design applied to the concept of the Language of the City (LOTC). Appropriation is a way to influence such language of the urban landscape through its various sign systems. I described and defined various types of appropriation and considered how they establish, or interact with, LOTC. In future investigations, it will be attractive to explore whether the LOTC may be enriched and how, what is the designer's intent and in which ways it allows a user's intervention without causing entropy.

In my view, assigning a responsibility to the Designer (Expert) for the User Experience of the User (Inhabitant) renders in the need to further examine and aim to find an understanding of the pragmatic use of the city. User research and user testing will allow to further grasp the concept of the LOTC and perception of the city language and its use by the public, as well as uncover values and attitudes of citizens towards historical or symbolic connotations. Demanding that experts create a functional and effective city system should not be only a subject of utopian literature[12].

---

[10] Kukal (2019) protests to the design flaws of new tramways Škoda 14T and 15T in Prague by not paying the fare on these particular vehicles.

[11] Lieberman et al. (2013) propose the following definition: End User Development (EUD) can be defined as a set of methods, techniques, and tools that allow users of software systems, who are acting as non-professional software developers, at some point to create, modify, or extend a software artifact.

[12] In his utopist text, Baczko (1989) talks about Lunol, a city of 650.000, placed on the Moon: "The foreigner never needs to ask here – the architecture talks to him with universal language of well-ordered forms...".

Still, after this reflection of the LOTC concept, many questions remain unanswered, for example: Can we distinguish particular differences in the language of different cities? What are their specifics and what do they have in common? Is the language of one city universally transferable to another? And most of all: What is the *user experience* from *using* the city – and how to cover it methodologically? Naturally, both languages and cities do change and evolve and it would also be interesting to look at cities from the perspective of the Theory of language change, for example. Another direction worth of an exploration would be an attempt to define a certain LOTC grammar, being inspired by the Christopher Alexander's Pattern Language (Alexander et al. 1977). In any case, the respect to the city users, their needs and ways of communication, must remain the pinnacle of interest of every municipality.

References

Alexander, C., Ishikawa, S., Silverstein, M.: A Pattern Language: Towns, Buildings, Construction. Oxford University Press, New York (1977). ISBN 9780195019193

Bolter, J.D., Grusin, R.A.: Remediation: Understanding New Media. MIT Press, Cambridge (2000). ISBN 0-262-02452-7

de Certeau, M.: The Practice of Everyday Life. University of California Press, Berkeley (1984). ISBN 0-520-06168-3

Barthes, R.: Semiology and Urbanism. In: The Semiotic Challenge. University of California Press, Berkeley (1995). ISBN 978-052-0087-842. http://www.columbia.edu/itc/architecture/ockman/pdfs/dossier_4/barthes_2.pdf

Brejcha, J.: Cross-Cultural Human-Computer Interaction and User Experience Design: A Semiotic Perspective. CRC Press/Taylor & Francis Group, Boca Raton (2015). ISBN 978-1-4987-0257-7. Commercially: http://www.crcpress.com/product/isbn/9781498702577

Baczko, B.: Utopian Lights. Paragon House, New York (1989). In: VACKOVÁ, Barbora. Prostor, moc a utopie: ideální město a jeho společnost. [Space, Power and Utopia: The Ideal City and its Society.] Masaryk University, Brno (2010). ISBN 978-80-210-5252-9

Börjesson, M., Jonsson, D.R., Lundberg, M.: An ex-post CBA for the Stockholm metro. Trans. Res. Part A: Policy Pract. **70**, 135–148 (2014). ISSN 0965-8564. https://doi.org/10.1016/j.tra.2014.10.006

Busse, M., Strang, V.: Ownership and Appropriation. Vol. English ed. A.S.A. Monographs. Berg Publishers, Oxford (2011). http://search.ebscohost.com/login.aspx?direct=true&AuthType=ip,shib&db=nlebk&AN=390453&lang=cs&site=eds-live&scope=site

Gautrand, J.C.: Eugène Atget: Paris. Cologne (Germany): Taschen, Bibliotheca Universalis (2016). ISBN 978-3836522304

Hendl, J.: Kvalitativní výzkum: základní teorie, metody a aplikace. [Qualitative Research: Basic Theories, Methods and Applications.] Portál, Praha (2016). ISBN 978-80-262-0982-9

Formánek, O.: Řekni to smajlíkem: Lidé kvůli používání emoji stanuli před soudem, z obrázků se stalo i politické téma. [Say it with the Smiley: People in front of the Court because of using emoji, pictures developed into a political topic.] Hospodářské noviny. commercially: https://archiv.ihned.cz/c1-66614550-emoji-rekni-to-smajlikem

Hoffman, F.G.: Conflict in the 21st Century: The Rise of Hybrid Wars. Potomac Institute for Policy Studies, Arlington (2007)

Holbová, M.: Select regional centers of moravia existed as major transit hubs from the years 1800 to 2012. Olomouc (2015). Diploma thesis. University of Palacký in Olomouc, Faculty of Nature

Jenks, C.: Visual Culture. Routledge, New York (1995). ISBN 0415106230

Klodnerová, K.: Appropriation in public space as a way of improving a quality of life in a city: on the example from Prague. Praha (2015). Diploma thesis. Charles University in Prague, Faculty of Humanities, Department of Electronic Culture and Semiotics. https://dspace.cuni.cz/handle/20.500.11956/71095?locale-attribute=en

Kukal, Z.: Jezdím načerno. [I am Riding Without the Ticket.] Aktuálně. Praha (2019). http://blog.aktualne.cz/blogy/prazskej-blog.php?itemid=34365

Lieberman, H., Paternò, F., Klann, M., Wulf, V.: End-user development: an emerging paradigm. In: Lieberman, H., Paternò, F., Wulf, V. (eds.) End-User Development. Human-Computer Interaction Series, vol. 9, Chapt. 1, pp. 1–7. Springer, Cham (2006). https://doi.org/10.1007/1-4020-5386-x_1

Lynch, K.: The Image of the City. Massachusetts Institute of Technology Press, Cambridge (1960)

Marcelli, M.: Mesto vo filozofii [The City in Philosophy]. Kalligram, Bratislava (2011). ISBN 978-80-8101-400-0

Matsubayashi, T., Sawada, Y., Ueda, M.: Does the installation of blue lights on train platforms prevent suicide?: a before-and-after observational study from Japan. J. Affect. Dis. **2013**(147), 385–388. ISSN 0165-0327. https://doi.org/10.1016/j.jad.2012.08.018

Mcquail, D.: Audience Analysis. Sage Publications, Thousand Oaks (1997). ISBN 07-619-1002-6

Mongin, O.: Urbánní situace: město v čase globalizace. Praha: Univerzita Karlova, nakladatelství Karolinum (2017). [orig.: La condition urbaine: La ville à l'heure de la mondialisation] ISBN 978-80-246-3442-5

Newman, O.: Creating Defensible Space. U.S. Department of Housing and Urban Development, Office of Policy Development and Research, Washington 1996

Norén, F.: H-Day 1967 – An alternative perspective on "propaganda" in the historiography of public relation. Public Rel. Rev. **45**(2), 236–245 (2019). https://doi.org/10.1016/j.pubrev.2018.10.004. ISSN 0363-8111

Norman, D.A.: The Design of Everyday Things. Basic Books, New York (2013). ISBN 978-046-5050-659

Rod, J., Graham, C., Gibbs, M.: Suicide effects. In: C&T 2011: Proceedings of the 5th International Conference on Communities and Technologies. ACM Press, New York (2011), s. 31-. https://doi.org/10.1145/2103354.2103359. ISBN 9781450308243. http://dl.acm.org/citation.cfm?doid=2103354.2103359

Rådhusklokkerne i København: Det Kongelige Bibliotek. c2008. http://www.kb.dk/da/nb/samling/ma/fokus/raadhus.html

Richarz, A.: The Amazing Psychology of Japanese Train Stations. Citylab.com. Washington D.C.: The Atlantic, 2018. https://www.citylab.com/transportation/2018/05/the-amazing-psychology-of-japanese-train-stations/560822/

Saarinen, E.: The City: Its Growth, Its Decay, Its Future. Pp. xvi, 380. Reinhold Publishing Corporation, New York (1943)

Segwaye zmizí z centra Prahy: Hlavní město začíná instalovat značky zakazující provoz vozítek. [Segways will disappear from the Center of Prague. The Capital begins to install the signs prohibiting the operation of such vehicles.] Český rozhlas. Praha, 25 November 2016. https://region.rozhlas.cz/segwaye-zmizi-z-centra-prahy-hlavni-mesto-zacina-instalovat-znacky-zakazujici-7250030

Sorkin, M.: Indefensible Space: The Architecture of the National Insecurity State. Routledge, New York (2007). ISBN 978-0415953689

Týcova dvě sklíčka opět na scéně (2012). [Týc's Two Glass Stencils Reappear.] Česká televize. Praha (2012). https://ct24.ceskatelevize.cz/kultura/1163530-tycova-dve-sklicka-opet-na-scene

Vacek, L.: Identita místa: Prostor jako vztah formy a času. [Identity of Place: Space as the Relationship of Form and Time.] Praha, FA ČVUT (2011)

A Systematic Review of Usability Evaluation Methods and Tools for ATM Interfaces

Joe Sahua$^{(\boxtimes)}$ ⓘ and Arturo Moquillaza ⓘ

Pontificia Universidad Católica del Perú, Avenida Universitaria 1801, San Miguel, Lima 32, Peru
{jsahuad,amoquillaza}@pucp.pe

Abstract. In this work, we present the results of a systematic review about methods for evaluate the usability on ATM interfaces and tools utilized. Following a Systematic Review Process, a total of 132 studies were found and 96 discounting duplicates, where 12 works were finally selected for the review. We also found the most used tools for usability evaluations and the frequency of them in the selected studies. Finally, we found that there exist some usability evaluation methods and process for some systems, but in the case of ATM, there is not studies was found. This work is intended to give ideas for usability evaluations on ATM interfaces, giving information of the current status of the Systematic Review and potential studies that can help to perform usability evaluations for ATM, especially, quantitative type researches. Based on this information, we intend to propose a usability evaluation process oriented to ATM applications.

Keywords: Systematic review · Usability evaluation method · Automated teller machine · Usability

1 Introduction

Nowadays, usability is determinant for the success of any software product, including the automated teller machines or ATM [1]. Usability offers some benefits, for example: (1) Increased user productivity, (2) Decrease in user errors, (3) Decrease in software training costs, (4) Lesser design changes in early stages of the project and (5) Reduction of user support [2].

Despite the importance and the increase of functionalities that have been added to the ATM, the interface usually shows usability defects, which could cause frustrating user experience [3]. The insufficient considerations about final user needs in the design of the ATM interfaces have produced some serious usability and accessibility problems, causing discomfort and operational errors. This may be happening by the fact that despite the existence of some principles and guides for web and mobile devices interfaces, there are few evidences yet about how to apply this principles and guidelines on ATM domain [4].

The importance of usability and know if a software possesses this characteristic has led some usability evaluations for ATM. However, some of these usability evaluations were made using adapted heuristics and guidelines due to the lack of standards and criteria for ATM domain.

© Springer Nature Switzerland AG 2020
A. Marcus and E. Rosenzweig (Eds.): HCII 2020, LNCS 12202, pp. 130–141, 2020.
https://doi.org/10.1007/978-3-030-49757-6_9

Having few guidelines and heuristics for ATM usability evaluation generate insufficient information about usability level of ATM applications and errors that may cause some problems to the users. Perform evaluations helps to know if the software fulfills the guidelines and heuristics that the evaluation method exposes, it also helps to find out the errors and problems on interfaces.

The main objective of this work is to provide information about the usability evaluation methods that can be used for ATM. Analyzing the studies that made or use some evaluation methods for ATM, allowed to identify the most common and important techniques and tools that may help to create new processes and protocols of usability evaluation for ATM, especially of the quantitative type in order to measure, compare and classify the level of usability of one or more ATM applications.

This paper is organized as follows: Sect. 2 defines some important terms for this study, Sect. 3 describes the systematic review process in detail, Sect. 4 details the results and answers to research questions are presented, and, finally, Sect. 4 shows some conclusions and future works.

2 Background

2.1 Self-service

Self-service is called to any activity that does not require interaction with human beings. This is not necessarily an activity carried out only on the Internet, it can also be done through a telephone (example: interactive voice response) or physically (example: ATM). In addition, the searches made in websites such as Google or Wikipedia are also considered self-services, although, care must be taken with these as they could provide erroneous information [5].

2.2 Automated Teller Machine (ATM)

An ATM, also called cash dispenser or automated teller machine, is an electronic computerized telecommunications device that allows clients of financial institutions to access their bank accounts securely. An ATM is a self-service banking terminal that accepts deposits, cash withdrawals or other functionalities. ATM are commonly activated by inserting a bank card into the card reader slot. For example, when a customer is trying to withdraw cash, the ATM first connects the bank's system to verify the balance, then dispenses the cash and sends a completed transaction notice [6].

2.3 Usability Evaluation Method

A usability evaluation method is a procedure composed by a set of well-defined activities to obtain data related to the interaction between the end user and the software, and how the specific properties of this software contribute to a certain degree of usability. These methods were initially developed to evaluate the WIMP interfaces (Window, icon, menu, pointing device), which are the most representative of desktop applications. One of the most representative examples is the heuristic evaluation method, proposed by Nielsen. Usability evaluation methods can be broadly classified into two different types [7]:

- Empirical methods: They are based on capturing and analyzing the usage data of a real end user. Real end users use the software or a prototype to complete a set of predefined tasks, while the evaluator records the results of their work. Analyses of these results can provide useful information to detect usability problems.
- Inspection methods: They are carried out by expert evaluators or designers and are based on the review of the usability aspects of Web artifacts, which are commonly user interfaces according to their set of guidelines.

2.4 Systematic Review

It is a form of documentary research that allows the study of the accumulated knowledge of a specific area, with the objective of inventorying and systematizing the production of knowledge of an area. The systematic review was born in the eighties, when in Latin America studies were mainly done in the area of social sciences, which required gathering information to be able to base policies and alternatives of action for social development. This can be used as a tool to recognize and interpret reality, a documentary methodological proposal and as a basis for the decision making in the field of research. There are multiple methodologies to run systematic reviews, but there is a common one among all, which consists of the following steps [8]:

- Contextualization: It takes into account the approach to the study problems, its limits, the documentary material to be used and criteria for contextualization.
- Classification: Definition of the parameters that will be used to systematize the information, the kind of documents to be studied, chronological aspects, study objectives, disciplines, lines of research, the conclusive level and the scope of these.
- Categorization: Hierarchy and generation of classes for the treatment of information. This can be classified into two categories: internal (derived directly from the study of documentation) and external (allow to find the socio-cultural contribution).
- Analysis: Discern what is the main reason for the creation of new knowledge in a specific area, discover trends and perspective of research.

3 Systematic Review Process

The present systematic review process was run based on the methodology for systematic review proposed by B. Kitchernham and Charters, which allowed us to objectively review information in various databases and digital libraries [9]. The selected articles were obtained from the following databases: Scopus, IEEE Xplore, ACM Digital Library and Springerlink. This methodology consists of the following steps [9]:

3.1 Research Questions

The main objective of this systematic review was to identify usability comparisons and evaluations made to ATM applications, self-service systems and other banking systems or applications. Other objectives were to find the improvements proposed based on the evaluations and comparisons made to the systems and find guidelines or heuristics of usability assessment for ATM domain.

The research questions were the following:

- What usability comparisons and evaluations have been made between ATM systems of different banks?
- What techniques and guidelines have been used to measure the level of usability of ATM interfaces?

In order to have better structured questions, a PICOC table was made (Table 1):

Table 1. PICOC.

Criterion	Description
Population	ATM system interfaces
Intervention	Usability comparisons, guidelines and heuristics used in the comparisons
Comparison	None
Outcomes	Usability comparisons made to ATM interfaces of different banks. Techniques, guidelines and heuristics used to measure the level if usability of ATM interfaces
Context	Academic context, software industry

3.2 Search Strategy

For the selection of the relevant studies, the most prominent terms for the research were defined and from them, some strings were built, which were subsequently used in the selected databases. The steps were the following:

Definition of Search String

From the proposed research questions, some terms were selected to conduct the systematic review. In addition to these terms, their synonyms and strongly related terms were selected, in order to obtain the most relevant and useful documents for the study. Publications dating from 2014 were considered, however, in some cases it was necessary to consider older articles due to their relevance for the study.

According to the above and the logical operators "AND" and "OR" the following search strings were obtained as follows:

- C1:
  "Comparisons" OR "Differences" OR "Differentiation" OR "Distinction" OR "Relation" OR "Evaluation" OR "Guidelines" OR "Principles"
- C2:
  "ATM" OR "Automated Teller Machine" OR "Automatic Teller Machine" OR "Cash machine" OR "Bank Software" OR "Financial Software" OR "Bank System" OR "Financial System"

- C3:

  "Usability" OR "User Experience" OR "UX" OR "Design" OR "UCD" OR "User Centered Design" OR "GUI" OR "Graphic User Interface"

  Therefore, the resulting search string was of the form:

C1 AND C2 AND C3

This resulting search was used in different selected databases, in order to find the most relevant and accurate information for the study.

Database Selection

Taking into account the databases recommended by the Pontificia Universidad Católica del Perú, the list was filtered to only those related to engineering and a specific search string was created for each database.

- Scopus

  ```
  TITLE (("Comparisons" OR "Comparability" OR "Versus" OR
  "Evaluation") AND ("ATM" OR "Automated Teller Machine" OR
  "Automatic Teller Machine" OR "Cash machine" OR "Bank Software"
  OR "Financial Software" OR "Bank System" OR "Financial System")
  AND ("Usability" OR "UX" OR "User experience" OR "Design" OR
  "UCD" OR "User Centered Design" OR "GUI" OR "Graphic User
  Interface"))
  ```

- IEEE Xplore

  ```
  ("Document Title":"Comparison" OR "Document
  Title":"Comparability" OR "Document Title":"Versus" OR
  "Document Title":"Evaluation") AND ("Document Title":"ATM" OR
  "Document Title":"Automated teller machine" OR "Document
  Title":"Automatic teller machine" OR "Document Title":"Cash
  machine" OR "Document Title":"Bank software" OR "Document
  Title":"Financial software" OR "Document Title":"Bank system" OR
  "Document Title":"Financial system") AND ("Document
  Title":"Usability" OR "Document Title":"UX" OR "Document
  Title":"User experience" OR "Document Title":"Design" OR
  "Document Title":"UCD" OR "Document Title":"User centered
  design" OR "Document Title":"GUI" OR "Document Title":"Graphic
  user interface")
  ```

- ACM Digital Library

  ```
  acmdlTitle:("Comparisons" OR "Comparability" OR "Versus" OR
  "Evaluation") AND acmdlTitle:("ATM" OR "Automated Teller
  Machine" OR "Automatic Teller Machine" OR "Cash machine" OR "Bank
  Software" OR "Financial Software" OR "Bank System" OR "Financial
  ```

```
System") AND acmdlTitle: ("Usability" OR "UX" OR "User
experience" OR "Design" OR "UCD" OR "User Centered Design" OR
"GUI" OR "Graphic User Interface")
```

- SpringerLink

```
(comparison* OR Comparability OR versus OR evaluation*) AND (ATM
OR automat* teller machine OR cash machine OR bank* software OR
financial software) AND (usability OR UX OR User experience OR
design OR UCD OR User-Centered Design OR GUI OR Graphic User
Interface).
```

Selection and Exclusion Criteria

In order for a contribution to be selected as relevant for the development of the study, the following points were taken into account:

Relationship with the following topics.

- Usability comparisons and evaluations made to banking applications of different banks.
- Guidelines or heuristics recommended for measuring usability of banking applications.
- Improvements in the usability of the main functionalities of an ATM.
- Positive or negative opinions of the usability of ATM.

For an article to be excluded and marked as not relevant, it must meet one of the following points.

- Provide improvements in hardware design.
- Refers to the term "ATM" in communications, biological, electronic, etc. contexts.
- Publications in languages other than Spanish and English.

3.3 Process Execution

Articles related to software products of financial institutions or other self-services and the design of their user interfaces were considered. In addition, some articles were selected despite their age (as of the year 2000) as they provided relevant information for the study.

Search and Selection Process

When the searches were performed in each database with their respective search string, multiple studies were obtained, each was reviewed to verify how relevant they were for the study. In addition, the list of results obtained was simplified since duplicates were found between one database and others (Table 2).

Table 2. Search results.

Database	Found	Duplicates	Relevant
Scopus	39	18	2
IEEE Xplore	4	2	0
ACM Digital Library	24	16	0
SpringerLink	65	0	10
TOTAL	**132**	**36**	**12**

4 Results

4.1 Report of Relevant Studies

This section shows the relevant studies found in the systematic review and how it contributed to the present study (in this case, which question helps answer). In addition, a summary of each study is shown.

Table 3. Relevant studies.

Topic	Author	Name	Tag
Usability guidelines and techniques	[4]	Developing an ATM interface using user-centered design techniques	A1
	[10]	Design of graphical user interfaces to implement new features in an ATM system of a financial bank	A2
	[1]	Methodologies for the design of ATM Interfaces: a systematic review	A3
	[11]	Skill specific spoken dialogues based personalized ATM design to maximize effective interaction for visually impaired persona	A4
	[12]	Token access: improving accessibility of Automatic Teller Machines (ATMs) by transferring the interface and interaction to personal accessible devices	A5
	[13]	Introducing user-centered systems design	A6
	[14]	Socio-cultural aspects in the design of multilingual banking interfaces in the arab region	A7
	[15]	Improving touchscreen accessibility in self-service technology	A8

(*continued*)

Table 3. (*continued*)

Topic	Author	Name	Tag
Evaluations and comparisons	[16]	Usability evaluation of model-driven cross-device web user interfaces	A9
	[17]	User-centered design approach for interactive kiosks: evaluation and redesign of an automatic teller machine	A10
	[18]	Usability evaluation of ticketing system of Metro Manila Train Network	A11
	[19]	Usability comparisons of seven main functions for automated teller machine (ATM) banking service of five banks in Thailand	A12

4.2 Answers to Research Questions

What usability comparisons and evaluations have been made between ATM systems of different banks?

In the systematic review, usability comparisons and evaluations made to ATMs of different banks were found. In Table 4 it can be seen that although only one article completely answers the question (in this case the article labeled A12), some could help to make comparisons. Studies with the tags A9, A10 and A11 carry out evaluations with the objective of observing if the interfaces evaluated are usable and find usability errors. Article A12 goes beyond the three mentioned above as it not only carries out evaluations of the seven main ATM functionalities of the five most important banks in Thailand, but also compared the interfaces based on the results obtained in the evaluation.

Table 4. Studies related to usability comparisons and evaluations.

Topics	Related studies
Comparisons	A12
Evaluations	A9, A10, A11

What techniques and guidelines have been used to measure the level of usability of ATM interfaces?

The systematic review sought the techniques and guidelines used to measure the usability of ATM interfaces. As can be seen in Table 5, there are studies in the literature that show techniques and guidelines to create user-centered interfaces not only for ATM, but for banking systems in general or other self-service technologies. Studies A1, A2, A3, A4 and A5 show ATM graphic interface design techniques, methodologies and features, article A6 proposes user-centered interface design, but for systems in general (not specifically ATMs), A7 is focused on banking systems and finally A8 exposes improvements for self-service interfaces with touch screens.

Table 5. Studies related to usability techniques and guidelines.

Usability techniques and guidelines	Related studies
For ATM	A1, A2, A3, A4, A5
For systems in general	A6
For banking systems in general	A7
For self-service technologies	A8

4.3 Evaluation Tools

After analyzing the selected studies, the tools used for the usability evaluation performed in each of these studies were listed. From Table 3, six studies were selected as they provided information on tools for usability evaluation:

1. Skill Specific Spoken Dialogues Based Personalized ATM Design to Maximize Effective Interaction for Visually Impaired Persona [11].
2. Token Access: Improving Accessibility of Automatic Teller Machine (ATMs) by Transferring the Interface and Interaction to Personal Accessible Devices [12].
3. Usability Evaluation of Model-Driven Cross-Device Web User Interfaces [16].
4. Usability Evaluation of Ticketing System of Metro Manila Train Network [18].
5. User-centered design approach for interactive kiosks: Evaluation and redesign of an automatic teller machine [17].
6. Usability comparisons of seven main functions for automated teller machine (ATM) banking service of five banks in Thailand [19].

The following Table 6 shows the comparative of usability evaluation tools reported in the literature per study.

From the previous table, the tools with the highest frequency of use in the selected studies were chosen (Table 7).

Finally, as we can see, an evaluation can use both the original ATM's own software or a prototype of it. Selecting one of these to perform a usability assessment is more than enough.

Table 6. Comparative chart of usability assessment studies reported in the literature and the tools used.

Tools	Studies					
	1	2	3	4	5	6
Questionnaire	X	X	✓	X	X	✓
Video cameras/screen recorders	X	X	X	✓	✓	X
Event logging software	✓	X	X	X	X	✓
ATM's own software	X	X	✓	✓	✓	X
Prototypes	✓	✓	X	X	X	✓
Heuristic evaluation	✓	✓	✓	✓	✓	✓
User evaluation	X	✓	X	X	X	✓

Table 7. Comparative chart of tools and its frequency of use in percentage.

Tools	Frequency	Percentage
Users evaluation	5	83.3%
Questionnaire	3	50%
ATM's own software	3	50%
Prototypes	3	50%
Video cameras/screen recorders	2	33.33%
Event logging software	2	33.33%
Heuristic evaluation	2	33.33%

5 Conclusions and Future Works

The systematic review showed us how important usability is when designing the graphical interface of not only ATMs, but of any system, including other self-services. The success of a software product and user experience in general, will depend not only on the functionality it provides, but on how usable it is.

This study managed to find guidelines and techniques used to design usable interfaces (not only ATMs, of various systems, including other self-services). These studies show steps, tips and recommendations for designing more user-centric and user-oriented interfaces.

There are guidelines to be able to make better designs and also usability evaluation methods, processes, and tools. However, it also shows very few methods, processes and comparisons of usability evaluation exclusive for ATM applications.

The results obtained in this systematic review has allowed us to know that the lack of usability evaluations for ATM causes the level of usability of these and the errors that they can count on their interfaces to be unknown. So, a question appears: How could we compare or improve interfaces, usability and user satisfaction if we don't have an initial measure, a starting point?

As future work, we will work on multiple evaluations to ATM applications of Peruvian banks, counting with different user profiles. These evaluations will follow the steps formulated in the usability evaluation and comparison process defined and proposed by us from the information obtained in this systematic review and an analysis of the judgment of experts in the ATM domain. Our future objective is to define, execute and validate a process that let to measure and compare the level of usability of one or more ATM applications.

Acknowledgments. We want to thank to participants from BBVA Perú, especially its ATM development team. Also, we thank to the "HCI, Design, User Experience, Accessibility & Innovation Technologies (HCI DUXAIT)" a research group from the Pontificia Universidad Católica del Perú (PUCP) for its support along the whole work.

References

1. Aguirre, J., Moquillaza, A., Paz, F.: Methodologies for the design of ATM interfaces: a systematic review. In: Ahram, T., Karwowski, W., Taiar, R. (eds.) IHSED 2018. AISC, vol. 876, pp. 256–262. Springer, Cham (2019). https://doi.org/10.1007/978-3-030-02053-8_39
2. Bias, R.G., Mayhew, D.J.: Cost-Justifying Usability: An Update for an Internet Age. Elsevier, Amsterdam (2005). eBook ISBN: 9780080455457
3. Curran, K., King, D.: Investigating the human computer interaction problems with automated teller machine navigation menus. In: Interactive Technology and Smart Education (2008). https://doi.org/10.1108/17415650810871583
4. Moquillaza, A., et al.: Developing an ATM interface using user-centered design techniques. In: Marcus, A., Wang, W. (eds.) DUXU 2017. LNCS, vol. 10290, pp. 690–701. Springer, Cham (2017). https://doi.org/10.1007/978-3-319-58640-3_49
5. Rosenbaum, S.: Creating usable self-service interaction. In: 2010 IEEE International Professional Communication Conference (IPCC), pp. 344–349 (2010). https://doi.org/10.1109/IPCC.2010.5530033
6. Zhang, M., Wang, F., Deng, H., Yin, J.: A survey on human computer interaction technology for ATM. Int. J. Intell. Eng. Syst., 20–29 (2013). https://doi.org/10.22266/ijies2013.0331.03
7. Fernandez, A., Insfran, E., Abrahão, S.: Usability evaluation methods for the web: a systematic mapping study. Inf. Softw. Technol. (2011). https://doi.org/10.1016/j.infsof.2011.02.007
8. Molina N.: Qué es el estado del arte? Ciencia & Tecnología Para La Salud Visual y Ocular (2005). https://doi.org/10.19052/sv.1666
9. Kitchenham, B., Charters, S.: Guidelines for performing systematic literature reviews in software engineering version 2.3. In: ICSE 2006: Proceedings of the 28th International Conference on Software Engineering, pp. 1051–1052 (2007). https://doi.org/10.1145/1134285.1134500
10. Meléndez, R., Paz, F.: Design of graphical user interfaces to implement new features in an ATM system of a financial bank. In: Marcus, A., Wang, W. (eds.) DUXU 2018. LNCS, vol. 10919, pp. 247–257. Springer, Cham (2018). https://doi.org/10.1007/978-3-319-91803-7_18
11. Shafiq, M., et al.: Skill specific spoken dialogues based personalized ATM design to maximize effective interaction for visually impaired persona. In: Marcus, A. (ed.) DUXU 2014. LNCS, vol. 8520, pp. 446–457. Springer, Cham (2014). https://doi.org/10.1007/978-3-319-07638-6_43

12. Zaim, E., Miesenberger, K.: TokenAccess: improving accessibility of Automatic Teller Machines (ATMs) by transferring the interface and interaction to personal accessible devices. In: Miesenberger, K., Kouroupetroglou, G. (eds.) ICCHP 2018. LNCS, vol. 10896, pp. 335–342. Springer, Cham (2018). https://doi.org/10.1007/978-3-319-94277-3_53

13. Ritter, F.E., Baxter, G.D., Churchill, E.F.: Foundations for Designing User-Centered Systems. Springer, London (2014). https://doi.org/10.1007/978-1-4471-5134-0

14. Alhumoud, S., Alabdulkarim, L., Almobarak, N., Al-Wabil, A.: Socio-cultural aspects in the design of multilingual banking interfaces in the Arab Region. In: Kurosu, M. (ed.) HCI 2015. LNCS, vol. 9171, pp. 269–280. Springer, Cham (2015). https://doi.org/10.1007/978-3-319-21006-3_27

15. Antona, M., Stephanidis, C. (eds.): UAHCI 2015. LNCS, vol. 9176. Springer, Cham (2015). https://doi.org/10.1007/978-3-319-20681-3

16. Bogdan, C., Kuusinen, K., Lárusdóttir, M.K., Palanque, P., Winckler, M. (eds.): HCSE 2018. LNCS, vol. 11262. Springer, Cham (2019). https://doi.org/10.1007/978-3-030-05909-5

17. Camilli, M., Dibitonto, M., Vona, A., Medaglia, C., Di Nocera, F.: User-centered design approach for interactive kiosks: evaluation and redesign of an automatic teller machine. In: ACM International Conference Proceeding Series, pp. 85–91 (2011). https://doi.org/10.1145/2037296.2037319

18. Canicosa, T., Medina, J., Guzman, B., Custodio, B., Portus, A.J.: Usability evaluation of ticketing system of metro manila train network. In: Ahram, T., Falcão, C. (eds.) AHFE 2017. AISC, vol. 607, pp. 591–602. Springer, Cham (2018). https://doi.org/10.1007/978-3-319-60492-3_56

19. Taohai, K., Phimoltares, S., Cooharojananone, N.: Usability comparisons of seven main functions for automated teller machine (ATM) banking service of five banks in Thailand. In: Proceedings - 2010 10th International Conference on Computational Science and Its Applications, ICCSA 2010 (2010). https://doi.org/10.1109/ICCSA.2010.50

Approaching Urban Experience Through Rhythmanalysis

Michal Smrčina[(⊠)] [iD]

Faculty of Humanities, Charles University, Prague, Czech Republic
michalsmrcina@gmail.com

Abstract. The paper revolves around the urban environment and its particular way of analysis. It aims to provide for a proper understanding of space and its meaningful design. It represents a theoretical basis of a more extensive research design that focuses on the dynamics of transit places, namely railway stations. There are three key parts. In the first one, I explain and contextualize rhythmanalysis. In the second one, I position it into the urban environment and discuss issues of spaces and places. The third part envisions the future case studies as it concerns the particular case of a railway station and shows possible approaches of the method from this distinct perspective. These research phases are illustrated by several hands-on examples.

Keywords: Genius loci · Homogenization · Railway station · Rhythmanalysis · Polyrhythmicity · Urban space

1 Introduction

Designing urban space and UX is usually subdued to various motivations. Practicing rhythmanalysis is, too. If we focus only on the urban environment, it is still important to keep this in mind, to understand it and identify what are our efforts aiming for. The hypothetical goal to optimize urban space design and usage might seem vague. Optimize for who, for what? As we proceed with rhythmanalysis and untangle visible or hidden rhythms, it becomes possible to glimpse the transient space and time with its bundles of rhythms and decide accordingly. One can use these tools to effectively produce space where commercial rhythms reign and public space is privatised. One may use it differently to come closer to a utopic space which is meaningful, just, democratic, sustainable, open and authentic with all its polyrhythmicity and resiliency. The first step is to fully understand it and act accordingly with the nature of the place to preserve or transform it so there is a certain balance between all the involved elements. The seamless, scheduled, completely predictable experience may not be always the best solution. A sensitive design doesn't reduce the pragmatics, usability, effectivity, but avoids any one-dimensional, isorhythmic dominance.

To explore the urban experience means both, to observe the urban environment rather indifferently from a vantage point and at the same time to actively immerse into it and sensitize oneself towards the most subtle perceptions. Following Henri Lefebvre's

© Springer Nature Switzerland AG 2020
A. Marcus and E. Rosenzweig (Eds.): HCII 2020, LNCS 12202, pp. 142–161, 2020.
https://doi.org/10.1007/978-3-030-49757-6_10

conception of rhythmanalysis, there is a possibility to reveal deep structures of the city organism, glimpse its dynamics and last but not least to see it not as an unchanging structure, but as a certain process, a becoming, a flux of myriads of rhythms that produce its time-space in every second. The city is ripe with diverse spaces and temporalities and its processes take infinite shapes in countless contexts. Rhythmanalysis offers a help to make sense of the environment whose unreduced complexity is often beyond any attempts to comprehend.

Lefebvre considered rhythmanalysis a method of investigating everyday life, of seeing power relations of modern society through rhythms which silently invade common routines. It was a part of a wider project that revolved around the quotidian in today's society, banality and emptiness, and possible emancipatory strategies. He conceived rhythmanalysis as a proper methodology or discipline to come, which only seems to happen recently and partially. Chen (2017: 7) elaborates on the original rhythmanalytical project and considers it a heuristic method, further explaining the adjective as "used to characterise the suggestive, experimental and procedural (trial and error) modes of operation that the method instigates". There is certainly some incompleteness and adaptability inherent to rhythmanalysis which haunts some scholars and hampers its acceptance as a regular method. Lyon (2018: 4) namedrops several authors which consider the rhythmanalysis as "orientation", "investigative disposition", "suggestive vein of temporal thinking rather than a definitive methodology" or "speculative invitation to think rhythmically". She hints that "the intangibility of rhythm itself may be part of the problem" (2017: 5). This elusive character has both pros and contras as it will be further outlined but mainly provides a means to reach phenomena of similarly elusive nature.

2 Seeing Through Rhythms

2.1 Notion of the Rhythm

Besides other things, rhythm represents a useful tool for approaching and analyzing time and space which makes it the principal element of rhythmanalysis.

To follow the notion of rhythm historically means to embark on a long journey, yet rhythm is certainly an ageless phenomenon. Yi Chen suggests its special position amongst the conventional "perceptual mechanisms": "rhythm is a meta-sense which synthesizes bodily and extra-bodily impressions" (Chen 2017: 2). While it is possible to escape the human-centred (or body-centred if you wish) perspective, our position as a perceiving subject often holds us there, despite the fact, that rhythms don't restrict themselves only to animate objects and operate throughout the latourian network of actants[1]. Their universal nature surpasses limits of a single discipline and together with an interconnectedness makes for one of their most appealing features.

Definitions of rhythms vary and so do rhythms. Oxford English Dictionary provides several definitions being it "a regularly occurring sequence of events or processes" or a "repeated pattern" ("Rhythm" 2020) etc. Considering that rhythms are fluid and ever-changing, it is wise to avoid too rigid or one-dimensional definition. Since this paper revolves around the rhythmanalysis, it follows Henri Lefebvre's notorious clarification

---

[1] Refering to the French philosopher and sociologist Bruno Latour and his concept.

on this matter: "Everywhere where there is interaction between a place, a time and an expenditure of energy, there is rhythm" (Lefebvre 2004: 15). Simply put, it is repetition that is central to rhythms but it is not a total repetition. "There is no rhythm without repetition in time and in space, without reprises, without returns, in short without *measure*. But there is no identical absolute repetition, indefinitely [...] there is always something new and unforeseen that introduces itself into the repetitive: *difference*" (Lefebvre 2004: 6). Through the repetition, new structures emerge while parts of the previous cycles are being preserved, eventually transformed. Sediments of the past are passed on to the future through various patterns that enhance or reduce them. One of the most prominent features of Lefebvre's approach to rhythms is also the abolition of the old division of space and time (or even dominance of one above the other), proclaiming thus indissolubility of time-space. Rhythmanalysis stands on such principles and harnesses their potential.

2.2 Meeting the Rhythmanalysis

The idea of rhythmanalysis provides researchers with a rich reservoir of concepts, which makes it difficult to briefly introduce it. Lefebvre's seminal book on the concept Éléments de rythmanalyse (1992) introduced this technique which doesn't cease to be a source of insights that are being further developed, even if it often means to abandon some of the original intentions.

For Lefebvre, one of the prospects of rhythmanalysis was certainly a critique of modern society, urbanity and abstract notions of time and space. In this regard, since it makes possible to interpret time and space as socially produced, it also holds the potential for social critique, to uncover the origins of the unhealthy symptoms and processes. Mulíček et al. (2015: 4) correctly observe that "Lefebvre perceives rhythm not as the object of study but instead as an analytical tool."

The rhythmanalyst sensitises himself to even the most subtle undulations of rhythms in time and space, he listens to them (often through the body in accordance with Lefebvre's argument for its centrality in the practice) and eventually uncovers various patterns in his surrounding environments, in society. As a research technique, rhythmanalysis provides a perspective of spatial-temporal ordering and experience that transcends the abstractions of time geographies (Edensor and Holloway 2008: 498). The relations between people and places unfold in time-spaces which are multidimensional, heterogeneous, emergent and often overlap, disappear and dynamically change. They speak of the interconnectedness and nature of such relations between places. Rhythms are not invariants but they stand for a certain unity in which many sensual registers meet. They may show us the complex ways in which not only society is constructed and functions.

There are various sites of rhythms, bundles which deserve closer focus and these rhythmic assemblages mutually influence each other in plenty of possible juxtapositions that might express more or less positive connotations of their constellations.

Several key elements of lefebvrian rhythmanalysis include linear and cyclical rhythms, centrality of body, polyrhythmia (and related eurhytmia or arrhythmia), isorhytmia and dressage.

A Brief Review of the Concept. It is not the aim of this paper to present an exhaustive overview of the history of the study of rhythms, respectively rhythmanalysis. This would come at the expense of the later parts that set the concept within more particular contexts. But it is a useful, yet short detour that shows that in a wider picture, these efforts weren't solitary. Elden (2006) provides a well-shaped introduction to Lefebvre's life and work, but the actual rhythmanalytical framework is bigger and other authors also deserve credit. Mostly, these efforts differed in areas where the study of rhythms was put to use. It might have been dance or art in general, it might have been the economy of work in Fordist societies, it might have been urban studies or even therapy, and it often was philosophy or science. Some authors precede Lefebvre and most probably inspired him (Bachelard, Dos Santos). Some appear in a similar period (Barthes, Perec) as Kärrholm recently noticed (Brighenti and Kärrholm 2018: 2). Further, due to the renewed interest in rhythmanalysis, the so-called *return of the rhythms*, some contemporary authors eagerly revise the overall rhythmanalytical project, expand it or even go beyond it and try to correct its shortcomings and test its limits in their own research. Not to mention that the spectrum of areas where rhythmanalysis is applied is immense and the experimental nature of the research renders it open to challenges.

Philosophical Anchoring. This part should serve to merely present a necessarily selective portfolio of findings and notions that widen the scope of theoretical foundations of rhythmanalysis and show that while the original conception holds some invariable basis, it remains open to various interpretations at the same time.

A widespread view on rhythmanalysis saw it as a phenomenological project. This stems from its focus on the concrete, lived experience rather than abstract notions of the triad of time, space, and rhythms. In cases where the body is given the central role as the perceiving subject, it is in the closest proximity to rhythms as they also flow through it. Yi Chen in her book Practising Rhythmanalysis tries to support the methodology with philosophical foundations and dedicates this endeavour a whole chapter. Similarly, she considers rhythmanalysis as a "form of phenomenology" (2017: 29) and shares Heidegger's position that "the expression 'phenomenology' signifies primarily a methodological conception" (Chen 2017). Yi Chen presents three currents that phenomenology shares with rhythmanalysis. Firstly, they proceed in ways that resist abstraction which eventually means they also escape disciplinary boundaries. Secondly, they abridge the gap between subjectivism and objectivism through their accent on unmediated perceptual cognition. Thirdly, there is the notion that rhythm as a meta-sense achieves phenomenological unity of sensual affects, it might be viewed as a glue-like, common principle.

Chen doesn't stop there and further develops the concept focusing on the theory of moments (also a matter of interest for Lefebvre) where she clarifies their nature and connection between moments and rhythms. Lastly, she envisages rhythmanalysis in the current of new materialism. Such a materialist focus considers rhythms as materiality but together with Deleuze and Guattari as the "conception of materiality that doesn't necessarily belong to tangible objects" (2017: 47). The alleged becoming of materialities is of emergent nature. Such are potentialities of affects (whose forms may be rhythms) that may compose an assemblage. Rhythmic assemblage substitutes the classical notion of agents that would produce particular rhythms – the focus shifts towards these assemblages, bundles of rhythms, fluid and vivid sites of many rhythms. Importantly, she accords with Latour's concept of *actants* which calls for treating things in their ontological state and eventually ascribes agency also to inanimate or inorganic phenomena. Such profound foundations nevertheless often represent a creative expansion of the original lefebvrian ideas.

A slightly different take on rhythmanalysis came from Brighenti and Kärrholm (2018) which corresponds with the aforementioned reluctance towards the abstract nature of rhythms. According to them, rhythms are never encountered as abstract entities: they always have a presence and are investments into a certain situation. We are thus never talking about abstract, disassociated rhythm per se. Also, they develop a neo-vitalistic conception that "[…] is neither simply a description of rhythms nor an analysis of rhythms; instead, the goal is to capture the inner life of rhythms as they enter actual territorial formations" (2018: 2).

Nevertheless, connections and points shared with rhythmanalysis may be found also elsewhere, in different yet at the same time related areas. It shows some similarities even to a project from a structuralist framework. Greimas' topological semiotics (Pour une sémiotique topologique, 1972) appeared at the same time as the first rudiments of rhythmanalysis entered Lefebvre's work. However, topological semiotics represented an effort to apply specific grammar on a city and conceive a complex semiotic model of space and discover its own generative, topological languages. It was a structuralist project, but its morphology and system were not rigidly static and focused also on processual phenomena, an imprint of society into space, interconnectedness of subjects etc.

2.3 Extending the Concept

Dealing with rhythmanalysis one must ask about its potential limitations or setbacks. It depends on the particular goals with which the researcher uses it but it is possible to generalize the critique and focus the critical exploration on its original conception by Henri Lefebvre. Most of the authors refrain from any direct critique and prefer to make use of desired parts of Lefebvre's oeuvre and subtly alter it to meet their needs and objectives.

Mattias Kärrholm and Andrea Mubi Brighenti show an exemplary approach in a self-explanatory named paper Beyond rhythmanalysis: towards a territoriology of rhythms and melodies in everyday spatial activities (2018). He critically evaluated rhythmanalysis to adapt it to his project that stems from urban, human geography. As he explains, the move beyond rhythmanalysis shouldn't mean to throw away its insights. "Instead, we suggest, a benefit could come from further developing and integrating such insights into an enlarged science of territories and territorial formations" (2018: 1). He analyzes the notion of rhythm present within interactions between time, space and energy, but he finds the clarification of the nature of such energy lacking in the original study. Thus, he aims to revive it with notions such as investment, intensity and credo. Shortly put, he adds to this notion of energy a qualitative dimension which enables to capture gentle nuances, atmospheres of rhythms, places. "[…] we suggest that the notion of rhythm could be explored not only in terms of the recurrent patterns of association it defines, but also with essential reference to the qualitative singular intensive situations to which it corresponds. Our project thus consists in an intensification of rhythmanalysis" (2018: 2). This correlates with his already mentioned idea of neo-vitalism that accentuates the inner life of rhythms.

Kärrholm systematically proposes points of constructive critique that revisits Lefebvre with a claim that some of his reflections are reduced to sometimes naive oppositions or contradictions. There is the dichotomy between linear and cyclical time, a quantitative and qualitative one, a "bad" time of modern society and a "good" time of our ancestors, of the world where things were seemingly better and more natural. Kärrholm correctly rehabilitates this with a remark that we should proceed more objectively, aware of various contexts of situations: "[...] we need a more rounded understanding of rhythms capable of remaining open and sensitive to rhythmic phenomena and the role they play, without trying to define their nature [...]" (2018: 7). This is similar to Lefebvre's notions of relations of rhythms that may be characterized as eurhythmia or arrhythmia. Such polyrhythmic constellations, and even prefixes of the words, also show some steering towards "an evaluative point of a view", being correlative to percipient's own judgement. To surpass these binaries and avoid premature evaluation of which rhythms are good and bad, it is vital to consider particular context, political or cultural circumstances.

Rhythmanalysis is linked to the obvious phenomenological background based on Lefebvre's insistence to analyze lived temporality (of the everyday). Kärrholm doesn't refuse these phenomenological foundations of social theory but complements the analysis of the absolute, direct, local, now-and-here by "ecology, i.e. the analysis of relative global elsewhere-at-other-times. [...] rhythms must encounter territories, the latter being complex creations that are as much phenomenal (imbued with meaning) as they are ecological (generated by operative relations)" (2018: 8). This calling for a more complex grasp of the analyzed phenomena matches Kärrholm's intention to territorialize rhythmanalysis.

Extending and developing rhythmanalysis introduces many creative opportunities. Lyon (2018: 79) presents an up-to-date review of gains, limits and future prospects of rhythmanalysis and includes another set of examples of current studies and of its various employments. There is the centrality of the body which Lefebvre asserted and questions on how to surpass it. It is a mean to grasp the often fleeting sensory data and to preserve the liveliness of the dynamic experience. The embodied way of doing rhythmanalysis closely relates to sensoric perceptions. Therefore, it complements traditional methods of social sciences that may show to be insufficient in this regard. The body can be both a tool and the object of analysis. Current society is strongly visual, the eye has dominated (not only) research for a long time and it remains to hold considerable value. However, there are also other senses that connect with the rhythmical framework, once again with rhythm as meta-sense. There are studies and analyses based in the auditory domain, there are some that deal with olfactory, with so-called smell-scapes and more. As for the concepts of eurhythmia and arrhythmia, the disruptions may often serve as a research tactic to make visible the hidden, to unravel deep structures. Such was the cultural-historical case study and conjunctural analysis of Thatcherite Britain carried out by Chen (2017: 53). Sometimes, the body may not be enough to capture the complexity of the analyzed rhythmical environment. Technology offers tools to enhance the analysis. There are various tech devices, information technologies, applications, algorithms or most recently there emerged even the possibility to access and harness the potential of big data and broaden the scope of rhythmanalysis. Similarly, art may be employed to meet such purposes. Not only new media, visual art, intermedia, audio recordings, but even literature. Mulíček and colleagues (2015) chose to assess a chronotopic approach to urban timespace using partly rhythmanalysis and also the literary concept of chronotope firstly used in social sciences by a philosopher and literary critic Mikhail Bakhtin. Some "augmentations" may also help to approach such rhythms and processes that "are not directly accessible in audible or other sensory forms" (Lyon 2018: 92) This was the objective of a project (Palmer and Jones 2014) that applied sonification[2] to a particular seaside area of Severn Estuary– a process that converted data coming from environmental or other processes (e.g. tidal patterns or docklands' soundscapes) into sound and captured and transformed thus both the non-human and human rhythms into an overall sonic form approachable by human perception. All these possibilities come up with new ways how to do rhythmanalysis.

While Lefebvre didn't hide the audacious ambitions to establish rhythmanalysis as a new science, its development and twists it undergoes these days speak more in favour of its universality, interdisciplinarity and the unique feature to capture the essence of otherwise elusive phenomena. Its fragmentary character, opened to customization and modification makes slightly difficult to establish it among others, now traditional disciplines or sciences.

3   Rhythms Enter the City

Preceding part's purpose was to set up a basis and introduce the diverse threads of the rhythmanalytical approach. While this reflexive work and introductory research are advised at the current level of development of the concept, it seems that it is the actual practice of rhythmanalysis on a particular case, the active, hands-on activity that proves to be the most rewarding. Only subsequently it is possible to assess some findings of more general nature. And only by narrowing the analysis it is possible to achieve something and avoid getting lost.

It is possible to follow rhythms in non-urban or even non-human environments which is in concord with the actant perspective of the analyses and universal nature of rhythm. But urban space represents an environment which is the closest to human, to the rhythmanalyst. It leads to results that are the most suitable to be put to pragmatic use and also quickly testable. Its density provides myriads of opportunities and allows the analysis to proceed from perspectives of almost all thinkable areas of social studies (not only).

At the beginning of the 21st century, it is legitimate to claim that we live in an urbanized world (United Nations 2019). In the contemporary world where the urbanity takes many shapes and seizes unprecedently large areas, there are calls for a reassessment of its image, or for literally for "establishment of a corresponding new diagram for the city of future" that would deal with its current fragmentation (Castello 2018: 1). As

---

[2] "Sonification is the use of sound to communicate information. It is particularly appropriate in situations where a constant monitoring of changing data is required but a visual data display may be distracting" (Palmer and Jones 2012).

Castello further refers to French philosopher of the city Françoise Choay, most of the numerous narratives employed to depict the contemporary urban environment fail to enunciate satisfactorily the patterns that best characterize a city today" (Castello 2018: 2). However, what are these patterns? The visible structure is usually the result of intentional processes or of less intentional processes that sediment and distil themselves into solid forms. Rhythms are naturally interwoven with these patterns and they both influence each other in a dynamic interplay. Rhythms are set into certain structures and patterns, but undulations constantly alter their forms. To identify the patterns is to get to penetrate also to the rhythms beneath. They both form a certain language of the city, if not its grammatic.

The city is a polyrhythmic ensemble of competing, overlapping rhythms that meet at the points of rhythmic assemblages. It is the polyrhythmicity that makes it rich, special, that gives the city poetic energy, inner dynamics and the possibility of a tolerant co-existence in maximal diversity. As I will further demonstrate, the notion of isorhytmia is not in utter contradiction to this, but in cases may appear unhealthy. This spectacle of the city and its rhythmic life was and is often depicted in literature or cinema. The fascination was especially apparent in the cinematography of the first half of the 20th century in "metropolitan symphonies" (Man with a Movie Camera, Berlin: A Symphony of a Big City, The City of Millions, Rhythm of a City – A Film from Stockholm, to name a few). The city's life was portrayed focusing on particular vibes of the cities, temporality and spatiality of streets, squares, their everydayness and the interconnected whole they form. Recently, there was even shot a futuristic short film, also a city symphony, set into the urban landscape of tomorrow by Liam Young called Seoul City Machine.

Nowadays, we must add to this organism another level of complexity. Edensor and Holloway (2008: 485) follow Highmore (2005: 141) on the point which suggests that the city is the most "complex exemplar of the dynamic interplay of forces" in space and authors agree that the thick temporal flows through major cities possess a density and complexity that produces a rich rhythmic stew. There are phenomena symptomatic for the contemporaneity that manifest themselves in this increasing complexity. The binary opposition between city and nature had been breached a long time ago, dissolving into heterogenous, blurred areas – be it for example rural areas that slowly become urbanized or urban wilderness in city centres. Public spaces transform too, discussions on their privatization don't cease, commodification and retailization of urban space is often evident and inadequately regulated. The emergence of information technologies and virtual spaces is quite omnipresent. However, another shift happens also on the corporeal level, besides the fields of data warehouses. A new shift in perspective, for example, relates to the existence of human exclusion zones or machine landscapes and occasional departures from human-centred design (Zolotaev 2019). All these changes bring forward new rhythmic constellations and demand restructuring of former rhythmic constellations which eventually calls for our fresh attunement to their flows.

Regarding the relationship of time and space in an urban environment and basically another view on the city, Mulíček and colleagues (2015) pay attention to Massey's paper (1999) where she rethinks conceptions of time and space in geography and "describes the city as an open time-space system of social relationships composed of partial subsystems and linking various groups and activities, emphasizing that most urban activities are not projects conducted by a single individual" (2015: 5). There is especially noteworthy the focus on the collectivity of rhythms even though sometimes it may be enough to analyse a single, individual rhythm. Still, rhythmanalysis usually considers the collective city rhythms, woven threads.

3.1 Hidden Hegemonies

In one of the recent studies, Kärrholm discusses retail rhythms and urban life. He also helpfully illustrates processes of synchronization, constellations of polyrhythmicity, isorhythmicity and more. Eventually, the author unveils dominant currents, their rhythmical dynamics and power relations: "Contemporary retail planners have become more skilled and powerful in the art of capitalising city rhythms" (2009: 426). In the analysis of retail rhythms and urban life, Kärrholm follows Lefebvre's idea that with the advent of industrial society new, linear, dominating rhythms of production were introduced (2009: 435). Modernist and post-war design of cities often lead to a shift where "most places were turned from polyrhythmic into isorhythmic places" (2009: 425).

The notion of isorhythmicity relates to Lefebvre's idea of *dressage* (2004: 38-39) where there is a seemingly perfect synchronization of bodies, their manoeuvres appear natural as they conform to prescribed models rooted by tradition or exerted by force. In isorhythmicity the subjects and their rhythms are finely tuned, equalized, they act as if they were under the control of a mighty conductor's baton (to use Lefebvre's likening). Dressage itself is close to the example of military practices and routines. It is a process of bodily entrainment which imprints the rhythm into the body through repetition and this becomes slowly learned and evident in the body and its behaviour, it complements the act of socialization, acculturation. These processes often take place under the prevailing rhythm of a clockwork time that is metaphorically (and hierarchically) situated in an elevated place, a "tower" above a city.

In the past, there were introduced synchronic strategies for effective production and flow of capital, that shaped the material world into a scheduled, seamless, frictionless environment (Foucault 2000) by way of territoriality (Kärrholm 2009). Not only the element of surprise, spontaneous development and novelty were suppressed in favour of controlled existence and planning, but homogenization lead to predictable landscapes and also timescapes of time-clock. Nevertheless, things aren't black and white. To claim that polyrhythmical space is good and isorhythmic bad would mean to regress to simplification and evaluative bias that hadn't been seen as fruitful already in the critique of Lefebvre's conception.

Nowadays, these changes are more differentiated, less explicit, yet the prevailing inner logic structures the hierarchy of rhythms, makes use of various synchronizations and feeds upon existing rhythms. The importance of the rhythms of consumption and retail increases. They often tend to be more subtle, manipulative, flexible than before and ready to adapt. They do the latter well, both under conditions of polyrhythmia and isorhythmia, blurring their imaginary division. They can "hierarchise polyrhythmic landscapes of local life according to a logic of consumption. Or, they might produce an isorhythmia, reducing complexity not primarily by turning orders into a singular order (as in the modernistic tendency of spatial homogenisation), but by inscribing different orders in a system guided by a common denominator (the rhythms of consumption)"

(Kärrholm 2009: 427). It is important to discern the level of complexity or to be cautious about monofunctional spaces.

Planned production of predictable space (through isorhythmia) is a matter of the past, similarly as the loose and unpredictable nature of public spaces is a matter of even more distant past. Today, we see a mixture of both and it is essential to seek a balance – to avoid a total, regulated environment, but also to set out at least some limits to remove the non-beneficial rhythms and chaos in general and steer the social, cultural and political development in the desired or the least harmful direction. Commercial rhythms are embedded in our world, they often rule all around them, but they need to be tamed and prevented from "reigning freely and continuing a kind of mallification of public places of the urban landscape" (2009: 436). Paradoxically, it is not even in their intention to create utterly isorhythmic, stabilised and predictable, dull areas. Because of their versatility and ability to absorb late trends and novelties, they can further exploit them according to their motivations. Without these, there would be a smaller profit, less dynamic flow of capital (even though possibly smoother) and no new desires. They appreciate the difference that comes from rhythmical repetitions but follow their own logic and eventually act like parasitic rhythms.

While some ideologies and rhythms are dominant, it doesn't mean there wouldn't be any subversive or counter-rhythms. As already de Certeau (2011) notes there is always resistance to such rhythms, no matter if individual or collective as a public initiative. It seems to me that there is no ideal equilibrium, no silence without the whispering murmurs in behind. To criticise the dominant rhythms doesn't mean to favour the subversive ones. Yet the subversive ones are the players that bring forth novelty and other perspectives. They colour the grey and the indifferent and show further horizons. They might grow stronger if constellations and contexts are right. How? Through intensities of exerted energies, by right temporal and spatial tactics, they can stand out. On the matter of subversiveness and space, Shaw (2017) comes up with a term dark spaces. These are not to be mistaken with Augé's non-places (2008) even though they connotate. Dark spaces are the ruptures that emerge in the surveilled, up-to-that-time continuous, noninterrupted junkspace, in the total predictability of rhythmical environment (and despite it). In the totality normalized public space, they might be considered marginalized, abnormal, extraneous, unwanted. If non-places are stripped of meaningful existence and seem to belong to nobody, it is such dark spaces that authenticate and return a calculated space to the lived one (*l'espace habité*, as Lefebvre wrote). This eventually makes the places credible, diverse, inhabited, fuels them with memories and injects with *genius loci*. The genius loci, introduced and analyzed by Norberg-Schulz (2010), enhances places, makes them authentic, unique and even poetic. Kärrholm's proposed "intensified rhythmanalysis" could be the right tool to access the melody, atmosphere of a place and with them to glimpse at genius loci.

3.2 Public Space and Seamless Experience

Public space is one of the most discussed and evident examples of the above mentioned ongoing rhythmical and power transformations. It is often used also by commercial subjects, its large shares may get privatized, it might exist on the basis of privileged access rights, or it might even be subjected to the process of homogenization of space. There are demands and expectations for urban space. A dream of seamless urban experience seems close to the tendency to project predictable, scheduled spaces.

When Edensor analyzes a tourist coach tour in Kerry, Ireland he also touches the essence of such seamless, smooth experience: "Particular tourist environments are designed to minimise experiential disorder through architectural and managerial techniques that endeavour to banish harsh sensations through the assembling of modulated soundscapes, tactilities, smells and scenes" (Edensor and Holloway 2008: 487). On the other hand, his experience and own research still achieve to see ruptures in the assumed totality of "seamless visual consumption of spectacle within an 'air-conditioned bubble' that limits sensory and experiential diversity". The conception of the seamless space is very close to the conception of junkspace (Koolhaas and Foster 2016), total environment and eventually, to provide an example, to some of the transit spaces or shopping malls. Rhythms usually don't naturally flow with such smoothness, without any obstacles. Polyrhytmicity and novelty develop from things that often lack seamlessness. But for example, capital or similarly based rhythms, would appreciate a non-interrupted flow of theirs. Reduced complexity might be one of the sinister symptoms and again, it is well visible on public spaces.

Not by any means I would call for non-critical nostalgic approach to (public) places of past, imagined without any faults. However, the conception of complexity which Kärrholm uses provides an interesting perspective on some of the healthy and resilient ones: "Traditional public places in Malmö are often the venue of several intermingling territorial productions. A square could, during the same week, or even day, be the place of markets, demonstrations, parking lots, skaters, gangs of youth, children playing, etc., all producing some sort of more or less stable territories. One possible description of public space as a space of sociability and accessibility (cf. Madanipour 2003) could thus be in terms of territorial complexities (Kärrholm 2005), where a lot of different territorial productions intermingle at a place in order to grant accessibility for different groups and usages" (2009: 434). He characterizes territorial complexity through three aspects of territorial productions: their large number, multi-layeredness, mutual non-hierarchical relations. Isorhythmia may occur and reduce complexity, influencing these aspects. Why is a total seamless urban experience not such a good choice and why should we strive for more complex environments are fundamental questions.

3.3 Who for and by Who?

The debates on public space are an endless but vital part of (not only) urban planning. One may ask questions such as who they are designed for and serve, who should decide about them, plan them and to what shape, which subjects should be granted rights in this process etc. So-called participatory planning is only one of the recent essays in this matter. These questions relate to the whole topic of urban user experience design. When it comes to the expression "optimal urban space design", how do we translate the optimal? It is usually a matter of finding the right balance between all subjects, acts or rhythms involved.

Intermezzo at Dejvice Railway Station Pub. To demonstrate the difference, a recent example from my own city comes to aid. Moreover, an example that is very close to transit places as it is one of an old railway station pub called Dejvická Nádražka, situated in the Prague quarter of Dejvice. The neighbourhood itself is one of those that head towards gentrification but still retains a local authentic character with old residents. As usually, gentrification removed or transformed ordinary places that were daily used, now there are typical symptoms of the process such as trendy cafés and shops. It is one of the factors that could strip the quarter of a polyrhythmic character and reduce complexity of its places. The railway station pub seems to be one of a few surviving remnants, even more as it is part of the transit space of railway, also close to other means of public transport. Since it is a pub, it is a place of socialization, but it also often hosts various cultural, mostly musical, events. These may not correspond with nature of the gentrified surroundings, but the place itself is visited by many social groups of different classes both from neighbourhood and the whole town and even though it may seem a little shabby and cheap compared to the nearby generic venues, it withholds a unique, historical character enhanced with rich social life. If such places and institutions vanish without adequate substitution, it will also be a loss for certain social groups that are left behind for economic, cultural or other reasons.

The rents in Dejvice area kept being raised and eventually, the municipality informed the owner of the pub about the prospect that his rent might also rise. The discussion that followed revolved around the question if some places, even if private, should be somehow privileged and supported (in this case the question was if the rent should be kept at the same level as before) by regulation or exception and helped to survive. Such places preserve diversity, serve a variety of people (or people that may feel excluded by the gentrification) and keep a genuine, rich and lived character of the place/quarter. In Pierre Nora's words, they are also genuine places of memory (Nora 1996). Sometimes, they are not competitive enough to survive on their own when rhythms around change. A homogenous quarter with monofunctional parts, neatly tailored rhythms and isorhythmic lives of the involved subjects stands in opposition to this, even though such description may seem exaggerated. In such cases, it is wise to analyze the environment, untangle its rhythms and consider the situation accordingly.

3.4 Faceless Space

A seamless urban experience – this ideal brings us back to the question, what for are all the efforts to design urban space, whom they serve, who or what gains the most from them and who might be disadvantaged because of them. It is good to consider the actual nature of places.

Shopping malls were at the centre of attention for a long time as one of the first examples of a total environment, a commodified space or a junkspace and also embodied the concept of seamlessness. There were even semiotic analyses of them – Gottdiener and Lagopoulos (1986) saw that the classical city centre no longer existed, processes of deconcentration and fragmentation took place instead and he distinguished the mall as a new form of public space that replaced the centre, took on its social function and a became a new "main street". There, he proceeded with the semiotic analysis of its motif, design elements, communication codes, signification acts and uncovered how the mall manufactured, recreated seemingly natural, desirable environment that benefited the merchandising. Despite the fact the situation changed since then, it seems similar to the above-introduced conceptions even though the semiotic analysis is more structuralist than rhythmanalysis but analyzes here quite the same phenomena and both approaches could complement each other. The original shopping mall spread and spilt over to other places, decentralized and now we might as well talk about retailization of many spaces, including the public space, whose primary function is different. Eventually, the persistent question appears once again: how to produce and preserve the authentic, lived places with all the healthy polyrhythmicity and balanced structure, as opposed to non-places, or places that only emulate the former ones but hide different isorhythmic or violently dominant inner logic, or places that don't often really serve the users, or could benefit from a different design. And once again, rhythmanalysis may show the interrelations and rhythms between the present actors or put narrowly between people and places (and temporalities).

4   Fragments of Rhythmanalytical Cookbook

As it is now clear, rhythmanalysis constantly oscillates between theorising its method and actual, applied research. For reasons listed below, I won't perform actual, thorough research here, but rather orbit the place of the railway station and show some options on how to proceed and what to make of it.

4.1   Theoretical Grounding

When it comes to narrowing down the subject of analysis, in this case to transit spaces and more specifically a railway station, one must also consider what kind of rhythms and what subjects he aims to observe and eventually design a rhythmanalysis that would fit these goals. For example, Chen (2017) doesn't follow classic agents that produce rhythms (similar to the concept of the pacemaker by Mulíček and colleagues 2015), but rather follows a more processual approach. She focuses on the sites of rhythmic production, the assemblages and follows the interrelated dynamics of their present interactions from which rhythms eventually arise.

Another author that significantly contribute to the current overview of the rhythm-analytical studies and methods is again Lyon (2018). She is more literal in the advice that one should start with a preliminary rhythmanalysis of a site, "an activity or the unfolding of an event to identify the rhythms that are present" (2018: 85). These should then inform the actual research design. And it seems to be true, that they even continuously inform the design during the whole analysis. As Lyon further, rightly points, the central consideration of rhythmanalysis lies in the question where and when we focus our attention.

Value of Disruptions. One of the essential dispositions when performing the rhythmanalysis is to be sensitised towards rhythms. One may achieve this delicate skill by training or be simply gifted, it takes patience, but eventually reveals rhythms that hadn't seemed to be present. Sometimes, a disruption, an arrhythmia comes to help. In a sudden absence, change, irregularity, the rhythms beneath the surface, the ones that went unnoticed may reveal. Besides the revelatory potential, the disruptions hold also a transformative potential for innovation, novelty, change of the established order. This is present throughout Lefebvre's work (2004) and more recently, it reminds of the mentioned dark spaces (Shaw 2017) considered as ruptures and their re-formative or even revolutionary potential. The disruptions may become the decisive places of power, of intervention. Lyon (2018: 87) follows Edensor in an apt view, that disruptions can be even used as a "heuristic device" for the inquiry in rhythms. These notions are valuable not only concerning rhythms but in social sciences in general.

A prime illustration of its importance comes from Yi Chen. She accompanies the work Practising Rhythmanalysis (2017) with two case studies and uses rhythmanalysis as a tool for cultural historical analysis – she "puts the method of rhythmanalysis to work to propose historiography that re-examines the notion of conjuncture" (Chen 2017: 15). She refers to cultural theorist Stuart Hall who theorised the conjunctural moment in the 1970s and analyzed ideological foundations of Thatcherism in Britain. Chen values his "intuitive understanding of the cojunctural shift at the level of rhythms" (2017: 13) and uses this disruption in a history, a time of a political and social change, new configurations and unrest as a vantage point for the analysis that allows to see certain ruptures and rhythms that came to be more visible in that time of conjuncture, disruption. On this background, she shows "how the conceptual tools of rhythmanalysis (polyrhythmia, arrhythmia, eurhythmia) and their particular ways of attending to the analyzed matters may be employed to accentuate certain historical realities that elude to certain historical discourses" (Chen 2017: 16).

4.2 Dialectics of Two Proceedings

Rhytmanalysis allows a certain level of arbitrariness in research. Chen chose for the cultural historical rhythmanalysis the conjuncture of the 1970s which she enhanced with two case studies. These two studies testify of two approaches that determine the nature of the particular analysis: "dialectic of two proceedings, crudely summarized as either moving from the concrete to abstract or the other way around, is central to the operation of rhythmanalysis" (Chen 2017: 160). These are complementary, not exclusive.

It is possible to start with a particular, singular cultural phenomenon and work with rhythms to enrich abstract theoretical claims. It is possible to start with a certain abstract cultural framework, a polyrhythmicity and try to unravel its complexity, following it to separate threads. Chen refers back to Lefebvre with a demand to discern two tendencies within polyrhytmia: "The tendency towards homogenization and that towards diversity" (2004: 99). This adequately speaks in favour of the notion that polyrhythmicity doesn't necessarily lead to diversity (but might).

Both case studies dealt with the conjuncture of the 1970s, but differently. The first study focused on bodily rhythms, walking practices in East London and changes in this urban environment. It started with the most visible manifestations of arrhythmia, rather on an abstract level of capitalist, social rhythms to which bodily rhythms succumbed and slowly disentangled the "unity". A metaphor of the centrifugal movement was used there. The second study dealt with British postal systems as sites of institutional rhythms that constitute a polyrhythmia of communication rhythms. There, the idea was oppositely to assemble and entangle multiplicity of temporal-spatial experiences and rhythmic orchestrations into a polyrhytmia – "to bundle up postal rhythms to portray a polyrhythmic conjuncture which extends beyond 'events', enabling non-linear historiography" (2017: 168). To sum it up, one way we may start with dismantling the complex or abstract, often overarching structure, ideology, period, environment. The other way, we opt for the opposite direction and eventually weave together the polyrhythmical ensemble made of countless lesser threads that may form alliances or refusals of rhythms, struggles for eurhythmia in times of disruption and reversely. As the examples suggest, the shape of the rhythmanalytical proceedings is a subject to the analyzed phenomena and it takes many shapes. Once again, the arbitrariness of rhythmanalysis is not a setback, but an advantage.

The Right Choice of Analysis
Besides the options on how to proceed with rhythmanalysis that are introduced above, there are even more essential ones. Lyon (2019: 34,79) provided an intriguing overview of up-to-date rhythmanalytical studies and assessed a provisional typology according to the strongest field of their interest. This reminds the researcher, that it is fundamental to remind himself/herself of the area in which the study might belong. Such areas involve for example rhythms and mobility, rhythms of place and place-making, work rhythms, working rhythms, rhythms of nature, cultural-historical analysis. Fundamental is also a book Geographies of Rhythm edited by Tim Edensor (2010) that encompassed many studies that employ rhythmanalysis or simply deal with rhythms and showed thus the diversity of the fields of relevant research and the possibilities.

5   Approaching the Railway Station

When it comes to applying the theory, it is necessary to switch back and test the introduced concepts. Now would be the time to start with the actual analysis. However, this paper emphasized rather the theoretical part and the actual empirical part is a matter of another work. Still, I conclude with a reflection that brings together several notions on a model case of a transit space, more specifically a particular railway station. In this final part, I situate the rhythmanalytical method into this environment but I restrain from its full application. What is essential here is to provide a mere outline of the actual analysis and case studies that will follow.

5.1   Railway Station: Praha – Smíchovské nádraží

The subject of my further inquiries is a Prague railway station Smíchovské nádraží which is yet about to undergo a thorough reconstruction. This deserves long-term continuous attention. I observe the rhythms in its current stage of existence that is about to end soon, slowly towards the end of 2020. I aim to use the potential of such an event of extensive urban change to be able to continuously compare the rhythms of the past and the rhythms that are yet about to appear. Besides a new railway station connected to a bus terminal and other public city transport, in a manner of multi-modal station, a whole new district, titled "Smíchov City" (there is no name to it in Czech language), is to be built around it.

Offices, new flats, shops and enterprises of a very different character from the current one are about to appear, as well as public spaces. This audacious project will certainly erase many old rhythms, change some existing and create plenty of new ones. There will be a great negotiation of space, of rhythmical, temporal and spatial relations which provides a very interesting subject for a broad rhythmanalysis, as many other grand disruptions had provided before.

Such a case reminds of the mentioned Chen's analysis of the new order in the British postal system and its rhythms in the 1970s as during that time many arrhythmias arose. Combined with "Beeching cuts" of the 1960s and 70s that drastically cut the country's railway system, many villages and small cities had to find ways to at least partly adapt to the situation and new rhythms of mobility. In this regard, it appears fruitful to analyze the resurrection of these British rails because some lines and stations that were affected by these decades-old closures might be soon reopened (Department for Transport 2020). The reconstruction of the Smíchov railway station and the development of a new quarter is also a matter of emerging arrhythmia and new constellations, but also slightly different as the original transit function is not only preserved but even expanded. To illustrate the extent of the project, it should host up to 3 300 new residents and supposedly also provide for 9 000 job positions. Not speaking of a park whose size should take up circa 14 000 m^2. Many new rhythmic bundles are about to enter this closely watched scene.

5.2 UX Perspective/Public Space/Features of Railway

What makes the railway station (and rail transportation in general) special and what are its features? Such are the first questions to ask, to characterize it. Its' primary function is the transport, but as historian Judt (2010) ponders in his historical reflection, "railways were never just functional". He points also to the dimensions of adventure, pleasure, or "archetypical modern experience". They used to be the so-called gateways to the city, the representative portals and massive edifices, harbingers of modernity. Nowadays, the transport function remains to be the chief one.

What does it mean for the user experience design? From the pragmatic perspective of usability, there are typical demands such as that all the assets there should be highly functional, have a considerably long lifespan, should be able to overcome physical or cultural barriers, easy to understand and intuitively use and more. The overall design should respect both flows of people in hurry and users that sojourn at the station for a longer time, no matter the reasons. The mood, atmosphere are also of great importance, even though they don't exclusively derive only from an aesthetic basis. All these aspects naturally stem from preliminary analyses and studies, but it is possible to enhance them with rhythmanalysis and attain a deeper understanding of the station and more subtle dynamics.

Also, as a public space, it has some standard requirements that are generally recognized (but not always satisfied) and on the other side, it is a subject to various risks, potential dangers and negative effects. Considering the mentioned transformation of the selected railway station, it is possible to discern some of the elements of possible endangerment and predict possible changes. There are some phenomena omnipresent in the current society and urban space. Kärrholm (2009) correctly identified the increasing dominance of retailization and commodification of public space on levels of rhythms and territorial production. Certain privatization or privilegization of public space is also one of such disquieting processes. The introduced seamless urban space, with its non-places and total environments, is often symptomatic of transit places. What is at risk? Loss of authenticity, diversity and democratic quality. A modern terminal understandably often lacks the character of the older ones. The memory of places, their historical value may also be lost, or in the better case museified. The radical reconstruction of the railway station and its transformation is about to bring arrhythmic situation or at least strong rhythmical changes. The rhythmanalysis can follow the on-going project and see how the rhythms behave, eventually evaluating it. It may or may not lose natural bonds with its surroundings and it might need to develop new ones, which takes time and can be planned only partially. In the end, the question is how to proceed in the best way during the development project and afterwards, to avoid radical desemantization and rhythmical cuts and how to achieve an optimal polyrhythmical transit space that underwent significant resemantization and rhythmical reprogramming. The sensitivity is one of the key elements as the rhythms will find their own, often unexpected ways despite the efforts to control and plan the environment.

5.3 Outlining Railway Station Rhythms

In terms of preliminary rhythmalysis, how do we regard the railway station? It could certainly be viewed from the perspective of rhythms of mobility, but for the purpose of my research, I believe it is better to integrate it within an overall framework of rhythms of places.

Since I keep the actual rhythmanalysis to the latter case studies, it is sufficient to simply sketch some of the approaches. However, each case demands own design of rhythmanalysis. Illustratively and without any aim to be a proper categorization, I imagine three figures of rhythmanalyst: *a flâneur*, *a storyteller* and *an analyst*.

To start with, it is possible to adopt a flâneur-like approach and to leisurely, haphazardly explore the railway station, letting oneself be guided by one's attention, preferences and chance. Similarly like Walter Benjamin's flâneur (or more originally Baudelaire's), one is both the active part of the environment and at the same time its' distanced observer. He is curious, in a way aimless and leisurely hanging around. A parallel with Lefebvre's famous observation of Rue Rambuteau from his Parisian balcony occurs. Another figure of flâneur is such when he represents a discursive body of knowledge, a spy whose wandering allows him to gather and taxonomize social dynamics, lively phenomena (and rhythms) that would otherwise escape the systematic analysis. Firstly, the flâneur-like approach helps in designing a specific type of rhythmanalysis, secondly, it is valuable in actually conducting it.

Similar to this might seem the approach of a storyteller, using literary devices to vividly describe the lived space and reach out to the reader to make him understand and feel the present dynamics. It is even possible to follow a selected persona, such as a railway employee and follow not only his rhythms but also the rhythms he encounters during a certain time range. Artistic approaches, audiovisual tools are of help here – it is a matter of the form of conveying the rhythms.

Nevertheless, these quite loose approaches will perhaps all make use of the perspective of the third figure, that of an analyst. His position is more methodologically grounded and he may opt for a combination of Chen's centrifugal (e.g. focus firstly on overall transit rhythms) and centripetal approach (e.g. a traveller, an employee) (2017) that were already described. Or it is possible to follow Kärrholm (2009) on the matter how selected phenomenon (in his case retail rhythms) operates with various types of synchronizations. In his study, he presented for example six "synchronization to rhythms of retailing, movements, events, activities, bodies or collectives" (2009: 427). What do rhythms of the station encompass, to which rhythms they succumb, how do they relate to an overall social or ideological framework such as the mentioned retailization or rhythms of capital and such? How do bodily rhythms interact with the rhythms of the station, how they influence each other? How to differentiate the rhythms of the station and railway rhythms in general? These are only a few of the matters that need to be decided in the beginning. It is necessary to start at some of the demarcation lines and follow the selected rhythms further.

The complexity and the fast-pace of the unfolding rhythms are dizzying. As Edensor showed (Edensor and Holloway 2008: 498) during a tourist coach tour, the rhythmanalyst in its heightened sensitivity may even widen the spectrum and think of rhythms of other flows that are normally sensually eclipsed. He may come to indirectly perceive a rhythm of a river that flows nearby, of trajectories of birds in the sky, of slow, nature or non-human rhythms that are not directly perceptible. However, it is wise to narrow this complexity and approach the rhythmical richness only through selected, often dominant veins of rhythmic assemblages present at the train station and its life cycles. From there, it is possible to untangle them, see their eurhythmic or arrhythmic constellations and more. Also, the analyst shouldn't follow only the explicit spatial or temporal rhythms, but also strive to see some of the inner rhythms – for example circulating rhythms of representations (symbolic imaginaries of the station, of the poetics of railway travel for example), melodies that accompany the rhythms and places and intensities of rhythms that eventually contribute to the atmosphere, mood or genius loci of the station. One may even go as far as to enlist the rhythmic patterns of solitary travellers that listen to music from mobile devices and carry a specific rhythm inside enhanced with the actual music. All in all, the crucial is to follow the preliminary delimited rhythm, a trajectory, a theme and possibly steer from it when there is a right opportunity, but not to get lost along the way.

6 Conclusion

6.1 Future Prospects

As it has been shown, recently there appeared several works that equipped rhythmanalysis with methodological foundations and more. There has also been a significant surge in terms of papers and studies that use rhythmanalysis to a smaller or larger extent. Many of them show countless possibilities of its applications as their areas and disciplines quite differ and they even might use different approaches.

This paper's objective was to provide an interpretative introduction to rhythmanalysis, provide a necessarily selective review of the method, show its limits and possibilities and set it in a context of urban space or more precisely railway station. While this has been done, case studies focusing on the above mentioned particular example of a transformation of a particular railway station will follow in future. These will deepen the theoretical foundations that were laid here. The particular case the studies focus on seems promising to bring exciting results and involve most of the concepts and ideas presented in this paper.

6.2 Final Thoughts

What does the ideal environment to which the rhythmanalysis should contribute look like? Answers will vary depending on the context. To Lefebvre, it seemed that the utopic cyclical time is more valuable than the linear time of modern times. In the omnipresent polyrhytmia, it seemed that eurhythmic state of affairs is more beneficial than the arrhythmia. Kärrholm showed that it is wise to avoid such definitive evaluative conclusions – while it seemed that in his study on retailization he values polyrhythmical environment over homogenous isorhytmia, the matters are even more complicated. Eventually, he saw the actual source of richness in variety of territorial orders and productions: "Several territorial orders also indicate several possibilities, and the danger of an exclusive onesided spatial use does not just lie in territorial homogenisation (of one territorial production becoming more stable), but in a place lacking superimposed territorial productions" (2009: 434).

In the end, it is the very context of the particular case of the distinct urban environment which we must consider and adapt the actual analysis to. Last but not least, the discussed matter of the policy of regulating urban space is to be carefully evaluated. To stick with the provided example – a particular railway station will face different perils and challenges than another station and obviously than a place of a different character. Rhythmanalysis allows us to remain flexible, versatile, sensitive and open to the dynamic conditions of everchanging urban environment and demands of subjects involved.

References

Augé, M.: Non-places: Introduction to an Anthropology of Supermodernity, 2nd English Language edn. Verso, New York (2008)

de Certeau, M.: The Practice of Everyday Life Reprint. University of California Press, Berkeley (2011)

Department for Transport: Re-opening Beeching era lines and stations. GOV.UK (2020). https://www.gov.uk/government/publications/re-opening-beeching-era-lines-and-stations. Accessed 07 Feb 2020)

Edensor, T. (ed.): Geographies of Rhythm: Nature Place Mobilities and Bodies. Ashgate Publishing, Burlington (2010)

Edensor, T., Holloway, J.: Rhythmanalysing the coach tour: the ring of kerry Ireland. Trans. Inst. Br. Geogr. 33(4), 483–501 (2008). http://doi.wiley.com/10.1111/j.1475-5661.2008.00318.x

Elden, S.: Some are born posthumously: the French afterlife of Henri Lefebvre. Hist. Material. 14(4), 185–202 (2006). https://brill.com/view/journals/hima/14/4/article-p185_10.xml

Foucault, M.: Dohlížet a trestat: kniha o zrodu vězení. Dauphin, Praha (2000)

Gottdiener, M.: Recapturing the center: a semiotic analysis of shopping malls. In: The City and the Sign, pp. 288–302. Columbia University Press, New York (1986)

Highmore, B.: Cityscapes: Cultural Readings in the Material and Symbolic city. Palgrave Macmillan, New York (2005)

Chen, Y.: Practising Rhythmanalysis: Theories and Methodologies. Rowman & Littlefield, New York (2017)

Judt, T.: The Glory of the Rails (2010). http://www.nybooks.com/articles/2010/12/23/glory-rails/. Accessed 29 Apr 2017

Koolhaas, R., Foster, H.: Junkspace with Running Room. Notting Hill Editions, New York (2016)

Lefebvre, H.: Rhythmanalysis: Space, Time, and Everyday Life. Continuum, New York (2004)

Lyon, D.: What is Rhythmanalysis? Bloomsbury Academic, New York (2018)

Massey, D.: Space-time, 'science' and the relationship between physical geography and human geography. Trans. Inst. Br. Geogr. **24**(3), 261–276 (1999). http://doi.wiley.com/10.1111/j.0020-2754.1999.00261.x

Mulíček, O., Osman, R., Seidenglanz, D.: Urban rhythms: a chronotopic approach to urban times-pace. Time Soc. **24**(3), 304–325 (2015). http://journals.sagepub.com/doi/10.1177/0961463X14535905

Nora, P.: Mezi pamětí a historií: problematika míst. In: Antologie francouzských společenských věd: Město. CEFRES. http://www.cefres.cz/IMG/pdf/nora_1996_mezi_pameti_historii.pdf. Accessed 27 Feb 2020

Norberg-Schulz, C.: Genius loci: krajina, místo, architektura, 2 vyd. Dokořán, Praha (2010)

Shaw, D.: Posthuman Urbanism: Mapping Bodies in Contemporary City Space. Rowman & Littlefield International, New York (2017)

United Nations: World Urbanization Prospects: The 2018 Revision. United Nations: Department of Economic and Social Affairs, Population Division (2019). https://population.un.org/wup/Publications/Files/WUP2018-Report.pdf. Accessed 18 Jan 2020

Zolotoev, T.: Landscapes of the Post-Anthropocene: Liam Young on Architecture without People. Strelka Mag (2019). https://strelkamag.com/en/article/landscapes-of-the-post-anthropocene-liam-young-on-architecture-without-people. Accessed 26 Aug 2019

Anon: Rhythm. Oxford Online Dictionary (2020). https://en.oxforddictionaries.com/definition/rhythm. Accessed 22 Feb 2020

Castello, L.: Revenge of the fragmented metropolis. In: Engaging Architectural Science: Meeting the Challenges of Higher Density: 52nd International Conference of the Architectural Science Association 2018. Australia: The Architectural Science Association and RMIT University, pp. 779–786 (2018)

Kärrholm, M.: Territorial complexity. Nord. J. Arch. Res. **18**(1), 99–114 (2005)

Kärrholm, M.: To the rhythm of shopping—on synchronisation in urban landscapes of consumption. **10**(4), 421–440 (2009). http://www.tandfonline.com/doi/abs/10.1080/1464936090 2853254

Brighenti, A.M., Kärrholm, M.: Beyond rhythmanalysis: towards a territoriology of rhythms and melodies in everyday spatial activities. City, Territ. Arch. **5**(1) (2018). https://cityterritoryarchitecture.springeropen.com/articles/10.1186/s40410-018-0080-x

Madanipour, A.: Public and Private Spaces of the City. Routledge, London (2003)

Palmer, M., Jones, O.: The Breath of the Moon (2012). http://www.digital-arts.org.uk/tide.htm. Accessed 19 May 2020

Palmer, M., Jones, O.: On breathing and geography: explorations of data sonifications of timespace processes with illustrating examples from a tidally dynamic landscape (Severn Estuary, UK). Environ. Plan. A: Econ. Space **46**(1), 222–240 (2014). https://doi.org/10.1068/a45264

Mobile Based Agricultural Management System for Indian Farmers

Ashmean Kaur Sran[1]($\boxtimes$) (iD), Sherrie Y. X. Komiak[1]($\boxtimes$) (iD), and Sabir Manzoor[2]($\boxtimes$) (iD)

[1] Faculty of Business Administration, Memorial University of Newfoundland, St. John's, NL A1C5S7, Canada
{aksran,skomiak}@mun.ca
[2] Faculty of Engineering and Applied Science, Memorial University of Newfoundland, St. John's, NL A1C5S7, Canada
smanzoor@mun.ca

Abstract. Agriculture is one of the most powerful tools to eradicate hunger and poverty from the world. Technology has been playing an essential role in the agricultural sector of developed economies, but when it comes to developing and under-developed nations, there is a need to bridge the gap between technology and agriculture. The efficiency in the crop productivity and optimum utilization of resources is a challenge that can be addressed with technological advancement. This study aims to create a knowledge-based system (KBS) in the form of a mobile application to help the Indian farmers for improvement in their agricultural practices and increasing crop productivity. A prototype mobile application, 'Farm-n-pedia,' is used to fulfill the informational needs of the farmers and provide a tool for agriculture management using a single platform. This agricultural knowledge mobile application provides accessibility and personalization, which is long desired by the farmers. It enables the users to access any information they want from all around the globe, get personalized expert guidance, know about the latest farming techniques and technology, and increase agricultural productivity.

Keywords: Agriculture app · Knowledge-based system · Crop management · Farming

1 Introduction

This paper proposes a prototype knowledge-based system (KBS) in the form of a mobile-based application of farming practices for Indian farmers aiming to increase crop productivity. Agriculture plays an essential role in the growth of the Indian economy, so it is often mentioned as the backbone of the economy after the Green Revolution of 1968. India is the seventh-largest country by area, and it is the second-most populous country having a population of 1.371 billion (2019) [1]. Indian Government is trying its best to address the food security challenge by engaging agricultural scientists in increasing food grain production [2]. Thus, the importance of farm output in the context of global competition has occupied an essential place in the national development plan. Agriculture

© Springer Nature Switzerland AG 2020
A. Marcus and E. Rosenzweig (Eds.): HCII 2020, LNCS 12202, pp. 162–174, 2020.
https://doi.org/10.1007/978-3-030-49757-6_11

employs more than 50% of the Indian workforce but contributes only 18% of India's Gross Domestic Product (GDP) [3].

Generally, ordinary people underestimate agriculture as an easy practice to grow and harvest crops, but it is just a myth as agricultural practices require high precision and knowledge. Still, we see many people with little knowledge of farming, getting involved in agricultural practices. It results in failure and resource wastage of the economy, which indirectly leads to socio-economic challenges [4]. A farmer needs to have the knowledge, be able to manage the optimal utilization of all available resources, and extract maximum productivity and profits [5]. Thus, we can say that training is an essential method to enhance the productivity and capacity building of people. The farmers need to be trained according to their individual needs, i.e., by figuring out individual needs and the skills that need to be focused on improving performance. The personalized assistance and huge knowledge banks provided on our mobile application can make it possible for the farmers to practice smart farming.

1.1 Motivation

A lot of research is done daily by the experts in the research laboratories all over the world, but the major constraint faced by Indian agriculture is the dissemination of knowledge that is generated to the end-users. The information should reach to the actual stakeholders, i.e., farmers and the field workers. There is a need to bridge the gap of knowledge between farmers and agricultural experts for improvement in farming practices and to increase farming productivity. More attention is required in the agricultural sector for its optimum growth. The farmers need a source for seeking information, problem-solving, and agricultural management. This necessity explains the motivation behind the development of the 'Farm-n-pedia' mobile application prototype.

1.2 Research Objective

Considering the interest of Indian farmers on how we can help them in making their lives easier, we came up with our research purpose. Our goal is to provide accessibility and personalization to the farmers in performing day-to-day farming activities.

Many farmers fail to put their required potential in agricultural activities because of the lack of knowledge and resources. With technological advancement in all economic sectors globally, we cannot deny the impact of technology in agriculture. Nowadays, mobile technologies offer optimal and integral solutions for agriculture. Hence, these technologies can help in improving agricultural activities and provide easily accessible solutions for problems like crop monitoring, crop management, machinery, working hours, weather forecasting, and many more to all the farmers. Using mobile technology, we aim to answer our research question, "What techniques can be used to provide accessibility and personalization to the farmers for performing their day-to-day agricultural activities?"

2 Literature Review

Under this section, we have researchers who focused on growth in the agricultural sector in terms of efficiency and productivity using Information Communication Technologies

(ICTs), technology as a source of quality information, and expert systems. Also, few researchers are more focused on the impact of the economic system upon the agriculture sector. Use of Information and Communication Technologies for improving agricultural practices has been a hot topic for researchers across the globe like Jain and Neeraj Kumar (2017), and Allahyari and Chizari (2010) from more than a decade. Jain and Neeraj Kumar [9] suggested an ICT model for developing and strengthening agricultural standards. They measured the knowledge level and attitude of farmers towards technology-based agrarian services. The findings showed that most of the farmers were unaware of the use of technology in farming practices. Allahyari and Chizari [6] conducted a study to identify the possibilities and roles of new technologies in the agricultural and rural sectors. The study revealed that most applications for technology in the countryside and agricultural sector were training activities for rural inhabitants, e-trade of input-output, transfer of knowledge between urban and rural areas, Geographic Information System (GIS) for natural resources management and official procedures. The research also emphasized the use of Information and Communication Technologies (ICTs) for the improvement of agricultural produce, reducing rural poverty, and the development of livelihood of the people.

A different school of thought did research focused on using technology as a source to provide information to the farmers for improving agricultural efficiency. Mittal (2016) and Mwakaje (2010) are some of the analysts who worked in this area. Mittal [10] did a study on the "Role of Information Technology (IT) in Agriculture and its Scope in India," which concluded that agricultural efficiency and productivity could be improved with quality information. Besides, to improve farmers' proficiency, IT brings qualitative improvement in their life by providing timely and quality information for better decision making. The people who are engaged in agricultural sectors such as field workers and farmers do not have access to the latest news for farming, which reduces the effectiveness of the farming community. This paper focuses on the scope of penetrating the most recent IT developments in the rural areas of India for their welfare and changing the importance of technological advancement for the rural population. Mwakaje [11] conducted a study in Tanzania about the usage of Information and Communication Technology (ICT) for providing market access to rural farmers. The research findings showed that farmers, relatives, and traders dominate market information sources. 23% of the farmers used ICT to access market information, information about the latest farming technologies and, weather forecasting. The farmers who used ICT gained higher prices for their produce than farmers who did not use ICT for accessing market information about weather, market, fertilizers, and others. Costs, accessibility, and reliability constrain the use of ICT.

Some scholars concentrated on studying the impact of the public, private and cooperative sector for improvement in agriculture without putting technology as the main idea of their research paper. Meera, Jhamtani and Rao (2004) [8] conducted a comparative analysis for examination of the performance of three projects working on agricultural development in India. The projects operated in different backgrounds and had distinct purposes, but all aimed at improving the delivery of information to rural people and farmers. The study describes each project, talks about the types of farmers involved, the variety of services that were provided to the farmers and looked at the backgrounds and performance of those who managed the projects. The services provided to farmers included advisory help, marketing information, information about rural development programs, and other useful information from private sources, central and state governments. The study focused on an individual company project, a cooperative project, and a state government project, where the state government provided users with valid access to land records, government development policies, and market information. Farm management information, accounting, and question-and-answer services were the most valuable in a cooperative project. In private company research, rural development programs, management of crop infection, and providing information to farmers were valued most.

Researchers like Pradeep Kumar and Mohd Shahid (2016) [7] followed a more concentrated school of thought, focusing on the impact of expert systems on agriculture. They did a critical review of the expert system for agriculture that integrates the accumulated expertise of various disciplines such as soil management and horticulture into a model that addresses onsite problems of the Indian farmers. The study claims that the main advantage of an expert system is to enhance the performance of an ordinary worker to an expert level. Furthermore, various applications like Kisan Suvidha, mKrishi and KrishiKosh [12] focus on providing aids to farmers, but they cover only a specific set of objectives. Several agricultural universities and research centers provide detailed knowledge, but then these are not available in remote areas. Besides, a problem of scalability arises as there are just a few experts, whereas the information-seeking farmers are large in number, so it is not a feasible approach. Agricultural Management is very crucial for efficiency in farming practices. Globally, the public and the private sector invest 6 million dollars (approx.) in improving farming, but they focus on the needs of large farmers [12].

3 Prototype

After referring to different studies focused on ICTs and current mobile applications, it is observed that IT is very important for the development of the agriculture sector. Besides, there is a scope of using a mobile app that addresses all these constraints faced by the farmers and provides personalized information to the end-users by creating a link between experts and farmers. In this paper, we are covering the prototype building of the app (Farm-n-pedia). The design of the app makes it suitable to work in line with the needs of Indian farmers. We propose to integrate the mobile app with massive databases from some online advisory systems of the Indian government and other legitimate websites to provide refined solutions to user-specific problems. We aim to cover the overall agricultural management system on a single online platform for delivering maximum ease to the farmers.

A knowledge-based system (KBS) [13] has been developed for Indian farmers to fulfill their informational needs and increase crop productivity by using a single platform. It uses a global positioning system (GPS), geographical information system (GIS), and mobile user interface to create a simulation of their farms for developing a personalized agriculture management system. Through the online system and the database of the Farm-n-pedia, farmers can get expert opinions for their daily problems and find the best possible solution. The app provides personalized responses for all the farmers, and it is a self-learning system, so it stores the issues and reactions in the repository for future reference too. The development and implementation of site-specific farming can be possible by combining advanced technology with agriculture. The geographic information systems (GIS) and global positioning system (GPS) are some of the techniques that are in use in western countries for enhancing their farming production and provide ease of use to the farmers [14]. It enables the pairing of real-time position information with accurate data collection, leading to the analysis and efficient manipulation of significant amounts of geospatial data. These technologies can be used in precision farming for farm planning, field mapping, soil sampling, guidance in operating the farm, various types of machinery like tractors, and harvesters, crop inspection for pest and insect infection, variable rate applications, and yield mapping. The GPS can allow farmers to work even during low visibility field conditions such as rain, dust, fog, and darkness.

3.1 Aim of Research

There is a strong need for this technology because many Indian farmers get less yield per hectare due to adverse weather conditions. This application allows the farmers to keep track of the progress of the crops and make informed decisions to harvest the produce timely. Weather information also plays an instrumental role in the field of precision agriculture as it helps the farmers to make cost-saving decisions as to when and how much to irrigate the fields. Weather forecasts by Farm-n-pedia support the farmers in determining the right time to use fertilizers in their fields. For example, imagine a farmer sprayed fertilizers in all fields, and soon after finishing the job, it starts raining. Then all the fertilizers will get washed away with the rain causing a significant loss of resources to the farmer. To save the farmer from this trouble and to advise a suitable time for irrigation, Farm-n-pedia will come to use. It determines the right period to apply fertilizers in the fields by the weather forecast. Furthermore, with the help of a portable tensiometer [15], the farmer can examine the current situation of the farmland and tells if the land is moist enough for the fertilizers to get worked into the soil.

3.2 Features

The application focuses on the problems of the farmers by getting input about their issue in either text or image form. Suppose a farmer is struggling with an insect infection in his fields, and he needs an immediate solution. The farmer will open the app and capture an image of the insect infecting the crops. KBS identifies the problem and uses an image processing algorithm to suggest whether the insect is harmful to the plant or not. If it is dangerous, then it will inform the farmer about the insecticide that will remove insect infection of plants [16]. It even helps the farmer in locating nearby stores (by using location-based data) to get the insecticide. In addition to it, Farm-n-pedia will store the data of insect infection in the database and inform the farmers in the nearby areas about the threat so that others can also be cautious and protect their crops.

- Farm planning, file mapping and better identification of fields
- Draw comparison between the production of different years

- Online support and local expert guidance for farming practices
- Crop inspection for insect and pest management
- Providing information in regional languages
- Optimizing land usage for production
- Weather conditions
- Keeping track of historical field data
- Learning the latest farming techniques
- Self-learning systems based on interaction with users
- Know consumer and market demand for crop production
- Suggesting methods to save resources like money, labor, land, and seeds
- Determining how to operate agricultural machinery like tractors and harvesters
- Determine soil fertility, soil sampling and crop recommendation based on the type of soil.

Farmers can also keep track of different crops produced and their profitability reports. With the application, the farmers can move around the fields, mention details of their crop production, and how much profit they earned from the piece of land by creating notes on the app's farm simulation. It will be saved virtually in the app cloud and linked to the exact location coordinates using the geolocation algorithm. Finally, the data can be converted into graphical representation to depict agricultural productivity to the farmers for enhanced efficiency [17]. This database can also serve as a platform for the government to track changes in agricultural production by farmers in different parts of the country.

4 Design

Our research model uses the Technology Acceptance Model (TAM) as its theoretical foundation. TAM theorizes that perceived ease of use and perceived usefulness determine an individual's intention to use a system as a mediator of actual system use [18]. The dependent variables are behavioral intention to use and the actual application usage and, the independent variables include accessibility, personalization, perceived usefulness, and perceived ease of use (Fig. 1).

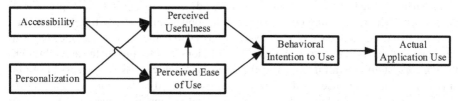

Fig. 1. Research model structured around TAM model

Based on the TAM model, many previous works have empirically evaluated the positive influence of perceived ease of use, perceived usefulness, behavioral intention to use, and actual application use on one another. Davis [18] defines Perceived Usefulness as the degree to which a person believes that using a particular system may improve its performance; and, Perceived Ease of Use as the degree to which a person believes that using an information system will be free of effort. It suggests that individuals will use a particular technology if they think that this use will provide positive results, focusing on the Perceived Ease of Use and Perceived Usefulness [19]. Venkatesh, Thong and Xu proposed that there must be a corresponding attitude towards real behavior before an action occurs, which means that attitude affects user acceptance behavior [20]. The behavioral tendency influences the actual usage of personalized products or services. Based on these conclusions, we find this model as most appropriate for this paper.

In this model, we aim to achieve accessibility and personalization through our mobile application 'Farm-n-pedia.' We intend to work on achieving the applicability of the TAM model as we progress towards improvement and actual usage of our mobile application. Accessibility refers to the ability to access information from the system when a person is on the go or moving to different locations [21]. The proposed app aims to have a higher level of accessibility compared to localized agricultural centers because the farmers can access any required information whenever they want. They do not need to go and find a local agriculture research center; instead, they can ask the app for the best solution to resolve their problems. Thus, it proposes to have a positive effect on the ease of access for the user. Personalization refers to the process of providing the user with expert guidance by using pre-programmed decision-making rules and algorithms [22]. The application gives personalized feedback to the user after carefully analyzing their problems. The app can provide a higher level of personalization to the user as opposed to the global web platforms. Thus, it aims to increase perceived usefulness for the user.

4.1 Methodology

The interface of the knowledge-based system in the mobile application is explained through the model, as shown under (Fig. 2):

5 Develop

A knowledge-based mobile application termed "Farm-n-pedia" is designed and developed specifically for the Indian farmers using Android mobile devices to address the requirements of the farmers' community and provide a way to increase their agricultural productivity. The functioning of existing mobile applications for assisting farmers was checked, and reviews of the end-users were evaluated to come up with a single platform that covers all needs of the farmers. Real-time solutions are provided to the users through the expert system, and all data is stored in the cloud, which makes it accessible from any device. The preferences of the farmers were considered in designing the interactive user interface, system technical design, and content development. It has been developed through several iterations of the mobile application. A user(farmer) with basic knowledge of operating a mobile phone was kept in mind while developing the app. An interactive and easy-to-learn mobile application is designed with relevant tutorials for providing ease of use to the end-user. All necessary information for the content development of the app was accumulated.

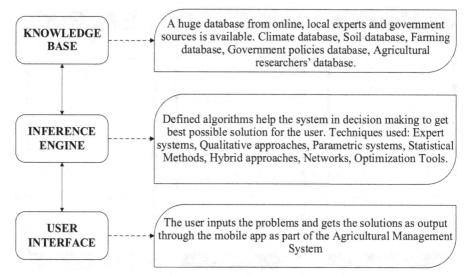

Fig. 2. Conceptual model for the agricultural management system app

5.1 Resources

We used Flutter [23] toolkit for our app development, and most of the coding is done in Dart and Python. Flutter is used to develop full-featured apps, including support for network, storage, cameras, expert systems, geolocation, and more. Other appropriate tools and technologies are also used to enhance the capabilities of the mobile application are used, and Android Studio is used for handling the whole app project and testing phase. During the first iteration, basic app functioning and session structure were tested. Further iterations were performed to test the system architecture, working of interactive app features including camera and videos. Advanced features like real-time data availability, farm view in maps were incorporated later in the prototype.

5.2 System Architecture and Implementation

The system architecture is designed for providing help in agricultural practices through the one-stop solution mobile platform Farm-n-pedia. In order to make the system user-friendly, an easily recognizable icon is designed. App navigation is made effortless for the user. A secure sign-in option is available to the user after opening the app, and then the user is connected to the app homepage where all features can be explored. A tutorial is provided at the beginning to go through the app for assistance. The user can access the follow-up pages according to their requirement from the homepage of the system.

As illustrated in Fig. 3(a), the user opens the homepage and then clicks on 'Crop Management' in Fig. 3(b), where the user can see the list of the farmlands. The user can edit or add new entries according to the need. Moreover, then by clicking on 'Farm 3' in Fig. 3(c), the user can see details of 'Labour Cost,' which was added prior by the user. The app shows a graphical representation of all the data that was stored by the farmer. Based on previous entries, the app suggests future expenditure for the farmland.

(a)	(b)	(c)

Fig. 3. Screenshots of the mobile application: (a) app homepage, (b) crop management tab with a list of farmland entries by the farmer, and (c) statistics of Farm 3

The icons are specially designed as readily recognizable by users across various farming communities. These icons are used in this mobile application to maintain a unique identity of features. These features are in itself quite extensive and fulfilling the needs of the farmers. Some typical icons like home, inbox, settings are used, which can be seen in most of the mobile applications. The layout of Farm-n-pedia makes it unique and compatible with all types of smartphones.

5.3   Framework

The app data is saved on the cloud to make it accessible for the user from any mobile device. The 'Encyclopedia' feature of the app is available offline to make information available to farmers all the time. The app is also available in a few regional languages to make it even easier for the farmers to understand. Some of the databases are built from resources provided by the government. The relevant information like change in a subsidy policy, weather, news, latest technological advancement for agriculture, and others are updated from time-to-time in the app. It is done based on the demand of the farmers. Access to a library with abundant learning resources is provided through internet connectivity. Information about types of crops, growth period, insecticides, and fertilizers for crops, machinery usage are some of the topics that are available in offline mode to the users. In addition to it, community and expert discussions about farming trends are available under the 'Discussion Forum.' Furthermore, if the user(farmer) wants to get a personalized solution for a problem, he can post a discussion thread in the Forum or open a chat with the expert. Hence, tailored solutions to all problems are provided through the mobile app as it bridges the gap between farmers and agriculture experts (Fig. 4).

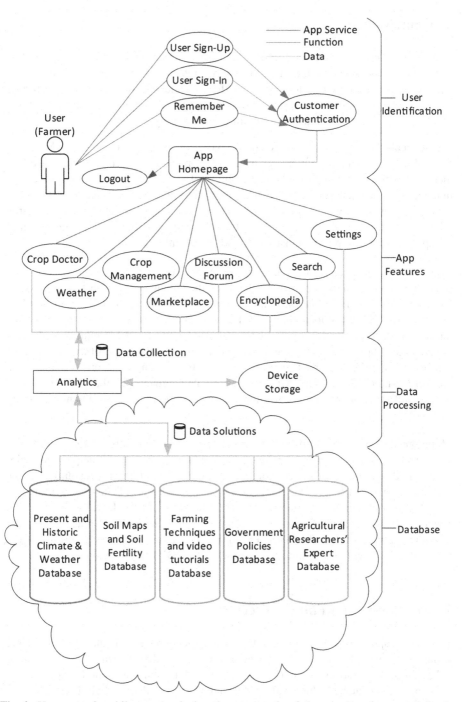

Fig. 4. Use case of mobile app (analyzing the commands of the user based on pre-defined algorithms in the system. Here, data input is linked to the database for farmer's specific needs.)

6   Contribution

The study focuses on studying the need and development of Farm-n-pedia, a mobile application to increase agricultural productivity. This paper aims to propose a prototype of the mobile app that serves as a single platform to address all the issues that a farmer faces in doing daily farm activities and provides an agricultural management system that will help the farmer in increasing agricultural productivity.

Theoretical- We proposed a research model based on the integration of the TAM model, accessibility, and personalization. As the mobile application is currently in the development phase, we intend to prove the applicability of the TAM model with improvement in the mobile application and its actual usage by the end-users. This model strengthens the application of the widely used TAM model and offers referential values for research related to the use of mobile technology in the sphere of agriculture. The development of the app provides new research insights for advancement in this area.

Practical- One critical aspect of the usage of mobile apps in farming is the involvement of human interface, indicating a dependence on the human element for transmission of knowledge to farmers so that they can work smartly and increase yield from farming. So, there is a necessity to realize how far technology can address the needs of the farmers so that better solutions can be developed to address those unmet needs. Our motive is to address the needs of the farmers, promote actual usage of the mobile app, and bring a significant impact on crop productivity. The impact of this research is an interactive app for the farmers that assist in regional languages, on-the-go access to any required information, willingness to adopt new technology, and improvement of farming techniques.

Managerial- This study contributes to an improvement in agricultural practices in India and aims to improve agricultural productivity for farmers. It will also help in the socio-economic development of the economy, and this app could bring a revolution to the agriculture sector in India. The companies that are engaged in IT and agriculture can work together on building similar platforms for helping farmers. It will generate much revenue in India and other developing countries where agricultural practices are not technologically advanced. This business idea will not only increase the profits of the corporates, but it will also lead to an increase in the GDP of the economy.

7   Conclusion and Future Direction

This mobile application is currently in the development phase, and it has some technical issues, which we are currently addressing. It establishes adequate support structures for Indian farmers who are essential for the sustenance of this innovative mobile application. This application can be further evaluated through actual evaluation with Indian farmers to assess the effectiveness of the mobile-based agricultural management system and to update and complete the design of the application thoroughly. It will also help us in testing the applicability of TAM model in the future. As such, the findings of this paper bring out the use of the latest google toolkit for app development and designing a platform as a one-stop solution to all problems that a farmer faces day-to-day in agricultural practices. It provides guiding principles for designing mobile applications; and also highlights other technological and contextual attributes that need to be considered in the designing process of a mobile application. It also provides guiding principles for designing both mobile solutions and on how to conduct design-based research in mobile learning.

References

1. United Nations: World Population Prospects 2019, no. 141 (2019)
2. Veeranjaneyulu, K.: KrishiKosh: an institutional repository of national agricultural research system in India. Libr. Manag. **35**(4/5), 345–354 (2014)
3. Madhusudhan, L.: Agriculture role on Indian economy. Bus. Econ. J. **06**(04), 1000176 (2015)
4. Murria, P.: Indian agrarian economy or suicide economy: is there any way out? Productivity **59**(1), 10–20 (2018)
5. Armstrong, L.J., Gandhi, N., Lanjekar, K.: Use of information and communication technology (ICT) tools by rural farmers in Ratnagiri District of Maharastra, India. In: Proceedings - International Conference on Communication Systems and Network Technologies, CSNT 2012, pp. 950–955 (2012)
6. Allahyari, M.S., Chizari, M.: Potentials of new Information and communication technologies (ICTs) in agriculture sector. J. Agric. Sci. Technol. **4**(4), 115–120 (2010)
7. Pradeep Kumar, S., Mohd Shahid, H.: Expert system for crop selection in agriculture: a critical review. Int. J. Adv. Res. Comput. Sci. **9**(2), 143–146 (2018)
8. Meera, S.N., Jhamtani, A., Rao, D.U.M.: Information and communication technology in agricultural development: a comparative analysis of three projects from India. Agricultural Research and Extension Network, AgREN, no. 135, p. 135 (2004)
9. Jain, D.S., Neeraj Kumar, P.: Assessment of knowledge level, need and impact of ICTs among farmers in different aspects of agriculture at talera block of Bundi District in Rajasthan. Int. J. Res. Commer. IT Manag. **7**(1041) (2017)
10. Mittal, S.C.: Role of information technology in agriculture and its scope in India. Indian Farmers Fertilizer Cooperation Ltd. (2016)
11. Mwakaje, A.: Information and communication technology for rural farmers market access in Tanzania. J. Inf. Technol. Impact **10**, 111–128 (2010)
12. Dwivedi, S., Parshav, V., Sharma, N., Kumar, P., Chhabra, S., Goudar, R.H.: Using technology to make farming easier and better: simplified e-farming support (SEFS). In: 2013 International Conference on Human Computer Interactions, ICHCI 2013, no. 248002, pp. 1–6 (2013)
13. K. Based and S. Technologies. Article Artificial Intelligence and Knowledge Based. **4**(1), 1–6 (2015)
14. GPS.gov: Agricultural Applications. https://www.gps.gov/applications/agriculture/. Accessed 25 Jan 2020
15. Topp, G.C., Davis, J.L., Bailey, W.G., Zebchuk, W.D.: The measurement of soil water content using a portable TDR hand probe. Can. J. Soil Sci. **64**, 313–321 (1984)
16. Nigam, A., Kabra, P., Doke, P.: Augmented reality in agriculture. In: International Conference on Wireless and Mobile Computing, Networking and Communications, pp. 445–448 (2011)
17. Information Solutions: Mobile services could enhance income of farmers. E-Governance Electronic Data Processing, pp. 1–2 (2015)
18. Davis, F.: Perceived usefulness, perceived ease of use, and user acceptance of information technology. MIS Q. **13**, 319 (1989)

19. Silva, P.: Davis' technology acceptance model (TAM) (1989). In: Information Seeking Behavior and Technology Adoption: Theories and Trends, no. 1989, pp. 205–219 (2015)
20. Venkatesh, V., Thong, J.Y.L., Xu, X.: Consumer acceptance and use of information technology: extending the unified theory of acceptance and use of technology. MIS Q. 36(1), 157–178 (2012)
21. Weik, M.H.: Mobility BT - Computer Science and Communications Dictionary. In: Weik, M.H. (ed.) p. 1027. Springer, Boston (2001)
22. Johnson, S.S., Evers, K.E.: Using individually tailored and mobile behavior change solutions to promote multiple behavior change. Am. J. Health Promot. 29(TAHP-4), TAHP-8–TAHP10 (2015)
23. Flutter - Beautiful native apps in record time. https://flutter.dev/. Accessed 25 Jan 2020

Interactive Pavement: Moving Spatial Surface to Dynamically Convey Information

Voraphan Vorakitphan[1]([⊠]) and Takashi Ohta[2]

[1] Graduate School of Bionics, Computer and Media Sciences, Tokyo University of Technology, Hachioji, Tokyo, Japan
boat_voraphan@hotmail.com
[2] Tokyo University of Technology, Hachioji, Tokyo, Japan
takashi@stf.teu.ac.jp

Abstract. We design an interactive pavement as an attempt to convert our living environment into a medium for conveying information. Our idea to create a pavement as a means for conveying information is developing a mechanism that generates a subtle wave-like movement on the pavement surface. We expect that a person standing on it will be able to detect the movement with his/her feet and know the implication instantly. The objective of this work is to show an example of a digital function smoothly integrated into our daily environment. We implement our first prototype and examine its effectiveness by making a series of observations and performing system evaluation tests. We verify that the prototype provides an intuitive haptic experience and participants can identify directional patterns without requiring further instruction.

Keywords: Interactive environment · Interaction design · Actuator arrays

1 Introduction

The usage of computers is now integrated into numerous aspects of our daily life. Even emerging information technologies such as artificial intelligence and virtual reality are on the rise and have become a part of our daily life. While there are a variety of digital functions, people use most personal applications on a smartphone. This is convenient if a user has a smartphone along, which is a common practice nowadays; however, they cannot do anything without it.

With this regard, concepts and campaigns to redesign digital functions from a user's point of view are being developed. In Society 5.0 [1], the emerging form of a society characterized as a "Creative Society" and employing digital transformation (DX) for realizing it was discussed. DX is an applicable current innovation, particularly for the Internet of Things (IoT) that digitalize everyday life. This contributes toward sustainability and social inclusion, and other breakthroughs to provide a better design for human and computer relations. This would cause revolutionary changes in industry and society beyond technological innovation.

A. Marcus and E. Rosenzweig (Eds.): HCII 2020, LNCS 12202, pp. 175–188, 2020.
https://doi.org/10.1007/978-3-030-49757-6_12

With this background, we propose a design for integrating a digital function into our living environment. Our idea is to make a pavement as a means for conveying information. We consider generating subtle movements on the pavement surface for conveying information to a person standing on it. If the person can feel and identify the different movements on the surface, a variety of notifications can be delivered, which can be perceived through his/her feet.

As an early phase of the research, our objective is to examine the concept's feasibility by implementing a prototype system. The prototype designed here is a unit of the pavement. It consists of flat tiles that are driven by actuators equipped under them. We examine the prototype to determine whether the information is perceptible by humans for basic understandings of the effectiveness of the approach. This would be a basis for us to improve the mechanism and interaction design. At the same time, this work is one attempt for a much broader research scope. We aim to demonstrate an example that allows a digital function to be smoothly integrated into our daily environment. Such a design could relieve people from the current situation in which most applications require a smartphone.

This paper is organized as follows. In Sect. 2, we introduce the concept of an interactive pavement. Then, we survey the related works in Sect. 3; we describe the design and implementation of the prototype in Sect. 4. We examine the validity of the system by performing functional and usability tests, which are described in Sect. 5. Discussions on results and future work are presented in Sect. 6.

2 Design Specifications

We considered designing a pavement such that it can convey multiple types of information interactivity. Generally, a person can be guided with a standard tactile pavement; it is beneficial for informing people about the static state of a place. However, such pavements fail to notify about the occurrence of a change in the surroundings. For example, they can help a blind person perceive the existence of a crossing but fail to notify about signal changes. If we can provide a subtle movement under the feet when a signal changes, it would help a person notice it.

If a pavement can be used for conveying information by generating movement on its surface, people will not need to use an application on a smartphone; instead, only walking or standing on the pavement would be required to obtain information. This design example integrates a digital function into our living environment. This is not only an integration in terms of a system, but an integration of a function in people's daily activity, i.e., walking. People do not walk on pavements with the specific intention of receiving information. They walk on it because they are simply going somewhere. The environment, i.e., a pavement in this case, provides information regardless of people's explicit action of requesting it. We believe such an integration of a digital function in daily human behavior, where operating a system is not intended, is a vital designing concept in creating an ambient system.

Here, we propose the design of an interactive pavement (Fig. 1), which can convey information by generating controlled movements on the surface. We expect that a person will not require any assistance to understand the information and will be able to instantly understand the meaning if the movement is appropriately designed.

Fig. 1. Interactive pavement

The pavement is expected to be able to convey a variety of information by different patterns formed on the surface, as shown in Fig. 2. A simple wave pattern, with varying speed and interval, can indicate movement in a particular direction (Fig. 2, above). Another pattern could be one of expanding circle from a certain point (Fig. 2, below) with varying propagating speed, area, and interval. These patterns can be to overlaid to express multiple types of information simultaneously. Furthermore, each pattern can express different types of information by itself depending on the context to which it is applied.

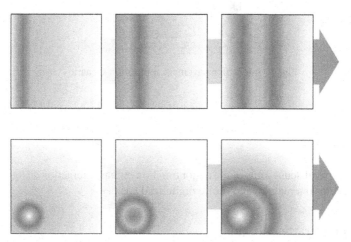

Fig. 2. Wave patterns of the interactive pavement: (above) pattern A: wave in one direction; (below) pattern B: enlarging circle

Some of the possible application scenarios are as follows. First, it can be used for notifying a change of a traffic light, especially to a visually impaired person waiting at a crosswalk (Fig. 2, a). If the area covered by the system is expanded to cover the entire crossing, it can be used to guide people in a particular direction while they walk. This would also be useful considering that nowadays many people concentrate on their smartphones and do not pay attention to their surroundings. Second, if the pavement is equipped with sensors to detect a car, it can be used to generate a warning (Fig. 2, b). To notify a person of unknown danger, movement with changing speed or intensity, corresponding to the circumstance, can be generated. Further, this can be useful for attracting people's attention to something placed along the pavement (Fig. 2, c). This would be possible by creating waves like ripples.

Figure 3 shows the scenarios of using an interactive pavement: (a) for guiding people on a crosswalk; (b) to notify people about an approaching car; and (c) to intrigue people to look at a visual element.

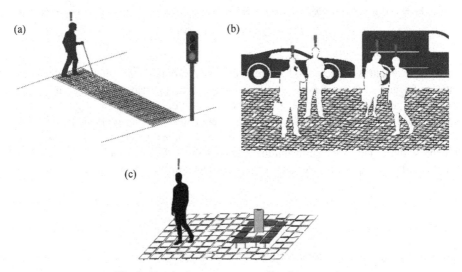

Fig. 3. Interactive pavement application scenarios

3 Related Works

In this section, we discuss some of the major trends in human interaction design, physical human-computer interaction, and future digitalized society.

3.1 Human Interaction Design

First, there have been a lot of studies on an haptic interface, which allows users to interact with a device by touch and most often responds to the movement of users. In this study, we focus on the tactile surface of an interactive pavement through which information can be naturally conveyed to users. In addition, we can make use of the characteristics of human perceptions as well as tactile step for the interactive pavement. There are two types of haptic systems [2], namely, active and passive; both use a programmable property.

As far as active devices are concerned, the power exchange between the user and the computer is entirely a result of response control. On the other hand, passive devices are sometimes equipped for programmable dispersion; this class belongs to devices with controllable brakes as a feature of position or time. Passive devices are used in our novel interactive pavement; our proposed method uses 3D-printed actuators as a source of pressure to rise, and to control the position of the interactive pavement. Therefore, information can be naturally conveyed to users through their feet by the physical movement of the surface. Moreover, the interactive pavement maximizes the significant and superior capabilities of a haptic interface for human feet by including motor control and engine control.

As another alternative to haptic interface, Iwata proposed an interface system consisting of a flexible display [3], an actuator array, and a projector. The actuator deforms a transparent screen on which an image is projected. The user can then directly touch the object and feel its form and rigidity. However, Iwata focused mainly on the physical rendering of digital content to address the restrictions of single-point haptic interfaces.

Leithinger et al. created a 2.5D shape display [4] for experiencing, designing, and operating 3D content in the real world by identifying a set of common shapes for interaction for displaying and controlling content. The 2.5D shape displays require user sensitive input that can be used for touching and pressing the surface of the interface to perform a wide range of applications.

Programmable maps to explore how children and adolescents with visual impairment can recognize and take advantage of the displayed tactile graphics using a programmable pin-array touchscreen have also been studied [5]. Pin-array displays have been shown to be efficient for interacting with tactile images for both sighted and visually impaired people. Moreover, their aim was to provide all students with an opportunity to improve their performance regardless of age or degree of visual impairment. Based on these results, a preliminary study suggested that children with visual impairment recognize and benefit from programmable tactile interfaces in academic and recovery contexts.

3.2 Physical Human-Computer Interaction

The interactive pavement is an advanced technique for physical human-computer interaction. Badeau et al. proposed another alternative to physical human-computer interaction [6], i.e., a passive mechanism and macro-mini architecture for effective and intuitive physical human-robot interaction. The macro-mini concept allows the use of a mini low-impedance passive (LIP) mechanism to effortlessly and intuitively control a macro high-impedance active (HIA) system such as a gantry manipulator. The mini LIP design is based on a three-degrees-of-freedom (3-DoF) translational parallel mechanism, making it simple and lightweight and adding no friction to the final effector of the HIA macro mechanism.

Siio created the InfoBinder [7], which consists of a push button and an ID. A monitor over a desk recognizes the ID. The system provides the user with access to physical objects such as a phone's virtual assets.

Bajcsy stated that robots should not regard human interaction as disruptions [8]. Instead, learning from such interactions is formalized as a dynamic system in which the objective function has parameters that are a part of the hidden state and these parameters are determined by physical human interactions. The results show that learning from physical interaction with less human effort lead to an enhanced robot performance.

3.3 Future Digitalized Society

In Society 5.0 [1], the emerging form of a society characterized as a "Creative Society" that has made digital functions possible was addressed. Digital function is an applicable current innovation, particularly with regards to IoT and robotics; it gives people enhanced capabilities that allow them to pursue their dreams, some of which lead to major contributions to the global agenda. These contribute toward sustainability and social inclusion, and other major breakthroughs to provide a better design for human-computer relations. Moreover, the world is facing an even greater wave of change with the fast-moving innovations in digital functions. This will cause revolutionary changes in the industry and society beyond technological innovation.

Narumalani [8] referred to the Global Cities Teams Challenge for cyber-physical structures to pursue novel research on effective integration of networked computing systems and physical devices that will have significant impact on smart and connected communities. He also provided another investment possibility in making electrical shuttles for safe and reliable mobility. He also described the Urban Scale Measurement, which gauges a city's "fitness" to measure carbon monoxide levels, ambient sound, and pedestrian and vehicular traffic in real environment through its major research infrastructure program or MRI. Using this example, environmental data is being measured in partnership with the City of Chicago in Chicago, Illinois; this data will be free and publicly available through the city of Chicago Data Portal.

The stated digital function in Society 5.0 [1] provided the foundation for smart and connected communities through investments in human-technology interactions and urban science. Such innovations include a mechanism that is controlled or monitored by computer-based algorithms, among others, across application areas such as the environment and public safety. In addition, digital technologies such as IoT and robotics will cause revolutionary changes in industry and society beyond technological innovation. For these reasons, digital function is necessary for our research.

In this study, we propose a design for integrating digital functions into the our living environment by applying our novel interactive pavement to a part of the living environment embedded into human life. This makes the real world an interface for receiving information. We expect this approach to provide a solution to the following: First, concentrating on the use of digital applications to a smartphone, and the second is not a digital function to use, or operate, but one that empowers users so that he/she senses the surroundings more instead of digital functions.

4 Prototype Implementation

4.1 Hardware

We implemented our first interactive pavement prototype using tiles and 3D-printed actuators for driving them. The system could deploy instruments such as motorized rod arrays to move the tiles for fully conveying information by physical movement in the form of wave patterns. Practically, we used a realistic tile in the shape of a square for our prototype. The actuator system consisted of 16 rods, each of which was individually enclosed in a tile surface of 3×3 in.

Servomotors and 3D-printed actuators were used to move the rods; the vertical length of the rods was 20 cm. We were constrained by the dimensions of the 3D-printed actuators to achieve minimum distance between each of them. The actuators were placed in a square grid with a spacing of 8 cm in each rod of the conversion process. We used four Arduino boards to power 16 rods. This approach was used for the system to achieve wave patterns to convey information to users.

In our prototype, the actuators were made from acrylonitrile butadiene styrene (ABS) by a 3D printer. Each joint of the actuator was connected with screws and the base of the interactive pavement was made of wood. This complete structure is shown in Fig. 4.

Fig. 4. Elements of the prototype

Figure 4 shows the following constituent elements: (a) 3D-printed motor holder, (b) 3D-printed slider holder, (c) 3D-printed linear slider, (d) steel linear rail shaft for joining the servomotor with the 3D-printed linear slider, (e) tile formed by paper, and (f) the base of the tile made of wood.

The actuator structure can be moved by connecting the 3D-printed motor holder (Fig. 4, a) with the 3D-printed linear slider (Fig. 4, c), as shown in Fig. 5. The steel linear rail shaft (Fig. 4, d) is used as a deformable joint slider to generate wave patterns by moving the tile surface. The tile can be controlled by the servomotor. These parameters related to the ease of deployment of the deformation structure as a linear actuator.

The servomotors were installed as actuators; their axis movement was controlled by the 3D-printed motor holder (Fig. 4, a), 3D-printed linear slider (Fig. 4, c), and steel linear rail shaft to create the linear motion of each rod (Fig. 4, d). The rods move from 0 to 90 degrees to create wave patterns respectively following by Fig. 5.

The linear actuator system has a hardware limitation that it cannot support the weight of a human body. To solve this issue in our first prototype, we attempted to create strong and independent materials as joints between the base (Fig. 4, f) and tiles (Fig. 4, e). Therefore, instead of using a servomotor to support the weight of a human body directly, it is possible to transfer the weight to the base to avoid damage.

Fig. 5. Overview of the interactive pavement

Figure 5 shows the overview of the rod when the interactive pavement is moving. The rod produces the power to hold the position of the steel linear rail shaft. When a user takes a step toward the rods, each rod must push itself outward to create wave patterns on the tile surface to convey information to users. A servomotor moves each rod according to the wave patterns described in Sect. 4.2.

The interactive pavement consists of 4×4 columns in one group, and an individual 4×1 column in a sub-group of rods. To align the interactive pavement, four Arduinos were used to monitor each sub-group of rods for physical movement.

To achieve this, the pavement surface was constructed using tactile-surface materials that convey information by physical movement in a dynamic form.

4.2 Software

Our software was run on a Windows computer with a frequency of 60 Hz and was developed in a C++ environment.

The control machine software was written in Arduino. The tiles were controlled by servomotor rods, which were controlled by four Arduinos. An Arduino controls 1 row in pattern A, in the straight (Fig. 8, a) and right (Fig. 8, b) directions. Rendering on the actuated surface was achieved by defining the operation of the servomotor by specifying the wave speed. The speeds were defined in three levels: (1) a non-wave speed, (2) an intermediate wave speed, and (3) a high wave speed; the wave speed changes depending on the delay function of 0, 80, and 160 ms, respectively.

The pavement moves in the required wave patterns by the movement of the servomotor rod array; the movement depends on the direction and rod's position. We programmed the wave pattern of the pavement like a sine wave. If the rod is flat, the sine angle will be 0° (Fig. 6, a) pattern encoded in the shaft of the motor, and is usually a value 0 with no load. In addition, if the rod is at a height, the sine angle will be 0, 45, 90, 45, or 0° like a sine wave movement (Fig. 6, b); the rod array will have corresponding angles to create sinusoidal movement.

However, when there is a load on the generator, these values are saturated. Therefore, we must first have good estimates of the sine angle variables to form a good estimate of

(a)   (b)

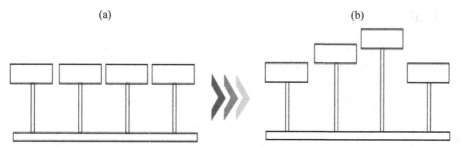

Fig. 6. Design space of the interactive pavement for presenting wave patterns.

the body weight. We do this during the calibration stage, where we run a data collection routine for each servomotor rod to collect the sine angle values. To characterize the linear proportion of the actuator, we ran the calibration several times: first without weights and then by adding different weights to the rod.

For a traffic light system for guiding people, our interactive pavement will be flat (or have no wave speed) when the light is red, moderate speed when it is green, and high speed when it is yellow to alert the users (Fig. 2). The system thus generates wave patterns to convey information in the real environment to users through the surface of the interactive pavement (Fig. 7).

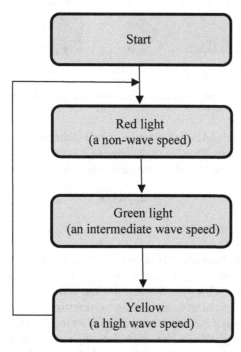

Fig. 7. Flowchart of the system design for traffic light application using physical movement for guiding people on a crosswalk.

5   Evaluation

As for the usability test of the prototype of the interactive pavement, we examined position error of the perceived objects for each servomotor and the accuracy rate. We also examined the behavior of novice users of the device. We especially focused on the behavior of first-time users.

5.1   Position Error of Pavement

We examined the performance of the interactive pavement prototype. We defined two directions in pattern A, as shown in Fig. 8, where pattern A was composed of 16 rods. In this experiment, this pattern is displayed in the straight (Fig. 8, a) and right (Fig. 8, b) wave directions. We performed the test a total of 100 times for the performance evaluation of each servomotor rod for a total of 16 rods, controlled by four Arduinos.

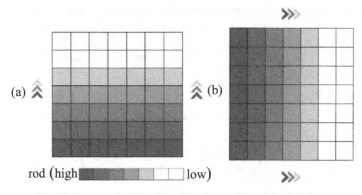

Fig. 8. Pattern A: (a) straight direction and (b) right direction.

We calculated the size and central position (center of the mass) of each servomotor rod of the interactive pavement. The size of the pavement is represented by the approximate diameter of the servomotor rod. The diameter is given by the following equation:

$$d = \sqrt{4S/\pi}$$

where d = approximate diameter

S = measured area

In Fig. 9, the errors for pattern A in straight (Fig. 8, a) and right (Fig. 8, b) wave directions for the perception of the central position of the pavement are shown to be from 0.5 mm to 0.6 mm. This indicates that the interactive pavement succeeded in the presentation of a pavement in terms of its range. Overestimation by the subjects seemed to be because the pavement was set above the servomotor rods. The size of the pavement was calculated from the position of the edge of the highest positioned rod. However, the subjects felt the edge through the pavement, which helped perceive the wave's directions.

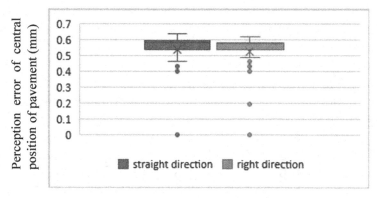

Fig. 9. Position error of the pavement surface.

5.2 Accuracy Rate

We examin ed the performance of the interactive pavement prototype. The subjects are 16 servomotors through 4 × 4 of pavements, controlled by 4 Arduino. We performed the test 100 times to determine the accuracy rate of each servomotor. The servomotor's accuracy rates for pattern A in the straight (Fig. 8, a) and right (Fig. 8, b) wave directions are shown below.

Considering the results of the accuracy rate in Fig. 10. and Fig. 11, we conclude that the use of four Arduinos to control the servomotor is successful, which can be increased in each row by 4 × 4. The experimental results collected are shown in Fig. 10 and Fig. 11; the accuracy rate for the straight direction of row 1 to row 4 is 85% and the error value is approximately 15%. The accuracy rate for the right direction of row 1 to row 4 is 92.5% and the error value is approximately 7.5%.

Although there are motors that cannot attain 7.5% to 15% error values for each pattern, the user could still identify the direction of the pavement as a consequence of human behavior; this indicates that the error value does not affect human perception and the device can still be used.

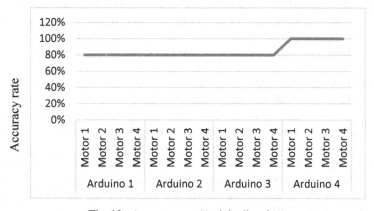

Fig. 10. Accuracy rate (straight direction)

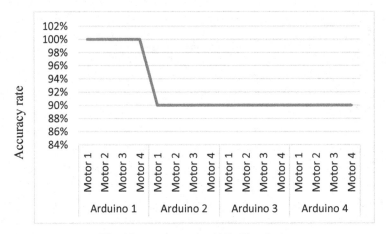

Fig. 11. Accuracy rate (right direction)

The pavement can be controlled using four Arduinos; an Arduino controls a row, in both directions for pattern A, i.e., straight (Fig. 8, a) and right (Fig. 8, b) wave directions. Considering the results, a user can identify pavement directions. The system achieves speed control of a wave to convey information to users in the real environment.

5.3 Observation of User Behavior

We examined the behavior of novice users of the device for the usability test of the interactive pavement prototype. We particularly focused on the behavior of first-time users. We demonstrated the interactive pavement in Tokyo University of Technology to recruit subjects for this purpose. The way first-time users interact without guidance or clarification was the main focus of this experiment. We observed the behavior of the participants in Tokyo University of Technology and recorded information for 10 participants. For this experiment, we used pattern A, particularly to guide the participants in the two directions naturally. We displayed the signs as straight and right wave directions. These were the instructions given to the users. We asked the participants about their behavior and noted their answers. We recorded the parts of the feet that the subjects used to interact with the pavement surfaces.

We categorized the subject's behavior into four classes:

(1) Touched the pavement with a bare foot.
(2) Touched the pavement with bare feet.
(3) Touched the pavement with one foot while wearing shoes.
(4) Touched the pavement with their feet while wearing shoes.

In Table 1, the results of the experiment show that 100% and 90% of the subjects who used bare feet could recognize the straight and right directions, respectively. In addition, 80% and 100% of the subjects who used both feet while wearing shoes could recognize the straight and right directions, respectively.

This finding indicates that the prototype system almost achieved the first goal of this research; it allowed users to feel the directions with their feet. They spontaneously used the surface of their feet even though the main function of the system was not explained to them.

The results of the experiment show that 80% of the subjects who used a bare foot could recognize both straight and right directions. In addition, 70% and 60% of the subjects who used one foot while wearing shoes could recognize the straight and right directions, respectively.

The subjects who used a bare foot and those who used one foot while wearing shoes seemed to touch it gingerly. Because the subject was an unknown direction, this behavior could be a natural response.

Another finding of the experiment was that multiple participants could use the surface simultaneously. The system provides haptic sensation at any part of the pavement surface and so it has the ability to support multiple users. Haptics was originally experienced by a single person; however, multiple users can share haptic sensations.

Table 1. Number of subjects who recognized the difference of information in pattern A for waves in the straight (Fig. 8, a) and right (Fig. 8, b) directions for each category.

Category	Number of subjects (straight direction)	Number of subjects (right direction)
1	8 (80%)	8 (80%)
2	10 (100%)	9 (90%)
3	7 (70%)	6 (60%)
4	8 (80%)	10 (100%)

6   Discussions and Results

The major advantage of the interactive pavement is that it allows natural interaction with users who could use a foot or both feet with/without shoes for the interaction. In Tokyo University of Technology, the participants spontaneously enjoyed the paving surface experience.

Another advantage of the interactive pavement is safety. The users of the pavement can wear shoes while the interaction is taking place. Generally, paving surfaces have control problems on the surface in contact with the foot/feet. The body weight or forces can be generated by the base that transferring the body weight to the base to avoid the damage from the body weight, which is sometimes dangerous. The contact surface of the interactive pavement is physically generated, so it is free from such control problems.

The major disadvantage of the pavement is the difficulty in its implementation. It requires a large number of actuators that have to be controlled naturally. The drive mechanism of the actuator must be robust enough for rough manipulation. Because the interactive pavement provides a feeling of a natural interaction, some users may apply a very strong force on the surface.

Another disadvantage of the pavement is the limitation in terms of conveying information as wave directions cannot be smoothly formed. The current prototypes cannot present a smooth edge on pavement surfaces. Furthermore, the space occupied by each linear actuator array is fixed in each rod. Therefore, some part of the pavement surface cannot fully convey the information to the users naturally.

7   Conclusions

This study presented the concept of an interactive pavement using a moving-tile mechanism to express information by physical movement. Our first prototype was developed to demonstrate the effectiveness of the idea. It was used for evaluation by anonymous users. The basic finding is that it provides an intuitive haptic experience. The participants of Tokyo University of Technology could identify directional patterns without the need for further instructions. Moreover, our prototype could convey information by physical movement to users. Performance evaluation tests showed its capability for stepping. The current prototypes have fabrication problems and limitations in terms of the type of 3D-mechanism and size of the systems. In our implementation, through a scenario, a guiding concept has been evaluated.

In the future, a new mechanical design for the actuators and base will be included; we will improve our current prototype to act as a guide for people, especially the visually impaired, as they walk on the streets or unknown places. Furthermore, we will include movement to notify users of a change in the situation and attract their attention to an aspect of city life. This would allow product planners and city planners to redesign products and cities using these dynamic physical models.

References

1. Center for Research and Development Strategy: Future Services & Societal Systems. In: Society 5.0 (2016)
2. Vincent, H., Oliver, R., Astley, C., Danny, G., Gabriel, R.: Haptic interfaces and devices. In: Sensor Review (2004)
3. Hiroo, I., Hiroaki, Y., Fumitaka, N., Ryo, K.: Project feelex: adding haptic surface to graphics. In: Proceedings of SIGGRAPH (2001)
4. Daniel, L., David, L., Anthony, D., Matthew, B., Hiroshi, I.: Direct and gestural interaction with relief: a 2.5D shape display. In: UIST (2011)
5. Fabrizio, L., Elena, C., Luca, B.: The effect of programmable tactile displays on spatial learning skills in children and adolescents of different visual disability. In: IEEE Transactions on Neural Systems and Rehabilitation Engineering, TNSRE (2016)
6. Nicolas, B., Clément, G., Simon, F., Thierry, L., Muhammad, E.A.: Intuitive physical human-robot interaction using a passive parallel mechanism. IEEE Robot. Autom. Mag. 25, 28–38 (2018)
7. Anzai, Y., Ogawa, K., Mori, H.: InfoBinder: a pointing device for a virtual desktop system. In: Symbiosis of Human and Artifact (1995)
8. Andrea, B., Dylan, P.L., Anca, D.D.: Learning robot objectives from physical human interaction. In: 1st Conference on Robot Learning CoRL (2017)

Usability Testing of Bank of China Automatic Teller Machine

Yingnan Weng[(⊠)], Shuxin Xia[(⊠)], Shuang Liang[(⊠)], and Marcelo M. Soares[(⊠)]

School of Design, Hunan University, Changsha, People's Republic of China
neroil.zero@outlook.com, 3512316636@qq.com, 783214479@qq.com,
soaresmm@gmail.com

Abstract. The objective of this study is to evaluate the usability of Automatic Teller Machine (ATM) of Bank of China (BOC). Several experiments were designed to identify the reasonability and validity of existing product's navigation and its usability. Eight users, ages twenty to forty participated in the study. Response measures included System Usability Scale (SUS), questionnaire according to Leventhal and Barnes Usability Model and an interview.

Keywords: Automatic Teller Machine (ATM) · Bank of China · Leventhal and Barnes Usability Model · System Usability Scale (SUS) · Card sorting · Questionnaire · Navigation · Mobile baking service

1 Introduction

An automated teller machine (ATM) is an electronic banking outlet that allows customers to complete basic transactions without the aid of a branch representative or teller. Anyone with a credit card or debit card can access most ATMs. There are two primary types of ATMs. Basic units only allow customers to withdraw cash and receive updated account balances. The more complex machines accept deposits, facilitate line-of-credit payments, transfers, and report account information and so on [1]. The Test Product we choose is the latter one, which is offered by Bank of China. On an ATM of Bank of China, you can use not only a credit card or a debit card of Bank of China but also any cards with a Union Pay sign.

On June 27, 1967, the world's first ATM was unveiled at Barclays Bank near London, which is half a century old. There are many opinions that in the context of the continuous development of biometrics, artificial intelligence and 5G technology, ATM will be more intelligent in the future. In China, government also emphasized that banks are encouraged to apply multi-factor authentication methods such as biometric identification in self-service teller machines to explore security and convenient payment services. In the intelligent transformation of bank branches, the new ATM is an indispensable part of it. The ATM can offer significant benefits to both banks and customers. Banks usually try to use technology for internal use and communication from the beginning and later as a tool to serve their customers. So we decided to do an experiment to test the usability of ATM used in Bank of China.

© Springer Nature Switzerland AG 2020
A. Marcus and E. Rosenzweig (Eds.): HCII 2020, LNCS 12202, pp. 189–199, 2020.
https://doi.org/10.1007/978-3-030-49757-6_13

2   Executive Summary

1. Eight individuals participated in the usability test of Automatic Teller Machine (ATM) of Bank of China.
2. The test aimed to assess ATM's usability according to Leventhal and Barnes Usability Model and identify the reasonability and validity of its navigation bar.
3. Participants are required to arrange navigation bar using card sorting.
4. After finishing the test, participants completed a System Usability Scale (SUS), a questionnaire and an interview about their experience.
5. The young show greater performance than the older age group.
6. This report presents summarizes, the product's goals, our usability test methodology, and our findings and associated with recommendations.

3   Methods

3.1   Subjects

At first, we observed and counted the number of people entering and leaving the self-help Bank of China in our campus on one-day and found that the ratio of male to female was basically 5:3. Avoiding the limitation of single type of subjects' occupation, we decide to recruit some people with a job and some students.

Finally, we recruited 8 participants. Five males and 3 females participated in the experiment. Their ages ranged from 20 to 40 years old (mean = 27.75). There are 4 students, 2 office worker, 1 engineer, 1 research associate. 4 participants reported high comfort with technology, 2 participants reported medium comfort, 2 participants reported low comfort. And there isn't participant reported Internet Banking experience. All participants go to banks about three to four times a month to perform common tasks (e.g. deposit, withdraw and transfer money, buying fund). None of the participants had experience of developing interactive electronic devices.

3.2   Experimental Design

We used Leventhal and Barnes Usability Model to make the whole experiment structure and user interface characteristics contain ease of learning, ease of use, task match, flexibility and user satisfaction (see Fig. 1) [17].

characteristic	measurement	how	interpretation	why
ease of learning	accuracy, speed and error rate	field observation	ranking by the points they get	easy to analyze
ease of use		questionaire		
task match	quantitatively measurement scales and qualitatively subjective opinions	card-sorting	ranking by the points they get	we can get subjective opinions and concrete data
flexibility		cognitive walkthrough		
user satisfaction	rating scales	questionaire(SUS) /interview	1~5 annoyed 6~10 normal above10 happy	it's accurate

Fig. 1. Experiment structure

Card Sorting. Those eight participants are required to freely classify cards on which functions offered by existing ATM are written and cards are allowed to be discarded if they think the function is unnecessary or add new cards if necessary [2]. In addition, they can change the name on cards if it is confused.. The cards used in this study is illustrated in Fig. 1. For some named that is hard to understand, necessary explanations are attached. And before sorting, existing first-class navigation frame is placed in advance (see Fig. 2).

Task process

1. Existing functions are printed in the cards with brief explanations.
2. Participants are allowed to modify the content or make a new card if they think the expressions are not clear.
3. Participants are asked to group items in a way that makes sense to them.
4. After sorting, participants are asked to name the resulting groups.
5. Once all participants have completed the exercise, enter the data in a spreadsheet, and examine the groupings.

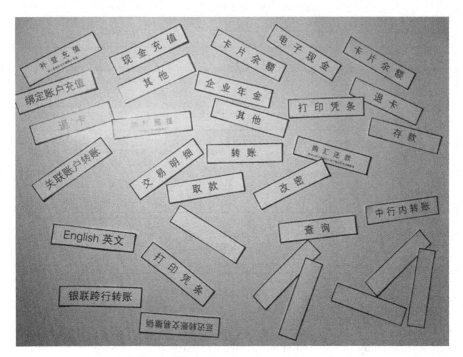

Fig. 2. Photo of card sorting experiment

Field Observation. Eight Participants are required to use ATM to transfer a sum of money from their own accounts to a specific account. Next, they try to use Bank of China Mobile Banking Service to complete the same operation. Time spent in two different platforms will be recorded and compared.

Task process

1. Ask participants to complete the task that transfer $200 to a designated account on ATM.
2. During the task, record the time they spend and where they hesitate.
3. Ask participants to complete the task that transfer $200 to a designated account on APP.
4. During the task, record the time they spend and where they hesitate.

Free Exploration. It was asked the volunteers to complete some tasks that they often perform in a real bank or try some new operations offered by Automatic Teller Machine (ATM).

There were a SUS after each task during the process of transferring money and free exploration.

During the whole process, participants were speaked to speak aloud what they are thinking or ask questions if coming across any barriers. Words and questions will be recorded for further analysis.

Questionnaire. We have prepared a questionnaire including twelve questions about users' feelings about using the ATM of Bank of China. Two questions are in one group, participants use number 1 to 5 to scale their feelings, these feelings include ease of using, satisfaction degree, comfort level and emotion.

The scores of each question will be recorded and be analyzed afterwards, the scores associated with different feelings can reflect how good or bad the usability of the ATM is.

Interview. We have prepared 3 open questions for participants to answer, these questions are associated with the usability of ATM, participants will give their answers on the paper given with 3 questions on it.

We will take back the answer sheet after participants finish the questions, and we will analyze the feedback to get a whole view point about the usability of ATM.
Task process

1. Express your feelings about using the ATM.
2. How dose it match your perception of using the ATM?
3. Do you agree the function of the ATM should be improved?

3.3 Experiment Procedure

There are six in-person sessions and two remote sessions through video call on WeChat.

Card Sorting. Prior to the experiment each subject was instructed about the purpose and procedure of the study. They are told that the whole process will be photographed,and only it is permitted, will the test begin. Several extra blank cards and a pen were provided for experimentation to add new functions or change the existing names. During the testing, moderator recorded participants' thinking and questions and offered some instructions if necessary.

Transfer Money. Six in-person sessions experiments were carried out on a Self-Service Bank of China in Hunan, China. The experiment environment was standardized. And the bank cards used belongs to themselves. After completing the operation of transferring money, they completed a System Usability Scale. Next, bank of China Mobile Banking Service experiments were operated in a offered unified mobile phone. Also a System Usability Scale is filled at the end of the operation.

Two remote sessions experiments were carried out in a Self-Service Bank of China in Beijing, China and Shanghai, China. Also the experiment environment was standardized and the bank cards used belongs to themselves. Bank of China Mobile Banking Service experiments were operated in a mobile phone whose model is the same as inperson sessions. After each task, a System Usability Scale is completed.

During the testing, moderator calculated time spent in two platforms, recorded participants' thinking and questions and offered some instructions if necessary.

Free Exploration. Two participants try to complete some basic operations such as Withdrawal, Deposit and Inquiry, they are able to finish the task without assistant. Four participants try to search for some unfamiliar functions, and Three of them made some mistakes, Two of them self-correction and another one completing the operation after help. The last two participants were worried about pressing wrong buttons, refusing doing unknown operations because they could not understand clear the words on the buttons.

Questionnaire. Six participants are tested in person, two participants are tested remotely by WeChat we give them the questionnaire and after some time, we collect those questionnaires with answers, during the whole process, they finish the questions with nobody influencing their thinking or disturbing them.

Interview. We have prepared three questions for eisght participants, we interviewed them one by one and write down their answers on our notebook. They all respond quickly. They are required to tell some basic information including their age, sex and occupation at the end of the interview.

4   Results and Discussion

4.1   Card Sorting

The summarized card sorting results are navigation, which are the same as the existing navigation frame. For less commonly used functions such as [Electronic Cash] and [Purchase Repayment], More than half of the participants move these two function to second-class navigation.

And nearly half of the participants remove the function [PIN change] because they proposed that this function increases the risk of account stolen (see Fig. 3).

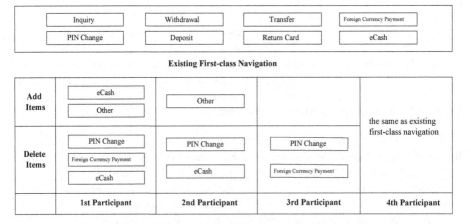

Fig. 3. Card sorting result of first class navigation

4.2 Transfer Money and Free Exploration

When finding the function [Unload to Primary Account], nearly two-third of the participants choose wrong buttons once or twice.

4.3 Questionnaire

Results of the questionnaire are shown in the table below (see Fig. 4), each number represents an average score which reflects participants' attitude towards the usability of the ATM [5].

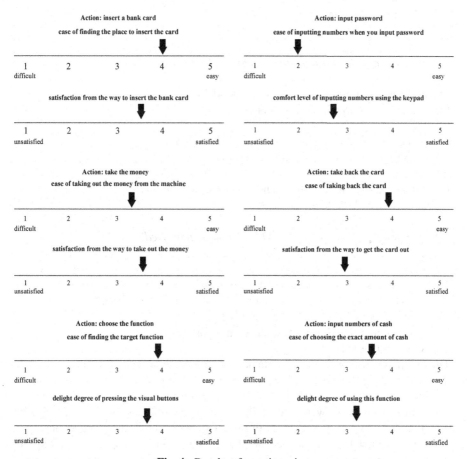

Fig. 4. Results of questionnaires

4.4 Interview

Here are results below:

Express your feelings about using the ATM

- The machine is clumsy but useful.
- The machine has too many buttons, too many choices, which makes me confused.
- The process is easy to understand and but the socket is hard to find.
- The interaction design is too old, it makes me try a lot times before getting what I want.
- I'm afraid of making mistakes, so I spend an amount of time reading the instruments
- It's convenient, fluent and quick.
- The ATM of China Bank is good.
- It's OK.

How dose it match your perception of using the ATM?

- The machine is a little difficult but understandable.
- I need an assistant to tell me which button to press.
- It's OK.
- The process,the interaction and steps satisfy my habit.
- It has many functions which I have never used.
- It's good.
- I don't like waiting in line, the machine is not clean enough.
- It matches perfectly with my perception.

Do you agree the function of the ATM should be improved?

- Yes.
- The operation is too complicated and there many useless buttons.
- I hope it can be more human-centered,easy to learn and easy to use.
- No, I think it's good enough, it satisfies my habit.
- I need a reminder to tell me to take the card before leaving.
- The look can be improved.
- The function is enough, the China Bank application can be a supplement.
- Yes, it should be improved.

After analyzing the answers taken down, we find 20% of the participants are slightly satisfied or satisfied with the usability of the ATM, others think the content shown on the display are much too complicated and they have to read instructions in order not to make mistakes which is time-consuming and can be annoying sometimes. About 30% agree that operation steps match their perception of using an ATM. And about 60% of the participants hold the idea that the usability of the ATM should be improved.

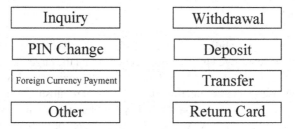

Fig. 5. Existing first-class navigation

5 Recommendations

1. In fist-class navigation, delete [Foreign Currency Payment], [e Cash] and [PIN change] and add a new item [Other] (Fig. 6). (Fig. 5 shows the existing first-class navigation)

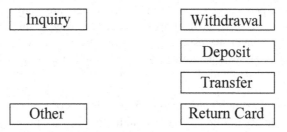

Fig. 6. Suggestions for revision for first-class navigation

2. Remove [Foreign Currency Payment and [e Cash] from first-class navigation to [Other] second-class navigation.
3. Remove the function [PIN change] from ATM to increase the account security.
4. Move [Unload to Primary Account] from [e Cash] second-class navigation to [Other] second-class navigation (Fig. 7).

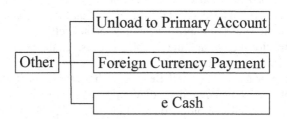

Fig. 7. Suggestions for revision for [Other] second-class navigation

5. Add necessary explanations to some less frequently used functions such as [Load from Primary Account], [e Cash Update] and [Load by Cash].

6 Conclusion

This study evaluated the usability of Bank of China ATM. The results indicate that its navigation should be rearranged in order that users can find the target functionality more easily. The redesign is supposed to aimed at solving the main usability criticisms and to implement new user-centered functionalities.People care mostly about security, ease of use, error tolerance and satisfaction when they are operating on the ATM. Designers can improve the usability of the ATM from the perspectives of these 4 factors.

7 Limitations and Future Works

1. Limited by time and money, we didn't have enough people to ensure the experiment is proper and the conclusion is completely reliable.
2. The style of the interface is also important for the usability, but we focusd on reasonability and validity of existing product's navigation rather than the interface style.
3. We didn't invite people aged over 40, but actually there are many people aged over 40 would like to use ATM and their response and their ways of thinking are different from those aged under 40, especially the aged, their comprehensive ability and learning capacity are degenerating. The lower comprehensive ability and learning capacity also seemed as with those aged under 20 or other the disabled, but we didn't get the sample either.
4. In the experiment, we didn't invite people from small city or rural village. Maybe they have different modes of thinking and would figure out more problems the interface had.
5. We don't have a test prototype, so we can't test the final edition of our design, that's regrettable.

The rapid development of Internet has led to many changes in our daily lives. Many users now prefer to using new technology and mobile electronic services in their lives, but still, the automatic teller machine have the responsibility to help people in many formal or business situations, and people like transferring and withdraw a large amount of money with automatic teller machine as well. So even now e-pay is developing very fast and convenient, we still need to test the usability of automatic teller machine. From my perspective, future works of improvement of automatic teller machine must be done to test the usability for the old and the disabled because as the population aging, the population of the old using automatic teller machine is growing, as for the disabled, sometimes they need to use ATM as well. Besides, with the evolvement and improvement of technology, more work is required to address the usability issues which will be key to successful implementation of biometrics within a general public application such as banking. Biometric method to test the usability of ATMs will be a trend. Moreover, bitcoin ATM is rapidly growing, the traditional machines are bound to transform and improve.

Acknowledgement. We would like to thank all the authors of the literature which we surveyed. We are also grateful to Coco Zeng who provided us precious advice and Professor Marcelo M. Soares who gave us the direction and guidance.

References

1. Lagan, J.: Investopedia for Automated Teller Machine (ATM), 14 April 2019
2. Gläscher, J., Adolphs, R., Tranel, D.: Model-based lesion mapping of cognitive control using the Wisconsin Card Sorting Test. Nat. Commun. **10**(1), 1–12 (2019)
3. Bangor, A., Kortum, P.T., Miller, J.T.: Determining what individual SUS scores mean: adding an adjective rating scale. J. Usability Stud. **4**(3), 114–123 (2009)
4. John Brooke, S.U.S.: A retrospective. J. Usability Stud. **8**(2), 29–40 (2013)
5. Pontes de França, A.C., Vitorino, D.F., de Oliveira Neves, A., de Lima, C.N., Soares, M.M.: A comparative usability analysis of virtual reality goggles. In: Marcus, A., Wang, W. (eds.) DUXU 2017. LNCS, vol. 10289, pp. 565–574. Springer, Cham (2017). https://doi.org/10. 1007/978-3-319-58637-3_44
6. Kang, Y.Y., Wang, M.J., Lin, R.: Usability evaluation of E-books. Displays **30**, 49–52 (2008)
7. Anderson, T., Jordan, P.W.: An Introduction to Usability (2019)
8. Hom, J.: The Usability Methods Toolbox Handbook (1998)
9. Camilli, M.: User-centered design approach for interactive kiosks: evaluation and redesign of an automatic teller machine (2011)
10. Zhang, M., Wang, F., Deng, H., Yin, J.: A survey on human computer interaction technology for ATM. Int. J. Intell. Eng. Syst. **6**, 20–29 (2013)
11. Coventry, L., De Angeli, A., Johnson, G.: Usability and Biometric Verification at the ATM Interface (2003)
12. Akatsu, H., Miki, H.: Usability research for the elderly people. OKI Tech. Rev. **71**(3), 54–57 (2004)
13. Norman, D.A.: Cognitive artifacts. In: Carroll, J.M. (ed.) Designing Interaction: Psychology at the Human Computer Interface. Cambridge University Press, Cambridge (1991)
14. Rogers, W., Cabrera, E., Walker, N., Gilbert, K., Fisk, A.: A survey of automatic teller machine usage across the adult lifespan. Hum. Factors **38**(1), 156–166 (1996)
15. Rogers, W., Gilbert, D., Cabrera, K.: An analysis of automatic teller machine usage by older adults. A structured interview approach. Appl. Ergon. **28**(3), 173–180 (1997)
16. Leshan, L.: Human-Computer Interface Design. Beijing Science Publishing House, Beijing (2004)
17. Leventhal, L., Barnes, J.: Usability Engineering: Process, Products and Examples. Pearson Education Inc., Hoboken (2008)

UX Design for Health and Well-Being

Transforming Patient Hospital Experience Through Smart Technologies

Haneen Ali[1]([⊠]) [iD], Astin Cole[2] [iD], and Gabby Panos[3]

[1] Health Services Administration Program and Department of Industrial and Systems
Engineering, Auburn University, Auburn, AL, USA
hba0007@auburn.edu
[2] Public Administration, Auburn University, Auburn, AL, USA
abc0074@auburn.edu
[3] Health Services Administration Program, Auburn University, Auburn, AL, USA
gzp0012@auburn.edu

Abstract. Due to advances made in telehealth, and the growing usage of information and communication technology in all growing sectors, patients have more
control over their healthcare experience through greater access to information and
their care providers. While the literature provides evidence supporting integrating more modern approaches, we find that patient rooms in hospital settings have
largely ignored advances made in information and communication technology
(ICT). This paper proposes a "smart" patient room layout designed not only to
help improve communication, safety, and satisfaction of both patients and nurses
but also to engage and empower patients by giving them access to technology and
educational resources, in-room entertainment. Three smart devices were proposed
in this paper as a way of transforming the quality, speed, accuracy, and experience of care services. First, a tablet was proposed to replace the original call light
device in patients' rooms. The second device discussed in this paper is a hands-free
device (smartwatch) worn by nurses to better prioritize patient calls, which will
improve patient safety, and improve nurse's workflow. The tablet and watch will
work in tandem with a third smart communication tool, voice assistance technology such as Amazon Alexa, to completely transform the patient experience and
allow patients to take control of their healthcare journey. Implanting this system
is expected to improve the quality, efficiency, and experience of both patients and
nurses. A high-fidelity prototype of the system will be developed and tested in the
university nursing simulation lab.

Keywords: Quality of care · Patient experience · Information and
communication technology · Call light technology · Patient satisfaction

1 Introduction

Call systems, defined as a bedside button typically tethered to the wall in a patient's room
directing signals to the nursing station, are primarily used by patients to indicate that they
have a need or a perceived need requiring the attention of the nurses on duty [25]. The

© Springer Nature Switzerland AG 2020
A. Marcus and E. Rosenzweig (Eds.): HCII 2020, LNCS 12202, pp. 203–215, 2020.
https://doi.org/10.1007/978-3-030-49757-6_14

patient call light system is not only considered an essential mode of communication in hospital settings, but it is also a "lifeline" that links care providers to their patients [26]. Effective communication technology is essential in providing exceptional patient care. Studies find that any breakdowns in patient-provider communication can lead to poor outcomes, such as patient complications or deaths, contributing over 7,000 incidents in 2015, totaling up to $1.7 billion in malpractice and legal damages [18]. The call light system plays an essential part in patient safety by communicating the hospitalized patients' needs to the medical staff [27]. In hospital settings, call light systems were found to be associated with difficulties and challenges such as determining patient care priorities, as well as the nature and purpose of call light alarm, in addition to usability issues [2, 3, 16], which can lead to causing harm to the patients and affecting patients and nurses outcomes. These challenges and usability issues such as greater instances of work redundancies, false alarms, nonessential alarms, low/no discriminability, prioritization, noise, and multiple call lights at the same time were linked to higher response time thereby contributing to adverse events such as falling, prolonged pain, and other general health outcomes [2, 17, 18], and was found to have a negative effect of patients and nurses outcomes [1, 3].

Literature suggests that greater usage of information and communication technology (ICT) can help advance the development of patient-provider communication by providing greater usability for both patient and provider than the current version of the call light system [3]. The most prevalent example of integrating ICT into living spaces is in the hospitality industry's "smart rooms" [10, 14]. Smart rooms refer to layouts that utilize ICT as a network of devices used to receive, process, and deliver information [10, 13, 14, 24, 28]. ICT can range from mobile devices such as tablets and smartwatches to voice-activated devices such as Alexa, as well as stationary devices such as AC/heaters which can connect to smart apps used by the other devices [10, 13, 23, 24]. ICT not only improves management functions and overall efficiency, but it also facilitates much higher levels of guest/resident satisfaction by providing prompt and customizable service [10, 23, 24].

In the health sector, ICTs refer to an arrangement of devices and services that facilitate patient-provider communication in the form of remote care (telehealth), interdisciplinary clinical support, as well as general knowledge transfer [23] Literature suggests that an integration of ICT-integrated patient rooms could improve health outcomes by providing patients with greater access to their health information, as well as online amenities that are mainstays in most households [9]. According to a report by the Institute of Medicines report, numerous design elements are critical in ensuring patient safety and quality care. For example, enabling access to health care information is a patient-centered outcome found to be affected by patient room layout [31]. Additionally, patient safety outcomes related to room layout include improving the availability of assistant devices to avert patient falls and addressing the sensitivities associated with the interdependencies of care, including workspaces and work processes [7]. Further, the patient room's general layout can impact patient care by ensuring rapid response to patient needs, eliminating inefficiencies in the processes of care delivery, and overall facilitation of the clinical work of nurses [7, 21, 23, 31].

Today, many technologies have become available for the healthcare industry that aims to reduce cost and medical errors and improve the quality of care. There is a need to improve both patient and staff experiences with patient-provider communication, to keep pace with the advances in communication technology [22, 31]. Further, there is also a need to update patient rooms to facilitate greater levels of comfort and access to health information. The study finds that one way of addressing these concerns simultaneously is by developing a smart system comprised of a tablet, a hands-free device such as smartwatches, and a voice assistant technology such as Alexa. Introducing ICT to the healthcare industry as a smart room layout has the capability of improving communication efficiency and nursing workflow, as such devices are compact, provide greater access to information, entertainment, and social interaction, and provide patients a diverse array of methods to engage with their providers [6, 10, 30]. In addition to improving patient satisfaction, the proposed system provides patients with easier access to alert staff of pain or discomfort, which helps to improve the patient safety function of the call light system [9]. Although the application of hands-free devices in the healthcare industry is in its early stages, the literature suggests that their use is promising, especially for communication, and can improve workflow [7, 15]. Smart apps. smartwatches, tablets, and voice assistant devices such as Alexa, allow staff to receive alarms and updates quickly, to engage with a patient remotely, and to organize and prioritize patient alarms based on more meaningful indicators such as current vitals, reported pain levels, and patient acuity [21].

The study proposes an interactive patient system composed of a tablet, smartwatch, and voice assistant technology to overcome the usability challenges with current call light systems, see Figs. 1 and 2. The objective of this design is to propose a communication system that allows patients to request assistance more efficiently through the use of the tablet or hands-free device and to improve the workflow of hospital staff by providing nurses with the tools necessary to effectively identify, organize, and prioritize multiple call light alarms through notifications designed to be more user-friendly and accessible overall. Successful implementation of the devices is expected to not only reduce staff workload by improving workflow but to also improve quality and efficiency of care and increase patient's and nurses' over-all satisfaction.

1.1 Smart Technology Application in Hospital Settings

While there are gaps in health literature that observe the effects of ICT-integrated patient rooms as a system of devices, there are multiple studies that observe the use of certain smart devices as individual components. One study shows positive results when a hospital utilized smart tablets and inpatient portals to keep patients up to date and engaged in their care. After identifying frequently asked patient questions, they were able to pinpoint the most valuable information to include in an inpatient portal [14] such as information about the provider (name), or case manager, time of the scan, lab results, time of last pain medication administration, meals menu, etc.

Smart Devices and Apps

Tablets are small portable computers that accept input directly on to its touch screen display rather than via a keyboard or mouse [9]. Tablets use apps and software that ranges from simple functions like telling time to complex programs that can analyze and predict consumer demands [23]. Tablets are increasingly utilized in hospital settings to facilitate teamwork among nurses, physicians, patients and to engage patients and care partners in their plan of care. Literature suggests that faced with time limitations, large amounts of information, and inadequate educational material, patients may not fully comprehend the nuances of their medical condition [9, 30]. In the U.S., 50% of adults have difficulty understanding medical jargon often used by physicians, and providers, unaware of this issue, may exacerbate their confusion through their use of unnecessarily complex terminology [23]. Patients that are less knowledgeable about their healthcare are also less likely to ask questions, as they may fear judgment or condescension if they express their confusion [23]. Literature suggests that patients are using smart apps to bridge knowledge gaps about their healthcare. The Pew Research Center reports that 77% of Americans own a smartphone [20], with claiming to have downloaded at least one health-related app [20]. Literature suggests that a patient who engages in their healthcare using educational apps found have a significantly better understanding of their health conditions as well as a significantly higher patient satisfaction score [31]. Smart apps provide educational opportunities in the convenience of a tablet. One example includes MyChart Bedside, an application included in the study that allows patients to view their EHR during an inpatient hospitalization [31]. It was designed to improve patient education and engagement and to strengthen patients' relationships with their care team. MyChart Bedside allows patients to view real-time information on their vital signs, laboratory results, medical procedures, and medications [31]. It also allows patients to learn about their care team, request services, and access educational information [23]. Pilot testing of the app showed a significant improvement in patients-provider communication including an improvement to how well patients understood their medications [31].

In addition to patient education, smart apps provide entertainment in the form of famous platforms such as Netflix, Hulu, and Spotify, which provide large selections of movies, television series, and music respectively. Consumers with access to amenities like those found in their homes were found to score higher levels of comfort and satisfaction [10]. Smart apps can also provide information for practical purposes, such as travel details, checking the weather, booking flights, and making hotel reservations [12]. These apps allow patients to stay up to date on their affairs from their hospital room. Perhaps more importantly, smart apps provide greater access for patients to interact with others, through social media platforms such as Facebook, Twitter, and Instagram, as well as video chat platforms such as Zoom, Skype, and Duo [23]. These apps allow patients to connect with friends and family members at their discretion, giving the patient greater control over the duration and timing of interactions than in physical circumstances [10]. In conjunction with the tablet and Alexa, smart apps can range from educational, entertainment, planning, and social options that provide patients with greater amenities and therefore facilitate greater patient satisfaction.

Smart apps not only offer greater access to information for patients but can also provide more effective communication tools through apps that organize, prioritize, and ultimately customize their call light experience.

While tablets and smart apps are shown to be useful tools for patients, and indeed many healthcare professionals, the literature finds that staffing demands require many nurses have access to both of their hands, thereby limiting the use of most mobile devices [12]. One of the components of the proposed solution includes the use of the smartwatch. A smartwatch is a mobile device consisting of a touchscreen display that is designed to be worn on the wrist. Recent research has explored the use of wearable/hands-free devices, such as smartwatches, in clinical settings. Literature finds that smartwatch provides similar benefits to the use of a tablet such as faster access to information, communication, and notification, but with greater mobility due to its wearable design. Additionally, because wearable technology is capable of vibrating, the notification function of the smartwatch notification is perhaps more effective than other mobile devices in that it provides the fastest and most varied modes of notification by incorporating visual, auditory, and tactile alarms [12]. In addition to improving patient-provider communication, the smartwatch allows providers to monitor a patient's vitals such as heart rate and blood pressure passively and without an invasive procedure. A notable example includes VITAL-ECG, a smartwatch that monitors patient vitals post-surgery [28]. This smart device improves the efficiency of healthcare delivery by reducing the time it takes for patients to be discharged from the hospital. Further, the device may improve patient health and safety by providing physicians and nurses with a faster way to analyze and report patient vitals to their providers [28].

In addition to smart technology that collects and reports information, many smart rooms are capable of voice assistant services that provide answers to common logistical queries and can manage other smart devices through a verbal comma. Amazon Alexa is a voice-activated device located placed on a horizontal surface that responds to queries made by the resident consumer [11]. With Alexa's new HIPAA-compliant version, the smart device is capable of virtually assisting patients by booking follow-up appointments, accessing hospital post-discharge instructions, and checking on the status of a prescription delivery [11]. Not only can Alexa improve data collection functions for nurse staff, as well as communication and overall satisfaction by patients, an Alexa device could also improve health and safety outcomes. A study found that providers using Alexa devices have less need to touch non-sterile devices such as keyboards and music players, thereby reducing the patient's exposure to communicable illnesses as well as germs and bacteria in general [11]. Further, in conjunction with the use of the tablet for patient use, and the smartwatch for nurse's use, Alexa provides additional accessibility to patients who are immobile and unable to use the tablet with their hands due to a neurological/musculoskeletal disorder.

2 Methods

The study employed a User-Centered Design (UCD) technique in consultation with the nursing faculty and nursing school simulation lab experts. The challenges were identified through the insights of nursing faculty, lab experts, and clinical nursing instructors. Over 25 h of the interview were conducted with nursing professionals aims at investigating the work routine, tasks assigned, call light systems, how these systems are being used, the challenges facing the nursing staff, etc. The results of the interview stage in addition to previous studies conducted to understand the challenges facing the staff while using the call light systems in other settings [2, 19] revealed numerous usability issues which may impact workflow and job satisfaction such as noise, lack of prioritization, and lack of individual notification. The proposed design employs hands-free communication devices (smartwatches) with action sequences to make prioritization easier, the staff will be able to access up-to-date information about the patients. Further, patients will have access to smart devices used not only for communicating their medical needs but also as an entertainment device.

2.1 Iterative Design

The smart system (Figs. 1 and 2) will incorporate smart devices in patients' rooms and hands-free communication devices for the staff to wear with multi-modal interfaces (visual, auditory/voice assistant device, and tactile) that will be able to prioritize alarms in a hospital setting by weighting the severity of patient condition and alarm/call type. The system will replace the traditional call button (in patients' rooms) with a smart device with a touchscreen (display) and a voice assistant technology to overcome accessibility and cultural challenges such as language barriers. Three iterations were completed. Heuristic evaluation and cognitive walkthrough were used with each prototype. Paper prototypes were created for the 1st design. The first design was tested by the research team and nursing students. Significant improvements were added to the design after the first cognitive walkthrough such as changing locations of Apps and adding more Apps for the patient, using the smart device in patients' rooms as an entertaining device in addition to communicating patients' needs and access medical records (orders, labs, etc.). A 2nd paper prototype was also created and tested by the research team in addition to nursing students. Multiple interviews with nurses were conducted to discuss the prototype. The major improvements for this stage included adding voice assistant technology (Alexa), and adding a feature which allows nurses to delete alarms from the smartwatch. The 3rd prototype was created using InVision software. The major improvements after the 3rd cognitive walkthrough included changing the location of the call light icons and other Apps on the patient's room device display.

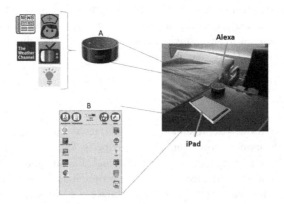

Fig. 1. In-patient room, two smart devices; A: Alexa, B: iPad

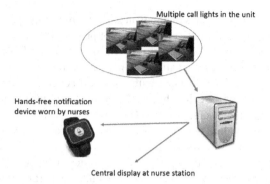

Fig. 2. In-patients' rooms devices will send notification to the unit's server and hands-free devises worn by nurses

2.2 Cognitive Walkthrough

Cognitive walkthrough is a usability inspection method that evaluates a design for its ease of learning and to identify factors that can lead to errors, which is often accomplished through exploration via simulation [30]. For this study, the cognitive walkthrough will consist of a trial of the proposed devices, testing specific tasks and processes for their usability, comprehensibility, and intuitive feel [32]. The steps for conducting a prototype include asking the following questions: (1) Does the design encourage the user to try to reach the intended effect? (2) Does the design allow the user to realize which action is appropriate at which time? (3) Does the user associate the appropriate action with the intended effect? (4) Upon performance, does that design reward the user by showing how the action performed contributes to the intended effect? [30] Literature suggests that if there are positive answers to all four questions, this is termed a "success" for the specified action, and a "failure if any of the questions lead to a negative answer [4].

3   Results

3.1   Interview Stage

Respondents to the interview agreed that patients use the call light system for unurgent requests. Further, it was found that nurses perceived unurgent calls as an interruption and as taking time and energy away from the patient's treatment. Nurses also mentioned that in some cases, they must make a trip to the nurse station to access the information about the call lights, with many mentioning how call lights tend to override each other during multiple alarms. The noise was found to be a prevalent issue for most respondents using the call light system. Due to the redundancies caused by usability gaps such as the system overriding multiple call light alarms, as well as the frequency of unurgent alarms, nurses perceive the noise from the auditory alarms as a distraction, given that they must ultimately report to the nurse's station rather than report directly to the sound. As a result, many nurses develop alarm fatigue, which could cause ignoring call light alarms, which may contribute to longer response times in addressing patient needs. These results were consistent with the literature [2, 3]. Regarding the patient, the current call light systems were found to have usability issues that may negatively impact the patient's experience. For example, the current call light system does not provide the patient with the ability to express their needs outside of pressing the call light button. Further, the usability issues which impact nurses can also affect the patient's experience. As longer response times have been found to be associated with increased adverse events such as falling, usability issues in the use of the call light can, therefore, contribute to decreases in patient satisfaction as well as patient safety [3, 17]. The results suggest that the current call light system falls short in providing nurses with the tools necessary to address patient needs in a timely manner, as usability issues have been linked to higher response times. The study, therefore, proposes an ICT system that incorporates the insights found in previous studies to transform the current patient room layout into a smart room design.

3.2 Design and Development

Design Stage 1. The first cognitive walkthrough was done with the original design interface of a call-light. The goals from the cognitive walkthrough at this stage was to investigate the size of the smartwatch that would be used by the nurse as well as decide on what call light display should be used, what type of tasks the two displays/devices should do/or provide, the action sequences, specific flow of alarming process, and what level of information should be provided for each alarm. At this stage, the same size and shape of the traditional call system were proposed with the addition of 4 buttons instead of one, see Fig. 3. The four buttons represent the top four reasons that patients use the call light system to call for a nurse [26]. There is a button for pain medicine administration, one for bathroom assistance, one for help rearranging the patient's position in bed, and one for assistance with intravenous problems or pump alarm. The first design was aiming to send notifications related to the reason for the call light in a prioritization list to the nurses' smartwatch. The smartwatch will show the room number, the reason for the call, and the time since the alarm was triggered. Urgent alarms such as pain and bathroom (depending on the severity of the patient) will be highlighted on the smartwatch display. Each of the four buttons makes a different sound on the nurses' smartwatch when the patient presses it. The sound of the alarm will increase if no one responds or if the response time exceeded a specific time.

A paper porotype was developed for the first evaluation of the display and discussed and tested using a specific scenario with nurses and with a nursing faculty expert in nursing clinical education and a nursing simulation lab expert. feedback was collected about the size of the device in the patient's room, it was proposed that the best device for this would be something bigger than the original call light design, like a tablet (see Fig. 4, A). The device would be wireless while the patient used it but would have a chargeable base on the side of the bed. One important improvement at this stage resulting from a brainstorm session with the research team is to use the device at the patient's room as an entertaining device as well as to call the nurses.

Design Stage 2. The improvements and feedback from the first walkthrough were integrated into the design. Another paper prototype was created for the second cognitive walkthrough. The goals from the cognitive walkthrough this time was evaluating the

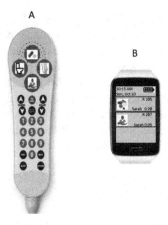

Fig. 3. Design stage 1: A: in-patient room device, B: Smartwatch display

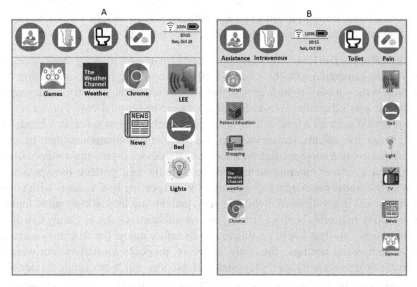

Fig. 4. In-patient room's device display; A: Design stage 2, B: design stage 3

patient's device display and the smartwatch display to uncover issues with the interface design, the specific flow of alarming tasks, and to uncover the usability problems with the design. The results from the cognitive walkthrough were to allow nurses to delete alarm from the smartwatch and provide a confirmation message of deleting the alarm to reduce the chance of deleting another alarm by mistake, and to add a voice assistant device such as Alexa for easier access. And, when the device is at a 50% charge, a notification will be sent to the display at nurse station to remind nurses to check the device and ask the patient to place it on the chargeable base.

Design Stage 3. A final prototype was created using InVision for the last cognitive walkthrough. Students and nurses were invited to imitate patients in hospital beds and use the prototype to determine which access points should be used for the call light buttons. From this walkthrough, it was determined that it would be easiest for the patient if two of the call light buttons were located on the top-left hand corner of the display and two on the top-right hand corner (see Fig. 4, B). It was also decided that a one-word description, such as pain or bathroom, would be added under the call light button icons to indicate what each button was for. Putting all the applications on the right and left side of the display is most easily accessible for patients.

3.3   Final Proposed Design

The final system: The smart call light system focuses on improving the communication process by eliminating many of the challenges and hence improving the quality and safety of care. We are proposing communicative devices used by the patient to communicate their specific needs through sending signals to the hands-free devices worn by the nurses. It will also be utilized as a form of entertainment for patients.

In-Patient Rooms Devices. The study proposes a smart system using three devices to improve communication with the medical staff and improving patient satisfaction. The first device in the patients' room is an iPad that will be used by the patient to communicate their specific needs directly to hands-free devices worn by hospital staff. Further, a voice assistant device such as Alexa will be installed in each room to serve as a hands-free support device for patients. Patients will be able to verbally communicate their needs by asking Alexa to call a nurse and deliver messages. The device in patients' rooms will also be utilized as a form of entertainment for patients. In the past, patients have passed the time in their hospital room by watching cable TV and playing board games with guests. With the current innovations in mobile devices, patients are increasingly more familiar with streaming platforms such as Netflix, and mobile games such as Candy Crush. As a result, patients are less likely to utilize, and therefore enjoy, the amenities currently available in hospital settings. The study, therefore, proposes a smart system whereby patients are able to not only notify hospital staff, but also watch streaming services like Netflix and Hulu, access the internet, shop, play video games, order food, and access any book at a touch of a button. Further, such a device could be used by the patients to watch patient education videos and hospital introduction videos. This allows patients greater access to health information and therefore more opportunities to retain pertinent health information. While the tablet and smart apps provide the foundation of the patient smart system, the voice assistant device, Alexa, will be used to overcome the accessibility and physical challenges in using mobile devices. Alexa will be installed in patients' rooms and will be assigned and adjusted to control the amenities of that specific room, such as climate control, TV, lights, and the call light smart app. As Alexa will be assigned to each patient's room, the device will be programmed to deliver a specific message to the nursing staff such as "Alexa, call the nurse", "Alexa, I am in pain", "Alexa, I need help to go to the bathroom", etc. Upon these commands, the device will then deliver a message which connects to a centralized console/unit that serves as a hub for the unit's Alexa devices. The operators will generate patient requests and assign prioritization weight. Alexa provides a wealth of opportunities for patients to engage with their healthcare, by providing an interfacing function to receive and respond to the patient's request and concerns. Further, because Alexa now comes in a HIPAA version, the study finds that the device provides adequate privacy protection safeguards for any sensitive information recorded by the device [19]. The study finds implementation of Alexa or a similar voice assistant device as a crucial component in ensuring the widest range of physical and cognitive accessibility for patients engaging in a call light system.

Nurse Device. Smartwatches will be used to deliver information about alarms and call lights in the unit to the nursing staff. The smartwatch will be used as a notification and communication device, providing hospital staff access to up-to-date information. A study conducted in a simulated nursing home setting aims at testing the smartwatches as notification and communication devices for the nursing staff show a significant improvement in the workflow, a decrease in perceived workload, and reduced response time [28].

The study notes that features providing prioritization as a key function which the current call light systems lack. An algorithm for alarm prioritizing will be developed through simulation modeling. Patients will be assigned to groups based on their severity, call lights will be given priorities based on the type of call light/alarm, information about walking distance (such as from the patient room to the medication cart, and from the patient room to the nurse station), walk speed, and estimated time for the nurse to complete the patient's request. The calls will be arranged in a priority queue and sent to the nurse. Prioritizing alarms will help the nursing staff in decision making by directing their attention to those patients with the most urgent needs. the algorithm to prioritize alarms is expected to reduce the workload and burnout for the nursing staff by keeping them informed about any changes in the patients' conditions and reducing the number of trips they must make to patients' rooms. The smartwatch will display the type of alarms, room number, the nurse assigned, time since the alarm was triggered, and will show the action sequences. Urgent alarms such as pain and bathroom assistance (depending on the severity of the patient) will be highlighted on the smartwatch display.

4 Future Work

The effects of implanting this system are expected to improve the quality, efficiency, and experience of both patients and nurses. A high-fidelity prototype of the system will be developed and tested in the university's nursing simulation lab. Nursing students and faculty will be recruited to perform hypothetical tasks created based on real case scenarios.

References

1. Ali, H., Ahmed, A.: Communicative technologies in nursing homes: a framework for evaluation. J. Med. Internet Res. (submitted, 2020) https://doi.org/10.2196/17254
2. Ali, H., Cole, A. Sienkiewicz, A., Ho, T.: Perspectives of Nursing Homes Staff on the Nature of Residents-Initiated Call Lights. SAGE Open Nursing (2020, in press)

3. Ali, H., Li, H.: Notification and communication technology: an observational study of call light systems in nursing homes. J. Med. Internet Res. (2020). https://doi.org/10.2196/16252

4. Følstad, A., Law, E., Hornbæk, K.: Analysis in practical usability evaluation: a survey study. In: Proceedings of the SIGCHI Conference on Human Factors in Computing Systems (CHI 2012), pp. 2127–2136. Association for Computing Machinery, New York (2012). https://doi.org/10.1145/2207676.2208365

5. Castle, N.G., Wagner, L.M., Ferguson, J.C., Handler, S.M.: Nursing home deficiency citations for safety. J. Aging Soc. Policy **23**, 34–57 (2011)

6. Chung, A.E., Griffin, A.C., Selezneva, D., Gotz, D.: Health and Fitness Apps for Hands-Free Voice-Activated Assistants: Content Analysis (2018)

7. Friend, T., Jennings, S., Copenhaver, M., et al.: Implementation of the Vocera communication system in a quaternary perioperative environment. J. Med. Syst. **41**, 6 (2017)

8. Gemou, M., Bekiaris, E.: Evaluation framework towards all inclusive mainstream ICT. In: Stephanidis, C. (ed.) UAHCI 2009. LNCS, vol. 5614, pp. 480–488. Springer, Heidelberg (2009). https://doi.org/10.1007/978-3-642-02707-9_54

9. Greysen, S.R., Khanna, R.R., Jacolbia, R., Lee, H.M., Auerback, A.D.: Tablet computers for hospitalized patients: a pilot study to improve inpatient engagement. J. Hosp. Med. **9**, 396–399 (2014)

10. Wu, H.-C., Cheng, C.-C.: Relationships between technology attachment, experiential relationship quality, experiential risk and experiential sharing intentions in a smart hotel. J. Hosp. Tour. Manag. **37**, 42–58 (2018). https://doi.org/10.1016/j.jhtm.2018.09.003. ISSN 1447-6770

11. Janhofer, D.E., Lakhiani, C., Chadab, T.M., Song, D.H.: "Alexa, Stop!" voice-controlled devices in the operating room. Plast. Reconstr. Surg. **143**(2), 460e–461e (2019)

12. Yuantoro, K., et al.: Development of monitoring and hospital patient alert systems using smartwatch application. ICP Conf Ser.: Mater. Sci. Eng. **403**, 01206 (2018)

13. Kalisch, B.J., Lee, H., Rochman, M.: Nursing staff teamwork and job satisfaction. J. Nurs. Manag. **18**(8), 938–947 (2010). https://doi.org/10.1111/j.1365-2834.2010.01153.x

14. Kelly, M.M., Coller, R.J., Hoonakker, P.L.: Inpatient portals for hospitalized patients and caregivers: a systematic review. J. Hosp. Med. **13**(6), 405–412 (2018). https://doi.org/10.12788/jhm.2894

15. Kent, B., et al.: Exploring nurses' reactions to a novel technology to support acute health care delivery. J. Clin. Nurs. **24**, 2340–2351 (2015)

16. Lasiter, S.: "The Button": initiating the patient-nurse interaction. Clin. Nur. Res. **23**(2), 188–200 (2013)

17. Meade, C.M., Bursell, A.L., Ketelsen, L.: Effects of nursing rounds on patients' call light use, satisfaction, and safety. Am. J. Nurs. **106**(9), 58–70 (2006)

18. New CRICO Comparative Benchmarking System report indicates claim frequency down; claim severity, management costs up. Med. Liab. Monit. **44**(3):1, 7 (2019)

19. Perez, S.: Amazon Alexa Launches Its First HIPAA-Compliant Medical Skills" TechCrunch (2019). https://techcrunch.com/2019/04/04/amazon-alexa-launches-its-first-hipaa-compliant-medical-skills/

20. Pew Research Center. (2018). Mobile fact sheet. http://www.pewinternet.org/fact-sheet/mobile

21. Raabe, L., Fleharty, B.: Embracing Technology as the Extension of Nursing Practice to Enhance the Patient Experience (2019)

22. Reiling, J., Hughes, R.G., Murphy, M.R.: The impact of facility design on patient safety. In: Hughes, R.G., editor. Patient Safety and Quality: An Evidence-Based Handbook for Nurses. Rockville (MD): Agency for Healthcare Research and Quality (US); Apr. Chapter 28 (2008)

23. Rouleau, G., Gagnon, M.P., Côté, J., Payne-Gagnon, J., Hudson, E., Dubois, C.A.: Impact of information and communication technologies on nursing care: results of an overview of systematic reviews. J. Med. Internet Res. **19**(4), e122 (2017)

24. Schoville, R.R.: Exploring the Implementation Process of Technology Adoption in Long-term Care Nursing Facilities. The University of Michigan (2015)
25. Stokowski, L.A.: Ring for the nurse! Improving call light management. Medscape website (2008). http://www.medscape.org/viewarticle/570242
26. Tzeng, H.M.: Perspectives of staff nurses of the reasons for and the nature of patient-initiated call lights: an exploratory survey study in four USA hospitals. BMC Health Serv. Res. **10**(1), 52 (2010)
27. Tzeng, H.M.: Using multiple data sources to answer patient safety-related research questions in hospital inpatient settings: a discursive paper using inpatient falls as an example. J. Clin. Nurs. **20**(23–24), 3276–3284 (2011)
28. Randazzo, V., Pasero, E., Navaretti, S.: VITAL-ECG: a portable wearable hospital. In: 2018 IEEE Sensors Applications Symposium (SAS), Seoul, pp. 1–6 (2018). https://doi.org/10.1109/sas.2018.8336776
29. Varga, N., Bokor, L., Takács, A.: Context-aware IPv6 flow mobility for multi-sensor based mobile patient monitoring and tele-consultation. Procedia Comput. Sci. **40**, 222–229 (2014)
30. Wharton, C., Rieman, J., Lewis, C,, Poison, P.: The cognitive walkthrough method: a practitioner's guide. In: Nielsen, J., Mack, R.L. (eds.) Usability Inspection Methods, pp. 105–140. Wiley, New York (1994)
31. Winstanley, E.L., et al.: Inpatient experiences with mychart bedside. Telemedi. J. e-health Official J. Am. Telemed. Assoc. **23**(8), 691–693 (2017). https://doi.org/10.1089/tmj.2016.0132
32. Liu, Y., Osvalder, A.-L., Dahlman, S.: Exploring user background settings in cognitive walkthrough evaluation of medical prototype interfaces: a case study. Int. J. Ind. Ergon. **35**(4), 379–390 (2005). ISSN 0169–8141. https://doi.org/10.1016/j.ergon.2004.10.004

Gamedesign and Physiotherapy: Contribution of Gamification and UX Techniques to Physical Teenagers' Recovery

Ernesto Filgueiras[1,2(✉)] and Gustavo Desouzart[3]

[1] CIAUD – Research Centre for Architecture, Urbanism and Design, Lisbon, Portugal
ernestovf@gmail.com
[2] Communication Laboratory – LabCom, University of Beira Interior, Covilhã, Portugal
[3] RECI I&D, Piaget Institute of Viseu, Viseu, Portugal

Abstract. Nowadays children and teenagers play videogames more and more regularly. The scope of these videogames is not limited to home entertainment but, is increasingly seen as a paradigm between overuse of technology and the motivational and skill enhancing potential that is increasingly being explored in the fields of education and of rehabilitation. The aim of the present study is verify the existence of studies that use the Videogame in the postural rehabilitation in school context; to verify the prevalence of using videogames with and without motion device in school-age children and teenagers and its relationship with back pain. Data collection was performed from March to May 2018 in schools in the city of Viseu, Portugal, which belonged to the 2nd and 3rd cycles of basic education. A questionnaire designed with sociodemographic information, use of videogames and body discomfort scale was applied. For the study, 124 participants were selected with $12,43 \pm 1,67$ years old, 77.4% of participants report feeling pain and there was a mean of $2,78 \pm 1,400$ that correspond to a moderate to severe episode. 44.4% reported feeling pain when playing Videogames. Videogame use by consoles was reported by 74.2% of participants, using the motion app, only 26.6% owns. There is a correlation, according Pearson test, between the fact of having the motion device and the number of times of use, being who has fewer hours on average than those who do not have the motion device ($p = 0,031$), having only the console. The therapeutic effects on the use of Videogames are little explored, focusing mainly on the elderly population and balance disorders. Therefore, it is necessary to verify the use of videogames in the motivational behaviors of children and teenagers to demonstrate the existence of benefits and provide a basis for future studies.

Keywords: Videogames and motion app · Back pain · Physical rehabilitation · Exergaming · School-age

1 Introduction

There are a large number of children who only perform physical activity, whether in physical education classes in school context. After that they return to the sedentary base

© Springer Nature Switzerland AG 2020
A. Marcus and E. Rosenzweig (Eds.): HCII 2020, LNCS 12202, pp. 216–228, 2020.
https://doi.org/10.1007/978-3-030-49757-6_15

of study, computer use, watching television or playing Videogames (which can lead to repetitive strain injuries, sleep disorders due to excessive use of online games and excessive time spent on them) [9]. Children and teenagers play videogames more and more regularly. The scope of these videogames is not limited to home entertainment, but is increasingly seen as a paradigm between overuse of technology and the motivational and skill enhancing potential that is increasingly being explored in the fields of education and of rehabilitation [1, 2].

The popularity of videogames among children and teenagers led researchers in various fields, such as developmental and social psychology, to focus their analysis on the usability of Videogames, but their research was geared between associating their use with negative outcomes in these areas for its consequences related to the use sedentary lifestyle and increased aggressiveness due to large number of violent games, bringing health and health complications social life, while research on positive outcomes are more limited [3, 4].

In recent years, the use of Videogames has changed its form, moving from a passive posture (i.e. a player sitting with the controller in hand) to an increasingly active posture (using motion software, where it is tracked the actual physical displacement of the player's body parts to control the game). This active control of the game requires a higher level of activity and participation [10].

The technological advance contributed significantly to the development of virtual games destined to the practice of physical activity, developed to employ human movement as input element, with the purpose of increasing caloric expenditure and interactivity [11, 12].

The benefits of games known as "Exergaming" have been discussed. These types of games reinforce the idea of spending a healthy leisure time. In motor rehabilitation it provides information for a thriving field of activity; However, the limited number of researches suggest that more scientific research and case studies be conducted using the videogame as a rehabilitation tool [13, 15].

Physical activity in playing "Exergaming" games can be considered as a good actual exercise, but it does not replace conventional aerobic exercise. The benefits of its use in rehabilitation as a therapeutic tool are improved balance, increased mobility, upper and lower limbs range of motion, and patient motivation [13, 14].

Integration of Videogames into conventional physical rehabilitation began about a decade and a half ago, and several articles have reported integrating conventional Videogames with physical rehabilitation schemes. However, most published studies focus on neurological rehabilitation (stroke, cerebral palsy and Parkinson's disease) using conventional games, not built for the specificities of the clinical condition [16].

The aim of the present study is to verify the prevalence of using Videogames with and without motion device in school-age children and teenagers and verify the existence of studies oriented to postural rehabilitation in school-age participants with videogame support.

2 Game Design and Rehabilitation

Virtual learning environments (VLE) are spreading in the various areas of knowledge. Its presence in Education and rehabilitation is providing new ways of conveying and accessing a large volume of information and knowledge [17, 18]. Videogames are one of the examples of VLE where they are being used to work on cognitive skills, visual attention, memory and problem solving, especially in children and the elderly [19, 20]. The process of producing a game starts with the concept definition, through game design, several steps take place until the final version of the game [21–23]. The central idea is to gamify the processes of interaction and learning through games and to implement them in real-world situations, often with the aim of motivating specific behaviors within game situations [24, 25]. Many authors see gamification as an innovative and promising concept, which refers to the use of game design elements that can be applied within various contexts [26–28].

Gamification is implemented in multifactorial contexts, such as at work, education, data collection, health, marketing, social networks, among others. Within all of these contexts, it is expected that gamification can promote the beginning or continuation of behavior directed to specific objectives, with a focus on the motivation of its users [17, 22, 24, 29–32]. In this case the gamification focuses on playful activities and experiences that the user unleashes in non-game contexts that are more similar to games, using game design elements [24, 28]. A basic assumption is that game design elements can be deliberately used to modify non-game contexts, such as work or learning environments, and therefore can purposefully address motivational mechanisms [24].

Virtual learning environments (VLE) are spreading in different areas of knowledge. The virtual reality interface is the technology responsible for this set of tools used in several areas, as it is able to provide greater interaction with the user, in which the possibility of visualizing different environments together with other sense organs, increases the sensitivity of the user. Games, for example, are being used as VLE to work on cognitive skills, visual attention, memory and problem solving [20, 33].

Due to the possibility of low-cost use of perception and performance technologies, a class of games called Active Videogames (AVG) or Exergame (EXG) emerged about a decade ago. This modality provides the user with the development of sensory and motor skills, thanks to the possibility of perceptual and performance emulation, provided by virtual reality mechanisms and tracking and performance technologies. EXG are an educational tool for Health Sciences, especially for Physical Education, since human movement is a fundamental characteristic in these types of games [13, 14, 34].

Exergames (EXG) is the combination of physical exercise with the game, allowing the use of games to be taken advantage of by physical exercise. This requires physically interacting with the game through various physical activities, such as dancing, running and boxing. This type of interaction has received more attention from an area of computing known as Human Computer Interaction [15, 34, 35].

A computational approach generated through game design was that of virtual reality. Virtual reality (VR) is an innovative technology that describes a scenario generated by an electronic device. This allows the creation of multisensory stimuli that transfer a complexity from the physical world to another controlled environment [36, 37].

The VR is an immersive, interactive, structured and presented experience using graphic images generated in real time by a computer or other electronic device. This interactive process shows itself as a dynamic developer, potentializing achievements and allowing new forms of creation [38].

The VR interface is the technology responsible for this set of tools used in education, as it is able to provide greater interaction with the user, in which the possibility of visualizing different environments together with other organs of sense, which can enable the increase user sensitivity. Adaptation to new technologies allows coupling with electronic devices to enhance cognitive functions, such as the development of strategic thinking, reasoning and perception [33, 34].

This approach through new technologies means an important analysis for the motor system in the field of neuroscience, which offers the opportunity to unify experimental data from the theoretical form of the structure. This approach allows the use of this technology through Videogames due to rehabilitation, where it allows the patient to make more precise and effective movements through a sensorimotor component [37, 39].

The use of Videogames as a strategy for rehabilitation has also been the focus of several studies today, but much remains to be done for scientific findings about its validity as an assessment tool or as a therapeutic resource [10].

In rehabilitation, it is necessary to address several aspects, such as motor control and motor learning, where the production of adequate movements is developed through the integration of cognitive processes with an appropriate sensorimotor. In this rehabilitation process, there is an approach through the awareness of cognitive processes, with the enhancement of the attention and motivation aspects [40, 41].

One way to integrate all these important aspects in motor rehabilitation, such as cognitive function and motor learning and control, can be the use of interaction with electronic devices [41].

AVG or EXG can be used as an alternative to promote participation in physical activity and improve quality of life, where they are receiving considerable attention from researchers and healthcare professionals as a rehabilitation tool in clinical, school and leisure environments to promote physical, psychological, and cognitive functioning. In fact, the positive effects of AVGs on health-related outcomes are increasingly being related among children and youth, namely in school environment [42, 43].

3 Intervention in School Environment

The school is the space responsible for the formalization of education and the teaching and learning process, and it is in the early years of school life, when the child is still growing, the best time to start the postural education work with a view to decrease musculoskeletal problems, increasing functional efficiency [12, 44].

There are several methods of intervention in the school environment, one of them being practiced by physiotherapy to prevent postural changes and consequent musculoskeletal pain in the spine [45, 46].

The intervention of physiotherapy in schools should be preventive, with early initiation, as the appropriate and inappropriate pattern of posture and movement begin to be shaped from childhood, being practiced in adolescence, becoming habitual [47].

In this regard, the physiotherapist is necessary within the school environment, in order to promote health education practices focused on the postural issue, through educational programs, postural orientations, lectures and/or health workshops and with exercise programs [45, 46, 48].

It is necessary to promote intervention actions in the school environment with the objective of promoting and preventing health, considering that most health problems and risky behaviors can be minimized or prevented by the increase in health literacy [49].

Preventive training programs are also another way of reducing the effects of improper posture on the body, and according to training a system is developed that generates a model of behavioral skills, attitudes, and knowledge necessary to promote changes in the behavior of children in regarding your habits and your health. Both components and practices favor a whole atmosphere of cognitive training that impacts their health [50].

The performance of health professionals in schools must, therefore, involve a salutogenic approach to create in schools a stimulating environment of creativity and critical sense, not just an intervention aimed at changes in risk factors [49].

Thus, it is important that teachers also address this issue with their students and do preventive work because they have daily contact, facilitating the identification and correction of habits in the school environment, while parents have the task of educating them in activities of daily living [50–52].

There is still a little explored component of physiotherapy intervention in postural changes, which requires the use of new technologies associated with exercise and Videogames. Despite few studies of this school-age intervention, it has proven to be beneficial in many respects [11].

Preventive measures are taken in the school environment, not only in prevention actions and postural education in schools, but also in a more practical intervention. As the prevalence of postural changes increases, there is a concern to find more and more effective measures. The promotion of behavioral changes, leading to more active and healthy lifestyles, is quite complex, which is why it is considered pertinent to seek solutions so that the daily lives of these children can be substantially improved [12, 52].

The effectiveness of a more active intervention using Videogames, for example, with the aim of improving postural behavior, preventing pain and increasing the participation, motivation and physical and sensorimotor interaction of children and adolescents can be a solution [12].

The benefits of using AVG or EXG in Physiotherapy, as a therapeutic tool according to the literature, improving balance, increasing locomotion capacity, increased range of motion of the upper and lower limbs, in addition to patient motivation [7, 12, 13, 35].

There are still other important studies such as:

- In relation to the elderly population, they show a significant improvement in balance [53];
- Case of cerebral palsy, he used the Wii, (including tennis, golf, boxing, bowling and baseball games), where he concluded an improvement in the process of visual perception, postural control and functional mobility [54, 55].
- With the purpose of analyzing the motor recovery of patients after stroke (stroke), using interactive VR games (virtual reality), which stimulated specific movements in the selected patients. At the end of the proposed protocol, an improvement in motor function was observed [56].

- Proprioceptive training with the proprioceptive disc and the Balance Board. At the end of the study, when comparing the groups, no significant differences were observed between them. Both improved performance in SEBT, in which Wii Fit achieved an improvement in performance in both members, while the other group obtained only in one member [57, 58].

These studies show, according to the results, that virtual reality and UX techniques is beneficial for both healthy individuals and individuals with neurological problems [8, 17, 36, 59].

4 Methods

Technological developments, which we have witnessed in recent years, have brought a series of devices that are increasingly being developed through an interface that allows the average user to interact with a computer, especially with regard to making computer games. a more natural way, which allows us to use virtual games in the field of interactive rehabilitation [6–8].

The aim of the present study is: (1) to verify the existence of studies that use the Videogame in the postural rehabilitation in school context; (2) to verify the prevalence of using Videogames with and without motion device in school-age children and teenagers and its relationship with back pain.

A preliminary survey in the first aim was conducted at the databases (Cochrane Library, MEDLINE and PEDro), followed by an analysis of text words contained in the title and abstract, and the index terms used to describe the article, revealed that there is no Scoping Review (published or forthcoming), on the effectiveness of contribution of physiotherapy using Videogame on the postural education, that took into account the validation of measurement instruments according to the PRISMA [60] and PICO [61] including randomized studies.

The keywords used in the search to identify titles, abstracts or articles in texts were "videogame or Videogame", "gamification", "videogame in the school age", "gamification in school age", "rehabilitation using videogame or Videogame", "rehabilitation using gamification", "postural education using videogame or Videogame", "postural education using gamification", "postural intervention using videogame or Videogame", "postural intervention using gamification", "physiotherapy or physical therapy using videogame or Videogame", "physiotherapy or physical therapy using gamification", "physiotherapy or physical therapy in postural intervention using videogame or Videogame", "physiotherapy or physical therapy in postural intervention using gamification", "physiotherapy or physical therapy in postural intervention using videogame or Videogame in school environment" and, "physiotherapy or physical therapy in postural intervention using gamification in school environment". The bibliographic references of the texts found were analyzed in order to define new searches. Only articles written in English and Portuguese, published in the last 5 years, which had the full article available free of charge for further analysis, were considered.

4.1 Eligibility Criteria

The following inclusion criteria were used for each study: (1) published in English and Portuguese between January 2015 and January 2020 as empirical peer-reviewed research, (2) used the use of at least one AVG or EXG (for example, Xbox-Kinect, Wii balance, Wii fit, playstation move, etc.), (3) the sample consisted of children and adolescents (mean age ≤ 19 years and ≥ 10 years) with musculoskeletal pain and/or postural changes (for example, back pain, scoliosis, etc.), (4) the main objective of using AVG or EXG was the rehabilitation or postural education of children and teenagers in school environment and (5) used quantitative measures in the evaluation of health-related results.

The PRISMA method (Preferred Reporting Items for Systematic Reviews and Meta-Analyses) was used to evaluate randomized studies on the study topic [60].

In the second aim, dating from March to June 2018, there were 230 students enrolled in the school, which attending the 2nd and 3rd Basic Education Cycle, of whom 125 were in the 7th and 9th grade (50 and 75, respectively).

Children and adolescents aged between 9 and 16 years who attended the 2nd and 3rd cycles of elementary school education in the city of Viseu, Portugal, were chosen for the sample of the present study.

A questionnaire designed with sociodemographic information, use of Videogames and body discomfort scale was applied. This study have taken three month from participant selection process, personal identification questionnaire fill, which included 13 questions related to socio-demographic analysis (gender, age, weight, height and participant identification number), the occurrence, intensity and location of musculoskeletal pain assessment according to Corporal Discomfort Scale [52, 62] in order to verify and categorize the pain felt (where 0 corresponded to no pain and 5 to the full amount of pain felt by the subject), and its duration (acute pain – under one month, subacute – from 1 to 3 months, and finally, chronic pain – over a 3 month period).

SPSS, 26.0 version was used in order to treat all the statistical data, for normality verification Kolmogorov-Smirnov test was applied before a descriptive analysis. This last, was calculated based upon standard methods. In order to analyze any characteristically difference between participants according of using Videogames with and without motion device, the parametric test of ANOVA was applied. The statistically level of significance was established in $p \leq 0.05$.

5 Results

In the first aim, the initial search produced 713 articles. After removing duplicates, the titles and abstracts of the other articles were selected according to the inclusion criteria. After a complete review of the remaining articles, only one study was included in this review (Fig. 1). PRISMA flow diagram of the studies during the review process. * Reasons for exclusion from the study included ineligible age; ineligible populations; ineligible AVG types; results Many studies were excluded for several reasons: the databases included: Complete academic research (n = 226), duplicate articles (n = 123); Cochrane Library (n = 57), PEDro (n = 95) and Medline (n = 211). There was a high agreement between the evaluators (95%) between the authors for the articles included.

According to the PRISMA (Fig. 1) analysis, it will not be possible to carry out a systematic review of the studies that used the Videogame for postural intervention in children and teenagers in a school environment.

This single study included in the eligibility criteria aimed to implement an exercise program using videogames through the Wii Fit platform, in order to verify if the intervention is effective in the postural alterations of 54 children and adolescents, in relation to the posture, flexibility and decreased back pain. After 8 weeks of intervention, significant results were obtained in the reduction of complaints of back pain ($p = 0.040$) and pain while in Videogame activity ($p = 0.033$), and improvements in posture and flexibility, but without significant difference. This study demonstrated that the exercise plan in the Wii platform allows positive effects on the variables and allows a greater incentive to the participants (12).

In the second aim, a sample of 124 participants were selected with $12,43 \pm 1,67$ years old, 62 males (50%) and 62 females (50%) belonging to the 5th (18,5%), 6th (31,5%), 7th (26,6%) and 9th grades (23,4%) due to colliding with growth stages.

The beginning and end of the 2nd and 3rd cycles were then chosen randomly. Body Discomfort Scale allowed us to find that episode among the 124 subjects, 77.4% of participants report feeling pain and there was a mean of $2,78 \pm 1,400$ that correspond to a moderate to severe episode.

Figure 1 shows the flow chart diagram of the study selection process:

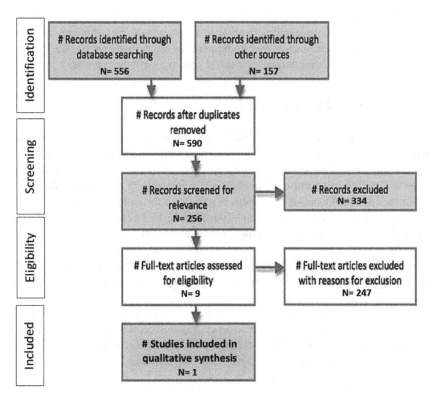

Fig. 1. PRISMA - study selection process

Regarding the sensation of pain while playing Videogames, 44.4% reported feeling pain. Videogame use by consoles was reported by 74.2% of participants, with the highest prevalence of Playstation (56.5%), followed by Wii (18.5%), other consoles (16.3%), Xbox (6.5%) and Nintendo Switch (2.2%). Regarding the motion app, only 26.6% owns, being 57.6% Playstation move, 33.3% Wii balance and 9.1% Xbox Kinect.

Regarding weekly hours, 60.9% of participants spend about 1–2 h playing Videogames, 22.8% spend about 3 to 5 h, 5.4% spend between 6 to 9 h and 10.9% of participants indicated a use of 10 h or more per week (Table 1).

Table 1. Use of Videogame console with and without motion app.

Console type	Console use	Use of motion app on this console
Videogame by console	**74,2%**	26,6%
Playstation/playstation move	**56,5%**	57,6%
Wii/Wii balance	**18,5%**	33,3%
Xbox/Xbox kinect	**6,5%**	9,1%
Nintendo Switch	2,2%	Without registration
Others	16,3%	Without registration

There is a correlation, according Pearson test, between the fact of having the motion device and the number of times of use, being who has fewer hours on average than those who do not have the motion device ($p = 0,031$), having only the console.

6 Discussion and Conclusion

In conducting a literature review, the results obtained in the studies show that the use of Videogames has shown excellent results as a therapeutic tool in various components.

According to the study by Agmon [63], the exercises performed by the elderly group through the Wii Fit platform demonstrated improvements in the Berg Scale after the intervention ($p < 0.01$) and improvement in gait speed through WT4min ($p < 0.108$).

According to the study Toulotte and Toursel [64], in a group also of the elderly, it was found after the training plan that the score in the Tinetti Test significantly decreased ($p < 0.05$).

In another study by Merians [65], in a 12-year-old patient with 12-year ataxic cerebral palsy, an average GMFM-66 (Gross Motor Function) score increased from 71.69 (±1.64) to 77, 46 (±2.06).

The therapeutic effects on the use of Videogames are little explored, focusing mainly on the elderly population and balance disorders. Therefore, it is necessary to verify the use of videogames in the motivational behaviors of children and teenagers to demonstrate the existence of benefits and provide a basis for future studies.

Acknowledgments. The authors would like to thank: (1) the participants in this study; (2) as well as the collaboration of students Ana Sofia, Tatiana Pinto and Carina Santos for their support in data collection and; (3) We would also like to thank the directors of the school groups in Viseu and Leiria, who allowed the study to be carried out.

References

1. Durkin, K., Boyle, J., Hunter, S., Conti-Ramsden, G.: Videogames for children and adolescents with special educational needs. Z Psychol. **221**, 79 (2015)
2. Harrington, B., O'Connell, M.: Videogames as virtual teachers: prosocial videogame use by children and adolescents from different socioeconomic groups is associated with increased empathy and prosocial behaviour. Comput. Hum. Behav. **63**, 650–658 (2016)
3. Tran, B.: Clinical use of videogames. In: Advanced Methodologies and Technologies in Media and Communications, pp. 76–89. IGI Global (2019)
4. Yılmaz, E., Yel, S., Griffiths, M.D.: The impact of heavy (excessive) video gaming students on peers and teachers in the school environment: a qualitative study. Addicta Turk. J. Addict. **5**(2), 147–161 (2018)
5. Rizzo, A.S., Kim, G.J.: A SWOT analysis of the field of virtual reality rehabilitation and therapy. Presence Teleoper. Virtual Environ. **14**(2), 119–146 (2005)
6. Lange, B., Rizzo, A., Chang, C.-Y., Suma, E.A., Bolas, M.: Markerless full body tracking: depth-sensing technology within virtual environments. In: Interservice/Industry Training, Simulation, and Education Conference (I/ITSEC) (2011)
7. Lamrani, R., Chraibi, S., Qassimi, S., Hafidi, M., El Amrani, A.: Serious game to enhance and promote youth entrepreneurship. In: Rocha, Á., Serrhini, M., Felgueiras, C. (eds.) Europe and MENA Cooperation Advances in Information and Communication Technologies. AISC, vol. 520, pp. 77–85. Springer, Cham (2017). https://doi.org/10.1007/978-3-319-46568-5_8
8. Lopes, O., Martins, T., Carvalho, V., Matos, D., Soares, F., Machado, J.: Ergonomics and usability in the development of a portable virtual gaming device applied in physiotherapy. Trans. FAMENA **40**(4), 95–106 (2016)
9. Hsu, S.H., Wen, M.-H., Wu, M.-C.: Exploring user experiences as predictors of MMORPG addiction. Comput. Educ. **53**(3), 990–999 (2009)
10. Taylor, M.J.D., McCormick, D., Shawis, T., Impson, R., Griffin, M.: Activity-promoting gaming systems in exercise and rehabilitation. J. Rehabil. Res. Dev. **48**(10), 1171–1186 (2011)
11. Bekker, T.M., Eggen, B.H.: Designing for children's physical play. In: CHI 2008 Extended Abstracts on Human Factors in Computing Systems, pp. 2871–2876. ACM (2008)
12. Filgueiras, E., Desouzart, G., Silva, A.: Teenagers postural effects through videogames therapeutic approach. In: Rebelo, F., Soares, M.M. (eds.) AHFE 2019. AISC, vol. 955, pp. 15–22. Springer, Cham (2020). https://doi.org/10.1007/978-3-030-20227-9_2
13. Staiano, A.E., Calvert, S.L.: Exergames for physical education courses: physical, social, and cognitive benefits. Child. Dev. Perspect. **5**(2), 93–98 (2011)
14. Göbel, S., Hardy, S., Wendel, V., Mehm, F., Steinmetz, R.: Serious games for health: personalized exergames. In: Proceedings of the 18th ACM International Conference on Multimedia, pp. 1663–1666. ACM (2010)
15. Sinclair, J., Hingston, P., Masek, M.: Considerations for the design of exergames. In: Proceedings of the 5th International Conference on Computer Graphics and Interactive Techniques in Australia and Southeast Asia, pp. 289–295. ACM (2007)
16. Bonnechère, B., Jansen, B., Omelina, L., Van Sint, J.: The use of commercial videogames in rehabilitation: a systematic review. Int. J. Rehabil. Res. **39**(4), 277–290 (2016)

17. Pan, Z., Cheok, A.D., Yang, H., Zhu, J., Shi, J.: Virtual reality and mixed reality for virtual learning environments. Comput. Graph. **30**(1), 20–28 (2006)
18. Kehrwald, B.: Understanding social presence in text-based online learning environments. Distance Educ. **29**(1), 89–106 (2008)
19. Gray, P.: Cognitive benefits of playing videogames. Psychol. Today Viitattu **19**, 2016 (2015)
20. De Lisi, R., Wolford, J.L.: Improving children's mental rotation accuracy with computer game playing. J. Genet. Psychol. **163**(3), 272–282 (2002)
21. Hayes, E.R., Games, I.A.: Making computer games and design thinking: a review of current software and strategies. Games Cult. **3**(3–4), 309–332 (2008)
22. Fernandes, K.T., Lucena, M.J.N.R., da Silva Aranha, E.H.: Uma Experiência na Criação de game design de Jogos Digitais Educativos a partir do design thinking. RENOTE-Revista Novas Technol. na Educ. **16**(1) (2018)
23. Browne, C., Maire, F.: Evolutionary game design. IEEE Trans. Comput. Intell. AI Games **2**(1), 1–16 (2010)
24. Sailer, M., Hense, J.U., Mayr, S.K., Mandl, H.: How gamification motivates: an experimental study of the effects of specific game design elements on psychological need satisfaction. Comput. Hum. Behav. **69**, 371–380 (2017)
25. Richter, G., Raban, D.R., Rafaeli, S.: Studying gamification: the effect of rewards and incentives on motivation. In: Reiners, T., Wood, L.C. (eds.) Gamification in Education and Business, pp. 21–46. Springer, Cham (2015). https://doi.org/10.1007/978-3-319-10208-5_2
26. Deterding, S., Dixon, D., Khaled, R., Nacke, L.: From game design elements to gamefulness: defining "gamification". In: Proceedings of the 15th International Academic MindTrek Conference: Envisioning Future Media Environments, pp. 9–15 (2011)
27. Zichermann, G., Cunningham, C.: Gamification by Design: Implementing Game Mechanics in Web and Mobile Apps. O'Reilly Media Inc, Cambridge (2011)
28. Werbach, K., Hunter, D.: For the Win: How Game Thinking Can Revolutionize Your Business. Wharton Digital Press, Philadelphia (2012)
29. Farzan, R., Brusilovsky, P.: Encouraging user participation in a course recommender system: an impact on user behavior. Comput. Hum. Behav. **27**(1), 276–284 (2011)
30. Hamari, J., Koivisto, J.: Why do people use gamification services? Int. J. Inf. Manag. **35**(4), 419–431 (2015)
31. Arai, S., Sakamoto, K., Washizaki, H., Fukazawa, Y.: A gamified tool for motivating developers to remove warnings of bug pattern tools. In: 2014 6th International Workshop on Empirical Software Engineering in Practice, pp. 37–42. IEEE (2014)
32. Mekler, E.D., Brühlmann, F., Tuch, A.N., Opwis, K.: Towards understanding the effects of individual gamification elements on intrinsic motivation and performance. Comput. Hum. Behav. **71**, 525–534 (2017)
33. Kastrup, V.: A apredizagem da atenção na cognição inventiva. Psicol Soc. **16**(3), 7–16 (2004)
34. Vaghetti, C.A.O., da Costa Botelho, S.S.: Ambientes virtuais de aprendizagem na educação física: uma revisão sobre a utilização de Exergames. Ciências & Cognição **15**(1), 64 (2010)
35. Gao, Z., Chen, S.: Are field-based exergames useful in preventing childhood obesity? A systematic review. Obes. Rev. **15**(8), 676–691 (2014)
36. Keshner, E.A.: Virtual reality and physical rehabilitation: a new toy or a new research and rehabilitation tool? J. NeuroEngineering Rehabil. **1**, 8 (2004). https://doi.org/10.1186/1743-0003-1-8
37. Luque-Moreno, C., Ferragut-Garcías, A., Rodríguez-Blanco, C., Heredia-Rizo, A.M., Oliva-Pascual-Vaca, J., Kiper, P., et al.: A decade of progress using virtual reality for poststroke lower extremity rehabilitation: systematic review of the intervention methods. Biomed. Res. Int. **2015**, 7 (2015)
38. Baracho, A.F.O., Gripp, F.J., de Lima, M.R.: Os exergames e a educação física escolar na cultura digital. Rev Bras Ciências do Esporte. **34**(1), 111–126 (2012)

39. Piron, L., Turolla, A., Agostini, M., Zucconi, C., Cortese, F., Zampolini, M., et al.: Exercises for paretic upper limb after stroke: a combined virtual-reality and telemedicine approach. J. Rehabil. Med. **41**(12), 1016–1020 (2009)
40. Shumway-Cook, A., Woollacott, M.H.: Motor into Clinical Practice. Lippincott Williams & Wilkins, New York (2007)
41. Sandlund, M., McDonough, S., Häger-Ross, C.: Interactive computer play in rehabilitation of children with sensorimotor disorders: a systematic review. Dev. Med. Child Neurol. **51**(3), 173–179 (2009)
42. Zeng, N., Pope, Z., Lee, J.E., Gao, Z.: A systematic review of active videogames on rehabilitative outcomes among older patients. J. Sport Health Sci. **6**(1), 33–43 (2017)
43. Garn, A.C., Baker, B.L., Beasley, E.K., Solmon, M.A.: What are the benefits of a commercial exergaming platform for college students? Examining physical activity, enjoyment, and future intentions. J. Phys. Act. Health **9**(2), 311–318 (2012)
44. Zapater, A.R., Silveira, D.M., de Vitta, A., Padovani, C.R., da Silva, J.C.P.: Postura sentada: a eficácia de um programa de educação para escolares. Cien Saude Colet. **9**, 191–199 (2004)
45. Prins, Y., Crous, L., Louw, Q.A.: A systematic review of posture and psychosocial factors as contributors to upper quadrant musculoskeletal pain in children and adolescents. Physiother. Theory Pract. **24**(4), 221–242 (2008)
46. Milhem, M., Kalichman, L., Ezra, D., Alperovitch-Najenson, D.: Work-related musculoskeletal disorders among physical therapists: a comprehensive narrative review. Int. J. Occup. Med. Environ. Health **29**(5), 735–747 (2016)
47. Santos, C., Cunha, A., Braga, V., Saad, I., Ribeiro, M., Conti, P., et al.: Ocorrência de desvios posturais em escolares do ensino público fundamental de Jaguariúna, São Paulo. Rev. Paul Pediatr. **27**(1), 74–80 (2009)
48. de Lemos, A.T., dos Santos, F.R., Gaya, A.C.A.: Lumbar hyperlordosis in children and adolescents at a privative school in southern Brazil: occurrence and associated factors. Cad Saude Publica. **28**(4), 781–788 (2012)
49. Minghelli, B.: Low back pain in childhood and adolescent phase: consequences, prevalence and risk factors–a revision. J. Spine **6**, 1000351 (2017)
50. Benini, J., Karolczak, A.P.B.: Benefícios de um programa de educação postural para alunos de uma escola municipal de Garibaldi, RS. Fisioter e Pesqui. **17**(4), 346–351 (2010)
51. Jennings, P.A., Greenberg, M.T.: The prosocial classroom: teacher social and emotional competence in relation to student and classroom outcomes. Rev. Educ. Res. **79**(1), 491–525 (2009)
52. Desouzart, G., Filgueiras, E., Matos, R., Dagge, R.: Postural education: correlation between postural habits and musculoskeletal pain in school age children. In: Rebelo, F., Soares, M. (eds.) Advances in Ergonomics in Design. AISC, vol. 485, pp. 255–263. Springer, Cham (2016). https://doi.org/10.1007/978-3-319-41983-1_23
53. Eggenberger, P., Wolf, M., Schumann, M., de Bruin, E.D.: Exergame and balance training modulate prefrontal brain activity during walking and enhance executive function in older adults. Front. Aging Neurosci. **8**, 66 (2016)
54. Zoccolillo, L., Morelli, D., Cincotti, F., Muzzioli, L., Gobbetti, T., Paolucci, S., et al.: Videogame based therapy performed by children with cerebral palsy: a cross-over randomized controlled trial and a cross-sectional quantitative measure of physical activity. Eur. J. Phys. Rehabil. Med. **51**(6), 669–676 (2015)
55. Atasavun Uysal, S., Baltaci, G.: Effects of Nintendo Wii™ training on occupational performance, balance, and daily living activities in children with spastic hemiplegic cerebral palsy: a single-blind and randomized trial. Games Health J. **5**(5), 311–317 (2016)
56. Cheok, G., Tan, D., Low, A., Hewitt, J.: Is Nintendo Wii an effective intervention for individuals with stroke? A systematic review and meta-analysis. J. Am. Med. Dir. Assoc. **16**(11), 923–932 (2015)

57. Cone, B.L., Levy, S.S., Goble, D.J.: Wii Fit exer-game training improves sensory weighting and dynamic balance in healthy young adults. Gait Posture **41**(2), 711–715 (2015)
58. Kim, K.J., Jun, H.J.: Effects of virtual reality programs on proprioception and instability of functional ankle instability. J. Int. Acad. Phys. Ther Res. **6**(2), 891–895 (2015)
59. Halton, J.: Virtual rehabilitation with videogames: a new frontier for occupational therapy. Occup. Ther. Now **9**(6), 12–14 (2008)
60. Moher, D., Shamseer, L., Clarke, M., Ghersi, D., Liberati, A., Petticrew, M., et al.: Preferred reporting items for systematic review and meta-analysis protocols (PRISMA-P) 2015 statement. Syst. Rev. **4**(1), 1 (2015)
61. da Santos, C.M.C., de Pimenta, C.A.M., Nobre, M.R.C.: Estrategia PICO para la construcción de la pregunta de investigación y la búsqueda de evidencias. Rev. Lat Am. Enfermagem **15**(3), 508–511 (2007)
62. Corlett, E.N., Bishop, R.P.: A technique for assessing postural discomfort. Ergonomics **19**(2), 175–182 (1976)
63. Agmon, M., Perry, C.K., Phelan, E., Demiris, G., Nguyen, H.Q.: A pilot study of Wii Fit exergames to improve balance in older adults. J. Geriatr. Phys. Ther. **34**(4), 161–167 (2011)
64. Toulotte, C., Toursel, C., Olivier, N.: Wii Fit® training vs. Adapted Physical Activities: which one is the most appropriate to improve the balance of independent senior subjects? A randomized controlled study. Clin. Rehabil. **26**(9), 827–835 (2012)
65. Merians, A.S., Jack, D., Boian, R., Tremaine, M., Burdea, G.C., Adamovich, S.V., et al.: Virtual reality–augmented rehabilitation for patients following stroke. Phys. Ther. **82**(9), 898–915 (2002)

UX Concerns in Developing Functional Orthodontic Appliances

Stefano Filippi[1]([✉]), Luca Grigolato[2], and Gianpaolo Savio[2]

[1] DPIA Department, University of Udine, Udine, Italy
filippi@uniud.it
[2] ICEA Department, University of Padova, Padua, Italy

Abstract. In the orthodontic field, UX concerns can take an important role in boosting innovation from the designers, engineers, dentists, dental technicians and patients' points of view. In the last months, these concerns spread over the development of functional orthodontic appliances for the correction of skeletal class II malocclusions. This paper focuses on two phases: the data collection before starting the development and the evaluation of the design results. The UX concerns developed through the involvement of the Quality Function Deployment and the irMMs-based UX evaluation method 2.0, including the meQUE questionnaire 2.0. This paper describes the UX role, the related activities and the impact of its involvement in the design process.

Keywords: User experience · Functional orthodontic appliances · Quality function deployment · irMMs-based UX evaluation method 2.0 · meCUE questionnaire

1 Introduction

Orthodontic field goes continuously towards innovation and well-being. Among the possible research directions, that to UX concerns can take an important role in developing innovative devices from the designers, engineers, dentists, dental technicians and patients' points of view. Our research group, composed by heterogeneous competencies ranging from conceptual design to orthodontics, rapid prototyping and UX design/evaluation, developed a functional orthodontic appliance for the correction of skeletal class II malocclusions.

UX concerns spread over the whole development process; nevertheless, this paper focuses on two phases: the data collection before starting the development and the evaluation of the design results. The UX concerns developed through the involvement of the Quality Function Deployment and the irMMs-based UX evaluation method 2.0, including the meQUE questionnaire 2.0.

Data collection highlighted customers' requirements that, in turn, allowed leading the design effort towards the correct goals and performing at best the benchmark of existing functional orthodontic appliances. The evaluation of the design results verified the achievement of the goals and gave suggestions for possible improvements.

© Springer Nature Switzerland AG 2020
A. Marcus and E. Rosenzweig (Eds.): HCII 2020, LNCS 12202, pp. 229–241, 2020.
https://doi.org/10.1007/978-3-030-49757-6_16

The paper runs as follows. The background section contains an overview on functional orthodontic appliances, as well as the description of the Quality Function Deployment method and of the irMMs-based UX evaluation method 2.0. The research activities section describes the two phases this work focuses on. The discussion section reasons about the results of the product evaluation and the conclusions close the paper, together with some perspectives for future work.

2   Background

2.1   Functional Orthodontic Appliances

Functional orthodontic appliances are devices used to correct malocclusions [1, 2]. These devices control and modify opening-closing patterns to adapt condyle shapes. They are placed inside the mouth; the therapy usually lasts from six months to two years. Among the different types of malocclusions defined by E. Angle [2], class II malocclusion is a deviation - either aesthetic, functional or both, from the ideal occlusion (mandible retruded respect to the maxilla).

It is acknowledged that the main issue for good medical results with these devices is the patient's compliance, especially because the treatment takes place with children [2]. Therefore, these devices are classified into non-compliance and compliance [1–3]. The first ones refer directly to fixed devices, usually cemented on the patients' teeth, all of this forcing full-time wear during therapy; the second ones refer to removable devices, more comfortable because they can be taken out while eating, etc.

Different kinds of devices exist, from Herbst [4] to MARA [5], Jasper Jumper [6], Forsus [1], Twin Block [7], Bionator and Frankel [2, 3]. Herbst and Twin Block are the most used as fixed and removable devices, respectively. Figure 1 depicts them.

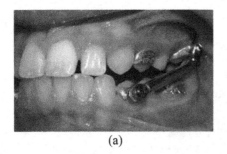   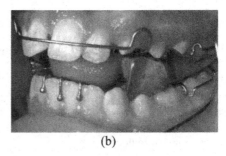

(a)   (b)

Fig. 1. The most used fixed and removable devices: Herbst (a) and Twin Block (b).

Herbst is a bilateral joint with a telescopic mechanism usually welded to orthodontic bands. Twin Block is a bilateral joint as well; it consists of acrylic inclined blocks. The other kinds of devices are redesigns aimed at resolving the drawbacks reported by these two main devices like the fact that size and shape can cause lack of compliance with patients and can make sores in the soft tissues of the mouth, hygiene can be affected due to plaque accumulation, positioning/removal procedures can be difficult and/or hurting and that most of the times the treatment effectiveness is quite moot [2, 8–10].

2.2   Quality Function Deployment

Quality Function Deployment (QFD) is a well-known method to understand the design problem and collect and organize data for the design process [11]. The method consists of a series of steps to translate qualitative information, the customers' requirements, into quantitative parameters, the engineering requirements. The House of Quality (HoQ) data structure collects the data and makes them easily accessible to the downstream design phases. The HoQ is suitable for systematic design and can work in synergy with other design tools such like morphology and TRIZ [12, 13].

At the beginning, data about users and about products similar to the one under development are collected, evaluated and rated. The identification of the customers represents the first step. Then, customers' requirements are described, translated into design requirements and evaluated through questionnaires. Meanwhile, a competitors' benchmarking is performed; existing products are identified and evaluated against the requirements in order to highlight satisfaction degrees. The results of these evaluations allow focusing on the most interesting competitors' product solutions and ranking the design requirements to distribute the design efforts as effectively as possible. It is worth to say that UX concerns are getting more and more importance among the customers' requirements.

2.3   IrMMs-Based UX Evaluation Method 2.0

The irMMs-based UX evaluation method 2.0 (irMMs method, hereafter) quantifies the UX of products [14]. The core of the irMMs method exploits interaction related Mental Models (irMMs) and evaluate the UX by comparing what is expected (before the inter-action) to what is real (thanks to the interaction). The irMMs method reached the release 2.0 thanks to the addition of the meQUE questionnaire 2.0.

The irMMs are cognitive processes that users generate in their mind before to act in order to satisfy a specific need in a specific situation of interaction. They consist of lists of users' meanings and emotions, including users and products' behaviors determined by these meanings and emotions [15]. The generation of an irMM develops through five steps, based on the Norman's model of the seven stages of the action cycle [16].

The adoption of the irMMs method happens through user tests. Users generate their irMMs respect to a specific need to satisfy and compare these irMMs to the real inter-action with the product. The adoption generates two lists of positive and negative UX aspects that describe the strong points and the criticalities of the experience, respectively. More specifically, the irMMs method consists of three sections that differ in the knowl-edge about the product of the users who undergo the tests. The first section considers users who do not know the product at all; they generate their irMMs based on previous experiences with different products only. This is the absolute beginners (AB) section. The second section considers again users who do not know the product; nevertheless, before the generation of the irMMs (and before to know the need to satisfy) they are allowed to interact freely with the product for some time. This is the relative beginners (RB) section. Finally, the third section considers users who already know the product. This is the relative experts (RE) section. Figure 2 summarizes the four phases of the irMMs method adoption: input setting, material and environment setup, test execution and data analysis. The tests for the three sections can run in parallel, providing that no influences among them happen in the meantime.

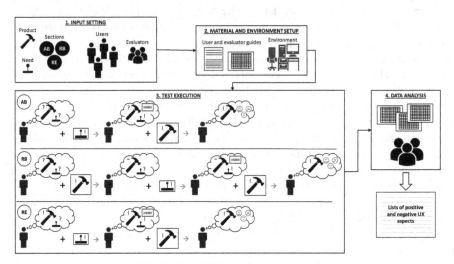

Fig. 2. The irMMs method adoption.

As soon as the tests come to the end, the evaluators generate the UX aspects thanks to some precise rules [14]. After that, the evaluators classify the UX aspects against the interaction topics they refer to (specific procedures, product components, etc.) and, for each topic, they split the UX aspects t into positive and negative and order them against the number of occurrences and the impact. If an UX aspect refers to product characteristics rarely involved in the interaction, its impact will be low; on the contrary, if the UX aspect deals with core procedures determining the cognitive compatibility of the product with the users' problem solving processes, the impact will be higher.

The irMMs method exploits the meCUE questionnaire 2.0 (meCUE, hereafter) to deepen the UX analysis from different points of view. This questionnaire provides a quantitative UX evaluation starting from the Components model of User Experience (CUE model) of Thuring and Mahlke [17]. As shown in Fig. 3 this model considers the perceptions of instrumental and non-instrumental product qualities and the emotional reactions as main components of the UX. The meQUE maps the CUE model into five modules named instrumental product qualities, non-instrumental product qualities, emotions, consequences of use and overall evaluation.

The integration of the meQUE in the irMMs method, proposed by Filippi and Barattin is summarized in Fig. 4 [14]. White boxes represent those activities of the irMMs method that remain as they are; four grayed boxes contain activities modified and seven grayed boxes with bold text indicate the new activities added by the integration. The integration implies changes in phase two (material and environmental setup), changes and additions in phase three (test execution) and additions in phase four (data analysis).

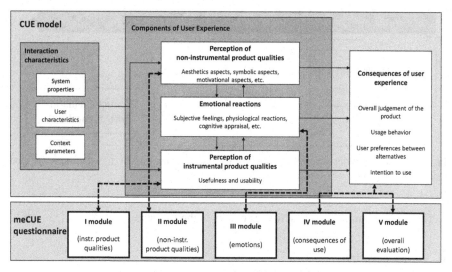

Fig. 3. CUE model and meCUE questionnaire.

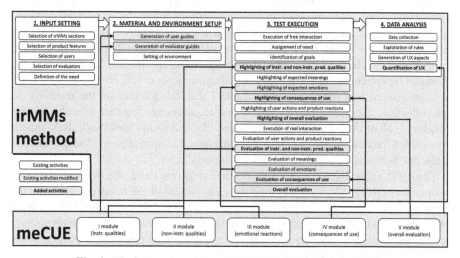

Fig. 4. The integration of the meQUE in the irMMs method [14].

3   Research Activities

The design process considered here consisted of four stages: observation, ideation, prototyping and testing [16]; Clearly, UX concerns were present throughout. Nevertheless, this paper considers them in those two activities where they had the heaviest impact, the data collection in the observation stage - before starting the development of the device, and the evaluation of the design results - named product evaluation - in the prototyping and testing stages. The QFD and irMMs method were involved, respectively. All of this is depicted in Fig. 5.

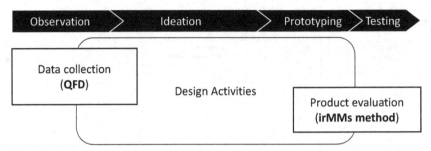

Fig. 5. The two activities where UX concerns had the heaviest impact, together with the tools used to manage them.

The description of the two activities occurs in the following.

3.1 Data Collection

The QFD analysis considered three kinds of customers, differently involved from the UX point of view. Three dentists, two dental technicians and five patients expressed their expectations using questionnaires. In addition, four among the most relevant competitors were evaluated focusing on the satisfaction of the customers' requirements: Herbst (labeled as Comp1 in the following), MARA (Comp2), Jasper Jumper (Comp3) and Forsus (Comp4). The dentists, as orthodontics specialists, performed this evaluation and found that no system satisfied the customers' requirements in full; for this reason, space for improvement was reputed to exist. Table 1 and Table 2 contain the result of the data collection. Table 1 shows the customers' requirements together with the relative importance, all of them classified by use phase. Table 2 shows how much the competitors satisfied the customers' requirements. This quantification uses a 1-5 scale, where 1 represents "not satisfy" and 5 is "completely satisfy".

The QFD analysis had a two-face result. From one hand, the ordered pieces of information in the HoQ allowed getting the clear picture of the requirements of all the customers and, consequently, generated the bases for the UX evaluation that occurred in the other activity this research focuses on. On the other hand, the QFD analysis gave precious indications for the development process in terms of priorities, aspects to focus on, quantitative targets to aim at, etc.

Regarding the first result, the UX-related requirements highlighted thanks to the QFD involvement can be summarized as follows.

- UX-Req1. Minimizing interfering with daily activities (speaking, eating, etc.) (highlighted by patients).
- UX-Req2. Being robust (dentists and dental technicians).
- UX-Req3. No injuring and/or harmful (patients).
- UX-Req4. Being good-looking (small, almost invisible, etc.) (patients).
- UX-Req5. Easy to mount and fix (possibly cemented to the teeth) (dentists).

Table 1. Customers' requirements with relative importance, classified by use phase.

Use phase	Customers' requirement	Customers	Relative importance
Position and fix	Easy to mount	Dentists	3.44
	Small number of parts	Dental technicians	3.81
Use	Easy to adjust	Dentists	3.56
	Assure physiological opening of mandible	Patients	5.00
	Assure physiological lateral movements	Patients	4.68
	Limited dimensions	Patients	4.14
	Limited weight	Patients	3.57
	No injuring and/or harmful	Patients	4.57
	Short cleaning time	Dentists	4.43
	Avoid plaque accumulation	Dentists	4.29
	Almost invisible	Patients	4.51
	Resistant	Dentists	4.83
	Reliable	Dentists	4.48
	No dentoalveolar movements	Dentists	4.62
Unmount	Easy to unmount	Dentists	3.63
	Unpainful removal	Patients	4.32

For what concerns the second result, designers had quite precise indications to carry their work on, focusing on the engineering requirements of real interest. The main ones were as follows.

- Ind1. Maximize robustness.
- Ind2. Minimize volume.
- Ind3. Minimize contact with soft tissues.
- Ind4. Minimize sharp geometries.
- Ind5. Minimize the number of pieces.

Designers tried to satisfy the customers' requirements with activities optimized by following these indications. The device was designed starting from a free-form, patient-specific concept developed in a previous study [18]. Once designed, the device was prototyped using a 3D printer, together with a pair of sample dental arches, in order to make the tests of the irMMs method feasible. Figure 6 shows the result of the designers' effort, represented both digitally and physically.

Table 2. Results of the benchmarking of the competitors.

Customers' requirement	Requirement satisfaction			
	Comp1	Comp2	Comp3	Comp4
Easy to mount	1	2	2	2
Small number of parts	2	2	2	3
Easy to adjust	2	3	3	3
Assure physiological opening of mandible	3	4	3	3
Assure physiological lateral movements	2	3	3	3
Limited dimensions	2	3	2	2
Limited weight	3	3	3	2
No injuring and/or harmful	1	2	3	2
Short cleaning time	2	2	2	2
Avoid plaque accumulation	2	3	1	1
Almost invisible	2	3	1	1
Resistant	2	2	2	2
Reliable	1	2	2	2
No dentoalveolar movements	1	2	1	1
Easy to unmount	1	2	2	2
Unpainful removal	2	2	3	3
Total	29	40	35	34
Mean value	1,88	2,56	2,25	2,19

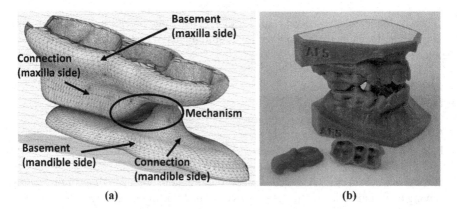

(a)   (b)

Fig. 6. The digital (a) and physical (b) representation of the developed device.

Four pieces, two for the left and two for the right side, compose the device. Each side consists of three zones: the mechanism, the basements and the connections (Fig. 6a shows them. The mechanism zone, designed on the specific patient's corrected mandible path obtained by elaborating data from video tracking, consists of a spherical pin in the lower side (mandibular side), which slides on a guide surface in the upper side (maxillary side), to accomplish the correction in a smooth way. The two basements (upper and lower sides) are the second zone and consist of an offset of the shape of the second premolar and first and second molar; these teeth are those the two basements will be cemented to. The third zone consists of free forms connecting the basements to the mechanism; their definition aims at minimizing the volume and at being as smooth as possible.

Designers were quite sure about the satisfaction of the customers' requirements for the following reasons.

- UX-Req1. The interocclusal positioning of the device parts should guarantee freedom of movements. Rounded edges and variably sloped contact surfaces should increase comfort, allowing painless daily use of the device and avoiding the mechanism to get stuck.
- UX-Req2. The four monolithic device pieces should increase robustness and avoid unexpected failures. The mechanism concept was chosen as simple as possible for the same reason, in accordance with Comp2, the best competitor from this point of view.
- UX-Req3. The smooth free forms surfaces spread over the device should make it safe for the patients, avoiding injuries and any other disease. All of this is helped also by the interocclusal position since this reduces the amount of material in contact with the soft tissues of the mouth.
- UX-Req4. Reduced volume and interocclusal positioning should make the device almost invisible; consequently, patients should be more prone to accepting it.
- UX-Req5. The offset solution mimicking the teeth shape of the basements should make the device implant straightforward.

Now, designers' belief needed to be checked against the final users' opinion. This is why the second activity of interest in this research, the product evaluation, took place.

3.2   Product Evaluation

The UX evaluation occurred through the four phases of the irMMs method adoption cited in the background section. How these phases occurred here is described in the following.

Input Setting. The product was the device just developed. The need was "implant it", if the user was a dentist or a dental technician, and "use it", if he/she was a patient". All sections (AB, RB and RE) were considered. Nineteen users (seven AB, six RB and six RE) were involved, selected among dentists, dental technicians and patients, all of them showing different levels of knowledge about class II malocclusions and other solutions available on the market. Finally, three evaluators took part in the tests, two designers and one UX specialist.

Material and Environment Setup. Physical models of the new device as well as of the upper and lower dental arches (Fig. 6b) were prepared to allow RB users getting confident with the product and all users performing the tests. User guides were customized focusing on the aspects highlighted by the QFD analysis during the data collection.

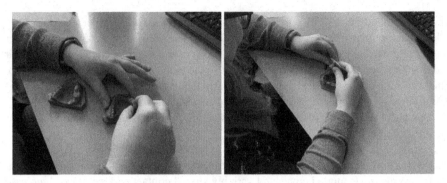

Fig. 7. Photographs taken during the test of an RE user.

Test Execution. At the beginning, the device was briefly described to the users, without showing the prototype. This description allowed them to express their expectations as mental models. After that, users compared their expectations with the actions allowed by the prototypes they interact with and with the feedback coming from them. All the tests ran smoothly. They took 25 min each in average. Figure 7 shows two photographs taken during the test of an RE user.

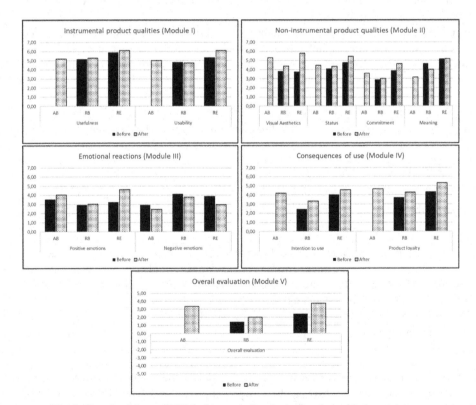

Fig. 8. Result of the meQUE, before and after the interaction with the prototypes.

Data Analysis. At the end, the content of nineteen user guides (every user reached the end of the test and filled one guide) was available for reasoning about the UX of the device. Figure 8 reports what was expected (before the interaction with the prototypes) and what had been real (after the interaction), all of this for every section (AB, RB and RE) and classified against the five modules of the meQUE. It is worth to say that data from AB users before the interaction refer only to emotions because of the irMMs method functioning.

The evaluators used these data to generate the lists of UX aspects, as expected by the irMMs method. The lists contain 9 positive and 35 negative UX aspects. The UX aspects are not reported here for space reason. Some of them are cited in the following to support the discussion.

4   Discussion

At first, the comparison between the data collected in the two moments allows making some considerations.

- The UX of the device was better than expected for every section for every module of the meQUE. The expected UX described in the mental models has always been overcome during the interaction with the device. The only exception regarded the meaning for the RB users. All of this lets start thinking about a good result of the design activities.
- The RE users were those who showed the major differences between the "before" and the "after". Since RE users should be the sternest judges, once again all of this witnesses the goodness of the device from the UX point of view.
- Regarding the modules of the meQUE, those with higher values on average referred to instrumental and non-instrumental product qualities (module I and module II). The device was reputed as particularly good for what concerns usefulness and usability, as well as visual aesthetics, status, commitment and meaning.
- Emotional reactions (module III) and consequences of use (module IV) had lower values, although a meaningful difference exist between the "before" and the "after". Nevertheless, it is quite difficult to associate positive emotions, intentions to use in the future, etc., to these kinds of devices; therefore, this result was somehow expected.
- The overall evaluation was very low in the mental models ("before") and the real interaction ("after") increased it just a bit. Probably, negative emotions and the reluctance to use these devices in general, influenced the judgment negatively.

The availability of the lists of UX aspects allowed verifying the effectiveness of the designers' effort in satisfying the customers' requirements (expectations) collected thanks to the QFD exploitation in the data collection phase and summarized in Sect. 3.1. These customers' requirements are recalled in the following, together with some reasoning about design drawbacks and possible suggestions for further device improvements.

- UX-Req1. Minimizing interfering with daily activities (speaking, eating, etc.). Despite the interocclusal positioning and the use of rounded edges and variably sloped contact surfaces, users felt the prototype quite uncomfortable and interfering with daily activities. For example, a negative UX aspect reported "the upper part of the device is ok but that spherical pin at the bottom is something my tongue cannot stop to interfere with" or "I am not sure I can bite properly with these smooth surfaces".
- UX-Req2. Being robust. The users perceived the robustness assurance guaranteed by the four pieces only partially. One of the negative UX aspects, expressed by an RE dental technician, was "I don't think that that pin is strong enough to withstand the forces occurring during mandible movements, its size should be increased".
- UX-Req3. No injuring and/or harmful. The device shape, as well as its positioning, made the users quite confident about using it safely. Nevertheless, some perplexities arose, like that expressed in the negative UX aspect "the freedom in the mandible movement (mouth opening without constraints) is of course something good; nevertheless, I feel that this freedom increases the risk to bite my tongue or the inside of my cheeks" or in another negative UX aspect "I think that the part of the device devoted to fixing is too thin. To me, the device risks to slip away more than often".
- UX-Req4. Being good-looking (small, almost invisible, etc.). People who used such kinds of devices in the past appreciated the design effort towards aesthetics and non-invasiveness. Only one user was a bit disappointed as witnessed by his negative UX aspect "that spherical pin is horrible. To me, people I could talk with can see it and think that I have something wrong in my teeth". Moreover, several users highlighted the importance of the color choice.
- UX-Req5. Easy to mount and fix (possibly cemented to the teeth). Dentists and dental technicians expressed no remarks from this point of view during the evaluation. This because the cemented device was somehow an explicit request. Conversely, some patients complained about this. For example, a negative UX aspect was "I expected an innovative device, easy to put on and off. Instead, it is only another fixed device" and another negative UX aspect was "it is not so simple to position as it seems".

5   Conclusions

This research addressed the importance of UX concerns in developing functional orthodontic appliances. The discussion section should have made clear this importance, both in terms of indications for an effective development and of suggestions for possible improvement of the design results. The device developed during this research seems to answer to the customers' requirements better than other existing devices.

The research activities in the near future will focus on the suggestions for possible improvements. A new release of the device, lighter and even more non-invasive than the current one will be developed. Overall, particular attention will be paid in trying to substitute the spherical pin, disagreeable to many users during the tests, with something arising more confidence about strength, safety and non-invasiveness. The result will undergo the irMMs method adoption, involving different dentists, dental technicians and patients.

Acknowledgments. This project was partially funded by the grant "FSE 2105-51-11 2018" by Regione Veneto.

References

1. Papadopoulos, M.A.: Non-compliance approaches for management of class II malocclusion. In: Skeletal Anchorage in Orthodontic Treatment of Class II Malocclusion, pp. 6–21. Elsevier (2015)
2. Proffit, W.R., Fields Jr., H.W., Sarver, D.M.: Contemporary orthodontics. Elsevier Health Sciences, Amsterdam (2006)
3. Bishara, S.E., Ziaja, R.R.: Functional appliances: a review. Am. J. Orthod. Dentofac. Orthop. **95**, 250–258 (1989)
4. Pancherz, H.: Treatment of class II malocclusions by jumping the bite with the Herbst appliance. A cephalometric investigation. Am. J. Orthod. **76**, 423–442 (1979)
5. Allen-Noble, P.S.: Clinical Management of MARA Appliance. Allesee Orthodontic Appliances (2005)
6. Jasper, J.J., McNamara, J.A.: The correction of interarch malocclusions using a fixed force module. Am. J. Orthod. Dentofac. Orthop. **108**, 641–650 (1995)
7. Clark, W.J.: The twin block technique a functional orthopedic appliance system. Am. J. Orthod. Dentofac. Orthop. **93**, 1–8 (1988)
8. Schiavoni, R.: The Herbst appliance updated. Prog. Orthod. **12**, 149–160 (2011)
9. McNamara, J.A., Howe, R.P., Dischinger, T.G.: A comparison of the Herbst and Fränkel appliances in the treatment of class II malocclusion. Am. J. Orthod. Dentofac. Orthop. **98**, 134–144 (1990)
10. Moro, A., et al.: Twenty-year clinical experience with fixed functional appliances. Dent. Press J. Orthod. **23**, 87–109 (2018)
11. Akao, Y.: QFD: Quality Function Deployment - Integrating Customer Requirements into Product Design (1990)
12. Ullman, D.G.: The Mechanical Design Process. McGraw-Hill, New York (2010)
13. Ulrich, K.T., Eppinger, S.D.: Product Design and Development. McGraw-Hill, New York (2012)
14. Filippi, S., Barattin, D.: Exploiting the meCUE questionnaire to enhance an existing UX evaluation method based on mental models. In: Marcus, A., Wang, W. (eds.) HCII 2019, Part IV. LNCS, vol. 11586, pp. 117–133. Springer, Cham (2019). https://doi.org/10.1007/978-3-030-23535-2_8
15. Filippi, S., Barattin, D.: Considering users' different knowledge about products to improve a UX evaluation method based on mental models. In: Marcus, A., Wang, W. (eds.) DUXU 2018, Part I. LNCS, vol. 10918, pp. 367–378. Springer, Cham (2018). https://doi.org/10.1007/978-3-319-91797-9_26
16. Norman, D.: The Design of Everyday Things. Revised and Expanded Edition. Basic Book, New York (2013)
17. Thuring, M., Mahlke, S.: Usability, aesthetics and emotions in human-computer technology interaction. Int. J. Psychol. **42**(4), 253–264 (2007)
18. Grigolato, L., et al.: Conceptual design of a functional orthodontic appliance for the correction of skeletal class II malocclusion. In: Rizzi, C., Andrisano, A.O., Leali, F., Gherardini, F., Pini, F., Vergnano, A. (eds.) ADM 2019. LNME, pp. 329–341. Springer, Cham (2020). https://doi.org/10.1007/978-3-030-31154-4_28

PLANTY GO: A Smart Planter System to Relieve Stress and Anxiety of Urban Youngsters

Weilun Huang$^{(\boxtimes)}$, Zhenyu Cheryl Qian, Jung Joo Sohn, and Yunran Ju

Purdue University, West Lafayette, IN 47906, USA
willemhwl94@gmail.com

Abstract. This paper introduces an application design named Planty Go which encourages young people to exchange their planting harvests in big cities to relieve anxiety. To achieve this target Planty Go offer youngsters a place to learn planting skills, exchange harvest, and make friends with people who also like planting. This paper also includes the process of the application design from research to evaluation. Different from other planting applications, Planty Go focuses on supporting the emotions of youngsters and planting experience. So this paper introduces how to identify the problem through primary research and how to solve those problems with the Planty Go. Finally, this paper introduced a Heuristic Evaluation which helps designers improve this design continually.

Keywords: Emotion design · Social application · Planting experience

1 Introduction

With the rapid urban development, more young people swarm into the metropolis from villages and small cites [1]. The accelerated living pace and high-intensity workload bring stress and anxiety to youngsters' daily life. Living alone in a metropolis leads to loneliness and also enhances the stress. Lots of psychological research [2] focused on investigating the causing factors, risks, and outcomes such as PSD (Posttraumatic Stress Disorder) since the 1970s [3]. In recent years, the therapeutic effect of a natural environment has been verified to relieve stress, and a lot of further evidence-based studies have been undertaken. Various experimental approaches [4, 5] have attempted to measure physiologically, which can verify the beneficial effects of natural stimuli quantitatively [5]. Indoor plants have drawn the attention of the scientific community because of their various benefits [4]. However, based on a preliminary questionnaire study we conducted upon 200 youngsters (age between 20–35) in big cities, we found that indoor planting is not popular among youngsters as we expected. Two major reasons exist: the lack of planting information and experience, and the fading of motivation to take good care of plants. This research aims to promote the indoor planting experience through adding social activities into planting process as an emotion-centered supporting approach, measures the effectiveness of the design, and suggests a direction for reducing psychological and physiological stress by encouraging young adults who are undertaking pressure to enjoy the process and result of planting.

© Springer Nature Switzerland AG 2020
A. Marcus and E. Rosenzweig (Eds.): HCII 2020, LNCS 12202, pp. 242–253, 2020.
https://doi.org/10.1007/978-3-030-49757-6_17

2   Related Studies

2.1   Planting to Relieve Stress

Based on the research of National Institute of Mental Health American (2017), 11.01% of youth (age 12–17) report suffering from at least one major depressive episode (MDE) in the past year [6] and 18.57% of adults are experiencing a mental health illness, equivalent to 45 million Americans [7]. The worst result of pressure and anxiety may lead to depression or PSD (Posttraumatic Stress Disorder) [3]. According to the data, the number of depression has already increased dramatically in American. Under this environment, multiple types of researches and products aimed to deal with pressure and loneliness. Planting is one of those approaches which could relax people effectively in several situations [8]. Such as working in an environment with live plants, people tend to be happier and more satisfied with their jobs [5]. Furthermore, looking at green plants could have positive effects on recovery from fatigue or stress [4]. There are three main benefits of planting. Firstly the visual stimulation with green plants helps people relax and even physiological relaxing [9]. The second part is that the process of gardening helps people enjoy life [10]. Paying attention to planting helps people escape from the stressful urban life and imagine themselves have returned to a cozy country lifestyle. Thirdly, the environment of planting, such as the fresh smell and atmosphere from the plants, also make people enjoy the life and also give people positive psychological affect. Those findings are not limited in the research area. As shown by data, planting has become popular in urban life. According to the Daily Chart [11], "the number of Google searches for succulents has risen tenfold since 2010, and other green plants have had similar spurts of popularity." However, the popularity of planting does not mean that young people do not have problems with cultivation and current planting application are helpful.

2.2   Peer-Product Review

There are many planting websites and mobile applications online which offer cultivated information and help users with planting such as Self Watering, Smart Pest Management, and Smart Sensing products [12]. In general, they can be divided into 4 types: planting information app, planters community, smart detection device and self-water device. Planting information application is the most popular category. Most designers try to solve the planting problem by informing users of planning knowledge, such as planting skills or information about a specific kind of plant. Some may use advanced technology like using an image process to identify a plant in the database and find information about this plant. Those applications are suitable for new planter who don't have any planting experience. Knowing some information about a plant always help people plant it. For planters online community applications such as Plantifier [13], they try to encourage users to help other users in their online community. The benefit of this kind of application is they can solve some problems which cannot be solved only by information. Sometimes a plant is ill, people go through information online, but they still can't make sure what illness it has. What they need is a real person who may be a processional botany scholar or an experienced planter who keeps the same plant with them. With the development of advanced technology, smart detection devices and self-water devices become more popular in the market. The price dropping also allows those devices to be affordable to everybody. Xiaomi Smart pot [14] is one of these products which detect the condition of a plant through sensors and send the information to a mobile application. Users also use the application to control the water device to keep the humidity of the soil.

By analyzing existed products in the market, we found all of them have advantages and disadvantages. However, we found almost none of them focus on the users' emotions and motivation. Actually, the current problem is not users can't find an instruction of planting. It's because some people did not take plants seriously. They always forget to water it or they don't want to search planting instruction. In this paper, Planty Go tries to solve the planting problem in an emotional way. It works on motivating people rather than just offer information.

2.3 Design Goals

Planty Go includes two design goals. One of them is employing the method of planting to relax youngsters and relieve anxiety. In this application, we added social society elements into consideration, encouraging users to exchange planting harvests in the social communities of the cities where they are living in. Most anxiety for youngsters in big cities come from loneliness. They need friends and a colorful social life. We hope during the process of exchange, people not only could make the deal, but they also could communicate and make friends with strangers who may have the same hobby with them.

The second goal is motivating users to plant by exchanging harvests. During the planting, the death of plants always ruins the experience of planting and makes people Frustrated. The reasons which lead plants dead may be the lack of planting knowledge or loss interest of planting. Planting is a long period of activity which may take a few months to get the result. During this long planting period, people tend to lose their interest. In order to help people keep their freshness and get motivate frequently, we encourage young people to exchange their planting harvests with nearby people. Compare with plants without harvest, planters will get more motivated when they get harvests. However, if people keep getting the same produce, the motivation will fade out gradually. So we encourage people to exchange crops, in which they can get various vegetables. By using the Planty Go, users will get engaged in planting and enjoy the process of planting.

In addition, Planty Go offers users useful and accurate information, but we realize that engagement and enjoyments are more crucial in planting. Because if users could enjoy planting and keep on planting it, of course, they can find some ways to solve the planting challenges. However, in lots of cases, plants died, it's not because people don't know how to solve it. It's because people don't want to spend too much time and effort into it.

3   Methods

To figure out how to solve the problem of planting and the anxiety of youngsters, we should understand the living condition of youngsters and we can find out where and how we can help them. We conduct three rounds of researches, step by step, to explore several key insights that finally help us to finish our design. At first, we distributed a survey to ask about some general questions. In the second round, we recruited five people to have interviews. Based on the ideas we got from the first round, we find a few insights through the interview. Finally, in the third round, we distributed a survey again to testify the validity of our findings to make sure those findings are not personal issues, they can be applied to a lot of people.

3.1 First Round Survey

In the first round survey, interviewees answered less than 18 questions. I divided the survey into 4 parts: demography (4 questions), city life (5 questions) and plant experience (3–7 questions). Besides, I have 2 questions to testify validity. I distribute my survey through 3 methods: Facebook survey help group, online survey pool and Instagram of plants related comment. Finally, I got 200 participants. We hope our final analyze as accurate as possible, we only analyze the surveys from our target users who are youngster (20–35) from big cities (New York, Los Angeles, Chicago, San Francisco, etc.). By filter dirty data and people who are not from our target age group, I got near 112 valid surveys.

After analyzing the data, I found several ideas. Not matter they are studying or they are working. Only 12% of youngsters in big cities claimed they don't have any pressure, which shows under pressure has been a normal phenomenon in big cities. And 72% the youngster who claimed they are under pressure said they have plants or ever had planted before. And 78% of them expressed plants help them feel relaxed in some sense. Facing anxiety the most popular ways are watching videos (52%), hanging out with friends (32%) and online social networks (28%). In the planting area, we found mobile application doesn't work well in this area. Only 25% of people said they used apps to help them cultivate before.

3.2 Second Round Interview

Based on findings from the survey, we want to know more reasons and details about why plants always dead under our cultivation and how to make planting really help people relieve pressure. To achieve this goal, we hire 5 volunteers to join our interview. Four of them are working in big cities and feel anxious. One of them is the owner of a green store. We offer 20$ to each volunteer to have 30 min interview.

We conducted interviews through video chatting. Voice is recorded in the interview. The interviewer also took note of their talking. After the interviews, we highlight sentences on scripts that could give us insights on design. Finally, we find several key insights which are important to us and could give us help on design methodology. They are

- Some people consider plants as an air filter. At first, they may not enjoy the process of planting. Other people may consider plants as real life. They will take plants with them even they are going to move to another city.
- Youngsters in big cities usually have their hobby. When planting is related to their other hobbies, they may have more interests in it.

- A lot of planters like shopping green stores. The shopping experience in green stores should be improved.
- Customers in green stores care about them they time spending on cultivation and is this plant easy to die.
- The outcome of planting is important. This outcome could be visual or functional.

3.3 Third Round Survey

Since the insights are all from these five volunteers, we cannot promise the accuracy of those insights. Could those insights be applied to most users? Or they are volunteers' personal biases. We design the third survey to test the validity of those insights. I divided the study into 3 parts. In the first part, I asked general questions to allow participants to understand the background of the survey. In the second part, we asked about their opinion about the statement of insight that we get through the interview. For each insight, we give participants 7 levels from totally disagree to totally agree. In the third part, I set 2 questions to test the validity. The first question asks "is cat a kind of animal? (a common sense question and everyone knows the right answer)" If the answer is negative, the survey will be considered as fault data. The second question asks the same question which has been asked before. If the gap between of two answers is more than 3 levels, this survey will be considered as dirty data.

I collected 200 surveys through Survey star [15]. 163 surveys are valid data that is used to analyze. Participants rated those insights on curve from 0 to 6. The totally disagree takes 0 points and totally agree takes 6 points. For each insight, we calculate their average scores. If the average rating is higher than 5, we consider this insight is reliable. The first three questions are higher than 5, we decided to design this application based on this insight.

3.4 Findings

Based on the researches we have done, here are some findings which inspire our design.

1. Missing the primary goal of helping the user to relax and enjoy the process. Most websites and apps always focus on displaying information about plants and cultivation rather than the people themselves. The long and tedious planting experience is easy to exhaust the youngsters' patience and interest.
2. Fail to capture the pleasure and provide continuous encouragement. During the process of cultivation, satisfaction with acquisition is insufficient. Some people consider the process of hard work as a relaxation; some do not. Continuous motivation during the whole process of planting is the key that decides how long the plant could survive.
3. Existing systems are unable to highlight the benefits of indoor planting. The young generation is easy to be distracted by a more vivid appearance of other media or items. After accustomed to the plants, people become numb to the results of planting, such as smell or visual appearance, which are not as engaging as in the first period. They seek more interactive stuff that could communicate with them.

4. The lack of functional experience instead of theoretical knowledge. Planting is such a complicated process that is influenced by the location, environment, seasons and soil condition. Following the online instruction and ignoring various effects from multiple factors, people will lose their plants eventually and make a conclusion planting applications are useless.

4 Design Process

Based on the findings from primary researches, the next step is ideation. We create several hypotheses to help people to fix problems that we identified previously. During this part, we had 3 main ideas and finally narrow down to one which is exchanging harvests in the community. After that, we design the sitemap for this application (Fig. 1). In the sitemap, we can easily check the navigation and info structure clearly.

Following the sitemap, we designed a low fidelity user interface (Fig. 2). Low fidelity UI showed an overall location and structure of the user interface. Later, we added colors and modify the detail and make the final high fidelity UI. Finally, we make an interactive prototype that demonstrates the interactions in the app.

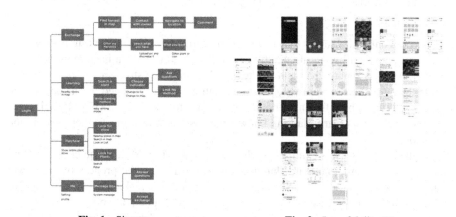

Fig. 1. Sitemap   **Fig. 2.** Low fidelity UI

5 Final Design

Following the design process, finally, Planty Go comes to the public which contains 5 main parts: Map-based Exploration, Planting Instruction Storage, Personal Management Page, Engage with the Community, and User Rewarding System.

5.1 Map-Based Exploration

While opening the app of Planty Go, the user will see a map in which he/she can find harvests he/she want to exchange (Fig. 3). The system does not allow users to ship or take hours to go to another side of the city to get any harvests. We want to limit the

Fig. 3. Exchange   **Fig. 4.** Workshop   **Fig. 5.** Store

distance and only allow users to exchange in a nearby community. Making friends with the same hobby and live in the nearby community lead users can have more activities together. And have more change to make users' relationship stronger.

On the map, there are not only harvests waiting to be exchanged. Users can switch to the workshop tab to find a workshop they want to take part in (Fig. 4). Joining a workshop help users learn planting knowledge, also users can meet other users in the workshop.

On the store tab, users can find nearby green stores (Fig. 5). It's a quick way to find a nearby store to buy plants or planting equipment. During the process of exchange, Planty Go encourages users to exchange at our certified store, which is in the midway of two users. In the shop, if users need anything, they can get help as soon as possible. As we said, it's not only a deal; it's a chance to communicate. We don't want users to meet at the sidewalk, meet, exchange and separate immediately. The store is a quiet space to allow users to talk and share. To encourage users to meet at stores, we may provide free service or items when they finish exchanges in the assigned store. From the stores' perspective, they are willing to cooperate with us, because they can get more potential customers coming to their store.

On the map page, users can switch between 2 views (map view and list view). The default page is the map page. But for some users, they care more about the item they may get rather than the location itself. They need more efficiency. In this case, they can switch to list of all item my can exchange with. There is also a filter function that helps users find their target item accurately.

5.2 Planting Instruction Storage

Except for the exchange, we also offer a place to learn to plant knowledge from other users' articles which are learning tutorials (Fig. 6). The tutorial page is an endless article page. On the tutorial page, we will recommend various articles written by other users based on users' hobby and habit. We will also filter and find high-quality articles which will be recommended to users. Except for professional articles online, we also include some articles from users' cities or which is close to the user. Planting knowledge relates to location, weather, season and climate. Users who are living in the same area must have the same planting environment. Their suggestions could be more helpful.

Fig. 6. Tutorial

Users not only can read tutorials written by others, but they can also share their own knowledge with others. Under articles, readers and the author could talk and ask questions. Since the distribution of articles is based on location. Users who are talking with others under his/her articles may come from the same cities. This is another chance to make friends with people who are in the same community.

5.3 Personal Management Page

As I introduced before, this planting app is based on social society. We hope to encourage people to make new friends on this app. So we have a plentiful personal page. Users can visit their own personal page to check what he/she has done in the Planty Go (Fig. 7). Users can also visit others' personal page to find what he or she has done here. If users find a proficient planter, they can also follow this user (Fig. 8). When he or she publishes a new article, this user will get a notification for the first time.

The Internet is a place we don't know each other. In the Planty Go, we hope people could know more about other people and trust other people. Harvest is an effect exam for planting skills. If users get a fresh and high qualified harvest, undoubtedly this planter is

Fig. 7. My page

Fig. 8. Follow other planter

professional. They can trust his articles and ask questions from him. On the other way, if users find a person writes tons of tutorials and he got a lot follower and likes, definitely they can exchange with him. His article and follower are a promise of a good harvest.

5.4 Engage with the Community

Actually, joining a workshop is the most efficient way to learn planting skills. However, because of some reason, only limited people have joined a planting workshop. We encourage people to join our workshops. Harvest is harder than just keep a plant that needs more professional knowledge. Planty Go's users do not sell the harvest for income, but for fun - a way to relax. They don't need to know how to keep every plant. Knowing about one plant and keeping it in the free time are enough for our users. Maybe just 1 or 2 workshops, they may get enough knowledge to keep their plants and get harvests. And in the workshop, users can also meet new people and make friends in workshops.

5.5 User Rewarding System

Planty Go has a rewarding system that allows users to collect coins. Sometimes, it's hard to find a person who needs what you have and you also want to get his harvest. So we use coins. Users can exchange your harvest with coins. And you later users can exchange coin with what they want. Another advantage of it is we can take coins as a reward for our users who join workshops or complete a task assigned by us.

6 Evaluation Study

After we finish the design, we need to figure out if the design work well or not. We want to know is there any using Disaster? Is any function is not user-friendly? In this evaluation, we employed the Heuristic Evaluation [16]. We recruited 5 professional designers to join the evaluation. An evaluation form was designed for evaluators. Each of them needs to use the application under the record, finish the form and have a short interview with us. In the interview, every evaluator may be asked to explain the form they finished and how they think about this design based on aesthetic, Use-friendly and problem-solving perspectives.

During the evaluation, we recruited 5 professional designers. Two of them are master design student major in interaction design, one of them are PhD student major in visual communication design two of them are user experience designers who are working in the industry. We invited them individually to a quiet computer lab to conduct the evaluation. Firstly, we introduce the background and product and target users to them, but we did not give any instructions about how to use it. And then evaluators play with our app by themselves. If they meet any question, they can get help from the host. During the evaluation, they are asked to answer to finish the evaluation form (Fig. 9). In the form, they are asked to rate each category from 0 to 4. 0 means no problem and 4 means a using disaster. After rating each category, they need to explain the reason and where his problem is. After the test, there was a small interview for them in which we asked them to explain more about some of the questions in the evaluation form. And they were asked 3 more questions: 1) Do you think using this app could help users relieve the pressure? Why? 2) Which part gives you the worst using experience? 3) If you are plating, will you use it? Why? Our recorder noted answers and the whole actions evaluators did during the evaluation.

	Problem describe	R1	R2	R3	R4	R5	Average
UI							
Color combination		1	0	0	0	1	0.4
Style consistency		1	1	1	1	1	0.8
Using Experience							
Speaking users languages		0	1	0	1	0	0.4
Feedback		1	0	0	1	1	0.6
Functions Reasonable		0	1	1	2	1	0.8
Navigation		0	0	0	1	1	0.4
Problem solving							
Attractiveness		1	2	1	2	2	1.6
Emotional encouraged		2	1	2	2	1	1.6
Duration		2	0	2	2	3	1.8

Fig. 9. Evaluation Form

Finally, we found in the user interface and user-experience part, most evaluators gave a low grade on it which mean UI and Using experience do not have huge problem. The biggest problem comes from "problem-solving". Here are some feedbacks from evaluators:

- Users need to meet to exchange harvest. This process this kind complicated and also required both of them are free.

- Planting for harvest is still a long time. Some plants may have harvest twice a year. Users will have nothing to do without harvest.
- It's hard to testify the effect of Planty Go.
- Most harvests are cheap. Nobody is willing to walk half an hour to exchange harvests.
- The format of the tutorial page is kind of different from other pages.
- Making friends with stingers through the process of exchanging harvest is wired.

Even for those designers, they are not sure if this design can really solve the problem or not. What we need is a long term field study to know about users real situation when are using this app.

7   Conclusion

This paper is a new attempt in planting the mobile application market, which adopts social elements in the application. By encouraging youngsters to engage the process of planting and make more real friends, users relax and relieve anxiety. Undoubtedly, emotional problems hard to be solved only by an application. But we still want to have some positive effects on youngsters. Besides, we try to solve the most frustrating problem in planting which is the death of planting in the mistime. We are trying to work on an emotional issue, so we should not create any bad emotions for our users. In this problem, we didn't always offer users planting information like most of the applications. Instead, we motivate users to exchange harvest with others. By enjoying this process, users would be more attractive to planting and solve planting problems by themselves. As mentioned before, in this age of information explosion, the main problem is not that people can't find planting information. The problem is if they want to spend time and energy on it.

The feedback from the evaluation proves the effect of the user interface. The interface and languages used in it are understandable. The Navigation is clear enough feedback is in time. However, we apply the Heuristic Evaluation, which means the evaluators are professional designers. We still need to evaluate a large number of real regular users who don't have too much design and computer science background to know about the real reaction from our users. To prove the validity of this hypothesis (using this planting social, mobile application to relieve anxiety), a long term experiment is needed. And the result could be affected by various factors such as the quality of design, the demography of users. So it's hard to test the result of the design.

References

1. Why Millennials Are Avoiding Small-Town America | Fast Forward | OZY. https://www.ozy.com/fast-forward/why-millennials-are-avoiding-small-town-america/34058. Accessed 05 Oct 2019
2. Drazdowski, T.K., Kliewer, W.L., Farrell, A., Sullivan, T., Roberson-Nay, R., Jäggi, L.: A longitudinal study of the bidirectional relations between anxiety symptoms and peer victimization in urban adolescents. J. Interpers. Violence 088626051882464 (2019). https://doi.org/10.1177/0886260518824647

3. Breslau, N.: Traumatic events and posttraumatic stress disorder in an urban population of young adults. Arch. Gen. Psychiatr. **48**(3), 216 (1991). https://doi.org/10.1001/archpsyc.1991. 01810270028003
4. Shibata, S., Suzuki, N.: Effects of indoor foliage plants on subjects' recovery from mental fatigue. North Am. J. Psychol. **3**(3), 385–396 (2001)
5. Dravigne, A., Waliczek, T.M., Lineberger, R.D., Zajicek, J.M.: The effect of live plants and window views of green spaces on employee perceptions of job satisfaction. HortScience **43**(1), 183–187 (2008). https://doi.org/10.21273/HORTSCI.43.1.183
6. 2017 State of Mental Health in America - Youth Data | Mental Health America. https://www. mhanational.org/issues/2017-state-mental-health-america-youth-data. Accessed 05 Oct 2019
7. Mental Health in America - Adult Data | Mental Health America. https://www.mhanational. org/issues/mental-health-america-adult-data. Accessed 05 Oct 2019
8. Elings, M.: People-plant interaction: the physiological, psychological and sociological effects of plants on people. In: Hassink, J., Van Dijk, M. (eds.) Farming for Health, vol. 13, pp. 43–55. Springer, Dordrecht (2006). https://doi.org/10.1007/1-4020-4541-7_4
9. Ikei, H., Song, C., Igarashi, M., Namekawa, T., Miyazaki, Y.: Physiological and psychological relaxing effects of visual stimulation with foliage plants in high school students, p. 6 (2014)
10. Clayton, S.: Domesticated nature: motivations for gardening and perceptions of environmental impact. J. Environ. Psychol. **27**(3), 215–224 (2007). https://doi.org/10.1016/j.jenvp.2007. 06.001
11. Instead of houses, young people have houseplants - daily chart. https://www.economist.com/ graphic-detail/2018/08/06/instead-of-houses-young-people-have-houseplants. Accessed 05 Oct 2019
12. Smart Indoor Garden Market Size | Industry Report, 2025. https://www.valuemarketresearch. com/report/smart-indoor-garden-market. Accessed 10 Oct 2019
13. Plantifier – Apps on Google Play. https://play.google.com/store/apps/details?id=air.be.tre ndsco.plantifier&hl=en_GB. Accessed 31 Jan 2020
14. Xiaomi Smart Flower Pot Flora Review - XiaomiToday. https://www.xiaomitoday.com/xia omi-smart-flower-pot-flora-review/. Accessed 31 Jan 2020
15. Wenjuanxing. https://www.wjx.cn/. Accessed 31 Jan 2020
16. Nielsen, J., Molich, R.: Heuristic evaluation of user interfaces. In: Proceedings of the SIGCHI Conference on Human Factors in Computing Systems Empowering People - CHI 1990, Seattle, Washington, United States, pp. 249–256 (1990). https://doi.org/10.1145/97243.97281

Prototyping a Mental Health Smartphone Application

Julian Hunter and Tania Roy(✉)

New College of Florida, Sarasota, FL 34243, USA
{julian.hunter16,troy}@ncf.edu

Abstract. Mental illness among young people has reached epidemic proportions. One solution proposed for addressing this issue is increasing their mental health literacy, which research has found to be negatively correlated with the chance of developing a mental illness. This study suggests that a smartphone app may be the best medium for raising the mental health literacy of young people. Most young people own smartphones, which have the technology to utilize both traditional and unique techniques for delivering information on mental illness. To explore the potential of a mental health literacy app, a literature review on existing mental health apps was conducted. In addition, 15 young adults equally divided into 3 focus groups were asked to discuss their knowledge of and opinions on mental health, technology design, mental health apps, and what they would theoretically like to see in a mental health literacy app. The results found a varied level of knowledge about mental health among the participants. In addition, participants offered several guiding principles for the development of mental health apps, such as suggesting they focus on providing users information, not a diagnosis. Further the results offer guidelines on the design of a mental health literacy app, the likely support it would receive from young people, and its necessity for this demographic.

Keywords: Mental health literacy · Design guidelines · Prototyping

1 Introduction

Mental health, defined as an "internal equilibrium which enables individuals to use their abilities in harmony with universal values of society" [1], impacts our cognitive and social capabilities, emotional intelligence, and coping skills. For this reason, the epidemic of poor mental health affecting young people must be taken seriously [2]. According to past research, mental illness is said to peak in adolescence and young adulthood, with approximately one in four adolescents having a mental illness and a large percentage of them carrying their conditions into adulthood. Appropriate resources and medical assistance need to be made be available to these young people to address this situation.

This paper theorizes that raising awareness and understanding of mental health through easily accessible applications may be the best course of action. This hypothesis is supported through a literature review exploring the nature of mental health literacy and the accessibility of applications for young adults and adolescents. To assist in developing

© Springer Nature Switzerland AG 2020
A. Marcus and E. Rosenzweig (Eds.): HCII 2020, LNCS 12202, pp. 254–267, 2020.
https://doi.org/10.1007/978-3-030-49757-6_18

guidelines for such an application, the literature review also examines research on the design and functionality of smartphone applications dedicated to providing non-clinical mental health treatment to this demographic. Using this information we then conducted focus groups investigating young adults' views on what a mental health literacy application should look like, both in design and functionality. Based on the information obtained, we developed a set of guidelines for future app developers and mental health advocates to follow when creating mental health awareness smartphone applications to assist in addressing the current epidemic young adults face.

1.1 Background

In the field of psychology, mental health literacy is often defined as "knowledge and beliefs about mental disorders which aid their recognition, management and prevention" [3]. Someone with good mental health literacy is able to identify signs of mental illness in themselves and others and the best means for treating these illnesses, including when professional help should be sought. It has been shown that communities high in mental health literacy tend to be comprised of individuals with good mental health [3, 4], probably because in such communities, residents are capable of recognizing signs of mental illness in one another, offering appropriate emotional support to one another, and recommending professional help when necessary.

Despite these benefits of teaching and improving mental health literacy in individuals, carelessly providing people knowledge on mental health can have detrimental side effects. For example, Kitchener's study of a mental health literacy course found that while participants in the course expressed higher mental health literacy in many regards, such as in identifying mental illness and in basic first aid, there was a notable number who still did not believe in recommending professional care, expressing a belief that the mental illness can be taken care of by the individual and his/her support group [3]. In other words, while mental health literacy is a valuable tool, it is important that it is taught as accurately as possible to mitigate unintended consequences. The course in Kitchener's study, for example, should have been stressed that support groups are not a replacement for clinical treatment.

In addition to these concerns, since this study is primarily concerned with the epidemic of poor mental health among young people, it becomes relevant to consider whether young people need to improve their mental health literacy, and if so, what kind of information do they need. While younger people have been shown to have better mental health literacy than older, it is still not at an ideal level [5]. Farrer et al. [5] found that even though younger people were more adept at identifying and generally had fewer negative views concerning mental illnesses than older, there were still clear issues in their mental health literacy. For example, this age demographic had difficulty identifying any mental illness that was not depression. Additionally, young people appear to stigmatize the act of seeking help while glorifying self-reliance in overcoming mental illness [6].

The study reported here posits that improving young people's mental health literacy will aid them in a mental health crisis. However, as the research has shown, providing mental health information without careful consideration of the delivery system may have unexpected negative consequences for the target audience. Therefore, the delivery of mental health literacy to young people must be carefully examined.

Delivery of Mental Health Literacy. If a lack of mental health literacy in young adults is one of the causes for the prevalence of mental illness in this age group, then it is likely that these young people may be unaware of the importance of mental health information. As a result, it is reasonable to theorize that they may be resistant to exposure to information they believe they do not need. This resistance might be addressed by developing a delivery method for mental health literacy that is engaging as well as safe and effective.

Much research has focused on determining the effectiveness of directly teaching people mental health literacy through training courses, where the material is presented in a traditional classroom situation [4, 7, 8]. Participants in these three studies all exhibited notable increases in their mental health literacy after the training courses fairly consistently across the studies. These results indicate that presenting the material in a clear and informative manner is an effective means of delivering mental health literacy, suggesting that a mental health literacy app using similar straightforward methods may be successful.

However, teaching the material is not the only issue that must be considered when attempting to raise the mental health literacy of the users of this app. In [4, 7, 8] the participants recruited to take the course were either personally motivated or were persuaded by some form of compensation. As this study is attempting to deliver this information to average young adults who may have no interest in mental health literacy, the material must be presented in a way that will encourage this demographic to improve their mental health literacy.

Studies have explored entertaining and engaging ways to educate individuals on mental health literacy. One popular approach has been to use narrative as a means of teaching mental health literacy in an engaging manner [9, 10]. Li's study [10], for example, student participants played a web-based game that involved a story In about a student navigating a school utilizing mental health literacy skills, such as good communication skills, to progress through the narrative. In Chang's study [9], the efficacy of narrative advertising, which consisted of teaching by presenting scenarios with actors who had goals they wished to accomplish, was tested. In both of these studies, the narrative-based approaches increased the participants' interest in the subject matter, reporting a reduced stigma toward and an improved understanding of mental illness.

A second approach, gamifying the teaching of mental health literacy, was also investigated in Li's [10] study. This study extended the narrative by including gameplay elements that appeared to further engage and entertain the participants as they learned the necessary material. Narrative advertising and gamification both lend themselves well to implementation on a smartphone app. In addition, meta-analyses of mental health smartphone apps have recommended gamification as a way to deliver non-clinical treatment [11, 12].

Gamification has also been suggested as a potentially effective way for appealing to young adults with mental issues whose situations, be it financial or personal, may not allow them to receive clinical treatment, as well as young adults who may not currently have mental issues but who could develop them in the future. It has been shown that young people in this demographic value their autonomy and find the commitment that comes with clinical treatment to be a deterrent [11]. According to Bakker [11] and Neilsen [12], gamification lightens the sense of commitment that treatment brings, further encouraging this demographic's awareness of their mental literacy. In addition, prevention is often a better solution to mental illness than treatment [11]. By including aspects such as gameplay in an app that can be enjoyed separately from its mental health benefits, users who believe themselves to be free of mental issues may still be drawn to use the app and raise their mental health literacy, perhaps preventing future mental illness by informing users on how to maintain ideal mental health and respond to mental illness [11, 13].

1.2   The Potential Functionality of a Mental Health Literacy App

The access young people have to smartphones and the advanced technology they currently offer reinforce the potential for functional and accessible mental health literacy smartphone apps. The approaches discussed for teaching mental health literacy, i.e. gamification and narration, are translatable into smartphone applications. In addition, meta-analyses of mental health smartphone apps have begun to explore this functionality, though only from the standpoint of implementing certain non-clinical treatments [11, 12, 14].

One potential feature highlighted by all the articles allowed users to record their thoughts and emotions. Doing so has several benefits. For one, it assists in raising emotional competency. By having an outlet for recording their thoughts and emotions, users become more adept at identifying and expressing these feelings. Secondly, evidence suggests that young adults are more comfortable admitting personal thoughts and emotions to a smartphone than to a clinician [14]. Thirdly, keeping such a record lends itself well to the implementation of cognitive behavioral therapy, which has been recommended to be a part of the non-clinical treatment that these apps should aim to offer.

Mindful cognitive behavioral therapy, a mental health protocol in which patients are to be taught to be mindful and aware of their own thought processes and emotions with the goal of eliminating negative ones, has been shown to be effective [15]. Encouraging the recording of mental processes not only raises mindfulness and awareness of one's mental state but users can also use their own writing to reflect and come to conclusions about their mental state, conclusions that will be supported by the mental health literacy training offered by the same app.

This feature could easily be supplemented by real-time engagement, another recommended feature [11]. Bakker et al.'s meta-analysis [11] recommends that mental health apps should be able to send periodic reminders to the user to both interact with the app as well as do other things, such as reflect on a recorded emotion. The article argues that this feature offers a benefit that traditional therapy does not: a mental health app on a smartphone gives the user access to constant treatment in the form of reminders to engage in healthy behavior.

Another common theme across the literature is the suggestion that mental health apps should recommend activities and social groups for the user [11, 12]. Both [11, 12] cite participation in support groups and productive activities as effective means for recovering from mental illness, and an app on a smartphone offers the potential for recommending relevant groups and activities based on information provided by the user, potentially affecting an immediate change in the user's mental state.

An additional common theme was the importance of tailoring mental health apps to individual users [11, 12, 14] by requesting personal information, such as demographics, interests, and mental state, among others. Because apps have this capability, the aid they offer will specifically relate to the user, in turn increasing the user's trust in it. This aid can include information relevant to the user's mental state as well as recommendations for specific social groups and activities that the user would enjoy.

Finally, a feature frequently recommended for most mental health apps was a means of immediate stress relief for users [11, 14]. By including this feature, Bakker, Rickwood, and Rickard argue that users become more engaged with the app. By gaining immediate short-term benefits, in this case immediate stress relief, or preventing panic attacks, users develop a trust in the app's ability to assist them long term. Thus, they are more likely to stay engaged with the app. Immediate stress relief methods that have been shown to be effective on smartphone apps include music therapy and breathing exercises [14].

Issues with Current Mental Health Smartphone Applications. These articles also analyzed the features and design concepts that are ineffective in the current mental health apps. One concern mentioned was the lack of discussion on the design philosophy behind these apps [12]. Søgaard and Wilson argue that few academics in the field of development of mental health apps are discussing the actual design of these apps, and as a result, the designs need improvement to ensure their effectiveness. Focusing primarily on the assertion that the apps were not user-friendly, these researchers recommended several improvements. For example, they suggested multimodal delivery of information, or delivering information through multiple types of media, not just text. In addition, they recommended that a slightly large, dark grey text with a multicolor background was the most effective. The article also stressed that easy navigability and concrete directions were vital for the success of a mental health app.

An additional concern was the lack of individuals with mental illnesses participating in user testing [12]. This article argues that while apps which aim to offer non-clinical assistance should not user test exclusively with mentally ill people, they are still a vital part of the demographic that the app is aiming to assist. Thus, mentally ill people should participate in the user testing as their input is valuable for creating an app suitable for as large a demographic as possible.

Finally, most of the literature agrees that diagnosing users with mental illnesses as well as developing apps that offer non-clinical treatment is generally not recommended [1, 14]. These articles argue that diagnosing a person requires clinical assessment, which involves a trained professional. Technology developed for non-clinical public use that does not involve a human potentially may offer an inaccurate assessment, perhaps one that may even make the user's situation worse. For example, a vulnerable user who is told that they have a mental illness may not react as advised, especially if they do indeed have a mental illness and/or do not have access to clinical treatment.

1.3 Current Study

Throughout this literature review, the importance of mental health literacy and how it can best be delivered have been discussed. Of critical importance is the accessibility of this information, and with the availability of smartphones to young people, we became interested in integrating the information discussed with effective teaching methods into a smartphone app. As past research has analyzed the design and functionality of mental health applications, the goal of the research reported here was to integrate the existing functionality and design of effective mental health apps with the theoretically effective means of delivering mental health literacy.

To obtain an understanding of the features needed in an effective mental health literacy app, this study conducted focus groups comprised of 4–6 young adults. These focus groups were asked to discuss their thoughts on today's technology design, mental health literacy, the effective means of raising mental health awareness, and their concept of an ideal mental health literacy app. With this information, future developers will have a greater understanding of the design principles that young people wish to see in their apps. Mental health advocates will also have a greater understanding of what young people believe their demographic needs to raise their mental health literacy. And for developers interested in creating an app dedicated towards improving the mental health of young people, this study will serve as a guideline, outlining young people's recommendations for such an app.

2   Methods

2.1   Participants

The participants consisted of 15 young adults divided into 3 focus groups. These young people were recruited through college email forums and personal requests. The demographic variables of the participants can be found in Table 1.

Table 1. Demographic information

Variable	Proportion
Race	15 participants
Caucasian	13
Hispanic	1
African American	1
Average age	21.5 years
Gender	
Female	5
Male	6
Non-binary	3
Did not disclose	1
Marital status	
Single	4
In-a relationship	6
Prefer not to say	5

2.2 Procedure

The focus groups met in a classroom specified by the researcher. Once all were present, the researcher asked the participants to complete the demographic survey. Next, they competed a survey asking for their experiences with mental health apps and their opinions of the importance of mental health awareness. Once the participants had completed these two surveys, the researcher began to facilitate dialogue among the members of the focus groups using a script. The script consisted of topics covering the participants' views on ideal technology design, mental health literacy, existing mental health apps, the features and design principles necessary for creating successful mental health literacy apps, privacy in regards to sharing personal information, and the capability of expanding mental health literacy training and non-clinical mental health treatment through technology in the form of AI and gamification, among others.

The participants were encouraged to talk among themselves on each topic for approximately 2–5 min at a time while the facilitator took notes, entering into the dialogue only when necessary to divert attention to a new topic or to further encourage dialogue on a given topic. Once all the topics had been discussed, which the facilitator ensured occurred within 40 min, the participants were asked to draw what they considered an ideal design for a mental health literacy app. Once this was completed, their participation in the project ended.

Using the notes from each focus group, a thematic analysis was conducted. Themes that were common across more than 2 participants were identified as especially important to the participants' desires for a mental health application. While discussing the results we refer to participants by the ID numbers such as 1A.

3 Results

3.1 Survey Results

In response to being asked if they have ever used a mental health application, 10 participants had not, and 5 participants had, with Headspace, Calm Harm, 7Cups, Youper, and Therapy Assistance Online (TAO) all being cited. When asked if they thought that mental health awareness would encourage people with mental health issues to seek treatment, 10 said they believed so, with 1 person indicating skepticism. When asked if they thought increased mental health awareness would help reduce the stigma attached to those with mental illness, 14 said they believed so, and 1 indicated skepticism. When asked if they thought that "people are generally caring and sympathetic to people with mental illnesses," based on a 1–5 Likert scale with 1 being Strongly Disagree, 6 people answered with a 2, and 8 with a 3, and 1 with a 5.

3.2 Designing Principles of Application

When asked about what makes technology user-friendly and easy-to-use, four participants agreed that an application's design should focus on the specific device that it will be used on because mindlessly adapting technology and apps to various platforms results in a loss of effectiveness (1A, 1C, 1F, 3D). Apps built for both smartphones and desktops were recommended to be designed specifically for their respective platform. By doing so, the text size and options of an apps are adapted to be viewable for the display being used, the buttons and other aspects of navigability better fit the platform's control scheme, and the experience of using the app is generally cohesive with the experience of using the platform in question. In addition, the participants recommended being able to customize an app's layout through editable color schemes, text sizes, etc. to allow the app to feel natural and personal for the user (1C, 2D, 2E). Several participants stated that color palettes that included a variety of blues were often preferred as these colors put users at ease and, thus, encouraged them engage more readily with such apps (1C, 2B, 2D, 2E).

Precise controls were generally agreed upon as crucial, notably in the context of smartphone apps (1C, 1E, 1F, 2D, 2E, 3B, 3C). Excessive numbers of hyperlinks, poorly placed scroll bars, and a lack of scroll bars for navigating through large amounts of text were all cited as design aspects that made apps difficult to navigate as the first two particularly could be frequently used accidentally. Additionally, several participants agreed that a well-designed concept has a core functionality that it accurately advertises and prioritizes (1A, 1B, 1C, 1D, 1E, 1F). These participants argued that when applications do not follow this principle, they become oversaturated with options. This oversaturation overwhelms users both from a functional standpoint as they are not sure what they should be using within the app and from a design point as these options often clutter the screen, making navigating especially difficult.

In addition to design choices, several aspects were cited as deterrents to using and enjoying an app. Almost every participant agreed that advertisements are an irritating deterrent for any app. As 3A suggested, this effect is less because advertisements are present in apps and more because of how they exist in them. This participant pointed out that many apps in mobile games interrupt the flow of gameplay directly and often the button that closes the advertisement is obscurely placed, making it difficult to continue using the app. They argued that if advertisements in apps appeared at less disruptive times and were easier to close, the user base would not mind them nearly as much. Moreover, several participants felt deterred by apps that lock selective content behind accounts and subscriptions (1A, 1C, 3B, 3D).

3.3 Participants' Understanding of Mental Health Literacy

Participants' knowledge of mental health literacy was mixed: approximately half of the participants were able to confidently define mental health and mental health literacy (1A, 1B, 1C, 1D, 1E, 1F, 2C, 3A), while the remaining half were hesitant and unclear as to what these terms mean (2A, 2B, 2D, 2E, 3B, 3C). These latter participants had general guesses and conceptions but reported feeling a lack of confidence in either giving concise definitions or distinguishing between mental health literacy and awareness. When discussing what they believed to be the best means for improving mental health literacy, participants consistently argued that personal interaction was the most effective (1C, 1F, 2B, 2C, 2E, 3A, 3B, 3C, 3D). While participants often specified one-on-one interactions where a person is offered new information regarding mental health, some participants also cited community-based events as effective as well (1D, 1E, 2C). A few participants also argued that schools, in particular middle schools and high schools, should offer some form of mental health literacy course (1F, 3A, 3C).

3.4 The Desired Qualities of Mental Health Technology

Several participants supported a mental health app focusing on providing users with information and mental health literacy training as they felt it was the safest, simplest, and most effective means of improving mental health through technology (2A, 2B, 2D, 3B, 3D). Applications with functionality to provide immediate assistance to users experiencing symptoms of mental illnesses, such as panic attacks and depressive episodes, were also supported by several participants (1B, 1D, 2D, 2E). One participant provided an example of a smartphone application with a breathing exercise that involved having the users rhythmically press a button in time with each breath to calm their breathing (1B). Applications that provided features that allowed users to record their emotions and thoughts in something comparable to a virtual diary were also credited as an effective means of helping users cope with their emotional issues as well as come to understand them on a better level (1B, 2C).

In regards to the question of how a mental health literacy application should ideally function, many participants supported the idea of connecting users through the application's functionality, emphasizing the previous point that discussing mental health literacy is one of the most effective means for improving it (2B, 2C, 3A, 3B, 3C, 3D). Ideas on how this functionality could be handled varied. A few participants discussed the potential for online chat rooms that the app could recommend to users based on their reported symptoms and situations (2B, 2C). These participants continued to argue that if this were a feature, the application should require users to take an empathetic communication course before being able to use it. On the other hand, several participants were in favor of a moderated forum that would be affiliated with a mental health app (3A, 3B, 3C, 3D). Users could use this forum to find solidarity and advice from people experiencing similar illnesses and experiences.

Participants endorsed applications tailored to the users though they often clarified that this process should not involve automatic changes that drastically altered the functionality and layout of the application without the user's knowledge or consent, arguing that this would make users lose a sense of trust and control over the application (1A, 1C, 1D). Worth noting is the one participant who argued against this tailoring, fearing that it would encourage a diagnostic mentality in the app (3B). When discussing the best platform for a mental health literacy application, most participants argued that an application aiming to provide information and resources about mental health to those in need of it should be available on as many platforms as possible (1A, 1B, 1C, 1D, 1E, 1F, 2A, 3A).

3.5 Important Considerations for Mental Health Technology

Most participants agreed that the apps should never be diagnostic nor attempt to deliver clinical treatment to its users, believing that a clinician is needed to make an accurate diagnosis (1E, 1F, 2A, 2B, 2D, 3A, 3B, 3C). A few of these participants argued that non-clinically diagnosing users puts them at risk as the diagnosis is likely to be incorrect and misleading (1E, 1F, 3B, 3C). Moreover, users may need immediate access to resources and support upon receiving a particularly serious diagnosis, and if an application delivers this diagnosis, these resources may not be made available to the user at a critical time.

A few participants stated that they specifically did not like apps that shamed users for not engaging with them because such messages create a general negative feeling towards the app (2B, 2D, 2E). Commonly given examples were apps that sent users notifications that insisted they were slacking in regard to personal work and missing out on potential growth by ignoring the app. Additionally, AI, which was usually introduced into the dialogue by the participants, was not endorsed (1A, 1C, 1E, 2B, 2C, 2D, 2E, 3A, 3B, 3C). Most participants felt as though mental health AI promises to do too much in terms of providing users with comfort and meaningful advice when many of the responses given are clearly automated and lack specificity for any given question.

The topic of privacy was met with mixed responses from the participants. Approximately half of the participants responded to this topic with an air of casualness, stating that privacy in the modern age was not a concern (1A, 1B, 1C, 1D, 1E, 1F). As such, they reported that they would feel comfortable sharing their emotions and thoughts with an app of this kind. Other participants expressed a clear interest in maintaining their privacy and protecting their personal information (2A, 2B, 2D, 2E, 3A, 3B, 3C). These participants expressed a clear lack of desire for sharing intimate thoughts and emotions, emphasizing the need for a feeling of safety when doing so with an app. These same participants reported that an app would have to include precautions such as locking virtual diaries behind passcodes to ensure the safety of their information before they would feel comfortable sharing it. Participants who recommended that these apps should allow users to share their information often qualified that this information should be able to be made private or public.

3.6 Designs Drawn

In the final portion of the study, each participant drew a potential app incorporating the various features and best practices discussed in the groups. We use the design from Participant, 2C, who imagined the app divided into to 3 main HUDs that can be accessed at a taskbar at the bottom of the screen (see Fig. 1), as a typical example. In this app "the home tracking page" displays a mood tracker where the user would access features such as an online diary; "news," the news page, includes information on current events relevant to mental health treatment and research in addition to providing the user access to mental health literacy training, and the "community page," which shows the users the various groups, potentially both online and offline, that they belong to, is where the user could potentially reach out to others.

Fig. 1. An illustration of a theoretical mental health/mental health literacy app drawn by Participant 2C

4 Discussion

4.1 Principal Findings

This study hypothesized that raising the mental health literacy of young people is an appropriate response to the crisis of mental illness they face. It was theorized that providing mental health literacy training over a smartphone app would be appropriate, as a large proportion of youths have access to this media and modern technology allows for a wide variety of functionalities that would support mental health literacy training. While the participants were mixed in their understanding of mental health literacy and in their confidence in their knowledge of mental health, they consistently agreed that raising a person's mental health awareness would raise their likelihood of seeking professional counseling and support when necessary as well as raise their empathy towards the mentally ill. These results suggest that while young people may be uncomfortable with the terminology and their knowledge about mental health, they still possess a foundational understanding of mental illness and the importance of being educated about it. This awareness bodes well for the popularity and use of a mental health literacy app.

In the discussion of design, fewer consistent themes were found, potentially reflecting a lack of thought in this area. However, two themes emerged as strongly consistent across the focus groups, the desire for precise controls that match the medium the app is being used on and the design philosophy that an app should maintain a core functionality and goal. The former seems to refer to a dislike for apps that are not based on a human-centered design approach and that, consequently, fail to adapt to the capabilities of a technologically savvy but naturally imprecise young adult. The latter seems to voice a dislike for modern apps that attempt to cover too many potential functions, losing their core purpose as a result. Research on young people's use of apps reveals that they prefer to use them for short intervals at a time consecutively throughout the day, a tendency that researchers have suggested lends itself to app designs that are unilateral and streamlined in their goals and functionality [16, 17]. The findings from this study support this claim.

In terms of what participants wished to see in a mental health app, few themes were found to be common. Participants supported the idea of a mental health app that provides short-term relief of mental illness symptoms such as breathing exercises that assist in alleviating anxiety. This theme may be explained by the previously proposed theory that young people use apps in short-time intervals. It is possible that during these short intervals, users want to gain the maximum benefits possible from the app. Immediate symptom relief would be a significant short term benefit and as such should be considered as a feature in any mental health and/or mental health literacy app.

Participants also agreed that an app of this nature should be available on multiple platforms. This suggestion seems to agree with their understanding of the importance of mental health literacy and the potential remedying effect it could have on those afflicted with mental illness. The rationale behind this common support seemed to be that if the app is offered on multiple platforms, more people may have access to it, and, thus, more people would be able to raise their mental health literacy. This finding further speaks both to the understanding that young people have of mental health literacy and the support that a mental health literacy app would likely have.

When discussing what participants would rather not see in an ideal mental health or mental health literacy app, most did not endorse AI. While many emphasized the importance of interpersonal connections when raising mental health literacy, they also stressed the lack of personal connection they often felt when engaging with AI. The participants felt as though AI was not helpful due to technological limitations, suggesting that young adults are not content substituting interpersonal contact with AI. Worth noting is that there did not seem to be an overall negative response among the participants for having a blank set-piece for voicing their thoughts and feelings as when the topic of journaling came up in the focus groups, it was not harshly criticized. It appears mental health AI technologies would have to be improved to provide more tailored responses to make them feel more human-like and helpful before young adults would feel comfortable engaging with them. Should the technology evolve to make this possible, future studies should re-investigate young adults' attitudes toward AI and mental health AI at that point.

Participants also did not support diagnostic mental health apps, insisting that clinicians are necessary for proper diagnosis. A few participants further argued that when clients are diagnosed, they should immediately be directed to appropriate resources, something an app cannot do. These arguments reflect the participants' understanding of mental health as well as support the research in the field.

Privacy proved to be a divisive topic among the participants, with approximately half of the participants exhibiting a laissez-faire attitude towards modern cyber privacy, while the remainder demonstrated their skepticism for apps requesting personal information such as one's thoughts and a desire to maintain their privacy concerning these personal feelings. This response seems to be a reaction to the pervading awareness among the younger generation of the availability of their information to corporations and random individuals the moment it is put online. While some appear to accept this outcome as an inevitability and, thus, do not mind if their personal information is available online, others prefer to keep their personal information private, hoping to maintain control over the information they are not comfortable sharing with others.

4.2 Conclusions

Young people are experiencing a mental health crisis, and they need assistance and resources to handle it. As a large number of young people have access to smartphones, a smartphone app addressing this concern is a potential remedy for this situation. It is apparent that smartphone apps have the technical capacity to deliver the information based on current mental health apps, which, although in the early stages of development, show a good deal of promise. While their effectiveness has been questioned by a several studies, many of the issues can be addressed through improved design and functionality.

This study hypothesized that an underutilized strategy for mental health-based apps was for them to focus on mental health literacy and that such an app would be able to address the mental health crisis among young people. This study suggests that young people do not possess an optimal level of mental health literacy and, as such, could benefit from an app of this kind. Moreover, participants seemed to understand the benefits of mental health literacy, suggesting an app would be supported. Participants also expressed opposition to diagnostic mental health apps, supporting research that suggests that future mental health apps should focus on empowering their users rather than offering diagnoses.

Worth noting was the inconsistency of the participants' opinions on cyber privacy. A follow-up study should focus on the opinions of young adults concerning this issue. Such a study would include a sample size large enough to allow for parametric analyses. These analyses would provide more concrete conclusions about and understanding of young adults' opinions on the important matter.

A more direct follow-up study that could reveal critical results would involve young adults offering feedback on a prototype mental health literacy app. This prototype would ideally include some of the guidelines provided by this study. The participants could be provide quantitative data in the form of surveys measuring their engagement with specific features and design aspects. Alternatively, qualitative data similar to that found in this study could be collected through a review of the app. Both would represent a significant step towards creating an app of this nature.

The findings from this study are ideally meant to be serve as an indicator of the interest young people have in mental health literacy as well as how interested they are in increasing their mental health literacy. They should also be seen as a set of preliminary guidelines on what young people wish to see in a mental health literacy app as well as mental health apps in general. While the generalizability of these results may be limited, future research collecting data through more expedient quantitative methods could address this issue. With future research in this field, a tool for mitigating the mental health crisis among young people could be added to the list of resources available to this demographic.

References

1. Galderisi, S., Heinz, A., Kastrup, M., Beezhold, J., Sartorius, N.: Toward a new definition of mental health. World Psychiatry **14**, 231–233 (2015). https://doi.org/10.1002/wps.20231
2. Merikangas, K.R., et al.: Lifetime prevalence of mental disorders in U.S. adolescents: results from the National Comorbidity Survey Replication– Adolescent Supplement (NCS-A). J. Am. Acad. Child Adolesc. Psychiatry **49**(10), 980–989 (2010)

3. Kitchener, B.A., Jorm, A.F.: Mental health first aid training: review of evaluation studies. Aust. N. Z. J. Psychiatry **40**, 6–8 (2006). https://doi.org/10.1111/j.1440-1614.2006.01735.x
4. Kitchener, B.A., Jorm, A.F.: Mental health first aid training for the public: evaluation of effects on knowledge, attitudes and helping behavior. BMC Psychiatry **2** (2002). https://doi.org/10.1186/1471-244X-2-10
5. Farrer, L., Leach, L., Griffiths, K.M., Christensen, H., Jorm, A.F.: Age differences in mental health literacy. BMC Public Health **8** (2008). https://doi.org/10.1186/1471-2458-8-125
6. Gulliver, A., Griffiths, K.M., Christensen, H.: Perceived barriers and facilitators to mental health help-seeking in young people: a systematic review. BMC Psychiatry **10** (2010). https://doi.org/10.1186/1471-244X-10-113
7. Bapat, S., Jorm, A., Lawrence, K.: Evaluation of a mental health literacy training program for junior sporting clubs. Australas. Psychiatry **17**, 475–479 (2009). https://doi.org/10.1080/10398560902964586
8. Jorm, A.F., Kitchener, B.A., Mugford, S.K.: Experiences in applying skills learned in a mental health first aid training course: a qualitative study of participants' stories. BMC Psychiatry **5**, 43 (2005)
9. Chang, C.: Increasing mental health literacy via narrative advertising. J. Health Commun. **13**, 37–55 (2008). https://doi.org/10.1080/10810730701807027
10. Li, T.M.H., Chau, M., Wong, P.W.C., Lai, E.S.Y., Yip, P.S.F.: Evaluation of a web-based social network electronic game in enhancing mental health literacy for young people. J. Med. Internet Res. **15**, 112–123 (2013). https://doi.org/10.2196/jmir.2316
11. Bakker, D., Kazantzis, N., Rickwood, D., Rickard, N.: Mental health smartphone apps: review and evidence-based recommendations for future developments. JMIR Ment. Health **3** (2016). https://doi.org/10.2196/mental.4984
12. Søgaard Neilsen, A., Wilson, R.L.: Combining e-mental health intervention development with human computer interaction (HCI) design to enhance technology-facilitated recovery for people with depression and/or anxiety conditions: an integrative literature review. Int. J. Ment. Health Nurs. **28**, 22–39 (2018). https://doi.org/10.1111/inm.12527
13. Jorm, A.F., Barney, L.J., Christensen, H., Highet, N.J., Kelly, C.M., Kitchener, B.A.: Research on mental health literacy: what we know and what we still need to know. Aust. N. Z. J. Psychiatry **40**, 3–5 (2006)
14. Van Ameringen, M., Turna, J., Khalesi, Z., Pullia, K., Patterson, B.: There is an app for that! The current state of mobile applications (apps) for DSM-5 obsessive-compulsive disorder, posttraumatic stress disorder, anxiety and mood disorders. Depress. Anxiety **34**, 526–539 (2017). https://doi.org/10.1002/da.22657
15. Gu, J., Strauss, C., Bond, R., Cavanagh, K.: How do mindfulness-based cognitive therapy and mindfulness-based stress reduction improve mental health and wellbeing? A systematic review and meta-analysis of mediation studies. Clin. Psychol. Rev. **37**, 1–12 (2015). https://doi.org/10.1016/j.cpr.2015.01.006
16. Kwasny, M.J., Schueller, S.M., Lattie, E., Gray, E.L., Mohr, D.C.: Exploring the use of multiple mental health apps within a platform: secondary analysis of the intellicare field trial. JMIR Ment. Health. **6** (2019). https://doi.org/10.2196/11572
17. Oulasvirta, A., Tamminen, S., Roto, V., Kuorelahti, J.: Interaction in 4-second bursts: the fragmented nature of attentional resources in mobile HCI. In: Proceedings of the SIGHCI Conference on Human Factors in Computing Systems, pp. 919–928 (2005)

Stress Heatmaps: A Fuzzy-Based Approach that Uses Physiological Signals

Alexandros Liapis[1](✉), Christos Katsanos[2], Nikos Karousos[1], Dimitris Sotiropoulos[3], Michalis Xenos[4], and Theofanis Orphanoudakis[1]

[1] School of Science and Technology, Hellenic Open University, Patras, Greece
{aliapis,karousos,fanis}@eap.gr
[2] Department of Informatics, Aristotle University of Thessaloniki, Thessaloniki, Greece
ckatsanos@csd.auth.gr
[3] Department of Electrical and Computer Engineering, University of Peloponnese, Patras, Greece
dsotiropoulos@uop.gr
[4] Department of Computer Engineering and Informatics, University of Patras, Patras, Greece
xenos@ceid.upatras.gr

Abstract. This paper presents a fuzzy logic model for Real-time Stress Detection (RSD) that allows continuous and in-depth evaluation of user's stress in a straightforward and systematic way by using physiological data. The RSD model takes as input signals' values (galvanic skin response, heart rate) and then generates the corresponding level for user's stress (low, mid-low, mid-high and high). To this end, skin conductance and heart rate signals were used to determine the stress levels classes. Results showed that the proposed tool-based stress detection mechanism can support a systematic evaluation of user's stress in real time. Given that stress is highly subjective and may largely depend both on context and user characteristics, such results are rather encouraging for such a challenging problem. From a UX evaluators' perspective, a preliminary study, involving three HCI experts, investigated the usefulness of the proposed RSD mechanism and revealed that it can substantially decrease time and effort required to make sense of user testing data. Furthermore, practitioners reported that using RSD they could conduct a more in-depth analysis compared to their current practices.

Keywords: User Experience · Usability testing · Physiological signals · Stress detection · Galvanic Skin Response · Heart rate

1 Introduction

Evaluation of User Experience (UX) extends beyond traditional usability approaches [1] and mainly aims at the prevention of frustration and dissatisfaction by focusing on positive emotions [2]. Measuring emotion through physiological signals (e.g. heart rate, respiration, skin conductance) is an approach that is attracting increased interest [3]. Research has shown that physiological signals are associated with emotions and can be used to support UX evaluation [4].

© Springer Nature Switzerland AG 2020
A. Marcus and E. Rosenzweig (Eds.): HCII 2020, LNCS 12202, pp. 268–277, 2020.
https://doi.org/10.1007/978-3-030-49757-6_19

Stress is a state with particular interest for UX evaluation. In [5], stress is described as a rapid increment of arousal levels, accompanied by changes in humans' behavior and physiology for reasons of preserving the integrity of an organism. Although for many people stress is a condition interwoven with a negative experience (distress), it can also be beneficial (eustress) [6]. Studies [7, 8] have shown that interaction with a product or a system that has usability issues can cause stress. Frequent exposure to distress situations can badly affect users' health [9].

Physiological signals have been used in many studies [10–13] as objective and continuous markers of stress. In specific, Electrodermal Activity (EDA), also known as Skin Conductance (SC) or Galvanic Skin Response (GSR), has been shown as a reliable indicator of stress [14]. The most powerful characteristic of a GSR signal is that a stressful stimulus will probably be depicted as a peak. Moreover, peak's height and instantaneous peak rate can reveal a user's stress level [15]. Heart Rate (HR) is also a signal that is highly correlated with stress [12]. Consequently, a combination of the GSR and HR signals appears to be a robust approach for measuring stress [16]. These two signals are used in the proposed fuzzy-based approach for stress detection and visualization.

Measuring of stress through physiological signals has been addressed in our previous work [13] by using traditional supervised machine learning methods such as Discriminant Analysis (DA), Decision Trees (DT) and Support Vector Machine (SVM). These methods entail processes, such as feature extraction and classification, that are successfully applied, in terms of emotions classification accuracies, at post-session time [13]. However, it also important for UX researchers and practitioners to have available a tool-based approach that supports stress detection in real-time.

The motivation for such an approach is that it can be used to support real-time marking of usability issues during the user session, which in turn can substantially reduce the post-session data analysis time. It can be also used to dynamically modify the user testing protocol for the current or subsequent participants based on real-time findings, which is particularly useful in formative UX studies. Such studies typically involve a small number of participants, and thus it is important to try to make every session count. Moreover, real-time stress detection may improve the effectiveness of facilitator's interventions during a Concurrent Thinking Aloud (CTA) session.

Due to recent technological advances, physiological signals can be captured using wristband devices with integrated sensors, such as Empatica or Microsoft Band. In a pioneering work [17], a sophisticated fuzzy logic system for continuously monitoring of emotions was proposed and tested in the context of play technologies. Fuzzy logic models use rules (if/then) to describe the desired system response and are appropriate when someone works with continuous data [18], like physiological signals. However, the potential of this approach for interaction contexts in which emotions (e.g. stress) are more subtle remains unexplored and is investigated in the present paper.

In specific, this paper presents a fuzzy logic approach for Real-time Stress Detection (RSD) that allows continuous and in-depth evaluation of stress in a straightforward and systematic way by using physiological data. The RSD model has been trained to take as input signals' values and then generates the corresponding value for user's stress levels (low, mid-low, mid-high and high). To this end, a physiological dataset including GSR and HR signals was used to determine the stress level classes. The output is presented as a heatmap constructed in real-time. Heatmap visualization is selected because it can support UX evaluators to identify regions of interest during an interaction session at a glance [19].

The rest of the paper is structured as follows. Section 2 presents the physiological dataset, while in Sect. 3, the applied methodology is presented. In Sect. 4, findings are presented. Finally, in Sect. 4, conclusions, limitations of the presented work and directions for future research are elaborated.

2 Database Acquisition

In this study, a dataset of physiological signals from a previously conducted usability evaluation study of the free web based Orthophotos viewing service[1] offered by the Greek National Cadastre and Mapping Agency (NCMA) was used. This web application was selected because a previous heuristic evaluation study, conducted by five experienced HCI experts, showed that it had usability issues related with stress.

The study took place in the facilities of our fully equipped usability lab. In specific, 24 participants (14 males), aged between 18 and 45 (Mean $= 32.3$, SD $= 7.5$) were asked to use the service in order to perform two tasks. None of them had previous experience with the evaluated interface. Every participant completed an appropriate consent form, along with some demographic information.

In the first task, which included two sub-tasks, they were asked to a) locate a well-known bridge in Patras (i.e., the bridge connecting Rio with Antirrio, known as 'Charilaos Trikoupis' bridge) and measure the distance between the first and the fourth pillar of this bridge and b) navigate in Patras old harbor and measure the length of the breakwater. In the second task, which also involved two sub-tasks, participants were asked to a) locate a popular square (i.e., Georgiou Square) in the Patras city center and measure its area and b) to modify the measured area to include some new parts of the square.

The wireless NeXus-10 physiological platform, along with BioTrace+ interface were used to record physiological signals (GSR, HR) with a sampling rate of 32 Hz. Temperature and humidity in the experimental room were continuously monitored in order to avoid any effect on the collected physiological signals. The desktop Tobii-studio recording environment was used to present the interaction scenarios to each participant. However, the collected eye-tracking data are not of interest in this paper and are not discussed hereafter. Further details about the interaction tasks and experimental details can be found in [20, 21].

3 Methodology

This paper employs a fuzzy logic system for real-time stress detection in a user testing context.

In fuzzy logic, the truth value of a variable can be any number between 0 and 1 both inclusive. It is employed to handle the concept of partial truth, where the truth value may range between completely true and completely false. Fuzzy logic is a fruitful approach

---

[1] http://gis.ktimanet.gr/wms/ktbasemap/default.aspx.

in emotion detection because their boundaries may be considered as a more complicated decision than a strict binary choice. In specific, a fuzzy logic system can be described by a set of inputs, outputs, membership functions (MFs), and rules. The MFs are responsible for converting the membership of a specific element into a percentage membership in the set. They analyze each input, define any overlap between inputs, and determine the output. MFs have various shapes with triangular and trapezoidal being the most widely used. MFs can be different for each input and output response.

In the present study, we used the normalized SC and HR signals as input variables to a fuzzy logic model (see Fig. 1).

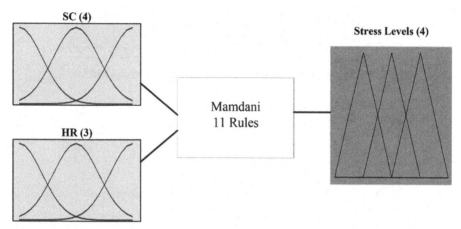

Fig. 1. Modeling stress levels from SC and HR. The proposed system uses 11 rules to transform the 2 inputs into the 4 stress levels (low, mid-low, mid-high, high). Values in parenthesis indicate the number of employed Membership Functions.

3.1 Membership Functions Creation

In order to create the MFs of the input variables, histograms for each signal were first created, an approach also used in [17]. Signals' values distribution supported the creation of the appropriate boundaries for each MF of the input variable.

Figures 2 and 3 present GSR and HR signals recorded in the context of the aforementioned UX evaluation study of a web-based service. It is interesting to visually compare them with GSR and HR data that had been recorded while participants interacted with a video game (Figs. 4 and 5 in [17]). For instance, the mean HR value in our study is 33.65 while in the video game case it is almost doubled. The distributions of values for both signals are also quite different. This shows that the interaction context plays an important role for emotion detection based on physiological signals. However, the creation of a generalizable emotion detection model constitutes a challenging task.

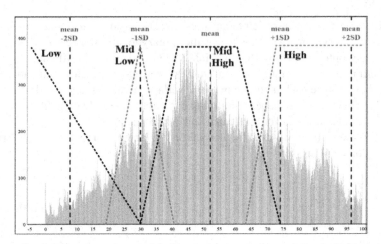

Fig. 2. Histogram of normalized GSR with descriptive statistics and MFs.

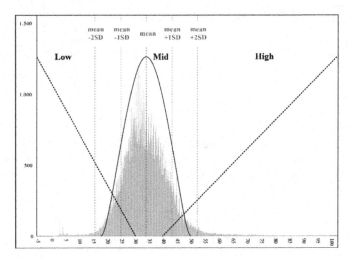

Fig. 3. Histogram of normalized HR with descriptive statistics and MFs.

3.2 Mamdani Rules Creation

Mamdani fuzzy inference was first introduced as a method to create a control system by synthesizing a set of linguistic control rules obtained from experienced human operators [22]. In such a system, the output of each rule is a fuzzy set. Since Mamdani systems have more intuitive and easier to understand rule bases, they are well-suited to expert system applications where the rules are created from human expert knowledge, such as medical diagnostics [23].

In our proposed model, Mamdani if/then rules were used to associate inputs (GSR, HR) with the desired output (four stress levels). For instance, one such rule states that "If

GSR is High and HR is Low then Stress is Mid-High". The proposed model integrates a set of 11 rules proposed by three experts and [17]. These rules are reported in the following:

1. If (GSR is Low) then (Stress is Low)
2. If (GSR is MidLow) then (Stress is MidLow)
3. If (GSR is MidHigh) then (Stress is MidHigh)
4. If (GSR is High) then (Stress is High)
5. If (HR is Low) then (Stress is Low)
6. If (HR is High) then (Stress is High)
7. If (GSR is Low) and (HR is High) then (Stress is MidLow)
8. If (GSR is High) and (HR is Low) then (Stress is MidHigh)
9. If (GSR is High) and (HR is Mid) then (Stress is MidHigh)
10. If (GSR is MidHigh) and (HR is Mid) then (Stress is MidHigh)
11. If (GSR is MidLow) and (HR is Mid) then (Stress is MidLow)

4 Analysis and Findings

After the development of the fuzzy model we proceeded to the evaluation phase. Figure 4 illustrates a GSR signal colored based on the defuzzied value (fuzzy logic output). The specific case shows a participant who starts the experimental session with high stress and as he/she flows in the task reaches the low stress level, and then goes to higher stress levels again. A visual inspection of the graph shows that all high stress instances (red color) occur in the mean + 1SD area, all low stress cases (cyan color) in the mean-1SD area, and the rest mid-level stress cases (yellow and green color) are mostly found in the mean ± 1SD area. Regarding the defuzzification values of the specific participant the stress profile may considered as mid-low (Mean = 2.05, SD = 0.70).

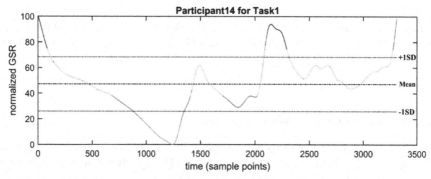

Fig. 4. Stress levels per GSR point for Participant 14 and Task1. **Cyan** (low stress), **green** (mid-low stress), **yellow** (mid-high stress) and **red** (high stress). Dotted lines represent participant's mean, mean + 1SD and mean-1SD values. (Color figure online)

4.1 Heatmap Mechanism

For each participant the fuzzy model was fed with a pair of signals points and returned a crisp value between 1 (low stress) and 4 (high stress) which represent a stress level (see Eq. 1). The model's output for a specific participant is presented as a stress level heatmap (see Fig. 5).

$$StressLevel_{(i)} = HeatMap\big(GSR_{(i)}, HR_{(i)}\big), \; i = 1 \ldots sample\,points \qquad (1)$$

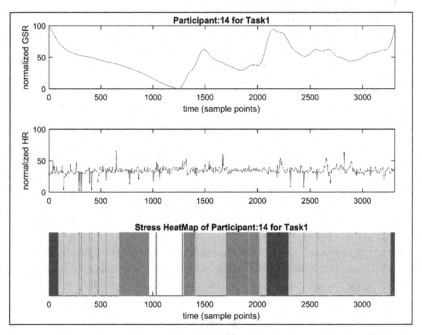

Fig. 5. Stress heatmap for Participant 14 and Task 1. **No color** (low stress), **green** (mid-low stress), **yellow** (mid-high stress) and **red** (high stress). The white area in heatmap is associated with the rule: *If GSR is Low and HR is Mid then Stress is Low.* (Color figure online)

4.2 Preliminary Findings from Practitioners

To evaluate the usefulness of the proposed approach, a dataset of 10 randomly selected participants along with their corresponding GSR and HR signals was selected and given to three UX evaluation experts in order to analyze them using the proposed RSD model.

Evaluators provided a detailed report which summarized their findings. The dominant finding was that RSD can substantially decrease time and effort required to evaluate UX from user testing data. Furthermore, they reported that when using RSD they could conduct a more in-depth UX evaluation compared to their current practice.

5   Limitations and Future Work

This paper presents a Real time Stress Detection (RSD) fuzzy logic model. RSD aims at the detection of stress levels during UX evaluation based on GSR and HR signals. Physiological signals (GSR and HR) of 24 participants were used as input variable to the RSD system. Eleven rules were used to associate inputs variables with four levels of stress (low, mid-low, mid-high, high). A preliminary study involving three HCI experts using the proposed model to analyze user testing sessions found that it can substantially decrease analysis time and effort. Furthermore, it can also support a more in-depth evaluation compared to their current practice.

Future work involves additional studies involving HCI practitioners using the proposed approach and providing feedback on how it performs in various evaluation contexts (e.g. application domains, user characteristics). In addition, we are already working on embedding the RSD model and heatmap visualization in a software entitled PhysiOBS[2] [24]. PhysiOBS is an observation analysis tool that combines physiological measurements, observation and self-reported data to support analysis of UX data. Currently the tool supports only post-study analysis of physiological signals.

Finally, we plan to investigate the alignment of the RSD model values with user's self-reported data for their perceived feeling of being stressed. Our previous studies [25, 26] found regions in the Valence-Arousal rating space that may reliably indicate self-reported stress that is in alignment with one's measured skin conductance while using interactive applications To this end, we will explore whether we can use Valence-Arousal ratings that have been already collected in [20, 21]. These data have been collected in Retrospective Thinking Aloud (RTA) sessions during which participants watched their corresponding interaction session (screen recording) and were asked to report time periods associated with a usability issue and use the Affect Grid [27] to rate their arousal and valence levels.

References

1. Remy, C., et al.: Evaluation beyond usability: validating sustainable HCI research. In: Proceedings of the 2018 CHI Conference on Human Factors in Computing Systems, pp. 216:1–216:14. ACM, New York (2018). https://doi.org/10.1145/3173574.3173790
2. Hassenzahl, M., Tractinsky, N.: User experience - a research agenda. Behav. Inf. Technol. **25**, 91–97 (2006). https://doi.org/10.1080/01449290500330331
3. Jangho, K., Da-Hye, K., Wanjoo, P., Laehyun, K.: A wearable device for emotional recognition using facial expression and physiological response. In: Proceedings of the International Conference of the IEEE Engineering in Medicine and Biology Society (EMBC), pp. 5765–5768 (2016). https://doi.org/10.1109/EMBC.2016.7592037
4. Georges, V., Courtemanche, F., Sénécal, S., Léger, P.-M., Nacke, L., Pourchon, R.: The adoption of physiological measures as an evaluation tool in UX. In: Nah, F.F.-H., Tan, C.-H. (eds.) HCIBGO 2017. LNCS, vol. 10293, pp. 90–98. Springer, Cham (2017). https://doi.org/10.1007/978-3-319-58481-2_8
5. Baum, A.: Stress, intrusive imagery, and chronic distress. Health Psychol. **9**, 653–675 (1990)

---

[2] https://alexliapis.wixsite.com/aliapis/physiobs

6. Le Fevre, M., Matheny, J., Kolt, G.S.: Eustress, distress, and interpretation in occupational stress. J. Manag. Psychol. **18**, 726–744 (2003)
7. Hernandez, J., Paredes, P., Roseway, A., Czerwinski, M.: Under pressure: sensing stress of computer users. In: Proceedings of the SIGCHI Conference on Human Factors in Computing Systems, pp. 51–60. ACM, New York (2014). https://doi.org/10.1145/2556288.2557165
8. Lovallo, W.R.: Stress and Health: Biological and Psychological Interactions. Sage Publications, Thousand Oaks (2015)
9. Pickering, T.G.: Mental stress as a causal factor in the development of hypertension and cardiovascular disease. Curr. Sci. Inc. **3**, 249–254 (2001). https://doi.org/10.1007/s11906-001-0047-1
10. Alberdi, A., Aztiria, A., Basarab, A.: Towards an automatic early stress recognition system for office environments based on multimodal measurements: a review. J. Biomed. Inform. **59**, 49–75 (2016)
11. Baltaci, S., Gokcay, D.: Stress detection in human-computer interaction: fusion of pupil dilation and facial temperature features. Int. J. Hum. Comput. Interact. **32**, 956–966 (2016). https://doi.org/10.1080/10447318.2016.1220069
12. Gjoreski, M., Gjoreski, H., Luštrek, M., Gams, M.: Continuous stress detection using a wrist device: in laboratory and real life. In: Proceedings of the 2016 ACM International Joint Conference on Pervasive and Ubiquitous Computing: Adjunct, pp. 1185–1193. ACM, New York (2016). https://doi.org/10.1145/2968219.2968306
13. Liapis, A., Katsanos, C., Sotiropoulos, D., Xenos, M., Karousos, N.: Recognizing emotions in human computer interaction: studying stress using skin conductance. In: Abascal, J., Barbosa, S., Fetter, M., Gross, T., Palanque, P., Winckler, M. (eds.) INTERACT 2015. LNCS, vol. 9296, pp. 255–262. Springer, Cham (2015). https://doi.org/10.1007/978-3-319-22701-6_18
14. Lunn, D., Harper, S.: Using galvanic skin response measures to identify areas of frustration for older web 2.0 users. In: Proceedings of the 2010 International Cross Disciplinary Conference on Web Accessibility (W4A), pp. 34:1–34:10. ACM, New York (2010). https://doi.org/10.1145/1805986.1806032
15. Setz, C., Arnrich, B., Schumm, J., Marca, R.L., Tröster, G., Ehlert, U.: Discriminating stress from cognitive load using a wearable EDA device. IEEE Trans. Inf. Technol. Biomed. **14**, 410–417 (2010). https://doi.org/10.1109/TITB.2009.2036164
16. de Santos Sierra, A., Ávila, C.S., Casanova, J.G., del Pozo, G.B.: A stress-detection system based on physiological signals and fuzzy logic. IEEE Trans. Ind. Electron. **58**, 4857–4865 (2011)
17. Mandryk, R.L., Atkins, M.S.: A fuzzy physiological approach for continuously modeling emotion during interaction with play technologies. Int. J. Hum Comput Stud. **65**, 329–347 (2007). https://doi.org/10.1016/j.ijhcs.2006.11.011
18. Cox, E.: Fuzzy fundamentals. IEEE Spectr. **29**, 58–61 (1992). https://doi.org/10.1109/6.158640
19. Courtemanche, F., Léger, P.-M., Dufresne, A., Fredette, M., Labonté-LeMoyne, É., Sénécal, S.: Physiological heatmaps: a tool for visualizing users' emotional reactions. Multimedia Tools Appl. **77**, 11547–11574 (2018). https://doi.org/10.1007/s11042-017-5091-1
20. Liapis, A., Katsanos, C., Karousos, N., Xenos, M., Orphanoudakis, T.: UDSP+: stress detection based on user-reported emotional ratings and wearable skin conductance sensor. In: Adjunct Proceedings of the 2019 ACM International Joint Conference on Pervasive and Ubiquitous Computing and Proceedings of the 2019 ACM International Symposium on Wearable Computers, pp. 125–128. ACM, New York (2019). https://doi.org/10.1145/3341162.3343831

21. Liapis, A., Katsanos, C., Xenos, M., Orphanoudakis, T.: Effect of personality traits on UX evaluation metrics: a study on usability issues, valence-arousal and skin conductance. In: Extended Abstracts of the 2019 CHI Conference on Human Factors in Computing Systems. pp. LBW2721:1–LBW2721:6. ACM, New York (2019). https://doi.org/10.1145/3290607.3312995
22. Mamdani, E.H., Assilian, S.: An experiment in linguistic synthesis with a fuzzy logic controller. In: Readings in Fuzzy Sets for Intelligent Systems, pp. 283–289. Elsevier (1993)
23. Mamdani and Sugeno Fuzzy Inference Systems - MATLAB & Simulink. https://www.mathworks.com/help/fuzzy/types-of-fuzzy-inference-systems.html. Accessed 03 Feb 2020
24. Liapis, A., Karousos, N., Katsanos, C., Xenos, M.: Evaluating user's emotional experience in HCI: the PhysiOBS approach. In: Kurosu, M. (ed.) HCI 2014. LNCS, vol. 8511, pp. 758–767. Springer, Cham (2014). https://doi.org/10.1007/978-3-319-07230-2_72
25. Liapis, A., Katsanos, C., Sotiropoulos, D.G., Karousos, N., Xenos, M.: Stress in interactive applications: analysis of the valence-arousal space based on physiological signals and self-reported data. Multimed Tools Appl. **76**, 5051–5071 (2017). https://doi.org/10.1007/s11042-016-3637-2
26. Liapis, A., Katsanos, C., Sotiropoulos, D., Xenos, M., Karousos, N.: Subjective assessment of stress in HCI: a study of the valence-arousal scale using skin conductance. In: Proceedings of the 11th Biannual Conference on Italian SIGCHI Chapter, pp. 174–177. ACM, New York (2015). https://doi.org/10.1145/2808435.2808450
27. Russell, J.A., Weiss, A., Mendelsohn, G.A.: Affect grid: a single-item scale of pleasure and arousal. J. Pers. Soc. Psychol. **57**, 493–502 (1989). https://doi.org/10.1037/0022-3514.57.3.493

Exploring Experience Activity Potential for Art Therapy to High School Students in International School, Guangzhou, China

Zhen Liu[1] (iD) and Meihan Liu[2](✉)

[1] School of Design, South China University of Technology, Guangzhou 510006, People's Republic of China
[2] Guangdong Country Garden School, Foshan, People's Republic of China
1713833630@qq.com

Abstract. Although the development of various technological products increases people's methods to approach diverse art forms, they also bring many distractions and addictions to recent people, especially to those young people who don't have much self-control ability. Those attractions causes students prefer to spend all weekend in virtual world, rather than participate in art exhibitions and museums, leading to lack of art appreciation ability and self-perception. This a worldwide issue, but few people have conducted such discussions both in theory and in practice. Therefore, a survey which aims to reveal the recent high school students real situation on artistic influence and a subsequent activity which hopes to improve those students' most serve problem revealed by the previous survey are prepared to conduct in an emerging group of Chinese high school students: international school students. Then those students who received further treatment on art will be retested on their art appreciation ability. The result will not only give a direction for more high school in China to improve their artistic influence education, but also highlight and reveal that serve issue to more people and schools. The survey by questionnaires reveals that high school students in Guangdong Country Garden international school lack artistic influence extremely. They completely don't have habit of paying attention to opera performance and visit the art exhibitions only a few times a year. This kind of usual practices leads to deficiency on cognitive power, perception ability and kinesthetic capability. In the survey, most students could describe their feelings to some concrete art works, but they could not describe their feelings on a film or an abstract painting successfully, which means they cannot perceive their own subtle emotional changes. Therefore, those students most severe problem is on their perception capability.

Keywords: Experience activity · Art therapy · Questionnaire · High school student · International school

1 Introduction

Although the development of various technological products increases people's methods to approach diverse art forms, they also bring many dis-tractions and addictions to recent

A. Marcus and E. Rosenzweig (Eds.): HCII 2020, LNCS 12202, pp. 278–293, 2020.
https://doi.org/10.1007/978-3-030-49757-6_20

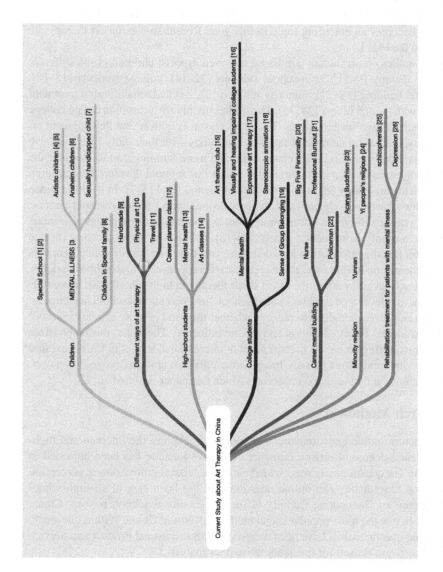

Fig. 1. The current study about Art Therapy in China (devised by the authors based on the literature).

people, especially to those young people who don't have much self-control ability. Those attractions causes students prefer to spend all weekend in virtual world, rather than participate in art exhibitions and museums, leading to lack of art appreciation ability and self-perception. This a worldwide issue, but few people have conducted such discussions both in theory and in practice.

Followed the development of economy and education in China, the exploration on art therapy becomes an emerging topic in this year. Recent studies on art therapy are illustrated in the Fig. 1.

Recent studies on art therapy are based on seven aspects: children [1–8], different ways of art therapy [9–11], high-school students [12–14], college students [15–18], career mental building [19–21], minority religion [22, 23] and rehabilitation treatment for patients with mental illness [24, 25]. The studies mainly focus in children and college students among above seven aspects. The main reason is with recent development on living quality, increasing number of families can satisfy with their daily lives and have enough finance for schooling. Therefore, more and more families start to consider the quality of education of their children, which seems that it could develop their children more complete personality [8] and own healthier mental level [3–7]. In addition, since college students have more chances and ability to do the survey for their own and exercise their essay writing ability, the information about art therapy in university is also intact and various, not only from mental aspect [15–18], but also for some physical disable students [16]. But the information between those two time periods for young people is scarce and there is no information about recent art therapy level of high school students, although there is an essay about the effect of art therapy in high school [13]. Moreover, as a recent newly developed popular kind of school, the international school in China, no information and survey are done to observe whether this kind of more expensive school could give students' better education and artistic influence. Therefore, this emphasizes the need for exploring recent art therapy level in international school in China and find out whether this kind of art therapy has positive effect on students' cognitive power, perception ability and kinesthetic capability, which this paper is aimed at.

2   Research Method

A semi-structure online questionnaire was adopted to explore the international high-school students' degree of artistic influence. The questionnaire has been uploaded to www.wjx.cn. The questionnaire was divided into three parts: cognitive power, perception question, and kinesthetic. The online questionnaire has been sent to all high-school students groups of Guangdong Country Garden international school, Foshan, China, via WeChat that is the most popular social media platform in China. Within one week, 34 completed questionnaires have been received. SPSS (Statistical Product and Service Solutions) software is used for the quantitative data analysis.

3   Research Result

3.1   Basic Background of Responding Students

Gender and Grade. As shown in Fig. 2, 34 questionnaire respondents are 18 boys and 16 girls, most of them are from Grade 10 (10.59%) and Grade 11 (32.35%) (Fig. 3).

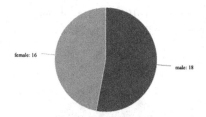

Fig. 2. The gender of respondents (responding students' view).

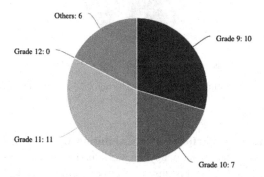

Fig. 3. The grade of respondents (responding students' view).

The Frequency Students Watch Movie a Year. The questionnaire respondents were asked to select their frequency of watching movies in a year. The results from Fig. 4 show that nearly half of (15) responding students watch movies more than 5 times in a year. Interestingly, there is no one selected 0 times. However, more than one third of (10) responding students reported that they view movies only 1–3 times a year.

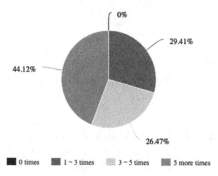

Fig. 4. The frequency students watch movie a year (responding students' view).

The Habit of Noticing New Opera Performance. The questionnaire respondents were asked to select their habit of noticing new opera performance. The results are shown in Fig. 5, which suggests that overwhelming (22) more than half responding students never notice new opera performance. Even (10) a quarter of students response they will notice sometimes, but just two students will always notice opera performance.

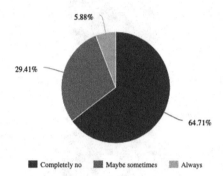

Fig. 5. The habit of noticing new opera performance (responding students' view).

The Frequency Students Participate in Exhibition in a Year. The questionnaire respondents were asked their frequency of participating in exhibition of a year. As shown in Fig. 6, the result is astonishing that about seven-eighths of (85%) responding students only participate in exhibition for 0–3 times in a year.

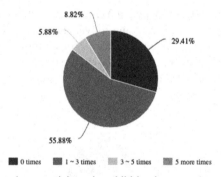

Fig. 6. The frequency students participate in exhibition in a year (responding students' view).

Students' Feeling about a Movie They Watched. The questionnaire respondents were asked to provide qualitative views of a movie they have been watching, as shown in Fig. 7. 34 of the responding students provided their feeling. As shown in Table 1, the result is unexpected, although more than half students view movies more than five times a year, their perception and analysis ability on movie are still primary. More than half students (64.70%) have no deeper feeling after watching the movie that their responds are all about "no any feeling" or "happy". But others students still can talk about some of them feelings about the film (35.28%), and half of the students in those students could give insightful and exciting analysis about the film.

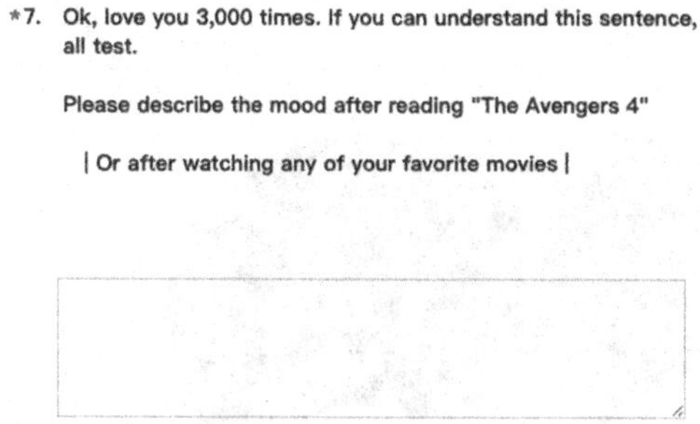

*7. Ok, love you 3,000 times. If you can understand this sentence, then we will officially start the sm
all test.

Please describe the mood after reading "The Avengers 4"

| Or after watching any of your favorite movies |

Fig. 7. The question about respondents' views on a movie they have been watching.

Table 1. Responding students' degree of feeling about a film with examples.

Degree of felling	Number of students	Percentage of students	Example
Unable to describe their own feelings	22	64.70%	Very happy, look good
Can describe some of their own feelings	6	17.64%	Excited + pity + joy? A bit difficult to describe, more complicated
Can describe their own feelings very specifically	6	17.64%	As for the end of a series, the feeling of the Avengers 4 is general. The rhythm is a bit of a hurry. The soundtrack is very suitable for the theme. The end of the fight is always a little mechanically fascinating, but the final emotional part is quite good, which can make the Marvel powder have a sense of substitution

Those above five questions embody that although many students have habit of watching movies, they artistic analysis ability has not been improved and they basically are lack of artistic influence on exhibition and opera.

3.2 Cognitive Power

Students' Cognitive Power on Identifying Picture. The questionnaire respondents were asked to select how many animals they can identify with this picture, as shown in Fig. 8. The results from Fig. 9 show that half of (50%) responding students reported that they can identify more than 8 species. Nearly half of (41.18%) the students saw 5–8 species. Few (8.82%) students stated that they just notice 1–5 species.

Students' Cognitive Power on Identify Scene in a Painting. The questionnaire respondents were asked to provide qualitative understanding for a painting that is 'Mädchen vor einem Spiegel - Girl Before a Mirror' by Pablo Picasso. 34 of the responding

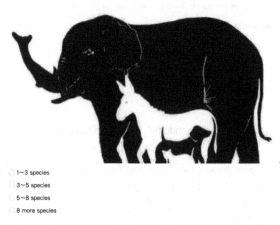

Fig. 8. The question about respondents' cognitive power on identifying picture.

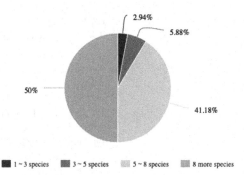

Fig. 9. The frequency students' ability on identify animals in the picture (responding students' view).

students provided their understanding. As shown in Table 2, the result is optimistic that nearly half of the students (47.05%) can give some basic understanding of the painting, especially some description of the scene by themselves. A quarter of students (23.52%) could give specific analysis about the painting, which includes their own feeling about the painting and the scene they imagine. But, the other quarter of the students (29.41%) still cannot describe the scene that they even give up on guessing the scene and imagine.

Students' Cognitive Power on Identifying Figures. The questionnaire respondents were asked to select what figures they can identify with this picture, as shown in Fig. 10. The results from Fig. 11 show that four-thirds of (73.53%) responding students reported that they can identify a cube which represent that basically all students can successfully identify the figure in the picture.

Those three questions above reflect that international high-school students' cognitive ability is good and expected.

Table 2. Responding students' degree of describing about a painting with examples.

Degree of describing	Number of students	Percentage of students	Example
Unable to describe the scene	10	29.41%	I don't understand
Can describe unclear scene	16	47.05%	Mother holding baby
Can describe the scene very specifically	8	23.52%	The image of two women, the feeling on the right is reflected by the mirror while the woman on the left is deep, holding the mirror and seems to be thinking

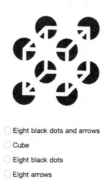

*10. What do you see at first glance in the picture below?

○ Eight black dots and arrows
○ Cube
○ Eight black dots
○ Eight arrows

Fig. 10. The question about respondents' cognitive power on identifying figures.

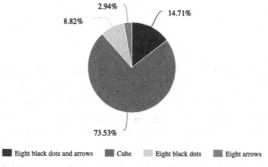

2.94%   14.71%
8.82%

73.53%

■ Eight black dots and arrows   ■ Cube   ▨ Eight black dots   ▨ Eight arrows

Fig. 11. The frequency students' ability on identify figure in the picture (responding students' view).

3.3 Perception Question

Students' Perception Power on Identifying Concrete Painting. The questionnaire respondents were asked to provide qualitative analysis for a painting that is 'Vain Courtship' by Sir Lawrence Alma-Tadema. 34 of the responding students provided their analysis. As shown in Table 3, the result is acceptable that nearly half of the students (44.11%) can give some basic understanding of the painting, especially some description of the scene by themselves and the feeling the painting gave them. More than a quarter of students (32.35%) could give specific analysis about the painting, which includes their own feeling about the painting and the scene and the emotion of characters they imagine about this oil painting. But, the other quarter of the students (23.52%) still cannot describe the scene that they just give some appraise about the color the painter used with no feeling of their emotional change when viewing this painting.

Table 3. Responding students' degree of felling about a painting with examples.

Degree of felling	Number of students	Percentage of students	Example
Unable to describe their own feelings or scene	8	23.52%	Nice, colorful, no feeling
Can describe some of their own feelings or scene	15	44.11%	Bright and comfortable, full of hope and beauty
Can describe their own feelings or scene very specifically	11	32.35%	It seems that a couple is admiring the scenery outside, but they are more like two strangers as they are not very close. The woman seems to look at the scenery again while the man is really admiring the beauty of the girl

Students' Perception Power on Identifying Less Concrete Painting. The questionnaire respondents were asked to provide qualitative analysis for a less concrete painting that is 'The Scream (Skrik)' by Edvard Munch very famous around the world. 34 of the responding students provided their analysis. As shown in Table 4, the result is unexpected that although this painting is very famous, nearly three quarters of the students (70.58%) cannot give some basic understanding of the painting, just use some very blur words to appraise the color of this drawing. Some students (17.64%) that own some basic knowledge could give specific analysis about the painting, which includes their own feeling about the painting and the scene and the emotion of characters they imagine about this oil painting. But, the other quarter of the students (23.52%) still cannot describe the scene that they just give some appraise about the color the painter used with no feeling of their emotional change when viewing this painting.

Table 4. Responding students' degree of felling about a less concrete painting with examples.

Degree of felling	Number of students	Percentage of students	Example
Unable to describe their own feelings or scene	24	70.58%	The sky is beautiful
Can describe some of their own feelings or scene	6	17.64%	Heavy, depressed, panic
Can describe their own feelings or scene very specifically	4	11.76%	Slightly depressed, slightly felt short-term worry, feeling duller

Students' Perception Power on Identifying Abstract Painting. The questionnaire respondents were asked to provide qualitative analysis for a very abstract painting that is 'Dominant Violet' oil and sand on canvas' by Wassily Kandinsky. 34 of the responding students provided their analysis. As shown in Table 5, nearly four-fifths (82.35%) cannot give any basic understanding of the painting that they just give up the chance of guessing the meaning of the drawing without any description. Only three students (8.82%) could give some guessing about the information the painting want to express. And also only three students (8.82%) describe correct theme of this drawing.

Table 5. Responding students' degree of felling about an abstract painting with examples.

Degree of felling	Number of students	Percentage of students	Example
Unable to understand the meaning	28	82.35%	I don't understand
Can describe some of their understand	3	8.82%	World Peace? (There are many flags and the colors are mild)
Can describe the major idea that the painter want to express	3	8.82%	Childlike fun

The analysis about above three questions shows that even international high-school students in China have acceptable ability on understanding and imagine concrete painting. Their perceptive capability on analysis abstract artworks is still very weak and their artistic knowledge is still extremely scarce.

3.4 Kinesthetic

Students' Kinesthetic Ability on Observing and Mimicking motion. The questionnaire respondents were asked to have a pair evaluation about the motion they imitated, which is a dance as shown in Fig. 12. The results from Fig. 13 show that one-third of (32.35%) responding students reported that they cannot imitate that dance due to lack of body coordinate ability. But the other two-third (67.65%) of students all received they peers' appraise that they can imitate exactly the same or even better.

*14. Please imitate the classic movement of our most handsome Kun Kun.

You can choose to show to the whole class, your friends look or look in the mirror

(Next, please rate your partner or yourself)

○ just singing, playing basketball, without dancing
○ God, there is potential for center debut.
○ Exactly imitating
○ Wow, I am handsomer than Kun Kun.
○ I have better adjectives _____ *

Fig. 12. The question about respondents' views on a pair evaluation for the motion they imitated.

Students' Kinesthetic Ability on Mimicking a Scene. The questionnaire respondents were asked to have a pair evaluation about a scene of a famous TV series they will imitate, as shown in Fig. 14. The results from Fig. 15 show that a quarter of (32.35%) responding students reported that their peer give positive feedback on their imitation. But the other nearly half (47.06%) of students all received they peers' laugh that they all cannot control their emotion and facial expression. This result is expected, since those students didn't received professional exercise before.

Students' Kinesthetic Ability on Expressing a Word by Body Language. As shown in Fig. 16, the questionnaire respondents were asked to have a game with their pair that they need to express a word from above list to their peer without any word, but just by their body language. The results from Fig. 17 show that more than a quarter of (32.35%) responding students reported that they successfully describe the word to their teammate precisely that their teammate guess correctly immediately. The other more

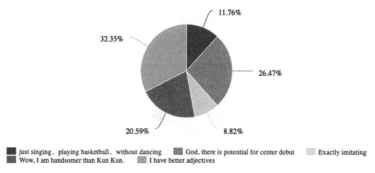

just singing，playing basketball，without dancing ■ God, there is potential for center debut ▨ Exactly imitating
■ Wow, I am handsomer than Kun Kun. ▨ I have better adjectives

Fig. 13. The frequency students' ability on imitation about a motion from a video (responding students' view).

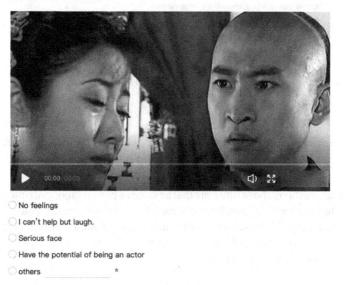

*15. Please perform the following episodes with deep affection and score:

Ziwei said with tears and said: "She said that you look at the snow together to see the stars and see the moon, from poetry and songs to the philosophy of life... I have not seen the snow with you, watching the stars, watching the moon, talking about life from poetry and songs. philosophy."

Erkang: "It's all my fault. I shouldn't watch snow with her, watch the stars, watch the moon, talk about life philosophy from poetry and songs... I promise you will only watch snow with you and see the moon in the future. From the poetry song to the philosophy of life..." (Part 2 Episode 10) | 16 seconds to 52 seconds |

○ No feelings

○ I can't help but laugh.

○ Serious face

○ Have the potential of being an actor

○ others   *

Fig. 14. The question about respondents' views on a pair evaluation for a scene of a famous TV series they will imitate.

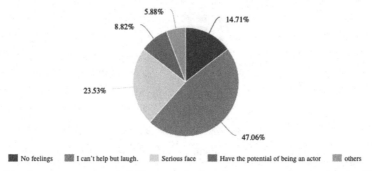

Fig. 15. The frequency students' ability on imitation about a scene from a famous TV series (responding students' view).

than a quarter (32.35%) of students consider their expression is precisely, but their peer cannot understand their expression which means their description by body language is not precise. Many other students are fall on this game that they cannot express a word by their body language. This result is expected.

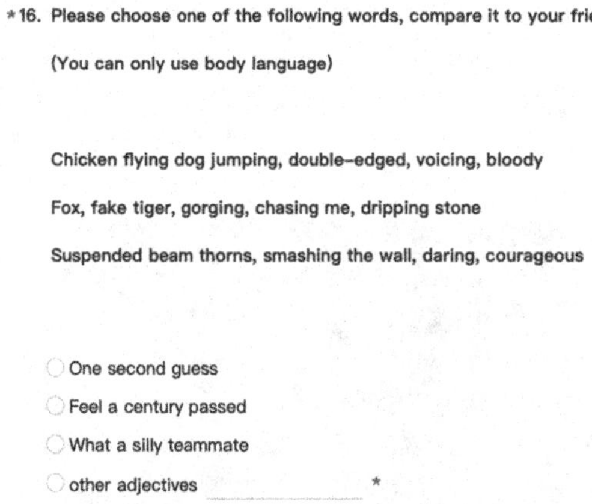

＊16. Please choose one of the following words, compare it to your friends, and let them guess.

(You can only use body language)

Chicken flying dog jumping, double-edged, voicing, bloody

Fox, fake tiger, gorging, chasing me, dripping stone

Suspended beam thorns, smashing the wall, daring, courageous

○ One second guess
○ Feel a century passed
○ What a silly teammate
○ other adjectives _____ ＊

Fig. 16. The question about respondents' kinesthetic ability on expressing a word by body language.

Those three questions above illustrate that as same as expectation, since most Chinese international high-school students have not received exercise on their body expression and kinesthetic during childhoods, only half of them own capability on mimicking motion and only one-third students could mimicking scene with lines. Those statistics point out that those students' kinesthetic ability still need to improve.

4 Discussion and Conclusion

Based on the results of the research, currently in China international high school, the intensity of artistic influence and art class is extremely insufficient that students even

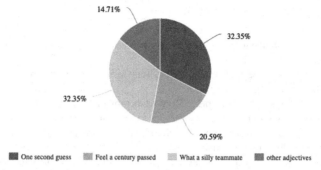

14.71%

32.35%

32.35%

20.59%

■ One second guess   ▥ Feel a century passed   ▦ What a silly teammate   ■ other adjectives

Fig. 17. The frequency students' ability on expression by body language on a word (responding students' view).

cannot distinguish the famous artwork "The Scream" and give some interpretations based on its name. This disability on catching the feeling of themselves when they view a painting leads them cannot analysis a painting deeply and connect the intention of the artist when drawing this painting with their own feelings. The lack of exercises in this aspect in art classes of students in China international high school is obvious, which result in lack of perceptive power for most students. Moreover, although the financial capabilities of those international high school students' families are superior, their families still not provide many artistic influences on them that the reason they don't have habit of viewing opera and exhibition is they parents also didn't pay much attention on artistic influence on their children. Therefore, the international high school should provide more chances for those students contact with other forms of art except from movies that it can organize more tour to museums and galleries. In addition, exercises in kinesthetic ability are scarcer. The reason is Chinese parents didn't pay much attention on the development on their children physical coordination and the society also all consider that acting is limited to actors. The most people ignore the significance of mimicking and the ability to express by body language. Therefore, most students will feel fear when they are asked to act and show limb incoordination when doing body language. This indicates that the international school should encourage students to act and establish more interesting clubs and lessons on acting. Besides those two aspects which students basically lack, the cognitive power of most students is expected, but it still can be improved until all students have the ability to distinguish the figures of a picture. Hence, based on the result of the study, the level of art therapy in international high schools in China is obviously insufficient that students still have difficulty on catching their own emotional change and physical coordination. And those high schools could mainly focus on developing their artistic influence and their acting ability to achieve the effect of art therapy which could bring significant positive effect on those student's personality and ability as shown in other related studies [14].

Acknowledgements. The authors wish to thank all the people who had provided their time and efforts for the study. This research is supported by "South China University of Technology Central University Basic Scientific Research Operating Expenses Subsidy (project approval no. XYZD201928)".

References

1. Liu, Q., Dong, X.: On the inspiration of art therapy to art courses in special schools. J. Leshan Norm. Univ. **3**, 133–137 (2015). (in Chinese)
2. Li, M.: An analysis of the application of art therapy in art teaching for special children. Pop. Art Acad. Ed. (2014). (in Chinese)
3. Yan, H., Chen, J.: The application prospect of art therapy in the treatment of children's mental problems. Chin. J. Child Health **05**, 50–52 (2015). (in Chinese)
4. Ma, C.: Analysis and research on intervention cases of art therapy for preschool autistic children. Master dissertation, China Academy of Fine Arts, Hangzhou (2016). (in Chinese)
5. Liang, Y.: Multi-factor investigation and analysis of autistic children and intervention analysis of painting art therapy. Art Technol. **1**, 9–10 (2016). (in Chinese)
6. Ba, J.: Discussion on children's art therapy from Arnheim's children's visual development concept. Ment. Health Educ. Prim. Second. Sch. **374**(27), 6–8 (2018). (in Chinese)
7. Li, T.: A review of the effects of art therapy on interpersonal relationships in children with developmental disorders. J. Suihua Univ. **4**, 148–151 (2015). (in Chinese)
8. Dong, X., Liu, X.: Analysis on the application of painting art therapy in special family parent education. Sci. Technol. Inf. **15**(25), 159–163 (2017). (in Chinese)
9. Wu, P.: From the perspective of psychology, the art therapy effect of manual creation is discussed. Mass Lit. Art (17) (2018). (in Chinese)
10. Li, X., Guo, T., Gao, Y., Zhu, S.: Effect of body art therapy on rehabilitation of patients with mental illness. Contemp. Chin. Med. **26**(4), 106–108 (2019). (in Chinese)
11. Zhu, P., Rao, Y.: To explore the practice research of garden tour as art therapy activity. Chin. Nation Expo (2) (2017). (in Chinese)
12. Li, J., Wu, X.: Application of expressive art therapy in high school career planning classroom teaching. Ment. Health Educ. Prim. Second. Sch. **387**(4), 22–24 (2019). (in Chinese)
13. Sun, L.: Study on the positive effect of art therapy on mental health education in colleges and universities. Eval. Art **15**, 143–144 (2017). (in Chinese)
14. Shi, L.: Some suggestions on how to integrate the concept of art therapy into high school art teaching. Art Educ. Res. **5**, 143 (2015). (in Chinese)
15. Zhao, M.: The role of art therapy community in psychological depression counseling of college students. Art Technol. (3) (2017). (in Chinese)
16. Hou, Q.: A study on the construction strategy of positive psychological field in art therapy for hearing impaired college students. J. Huaibei Norm. Univ. Philos. Soc. Sci. (2017). (in Chinese)
17. Weng, J.: The influence of expressive art therapy on college students' sense of belonging. J. Fujian Med. Univ. (Soc. Sci. Ed.) **20**(1), 37–43 (2019). (in Chinese)
18. Li, X.: Research on the application of three-dimensional animation art therapy in psychological counseling of college students. Master dissertation. Xi'an University of Technology, Xi'an (2018). (in Chinese)
19. Wang, X., Du, J, Liu, J., Xing, Y., Xi, X.: The effect of group expressive art therapy on nurses' personality. Chin. J. Health Psychol. (1), 7 (2017). (in Chinese)
20. Wang, X., Zong, C., Man, Z., Du, J., Liu, J.: Application of group expressive art therapy to the intervention effect of nurses' job burnout. Chin. J. Health Psychol. (8) (2017). (in Chinese)
21. Wang, X.: Application of art therapy in police mental health counseling. Cult. Issue **36**, 121–123 (2015). (in Chinese)
22. Li, S.: The ancient Yunnan Ahali teaches the charm art and the supersensory art therapy). J. Guangxi Norm. Univ. Natl. **4**, 33–35 (2015). (in Chinese)
23. Li, S.: The classic cases and general principles of Yi religious art therapy in Yunnan. J. Henan Inst. Educ. (Philos. Soc. Sci. Ed.) **6**, 19–23 (2017). (in Chinese)

24. Cao, Y., Lu, J.: The application of diversified art therapy in the rehabilitation of schizophrenic patients. Qilu Nurs. J. **22**(9), 12–14 (2016). (in Chinese)
25. Liao, S., Yao, W., Zhu, Q., Xie, Y.: The effect of painting art on post-schizophrenic depression. Chin. J. Health Psychol. **1**, 34–36 (2015). (in Chinese)

The Development of a Point of Care Clinical Guidelines Mobile Application Following a User-Centred Design Approach

James Mitchell[1]([✉]) [ID], Ed de Quincey[1] [ID], Charles Pantin[1], and Naveed Mustfa[2]

[1] Keele University, Staffordshire, UK
j.a.mitchell@keele.ac.uk
[2] Royal Stoke University Hospital, University Hospital North Midlands NHS Trust,
Stoke-on-Trent, UK

Abstract. This paper describes the development of a point of care clinical guidelines mobile application. A user-centred design approach was utilised to inform the design of a smartphone application, this included: Observations; a survey; focus groups and an analysis of popular apps utilised by clinicians in a UK NHS Trust. Usability testing was conducted to inform iterations of the application, which presents clinicians with a variety of integrated tools to aid in decision making and information retrieval.

The study found that clinicians use a mixture of technology to retrieve information, which is often inefficient or has poor usability. It also shows that smartphone application development for use in UK hospitals needs to consider the variety of users and their clinical knowledge and work pattern. This study highlights the need for applying user-centred design methods in the design of information presented to clinicians and the need for clinical information delivery that is efficient and easy to use at the bedside.

Keywords: Clinical guidelines · User-centred design · Mobile applications

1 Introduction

Since its inception, Smartphone use has increased exponentially [1] and following the launch of the iPhone in 2007 [2] and the App Store in 2008 [3] mobile application usage has seen dramatic growth [4]. The iOS App Store recently surpassed one billion downloads with more than two million Apps available [5]. Due to the growth in use, smartphones and mobile applications have become increasingly necessary tools for both clinical practice and education [6, 7]. Examples include the use of innovative digital delivery methods of delivery for Clinical Guidelines; Clinical Decision Support, and Calculations tools [6–8].

Some research has suggested that there are potentially negative aspects to smartphone use in clinical settings, most notably relating to patient perception [9] and accuracy of information [10]. However, it is generally accepted that smartphone use to enhance clinical care and healthcare practice is largely positive [6–8] with numerous studies

© Springer Nature Switzerland AG 2020
A. Marcus and E. Rosenzweig (Eds.): HCII 2020, LNCS 12202, pp. 294–313, 2020.
https://doi.org/10.1007/978-3-030-49757-6_21

providing evidence of the positive impact these devices and their applications have on reducing medical errors [11] improving learning [9] and creating a more efficient process for patients [12, 13].

In a clinical setting, relevant and accurate information is critical, it must be easy and convenient to access, benefiting both clinical practice, and clinical education [6–8]. This is especially true for information such as clinical guidelines [14] which are used to support clinicians in making decisions on how to diagnose, treat and care for patients. There is therefore clear potential for research combining methods for the design and development of medical applications and the delivery of medical guidelines.

1.1 Background/Problem Statement

Clinical guidelines are provided to all UK hospitals [14]. Some UK hospitals develop trust level guidelines to deliver more specific and concise information [15]. They are often bespoke, authored by clinical teams 'in house' to support patient care.

Local point of care clinical guidelines are generally available as basic web pages, PDFs or documents [14, 15]. Despite widespread availability and use, accessing clinical guidelines and information can be highly inefficient and restrictive [16, 17]. Clinicians require agile access to clinical guidelines and an efficient delivery method.

At present, there are no 'standards' (clear methods, designs, or recommendations) relating to clinical guidelines for use on mobile devices. Previous studies have investigated the delivery of clinical guidelines on mobile devices, but rarely implement well known heuristics for design [18–20] and often fail to involve users in each aspect of the design and development process, leading to poor usability. Common issues include focussing on navigational design (likely due to the complexity of the information) while continuing to present the guidelines to users in the original format – not optimised for mobile devices (intended for books or larger screens) or limited formats were the information is significantly reduced [21–23].

The research described in this paper, therefore, aimed to investigate and develop efficient methods for presenting and authoring clinical guidelines for use on mobile devices. This has been achieved via following a user-centred design (UCD) approach [24, 25]. UCD has been proven to provide positive outcomes when developing software [21, 24]. By producing clinical guidelines specifically developed for mobile devices, we hope to address many of the issues related to efficiency and ease of access, creating a more usable app.

2 Study Design

The 'Bedside Clinical Guidelines (BCGs)' have supported care at the bedside since 1996 and are currently utilised across 14 NHS Trusts throughout the UK, and aim to provide "consistent, evidence-based management of patients in acute hospital settings" [15] for 'in the moment' bedside use. The 142 guidelines give information on issues faced daily on the ward with breadth from consent to cardiovascular disease, from venous thrombolism to verification of death. Each guideline has a depth from drug dosage through contacting radiology to discharge policy. They are reviewed annually. The BCGs are currently available as an eBook (a pdf of the print edition) on each participating NHS Trust Intranet [15].

Table 1. Summary of methodology and durations for the software development lifecycle

	Study stage	Methodology	Purpose	Participants	Duration
1	Initial ideation	Research group meetings and observations	Develop initial ideas	4	1 Month
2	Requirements	Research group meetings, observations, survey	Identify functional requirements	20	3 Months
3	Development 1	App development	Initial prototype based on findings	4	3 Months
4	Usability testing	Heuristic evaluation	Evaluation on basic usability	1	2 Weeks
5	Development 2	App development	Further development of the prototype to address heuristic evaluation	4	3 Months
6	Focus group 1	Focus groups	User feedback and further requirements elicitation	21	1 Day
7	Development 3	App development	Further development of the prototype to address focus group 1	4	2 Months
8	SUS	Usability study	To gather feedback from users	~11	1 Day
9	Focus group 2	Focus groups	User feedback and further requirements elicitation	17	1 Day
10	Development 4	App development	Further development of the prototype to address focus group 2	4	3 Months (Ongoing)
11	SUS	Usability study	To gather feedback from users	11+	1 Day
12	Usability testing	Think aloud	User evaluation	~30	2–3 Months
13	Field test	On site field testing	To gather use data and user feedback	~10	~2 week
14	Pilot test	Live pilot testing with patients	To gather use data and user feedback	~30	~3 Months

Each stage of the study uses aspects from UCD methodology [24, 25], best practice design analysis and evaluation [18–20, 24, 25], and software development methodologies [26]. This included observations on clinical technology use, a survey to understand the technology and apps clinicians use, heuristic evaluations to ensure apps meet basic usability standards before testing; focus groups to gather feedback; System usability scales (SUS) [27] to measure any improvements in usability or any aspects that diminish usability.

These methods were used to inform the design of a prototype application which presents the BCGs on a mobile device. This paper discusses stages 1–11. Stages 12-14 are currently in progress.

Ethical approval was granted by Keele University Research Governance in the Faculty of Natural Sciences (ERP2370) and from Research and Development at the University Hospitals of North Midlands NHS Trust.

3   Results and Analysis

3.1   Observations (Study Stage 2: Requirements)

Observations, conducted following published methods [28, 29], were used to identify if (and how) clinical guidelines were being used. They also aimed to establish any current technology utilisation within the hospital, and the clinician's interactions with technology. This informed requirements for a smartphone application. The 'jotting note' method [30] was adopted for recording observations.

Clinicians across multiple departments at the Royal Stoke University Hospital were observed over three months between May and July 2019. Observations were conducted over several sessions in five wards: Respiratory; General Medicine, Accident and Emergency, Paediatric Accident and Emergency, and Resuscitation. Notes taken during each observation were analysed for consistent themes (Table 2).

Table 2. Key observations

Observation finding 1	Clinicians are interrupted on a regular basis even when using technology
Observation finding 2	Junior clinicians use technology more often than senior clinicians
Observation finding 3	Junior clinicians appear to use technology to establish knowledge. Senior clinicians utilise technology for knowledge affirmation
Observation finding 4	A mixture of personal and hospital technology was used during observations. Personal devices were often used for clinical knowledge retrieval, whereas hospital technology was used to retrieve patient data
Observation finding 5	Nearly all clinicians who utilised technology on their personal devices during observations used dedicated apps rather than an internet browser

One key finding from observing clinicians was that some departments embrace technology in all aspects of clinical practice, and some only for information retrieval. Multimodal technology use was evident, perhaps due to the lack of availability of some systems on mobile devices.

Clinicians were often interrupted during their interaction with technology, normally by colleagues requiring information or patient-specific questions. In many cases, Clinicians repeated steps within software applications due to time-outs or losing their train of thought. While it was visibly frustrating for the clinicians that they had to re-engage with the technology e.g. login or restart the application, it was accepted that this is how the technology behaves. However, there are detrimental effects e.g. loss of time or frustration associated with such less optimal solutions [31].

It was clear during observations that technology plays a key role in ensuring that clinicians have access to a wide range of up to date knowledge. All clinicians utilise the same technology for patient information retrieval. Hospital devices are used for patient information, but personal devices are often used for knowledge retrieval. Clinicians preferred using smartphone apps over web-based services (via an internet browser) when accessing information on their personal devices. This is likely due to the native features of the application in comparison to the web-based versions. An example of this is the British National Formulary (BNF) application, which utilises core-data storage to allow offline access. This mixed-use of technology within this location has been supported by other studies [7, 8, 33].

In addition, junior clinicians use technology to establish and increase their knowledge base, while senior clinicians use it to affirm their knowledge. Junior clinicians use of smartphone applications and web-based services such as the National Institute for Clinical Excellence (NICE) was greater. Other studies support that junior clinicians utilise technology more than their senior counterparts [32]. The observations highlighted the clinical workflow which any design must consider.

3.2 Survey (Study Stage 2: Requirements)

Survey Background. Previous studies have investigated mobile device and app usage among both clinical students and clinicians. Table 3 shows a summary of the results from previous studies [7, 8, 33] on device and App usage amongst clinicians, and nursing and medical students, categorised by 'year published' and where necessary, study limitations. Smartphone usage has become almost universal between 2012 and 2015 in all groups. While App usage has increased in all groups, this appears to be less in nursing students.

Table 3. Summary of the results from 3 key investigations discussed within this study

Study	Year	Smartphone use or ownership	Device use	App use for practice	Study groups
Payne, et al. [7]	2012	76.50%	iPhone 65.7% Android 18.7%	39.90%	Only students and junior clinicians
Mobasheri, et al. [8]	2015	98.90%	iPhone 75.6% Android 21.5%	89%	All clinicians
O'Conner and Andrews [33]	2015	98%	iPhone 48% Android 52%	47%	Only nursing students

Survey Aims and Objectives. The aim was to analyse technology use and identify design patterns and functionality in their preferred mobile apps amongst staff in trusts using BCGs.

A questionnaire was developed to answer the following research questions (RQ):

RQ1. Is smartphone ownership consistent across all groups surveyed (Consultants, Mid-Level, Junior and Students)?

RQ2. Is there a significant difference in the use of iPhone, Android and Other devices by Clinicians/Students?

RQ3. Has smartphone use changed significantly since prior research was conducted; do more or fewer clinicians/students now use smartphones on a regular basis to support their practice?

RQ4. Is there any consistency regarding which smartphone applications clinicians and students use?

RQ5. Is there a relationship between the clinical role and smartphone app use?

RQ6. Does age affect the use of smartphone applications for clinical use?

Survey Design, Distribution and Analysis. The questionnaire collected data relating to the respondents' device ownership (RQ 1, 2, 3), their role within the hospital (RQ 1, 2, 3, 4, 5), website use (RQ 4, 5); app use (RQ 4), time in role and local guideline use (RQ 4, 5) and respondents age (RQ 6). Specific App use (e.g. App Name) was collected via an open-ended response (RQ 5, 6). No honorarium was offered in exchange for completing the survey.

The survey was distributed via emails from clinical leads to clinicians in three North West UK NHS Trusts (n = ~1400) and medical students (3rd, 4th and 5th years) at Keele University (n = ~300).

Data analysis comprised of coding, frequency analysis, and cross-tabulation. Tests were completed in IBM SPSS Statistics version 24 for Mac. Where appropriate, the Chi-squared (X^2) test was used to compare data with results from alternative sources or when comparing between clinical groups, age groups, and devices. A P-level of <0.05 was considered statistically significant.

Survey Results. The questionnaire received one hundred and forty-six responses (n = 146). Results were analysed by age and role (Medical students 45% (n = 65), Junior/Mid-Level clinicians 23% (n = 34), and Consultants with 32% (n = 47) (Figs. 2 and 4).

Device ownership and manufacturer (RQs 1, 2 and 3). Table 4 shows the actual number of clinicians; their role, and their preferred smartphone.

Only 2 (1.4%) clinicians did not use a Smartphone for clinical practice, both were consultants between the age of 56 and 65.

iPhone ownership was ~72% (n = 106), while android device ownership was 26% (n = 38) (Fig. 1). All roles demonstrate ownership preference for iPhone over android (p = <0.05). This result is significantly different (p = <0.0001) to general smartphone device ownership research showing general ownership of Android and iPhones to be ~49% for each device [34, 35] and supports previous research [8], which found that 75.6% of doctors own iPhones.

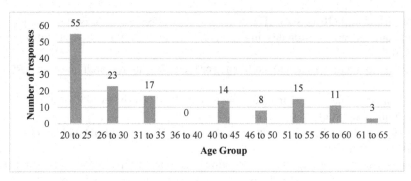

Fig. 1. Age range of respondents (RQ 6)

Table 4. Mobile device breakdown for clinical role and device type.

		Device			
		Android	iPhone	None	Other
Role	Consultant	13	32	1	1
	Mid-Level	4	12	0	0
	Junior	5	13	0	0
	Student	16	49	0	0
Total		**38** (26.4%)	**106** (73.6%)	**1** (0.7%)	**1** (0.7%)

Mobile App Usage (RQs 3, 4 and 5). Survey participants were asked to identify '*any apps you use on a regular basis to support you in your role*'.

9% (n = 13) do not use smartphone apps to support their role of whom 10 were consultant clinicians, representing 15% of the total number of Consultant respondents. Of the 13, eleven accessed the web-based tools provided by their NHS Trust regularly.

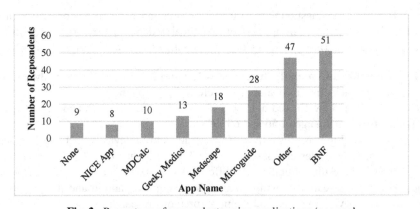

Fig. 2. Percentage of respondents using applications 'per app'

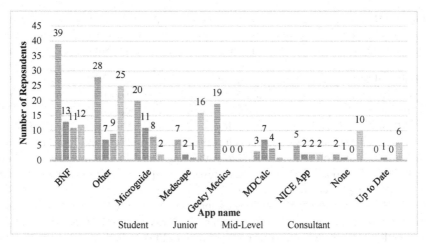

Fig. 3. Application use across clinical roles 'per app'.

Survey participants named a variety of apps (Figs. 2 & 3). The most 'popular' were Apps supporting prescribing, BNF App (51%: n = 75 of respondents) and Microguide (28% (n = 41) of respondents). The use was greatest amongst more junior clinicians who prescribe most drugs on a ward.

There was a wide range of other Apps with 47% (n = 69) reporting using an app which was not used by others in the survey. The Apps used related to their roles. These Apps included UpToDate (6 of the 7 users were consultants) for management of a wide spectrum of diseases; calculation tools e.g. MDCalc; clinical tools based on a specific clinical discipline; learning tools, and applications for general administration. 'Geeky Medics' was used by 60% (n = 28) of students to support their study and clinical practice.

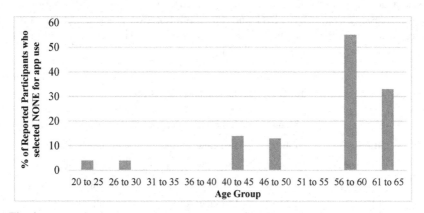

Fig. 4. Respondents who reported not using apps for clinical practice on a regular basis

Figure 4 shows that significantly higher percentages (p = <0.0001) of older clinicians (*56 to 60 and 61 to 65*) do not use Apps. In comparison, relatively few clinicians below the age of 56 reported 'None' for using apps on a regular basis to support their practice.

Discussion of Survey Findings. Smartphone ownership is consistent across all groups surveyed. The early adoption of iPhone app development for web-based clinical service tools such as Medscape, the BNF, and Microguide (launched 2009 [36], 2012 [37], and 2013 [38] respectively) may have influenced the device bias towards the iPhone. Medscape (as an example) was not launched on Android devices until four years after it was made available on iPhone, potentially allowing brand loyalty and user adoption to grow. There is also an element of 'peer pressure' [39], potentially leading to higher adoption rate of a particular manufacturer.

Over half of those surveyed regularly use prescribing Apps (BNF and Microguide). A large number of clinicians use Apps which are not widely used by other clinicians.

The pattern use relates to the role of the clinician (Figs. 2, 3, 4).

The 'App Store' rankings for the 'most mentioned' apps identified in the survey, reinforce the findings of the survey. At the time of writing, the most mentioned app from the survey (BNF) has an Apple '*App Store*' ranking of 10th in the UK and a Google '*Play Store*' ranking of 15th. Removing apps for consumer use (such as MyGP or NHS A&E Wait Times), the BNF would rank 1st. Microguide is the next 'non-consumer' ranked app in both stores, placed in the top 50 of both stores.

While 'App Store' ranking is not significant to design or usability, 'App Store' rankings and reported 'use' by clinicians/students correlate.

App Analysis. It is important to establish design patterns to inform the framework of the prototype, this will allow for consistent usability when clinicians adopt new apps for their practice [40].

The most popular apps reported by clinicians in Figs. 2 and 3 were analysed for consistent design features. The analysis investigated the type of menu, information access type for accessing sections, i.e. lists, and if a search function was available all common features which form the framework of the majority of apps. This analysis then informed the design of the prototype app described in Sect. 4.1.

Table 5. Popular app analysis (Basic)

App	Menu	Information access	Search
BNF	Tabbed	ListView A to Z	Yes, filter based
MicroGuide	Slide out	ListView by Category	Yes, full search
MedScape	Tabbed	ListView A to Z	Yes, filter based
MDCalc	Tabbed	ListView A to Z	Yes, filter based
NICE app*	Tabbed	ListView A to Z	Yes, filter based
GeekyMedics△	Main menu	ListView by Category	Yes, filter based

No longer available, △Student Learning Tool only

As Table 5 shows, the most popular apps all utilise a 'List View', either by category or in an alphabetical format. The apps also utilise a filter-based search function, rather than a full search. Finally, these Apps predominantly adopt a tabbed menu system as opposed to allowing users to quickly access other system features e.g. Settings or alternative views.

3.3 Summary

The results and findings during these study stages (1 & 2) have indicated that clinicians utilised a mixture of technologies and a cross-platform approach will, therefore, need to be considered. App design should allow clinicians to utilise features during clinical workflow, avoiding any design that will require the clinicians to engage for a long period of time e.g. manual calculations. This can be addressed by implementing the design aspects discussed in the App Analysis, integrating features such as a filter for efficiency, and easy access to the features any new app will offer. These findings informed the design and evaluation of a prototype application discussed in the next section.

4 Design and Evaluation

A review of the BCGs shows that the authored word versions already contain different types of information within a formal structure which need remodelling, plus new requirements, identified in Sect. 3, for presentation as an App.

4.1 Prototype Version 1 (Study Stages 3–5)

Technology Selection. This study (Table 4) supports a cross-platform development approach. Hybrid Application Development methods [41, 42] produce an application which employs web technologies such as HTML, CSS and JavaScript. The hybrid application files are then integrated within the native platform technologies. This produces an application that can be distributed across multiple platforms, whilst still having access to the fundamental technologies offered within the native system. This enables conversion to various platforms, offering a multimodal approach when distributing future versions of the app. Any future development can be integrated into other healthcare systems e.g. electronic health records (EHRs) which are often web-based.

Design Overview. Results from the review of BCGs in word format, the observation and survey studies inform the design of the initial BCG prototype application.

Figure 5 shows the initial prototype design of the application. Note the menu button in the top right, implemented during this prototype stage as the app functions were limited and did not require a 'tabbed' menu as the survey and app analysis suggested. Several design aspects were considered, these included how Warnings/Alerts were presented; Filtering/Highlights search text; Algorithms for diagnosis; Diagnostic Aids; Calculations; Evidence for each guideline; and the main menu to access individual guidelines.

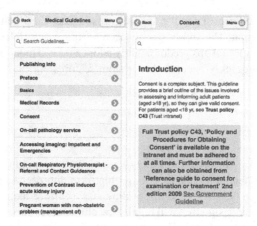

Fig. 5. The initial prototype of the BCG app.

A heuristic evaluation [18–20] of the prototype refined several aspects, these included: Guideline sections requiring more distinction; warnings required more prominent colours; sections and headers also required more distinction; guideline information was not presented similarly to what clinicians were used to.

A second prototype was then developed shown in Fig. 6. The sections were more distinguishable, and colours were utilised to ensure menu and guideline sections were more obvious to the user. Warnings were made more prominent by utilising red for the background and text.

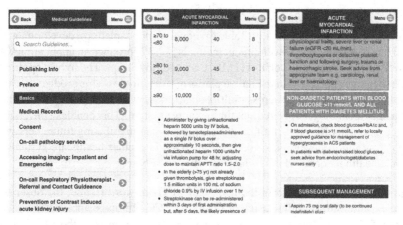

Fig. 6. The second prototype of the BCG app after a basic heuristic evaluation

Flowchart Prototype. The BCGs contain a number of decision algorithms for use during clinical practice. Figure 7 shows a standard decision algorithm to determine if a patient should be referred to the on-call respiratory physiotherapist. Decision algorithms are key components of guidelines and due to their size and complexity, pose a usability issue (highlighted in Fig. 7) when designing for mobile.

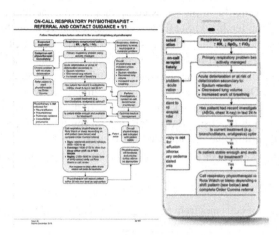

Fig. 7. Example of a decision algorithm

Figure 8 shows the apps prototype decision algorithm designed for displaying on a smartphone. The prototype version was developed using JavaScript, HTML 5 and CSS3. The design displays the selection or path the clinician has followed, and therefore limits the algorithm to only the required information.

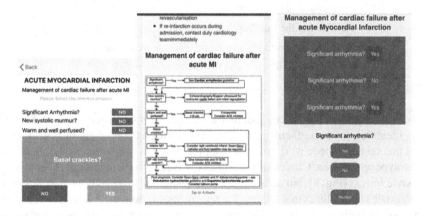

Fig. 8. Designs for the smartphone algorithm, right was an iteration of the initial design (left).

Focus Group Evaluation of Prototype Version 1 (Study Stage 6)

The prototype in Figs. 6 and 8 was demonstrated to clinicians in a focus group of 21 clinicians in a single session (student, junior and senior) at the Royal Stoke University Hospital. The main aim being to obtain functionality and design feedback for the prototype application from target users. The focus group was conducted utilising open discussion [43, 44]. These open discussion sessions were audio-recorded and transcribed. The transcripts were then analysed using thematic analysis [45].

It was apparent during the initial focus group that another method would have to be adopted for large group feedback. Sessions were time-sensitive (scheduling constraints inherent in clinical roles) and individual sessions or smaller groups, though preferred, were not possible. Idea writing [46, 47] was therefore adopted for the second focus group of 17 clinicians, which allowed all participants to contribute in a structured manner within the time constraints. During this session, clinicians interacted with a prototype of the application and were asked to feedback on each aspect of the design which was presented as a 'concept'. Although this limited open discussion (by design), it allowed for more specific feedback regarding the design of the BCG app.

Table 6 shows an example of feedback provided by clinicians during the idea writing session.

Table 6. Example of outcomes from an idea writing session conducted with clinicians

Flowchart concept	• Having the full pictographic flow chart is good because you can view the whole decision tree
	• Having a single question at a time is good for focus but it would be good to view the whole tree and highlight your position on it rather than being stripped down to only seeing "question yes no"
	• Nice clear format, I like that it can be changed to yes no
	• Clear format, would be more appropriate if we can get the full photographic picture
	• Viewing the full flowchart is ideal
	• Need an option to view the full chart as well as yes no options
	• Have both full view and the 'answer' view

The feedback from both focus groups was analysed for consistent themes. The key themes identified from the focus groups are that clinicians appreciate the clean, clear layouts that do not impede workflow. An example of this is the flowchart design within the prototype application. Clinicians provided positive feedback regarding the prototype Q&A style format (Fig. 8), but also suggested retaining the original flowchart design to give a gestalt view. Clinician's feedback also suggested the use of acronyms (e.g. PE for Pulmonary Embolism) when searching or filtering guidelines. This is in contrast to standard usability guidelines [48, 49] and reflects the challenges faced when designing for experts. Clinicians suggested that warnings require a hierarchy based on their severity with the use of more noticeable colours

Thus, changes that would be required in the next iteration of the prototype BCG app:

1. Decision algorithms to be displayed in-line with the guideline information.
2. The original 'flowchart' decision algorithm is provided.

3. Acronym use is prevalent in medicine, but not all clinicians have knowledge of acronyms. Methods to address both experts and novices should be adopted.
4. Guideline decision tools such as calculations should be automated.
5. Warnings should be clearer and adopt better salience for the user.
6. Guideline length would need reducing.

Usability Testing of Initial Prototype (Study Stage 8)
The System Usability Scale (SUS) [27] was used to establish the usability level of the prototype application (Version 1 created during study stage 5) from the clinicians' viewpoint. It also provided a baseline to measure future changes in the design and how they impact the usability. During 2 sessions, 26 clinicians were asked to complete information retrieval scenarios, developed in collaboration with senior clinicians at the Royal Stoke University (example shown in Fig. 9) and then complete the SUS.

In the management flowchart of Hyperkalaemia, what is the recommended action where Plasma K+ 6.0-6.4 mmol/L and Acute ECG changes are present?

Fig. 9. Example information retrieval scenario used in testing.

The app was shown to have a high usability score, with an overall score of 81 out of 100 (calculated utilising the methods described in [27]). Question 5 'how integrated features of the system are' showed the widest gap between ideal and current usability scores. This agrees with the focus groups.

This SUS score indicates an initial high level of usability; however, the focus groups identified several specific areas of improvement which are described in the following section.

4.2 Prototype Version 2 (Study Stage 10)

Design Overview. It was evident through feedback from the Focus Groups that the guideline length would need to be reduced. Research agrees with this feedback, as it helps to avoid unnecessary scrolling and prevents potential impact on clinical workflow, especially in regard to memorability and usability [50]. Design aspects including accordions were utilised to support this. Design patterns such as accordions [51] were utilised to support this (Fig. 10) which greatly reduced the length of some guidelines.

The BCGs contain tables for easy presentation in the book format, however these can be problematic on mobile devices due to constraints inherent in their design and size [52]. Figure 11 shows a guideline table converted to a diagnostic tool. The table requires clinicians to manually complete calculations. The BCG app version calculates the outcome and provides clinicians with clear and precise recommendations.

Acronyms are not understood by some clinical staff [53, 54]. Figure 12 shows acronyms displayed on popovers to potentially reduce errors due to misunderstandings [53, 54].

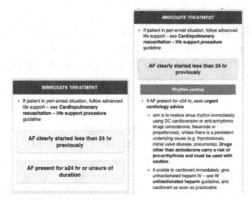

Fig. 10. Left image shows the closed format of the BCG accordion, right image shows how the accordion displays the contained information.

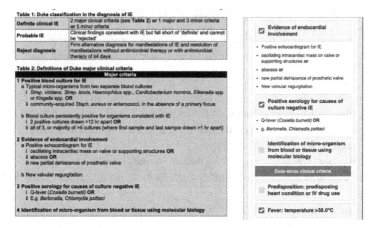

Fig. 11. Left image shows the original table format of the BCG classification tool (Dukes classification for infective endocarditis), the right image shows the BCG App version which allows users to select criteria and display a single recommendation.

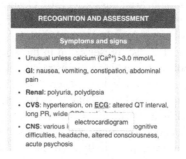

Fig. 12. Concept for displaying acronym details.

Clinical Guideline Warnings. The BCG Medical Guidelines contain over three-hundred warnings in a black box design. The focus groups, expert clinicians and authors were consulted on the design of a simple method of displaying a reduced number of warnings to avoid alert fatigue [55–57]. Figure 13 shows the original and new warning designs. The use of colour and icons improves the impact of the warnings [58].

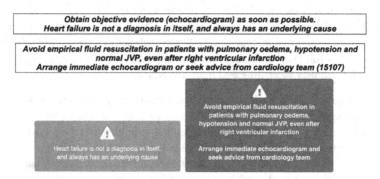

Fig. 13. Top images show the original warnings in the acute heart failure guideline. Bottom images show the BCG App versions, one with less text.

4.3 Summary

The user feedback has led to the design of the BCG App. Usability testing has shown promising results. Focus group participants described the app as "a much more efficient approach to presenting this information", "clear and easy to navigate", "easy to understand", "clean" and "Familiar". Usability testing using cognitive walkthroughs will inform further improvements before the app is used in live pilot testing.

5 Conclusion

This study has reaffirmed that smartphone ownership is consistent across all clinical roles (with iPhone ownership being dominant). Medical app usage in a clinical setting is becoming ubiquitous. This has implications for not only Doctors and app developers but also for Hospitals, Trusts and their patients as the majority of the applications reported in this study were not officially authorised by the NHS.

It is clear from the observations, survey and app analysis, there is a need to consider the wide variety of tools needed by a clinician when developing applications. Clinicians use several tools which would benefit from being integrated into a simple, easy to use system, which presents the information in line with elements such as calculators or decision algorithms. Mobile Medical apps like this require ease of use at point of care and integration into clinical workflow.

There is a real need for further investigation in this area and for doctors and app developers to work more closely to align needs and to develop standards. Applying a user centred design to the information presented to clinicians can yield improvements to usability results and this research shows that co-designing applications of this nature help to maintain accuracy and produce a usable system. When designing for mobile, it is important to design not only for the inherent strengths and weaknesses of the device but also for the context of use. Designing for "in the moment use" in a Hospital means designing for interruption and designing for users with specific expertise means including functionality that is counter-intuitive to standard design guidelines e.g. using acronyms. Reflecting on the use of UCD itself in this domain, there are severe constraints related to limited access to clinicians and so traditional methods have required adaption. Future work, therefore, will consider the use of implicit feedback (usage logs) to gather feedback to inform user modelling and interface adaptation.

Study Limitations. Although this survey was conducted across multiple locations, it was limited geographically (NW England) and to single locations within the trust. Increasing the study's reach; having multiple sites in multiple trusts, would enable a thorough analysis across each trust and enable comparisons at both single-site and trust level. This survey limitation may be affected by recommended apps dominating within that area. It may also be affected by bias, clinicians stating what they 'should' say compared what they actually use for clinical practice. Focus groups based on local information and not from further trusts, although focus groups at further NHS Trusts are planned.

Funding. This study was funded in part by the Keele University Acorn Fund and the University Hospital North Midlands NHS Trust Charity.

Acknowledgements. The authors thank Professor Barbara Kitchenham and Dr Sandra Woolley for their advice, and all of the clinicians and students who participated.

References

1. Statista: Number of smartphone users worldwide 2014–2020 (2019). https://www.statista.com/statistics/330695/number-of-smartphone-users-worldwide/. Accessed 7 May 2019
2. Apple: Apple Reinvents the Phone with iPhone (2007). https://www.apple.com/uk/newsroom/2007/01/09Apple-Reinvents-the-Phone-with-iPhone/. Accessed 7 May 2019
3. Apple Newsroom: Apple Introduces the New iPhone 3G (2008). https://www.apple.com/newsroom/2008/06/09Apple-Introduces-the-New-iPhone-3G/. Accessed 7 May 2019
4. Statista Topic: Mobile app usage (2019). https://www.statista.com/topics/1002/mobile-app-usage/. Accessed 7 May 2019
5. Apple Newsroom: The App Store turns 10 (2018). https://www.apple.com/newsroom/2018/07/app-store-turns-10/. Accessed 7 May 2019
6. Mosa, A.S.M., Yoo, I., Sheets, L.: A systematic review of healthcare applications for smartphones. BMC Med. Inform. Decis. Mak. **12**(1), 67 (2012). https://doi.org/10.1186/1472-6947-12-67
7. Payne, K.F.B., Wharrad, H., Watts, K.: Smartphone and medical related App use among medical students and junior doctors in the United Kingdom (UK): a regional survey. BMC Med. Inform. Decis. Mak. **12**(1), 121 (2012). https://doi.org/10.1186/1472-6947-12-121

8. Mobasheri, M.H., King, D., Johnston, M., Gautama, S., Purkayastha, S., Darzi, A.: The ownership and clinical use of smartphones by doctors and nurses in the UK: a multicentre survey study. BMJ Innovations **1**(4), 174–181 (2015)
9. Shenouda, J.E., Davies, B.S., Haq, I.: The role of the smartphone in the transition from medical student to foundation trainee: a qualitative interview and focus group study. BMC Med. Educ. **18**(1), 175 (2018). https://doi.org/10.1186/s12909-018-1279-y
10. Lewis, T.L., Wyatt, J.C.: mHealth and mobile medical apps: a framework to assess risk and promote safer use. J. Med. Internet Res. **16**(9), e210 (2014)
11. Melton, B.L., et al.: Reducing prescribing errors through creatinine clearance alert redesign. Am. J. Med. **128**(10), 1117–1125 (2015)
12. Demiris, G., et al.: Patient-centered applications: use of information technology to promote disease management and wellness. A white paper by the AMIA knowledge in motion working group. J. Am. Med. Inform. Assoc. **15**(1), 8–13 (2008)
13. Archer, N., Fevrier-Thomas, U., Lokker, C., McKibbon, K.A., Straus, S.E.: Personal health records: a scoping review. J. Am. Med. Inform. Assoc. **18**(4), 515–522 (2011)
14. NICE: Find guidance (2020). https://www.nice.org.uk/guidance. Accessed 1 Feb 2020
15. Pantin, C., Mucklow, J., Rogers, D., Cross, M., Wall, J.: Bedside clinical guidelines: the missing link. Clin. Med. **6**(1), 98–104 (2006)
16. Littlejohns, P., Wyatt, J.C., Garvican, L.: Evaluating computerised health information systems: hard lessons still to be learnt. BMJ **326**(7394), 860–863 (2003)
17. Burton, Z., Edwards, H.: A little less conversation, a little more high impact action. Future Healthc. J. **6**(Suppl 1), 201 (2019)
18. Nielsen, J.: 10 usability heuristics for user interface design. Nielsen Norman Group **1**(1), 1–2 (1995)
19. Nielsen, J.: How to conduct a heuristic evaluation. Nielsen Norman Group **1**, 1–8 (1995)
20. Gerhardt-Powals, J.: Cognitive engineering principles for enhancing human-computer performance. Int. J. Hum. Comput. Interact. **8**(2), 189–211 (1996)
21. Kwa, A., Carter, M., Page, D., Wilson, T., Brown, M., Baxendale, B.: Nottingham University hospital guidelines app–improving accessibility to 650 hospital clinical guidelines. In: Contemporary Ergonomics and Human Factors 2015: Proceedings of the International Conference on Ergonomics & Human Factors 2015, Daventry, Northamptonshire, UK, 13–16 April 2015, p. 220. CRC Press, Boca Raton (2015)
22. Payne, K.F., Weeks, L., Dunning, P.: A mixed methods pilot study to investigate the impact of a hospital-specific iPhone application (iTreat) within a British junior doctor cohort. Health Inform. J. **20**(1), 59–73 (2014)
23. Cossu, F., et al.: Supporting doctors through mobile multimodal interaction and process-aware execution of clinical guidelines. In: 2014 IEEE 7th International Conference on Service-Oriented Computing and Applications, November 2014, pp. 183–190. IEEE (2014)
24. Abras, C., Maloney-Krichmar, D., Preece, J.: User-centered design. In: Bainbridge, W. (ed.) Encyclopedia of Human-Computer Interaction, vol. 37, no. 4, pp. 445–456. Sage Publications, Thousand Oaks (2004)
25. Usability.gov.: User-Centered Design Basics (2020). https://www.usability.gov/what-and-why/user-centered-design.html. Accessed 1 Feb 2020
26. Fowler, M., Highsmith, J.: The agile manifesto. Softw. Dev. **9**(8), 28–35 (2001)
27. Brooke, J.: SUS-a quick and dirty usability scale. Usability Eval. Ind. **189**(194), 4–7 (1996)
28. Potts, C.: Software-engineering research revisited. IEEE Softw. **10**(5), 19–28 (1993)
29. O'reilly, K.: Ethnographic Methods, pp. 101–104. Routledge, Abingdon (2004)
30. Emerson, R.M., Fretz, R.I., Shaw, L.L.: Writing Ethnographic Fieldnotes. University of Chicago Press, Chicago (2011)
31. Scott, J.E.: Technology acceptance and ERP documentation usability. Commun. ACM **51**(11), 121–124 (2008)

32. Patel, R.K., Sayers, A.E., Patrick, N.L., Hughes, K., Armitage, J., Hunter, I.A.: A UK perspective on smartphone use amongst doctors within the surgical profession. Ann. Med. Surg. **4**(2), 107–112 (2015)
33. O'Connor, S., Andrews, T.: Co-designing mobile apps to assist in clinical nursing education: a study protocol. In: Nursing Informatics, pp. 963–964 (2016)
34. Statista, Mobile OS: market share in the United Kingdom 2011–2019 (2019). https://www.statista.com/statistics/262179/market-share-held-by-mobile-operating-systems-in-the-united-kingdom/. Accessed 18 May 2019
35. StatCounter Global Stats: Mobile Operating System Market Share United Kingdom (2019). http://gs.statcounter.com/os-market-share/mobile/united-kingdom. Accessed 20 May 2019
36. MobiHealthNews: WebMD launches Medscape CME app for iPhone (2009). https://www.mobihealthnews.com/3351/webmd-launches-medscape-cme-app-for-iphone/. Accessed 27 May 2019
37. NICE: Free BNF prescribing app launches (2012). https://www.nice.org.uk/news/article/free-bnf-prescribing-app-launches. Accessed 26 May 2019
38. microguide.eu.: About Us - Antimicrobial stewardship improved by MicroGuide No 1 medical guidance (n.d.). http://www.microguide.eu/about-hsp/. Accessed 25 May 2019
39. Rahim, A., Safin, S.Z., Kheng, L.K., Abas, N., Ali, S.M.: Factors influencing purchasing intention of smartphone among university students. Procedia Econ. Finance **37**, 245–253 (2016)
40. Nielsen, J.: The usability engineering life cycle. Computer **25**(3), 12–22 (1992)
41. Nielsen Norman Group, Mobile: Native Apps, Web Apps, and Hybrid Apps (2013). https://www.nngroup.com/articles/mobile-native-apps/. Accessed 21 Feb 2020
42. Panhale, M.: Beginning hybrid mobile application development. Apress, New York (2016)
43. Gibbs, A.: Focus groups. Soc. Res. Update **19**(8), 1–8 (1997)
44. Kitzinger, J.: Qualitative research: introducing focus groups. BMJ **311**(7000), 299–302 (1995)
45. Fereday, J., Muir-Cochrane, E.: Demonstrating rigor using thematic analysis: a hybrid approach of inductive and deductive coding and theme development. Int. J. Qual. Methods **5**(1), 80–92 (2006)
46. Austin, M.: Needs Assessment By Focus Groups (No. 9401). American Society for Training and Development, Alexandria (1994)
47. VanGundy, A.B.: Brain writing for new product ideas: an alternative to brainstorming. J. Consum. Mark. **1**(2), 67–74 (1984)
48. Lin, H.X., Choong, Y.Y., Salvendy, G.: A proposed index of usability: a method for comparing the relative usability of different software systems. Behav. Inf. Technol. **16**(4–5), 267–277 (1997)
49. Spencer, R.H.: Translatability: understandability and usability by others. Comput. Hum. Behav. **4**(4), 347–354 (1988)
50. Harms, J., Kratky, M., Wimmer, C., Kappel, K., Grechenig, T.: Navigation in long forms on smartphones: scrolling worse than tabs, menus, and collapsible fieldsets. In: Abascal, J., Barbosa, S., Fetter, M., Gross, T., Palanque, P., Winckler, M. (eds.) INTERACT 2015. LNCS, vol. 9298, pp. 333–340. Springer, Cham (2015). https://doi.org/10.1007/978-3-319-22698-9_21
51. Tidwell, J.: Designing interfaces: patterns for effective interaction design. O'Reilly Media Inc, Sebastopol (2010)
52. Monkman, H., Griffith, J., Kushniruk, A.W.: Evidence-based heuristics for evaluating demands on eHealth literacy and usability in a mobile consumer health application. In: MedInfo, pp.. 358–362, August 2015
53. Duncan, E.M., et al.: Learning curves, taking instructions, and patient safety: using a theoretical domains framework in an interview study to investigate prescribing errors among trainee doctors. Implement. Sci. **7**(1), 86 (2012)

54. Rees, G.: Staff use of acronyms in electronic care records. Mental Health Pract. **16**(10), 28–31 (2013)
55. Ancker, J.S., et al.: Effects of workload, work complexity, and repeated alerts on alert fatigue in a clinical decision support system. BMC Med. Inf. Decis. Making **17**(1), 36 (2017). https://doi.org/10.1186/s12911-017-0430-8
56. Embi, P.J., Leonard, A.C.: Evaluating alert fatigue over time to EHR-based clinical trial alerts: findings from a randomized controlled study. J. Am. Med. Inform. Assoc. **19**(e1), e145–e148 (2012)
57. Carspecken, C.W., Sharek, P.J., Longhurst, C., Pageler, N.M.: A clinical case of electronic health record drug alert fatigue: consequences for patient outcome. Pediatrics **131**(6), e1970–e1973 (2013)
58. Wogalter, M.S., Conzola, V.C., Smith-Jackson, T.L.: Research-based guidelines for warning design and evaluation. Appl. Ergon. **33**(3), 219–230 (2002)

Design and Usability of an E-Health Mobile Application

Maria Rita Nogueira[1]([✉])(iD), Paulo Menezes[1,2](iD), Sérgio Carvalho[3](iD),
Bruno Patrão[1,2](iD), Inês A. Trindade[3](iD), Raquel Guiomar[3](iD), Joana Duarte[3](iD),
Teresa Lapa[3](iD), José Pinto-Gouveia[3](iD), and Paula Freitas Castilho[3](iD)

[1] Institute of Systems and Robotics, University of Coimbra, Coimbra, Portugal
{maria.nogueira,paulomenezes}@isr.uc.pt
[2] Department Electrical and Computer Engineering, University of Coimbra,
Coimbra, Portugal
[3] Centre for Research in Neuropsychology and Cognitive Behavioral Intervention,
University of Coimbra, Coimbra, Portugal

Abstract. Health applications have increasingly been used to improve
physical, mental and social well-being. Chronic pain (CP) is defined as
pain that lasts for a period of three months and causes sporadic or
constant discomfort. In Portugal, the treatments for this type of pain
are almost exclusively pharmacological and with known limited effects.
Endowing patients with self-management skills, will help them cope with
pain in a more effective way. Psychological treatments (e.g. mindfulness-
based interventions) may play a relevant role here, because they intervene on a cognitive, emotional and behavioural level, which in turn helps
the chronic pain patient to deal with pain-related disorders and suffering. The current availability of connected and powerful smartphones and
tablets creates an opportunity to propose alternative pain management
solutions that may be used immediately when pain appears, which has
been the argument that favoured the pharmacological solutions. For this
we propose a mobile application that guides patients on the mindfulness
practice and to self-manage the sensed pain. Learning to gradually adequate pain management may have several advantages such as: reduced
the number of consultation visits and consequent waiting lists; increased
cost-effectiveness; self-management of chronic pain at the patient's pace
and according to their needs; extend access to the treatment to patients
that reside in low density regions. Being an alternative to traditional
treatment, the proposed treatment will be under the guidance of qualified health professionals that will supervise treatment sessions and perform the required assessments. By promoting patients' self-management,
the control and monitoring of the chronic pain condition is expected to
improve greatly, which in turn may prevent the aggravation of the clinical
condition. This research and the mobile application are being developed
in a collaboration between the Centre for Research in Neuropsychology

Supported by Institute of Systems and Robotics of University of Coimbra and Centre
for Research in Neuropsychology and Cognitive Behavioral Intervention of University
of Coimbra.

A. Marcus and E. Rosenzweig (Eds.): HCII 2020, LNCS 12202, pp. 314–328, 2020.
https://doi.org/10.1007/978-3-030-49757-6_22

and Cognitive Behavioral Intervention of the University of Coimbra and the Institute of Systems and Robotics.

Keywords: Chronic pain management · Mobile application · E-health · Design · Usability · User experience

1   Introduction

Relaxation training and Mindfulness are practices that provide a mental capacity which helps us to be less reactive to what is happening in the that moment [4]. These mental practices [5] focus on the self-regulation of attention with an attitude of openness and self-acceptance [1]. Mindfulness is used by a large number of people in the world (including non-patients) to improve health and well-being [2,3]. An initiation to the mindfulness practice should normally start by an understanding of the Four Foundations of Mindfulness [13], which are primarily based on Satipattana Sutta [12,14,15]. Although the evidence of the benefits of mindfulness in mental and physical health have been tested and shown [16–20], it has a larger and longer history that predates the recent interest of researchers and its growing use in clinical practice. Mindfulness comes from an eastern Buddhist tradition, and it derives from the Pali (ancient sanscript) word "Sati", which translates into "acting to things as they are" or put simply: mindfulness. For the last four decades, researchers and clinicians have put forward different westernized definitions of mindfulness in order to scientifically study it [18], and the commonly accepted conceptualization of mindfulness was suggested by Kabat-Zinn: mindfulness is paying attention on purpose, in the present moment and non-judgmentally [20]. Mindfulness practice can be especially advantageous and significantly improve the lives of those who suffer from Chronic Pain (CP). CP affects hundreds of millions of people worldwide [26] and it places a significant economic burden on healthcare systems [27]. Pain has an impact on different aspects and patients commonly experience depression, sleep disturbance, fatigue, and reduced physical and mental functioning [26]. These aspects usually affect daily routines, mental and physical health, social activities, relationships, productivity and well-being in the workplace. There are multiple health benefits associated with mindfulness, because these practices can improve as physical and emotional well-being, pain acceptance, improve focus and concentration, reduced impulsive reactions, and gain physical awareness [6,7,10,11].

This article describes an E-health mobile application, which supports a therapy based on digital tools and exercise plans, inspired on pain self-management strategies. It is expected that this system will help chronic patients to be more optimistic regarding their pain and life in general, and for this reason our proposed solution needs to consider the end-users' needs and expectations (Human-Centered Design principle) [58]. From the point of a view of Design and Usability, our focus is based on a dynamic experience [28], always bearing in mind chronic patients and thinking of a solution that allows natural interaction. These end-users in particular, are more likely to experience impatient behaviour, and so the non-intuitive options may, in turn, make users want to abandon the use of the application [38]. As this health application is targeted at a particular range of people, which are commonly more vulnerable to stress, the application should be dynamic and have particular attention to user experience details [41,42]. Our system, as a human-centred system, is defined around human features, e.g. physical, perceptual, cognitive, and emotional, and these features are important for an interaction with the artefact system [43]. One of our main objectives is to provide a useful and user-friendly application, with a simple visual design [39]. Through different user tests with chronic patients, we will improve on how accurate the application is, while helping chronic pain [40]. These user tests will be conducted with chronic patients aged between 18 and 65 years old, with the help of psychologists, therapists and researchers in the area of technology, psychology, usability and design. The tests will be defined and/or adapted to suit the requirement of the application and context of use. Based on the results, attractiveness will give the high score in relation to other elements, such as ease to use, efficiency, and stimulation.

This paper is organized as follows. Related work (Sect. 2) which describes the most relevant works and contributions to the development of this project. Methodology (Sect. 3), this section is divided in two subsections: user-research methodology (this subsection explains our system decisions, based on our end-users (chronic patients); and system development methodology (describes the process of the application system development). Section 4, which presents the proposed concept, is organized into a set of relevant characteristics of the application, such as treatment application process, exercises description, interaction design and monitoring, user interface and visual identity explanation. Conclusion (Sect. 5) presents our final reflections.

2   Related Work

A review of the literature on the topic of Chronic Pain, mobile applications or other platforms, identifies different procedures to tackle chronic pain. We selected the most relevant case studies concerned the following points: To provide well-being and improve the living standards of chronic patients, through didactic material [31,35,36]; The application purposes are to detect local pain and collect data about the evolution of pain [29,30,32–34]; The application's allows the sharing of knowledge and of chronic patients' experience [29,32,34,37]; The system provides medical and health professionals with support and feedback [31]. The research group tried and tested the different software products and raised the following issues. Any E-health application should provide the target audience, the patients, with a close contact with the healthcare professionals so the patients feel accompanied, even if only virtually. Users with chronic pain usually want to find documentation, material or measures that will help them better. Unfortunately, there are few applications which provide didactic material or examples of exercises to reduce the sense of pain and help to improve the well-being of patients. In the majority of cases, the applications' main task is to register local pain and in some cases [29,30,32–34] assessing pain intensity. When a patient is constantly evaluating their pain, it can have a significant impact at a given moment, and the patient could alleviate their pain through a more effective method. In the case of the "Pain Scale" application [31], the system provides many exercise possibilities for each locus chronic pain (e.g. neck, shoulder, chest), while in the case study "Kaia" [36] it only focuses on the back pain. Some of the applications mentioned present physical exercises, such as stretching exercises and yoga [31,35,36], but none of those applications address techniques of mindfulness meditation. In terms of functionality, these case studies do not have a treatment concept for a certain period of time, but different categories of material which the patients could try. In this regard, there is a lack of a system which includes the different points covered above, such as: treatment with a common thread, in other words, a treatment is carried out in organised, different steps; healthcare professional support, even if the support is virtual; didactic material which explains the different approaches to deal with pain. This is precisely the point we have been developing, a system that integrates the different needs and at the same time gives patients a tool that helps them to learn more about their pain and deal with situations of severe pain on a daily basis. When dealing with this subject we must also inevitably describe the method(s) by which the objectives have been or will be implemented, and explain our proposed system, in subsequent sections.

3 Methodology

This section describes the methodologies and focuses mainly on User Research Methodology and, thereafter, System Development. The first subsection, User-Research Methodology (Sect. 3.1) explains the user research methodology we used and which helped us to better identify our end-users' needs, in other words the chronic patients' needs. In order to understand the most useful user-research method, we followed the following methods: Attitudinal vs. Behavioral and Quantitative vs. Qualitative. The second subsection, the System Development (Sect. 3.2) describes the used method of each development system.

3.1 User-Research Methodology

User Research is an expansion and generalization of usability and engineering, where the goal is not merely to study and optimize interaction design, but to know as much as possible about users and their needs in general [44]. The following user research methods are easy to use and can help us to understand the problems and issues in our target audience.

The first user research method is the Attitudinal vs. Behavioral method. This method is based on the idea of "What people say" versus "What people do" [45], therefore we need to understand and to measure the chronic patients' convictions. We will test a pilot version of our E-health application (in a first phase), with 15 chronic patients, and observe the users' engagement and subsequently analyse their behaviour and attitude. These first user tests will help us to improve the usability, user experience and interface design of our E-health mobile application. To evaluate the attitudinal parameter we focused on personal surveys answered by the users. These surveys are divided into three structured type questions: Nominal questions (e.g. The user sees the call to action "Start"); Filtering question (e.g. What is the easiest exercise? What is the favourite exercise?) Ranking questions (e.g. During the interaction with the mobile application which details do you like most? Rank in order of preference, rated on a scale from 1 "Prefer Less" to 5 "Much Prefer") [48]. Generally, such responses should aim to understand which are the users' preferences. We expect that the experience with this survey demonstrates which of the approaches have clear advantages over the others, not only for chronic patients, but also for therapists, healthcare professionals, organisations, e-Health tools and other applications. This identified approach will be applied in future developments, and hopefully increase the results of the exercises, even if applied in other health areas. For the behavioural parameters, during these first user tests we will be analyse how the users interacted with the application, from the very first moment the user started using our system until the end of user tests. The methodology to be used for the behavioural research is based on the use of an eye tracking system and A/B testing. The first methodology will enable us to clearly perceive how users visually interact with the system and using touch screen technology. The A/B testing will presents different visual features and interaction design of the same exercise.

As shown in Fig. 1, there are three possibilities for the "Breathing exercise", with different visual formats and interaction designs e.g. therapist on video, or animation video and audio guided exercise. Both of these formats share the same audio characteristics and objective exercise, nonetheless the case with a real therapist shows exactly how the patient should behave and which posture to adopt. Following this same idea, through animation graphics we provide the Breathing exercise with a therapist avatar, in a relaxed environment. However, these two possibilities mentioned could distract the user, during the practice, and for this reason we also provide an audio-only option. Although in our opinion, there is a lack of attractive images in health educational materials [59], in this specific case we will perform usability tests in order to understand which visual material work best with chronic pain patients for this treatment and learning process. Through this method we will understand which format will get better results during the treatment and with which format the users prefers. This part of the study (understanding behavioural characteristics) focuses on engagement and the end-user's level of involvement with a system [47,49]. These behavioural characteristics under analysis could be the frequency, intensity, or depth of interaction over some time range [47]. For this project, examples might helps us understand the number of application visits per user (chronic patient) per day, or the number of module exercises done per user per week, or the number of treatment processes finished. Handheld devices are used as they have been recognised to lead to greater engagement levels [46], especially in the health sector.

Fig. 1. Breathing exercise with different visual features and interaction design

Quantitative and Qualitative Analyses are commonly referred to as Behavioural research methods [50–52]. Quantitative analysis is supported by items that can be numerically measured, as "How many users click here?" or "What percentage of users could find the call-button?". Qualitative research is often entitled as being "soft research" [53] and seeks to respond to the behavioural questions of the users and are open to different results and interpretations (in contrast to the numbers calculated with quantitative research). Quantitative research should be used in tandem with qualitative research methods that provide insight into why application users behave the way they do. The qualitative data enables us to assess the users' feedback on different prototypes and to understand how the target audience assesses the usefulness of the different stimulus material [54]. Why didn't the user see the call for the action? Are there other features that the users could detect on the application? This research usually is based on surveys, questionnaires and conversations with the users.

3.2 System Development

In this section we will focus on our system development process, including data collected, software development and design. Firstly, data collected includes: Usage frequency; Model type of mobile device used; Time between period of utilisation, fast backward steps or undo actions; Process feedback routinely. The above data will report chronic pain types to try and establish any possible correlations with those types, or reported pain intensity. The above data will be used to refine the interaction mechanisms and thus expected to improve the attained user experience. High interaction of the mobile application providing real-time feedback and prompts, is expected to contribute to promote user adherence and engagement. The software created uses a Learning Management System (LMS) which is organized and managed within an e-learning integrated system. LMS's process and disseminate educational material and support administration and communication associated with teaching and learning [56]. In this case, we have focused on the patients education and to provide them with access to the enhanced material and to share other form of treatment, through learning material. The mobile application's design and visual identity were created to provide a clear and light atmosphere during the user experience. All visual content is unique and designed exclusively for this research project. The software used for design content development is Adobe Creative Cloud.

4 Proposed Concept

Our study and mobile application shall be directed at the following target group: Women and Men; Aged between 18 and 65; Chronic pain diagnosis at least for the last three months; Access to mobile application and willingness to do the treatment assiduously (at least once a week). The exclusion criteria will be: currently undergoing other psychological intervention; psychiatric problem (e.g. severe depression, psychotic illness, bipolar disorder, non-suicidal self-injury, e suicide ideation); pain due to malignancy.

Navigation System. The E-health mobile application will give chronic pain access to eight modules throughout the 8-week intervention. They will be advised to follow the modules in a given order (1 module per week). The modules' contents will have different learning objectives: improving the corporal and sensory awareness in the treatment through different practices; understanding the link between mind and body, introducing the concept of Mindfulness (e.g. mindfulness and compassion practice); promoting availability and identify life values; develop the acquired skills. All modules will be composed of different types of content, such as video animation exercises, interactive quizzes, real therapists on video, audio exercises, narratives, complementary texts and downloadable extra exercises targeting specific topics. All data will be linked to a data hub tracking end-users' interactions with the mobile application (i.e. number of log-ins, duration of interaction with application, navigation scheme done by the user, exercise time done by the user, number of visualization of exercises and feedback on each module). Users will be automatically prompted to complete each week's module. Our first pilot test integrates 8 modules of treatment and a "Starting session" which aim to clarify the users how to perform the virtual treatment correctly.

After the registration form has been accepted, the "Starting Session" appears in the first interaction with the application, see Fig. 2. This session shares some informational content, such as introductory videos with the project team. This team is composed by psychologists, therapists, doctors and researchers who explained in this "Starting Session" the mobile application main goals and treatment objectives. This first contact will help patients to better understand, not only the aforementioned goals, but also the program workflow, how to adapt this treatment's practices and exercises to personal needs, and even details like the ideal body postures to adopt, or how to achieve a better self-presence grasp. The concept of self-presence has gained significant interest [57] in particular in the use of virtual environments for different types of exercises of mindfulness, relaxation, breathing, or other, helping the users reach higher intensity rewarding levels. From the very first contact between the user and the system, the application will show the involved health professionals, to help the patient feel accompanied and supported by real people, and not only by a mobile device. After the "Starting Session", the user begins his first treatment module. Once logged in the mobile application, the user gains access to a landing page which shall lodge a quick introduction to the current module. After this introduction, the user is presented with the current practices, topics covered and even homework, as shown in Fig. 3. In this way, the user will know about the next exercises and the most important information-seeking tasks. The user only has access and guidance to the exercises belonging to the current module and therefore the user cannot skip exercises or steps. When a module is finished, the user has the possibility of evaluating it, and assess the pain, as shown in Fig. 4. Although these steps may be skipped, the users will be encouraged to fill them so that the feedback system may benefit from this type of assessment. While following a module, users will receive notifications about new exercises and practices, as they become available, and these notifications will be repeated until they are completed.

During treatment, the user will receive notifications about new exercises, or practices, from the system application, and the user will be also reminded about the exercise, until it is completed. Also in landing page, the user has other key navigation elements: on the left hand corner of the screen there is a "calendar", where the system displays the current weekly calendar with specific suggestions for performing exercises and practices (the user could change the dates proposed by the system); on the right hand corner of the screen there is the "feedback", this screen provides detailed information. At the bottom, and apart from the standard option of "module" which has been explained, the tabbed navigation the system provides: "user profile", this screen shows the user activity from the beginning of treatment and information for each module done; "settings", this function includes information about network connectivity options, user notifications and other system details. The reduced number of interaction elements will help users to interact with the application in a more efficient way by enabling the rapid localization of the functionality of interest at any instant. The main focus of this application is to give the users an overview of the tools available to control their pain and suffering. For this reason, the landing page shares immediate solutions to help the patient feel better. In Fig. 4, we show the system architecture of the mobile application which help us to maintain the system [55]. Thus, the skills of the user experience (UX) designer, information architect, user researcher, and visual designer are in high demand.

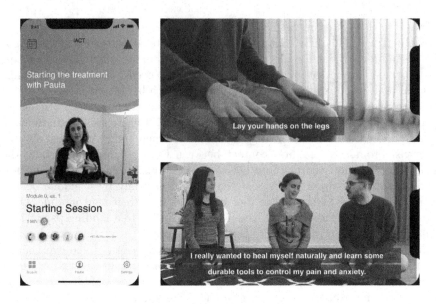

Fig. 2. Starting session screens

Design and Usability. This section describes the design application of our work. We focused on the interface design with the goal of offering an intuitive, attractive and user-friendly experience. We created an identity design which found itself between design and psychology and has adopted a simple visual approach. We developed minimal graphics and we have combined this visual communication with white spaces and Bézier curves [62]. This visual structure and scheme design ensure that the spotlight is on the content and the system functions with convenient navigation and effective visual communication for the end-user. Not only did we use illustrations and motion graphics in the visual content treatment, but also on the mobile navigation. Motion graphics helps the end-user to be more successful and to understand complicated things [63]. The application of this kind of visual content and interaction design creates a bridge between the user interface and user's action. In the sense that connection between patients and system design catch the attention of the end-users and also reduces their time while exploring the application along with giving them a more pleasant and intuitive experience. As already mentioned, the visual content is composed by motion graphics and illustrations and part of such content, at advanced modules, sometimes does not have a narrative storyline. This visual communication, without narrative storyline has long been considered as an effective manner of attracting the attention to health education [58,59]. Also, some of exercises and practices require greater physical concentration and focus on the human body parts. Therefore, these exercises may require a visual composition and more straightforward narratives, thereby this work aims to reduce or even eliminate unnecessary elements and fewer cognitive distractions [60].

Fig. 3. Landing page and exercise introduction

Nevertheless, the development of some exercises fields, such as Mindfulness and QiGong practice are always dependent on results of user-tests mentioned on Sect. 3.1.

The choice of colour was based on psychology of colour principles, and on the visual effect it has on the end-users interaction. Colour presence in a learning environment has an impact on the actions and human behaviour [64]. Focusing on the Human-Computer Interaction and Human Behaviour, certain colours have been linked with emotions or particular ideas and have a major influence on heart which affect the patients' perception [65]. The same colours could have different results in each patient, due to individual characteristics such as relation with the past of each one, temperament, living environment, and these contributions will affect the end-users color reaction [66]. According to a recent study cited by [67], there is a clear benefit when the participants involved are exposed to the blue color in terms of an impact on the psychological effects and social interaction. The use of colours such as red, orange, and yellow will increase more energy and stimulation, while blue, green, and violet creates a sense of relaxed atmosphere, calm and state of "flow" [68]. In this way, the application interface combines mainly colour tones such as blue, green and a few earthy and nature tones.

The user flow doesn't want longstanding users to be tired by repetitive tasks and as shown in Fig. 4, presents graphically how different screens, or pages, are connected and how a user can step through various screens of the system. A further crucial aspect is the consistency when mapping out end-user pathway and minimized the number of "interaction" points to simplify the navigation system. We did not want chronic patients (eventually many of them suffering from constant pain) to spend a lot of time entering personal and health data, every couple of hours. For that, users add their details in the initial application form which is divided into a number of categories and periodically the user is only asked to measure the treatment, usually at the end of each module. As shown in Fig. 5, we present three navigation screens sequences, which the first one shows a practical exercise, the middle screen presents the completion of the exercise and the last one the measure process of each module. This feedback process of the patients, help us to have a better understanding of their experience

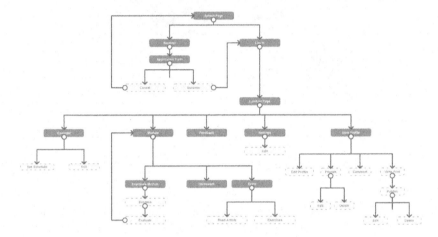

Fig. 4. Mobile application user flow

Fig. 5. Practical exercise and evaluate module

with the application and the treatment, module by module. Our system will be dependent on the end-user attention and for that reason we developed a system according to cognitive engineering and User-Centered Design [69], to achieve the best possible human-computer interaction.

5   Conclusion and Discussion

In this article, we described an E-Health mobile application to a particular target audience. To fully understand the end-users needs, we placed ourselves on a chronic patients' side and we searched the main goals concerning their pain and how they cope with it on their daily lives and we chose the following priorities for using the assistance of a mobile application. The position adopted in this research allowed to think ahead about the end-users' needs, requirements and user experience.

Future work is needed to investigate the following issues:

1. After the first user tests we will develop the whole application according to the results obtained, especially as regards the system navigation and visual content.
2. Further analysis is needed to considers new mobile operating system needs, such as interaction with multi-touch gestures (e.g. the tap, flick, and pinch), device orientation, location, awareness and positioning techniques, in accordance with user interaction.
3. Optimise the application usage control and data collected method. Defining these monitoring features will increase both reliability and efficiency of mobile application usability.

Embracing this research project could provide support to different audiences in understanding the aspects that must be recognized when developing advantageous, user-friendly and health applications. To conclude, we believe this project will provide new digital approaches in the fields of health.

References

1. Bishop, S., et al.: Mindfulness: a proposed operational definition. Clin. Psychol. Sci. Pract. **11**(3), 230–241 (2004)
2. Montero-Marin, J.: Psychological effects of a 1-month meditation retreat on experienced meditators: the role of non-attachment. Front. Psychol. **7**, 1935 (2016)
3. Navarro-Haro, M., et al.: Meditation experts try Virtual Reality Mindfulness: a pilot study evaluation of the feasibility and acceptability of Virtual Reality to facilitate mindfulness practice in people attending a mindfulness conference. PloS One **12**(11), e0187777 (2017). Public Library of Science, Location
4. Christopher, G.: What is mindfulness. Insight J. **22**(3), 24–29 (2004)
5. Zeidan, F., Johnson, S., Diamond, B., David, Z., Goolkasian, P.: Mindfulness meditation improves cognition: evidence of brief mental training. Conscious. Cogn. **19**(2), 597–605 (2010). Elsevier, Location

6. Teasdale, J., Segal, Z., Williams, M., Ridgeway, V., Soulsby, J., Lau, M.: Prevention of relapse/recurrence in major depression by mindfulness-based cognitive therapy. J. Consult. Clin. Psychol. **68**(4), 615 (2000). American Psychological Association

7. Carlson, L., Ursuliak, Z., Goodey, E., Angen, M., Speca, M.: The effects of a mindfulness meditation-based stress reduction program on mood and symptoms of stress in cancer outpatients: 6-month follow-up. Support. Care Cancer **9**(2), 112–123 (2001). https://doi.org/10.1007/s005200000206. Springer

8. Kabat-Zinn, J., Lipworth, L., Burncy, R., Sellers, W.: Four-year follow-up of a meditation-based program for the self-regulation of chronic pain: treatment outcomes and compliance. Support. Care Cancer **9**(2), 159–774 (1986)

9. Miller, J., Fletcher, K., Kabat-Zinn, J.: Three-year follow-up and clinical implications of a mindfulness meditation-based stress reduction intervention in the treatment of anxiety disorders. Support. Care Cancer **17**(3), 192–200 (1995). Elsevier

10. Reibel, D., Greeson, J., Brainard, G., Rosenzweig, S.: Mindfulness-based stress reduction and health-related quality of life in a heterogeneous patient population. Gen. Hosp. Psychiatry **23**(4), 183–192 (2001). Elsevier

11. Grossman, P., Niemann, L., Schmidt, S., Walach, H.: Mindfulness-based stress reduction and health benefits: a meta-analysis. J. Psychosom. Res. **57**(1), 35–43 (2004). Elsevier

12. Silananda, U.: The Four Foundations of Mindfulness. Simon and Schuster, New York (2002)

13. Williams, M., Kabat-Zinn, J.: Mindfulness: diverse perspectives on its meaning, origins, and multiple applications at the intersection of science and dharma. Contemp. Buddhism **12**(1), 1–18 (2011). Taylor Francis

14. Silananda, U.: Psychology of Buddhism and healing method of Japanese self-reflection. Trames **23**(4), 335–351 (2019). Taylor Francis

15. Cullen, M.: Mindfulness-based interventions: an emerging phenomenon. Mindfulness **2**(3), 186–193 (2011). https://doi.org/10.1007/s12671-011-0058-1. Springer

16. Tirch, D., Silberstein, L.R., Kolts, R.L.: Buddhist Psychology and Cognitive-Behavioral Therapy: A Clinician's Guide. Guilford Publications, New York (2015)

17. Olendzki, A.: The roots of mindfulness. In: Germer, C.K., Siegel, R.D., Fulton, P.R. (eds.) Mindfulness and psychotherapy, pp. 241–261. Guilford Press, New York (2005)

18. Shapiro, S.L., Carlson, L.E., Astin, J.A., Freedman, B.: Mechanisms of mindfulness. J. Clin. Psychol. **62**(3), 373–386 (2006)

19. Eberth, J., Sedlmeier, P.: The effects of mindfulness meditation: a meta-analysis. Mindfulness **3**(3), 174–189 (2012). https://doi.org/10.1007/s12671-012-0101-x

20. Kabat-Zinn, J.: Wherever You Go, There You Are: Mindfulness Meditation in Everyday Life. Hyperion, New York (1994)

21. Hutcherson, C., Seppala, E., Gross, J.: Loving-kindness meditation increases social connectedness. Am. Psychol. Assoc. **8**(5), 720 (2008). Elsevier

22. Ozawa-de Silva, B., Dodson-Lavelle, B., Raison, C., Negi, L., Silva, B., Phil, D.: Compassion and ethics: scientific and practical approaches to the cultivation of compassion as a foundation for ethical subjectivity and well-being. J. Healthc. Sci. Humanit. **2**(1), 145–161 (2012)

23. Hoyt, M.: Teaching with mindfulness: the pedagogy of being-with/for and without being-with/for, science and the humanities. J. Curriculum Theorizing **3**(1), 126–142 (2016)

24. Thera, N.: The Four Sublime States: Contemplations on Love, Compassion, Sympathetic Joy, and Equanimity, vol. 30, pp. 4–29. Buddhist Publication Society, Kandy (2008)

25. Bhikkhu, T.: Mindfulness defined (2007). Accessed 30 Nov 2007
26. Ashburn, M., Staats, P.: Management of chronic pain. Lancet **353**(9167), 1865–1869 (1999)
27. Gouveia, M., Augusto, M.: Custos indirectos da dor crónica em Portugal. Revista Portuguesa de Saúde Pública **29**(2), 100–107 (2011)
28. Buchenau, M., Suri, J.: Experience prototyping. In: Proceedings of the Conference on Designing Interactive Systems: Processes, Practices, Methods, and Techniques, pp. 424–433 (2000)
29. Catch my pain. https://www.catchmypain.com/
30. My pain diary. http://mypaindiary.com/
31. Pain scale. http://www.painscale.com/
32. Manage my pain. http://www.managinglife.com/
33. Chronic pain tracker. http://www.chronicpaintracker.com/
34. Flaredown. http://www.flaredown.com/
35. Curable. http://www.curablehealth.com/
36. Kaia. https://www.kaiahealth.com
37. My chronic pain team. http://www.mychronicpainteam.com/
38. Nogueira, M., Menezes, P., Carvalho, S., Castilho Freitas, P.: ACTwithpain - building an online platform for helping Chronic Pain Patients. In: Exp.AT 2019 (2019)
39. Buxton, B.: Sketching User Experiences, Getting the Design Right and the Right Design, pp. 115–125, 440–475. Morgan Kaufmann, Burlington (2007)
40. Wu, J., Wang, S., Lin, L.: Mobile computing acceptance factors in the healthcare industry: a structural equation model **27**(3), 66–77 (2006)
41. Sedrati, H., Nejjari, C., Chaqsare, S.: Mental and physical mobile health apps: review, **5**(10) (2016)
42. Andersson, J., Kjerrman, V.: Patient Empowerment and User Experience in eHealth Services. A Design-Oriented Study of eHealth Services in Uppsala County Council (2013)
43. Salvendy, G.: Handbook of Human Factors and Ergonomics. Wiley, Hoboken (2012)
44. Kuniavsky, M.: Observing the User Experience: A Practitioner's Guide to User Research. Elsevier, Amsterdam (2003)
45. Rohrer, C.: When to use which user-experience research methods. Nielsen Norman Group (2014)
46. Bastien, C.: Usability testing: a review of some methodological and technical aspects of the method. Int. J. Med. Inf. **79**(4), e18–e23 (2010)
47. Rodden, K., Hutchinson, H., Fu, X.: Measuring the user experience on a large scale: user-centered metrics for web applications. In: Proceedings of the SIGCHI Conference on Human Factors in Computing Systems. ACM (2010)
48. Hornbæk, K.: Current practice in measuring usability: Challenges to usability studies and research. Int. J. Hum. Comput. Stud. **64**(2), 79–102 (2006)
49. Attfield, S., et al.: Towards a science of user engagement (position paper). In: WSDM Workshop on User Modelling for Web Applications (2011)
50. Benbasat, I., Zmud, R.W.: Empirical research in information systems: the practice of relevance. MIS Q. **23**(1), 3–5 (1999)
51. Peffers, K., Tuunanen, T., Rothenberger, M.A., Chatterjee, S.: A design science research methodology for information systems research. J. Manage. Inf. Syst. **24**(3), 45–77 (2007)
52. Huysmans, P., De Bruyn, P.: A mixed methods approach to combining behavioral and design research methods in information systems research. In: ECIS (2013)
53. Qualitative Research Approach. https://www.statisticssolutions.com/qualitative-research-approach/. Accessed 12 Dec 2019

54. Martin, B., Bruce, H.: The Pocket Universal Methods of Design: 100 Ways to Research Complex Problems, Develop Innovative Ideas, and Design Effective Solutions. Rockport Publishers, Gloucester (2018)
55. Bandi, A., Fellah, A.: Design issues for converting websites to mobile sites and apps: a case study. In: 2017 International Conference on Computing Methodologies and Communication (ICCMC), pp. 652–656. IEEE (2017)
56. McGill, T.J., Klobas, J.E.: A task-technology fit view of learning management system impact. Comput. Educ. **52**(2), 496–508 (2009)
57. Heeter, C., Lehto, R., Allbritton, M., Day, T., Wiseman, M.: Effects of a technology-assisted meditation program on healthcare providers' interoceptive awareness, compassion fatigue, and burnout. J. Hosp. Palliat. Nurs. **19**(4), 314–322 (2017)
58. Adam, M., McMahon, S.A., Prober, C., Bärnighausen, T.: Human-centered design of video-based health education: an iterative, collaborative, community-based approach. J. Med. Internet Res. **21**(1), e12128 (2019)
59. Houts, P., et al.: The role of pictures in improving health communication: a review of research on attention, comprehension, recall, and adherence. Patient Educ. Couns. **61**(2), 173–190 (2006)
60. Shneiderman, B., Bederson, B.: Maintaining concentration to achieve task completion. In: Proceedings of the: Conference on Designing for User Experience. AIGA: American Institute of Graphic Arts (2005)
61. McCrickard, D.S., Chewar, C.M.: Attuning notification design to user goals and attention costs. Commun. ACM **46**(3), 67–72 (2003)
62. Logas, J., Mitchell, W., Khan, M., Freeman, L., Zeagler, C., Jackson, M.M.: A toolkit for animal touchscreen slider design. In: Proceedings of the Fifth International Conference on Animal-Computer Interaction (2018)
63. Skjulstad, S.: Communication design and motion graphics on the Web. J. Media Pract. **8**(3), 359–378 (2007)
64. Savavibool, N.: The effects of colour in work environment: a systematic review. Environ. Behav. Proc. J. **1**(4), 262–270 (2016)
65. Abbas, N., Kumar, D., Mclachlan, N.: The psychological and physiological effects of light and colour on space users. In 2005 IEEE Engineering in Medicine and Biology 27th Annual Conference, pp. 1228–1231 (2006)
66. Health Research.: Color Healing Chromotherapy, An exhaustive survey compiled by health research from 21 works of the leading practitioners. In: Health Research P.P. Box 860, Pomeroy (1999)
67. de Bell, S., Graham, H., Jarvis, S., White, P.: The importance of nature in mediating social and psychological benefits associated with visits to freshwater blue space. Landscape Urban Plann. **167**, 118–127 (2017)
68. Gutierrez, K.: Ways Colour Psychology Can Be Used to Design Effective eLearning. SHIFT's eLearning Blog (2014)
69. Norman, D.A.: Cognitive engineering. User centered system design (1986)

Preliminary Findings Regarding the Effect of an Interactive Wall to Promote Hand Hygiene Among Healthcare Workers

Beatriz Pereira[1], Hande Ayanoglu[1,2], and Emília Duarte[1,2(✉)]

[1] IADE, Universidade Europeia, Av. D. Carlos I, 4, 1200-649 Lisbon, Portugal
`beatrizrpereira215@gmail.com`,
`{hande.ayanoglu,emilia.duarte}@universidadeeuropeia.pt`
[2] UNIDCOM/IADE, Av. D. Carlos I, 4, 1200-649 Lisbon, Portugal

Abstract. Interactive walls offer promise for behaviour change due to their ability to engage and maintain the attention and interest of users, in a fun and appealing way. This paper presents an interactive wall designed to promote compliance with World Health Organization's hand hygiene guidelines and discusses its acceptance and user experience by healthcare workers. Although hand hygiene is considered the most effective method to prevent healthcare-associated infections, compliance rates with hand hygiene guidelines still remain below recommended levels, raising morbidity, deaths and healthcare costs. Thus, keeping healthcare workers motivated and involved in maintaining best hand hygiene practices is at the heart of this problem. The study was conducted at a Portuguese hospital and pre- and post-intervention data was collected. Preliminary results gathered about risk perceptions, consequences of non-compliance with hand hygiene guidelines and user experience, suggest that a solution like this, which is based on prospective memory and disgust emotions, triggered by visual reminders, easy to learn and use, and involving gesture-based interaction, can be a good approach to complement existing initiatives to improve compliance with hand hygiene guidelines in hospital settings.

Keywords: Interaction design · Design for Health · Healthcare-associated infections · Hand hygiene · Interactive wall

1 Introduction

Hand hygiene is a generic term referring to any action involving hand washing or disinfection. It's aim is to decrease colonization with transient flora [1] and has been highly recognized over the past two decades as the most effective method for preventing Healthcare-Associated Infections (HCAIs) [2]. According to the World Health Organization (WHO), HCAIs are a serious problem worldwide, with a significant impact on patients, as well as on the health sector's sustainability, being associated with numerous deaths per year [1]. Although hand hygiene practice is crucial, compliance rates with

© Springer Nature Switzerland AG 2020
A. Marcus and E. Rosenzweig (Eds.): HCII 2020, LNCS 12202, pp. 329–341, 2020.
https://doi.org/10.1007/978-3-030-49757-6_23

its guidelines are considerably below what is recommended by the WHO, ranging from 40% to 60% worldwide [1, 3].

In the broad field of Design for Health and Wellbeing, there are many solutions that aim to promote wellbeing and, therefore, reduce the negative outcomes associated with unhealthy/risky behaviours [4]. However, keeping the Healthcare Workers' (HCWs) engaged and motivated in maintaining the best hand hygiene practices remains a challenge, mostly because of the many well-known barriers. Previous studies on hand hygiene compliance have found that forgetfulness associated with routine/automation is one of the main causes for poor compliance [3].

Recent research shows that innovative technology-enabled tactics with visual reminders, based on behavioural theories, can meet the emotions of professionals and be effective for behavioural change [5, 7].

We, therefore, designed an interactive wall with visual reminders, based on prospective memory and emotion of disgust, to act on the forgetfulness caused by the routine and automation associated with hand hygiene protocols. This solution was designed to be used as a complementary action, together with other strategies already in use in many hospitals since the multi-action approaches are found to be the most effective [7].

Given the complexity of hospital organizational structure and infection control's multidimensional nature, which includes distinct groups of professionals, it is essential to fully involve the user in all the phases of the design process, according to a Human-Centered-Design (HCD) approach. The purpose of the current study was, therefore, to evaluate the general acceptance and user experience of an interactive wall applied at the Hospital Beatriz Ângelo, in Lisbon.

1.1 Hand Hygiene and Obstacles to Compliance

Numerous studies conducted over the past two decades have shown that the proper follow-up to hand hygiene practices can effectively reduce the transmission of HCAIs, promoting patient health and safety [8]. HCAIs consist of infections that occur in the patient during the care process in a hospital or a health service, not present at the time of admission [1].

To optimize compliance with hand hygiene practices worldwide, the WHO has established guidelines that consist of five moments (opportunities) where hand hygiene should be performed [1]: (1) before touching the patient, (2) before aseptic procedures, (3) after exposure to body fluids, (4) after touching the patient, and (5) after touching the physical environment around the patient. However, while hand hygiene practice is critical, adherence and appropriate implementation by healthcare workers are significantly lower than expected.

Several barriers and obstacles to the proper execution of hand hygiene practices have been identified over time; e.g., lack of training and practice of the techniques [4]; absence and/or failures in the observation and monitoring; failures in the implementation of multimodal strategies for a positive institutional culture around hand hygiene [9]; forgetfulness/automation and lack of time due to patient care priorities [10] or scarce or inconvenient access to hand hygiene supplements [9, 12, 13]. While hand hygiene seems to be simple, its practice is related to human behaviour (which is very difficult to change), constituting a huge challenge, directly reflected in the current failure of its successful practice [12].

1.2 Prospective Memory and Visual Clues/Reminders

Prospective memory, being the opposite of retrospective memory, involves remembering to perform a planned action that is expected to be performed later, with failures here affecting patient safety [13]. Reason [14] identifies several cognitive factors that could potentially contribute to omissions of prospective tasks that contribute to non-compliance with hand hygiene, such as the overload of information in the individuals' short-term memory, failure to perceive hand hygiene as an important task in their daily routines and the fact that they perceive hand hygiene procedures as a highly repetitive and tedious task.

To minimize the impact of possible gaps in prospective memory, authors argue that the use of external cues/reminders can support behavioural changes, leading to the desired action without relying on the prospective memory, combining both the trigger for the action and the content of the desired action [5]. These authors distinguish between two different types of visual cues/reminders: the focal cues, which overlap with information relevant to the task in progress, and non-focal cues that, though present in the environment, are not part of the information considered by the person in the moment of action. Zandt [15] claims that the two most important aspects for the success of visual cues are conspicuity and visibility. Conspicuity refers to placing the visual reminder or clue so that it clearly stands out from the background. Visibility refers to the ability to see the reminder under all expected viewing conditions. These authors also argue that multimodal reminders/clues, such as the combination of visual and audio warning signs, are more effective than just one-way reminders (e.g., only visual), but that their effectiveness depends on the project characteristics.

1.3 Emotion of Disgust as a Strategy to Promote Hand Hygiene

Disgust emotion is a negative emotion associated with repulsion and disapproval. It has been suggested as a factor involved in the chain of events that lead to performing hand hygiene [16], because it can trigger the need of self-protection from diseases [17].

Recent research shows that reminders based on behavioural theories and directed at professionals' emotions can be more effective [5]. Whitby and colleagues [18] state that hand hygiene is a ritual behaviour, performed mainly for self-protection against HCAIs, whenever the hands are visually dirty, supposedly dirty or "emotionally dirty". Therefore, stimuli that cause discomfort or aversion can motivate the practice of hand hygiene procedures. These can be bodily secretions, such as faeces and mucus, items that look dirty and certain animals. This could help to explain why the first moment of hand hygiene is the most often ignored opportunity, with a lower rate of adherence compared to the last moment [14, 17].

Pellegrino and colleagues [5] carried out a two-part study, in which the first part consisted of showing disgusting videos (for example, someone splashing with residual liquid). In the second part, disgust/aversion posters were placed in two bathrooms and two standard educational posters in two other public bathrooms. When comparing the results, they found that the intervention based on posters that caused aversion was significantly better in promoting hand hygiene, suggesting that this type of intervention can increase the likelihood that individuals will remember to act according to planned behaviour.

Other non-scientific interventions also based on the emotion of disgust were carried out. For example, at the Cedars-Sinai medical centre, in Los Angeles, USA, an image of a doctor's hand full of bacteria was used as a screensaver on hospital computers, making invisible contamination of the hands visible. In this intervention, compliance with hand hygiene at this hospital increased to almost 100% [17]. Based on the same type of intervention, a school spread pictures of objects full of bacteria that students regularly touched. This intervention resulted in a significant increase in the use of disinfectant alcohol before students went to lunch [17].

1.4 Interactive Warnings and Reminders

As claimed by previous studies [19–21], technology will transform conventional methods of risk communication and such technology-based solutions may be more effective than their static/printed counterparts, because people are less attuned to stimuli that do not change, especially in heavily repetitive situations.

An interactive strategy based on interactive visual reminders, through the application of prospective memory and the emotion of disgust in creating animations can, therefore, have several advantages over conventional posters applied in hospitals: (i) They are more effective in attracting the attention of professionals, due to their salience, not only visual but multimodal. (ii) They are also effective in maintaining the attention and interest of users given the way they make content available at levels of progression and depending on the response to certain user actions, keeping some degree of curiosity and surprise. (iii) The versatility of the solutions, allowing total customization through the integration of different animations depending on the services and/or the professionals, will also enable work on issues of comprehension and memory, as well as overcoming obstacles in terms of attitudes and beliefs. (iv) As it is a playful strategy and allows professionals to interact with animations, it will not only attract more attention than a simple static poster, overcoming the problem of monotony and habituation, but will generate greater motivation and engagement, especially if associated with a serious game strategy.

2   Method

2.1   Participants

The study was conducted at Hospital Beatriz Ângelo, Loures, Portugal. Two anonymous questionnaires were distributed via e-mail to the healthcare workers from this hospital, recruited through the Infection Control and Antimicrobial Resistance Group. One questionnaire was about hand hygiene and the other about the user experience with the interactive wall. The first questionnaire was applied pre- and post-intervention, while the second one was only applied afterwards.

A total of 84 participants answered the pre-intervention questionnaire. Participants who gave negative answers to the first question "Do you regularly attend the restaurant and cafeteria areas, located on floor −1 of this hospital?" (area of intervention) were excluded, reducing the sample to 73 respondents.

A total of 22 participants answered the post-intervention questionnaires. Participants who gave negative answers to the first question "Have you used the interactive solution (projection) available in the cafeteria/restaurant access zone of the hospital during the last two weeks?" (area of intervention) were subtracted, resulting in a total of 13 valid responses to the questionnaires.

2.2 Materials and Procedure

Questionnaires. A questionnaire about hand hygiene related questions was distributed via e-mail to all the Hospital staff. This questionnaire was applied twice, pre- and post-intervention, to assess differences regarding: (i) willingness to comply with hand hygiene protocols, (ii) perception of the importance of hand hygiene for patient safety, (iii) perception of the severity of the consequences of non-compliance with the hand hygiene protocol, and finally, (iv) perception about control in the transmission of infectious diseases. The questions, adapted from Wogalter and colleagues' study [22], are shown in Table 1. They made their judgments using a 5-point rating scale.

A second questionnaire was applied post-intervention to measure the user experience with the interactive wall: a) Attractiveness: General impression of the product: do users like it or not? b) Transparency: is it easy to become familiar with the product and learn to use it? c) Efficiency: can users solve their tasks without unnecessary effort? Reacts fast? d) Control: does the user feel control under the interaction? Is it safe and predictable? e) Stimulation: is it exciting and motivating to use the product? Is it fun to use? f) Innovation: Is the product design creative? Does it capture users' interest? The questions, based on a scale validated by Laugwitz, Held and Schrepp [23] and translated into Portuguese by Cota, Thomaschewski, Schrepp and Gonçalves [24] are shown in Table 2.

Prototype. The interactive wall measured 1.80 m wide and 1.50 m high and was projected by means of an EPSON EB-S05 projector. The animation was created in Unity 5. A Kinect motion sensing device, connected to a Windows PC via a USB port, was used to detect the presence of healthcare workers and allow interaction (i.e., gestures). The Kinect programming was made using in C# and the Visual Studio 2015 IDE (integrated development environment). Two speakers were used for the animations' sound.

Participants were able to interact, individually, with the interactive wall using hand gestures and displacement. The interaction was composed of two parts, the first one in which they were automatically exposed to an interface (a screensaver) with an awareness phrase - "Spread the word, not germs. Wash your hands!" accompanied by the sound of someone sneezing. At this point, animated bacteria followed the participants if they moved in the surrounding area covered by the Kinect (Fig. 1). If no motion was detected by the Kinect, the animation would remain in the first moment (screensaver).

If a motion was detected and then the participant remained still for more than five seconds in front of the wall, in an area indicated by a sticker on the floor, an animated image of a healthcare worker's hand holding a patient's hand appeared and began to get contaminated by insects (i.e., cockroaches), used as a representation of germs. This image was complemented by the sentence – "Did you know that in this Hospital the hand

Fig. 1. Screen saver

Fig. 2. Repulsive image with insects

hygiene rate is only 76%?" (Fig. 2) and, simultaneously, there was a sound associated with the insects. The number of insects kept rising unless the participants decided to start the hand hygiene procedure (i.e., "press" a button with an icon of a hand sanitiser solution dispenser). In response to this action, the number of insects would start to diminish until they vanished from the animation (Fig. 3).

Fig. 3. Repulsive image without insects

Fig. 4. Image with instructions

To help participants interact with the wall, some instructions were shown; e.g., stretching the arm horizontally until you noticed that the button for the alcoholic solution dispenser had been selected (confirmation by changing the colour). By selecting the button, and as the amount of alcohol in the dispenser decreased, the insects began to disappear from the screen (Fig. 4). The objective was to awaken the desire or need to interact with the wall so that the germs disappeared from the projection. If Kinect did not detect movement in the area of the alcohol dispenser button, the interface would show the phrase – "Do not let your patient's safety fall into your hands" and the instruction for interaction would be shown again.

The computer system automatically counted the number of interactions per day, as well as the number of incomplete interactions (only the first moment), half complete (till the instructions for interaction in the second moment) and complete (activate dispenser to eliminate germs).

Settings. The interactive wall prototype was installed, for two weeks, in a hallway from the Beatriz Ângelo Hospital leading to the cafeteria. The hallway measured 2,80 m wide and 3 m long. A "Stop here" sticker was placed on the floor to make the interactive wall more noticeable. Figure 5 shows the settings used.

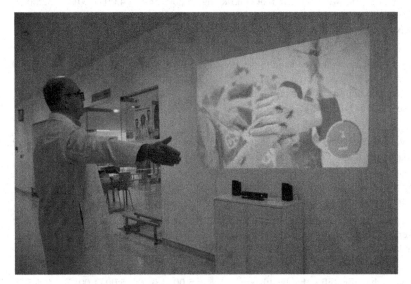

Fig. 5. The arrangement of the apparatus in the hallway

3 Results

3.1 Number of Interactions

The results obtained through the automatic counting of interactions by the system show that during the two weeks that the solution was available, there were 582 interactions initiated. These interactions correspond to the number of times that the system (Kinect) detected the presence of a professional or movement within the detection area. The system also counted 427 unfinished interactions, corresponding to occasions when the professionals were detected and stopped for more than 5 s to observe or perceive the interaction, but did not proceed until the final interaction. The large number of unfinished interactions may be related to the heavy workload and little break time.

Finally, 107 completed interactions were counted, in which the professional interacted from beginning to end, successfully ending and reaching the final goal (i.e., to make the insects disappear from the wall).

3.2 Pre- and Post-questionnaires

The healthcare workers' perceptions gathered before and after the intervention, through the pre- and post-intervention questionnaires, are shown in Table 1.

Table 1. Results of the pre- and post-intervention questionnaire

Questions	Pre (n = 73)	Post (n = 13)	MW Test	
	Mdn (IQR)	Mdn (IQR)	U	p
1- In your opinion, what is the risk of contracting an infection associated with healthcare? Scale: 1-Nothing risky; 2-Slightly risky; 3-Risky; 4-Too risky; 5-Extremely risky	3.00 (2.00)	4.00 (1.00)	328.0	0.63
2- In your opinion, when the hand hygiene protocol is not followed in a hospital context, what is the probability of transmitting infectious diseases? Scale: 1-Unlikely; 2-Slightly Unlikely; 3-Neutral; 4-Slightly likely; 5-Extremely likely	5.00 (0.00)	5.00 (0.00)	383.5	0.116
3- In your opinion, how serious can the consequences of non-compliance with the hand hygiene protocol be? Scale: 1-Not serious at all; 2-Slightly serious; 3-Serious; 4-Very serious; 5-Extremely serious	5.00 (1.00)	5.00 (1.00)	390.0	0.292
4- In your opinion, how strict should healthcare workers be in complying with hand hygiene procedures? Scale: 1-Not strict at all; 2-Slightly strict; 3-Strict; 4-Very strict; 5-Extremely strict	5.00 (0.00)	5.00 (1.00)	451.0	0.746
5- What is the probability that healthcare workers, in this hospital in general, perform hand hygiene? Scale: 1-Unlikely; 2-Slightly unlikely; 3-Neutral; 4- Slightly likely; 5-Extremely likely	5.00 (1.00)	5.00 (1.00)	465.5	0.972
6- How likely are the strategies implemented by the hospital to improve my adherence to hand hygiene procedures? Scale: 1-Unlikely; 2-Slightly unlikely; 3-Neutral; 4-Slightly likely; 5-Extremely likely	5.00 (0.00)	4.00 (1.00)	321.0	0.23
7- To what extent do I have control over the risks of transmitting infectious diseases? Scale: 1-No control at all; 2-Slight control; 3-Control; 4-A lot of control; 5-Full control	4.00 (1.00)	4.00 (1.00)	426.5	0.538

We were interested in understanding whether their perceptions about the risk, severity and control associated with infectious diseases, and awareness related to the importance of hand hygiene increased or decreased after having interacted with or noticing the wall.

Overall, the results indicate that the healthcare workers are very aware of the risk of contracting IACs, as well as the importance of compliance with hand hygiene guidelines to prevent them. A Mann Whitney U test was conducted to assess whether or not participant perceptions regarding hand hygiene were significantly affected by the interactive wall. Table 1 displays the results of the test. Although the median values attained by pre- and post-questionnaires are different for two questions (1 – Risk of contracting infection and 6 – Effectiveness of hospital interventions), the results reveal the interactive wall was not significant in any of the items assessed.

3.3 User Experience Questionnaire

The Experience Questionnaire (UEQ) was applied to evaluate the healthcare workers' user experience when interacting with the interactive wall. Only the responses from the participants that confirmed having interacted with the wall were considered. Table 2 shows the user experience evaluation results through the UEQ.

Table 2. Results from the user experience questionnaire (UEQ) (n = 13).

Item	Scale	Mean	VAR	SD		Left	Right
1	Attractiveness	0.5	3.4	1.9	→	Annoying	Enjoyable
2	Perspicuity	0.9	2.4	1.6	↑	Not understandable	Understandable
3	Novelty	0.6	4.9	2.2	→	Creative	Dull
4	Perspicuity	1.2	2.5	1.6	↑	Easy to learn	Difficult to learn
5	Stimulation	−0.1	3.7	1.9	→	Valuable	Inferior
6	Stimulation	0.2	3.3	1.8	→	Boring	Exciting
7	Stimulation	0.2	3.6	1.9	→	Not interesting	Interesting
8	Dependability	0.2	3.5	1.9	→	Unpredictable	Predictable
9	Efficiency	0.4	4.3	2.1	→	Fast	Slow
10	Novelty	1.5	3.1	1.8	↑	Inventive	Conventional
11	Dependability	0.2	1.9	1.4	→	Obstructive	Supportive
12	Attractiveness	0.0	3.5	1.9	→	Good	Bas
13	Perspicuity	2.2	1.0	1.0	↑	Complicated	Easy
14	Attractiveness	0.6	4.9	2.2	→	Unlikeable	Pleasing
15	Novelty	0.5	3.6	1.9	→	Usual	Leading edge
16	Attractiveness	0.4	3.1	1.8	→	Unpleasant	Pleasant
17	Dependability	1.1	1.7	1.3	↑	Secure	Not secure
18	Stimulation	0.1	2.4	1.6	→	Motivating	Demotivating
19	Dependability	−0.1	2.4	1.6	→	Meets expectation	Does not meet expectation
20	Efficiency	0.2	4.6	2.2	→	Inefficient	Effective
21	Perspicuity	1.1	1.7	1.3	↑	Clear	Confusing
22	Efficiency	1.6	1.4	1.2	↑	Impractical	Practical
23	Efficiency	0.8	2.0	1.4	→	Organized	Cluttered
24	Attractiveness	0.5	4.6	2.1	→	Attractive	Unattractive
25	Attractiveness	0.6	4.3	2.1	→	Friendly	Unfriendly
26	Novelty	0.8	3.0	1.7	→	Conservative	Innovative

The UEQ questionnaire consists of six main scales with 26 items: (1) Attractiveness; (2) Perspicuity; (3) Efficiency; (4) Dependability; (5) Stimulation; (6) Novelty. The scale ranges from 1 to 7, where answers between 1 and 3 (−3) are considered an extremely bad/negative evaluation; 4 is considered a neutral/average (0) answer and 5 to 7 (+3) are considered good/positive evaluations [26]. Note that, in some cases, the assessment on the left is positive and, in others, it is negative because each item is represented by two terms with opposite meanings. Regarding the order of terms, it is random per item: half of the items on a scale start with the positive term and the other half with the negative. The arrows in the second column indicate whether the gathered value is positive (↑), negative (↓) or neutral (→).

Bearing in mind that values ranging from −0.8 to 0.8 are considered neutral [25], results show that only seven of the 26 items attained positive evaluations, while the remaining 19 items attained a neutral/average evaluation. No negative evaluations were gathered. According to Cota, Thomaschewski, Schrepp and Gonçalves [24], very extreme values are rarely observed. Therefore, a value close to 2 represents a very positive participant impression.

Perspicuity was the most positively evaluated scale, with four items having the highest means (item 13 – M = 2.2; item 4 – M = 1.2; item 21– M = 1.1; item 2 – M = 0.9). Item 13 was the one with the highest mean value, which means the participants considered the wall as easy to use, easy to learn, clear, and understandable. Other positively evaluated items were item 22 (M = 1.6), from the efficiency scale; item 10 (M = 1.5), from the novelty scale and item 17 (M = 1.1.), from the dependability scale. This means the participants also evaluated the wall as practical, inventive, and secure. The lowest evaluations were attained by item 5 (M = −0.1), from the stimulation scale, and item 19 (M = −0.1) from the dependability scale. Other items with an average close to zero were 12 (M = 0), from the attractiveness scale; items 18 (M = 0.1), 6 and 7 (M = 0), all from the stimulation scale; items 8 and 11 (M = 0.2), from the dependability scale and, finally, item 20 (M = 0.2), from the efficiency scale.

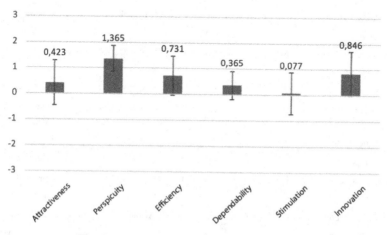

Fig. 6. Overall results for UEQ items, per scale.

When looking into the results analysed by scale (Fig. 6), it appears that the "Stimulation" (0.077), "Dependability" (0.365), "Attractiveness" (0.423) and "Efficiency" (0.731) scales had values <0.8, being assessed by the healthcare workers as neutral. The "Innovation" (0.846) and "Perspicuity" (1.365) scales are rated by healthcare workers as positive, with values >0.8.

Thus, according to the results related to the scales described above, it is reasonable to state that, in general, the healthcare workers considered the experience mostly neutral. The fact that positive values are also found, indirectly suggests that the interactive solution was considered acceptable, allowing us to consider future improvements to be implemented to raise the quality of the prototype and increase the neutral values to more solid ones in the future.

4 Discussion

The present study investigated the influence of an interactive wall on the healthcare workers' perceptions about hand hygiene and its association with HCAIs. The user experience with the wall was also assessed.

The wall was intended to work as an interactive visual reminder based on prospective memory and the emotion of disgust, to act on healthcare workers' forgetfulness to comply with the hand hygiene protocols. The idea behind this strategy was to cause discomfort and aversion in the healthcare workers, leveraging them to act and interact with the wall, working as a trigger for subsequent interaction with other means in use, as part of a broader strategy. Pellegrino [26] claims that strategies based on static visual reminders, such as posters, are effective and recommended in many interventions to improve hand hygiene, working more as educational tools than motivational ones. Education alone, however, is not able to increase adherence. Thus, more sophisticated means are required to influence behaviour related to hand hygiene, taking into account behavioural theories, as they do not function only as mere reminders.

A substantial amount of interaction with the interactive wall was registered, suggesting that it raised some interest in the hospital staff. However, the wall did not significantly affect the healthcare workers' perceptions regarding hand hygiene assessed via the pre- and post-intervention questionnaires. This, somewhat surprising, null finding is most likely due to the type of questions, which may have produced a ceiling effect, and the sample size for the post-intervention questionnaire.

The results from the UEQ indicate, globally, a neutral evaluation of the wall. The limitations of the Microsoft Kinect technology, which are well-known, such as not detecting rapid movements or not detecting people unless they are right in front of the camera, can explain this result, since it is associated with some frustration in the users, leading to lack of interest.

However, overall, the findings indicate that the interactive wall can be an effective method of calling attention to the importance of hand hygiene. Perhaps further investigation with longer periods of exposure to the wall; more and richer content being shown; more effective technology being used and other instruments to collect data, would lead to different findings.

Acknowledgments. This study was supported by UNIDCOM under a grant from the Fundação para a Ciência e Tecnologia (FCT) No. UID/DES/00711/2019 attributed to UNIDCOM – Unidade de Investigação em Design e Comunicação, Lisbon, Portugal. The authors would like to thank Hospital Beatriz Ângelo and its Local Coordination Group of the Program of Prevention and Control of Infections and Antimicrobial Resistance, and specifically Dr. Carlos Palos for his assistance in the data collection. We would also like to express our gratitude to José Graça, from IADE's Games and Apps Lab, for his support and generous assistance in programming the interactive wall.

References

1. World Health Organization: A Guide to the Implementation of the WHO Multimodal Hand Hygiene Improvement Strategy, pp. 12–48 (2010)
2. Geilleit, R., et al.: Feasibility of a real-time hand hygiene notification machine learning system in outpatient clinics. J. Hosp. Infect. **100**(2), 183–189 (2018)
3. Kurtz, S.L.: Identification of low, high, and super gelers and barriers to hand hygiene among intensive care unit nurses. Am. J. Infect. Control **45**(8), 839–843 (2017)
4. Pereira, P., Duarte. E.: Designing a gamification strategy to promote hand hygiene compliance. In: Duarte, E. (ed.) Design Doctoral Conference 2016: Transversality - Proceedings of the DDC 3rd Conference, pp. 128–135. Edições IADE, Lisbon (2016)
5. Pellegrino, R., Crandall, P.G., Seo, H.S.: Using olfaction and unpleasant reminders to reduce the intention-behavior gap in hand washing. Sci. Rep. **6**, 1–9 (2016)
6. Jenner, E.A., Jones, F., Fletcher, B.C., Miller, L., Scott, G.M.: Hand hygiene posters: motivators or mixed messages? J. Hosp. Infect. **60**(3), 218–225 (2005)
7. Kolola, T., Gezahegn, T.: A twenty-four-hour observational study of hand hygiene compliance among health-care workers in Debre Berhan referral hospital, Ethiopia. Antimicrob. Resist. Infect. Control **6**(1), 109 (2017). https://doi.org/10.1186/s13756-017-0268-y
8. Alshehari, A.A., Park, S., Rashid, H.: Strategies to improve hand hygiene compliance among healthcare workers in adult intensive care units: a mini systematic review. J. Hosp. Infect. **100**(2), 152–158 (2018)
9. Pittet, D.: Hand hygiene: improved standards and practice for hospital care. Curr. Opin. Infect. Dis. **16**(4), 327–335 (2003)
10. Larson, E.: A tool to assess barriers to adherence to hand hygiene guideline. Am. J. Infect. Control **32**(1), 48–51 (2004)
11. Nicolay, C.R.: Hand hygiene: an evidence-based review for surgeons. Int. J. Surg. **4**(1), 53–65 (2006)
12. Jumaa, P.A.: Hand hygiene: simple and complex. Int. J. Infect. Dis. **9**(1), 3–14 (2005)
13. Nevo, I., et al.: The efficacy of visual cues to improve hand hygiene compliance. Simul. Healthc. **5**(6), 325–331 (2010)
14. Reason, J.: Combating omission errors through task analysis and good reminders. Qual. Safety Health Care **11**(1), 40–44 (2002)
15. Proctor, R.W., Zandt, T.V.: Human Factors in Simple and Complex Systems. CRC Press, Boca Raton (2008)
16. Scott, B., Curtis, V., Rabie, T., Garbrah-Aidoo, N.: Health in our hands, but not in our heads: understanding hygiene motivation in Ghana. Health Policy Plan **22**(4), 225–233 (2007)
17. Porzig-Drummond, R., Stevenson, R., Case, T., Oaten, M.: Can the emotion of disgust be harnessed to promote hand hygiene? Experimental and field-based tests. Soc. Sci. Med. **68**(6), 1006–1012 (2009)

18. Whitby, M., Mclaws, M.L., Ross, M.W.: Why healthcare workers don't wash their hands: a behavioral explanation. Hosp. Epidemiol. **27**(5), 484–492 (2006)
19. Wogalter, M.S., Mayhorn, C.B.: The future of risk communication: technology-based warning systems. In: Wogalter, M.S. (ed.) Handbook of Warnings. Laurence Erlbaum Associates, Inc. Publishers, Mahwah (2006)
20. Hou, C., et al.: How to increase hand hygiene adherence for nurses with an electronic warning system. Am. J. Infect. Control **45**(6), 59 (2017)
21. Marra, A.R., Edmond, M.B.: New technologies to monitor healthcare worker hand hygiene. Clin. Microbiol. Infect. **20**(1), 29–33 (2014)
22. Wogalter, M.S., Young, S.L., Brelsford, J.W., Barlow, T.: The relative contributions of injury severity and likelihood information on hazard-risk judgments and warning compliance. J. Safety Res. **30**(3), 151–162 (1999)
23. Laugwitz, B., Held, T., Schrepp, M.: Construction and evaluation of a user experience questionnaire. In: Holzinger, A. (ed.) USAB 2008. LNCS, vol. 5298, pp. 63–76. Springer, Heidelberg (2008). https://doi.org/10.1007/978-3-540-89350-9_6
24. Cota, M.P., Thomaschewski, J., Schrepp, M., Gonçalves, R.: Efficient measurement of the user experience: A Portuguese version. Procedia Comput. Sci. **27**, 491–498 (2014)
25. Mispa, K., Mansor, E.I., Kamaruddin, A.: Evaluating children's user experience (UX) towards mobile application: the fantasy land prototype. In: ACM International Conference Proceeding Series, pp. 46–54 (2019)
26. Pellegrino, R.: Effect of Sensory Cues on Hand Hygiene Habits Among a Diverse Workforce in Food Service. Unpublished thesis (2015). https://scholarworks.uark.edu/etd/1109

Research on Usability Evaluation and Redesign of Treadmill Man-Machine Interface

Du Qin, Wan Tiantian$^{(\boxtimes)}$, Zhang Xinrui, Dai Roujing, and Marcelo M. Soares

School of Design, Hunan University, Hunan, People's Republic of China
1119487321@qq.com, 893285247@qq.com, 1426710239@qq.com,
472304601@qq.com, soaresmm@gmail.com

Abstract. The objective of this study was to propose a redesign solution to improve the user experience of the treadmill by evaluating the product usability. It was used the following methods: First, the human-machine interface between the user and the treadmill was evaluated using the subjective and objective multidimensional usability assessment method. Among them, the objective usability assessment is based on behavioral indicators (task completion time, task success rate) for analysis; subjective usability assessment uses a questionnaire based on user subjective evaluation. Secondly, combined with the subjective and objective evaluation of experimental results, the treadmill human-machine interface improvement suggestions are proposed and redesigned. Through the results of the experiment, we find that the human-machine interface of the treadmill has great problem with information management and button design. The interface contains too much information in each level and ranks in confusion. Besides, it shows low usage rate on certain buttons, which means a bad design on the usage flow. For a improvement, we select the features of the interface and redesign the interface by ranking the features by the users habits and importance of the features. We redesign the physical buttons into a touch screen but retain the position of each functional button. At the same time, we adjust the vibration feedback for users to reduce distracted from running.

Keywords: Interactive interface · Usability assessment · Subjective evaluation · Objective evaluation · Redesign

1 Description

With the improvement of living standards, people's demand for health and fitness is increasing. In the vicinity of the university town, the number of gymnasiums has also exploded. As a standing fitness equipment in the gym, the treadmill is the first choice for indoor fitness. Using the treadmill can not only avoid unexpected situations that may occur during outdoor sports, but also ensure the safety of the user. The running strength can be adjusted according to the user's wishes, and the physical condition can be feedback and monitored in time. However, as the treadmill continues to evolve, many complex functions have emerged. Although these functions meet the user's additional needs in addition to running, they bring problems to the convenience of operation. In

© Springer Nature Switzerland AG 2020
A. Marcus and E. Rosenzweig (Eds.): HCII 2020, LNCS 12202, pp. 342–350, 2020.
https://doi.org/10.1007/978-3-030-49757-6_24

order to further improve the user experience of the running machine, this paper uses the usability evaluation method to conduct human-computer interaction research on its operation community, aiming at designing a product interface that is convenient, simple and comfortable to use.

2 Previous Research

Through our preliminary investigation around the campus of Hunan University, we found that the existing treadmills are mainly divided into mechanical treadmills and automatic treadmills. Among them, chain gyms like SunPig, Yijia and Mariss all have joint designed automatic treadmills models. They are Yipao M8, Yipao M9 and HUIXIANGN HF6.0. Comparing the three models, we found existing treadmill interface mainly consist of operation buttons, digital display screens, and other functional modules. By reading paper of the related research [1], there are two types of mainstream buttons for treadmills, contact buttons and touch screen buttons.

The success rate of the contact button is high but the service life of the button is short. For the characteristics of the contact buttons, it is suitable for speed shortcuts, slope shortcuts, etc.

The touch screen button has a relatively long service life and has little wear during use. The disadvantage is that the success rate and accuracy are not high, so it is used for speed adjustment and volume adjustment, which is not required to operate accurately during running. Slope adjustment, etc.

As our field observation, we randomly chose 42 users (19 females and 23 males) in the gym to observe. When running on a treadmill, 69.05% users use their index finger and 23.81% users use their thumb to perform the interface operation. According to relevant research [2], the length of the button should be <19 mm when operating with thumb and <10 mm when operating with other fingers. Therefore, the size of circular button should be 8–18 mm and the size of rectangular button should be 10 * 10 mm, 10 * 15 mm or 15 * 20 mm. The existing design size is mostly designed according to the male finger size. The key spacing between the buttons should be designed to avoid user misoperation, and the size of the operation interface should be considered to avoid waste of space.

In addition to the above elements, the treadmill interface has some information elements such as text symbols. The font, size, color and other elements of the text also play crucial roles in the design of the interface. The main factors affecting the size of the text are the user's observation distance, the degree of character clarity, the speed required to obtain the information, etc. The relevant calculation formula is given in ergonomics: character height = (1/200 − 1/300) line of sight. After measuring, we concluded that the line of sight is 800 mm and the minimum of the character height is 2.67 mm when running on a treadmill. In a certain actual design, in order to increase the user's comfort, the height of the text will be increased according to the actual situation. Fonts generally choose between the imitation of the Song and the black body, and the English language uses the Arial font.

3   User Classification

The test. It is a commercial treadmill widely used in the university city gym. Therefore, the users are all students in the university city. For the treadmill, the users can be classified into: primary users, intermediate users and advanced users.

1) Primary users. Such users include those who have never used a treadmill and those who have only tried a treadmill. The characteristics of such users are that they do not know much about the operation mode and use process of the treadmill, and choose to use the corresponding operation according to self-awareness and intuitive understanding of the treadmill. For this type of user, designing relevant operational experiments for them can test whether the current design meets their usage habits and usage expectations. Good design can reduce the time and the psychological burden of their use, and can also reduce their error rate when using.

2) Intermediate users. This type of user is a general user. People who have used more than two treadmills, they probably know how to use the treadmill, have the habit of using the treadmill, in the process of using the treadmill, have formed a stereotype, can be used to test whether the M8 meets the industry common standards Whether it is compatible.

3) Advanced users. These users have not only used more than five treadmills, but also have a good understanding of the functions of most treadmills. Before we redesign the M8 human-computer interface, we can conduct in-depth user interviews to improve the design.

Since we tested the M8, the most used treadmill in the gym around the school, to evaluate the usability, we chose the gym for testing, and after the initial understanding of the treadmill use by the recruited users, the experimental design was carried out.

4   Research Methods

4.1   Usability Assessment Principles

According to cognitive psychology, some scholars have proposed the following basic principles of human-computer interaction design.

1) The principle of consistency, that is, from the task, the expression of information, the interaction control operation, etc., as much as possible to the user's understanding of the familiar model.

2) Compatibility, compatibility between user expectations and the reality of interaction design, based on the user's past experience.

3) Adaptability, the user is in a dominant position, and the interface must adapt to the needs of the user.

4) Guided, guide the user through the task prompt information and feedback information.

5) Structural, interactive design should be a structured design to reduce the complexity of the use process.

6) Economical, interactive design in order to achieve an operational task with a minimum of steps.

Relevant scholars summarized and proposed human-machine interaction interface design recommendations [3].

1) Specific to abstraction, provide specific objects to the user through the interface, let the learner summarize the abstract concept from the specific object, and finally use the simulation system to guide the abstract concept.
2) The visual display is invisible, using clear objects such as diagrams, animations, numbers, and colors to display invisible abstract content.
3) Simulation guides innovation, inspiring users' thinking and encouraging users to participate as much as possible, inspiring users' desire to learn to use.
4) Make full use of recognizing and revisiting, reducing the memory burden when users use the operation.
5) Consider the individual differences between users, using the language that users are accustomed to.

The above five points exemplify the design principle of cognitive psychology from "easy to difficult, gradually strengthened".

4.2 Method of Objective Usability Assessment

The objective usability evaluation method adopts the task completion time, that is, the time for completing each task in the experiment and the time for completing all tasks; the success rate of the task, that is, the ratio of the number of participants successfully completing the task to the total number of participants.

4.3 Methodology of Subjective Usability Assessment

The subjective usability assessment method is that after the test is completed, the questionnaire is filled in and interviewed. The content includes [4]: (1) Whether it is convenient to complete the task; (2) Whether the use process is satisfactory (3) Whether the human-computer interaction interface information is clear; (4) Whether the machine interaction interface is beautiful; (5) Whether the human-computer interaction interface can effectively correct faults and avoid mistakes. The questionnaire uses a 5-level scale, i.e., 1 means very disagree, 2 means disagree, 3 means general, 4 means consent, and 5 means very agree. Subsequently, the experimenter conducted user interviews on the subjects, clarified the operational problems encountered in the experiment, and provided suggestions for the design of the treadmill human-machine interface.

5 The Experimental Process

5.1 Participants

A total of 7 subjects with normal vision (naked or corrected visual acuity of 1.0 or higher, no high myopia) participated in the experiment, including 3 males and 3 females, aged

20 to 25 years. All participants had a treadmill fitness experience at the gym. Before the experiment, each subject read and signed the informed consent form, and informed the relevant experimental procedures and points of attention.

5.2 Data Collection

Evaluation Object. Yipao M8 treadmill human-computer interaction interface consists of two major functional areas of the display and button area. The display mainly displays motion information such as speed, time and heart rate as well as video content; the button area mainly has function keys such as speed adjustment, sound adjustment, stop, start, and emergency stop.

Experimental Procedure. The survey mainly used observation methods, questionnaires and think loud to evaluate the availability of treadmills. The observation method is to record the different users using the treadmill to complete the task (Table 1), the specific implementation process, and ask the different users (Table 2) to find the shortcomings of the M8 treadmill.

Table 1. Description of the experiment task

Task number	Mission details	Key operation
Task 1	Select "calorie mode" to start running	Click on "Sports Center", select "Calories Mode", select the target calories, and click "Confirm"
Task 2	Adjust the speed to 7.5	Press the "speed increase" button
	Adjust the slope to 7	Press the "Slope Increase" button
Task 3	Choose relaxation mode	Press the "relax" button
	Stop running	Press the "stop" button

Table 2. Information table of the object to be tested (fill in the exercise habits, delete it in brackets)

Number	Age	Gender	Sports habit	User classification
A	21	Male	Run everyday	Expert user
B	21	Male	Run twice or three times a week	Intermediate user
C	21	Female	Run occasionally	Intermediate user
D	20	Female	Run once a week	Intermediate user
E	21	Male	Don't run normally	Primary user
F	21	Female	Don't run recently	Primary user

5.3 Objective Usability Assessment Results and Analysis

Task completion time (Refer to the conclusions measured here, compare and analyze the length of each task and the reasons) (Table 3).

Table 3. Average task completion time for all subjects to complete each experimental task

	Task 1	Task 2	Task 3
Average time (S)	34.8 s	23.7 s	18.2 s

Mission Success Rate (**Compare** the success rate here, analyze the reasons, and talk about the improvement suggestions) (Table 4).

Table 4. The success rate, failure reason classification and statistics of the subjects who completed the various experimental tasks

A	task 1	failed	40s	0:19	touched the 'start' button on the screen	couldn't find where the calory mod is
				0:36	dragged the point that represent user and called out the adjust menu by mistake	thought that the point can be operated
				0:37	touched the 'stop' button on the screen by mistake	misoperation
	task 2	success	26s		no obvious mistakes	
	task 3	success	8s	2:45	touched the screen but no respond	the operation was not sensed by the screen
B	task 1	success	20s	0:34	touched the 'application' button on the screen	couldn't find where the calory mod is
	task 2	success	11s		no obvious mistakes	
	task 3	success	10s		no obvious mistakes	
C	task 1	failed	17s	0:29	touched the 'start' button on the screen and gave out to find the calory mod	couldn't find where the calory mod is
				0:44	touched the '6' button of the speed on the screen repeatedly	couldn't get the feedback of touching the screen and speed changing
	task 2	success	23s	1:01	touched the '7' button of the slope on the screen repeatedly	couldn't get the feedback of touching the screen and slope changing
				2:14	touched the '4' button of the speed on the screen	try to slow down the speed and relax by manual
	task 3	success	59s	2:29	touched the '34' button of the slope on the screen	try to gentle down the slope and relax by manual
D	task 1	failed	55s	0:12	asked how to use the safety clip	for non-experience user, there is no guide of the safety clip
				0:51	missed the calory mod and return to the main page	

(continued)

Table 4. (*continued*)

D	task 2	success	55s	1:28	touched the 'settings' button on the screen	couldn't find where to adjust the speed and the slope
				1:30	touched the 'machine management' button on the screen	
				1:46	touched the 'pause' button on the screen	
	task 3	success	21s	no obvious mistakes		
E	task 1	failed	15s	0:07	touched the 'start' button on the screen and gave out to find the calory mod	couldn't find where the calory mod is
	task 2	success	14s	no obvious mistakes		
	task 3	success	4s	no obvious mistakes		

5.4 Subjective Usability Results and Analysis

convenience

	1. I can easily recover when I meet error with using the treadmill.	2. I can get clear error feedback when I meet error with the treadmill.	3. I can quickly find message that I need.
A	3	3	3
B	3	3	1
C	2	2	1
D	2	2	1
E	2	3	3
F	2	4	3
average	2.33	2.83	2
midian	2	3	2
mode	2	3	2
variance	0.22	0.47	1

convenience

	1. Generally, I feel convenient when I use the treadmill.	2. I feel convenient when I use the touch screen.	3. I feel convenient when I use the press-button.
A	4	4	3
B	3	4	3
C	2	2	1
D	4	1	1
E	3	3	3
F	4	2	4
average	3.33	2.67	2.5
midian	3.5	2.5	3
mode	3.5	3.5	3
variance	0.56	1.22	1.25

satisfaction

	1. Generally, I am satisfied with the treadmill.	2. I feel satisfied when I'm running.	3. I feel satisfied when I'm adjusting the slope.	4. I feel satisfied when I'm adjusting the speed.	5. I think the treadmill satisfying my need.
A	4	4	5	4	4
B	4	3	2	2	3
C	2	3	2	2	3
D	3	4	4	3	4
E	4	4	4	4	4
F	4	4	4	2	4
average	3.5	3.67	3.5	2.83	3.67
midian	4	4	4	2.5	4
mode	4	4	4	2	4
variance	0.58	0.22	1.25	0.81	0.22

	1. I think the treadmill can respond me nicely.	2. I can understand the words and images on the interface.	3. I I can easily learn how to use the treadmill.	4. I am satisfied with style of the treadmill.
A	4	4	4	5
B	4	2	2	2
C	2	2	1	2
D	4	2	1	2
E	4	3	3	3
F	3	4	5	3
average	3.5	2.83	2.67	2.83
midian	3.5	2.5	2.5	2.5
mode	4	2	1	2
variance	0.58	0.81	2.22	1.14

5.5 Language and Body Language

1) 4 of the participants asked how to use the safety clip.
2) All participants asked where is the calory mod, and half of them gave up in the end.
3) of the participants used the touch screen almost through the whole test, 1 of them used press-button and 2 of them used the buttons only when they adjusted the slope and speed.
4) When using the press-button, one of the participants bent down because of her bad sight.
5) One of the screen users held his hand on the upside of the screen.

6 Treadmill Man-Machine Interface Redesign

Based on the results of subjective and objective multidimensional usability assessment, the suggestions for improving the man-machine interface of the treadmill are as follows:

1) The button area is replaced by a touch screen, the position is unchanged, and the screen vibration feedback is adjusted. Since the button area is close to the armrest, it is easy to operate accurately during running, but the button life is too short, so the touch screen is used instead. The gym is noisy and difficult to concentrate when running, so the touch screen will respond with vibration every time you adjust.
2) Reasonable design of running speed and slope function. The operation of the two is confusing, and is distinguished by words, colors, and patterns;
3) Visual display of running speed and slope. M8 treadmill button area adjusts the slope speed. Each time you press it, you can only adjust 0.1. Therefore, increase the running speed bar and slope bar in the button area to adjust the speed and slope to the user satisfaction value quickly.
4) Optimize the interface layout. The interface visual center of gravity is prioritized according to the visual habit and the importance of the function.
5) Increase the position where the phone is placed. Almost everyone in modern colleges and universities are mobile phones, and mobile phone slots are properly designed on treadmills to fully meet the needs of users.

According to the above suggestions, redesign the treadmill man-machine interface (Figs. 1 and 2).

Fig. 1. The original man-machine interface design.

Fig. 2. The redesigned man-machine interface.

References

1. Zhu, Y.Z.: Study on the Human-Machine Interaction Interface of the Treadmill. Zhejiang University (2015)
2. Wang, X.: A study of keys design based on user knowledge. Hefei University of Technology (2009)
3. Zhao, J.H.: Design Psychology. Beijing Institute of Technology Press (2006)
4. Ou, T.Y., Perng, C., Hsu, S., Chiou, W.-C.: The usability evaluation of website interface for mobile commerce website. Int. J. Netw. Virtual Organ. **15**, 152 (2015). https://doi.org/10.1504/IJNVO.2015.070425

Can an Environmental Feature Influence Interview Anxiety?
A Virtual Reality Study

Elisângela Vilar[1]([⊠]), Paulo Noriega[1], Tânia Borges[1,2], Francisco Rebelo[1], and Sara Ramos[2]

[1] Faculdade de Arquitetura, CIAUD, Universidade de Lisboa, Rua Sá Nogueira, Polo Universitário, Alto da Ajuda, 1349-055 Lisbon, Portugal
ebpvilar@edu.ulisboa.pt, paulonoriega@gmail.com, taniaborges20@gmail.com, frebelo@fa.ulisboa.pt
[2] ISCTE - Institute of Lisbon, Avenida das Forças Armadas, 1649-026 Lisbon, Portugal
sara.ramos@iscte.pt

Abstract. This paper presents a study using a virtual reality-based methodology that aims to investigate the effect of nature-like surroundings on interview anxiety. For this, sixty-three volunteers were asked to participate in a study in which a job interview was simulated in a virtual environment. An experimental condition – an office with a nature-like surroundings, and a control condition – without nature-like surroundings, were considered in a between subject design experiment. Self-perceived anxiety and emotional arousal were the dependent variables. Main findings suggests Main results suggest that nature-like surroundings can positively influence IA for men, whereas it negatively influences IA for women. Nature-like surroundings lowered men's concerns regarding their communication and behavioral IA and on the other hand enhanced female's performance IA. These findings are of great interest and can be seen as a step forward towards the understanding of gender differences amongst automatic nonconscious emotion regulation strategies.

Keywords: Virtual reality · Interview anxiety · Emotion regulation · Interior design

1 Introduction

Job interview, possibly, is the most used technique for a recruitment and selection [1] and the most daunting to the candidates. According to Huffcutt, Van Iddekinge, & Roth [2], anxiety is an inherent part of the job interview process and it also has the potential to interfere on hiring the individual who better fits the job and organization, mainly considering the fast paced and stressful work environment that many organization has in these days. For another hand, it can become problematic when it impedes the candidate from getting through to the next phase of the selection process without proving his/her value. Research has shown that highly anxious individuals receive significantly lower performance ratings by the interviewer than low-level anxious individuals [3–5].

© Springer Nature Switzerland AG 2020
A. Marcus and E. Rosenzweig (Eds.): HCII 2020, LNCS 12202, pp. 351–369, 2020.
https://doi.org/10.1007/978-3-030-49757-6_25

According to Cook and colleagues [3], anxious individuals are less likely to get a second interview, which is positively and significantly correlated to getting a job offer [3].

Research shows that some indicators of anxiety can lead the interviewer to believe the applicant is less competent, less qualified, and less proactive and motivated than any other competing candidate, although this may not necessarily be the case [3, 6].

Thus, in the context of job interviews, the interviewee frequently experiences state anxiety, recently described as interview anxiety (IA), as such a situation is highly stressful, evaluative and future threat-related [7, 8].

According to Bechtel and Churchman [9], physical environments are antecedent factors that have the capacity to either operate as stressors of human adaptive capacities or as coping resources. Empirical evidence has revealed that individuals can be more influenced by the salient physical artifacts in organizational settings than the actual occupant [see 10, 11], and that these influences are often unconscious (Cave, 1998, cited by [9]). Evidence suggests that environmental features such as nature-like surroundings convey a pleasing and calming experience [12], which can be essential for decreasing IA.

In this context, the main objective of this paper is present a study carried out to verify the effect of environmental features, namely nature-like surroundings, on IA. The main hypothesis is that nature-like surroundings can positively affect (i.e., lower) IA during a simulated interview.

For this, a Virtual-Reality (VR) based methodology was considered. VR can be defined as a paradigm of a human-computer interaction in which users are active participants in a computer generated three-dimensional world [13]. According to Berto (2014) studies have proved the effectiveness of using immersive VR as a valid stimulation of various positive visual and auditory stimuli that affect individuals' emotional responses, self-efficacy, and mood. The use of VR as a method in the present work can increase the psychological fidelity of the job interview in a laboratory setting with less cost and higher control of variables.

2 Methodology

The main objective of the present work was to investigate the effect of environmental features, namely nature-like surroundings, on interview anxiety (IA).

A between-subjects design was used considering two conditions: (i) An experimental condition – an office with a nature-like surroundings in which (a) plants with foliage and (b) a window with a view for an external green area were present in the virtual environment; and, (ii) A control condition – without nature-like surroundings.

Considering these, two hypothesis were formulated:

H1 – Participants will present lower self-perceived anxiety scores in the nature-like surroundings (experimental condition).
H2 – Participants will present lower physiological emotional arousal levels in the nature-like surroundings (experimental condition).

2.1 Participants

Sixty-three university students (38 women) from Psychology and Management of Human Resources degrees, participated voluntarily and gained partial credit on their respective course. They were aged between 19 and 30 (M = 21.73, SD = 2.48) and had on average experienced 2.16 (SD = 2.71) job or internship interviews. Participants were randomly assigned to two groups: the experimental condition or the control condition. In the experimental condition the participants (n = 31; 17 women and 14 men) were aged between 19 and 25 (M = 21.71, SD = 1.8) and had on average experienced 1.38 (SD = 1.66) job or internship interviews. In the control condition, the participants (n = 32; 21 women and 11 men) were aged between 19 and 30 (M = 21.74; SD = 3.06) and had on average experienced 2.97 (SD = 3.32) job or internship interviews. Trait anxiety was considered as a control variables, so participants with trait anxiety level score above the normal population (superior to 47 and 49, for men and women, respectively) were excluded from the sample [see 14 for normative population data]. Due to the exclusion criteria, 11 participants were removed from data analysis.

2.2 Measures

Sense of Presence. The sense of presence was evaluated through an adapted version of the Presence Questionnarie [15] as a manipulation check. Answers were collected in a seven-point Likert scale (1 indicating 'Never', 'Very low' or 'Very little' and 7 representing 'Always', 'Very much' or 'A lot'). As the Portuguese validated version was not available, a translation and retroversion method was used to guarantee the best conversion of the questionnaire.

Self-perceived Anxiety. Two self-reported measures were applied to evaluate the level of anxiety: STAI-Y-Form and MASI. Regarding STAI [16], the trait scale was applied before the job-interview in order to eliminate high trait anxiety participants. The MASI specifically measures IA. This questionnaire was created and validated by Mccarthy and Goffin [5] and has been recently used for job interview situations in VR [17]. Answers were collected in a 5-point scale (with 1 indicating "strongly disagree" to 5 signifying "strongly agree"). This questionnaire was used at the end of each interview.

The SAD Scale [18] and the BFNE [19] were used to evaluate trait of social anxiety. The SAD evaluates the level of discomfort, fear and anxiety experienced in social situations as well as their purposeful avoidance in a 5-point Likert scale [20, 21]. The BFNE estimates the level of preoccupation about being negatively evaluated [19]. The questionnaire contains 8 statements; participants are asked to rate how well each statement describes them in a five-point Likert scale.

Emotional Arousal. Participants' EDA is an established indicator of the sympathetic activation of the autonomous nervous system. The measurement of EDA as skin conductance is able to indicate one's emotional arousal [22]. More specifically, the data of the tonic level of the electrical conductivity of the skin, or SCL, was collected through an exosomatic measurement with Direct Current, using the Biopac MP1000 system (Biopac Systems, Inc) with the module GSR 100C as a response amplifier.

2.3   Virtual Environment (VE) and Virtual Character (VC)

The VE was developed based on architectural, psychological and computer engineering understandings that outlined the subsequent requirements for the VE development. In this way, VE was designed considering that it should represent a context of an organization, with a two-linked rooms (a waiting room and an office room), uniform light/shadow effects for conditions with artificial lighting and sunlight, with decorative elements to increase depth perspective, and use solid colors instead of non-identifiable/visible textures on walls, floors or furniture. The VE was previously validated in a pilot study [23]. Figure 1 shows images from the VE for the waiting room and office room for experimental and control conditions. A VC was also inserted. It was a male free model retrieved and animated via Blender® Software (Version 2.74) and integrated into to Unity3D® platform.

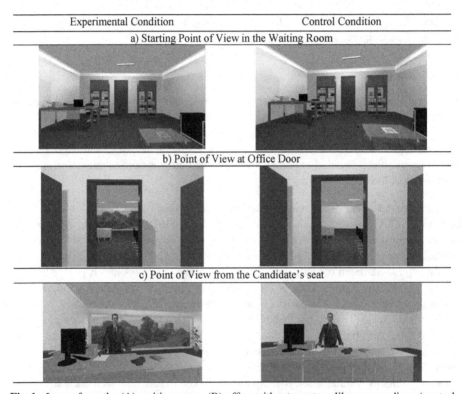

Fig. 1. Image from the (A) waiting room, (B) office without a nature-like surroundings (control condition), and (C) office with a nature-like surroundings (experimental conditions). (Color figure online)

2.4   Materials

All physiological data were collected using Ag-AgCl electrodes with a 0.6 mm diameter and K-Y lubricant gel was used to increase conductivity [24]. The Biopac (Biopac

Systems, Inc.) received participants' arousal activity with GSR 100C modules and the SCL was registered by the Acknowledge 3.7.2 software (Biopac Systems, Inc.) that was installed in an Asus® computer, with an Intel®-Core™ processor with 2,80 GHz, 4 GB of memory RAM, and a Microsoft Windows® 7 Enterprise – Service Pack 1 operation system, 2009 version (Microsoft Corporation).

In order to register events throughout the data collection in real time, the EDA was visualized through a LG W2453TQ 24 in. Monitor DVI with a resolution of 1920 × 1080. Throughout the experiment, participants remained seated and viewed the VE (first-person egocentric viewpoint) via a head-mounted display (HMD): the Oculus Rift Development Kit 2 (DK2). The simulation ran in an AlienWare M18X Computer (Intel® Core i7-3610QM) with 16 GB RAM, an 18.4-in. display (1920 × 1080), and dual graphics of 2 GB GDDR5 Nvidia GTX 675 M SLI 1 SR. A Logitech® keyboard K120 was used as a navigation device. The researcher watched the participant - VR interaction (on the AlienWare Computer's monitor) in order to manage the entire experiment. Figure 2 shows the experimental setup.

Fig. 2. The experimental setup: a) the participant's setup; b) the entire experimental setup with the researcher on the left and participant on the right.

2.5 Experimental Design and Procedure

The current study was conducted in two parts with a 3-month gap. In the first part, participants were recruited in a classroom setting. Participants were informed the study aimed to evaluate a VR simulation that would collect data regarding their behavior in an organizational context. They were not aware about the real objective of the study. Those who wished to participate signed a consenting form and answered three questionnaires: 1) the trait anxiety subscale of the STAI, 2) FNE Scale and 3) SAD Scale. After, demographic details (age, gender), name of course, number of internship or job interviews and lastly a contact (of their choice) to schedule the second part of the experiment were provided. Participants were instructed to answer the set of questionnaires individually and in silence. The measures provided participants' trait characteristics enabling to exclude clinically anxious individuals.

For the second part of the study, experiments were scheduled individually and lasted approximately 35 min. On arrival to the laboratory, participants were randomly assigned to one of two conditions (n = 31 in the nature-like surrounding office and n = 32 in the control office; between-subjects design). All participants fulfilled three phases: 1) a VR configuration and a training session, 2) a VR job interview session and 3) self-reported questionnaires.

After signing the informed consent form, participants were asked to wash their hands with a nonabrasive soap prior to having the electrodes attached. The electrodes, with K-Y lubricant gel, were then put on the participant's distal phalanges of the index and middle finger of their non-dominant hand. At this moment the recording of the SCL began. Next, the experimental procedure (i.e., the 3 phases) was explained and the materials (the Oculus 2DK and keyboard) that the participant would use were presented.

The first phase began with a VR configuration. The keyboard and Oculus Rift DK2 head strap was adjusted to each participant to maximize comfort. The latter was next configured through the "Oculus Configuration Utility" tool and the "Demo Scene" to ensure the participant was positioned correctly in the VE.

Next, the investigator introduced the VR training session. This session aimed to familiarize the participant with the VR simulation and the experimental setup (i.e., the navigation and visualization devices). The navigation was free and controlled by the participant through the keyboard arrows. Additionally, this session allowed a preliminary check for any indications of simulator sickness. The VE used for this phase consisted of a room with a closed door and a meeting table in the center. Only after the investigator ensured the participant's full use of the equipment could the participant go on to the next phase. Next, between the end of the first and beginning of the second phase, the SCL baseline was registered during approximately 2 min.

The second phase was the VR job interview session. Participants were first given the anxiety eliciting job interview narrative to read [25]. The narrative was presented in a presentation format and on paper. In addition to the narrative, the fictitious Company's Brand (Bworker) and the succeeding instructions were presented: *"You will find yourself near the sofa in the waiting room. The receptionist will inform you through a loudspeaker when you can enter Dr. Vilar's office. When called, go towards the office door that is in front of you, it will open automatically. Enter the office and sit on the chair in front of Dr. Vilar who will interview you. He will ask you some questions. Act as if you were in a real interview and answer directly to what is asked. You have a maximum time of 1 min to answer each question after which Dr. Vilar will interrupt you and go on to the next question. Good luck!"* Participants took approximately 4 min to read the narrative. Once they were ready to start the VR simulation, the Oculus 2DK were placed and the job interview simulation began.

In the job interview simulation (Fig. 1), a green colored magazine on the table in the waiting room indicated the participant would go in to a nature-like surrounding office (experimental condition). On the other hand, a yellow colored magazine in the same position and table indicated that the participant would go in to the control office condition. All participants waited for at least 30 s in the waiting room to be called. This allowed participants to experience a similar waiting time as in a real interview and begin in a neutral VE. They were called (by pressing the key 'Z') to go into the corresponding office (nature-like surrounding or control office). As soon as the participant entered the door, he/she was asked to sit in front of the interviewer who instantly said, "Please, sit down", indicating the chair in front of him and sitting down at the same time. The interviewer asked participants the same list of 8 questions, in the same order (see Table 1).

Table 1. Interview questions presented across all conditions.

No	Interview question
1	Tell me, what are your expectations and goals?
2	Tell me about a time when you made a mistake and overcame it?
3	What did you learn from the experience?
4	What was the last book you read?
5	What was it about?
6	How do you cope under pressure?
7	What type of leader are you?
8	What are your plans for the future?

The questions shown in Table 1 were formulated based on previous VR job interviews [17, 26]. The interviewer did not give facial or body reactions. Furthermore, when the participant's answers were shorter than 30 s, concluding expressions were implemented (e.g., OK, I am going to go on to the next question; Thank you). When the participant's answers exceeded 60 s, breaking-off expressions were given (e.g., Sorry to interrupt you, we have to go on to the next question; OK I will go on to the next question). At the end of the interview, the participant was thanked and informed he/she would be contacted soon. Once the simulation ended, the Oculus 2DK was removed as well as the electrodes. The investigator used a keyboard map to control all interaction moments of the VC with the participant.

After the interview, the participants had the third and final phase. They were asked to respond to the MASI questionnaire [5] and the PQ [15]. Subsequently, a debriefing was given to all participants regarding the study's main objective.

3   Results

3.1   Data Analysis

In order to measure participants' EDA, average SCLs were examined during the baseline period, the narrative, the waiting room and the interview. The baseline period chosen is characterized by the last 2 min of a resting mode. The narrative period consists of the whole interval of time used by the participant for this task. The waiting room period accounts for the moment of entry in VR until the moment in which the participant was called to go into Dr. Vilar's office (i.e., interview room). From this instant onwards, a 30 s interval (15 s before and after) was considered at the following specific events: Call for Interview, First Question of Interview, Last Question of Interview and End of Interview.

To reduce inter-individual variances and assure the correct proportion of intra-individual ranges, Lykken, Rose, Luther, and Maley's [27] range correction was applied for each period. Through this correction, the inter-individual physiological differences, which do not relate to the psycho-physiological processes from the experimental procedure, are eliminated [27].

The significance level for all of the statistical comparisons was set at $p < .05$. By default all analysis were conducted using the subject as the unit of analysis and the SPSS software (Version 19, IBM SPSS Statistics). Normality and homogeneity variance assumptions were verified and analysis was conducted accordingly. Posterior to manipulation check of experimental conditions, the following dependent variables were deemed relevant to our study: self-perceived anxiety scores and physiological arousal. The control variables, such as gender and interview experience, were also considered in the analysis for each dependent variable.

3.2 Manipulation Check

In order to evaluate the equivalency between conditions, mean comparison tests were conducted for the trait anxiety scale of STAI-Y form, BFNE and SAD. The average comparison of trait anxiety scores between conditions did not reveal a significant difference ($M = 37.48$, $SD = 7.00$, for the experimental condition; $M = 34.18$, $SD = 5.85$, for the control condition, $t(51) = 1.87$, $p = .07$, $d = .49$). The FNE scores also showed a nonsignificant difference between conditions ($M = 2.62$, $SD = .86$, for the experimental condition; $M = 2.32$, $SD = .68$, for the control condition, $t(51) = 1.21$, $p = .23$, $d = .39$), as well as the SAD scores ($M = 68.48$, $SD = 17.03$, for the experimental condition; $M = 63.39$, $SD = 13.65$, for the control condition, $t(51) = 1.87$, $p = .14$, $d = .33$). These results indicate the participants were equally distributed between conditions regarding trait-anxiety and social anxiety levels.

Regarding sense of presence, the experimental condition reported an average PQ score of 5 ($SD = .43$) while the control condition scored an average of 5.02 ($SD = .63$). The average PQ between conditions did not reveal significance ($t(50) = -.02$, $p = .90$, $d = .04$), indicating participants experienced an approximately equal level of presence. Also, given that the PQ ranged from 1 to 7, we can consider participants experienced a positive level of presence.

3.3 Self-perceived Anxiety Scores

Regarding self-perceived anxiety scores, we hypothesized that participants in the nature-like surrounding would report lower self-perceived anxiety scores than the control surrounding. We also expected that this effect would be evidenced despite differences in gender and the number on interviews previously experienced. Table 2 presents average and standard deviations of the MASI scores across conditions, gender and experienced interviews as main effects.

Table 2. Average (Standard Deviation) Scores and Sample Size (n) of Communication Anxiety (CA), Performance Anxiety (PA), Behavior Anxiety (BA) and MASI Composite among main effects of condition, gender and experienced interviews.

	Condition		Gender		Experienced interviews	
	Experimental	Control	Women	Men	Zero	One/two
	M (SD)	M (SD)	M (SD)	M (SD)	M (SD)	M (SD)
CA	3.19 (.98)	3.01 (.87)	3.20 (.96)	2.92 (.84)	3.41 (.82)	3.12 (.86)
PA	3.5 (1.01)	3.15 (.61)	3.52 (.82)*	2.98 (.76)*	3.52 (.79)	3.18 (.90)
BA	2.99 (.87)	2.99 (.76)	3.14 (.75)*	2.80 (.86)*	3.40 (.57)*	2.86 (.86)*
MASI composite	3.20 (.82)	3.05 (.60)	3.28 (.70)*	2.90 (.68)*	3.44 (.53)	3.06 (.78)
n	28	23	31	20	18	19

Note. Average values are based on a scale of 1–5, with 1 signifying totally disagree and 5 indicating totally agree.
*Score significant at p < .05, **Score significant at p < .001.

Independent t-tests for MASI scores were conducted to evaluate average differences between the experimental (nature-like surroundings) and the control condition. The analysis of MASI's dimensions separately showed participants in the experimental condition reported on average more Communication Anxiety (CA) than the participants in the control condition, however no significant difference was revealed, t(50) = .71, p = .49, d = .01. Likewise, participants in the experimental condition also reported a higher average Performance Anxiety (PA) than the control group. Though the average PA scores did not reach significance, it did reach a medium sized effect (t(38, 61) = 1.52, p = .14, d = .49). Thirdly, average Behavior Anxiety (BA) scores between conditions were approximately equivalent; no statistical difference was obtained (t(51) = −.01, p = .99, d = .002). Concerning the MASI Composite, which combines CA, PA and BA, the experimental condition reported a higher average score than the control condition although this difference did not reach significance (t(43, 20) = .78, p = .44, d = .24). Overall, participants' self-perceived anxiety scores were higher in the nature-like surrounding than in the control surrounding, despite the fact that no significant differences among conditions were obtained.

Subsequently, a two-way MANOVA was performed with condition and gender as independent variables. The dependent variables were CA, PA, BA and the MASI composite. Women consecutively reported higher anxiety scores when compared to men (Table 2). No main effect of gender was found on CA (F(1, 48) = 2.16, p > .05, ηp^2 = .04). Yet, the analysis did reveal a main effect of gender on PA (F(1, 48) = 8.59, p = .005, ηp^2 = .15), BA (F(1, 48) = 4.31, p = .04, ηp^2 = .09), and MASI Composite (F(1, 48) = 7.2, p = .01, ηp^2 = .13). Interestingly, the condition × gender interaction also revealed significant statistical differences among all dependent variables; i.e., CA (F(1, 48) = 7.54, p = .01, ηp^2 = .14), PA (F(1, 48) = 12.17, p = .001, ηp^2 = .20), BA (F(1, 48) = 9.36, p = .004, ηp^2 = .16) and MASI Composite (F(1, 48) = 15.22, p < .001, ηp^2 = .24). Average scores reported for each dependent variable are shown separately in Fig. 3.

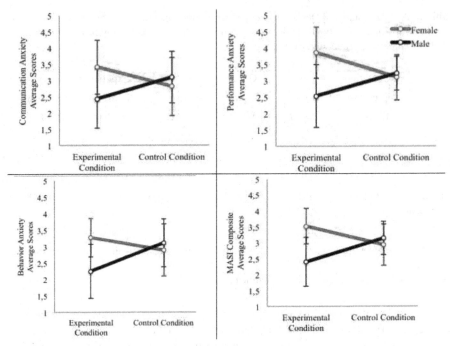

Fig. 3. Average Scores and Standard Deviations of (a) Communication Anxiety (CA), (b) Performance Anxiety (PA), (c) Behavior Anxiety (BA) and (d) MASI Composite Anxiety among interaction between conditions (Experimental and Control) and gender (women and men). (Note. Average values are based on a scale of 1–5, with 1 signifying totally disagree and 5 indicating totally agree.)

These results show that women and men significantly experienced the same VE differently. Women reported more anxiety in the experimental condition than in the control condition. They experienced significantly higher levels of PA (t (29) = 2.84, p = .01, d = 1.02) and MASI Composite (t(29) = 2.58, p = .02, d = .91) in the experimental (nature-like surrounding) condition compared to the control condition. Results regarding CA and BA between conditions did not reach significance, however average scores are predominantly higher in the experimental condition than in the control condition (p > .05). Such results indicate that the nature-like surroundings for the women were significantly counterproductive in terms of PA and IA in general (i.e., MASI Composite). On the other hand, men experienced the nature-like surrounding inversely; generally they reported lower IA in the experimental condition than in the control condition. Men reported significantly lower levels of CA (t(18) = −2.07, p = .05, d = −0.97), BA (t(19) = −2.67, p = .02, d = −1.18), and MASI Composite (t(19) = −2.99, p = .01, d = −1.31) in the experimental condition in comparison to the control condition. Thus, on the contrary to women, the experimental condition decreased men's CA, BA, and IA in general (i.e., MASI Composite).

Table 3. Average (Standard Deviation) Scores and Sample Size (n) of Communication Anxiety (CA), Performance Anxiety (PA), Behavior Anxiety (BA) and MASI Composite among interaction condition × number of experienced interviews.

| | Experimental condition | | Control condition | |
| | Zero experienced interviews | One/two experienced interviews | Zero experienced interviews | One/two experienced interviews |
	M (SD)	M (SD)	M (SD)	M (SD)
CA	3.22 (.98)	3.05 (.99)	3.65 (.54)	3.20 (.74)
PA	3.57 (1.01)	3.25 (1.06)	3.46 (.43)	3.11 (.72)
BA	3.40 (.46)	2.65 (1.00)	3.40 (.71)	3.09 (.65)
MASI composite	3.39 (.70)	2.98 (.93)	3.50 (.21)	3.14 (.61)
n	10	10	8	9

Note. Average values are based on a scale of 1–5, with 1 signifying totally disagree and 5 indicating totally agree.

3.4 Physiological Arousal

The tonic level of the electrical conductivity of the skin (SCL) was measured as an indicator of physiological arousal related to an emotional event. We hypothesized that the nature-like surrounding would lower SCLs in comparison to the control surrounding, and that this effect would be observed despite gender and number of experienced interviews. Average SCLs will be reported regarding seven specific moments: 1) baseline (2 min), 2) narrative (whole duration), 3) waiting room (whole duration), 4) call for the interview (30 s interval), 5) moment of first question (30 s interval), 6) moment of last question (30 s interval), and 7) moment of the end of interview (30 s interval). Figure 4 shows the average SCLs between the experimental (nature-like surroundings) and control condition.

The arousal levels are approximately equal until the first moment of the interview, i.e., the beginning of the interview. From the beginning of the interview onwards, the experimental condition (nature-like surroundings) tended to gradually report lower average SCLs in comparison to the control condition. A mixed ANOVA (using a Greenhouse-Geisser correction) with the experimental phase (baseline, narrative, waiting room, call for interview, first question, last question and end of interview) as a within-subject variable and condition (experimental or control) as a between-subject variable was conducted. Results revealed that a significant main effect of the experimental phases on the average SCL, $F(2, 89.91) = 45.44$, $p < .001$, $\eta p^2 = .50$. All participants had significantly different average SCLs between each experimental phase. On the other hand, neither the effect of condition (experimental vs. control), $F(1, 45) = 0.34$, $p = .56$, $\eta p^2 = .01$, nor the interaction experiment phase × condition, $F(2, 89.91) = 0.32$, $p = .73$, $\eta p^2 = .01$, were significant.

Further pairwise comparisons of SCL between experimental phases evidenced that participant's arousal levels were significantly higher during the narrative, in the waiting room and during the interview compared to the established baseline ($p < .001$).

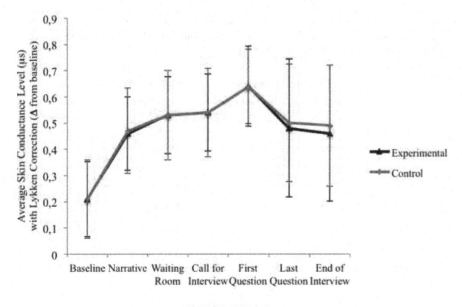

Fig. 4. Average and Standard Deviation of skin conductance levels (μs) between conditions across the main experiment phases (baseline, narrative, waiting room, call for interview, first question, last question and end of interview).

This indicates that the experience as a whole was emotionally arousing across conditions. Secondly, participants significantly experienced higher arousal levels when using VR (i.e., from the waiting room onwards) than when they did not (i.e., narrative moment) (p < .001), demonstrating the potential of VR creating higher emotional experiences. Thirdly, regarding the participant's arousal throughout the simulation, there was a significant increase from the baseline, to the narrative, to the waiting room phase (p < .001). Then, participants' average SCL was at its peak at the beginning of the interview (i.e., when the first question of the interview was asked) and significantly higher than all the other experimental phases (p < .001). Figure 4 shows a significant decrease towards the end of the interview (i.e., last question of the interview) and from the last question of the interview to the actual end of the interview, in which despite a decreasing tendency no significant differences were found (p > .05).

Likewise to the self-reported anxiety analysis, the effect of gender and number of interviews experienced were considered. It was expected that average SCLs would be lower in the nature-like surrounding than in the control surrounding, regardless of gender and number of interviews experienced. Table 4 shows the average SCLs among gender and number of experienced interviews as main effects.

Regarding gender, women predominantly reported higher average SCLs from the baseline phase until the first interview question phase than the men. However, from the first to the last interview question the women's average SCL decreased more comparatively to men. Also, women had lower average SCLs in the last two experimental phases

Table 4. Average (Standard Deviation) skin conductance level (μs) and Sample Size (n) between gender as well as number of experienced interviews for each experimental phase (i.e., baseline, narrative, waiting room, call for interview, first question, last question and end of interview).

	Gender		Number of experienced interviews	
	Women	Men	Zero	One/two
Baseline	.22 (.12)	.21 (.16)	.19 (.12)	.25 (.18)
Narrative	.46 (.14)	.43 (.16)	.46 (.14)	.44 (.19)
Waiting room	.55 (.13)	.51 (.21)	.53 (.13)	.51 (.22)
Call for interview	.58 (.17)	.57 (.22)	.58 (.18)	.57 (.22)
First interview question	.65 (.13)	.62 (.18)	.63 (.13)	.53 (.19)
Last interview question	.49 (.22)	.52 (.28)	.50 (.22)	.52 (.29)
End of interview	.48 (.23)	.51 (.28)	.49 (.23)	.51 (.28)
n	28	18	15	17

(last interview question and end of interview) than men. Additionally, between women a greater difference was noted in the experimental condition than in the control condition. Meanwhile men registered an approximate mean difference between conditions (see Table 5). A mixed ANOVA (with a Greenhouse-Geisser correction) was completed with condition (experimental and control) and gender (women and men) as between-subject variables and experimental phases as a within-subject variable. Results did not reveal a main effect of gender amongst experimental phases ($F(1.98, 85.11) = 0.32, p = .73$, $\eta p^2 = .01$) nor an interaction effect of condition $\times$ gender ($F(1.98, 85.11) = 0.24, p = .79$, $\eta p^2 = .01$).

The effect of the number of experienced interviews participants had in the past was further investigated. The average arousal levels between participants who had no experience and who had one or two interviews are presented in Table 5. Participants with no experience were more aroused than experienced participants during the narrative moment, the waiting room and at the moment of the first interview question. Between experimental conditions, participants with no experience reported lower arousal levels in the experimental condition in comparison to the control condition from the moment the interview began. Similarly, participants with one or two experienced interviews also reported lower levels of arousal in the experimental condition than in the control condition. A mixed ANOVA (with Greenhouse-Geisser correction) was conducted with condition (experimental and control) and number of experienced interviews (zero and one/two) as between-subject variables and experimental phases as a within-subject variable. Alike to the previous analysis, no main effect of the number of experienced interviews was observed across all experimental phases ($F(2.05, 59.49) = .27, p = .77$, $\eta p^2 = .01$). The interaction condition $\times$ number of experienced interviews also had non-significant differences ($F(2.05, 59.49) = .61, p = .58, \eta p^2 = .02$).

Table 5. Average (Standard Deviation) skin conductance level (μs) and Sample Size (n) of interaction condition x gender and interaction condition × number of experienced interviews for each experimental phase (i.e., baseline, narrative, waiting room, call for interview, first question, last question and end of interview).

	Experimental condition		Control condition		Experimental condition		Control condition	
	Gender				Number of experienced interviews			
	Women	Men	Women	Men	Zero	One/two	Zero	One/two
Baseline	.22 (.11)	.21 (.11)	.22 (.14)	.22 (.18)	.21 (.13)	.21 (.08)	.17 (.12)	.29 (.24)
Narrative	.48 (.11)	.36 (.15)	.45 (.18)	.47 (.16)	.47 (.12)	.38 (.13)	.45 (.16)	.50 (.23)
Waiting room	.57 (.11)	.44 (.21)	.53 (.14)	.54 (.22)	.53 (.11)	.48 (.17)	.53 (.15)	.55 (.27)
Call for interview	.56 (.12)	.46 (.20)	.54 (.15)	.55 (.20)	.53 (.22)	.53 (.22)	.62 (.11)	.62 (.22)
First interview question	.67 (.14)	.56 (.21)	.64 (.12)	.65 (.17)	.62 (.14)	.59 (.19)	.64 (.12)	.67 (.19)
Last interview question	.49 (.25)	.48 (.36)	.50 (.20)	.55 (.26)	.42 (.26)	.47 (.30)	.59 (.10)	.58 (.29)
End of interview	.47 (.27)	.45 (.33)	.48 (.20)	.54 (.27)	.39 (.28)	.46 (.29)	.60 (.08)	.57 (.29)
n	14	6	14	12	8	9	7	8

The effect of the number of experienced interviews participants had in the past was further investigated. The average arousal levels between participants who had no experience and who had one or two interviews are presented in Table 5. Participants with no experience were more aroused than experienced participants during the narrative moment, the waiting room and at the moment of the first interview question. Between experimental conditions, participants with no experience reported lower arousal levels in the experimental condition in comparison to the control condition from the moment the interview began. Similarly, participants with one or two experienced interviews also reported lower levels of arousal in the experimental condition than in the control condition. A mixed ANOVA (with Greenhouse-Geisser correction) was conducted with condition (experimental and control) and number of experienced interviews (zero and one/two) as between-subject variables and experimental phases as a within-subject variable. Alike to the previous analysis, no main effect of the number of experienced interviews was observed across all experimental phases ($F(2.05, 59.49) = .27$, p = .77, $\eta p^2 = .01$). The interaction condition × number of experienced interviews also had non-significant differences ($F(2.05, 59.49) = .61$, p = .58, $\eta p^2 = .02$).

4 Discussion and Conclusion

The present study attempted to answer the research question: Can nature-like surroundings influence IA? We expected that nature-like surroundings (window with nature view and indoor foliage plants) would produce lower self-reported anxiety scores (Hypothesis 1) as well as lower arousal levels (Hypothesis 2) comparatively to control surroundings (absence of window and indoor plants). It was also expected this effect would be observed independently of gender and number of experienced interviews (Hypothesis 3).

Overall, participants' self-reported IA was higher in the nature-like surrounding than in the control surrounding. Although this difference was not significant, this result could suggest nature-like surroundings negatively influence IA, hence rejecting our first hypothesis. However, further analysis controlling gender effects revealed meaningful findings that could explain the adverse effect of nature on IA. Women reported in general higher anxiety scores than men, especially in terms of performance, behavior and general IA. Respectively, women were significantly more worried about being good enough, had negative thoughts, feared failure and also recognized more of their own fidgeting, shaking hands and accelerated heartbeat. Such main effects of gender on anxiety are in agreement with the existing literature. It is well established among anxiety literature that women consistently self-report and demonstrate greater levels of anxiety than men [28]. They are also twice as much more likely than men to be diagnosed within a variety of anxiety disorders [29]. High femininity is related to fear [30], high levels of worry and rumination [31–33].

The focus of this study was the decreasing effect of women as well as men's IA when in a nature-like surrounding. Results revealed that women experienced significantly more PA and general IA with nature-like surroundings than in control surroundings, opposing our hypothesis (H3a). On the other hand, men corroborated our hypothesis (H3a) as they reported lower levels of anxiety in the nature-like surroundings comparatively to the control surroundings. Such findings do not echo extant literature that has described reduced self-reported anxiety across gender in natural contexts [34]. Possible reasons for the interaction effect of nature-like surroundings and gender are discussed next.

The first possible reason of gender differences between nature-like surroundings is the type of emotional regulation strategy that is used between women and men. Nolen-Hoeksema [31] reviewed that women (both adult and children) used more types of emotion regulation strategies than men. These included rumination, reappraisal, problem solving, acceptance, avoidance, distraction as well as seeking social support or religion [31]. Contrariwise men have reported to use more engaging, automatic, nonconscious emotion regulation strategies than women [35]. In the emerging literature of automatic nonconscious emotion regulation strategies, Williams and colleagues [36] have suggested that nonconscious emotion regulation strategies are more efficient approaches and are less susceptible to interference from cognitive load, like distraction and fatigue. In the present study, men may have used such strategy to regulate their emotional state and reduce interference and/or positively bias anxiety information processing at the second stage – the primal mode [37]. Men seemed to have successfully used the nature-like surrounding as a positive bias in this specific emotion-eliciting situation, i.e., the job interview. Fo women, a negative biased interpretation of additional environmental cues (nature-like surrounding) may have led to negative aesthetics perception, for example, perceived interviewer's status as high, thus the higher IA levels.

Further reasons that could explain distinct emotion coping strategies used among gender is their connection towards natural environments. However, to our knowledge only Richardson and Mitchell [38] have reported a similar pattern of gender differences among green space and physical health (i.e., cardiovascular and respiratory disease) [38]. They found green spaces tended to foster decreased physical health problems in men but not in women. This reinforces the underlining effects of nature that allow men to be more rapidly engaged in impulsive, reward-seeking behaviors in the face of adverse emotions or physical symptoms. Men have inclusively produced higher results during cognitively taxing tasks in the presence of nature than women [39].

The self-reported anxiety scores were also controlled in terms of individual's experienced in interviews. Generally, participants with no experience reported higher anxiety than participants who had experienced one or two interviews. Special emphasize was made regarding BA; participants without experience were significantly more preoccupied with their physical activity (e.g., fidgeting, handshaking, rapid heartbeat) than individuals with experience. Notwithstanding this expected training effect, we hypothesized that the nature-like surrounding would positively influence IA, regardless of experience. No interaction between number of interviews experienced and experimental conditions was noted. Individuals with no experience were always more anxious than individuals with experience, across conditions. Thus, we can conclude that the experience candidates have in interviews does not affect the potential of nature-like surroundings positively affecting IA. These findings are consistent with Feiler and Powell [40] which did not find moderation of experience in interviews between IA and interview performance.

Through the physiological analysis, the average skin conductance level differences were greater in the nature-like surrounding than the control surrounding. Hence, arousal levels decreased and recovery of arousal activity tended to be greater in the interview simulation where nature was present than when it was not, as expected and as is defended by Ulrich's Stress Recovery Theory [12]. Although this difference failed to reach significance and thus is not able to confirm our second hypothesis, it is important to emphasize that results do show a tendency in the predicted direction. Failure to reach significance may be related to the insufficient duration participants were exposed to nature-like surroundings. Another possible reason may be that nature stimuli in our study were present during the stress-eliciting situation, unlike other stress recovery studies where participants experienced or visualized nature posterior to stress-elicited situations [e.g., 41]. Thus, it seems plausible that more time may have been needed for the individual to adapt to the interview situation and then recover.

Further, it is also worth highlighting that all participants experienced a similar emotionally arousing pattern that is consistent with the IA pattern that has been described in previous studies [42]. The beginning of the interview was in fact the most highly arousing moment and participants tended to decrease arousal activity. This pattern supports the use of VR in laboratory settings for interview simulations as well as scholar's recommendations regarding the VR methodology for studies of human computer interaction [26].

Part of our third hypothesis expected that both gender and the number of experienced interviews would not affect the influence of the nature-like surrounding on arousal levels. Consistent with self-reported data, women showed higher physiological activity (arousal levels) than men at the beginning of the interview and a greater decrease in arousal by the end of the interview. This difference was not significant indicating there were no interaction effects across gender, supporting our hypothesis. In addition, between genders a greater difference in decreased arousal levels was noted in the nature-like surroundings than in the control surroundings suggesting a tendency of lower arousal levels when the candidate is present with nature-like surroundings as we expected. Physiological data for gender differences show inconsistency among literature and scholars recently defend that they depend among the methodology used as well as the women's hormonal status [29]. Our results go on to support Katkin and Hoffman's [43] view that when women and men respond to fearful stimuli they report similar levels of reactivity based on skin conductance.

Furthermore, findings confirm that the number of experienced interviews did not affect the influence of nature-like surroundings on physiological reactivity. Consistent with self- reported data, participants with no experience were more aroused, thus more anxious, than participants with one or two experienced interviews during the peak of the interview simulation (i.e., beginning of interview).

Acknowledgements. This research is supported by FCT grant n. UID/EAT/04008/2019

References

1. Macan, T.: The employment interview: a review of current studies and directions for future research. Hum. Resour. Manag. Rev. **19**, 203–218 (2009)
2. Huffcutt, A.I., Van Iddekinge, C.H., Roth, P.L.: Understanding applicant behavior in employment interviews: a theoretical model of interviewee performance. Hum. Resour. Manag. Rev. **21**, 353–367 (2011)
3. Cook, K.W., Vance, C.A., Spector, P.E.: The relation of candidate personality with selection-interview outcomes. J. Appl. Soc. Psychol. **30**, 867–885 (2000)
4. Feiler, A.R.: A self-regulation perspective of applicant behaviour in the employment interview (2014)
5. Mccarthy, J., Goffin, R.: Measuring job interview anxiety: beyond weak knees and sweaty palms. Pers. Pscyhol. **57**, 607–637 (2004)
6. Silvester, J., Anderson-Gough, F.M., Anderson, N.R., Mohamed, A.R.: Locus of control, attributions and impression management in the selection interview. J. Occup. Organ. Psychol. **75**, 59–76 (2002)
7. Anderson, N.: Editorial – the dark side of the moon: applicant perspectives, negative psychological effects (NPEs), and candidate decision making in selection. Int. J. Sel. Assess. **12**, 1–8 (2004)
8. Hulsheger, U.R., Anderson, N.: Applicant perspectives in selection: going beyond preference reactions. Int. J. Sel. Assess. **17**, 335–345 (2009)
9. Bechtel, R.B., Churchman, A.: Handbook of Environmental Psychology. Wiley, Hoboken (2002)
10. Elsbach, K.D., Pratt, M.G.: The physical environment in organizations. Acad. Manag. Ann. **4**, 181–224 (2007)

11. Elsbach, K.D., Bechky, B.A.: It's more than a desk: working smarter through leveraged office design. Calif. Manag. Rev. **49**, 80–102 (2007)
12. Ulrich, R.S., et al.: Stress recovery during exposure to natural and urban environments. J. Environ. Psychol. **11**, 201–230 (1991)
13. Vilar, E.: Using Virtual Reality to Study the Influence of Environmental Variables to Enhance Wayfinding within Complex Buildings (2012)
14. Silva, D., Campos, R.: Alguns dados normativos do Inventário de Estado-Traço de Ansiedade – Forma Y (STAI-Y), de Spielberger, para a população portuguesa.itle. Rev. Port. Psicol. **33**, 71–89 (1998)
15. Witmer, B.G., Singer, M.J.: Measuring presence in virtual environments: a presence questionnaire. Presence Teleop. Virt. Environ. **7**, 225–240 (1998)
16. Spielberger, C., Gorsuch, R., Lushene, R.: Manual for the State-Trait Anxiety Inventory. Palo Alto, CA (1970)
17. Kwon, J.H., Powell, J., Chalmers, A.: How level of realism influences anxiety in virtual reality environments for a job interview. Int. J. Hum. Comput. Stud. **71**, 978–987 (2013)
18. Watson, D., Ronald, F.: Measurement of social-evaluative anxiety. J. Consult. Clin. Psychol. **33**, 448–457 (1969)
19. Leary, M.R.: A brief version of the fear of negative evaluation scale. Pers. Soc. Psychol. Bull. **9**, 371–375 (1983)
20. Pinto Gouveia, J., Fonseca, L., Robalo, M., Allen, A., Matos, P.M., Gil, E.: Ansiedade Social: Utilização dos questionários de auto-resposta SAD, FNE, e SISST numa população portuguesa. Psiquiatr. Clínica **7**, 43–48 (1986)
21. Pinto-Gouveia, J.: Ansiedade social: Da timidez à fobia social. Quarteto Editora, Coimbra (2000)
22. Dawson, M.E., Schell, A.M., Filion, D.L.: The electrodermal system. In: Cacioppo, J.T., Tassinary, L.G., Berntson, G.G. (eds.) Handbook of Psychophysiology, pp. 159–181. Cambridge University Press, New York (2007)
23. Borges, T., Vilar, E., Noriega, P., Ramos, S., Rebelo, F.: Virtual reality to study job interview anxiety: evaluation of virtual environments. In: Rebelo, F., Soares, M. (eds.) Advances in Ergonomics in Design, pp. 25–33. Springer, Cham (2016). https://doi.org/10.1007/978-3-319-41983-1_3
24. Grey, S.J., Smith, B.L.: A comparison between commercially available electrode gels and purpose-made gel, in the measurement of electrodermal activity. Psychophysiology **21**, 551–557 (1984)
25. Borges, T., Ramos, S., Vilar, E., Noriega, P., Rebelo, F.: Interview anxiety narrative validation for a virtual reality-based study. Procedia Manuf. **3**, 5934–5940 (2015)
26. Villani, D., Repetto, C., Cipresso, P., Riva, G.: May I experience more presence in doing the same thing in virtual reality than in reality? An answer from a simulated job interview. Interact. Comput. **24**, 265–272 (2012)
27. Lykken, D.T., Rose, B., Luther, B., Maley, M.: Correcting psychophysiological measures for individual differences in range. Psychol. Bull. **66**, 481–484 (1966)
28. Egloff, B., Schmukle, S.C.: Gender differences in implicit and explicit anxiety measures. Pers. Individ. Dif. **36**, 1807–1815 (2004)
29. McLean, C.P., Anderson, E.R.: Brave men and timid women? A review of the gender differences in fear and anxiety. Clin. Psychol. Rev. **29**, 496–505 (2009)
30. Carey, M.P., Dusek, J.B., Spector, I.P.: Sex roles, gender and fears: a brief report. Phobia Pract. Res. J. **1**, 114–120 (1988)
31. Nolen-Hoeksema, S.: Emotion regulation and psychopathology: the role of gender. Annu. Rev. Clin. Psychol. **8**, 161–187 (2012)
32. Robichaud, M., Dugas, M.J., Conway, M.: Gender differences in worry and associated cognitive-behavioral variables. J. Anxiety Disord. **17**, 501–516 (2003)

33. Zlomke, K.R., Hahn, K.S.: Cognitive emotion regulation strategies: gender differences and associations to worry. Pers. Individ. Dif. **48**, 408–413 (2010)
34. Shoemaker, C.A., Randall, K., Relf, P.D., Geller, E.S.: Relationships between plants, behavior, and attitudes in an office environment. Horttechnology **2**, 205–206 (1992)
35. Barrett, L.F., Lane, R.D., Sechrest, L., Schwartz, G.E.: Sex differences in emotional awareness. Pers. Soc. Psychol. Bull. **26**, 1027–1035 (2000)
36. Williams, L.E., Bargh, J.A., Nocera, C.C., Gray, J.R.: The unconscious regulation of emotion: nonconscious reappraisal goals modulate emotional reactivity. Emotion **9**, 847–854 (2009)
37. Beck, A.T., Clark, D.A.: An information processing model of anxiety: automatic and strategic processes. Behav. Res. Ther. **35**, 49–58 (1997)
38. Richardson, E.A., Mitchell, R.: Gender differences in relationships between urban green space and health in the United Kingdom. Soc. Sci. Med. **71**, 568–575 (2010)
39. Shibata, S., Suzuki, N.: Effects of the foliage plant on task performance and mood. J. Environ. Psychol. **22**, 265–272 (2002)
40. Feiler, A.R., Powell, D.M.: Interview anxiety across the sexes: support for the sex-linked anxiety coping theory. Pers. Individ. Dif. **54**, 12–17 (2013)
41. Felsten, G.: Where to take a study break on the college campus: an attention restoration theory perspective. J. Environ. Psychol. **29**, 160–167 (2009)
42. Young, M.J., Behnke, R.R., Mann, Y.M.: Anxiety patterns in employment interviews. Commun. Reports. **17**, 49–57 (2004)
43. Katkin, E.S., Hoffman, L.S.: Sex differences and self-report of fear: a psychophysiological assessment. J. Abnorm. Psychol. **85**, 607–610 (1976)

Voice-Based Bodyweight Training Support System Using Smartphone

Ruiyun Wang[✉], Shin Takahashi, Buntarou Shizuki, and Ikkaku Kawaguchi

University of Tsukuba, 1-1-1 Tennodai, Tsukuba, Ibaraki, Japan
wang@iplab.cs.tsukuba.ac.jp, {shin,shizuki,kawaguchi}@cs.tsukuba.ac.jp

Abstract. Bodyweight training has grown in popularity; it is desirable to be fit and strong. However, training can be dangerous if performed incorrectly. Several systems are used to correct pose during training. However, most require wearable sensors that may interfere with training, or an expensive depth camera. We offer a new form of training support using a smartphone camera and a server. We use a verbal interface to help users to correct their pose and to encourage them. We describe our new system and experimentally evaluate it.

Keywords: Training · Verbal interface · OpenPose · Bodyweight training

1 Introduction

Bodyweight training is any work performed against gravity, and includes pushups, pullups, and squats used to increase strength and stamina [1]. Bodyweight training has grown in popularity because it requires minimal or no equipment. However, errors in pose or training intensity compromise the possible benefits and may negatively affect the joints. To avoid injury, it is desirable to observe and evaluate poses assumed during training.

Few convenient and inexpensive methods are available to correct pose and ensure appropriate exercise intensity. Support systems using wearable sensors or depth cameras (such as Microsoft Kinect) are expensive. Body-attached sensors may interfere with training.

Here, we develop a new bodyweight training support system using only a smartphone and a server; users receive verbal corrections and encouragement during training. We use OpenPose [2] to obtain skeletal data from RGB (Red–Green–Blue) images taken by the smartphone camera; these data aid pose recognition and correction. Feedback is aural (delivered by the smartphone). We constructed a prototype and evaluated it experimentally.

2 Related Work

Training support is a popular research topic. Depth cameras, wearable sensors, RFID (Radio Frequency IDentification) technologies, and RGB cameras have

© Springer Nature Switzerland AG 2020
A. Marcus and E. Rosenzweig (Eds.): HCII 2020, LNCS 12202, pp. 370–379, 2020.
https://doi.org/10.1007/978-3-030-49757-6_26

been used to detect user movements during training. For example, Eyes-Free Yoga [3] (an accessible yoga exergame) uses Microsoft Kinect to enable low– or no–vision subjects to correct their poses based on skeletal tracking and verbal feedback. Lee et al. [4] developed a rehabilitation system based on the Kinect sensor to assist patients with movement disorders to perform "Tai Chi" exercises at home. The FitCoach [5] is a virtual fitness coach using an accelerometer and a gyroscope powered by a smartphone or smartwatch to evaluate the quality of user exercises. The differences in body movement strength and speed between exercise repetitions are evaluated. RunBuddy, developed by Hao et al. [6], measures the breathing rhythm during running using an acceleration sensor and a wireless earphone connected to a smartphone. The physiological state can be estimated by reference to the breathing rhythm. The TTBA, an RFID-based motion tracking system proposed by Ding et al. [7], uses a single dumbbell tag to recognize vertical and circular motion. Recently, an RGB camera has been used to read two-dimensional gestures and thus support training. Qiao et al. [8] developed a real-time gesture grading system employing a single RGB camera. The differences between the standard and user joint trajectories are compared and the gesture grade calculated and shown on a screen.

Unlike previous works, we focus on low cost and convenience; we develop a voice-based bodyweight training support system using a smartphone camera. We deliver real-time verbal feedback to users.

3 System Overview and Implementation

We use the GUI (Graphical User Interface) smartphone application to support bodyweight training (Fig. 1); we deliver verbal corrections and encouragement via a smartphone. For example, in Fig. 2, user pose (a) is captured and evaluated during training. The verbal correction is *"Do not bend your knee"*. If the pose is then corrected, the user is told the time for which s/he is required to assume a high-quality pose. Successful training in a certain pose is followed by: *"Good job, go to the next pose"*. Before training commences, smartphone imaging during training must be established. Pose support requires whole-body images; the smartphone must thus be 2 to 3 m distant from the user. Users could also confirm the correct poses through the description using texts and figures in the GUI application before training.

Figure 3 shows the system architecture; the steps are: Attribute Pose Data Acquisition, Pose Recognition, and Pose Evaluation. The smartphone camera images poses assumed during training, evaluates them with the aid of the server, and sends verbal feedback to the user. We used OpenPose (a real-time, two-dimensional pose estimation method) to track the skeleton in RGB images; OpenPose recognizes body joints and yields their X and Y positions; we derived rules for training pose recognition and evaluation. The attribute pose data are the distances from the joints to the center of the body and the angles between the vectors.

We constructed a prototype. The smartphone was a Samsung Galaxy S10 running Android Ver. 9; the software prototype was implemented using QT

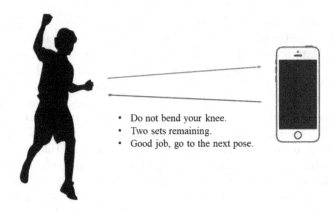

Fig. 1. Use scene.

for Android. We used Python API to run OpenPose in the server; all images were analyzed by NVIDA GeForce RTX 2060 at a speed of about 16.0 fps. The smartphone and the server were connected to the same local area network; a UDP connection was used to transfer images.

Fig. 2. The four poses used in the evaluation experiment, in the order in which they were performed.

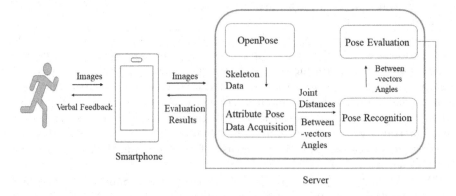

Fig. 3. The system architecture.

3.1   Attribute Pose Data Acquisition

We used OpenPose to acquire skeletal coordinates. OpenPose accepts RGB image inputs, and outputs the two-dimensional positions of 25 key anatomical points. We used the coordinates of 15 key points on the trunk (Fig. 4) to calculate attribute pose data (joint distances and angles between vectors); all data were employed for pose recognition. For pose evaluation, we used only pose-specific angles, thus, not all the angles. The joint distances and the between-vector angles used are shown in Fig. 4. The distances between the elbows, arms, knees, and ankles, and the center of the body, are indicated by red lines. We calculated 12 different angles: (n_0, n_1), (n_1, n_2), (n_2, n_3), (n_0, n_4), (n_4, n_5), (n_5, n_6), (n_7, n_8), (n_8, n_9), (n_9, n_{10}), (n_7, n_{11}), (n_{11}, n_{12}), (n_{12}, n_{13}).

3.2   Pose Recognition

Pose recognition employed the k-nearest neighbor algorithm [9], which is a simple but very accurate non-parametric method. The joint distances and between-vector angles served as the attributes.

3.3   Pose Evaluation

We evaluated pose accuracy, the time for which the pose was maintained, and the number of pose repetitions. For example, for pose (a) of Fig. 2, evaluation proceeds as follows:

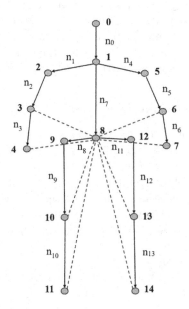

Fig. 4. Attribute pose data.

1. Check whether the angle between the thigh and the back (n_7, n_9) is 90°.
2. Check whether the angle between the shin and the thigh (n_9, n_{10}) is 180°.
3. If pose (a) was correct, was it maintained for 10 s?
4. Was pose (a) repeated four times?

In the implementation, we considered the recognition accuracy of OpenPose and set angle ranges.

4   Experiment 1: OpenPose Recognition Accuracy

To verify OpenPose recognition accuracy in terms of supporting bodyweight training, we performed a preliminary experiment using OpenPose to analyze images taken during training.

4.1   Participants

We recruited three graduate students (two males and one females) aged 24 to 27 years, of height 172 to 185 cm.

4.2   Procedure

The participants assumed bodyweight training poses and images were taken during training. We used OpenPose to identify and display key bodily points; we checked whether all points were correctly detected and displayed.

The smartphone camera was positioned vertically 2 and 3 m in front the participants. The three participants assumed six poses at two different distances; we collected 180 whole-body images totally. The participants first assumed three poses, including pose (c) of Fig. 2, while facing the camera. Next, they assumed three poses, including poses (a) and (b) of Fig. 2, with the camera to their right.

4.3   Results and Discussion

We calculated the percentage of the each key point that could be detected correctly in the 180 images. The recognition accuracies of the three poses when facing the camera are shown in Table 1. The accuracies when the camera was to the right are listed in Tables 2 and 3.

Recognition accuracy was high when participants faced the camera. When the camera was on the right, key left-side points were poorly detected because the camera could not see them. We assumed that bodyweight training poses were symmetrical; thus coordinates of the left side could be calculated and very accurate data could be obtained.

In addition, we also found that when the camera was closer to the participants (who then tended to fill the image), recognition accuracy decreased.

Table 1. The recognition accuracy of the three poses evaluated from the front.

Distance/m	Head	Shoulder	Elbow	Wrist	Hip	Knee	Ankle	Average
2	100	100	100	97.8	100	100	96.7	99.2
3	100	100	100	100	100	100	100	100

Table 2. The right side recognition accuracy of the three poses evaluated from the right.

Distance/m	Head	Center	r-Sho	r-Elb	r-Wri	r-Hip	r-Kne	r-Ank	Ave
2	100	83.3	100	90	90	70	80	53.3	83.3
3	100	100	100	100	100	96.7	100	100	99.6

5 Experiment 2: System Evaluation

We explored whether the proposed system delivered useful and convenient training support.

Table 3. The left side recognition accuracy of the three poses evaluated from the right.

Distance/m	l-Sho	l-Elb	l-Wri	l-Hip	l-Kne	l-Ank	Ave
2	90	0	0	50	46.7	26.7	35.6
3	100	0	0	100	66.7	53.3	53.3

5.1 Participants

We recruited eight graduate students (P1–P8) (five males and three females between the ages of 23 and 27 years). Since the proposed body-weight training system was designed for the beginners in bodyweight training, all of the participants had little or no experience in bodyweight training.

5.2 Procedure

We first explained the purpose and flow of the experiment. We asked each subject to confirm that s/he was in good physical condition; we wished to be sure that all training tasks would be completed. All participants performed four types of bodyweight training (Fig. 2). Each training exercise required about 10 s; we scheduled four repetitions. The entire process required about 8 min. Figure 5 shows the experimental conditions during evaluation.

The flow of the experiment and the specific support method are described using the pose (a) in Fig. 2 as an example. Given the limitations of OpenPose, we accepted angles from 80° to 100° as 90° and 170° to 190° as 180°. Each participant pressed the GUI start button. The words: "*Please set the smartphone*" were spoken. Each participant trained while learning how to assume pose (a). If the pose was correct, a voice began to count the seconds. If the angle between the thigh and the back was incorrect, the voice said: "*Please raise your foot*". If the angle between the thigh and shin was incorrect, the voice said: "*Do not bend your knees*". If the pose remained incorrect, the second-count ceased until the user correctly adjusted his/her pose. After correction, the second-count recommenced. As each set was completed, the words "*One set*", "*Two sets*", "*Two sets remaining*", and "*The last set*" were vocalized. After all sets were completed, the voice said: "*Good job, go to the next pose*" and the user moved on. When all training was completed, the experiment was terminated using the words: "*Good job, the training is finished*".

After the experiment was completed, a questionnaire was administered (Table 4).

5.3 Results

The answers to questions Q1–Q5 are listed in Table 5. The answers to questions Q6 and Q7 were as follows (translated from the Japanese):

P1: *After becoming accustomed to all of the training actions, I think that the voice-only training support is convenient and effective.*

P2: *The proposed system very effectively supports bodyweight training, but I want more types of supported training actions.*

P3: *It is convenient because I can use it at home, but it seems that identification accuracy is poor. I wonder if training is in fact effectively supported. Also, the system cannot be used in a small room.*

P4: *It is very important to correct posture, but the whole body must be photographed; the system cannot be used in a small room.*

Table 4. The questionnaire.

No	Questions	Answers
Q1	Your gender and age	Free description
Q2	Do you usually do bodyweight training?	5·4·3·2·1 Always ⇔ Never
Q3	The system could support bodyweight training	5·4·3·2·1 Strongly agree ⇔ Strongly disagree
Q4	The system was convenient	5·4·3·2·1 Strongly agree ⇔ Strongly disagree
Q5	I want to use the system again	5·4·3·2·1 Strongly agree ⇔ Strongly disagree
Q6	Do you have any advice about this system	Free description
Q7	Please tell us your sense of use	Free description

Table 5. The questionnaire results.

	Q1	Q2	Q3	Q4	Q5
P1	23 Female	2	5	5	5
P2	23 Female	3	5	5	5
P3	26 Male	3	3	3	3
P4	25 Male	3	5	4	4
P5	24 Male	2	5	4	4
P6	24 Female	1	4	4	5
P7	25 Male	3	4	4	4
P8	27 Male	1	4	5	4
Average		2.25	4.38	4.25	4.25

Fig. 5. Experimental conditions during evaluation.

P5: *The voice can help me correct poses and I don't need to look at the screen, so it is useful. It would be better if there was a function to score after the training was completed.*

P6: *The verbal corrections increase my desire to assume a correct posture. Even when I become tired, it is easy to continue training a few seconds after the verbal notification.*

P7: *More training actions would be good. Also, the correct posture ranges should be adjusted by a user depending on the individual physical situation.*

P8: *Only simple postures are supported. It is difficult to support more complex postures.*

5.4 Discussion

On Q3, all participants awarded scores of 4 or more (average 4.38), indicating that posture evaluation and correction were effective. Q4 and Q5 explored system convenience; the average score was 4.25, indicating the system was easy to use. The answers to Q6 and Q7 showed that it was difficult to support more complex training poses; this is a topic for the future. The voices should convey more information. A video offering more specific descriptions of poses before training might be useful. Visual and verbal feedback could be combined. An overall training score was requested; we will soon implement this to encourage users to keep exercising. The score will be based on the differences between the user and standard poses; the training time; and the number of pose repetitions. As a user scores more highly, rewards will be given to enhance motivation.

Different voices should be used for correction. Also, the current verbal feedback works for poses with long, but not short, hold times. Brief comments are required to correct short wrong poses. Also, if the user found it difficult to finish a pose, that pose could not be skipped. The system must deliver feedback when a user cannot complete his/her current training. We will ask the user if s/he finds it difficult to complete the pose, and skip that pose if the answer is "Yes". In addition, there is a need to distinguish a wrong posture from the state of training cessation. Finally, we explored only posture evaluation; real-time posture identification is required in future.

6 Conclusion

We present a voice-based, bodyweight training support system using a smartphone and a server. We used skeletal data from OpenPose for pose recognition, evaluation, and correction. We developed a prototype and evaluated it experimentally. The system was convenient and effective.

In future, we will improve the voices used, deliver more accurate pose corrections, and enhance motivation. We will improve real-time recognition and finally develop a system supporting all facets of bodyweight training.

References

1. Harrison, J.S.: Bodyweight training: a return to basics. Strength Cond. J. **32**(2), 52–55 (2010)
2. Zhe, C., Tomas, S., Shih-En, W., Yaser, S.: Realtime multi-person 2D pose estimation using part affinity fields. In: Proceedings of the IEEE Conference on Computer Vision and Pattern Recognition, Honolulu, USA, pp. 7291–7299. IEEE (2017)
3. Rector, K., Bennett Cynthia, L., Kientz Julie, A.: Eyes-free yoga: an exergame using depth cameras for blind & low vision exercise. In: Proceedings of the 15th International ACM SIGACCESS Conference on Computers and Accessibility (ASSETS 2013), Bellevue, Washington, pp. 12:1–12:8. ACM (2013)
4. Lee, J.-D., Hsieh, C.-H., Lin, T.-Y.: A preliminary study of using kinect-based physical rehabilitation system to perform Tai Chi exercises with FLS evaluation. Neuropsychiatry, Int. J. Clin. Skills **8**(1), 165–175 (2018)

5. Guo, X., Liu, J., Chen, Y.: FitCoach: virtual fitness coach empowered by wearable mobile devices. In: Proceedings of the IEEE Conference on Computer Communications (IEEE INFOCOM 2017), GA, USA, pp. 1–9. IEEE (2017)
6. Hao, T., Xing, G., Zhou, G.: RunBuddy: a smartphone system for running rhythm monitoring. In: Proceedings of the 2015 ACM International Joint Conference on Pervasive and Ubiquitous Computing (UbiComp 2015), Osaka, Japan, pp. 133–144. ACM (2015)
7. Ding, F., Zhang, Q., Zhao, R., Wang, D.: TTBA: an RFID-based tracking system for two basic actions in free-weight exercises. In: Proceedings of the 14th ACM International Symposium on QoS and Security for Wireless and Mobile Networks (Q2SWinet 2018), QC, Canada, pp. 7–14. ACM (2018)
8. Qiao, S., Wang, Y., Li, J.: Real-time human gesture grading based on OpenPose. In: 10th International Congress on Image and Signal Processing, BioMedical Engineering and Informatics (CISP-BMEI), ShangHai, China, pp. 357–358. IEEE (2017)
9. Hastie, T., Tibshirani, R.: Discriminant adaptive nearest neighbor classification. IEEE Trans. Pattern Anal. Mach. Intell. **18**(6), 607 (1996)

Exploring Information Support in Mobile Terminal Guidance in the Context of Medical Service

Wu Yue and Xin Chen[(⊠)]

Shenzhen University, Shenzhen 518060, Guangdong, China
wuyue@ed-alumni.net, xinchen@szu.edu.cn

Abstract. The healthcare industry is closely associated with citizens' well-being. In the context of the experience economy, healthcare experience has drawn substantial attention in the past decades. However, the role of information and knowledge support in improving healthcare experience is largely neglected. To fill this gap, this paper explores how to use mobile application to enhance information support between participants (patients, companions and staffs) and ultimately improve healthcare experience. Specifically, our study is based on the discussion of refractive surgery services in an ophthalmic hospital in Guangzhou, China. We design a mobile terminal guidance application which provides patients with instructions that are clear and easy to understand, shares real-time patients' surgery progress to their companions, and helps participants to exchange medical records efficiently. This application will greatly improve the effectiveness of communication among patients, companions and medical service providers, reduce doctor-patient conflicts, and even help achieve better treatment results.

This study includes four phases. First, we attempt to understand how participants feel and why they feel so by means of observation and interview. Second, we discuss how participants affect each other and identify our design objectives by user journey map and relationship map. Third, we provide solutions for how to accomplish the design objectives, and how to integrate solutions into one mobile application by quick validations and storyboard. In the last phase, we explain how the design works by service blueprint.

Keywords: Medical service · Service design · Healthcare experience · Information support

1 Introduction

Since healthcare industry has been closer to our health and well-being and healthcare design has also drawn more and more attention (Petrie 2011), people nowadays not only seek medical treatment when they are ill, but also make efforts to improve their quality of life by means of medical treatment when they are healthy. Medical products and services have become more closely linked to people's life. However, the innovation design of medical products and services in China is still in its infancy and there are still

© Springer Nature Switzerland AG 2020
A. Marcus and E. Rosenzweig (Eds.): HCII 2020, LNCS 12202, pp. 380–390, 2020.
https://doi.org/10.1007/978-3-030-49757-6_27

many imperfections. Therefore, it is worth exploring a more rational and humanized medical service system.

Vezzoli et al. (2014) proposed that service design should be responsible to create a system-level sustainability in society, ecology and economy. In this context, public service design mainly creates a wide range of social benefits to attain social sustainability. Mitigating stakeholders' negative emotions in the process of experiencing public service by resorting to soft-level services has been the focus of contemporary social innovation. That is to say, public service design can coordinate the relationship between human-beings and the environment, as well as the relationship between person and person, thus improving the user experience of public services (Hartman et al. 2010).

As an essential part of public services and public affairs management, medical service includes core diagnosis and treatment technologies. For example, Baker et al. (2017) reported that the medical Internet of Things were facing challenges in security, privacy, wearability and low power, and put forward suggestions for future research. Moreover, medical service nowadays also focuses on participants' experiences, emotions and feelings (McColl-Kennedy et al. 2017). In a study conducted by Bourne (2010), it was found that the innovation of medical technologies could not completely improve patient experience and satisfaction, and therefore more emphasis should be laid on experience and emotions. In an investigation into patient experience of ambulatory healthcare facilities, Lee (2011) established a conceptual framework and adopted a case-study approach from the perspective of service design to test the hypothesis of the framework. Bowen et al. (2010) demonstrated the experience-based design and innovation of participatory medical services in the UK. One to one interviews and video diaries were employed in the process their investigation. It is found that today's research into medical experience satisfaction focuses more on patients' experience and emotions. Chen et al. (2019) discussed the relations between patient satisfaction and results of the patient satisfaction scale by using backtracking analysis and linear regression model. Berkowitz (2016) explored different factors that impacted the measurement complexity of patient satisfaction. However, we believe that medical service should be regarded as a system in which all stakeholders are well satisfied so as to ensure the sustainability of medical service.

Among the factors that affect the satisfaction of stakeholders, the transfer of information and knowledge at the level of immaterial form plays an important role. In the process of medical services, the information asymmetry between medical service providers and users have a strong impact on the emotions and behaviors of the both parties (Sebastian et al. 2016). Studies have pointed out that patients and their families used to obtain unofficial and vague information about the diseases through a variety of channels. Now they hope to obtain confirmation and guidance from the medical staff, but such needs are often ignored by the medical staff. Moreover, patients want to obtain specific information about the environment, operating procedures, and cooperation requirements in special diagnosis and treatment such as surgery and gastroscopy beforehand, but this type of information is often neglected by medical service providers (Richards and McDonald 1985). However, some studies have pointed out that patients who obtain adequate information tend to maintain a positive attitude in decision-making of diagnosis and treatment. When patients are well-acquainted with their surgeries in advance, they can be less anxious and injected less postoperative analgesics (Williams 1993).

We also found that adequate information support not only contributes to better treatment results, but also develop harmonious relationships between medical service providers and users. Conversely, mistrust and conflicts would be easily triggered between the two parties when they lack information support. Moreover, inadequate information and knowledge will cause medical staff to undertake additional responsibility of consulting, thus increasing their workload and pressure. One of the negative impacts is that healthcare professionals are often disturbed and interrupted when they are concentrating on their work, which easily makes them annoyed and not in a good mood. Therefore, effective information and knowledge as well as guidance should be delivered timely to support the patients and companions, which will indirectly create a more satisfactory work environment for healthcare professionals.

In this paper, a mobile terminal guidance application is introduced and applied to a refractive surgery which has a relatively fixed treatment process, aiming to discuss how to efficiently enhance information and knowledge support in a complex medical service process so as to improve the experience for every participant groups.

2 Research Method

Three research methods are employed in this study: observation, interview and user journey map. The first method is observation. One of the authors observed companions, staffs and other patients as a patient in a refractive surgery. In order to understand the feelings of patients, companions and staffs during the surgery, we carried out interviews among three patients, two healthcare professionals and five companions. Moreover, interviews were adopted to explore the feelings of 245 patients and healthcare professionals in each link of the surgery. Finally, aiming to visualize medical processes and results of the interviews, we drew a user journey map to assist in analyzing and defining relevant problems.

2.1 Observation

One of the authors first experienced the entire surgery process as a patient, and found herself recovered quickly and remained conscious throughout the surgery. At the moment the surgery was completed, she felt her eyesight was almost normal with slight tingling and photophobia, and meanwhile she was conscious enough to take care of herself. The mild twinge disappeared the next day after the surgery and her eyesight got slightly hazy, but it did not result in any impediment to her life. Two weeks after the surgery, the haze disappeared. One month after the surgery, she recovered with a normal eyesight, feeling clear and comfortable.

As a patient, she concluded eight facts after her observation. 1) Patients gathered in the front desk, consulting the staff about their surgery in a disorderly manner, which made the front desk staff feel it difficult to handle. 2) The crowd in front of the consulting room disturbed the doctors. 3) In the examination room, overwhelming examination items but insufficient guidelines got patients confused, which made staffs frustrated to keep order. 4) Too many paper materials were generated during the surgery, which was a huge workload for patients and companions. They were usually reluctant to sort these materials out. 5) Healthcare professionals also needed to write a lot of surgery records repeatedly, which was high-workload for them. 6) Most of the companions appeared next to the patients who were wearing orange goggles after the surgery. 7) Companions felt bored while waiting for the patients during examination. 8) Patients and companions often felt helpless during the surgery.

2.2 Interview

Answers given by the three patients, five companions and two staffs to the question "During the surgery, how do you feel now and why?" are summarized as follows.

Patient A: To be honest, I feel anxious to keep asking the staffs about what I should do next because I can tell they are kind of impatient. But I am not able to get the information from elsewhere, and I have no concept of how my surgery works and don't how to cooperate. I am worried about what I should do in case of emergency.

Patient B: Some instructions of this hospital are misleading and need updating. It took me a very long time to find the location of the pharmacy.

Patient C: I am waiting for my surgery now and I feel quite nervous and helpless because I don't know what the surgery would be like. Actually, I really hope that my relatives or close friends could be with me. I think I can get some mental support from them.

Companion A: Well, I am getting bored now and I don't know how long the surgery will last.

Companion B: I feel helpless because the information about the surgery is limited and I can't feel very engaged in it.

Companion C: I am not satisfied with the staffs' attitude. They seem to be impatient with everything.

Companion D: I am worried about my work now. I am very busy but I really want more information about my daughter's surgery and I hope I can be her surgery companion. So, I have already taken that surgery day off to accompany her. Now I am going to follow up my project with a colleague.

Companion E: I feel confused about the surgery and I hope to be informed of more professional knowledge.

Staff A: Patients and companions are often in chaos. I sometimes feel agitated and lose my patience when answering their questions.

Staff B: As a doctor, I think the conversations between patients and me should be more related to professional medical knowledge instead of the location of the pharmacy or their payment and registration. And I don't want to be interrupted at work.

In summary, patients will be less anxious when they have companions as their mental support. The reason why patients get nervous is because they do not know much about the surgery and how to cope with it. As for the busy companions, they are more inclined to accompany the patients on the day of surgery. Although companions are not able to stay with the patients in the operation room, they have concern with the progress of the surgery. Some of the companions claimed that the doctors showed impatience when they were consulting professional knowledge about the surgery. Healthcare professionals are eager to solve the problem of being interrupted at work.

2.3 User Journey Map

In order to clearly and fully know about how patients and staffs feel about the medical service in the surgery, we recorded the emotions of the patients and the medical staff in each link of the surgery and summarized them into a figure for pain point analysis. In each link, we asked the patients and medical staff to mark their emotion values with stickers in the emotion range of "smiley (most happy)" to "crying (most unhappy)", and carried out quick interviews on their emotion values. Finally, we chose the area with most stickers as the mean of each character in each link. The results of the interviews were summarized in the following figure (see Fig. 1).

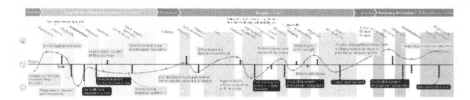

Fig. 1. User journey map

It can be seen from the figure above that what affects the patients' emotions most is the bad attitude of healthcare professionals, which makes it difficult for patients to communicate with doctors about their concerns over the surgery. Moreover, patients tend to become anxious when they cannot remember so many precautions at once and it is difficult for them to find the exact locations in the hospital such as the pharmacy and the examination room in a short time. Furthermore, patients claim that it is easy for them to get so many paper documents lost, which might increase their anxiety about the surgery. What also negatively impacts the patients' experience of surgery is their nervousness of the upcoming surgery. Meanwhile, patients (users) have a more positive attitude towards online processing (registration and payment), which demonstrates that they are more inclined to interact with mobile terminals to some extent.

For healthcare professionals, the factors negatively affect their emotions include the difficulties in keeping patients' order during the treatment, excessive repetitive work and interruptions.

3 Findings

By analyzing the results of the investigation (see Fig. 2), we conclude the current pain points of doctors, patients and companions and the interactions between the three. For patients, the pain points are not knowing much about the surgery, the difficulties in finding various places in the hospital quickly, and obtaining no archives of the surgery as well as feeling it hard to remember the precautions. These pain points result in nervousness and helplessness of the patients. For medical staff, the pain points are repeated interruptions and excessive repetitive mechanical writings, which might get the medical staff irritated.

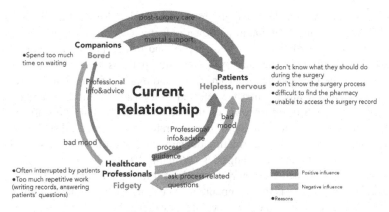

Fig. 2. Relationship mapping

For companions, the pain point is that the waiting time is too long, which makes them bored.

The negative effects of bad experiences are also passed on between the three parties. Since the patients know few about the medical process, they tend to interrupt and ask the medical staff's questions about the medical process. These questions not only occupy too much time for the patients to communication with doctors on their medical treatments, but also distract the medical staff from their work and get them irritated. The medical staff in a bad mood are more likely to deliver negative emotions to the patients and companions when providing guidance on the medical process and advice on the surgery. Moreover, the companions hope to reduce the accompanying time. However, when the patients feel nervous and helpless, they will rely more on their companions and seek mental support. This is a conflict of needs between the two parties.

The root cause of the bad experiences of patients and companions is inadequate information support. Since it is known from Sect. 2.3 that patients are more inclined to interact with mobile terminals, what we should explore next is how to promote communication between patients, companions and doctors, and enhance information support by means of mobile terminals, thus improving the three parties' (patients, companions and staffs) service experiences during the surgery.

4   Analysis and Discussion

In the stage of formulating the concept, in order to find the relationship that is closer to the needs of service participants, we first verified two hypotheses based on the investigation, proposed the expected relationships between the three service participants, and then determined the design objective and strategy, that is, to enhance information support medical service participants through mobile application. Finally, we built a prototype of the medical service based on mobile application through a storyboard and we acquire feedback from different service participant groups by conducting interviews.

The first hypothesis is that the nervousness of the patients is mainly due to a lack of information and professional knowledge about the surgery, not the fear of the surgery itself. To verify this, we conducted interviews in the hospital. Firstly, three patients were asked how they felt at the moment, and then a doctor was invited to tell the patients more professional knowledge about the surgery and to accept patients' consultation. After learning more about the surgery, those three patients were requested to share their feelings at the moment again. From their responses, we found that they were less anxious and became calmer. Then we referred to relevant literature to learn that the patients expect to confirm information on the surgery from the medical staff and know more about the surgery process and how to cooperate with the medical staff effectively. Effective communication and information delivery have significant effects. It can even reduce the use of postoperative analgesics (Williams 1993). Hence, we conclude that patients should be provided with more channels of information support.

The second hypothesis is that companions hope to take care of the patients after the surgery. We asked two companions how would they feel if they could be informed of the estimated completion of time the surgery. The two claimed that it would be convenient and save their time. Therefore, we conclude that companions should be informed of the estimated completion of time the surgery.

After verifying the two hypotheses, we began design the corresponding strategies which are illustrated in the following sections.

4.1 Expected Relationship

Based on the verified hypotheses, Fig. 3 presents an expected relationship diagram in which we demonstrate the design objectives and strategies.

Aiming to enhance information support for patients, we propose design objectives which are to efficiently find different places in the hospital, reduce anxiety, get more surgical communication opportunities between patients and the medical service providers, and conveniently check the design objectives of the surgical files and precautions for review. The corresponding design strategies are to provide real-time navigation in the hospital and clear surgery process guidance, let the patients and companions know more about how the surgery works and ways to cooperate effectively by means of surgery games, channels for consultation after the surgery, and private surgical qualification assessment as well as medical information exchange on the mobile application.

We aim to solve the pain points of staffs by enhancing information support for patients. We propose design objectives which are to reduce interruptions at work and repetitive communication and writings. The corresponding design strategies are to provide medical process guidance intended for the patients and a mobile application in which medical service providers can connect with each other as well as exchange medical information and records with patients.

In order to enhance information support for companions, we propose design objectives which are to strengthen the communication between patients and their companions on the accompanying time arrangement and to save time and energy of the companions before the surgery. The corresponding design strategies are to design the real-time sharing of surgery progress and to inform companions of the estimated completion time of the surgery.

Information support can help build a harmonious relationship between patients, staffs and companions. When the patients consult the surgery in an orderly fashion, the staffs

Fig. 3. Expected relationship

will not get irritated and the patients themselves can therefore gain more professional medical guidance and advice on the surgery. Hence, the companions will also feel at ease and satisfied. After the patients get clear guidance on the surgery process and learn more about the surgery, the nervousness and helplessness will be mitigated, and the need for being accompanied will be reduced. This can not only reduce the waiting time of the companions but also meet the needs of the companions.

4.2 Storyboard and Feedback

We visualize the scenarios when patients, companions and staffs are using this mobile application into a storyboard (see Fig. 4). We also carried out interviews to among 4 patients, 3 companions and 3 staffs to collect feedback after they had seen the storyboard.

In response to the detailed support and guidance that this mobile application offers to patients, we name it Surgery Secretary and build a storyboard to present our service prototype. The application enables patients to learn about their surgery schedules and make preparations in advance. When patients feel confused in the medical process, they can access very clear guidance on Surgery Secretary. Patients are also able to efficiently find their destinations in the hospital by following the navigation. Patients can conveniently review surgery related information including medical records and dos and don'ts. Companions can see the progress of patient's surgery when they are not

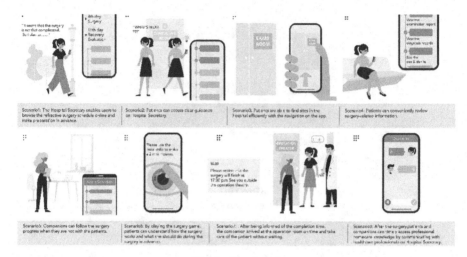

Fig. 4. Storyboard

with the patient. By playing the surgery games, patients can understand how the surgery works and what they should do after the surgery so as to mitigate their nervousness. Companions can not only be informed of the estimated surgery completion time on this application, thus saving their waiting time, but they can also get professional healthcare advice by communicating with doctors via the application.

From the results of the interviews, it is found that the patients and companions are satisfied with the application, stating that they feel relieved and calmer after learning about enough information through the application. As for the staffs, they emphasized that it would be better if they can share medical information among themselves in this application. Some staffs realized the importance of information support and they were not aware of the information support demands from patients until this interview.

4.3 Service Blueprint

In order to further plan the operation mode of medical service, we use a service blueprint (see Fig. 5) to specify the touch points among patients, frontstage staffs and backstage staffs.

We are more focused on the touch points of patients and front-end staffs. In the service blueprint, the mobile application bears some touch points of the front-end staffs such as registration, payment and medical records keeping. That is to say, patients can finish their registration and payment on the application instead of queuing up in the hospital. They can also review their medical records online, which not only save patients' time but also reduces staffs' workload. The information of each step of the surgery is clearly presented on this application in detailed. Moreover, new touch points have been created, like panoramic navigation which can help patients and companions to find their directions in the hospital.

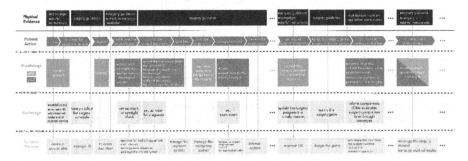

Fig. 5. Service blueprint

5 Conclusion

Through investigation, analysis, and discussion, we design a mobile application named Surgery Secretary to improve the information exchange volume and information exchange efficiency of the three stakeholders (patients, companions and staffs) in surgical services. On this basis, patients can get more support and care about surgery-related information and knowledge, companions can reduce their accompanying time, and staffs can work in a more orderly environment. At the same time, the guidance system can catalyze more potential consumers (patients), improve the efficiency of patient consultation, and improve the competitiveness of the surgery services among similar surgeries, thus creating greater profits for the hospital. Therefore, the increasing demand for medical materials can allow suppliers to generate more profits, and the government would be also delighted to see hospitals contribute to the society by promoting public services. The mobile terminal guidance system thus coordinates the interests of all parties and creates sustainable values.

We conclude that the role of information support is underestimated in medical services and patients' demand for adequate information is easily neglected by medical service providers. Meanwhile, we also learn that negative impacts will transfer between patients, companions and staffs when there is no adequate information support for the patients. It may even become a vicious circle that seriously affect the operation mode of the medical system. Therefore, if you are a manager or designer in the field of medical experience, please think about the information gap in three aspects including information transparency, medical records exchange between medical service providers and users as well as professional knowledge and information about surgery process for medical service users.

In the process of this research, we also notice that offline information support also has impacts on medical experience. The limitation of this research is that there is no enough discussion on how to combine the offline medical guidance and the online information support. Therefore, we will attempt to pay more attention to this field in our future works. Finally, we hope that our design can be implemented. Hence, more feedback can be collected to facilitate the iteration of our design.

References

Petrie, A.: The industrial design Rx for health care: new frontiers in design. Innov.-Dulles VA **30**(2), 14 (2011)

Vezzoli, C., et al.: Product-Service System Design for Sustainability. Greenleaf Publishing, Sheffield (2014)

Hartman, A., et al.: Participatory design of public sector services. In: Andersen, K.N., Francesconi, E., Grönlund, Å., van Engers, Tom M. (eds.) EGOVIS 2010. LNCS, vol. 6267, pp. 219–233. Springer, Heidelberg (2010). https://doi.org/10.1007/978-3-642-15172-9_21

Baker, S.B., Xiang, W., Atkinson, I.: Internet of things for smart healthcare: technologies, challenges, and opportunities. IEEE Access **5**, 26521–26544 (2017)

McColl-Kennedy, J.R., Danaher, T.S., Gallan, A.S., Orsingher, C., Lervik-Olsen, L., Verma, R.: How do you feel today? Managing patient emotions during health care experiences to enhance well-being. J. Bus. Res. **79**, 247–259 (2017)

Bourne, R.B., Chesworth, B.M., Davis, A.M., Mahomed, N.N., Charron, K.D.: Patient satisfaction after total knee arthroplasty: who is satisfied and who is not? Clin. Orthop. Relat. Res.® **468**(1), 57–63 (2010)

Lee, S.: Evaluating serviceability of healthcare servicescapes: service design perspective. Int. J. Des. **5**(2) (2011)

Bowen, S., Dearden, A., Wright, P., Wolstenholme, D., Cobb, M.: Participatory healthcare service design and innovation. In: Proceedings of the 11th Biennial Participatory Design Conference, pp. 155–158, November 2010

Chen, Q., et al.: The association between patient satisfaction and patient-reported health outcomes. J. Patient Exp. **6**(3), 201–209 (2019)

Berkowitz, B.: The patient experience and patient satisfaction: measurement of a complex dynamic. Online J. Issues Nurs. **21**(1) (2016)

Sebastian, N., Jesha, M., Sheela, P.H., Arya, S.N.: Gaps in doctor patient communication: a community based study. Int. J. Community Med. Public Health **3**(1), 264–269 (2016)

Richards, J., McDonald, P.: Doctor-patient communication in surgery. J. R. Soc. Med. **78**(11), 922–924 (1985)

Williams, O.A.: Patient knowledge of operative care. J. R. Soc. Med. **86**(6), 328 (1993)

DUXU for Creativity, Learning and Collaboration

Teaching Discussion on Information Visualization Design

Xiandong Cheng[1][(✉)], Hao He[2], Yan Ren[3], and Shengqi Ba[4]

[1] Beijing City University, No. 269 Bei Si Huan Zhong Lu, Hai Dian District, Beijing, China
doudesign@126.com
[2] Central Academy of Fine Arts, No. 8 Hua Jia Di Nan Street, Chao Yang District,
Beijing, China
[3] Tencent (Beijing), Beijing, China
[4] Eighty-Seven Studio, 314 Carshalton Road, Carshalton, England, UK

Abstract. When it comes to "visualization", it has become the main method of information interaction in the network. At the same time, many disciplines interpret the concept of information visualization from different professional perspectives, in which some emphasize is about generation and access of information, some focus on the change and interaction of information, some aim to exchange and commercial use, etc. As a result, this phenomenon causes the confusion about concept, design process and design results of information visualization in many students and designers in this field. In the teaching, it is found that students cannot distinguish the relationship among information visualization, data visualization, science visualization, user experience visualization etc.

Besides, it is difficult for them to design accurately when the commercial factors also influence. The processes of learning and design have been only carried out from a visual perspective, which is lack of usability in logical relationship of information. Is this phenomenon worthy of educational reflection in Art Design Major? In this paper, it summarizes the concept and design method of information visualization design for the field of art design, which combines the scientific presentation of information with artistic expression.

Keywords: Information · Visualization · Art design · Education

1 Research Background

1.1 "Image Society" Calls for Information Visualization

Due to the influence of Internet-driven intelligence and information explosion in the 21st century, it has brought people into the information era (image society). At present, the popularity of the current artificial intelligence and the 5G networks has also accelerated the production, acquisition and exchange of information, in which many fields of human activities have been changed, including art design. As a result, it undoubtedly puts forward a new subject for contemporary Chinese art and design education, which is an outdated model, aging in curriculum and duplicated teaching materials. Since the

© Springer Nature Switzerland AG 2020
A. Marcus and E. Rosenzweig (Eds.): HCII 2020, LNCS 12202, pp. 393–404, 2020.
https://doi.org/10.1007/978-3-030-49757-6_28

Industrial Revolution, the design has become the leading edge of social change. If the first two industrial revolutions tied people to machines and work while increasing efficiency, quality and wealth, the third Industrial Revolution succeeded in "consuming" people on the Internet with an information-led interactive platform. Due to the high speed of the popularity for the network, it makes the visual design of information have more emphasis on the performance of visualization. Although the process of all changes brings progress, it also brings negative effects. In terms of information visualization, only emphasizing vision is one of the negative aspects.

The development of science and technology in the 21st century boosts the development and reform of information in perspectives of generation, dissemination and application. With the participation of Internet, intelligence has brought many aspects of our life/work/learning/entertainment into the "information age". Nowadays, information impacts our lives through the Internet. It flows into our eyes, visually crowds our lives and affects our behavior. The information age is also an "image society". Although visualization had been a part of human communication, it is not only a form of communication, but also the most important route of information dissemination and application in this era.

With the popularity of intelligent devices and the continuous upgrading of network bandwidth, information visualization is ubiquitous. The widely used portable high-resolution screens has shifted information acquisition from the desktop to everyone's pocket, which makes it easier to present visual information for storytelling than ever before. The rapid rise of 5G will also accelerate the process of information production, licensing and exchange ("information consumption"). Many areas have changed, such as people's lifestyle and ways of thinking, the industrial production, business behavior and financial investment, etc. Therefore, information visualization has been valued and studied by many disciplines, and information visualization design has become a comprehensive interdisciplinary. In many cases, information design is one of the approaches in art design fields. In this article, we will try to discuss the design method and concept of information visualization from the perspective of art design, as well as the research on the course of art design.

1.2 Misunderstanding of Information Visualization Design

Information visualization design is a field, which is constantly upgrading and changing with the development of the times. Thus, it may cause many people in the industry finding it challenging to understand and follow. Information is the interpretation of data. Data is the carrier of information. When information is overloaded, data must be advanced. Many disciplines interpret information visualization from different professional perspectives. Some emphasize the generation and acquisition of information, some emphasize the change of information data, some emphasize the exchange and application of information. This phenomenon leads to many theories and methods of information visual design in many information visual design projects. The designer is only responsible for the artwork, which makes the designer lose the professional voice and participation consciousness in the information visual design. In addition, many Art and Design related faculties in colleges in China are lacking understanding of concepts about the professional perspective in the course. At present, visual communication is still the only approach used in the teaching of information visualization design, which is difficult to form the designer's deep understanding and utilized their design ability on information visualization.

Through two years of teaching and research experience on information visualization design, it is noticeable that many Art & Design students and professional designers have problems in understanding the concept and design methods of information visualization [1]. They often use the habitual thinking of visual communication to deal with information visualization projects. They overemphasize on aesthetic approach rather than informative content that weakens the role of information visualization. Fully understanding the objectives of information, data, visualization, design and also other aspects of the content and interrelationship will provide a professional approach in information visualization design. The attractive visual presentation is to strengthen the role of information, rather than distract the attention away from information content, which reduce the function of visual design of information. Alluring visual presentation and memorable storytelling can raise more attention to information, especially un-visualized information (implicit information). A well-presented visualization of information data will be more effective and informative for people.

2 Information/Data/Visualization

2.1 About Information and Data

There is a natural connection between information and data, but differences also exist. Many information visualization projects take data as the main element to present the content of information; therefore, information visualization design requires having a certain understanding about the relationship between information and data. Information is the interpretation of data, and data is the carrier of information. For example, data that shows a person's name, height, etc. In between, it can be called a piece of information, made up of a set of data. The difference is that information can be represented by data, but not all data can represent information. The same data may have different interpretations. Information is abstract. The same information can be represented in different ways.

Information has a complex definition because of its various expressions (voice/picture/temperature/volume/color, etc.) and various types of information (electronic information/financial information/weather information/biological information, etc.)

Communication science defines information as the uncertainty eliminated in communication, that is, the increased certainty in communication. Claude Elwood Shannon, founder of Informatics, defined information as "the difference between two kinds of uncertainties". In other words, *"information = uncertainty before communication - uncertainty after communication"* [1].

In the field of Humanities and Social Sciences, information is the cognition/thought/emotion/will, that people want to express. They are immaterial that only can be effectively spread through languages [1].

Information needs to be presented and applied by the carrier, and data is the carrier of information, which can be simply understood as: data is the record that reflects the attributes of objective things, and is the specific form of information. After data be processed, it became information. Information needs to be digitized into data to be stored and transfer. Data is record that reflects the attributes of objective things. "Data paints a picture of the real world," stated by Dr. Nathan Yau of UCLA in Data Points: Visualization That Means Something. Just as a photograph captures an instant, data is a snapshot of the real world" [2].

Data is the form and carrier of information. It can be symbol, text, number, sound, image, video, etc. Information is the connotation of data. Information carries on data and makes a meaningful interpretation of data. When information needs to be spread/analyzed or other utilization, information needs a certain objective carrier. This must relay on the existence of materials to carry this form of information. Objects, such as stone/Wood/paper/hard disk/CD/U disk, can record and store information through stone carving, wood carving and paper printing, until electronic devices, such as CD in modern days. Human beings take objects as information carriers. Wave signals of matter, such as mechanical wave/acoustic wave/electromagnetic wave/light wave, only can be heard and seen when sound wave propagates sound and image is propagated by light wave. We watch TV/listen to radio/communicate by mobile devise that information is transferred by radio waves. In fact, Wi-Fi is a type of high-frequency radio signal. Symbol carriers, such as natural language/text/numbers/graphics, can be heard/seen, and are commonly used.

2.2 About Visualization

Visualization refers to the technology and method that can be used to create graphics/images or animations for communication. Historically, it includes cave paintings/Egyptian hieroglyphs, etc. Nowadays, the application areas of visualization are expanding in science/education/industrial/medical/business/life utility program/entertainment, etc. Visualization is to build 'a mental model' or 'mental model of something'. Visualization transforms information from abstract to concrete [1]. Visualization transforms rational knowledge into perceptual knowledge.

The fundamental steps of visualization process seem like a unique pipeline, that the main steps interact with each other. It can be divided into three parts: collection, process and analysis. The most important part is analysis, which can develop the understanding of the relevant content to benefit and complete an effective visualization [3].

2.3 Information Visualization/Data Visualization/Knowledge Visualization

Visualization is an effective way to solve this problem by visually making information/data/knowledge easier to understand. Information visualization and data visualization are the formats of visualization. Information visualization aims to present data in a visual way. Information visualization is a graphic presentation combined of data and Design, which is conducive to information dissemination efficiently and effectively to the audience from individuals or organizations. Data visualization is a scientific study of data presentation. A data set represents a single element, and a large number of data sets constitute a data image at the same time, each attribute value of the data presents multi-dimensional data.

Knowledge visualization is to promote the dissemination and innovation of knowledge through visual presentation. Visual presentation is a key part of knowledge visualization designs and applications. Therefore, the value of realization in knowledge visualization depends on its visual representation formats. Knowledge visualization is based on graphic design and cognitive science, which is closely related to visual representation. Visual representation is one of the key factors of knowledge visualization.

3 Design Principles and Methods

3.1 Easy to Use and Good-Looking

Although information visualization is an interdisciplinary field, visual design still plays a dominate role in the design process, because the main principles are to be 'easy to use' and 'good-looking', or in other words "usability/legibility and aesthetics".

Based on the complexity and diversity of information content and related data, "easy to use" in information visualization design refers to respect the actual content of information. The accurate and effective expression of information content and related data is also the fundamental principle of information visualization design. In addition, "good-looking" is an important principle in vision, however this can not be over-emphasized, as it may distract the reader to understand the information and cause the information to be misread. The purpose of using graphics/image technology methods is to help people understand and analyze, rather than losing track in information visualization. The "good-looking" principle aims to a vivid visual expression, which assist to an accurate and comprehensive expression of information and deliver the role of information visualization, so as to help people understand/memories/analyze and utilize it. The design process should always focus on the expression of information content/related data, in which based on the accurate application of graphics/images and other design elements, instead of overwhelmed artistry and excessive decoration. In the mean time, user experience must to be taking into concern.

"Easy to use" is namely "usability/legibility ", and "good-looking" is namely "aesthetics". On this basis, more detailed requirement on information visualization design has been formed.

The Unity of Consciousness and the Collaborative Work Method. The rigorous and accurate agenda in information collecting/processing/analyzing through designers collaborate with information data workers to achieve the unity of understanding, so designers are able to have a great insight of information/data.

Goals and Users. Designers need to have a clear vision about the project expectation and target users on the information visualization project, so that the information visualization design can achieve the goal of the project with an excellent user experience. James Kalbach's *"Mapping Experiences"* is one of the great references in user experience.

Evaluation and Analysis. Evaluate the volume/complexity of the information content and related data, whilst analyzing the explicit and implicit relationships of the information, to clarify the certainty of the known information and the uncertainty of the unknown part after visualization.

Terminal and Scenario. At the initial stage of design, it is necessary to plan the final release terminal and application scenario. For example, traditional paper media needs to work around printing and printing technology, and modern electronic media requires configuration, such as different display standards/system versions between hardware devices, to projecting on multiple media outlets. These need to be planned in advance at the beginning of the project after in depth understanding of the goals and users, so to avoid the interface loopholes between the design outcome and the later presentation.

Function. The function planning of information visualization design also needs to be arranged ahead at the initial stage to cooperate with the expectation/target user/terminal to deliver the function of information visualization, especially, when the target user is a specific group with limited ability to interact with the information. It is vital to figure out solutions to cross the barrier to reach out these special users, so as to achieve the "good use" of the information visualization design. The chapters above are the summary of information visualization design principles; designers can use these as theoretical reference. And the next chapter suggests the practical details in the design process of specific methods.

3.2 Minimal/not Simple

Information visualization includes all the developments and advances in data visualization, information graphics, knowledge visualization, scientific visualization, and visual design. Therefore, create on the basis of the fundamental principles of the design that the methods are corresponding to the principles.

Define the Design Task and Cognitive Ability. With an in depth understanding of the task on information visualization design with creative ability and realistic project cycle, that information visualization can be classified into three approaches of outcomes: complete presentation/key presentation/interesting presentation.

'Complete presentation' is to deliver the information task in a accomplished, comprehensive and accurate way of visual design, which is relatively conservative in design without highlights of the key points, demonstrating a statement with the same weight to present all information, and may relatively be inefficient for some users to read/judge other than professional users. This method is suited for designers who have obstacles to analyze, but prefer the full presentation to avoid misreading of the information.

The 'key presentation' is to introduce the analyzed content of the information according to the use and needs of specific users, which could be very user- friendly to specific target groups. It has to have an accurate grasp of the analytical result; otherwise it could cause information to be misleading to the users. On the other hand, this method may cause non-target users to have an incomplete understanding of the information. This method requires designers to have an accurate insight of the information.

The 'presentation of interest' is to exhibit the information visualization in an interesting approach, such as the work "How to Build a Human" by American freelance designer Eleanor Lutz, which uses the animation of circle rotation to show the development of the embryo in the mother.

He made this using 44 animations that are 9 frames each. It wasn't able to show size properly though. For example, the 24-week fetus is about 40 times heavier than a 12-week fetus (but you can't tell that from this drawing) [4] (see Fig. 1).

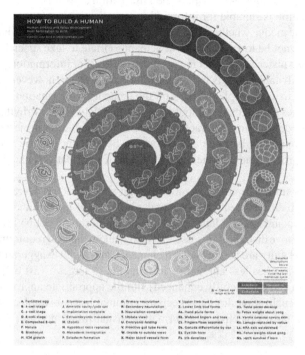

Fig. 1. How to Build a Human (design by Eleanor Lutz) Form: tabletopwhale.com

This method largely involved by designers' originality and creativity in the design. The style is eye-catching and informative, that requires the designer have a great grasp of the information content and design ability with respect to the accuracy of the information, also emphasizing the design style to present the information.

Visual. The volume of information, which affects the design expression and elements, determines the visual of information visualization The function of visual can make the visual design of information meet the aesthetic approach, and more importantly, it visually helps people to understand the information, in which visual elements play an important role (color/graphics/image/animation/characters, etc.)

Color, The use of colors in the visual design of information must represent to a certain context to indicate key information vividly. In ordinary circumstance, the main color scheme recommends to be controlled within three tones, and the auxiliary colors remain within minimal amount. The visual volume of auxiliary colors should not exceed the main colors. When in dynamic and interactive items, auxiliary colors should unify in transition color, and a slight diversity in color display in the interaction area should also be in consideration. For instance, the changed or important information and data should be in catchy colours, and the less important one can be diluted.

Graphics/images, information visualization project with a large amount of information can be designed by geometric (abstract) graphics combine with data charts, and projects with less amount of information can be designed by quasi-materialized (concrete) graphics or images to display the information content.

Image/animation is suitable for information visualization projects in which the terminal is electronic media, whether it is streaming media or interactive media, images and animation should not be too exaggerate. It is inappropriate to take special effects as the main design focus instead of respect the presentation logic of information to design. The intent of using a dynamic path is to present information better, however catchy special effects are easily irritate people to focus on the content of information. Therefore, the transition of images and animation should be smooth, relatively slow rhythm, conducive to reading and understanding. Interactive projects are suitable for projects with a large number of information, where the animation can be introduce in the needs to match the interactive purpose, and the linear presentation of information is applicable within image elements.

Characters in information visualization design should be considered based on the tone of the information content and the standard display of the terminal. For example, the minimum Standard English letter in the paper media should not be less than 5Pt.

The chapter above discussed the essential design elements and requirements. To sum up, simplicity and unity are the key design elements, and avoid exaggerating decorative design. If the project has less amount of information or target a vast majority groups, decorative design can be carefully enhanced with the appropriate approach. The secret of information visualization design is keeping minimal but not simple, which requires designers have a clear objective of information visualization design (You can see in figure below).

3.3 Types of Data Graphs

Information contains data that designers need to understand the type and scope of data charts in information visualization design to avoid misinterpretation in data expression [5]. Common data charts can be divided into three categories: Series/Coordinates/Components (see Figs. 2, 3, 4 and 5).

Example: Statistics of five basketball players starting for the Miami Heat. Apart from names, each data point has five dimensions, which are points, rebounds, assists, steals, and blocks (see Fig. 6). Radar charts are suitable to display multi-dimensional data, when every dimension data is sortable (i.e. nationality cannot be sorted within this case). However, radar charts are only applicable where the data has more than four but less than six dimensions, because below or over this range, data cannot be distinguished. Due to this fact, this chart has limited occasions that it can be used.

The larger the space in which the individual player's data projected, the more contribution this individual delivered to the team. In this sense, it suggests the importance of the individual to the team. Based on the data, it suggests that LeBron James (red area) is the most important player in the team of Heat (see Fig. 7).

It is noticeable that many users are not familiar with the radar chart, and find it is difficult to interpret. It is important for designers to provide description and explanation of the data to make it a user-friendly experience.

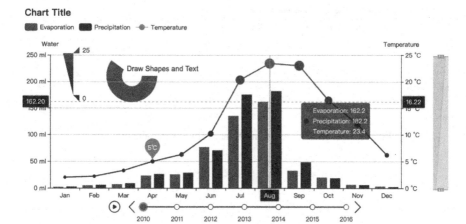

Fig. 2. Frequently-used components

Fig. 3. Series

Fig. 4. Coordinates

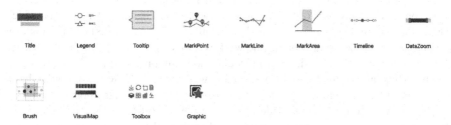

Fig. 5. Components

2011/12 Miami Heat Starting Lineup-Contribution to Team Total

Player	Points	Rebounds	Assists	Steals	Blocks
Chris Bosh	17.2	7.9	1.6	0.8	0.8
Shane Battier	5.4	2.6	1.2	1.0	0.5
LeBron James	28.0	8.4	6.1	1.9	0.8
Dwayne Wade	22.3	5.0	4.5	1.7	1.3
Mario Chalmers	10.2	2.9	3.6	1.4	0.2
Team Total	98.2	41.3	19.3	8.5	5.3

Radar charts

Fig. 6. Data of 2011/12 Miami Heat starting lineup-contribution

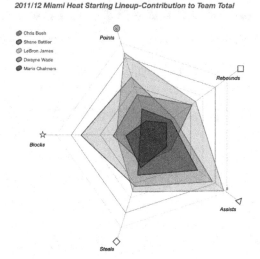

Fig. 7. Radar charts. (Color figure online)

3.4 Design Tools and Cases

The development and innovation of technology shaped information visual design. People with skills can create this type of work. Designers should consider various design tools to create and deliver the project with full respects of users and information through an appropriate presentation.

This is a very visual project; the amount of information is low, but accurate. The works on the three diseases of HPV (which causes cervical cancer), Adenovirus (which causes the common cold), Dengue (a close relative of the Zika virus) can be found in medical information visual design. The work is a dynamic GIF image, the 3D part of the image is realized by modeling (molecular modeling program) [6], later processed by Photoshop, and its finally published version was drawn by HTML5. The work has a strong visual impact, static very much like a poster, leaving a deep memory (see Fig. 8).

This is an information visual design of the men's 100-m event. Through multi-dimensional comparison, the work shows the changes of the men's 100-m performance in the 1986–2012 Olympic Games. There is a visual design case with less information in a single race. It is combined 3D with 2D. The graphical chart design is combined

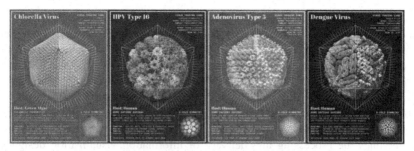

Fig. 8. Virus trading cards (design by Eleanor Lutz) Form: tabletopwhale.com

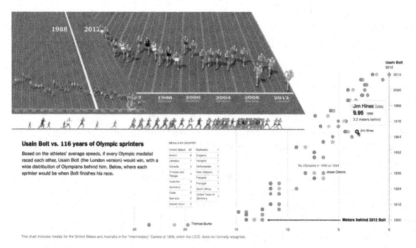

Fig. 9. London Olympics 2012 - Usain Bolt's Gold in the 100 m sprint (contributors: Kevin Quealy, Graham Roberts, Amanda Cox, Rose Eveleth, Chang W. Lee) Form: New York Times

with the 100-m track, and the vision is presented in a realistic method. In the complex data comparison, the chart form is selected, and the information is presented with simple shape/color/value (see Fig. 9).

4   Summary

Information visualization design is a comprehensive science, covering a lot of professional knowledge and skills. Every information visualization project needs to integrate all aspects of knowledge and professional sight related to designing the information content. Designers are required to collaborate with other professionals to accomplish this, in which the authenticity and accuracy of information should be respected. In addition, information visualization design should prioritize the preference of target audience user. Although the required skills are various, the purpose of defining information visualization design as a structured information presentation is to be effectively and clearly delivered to users.

Nowadays, information flow is consistently growing and changing, that distinguishability and anti-interference ability are getting poorer transmissibility and un-user-friendly in many cases. Therefore, information visualization design must be able to bring target users a straightforward insight of designated information. Humanity meeting user preference and acceptance are the key success factors of information visualization design.

Designers need to have a fine judgment to use visual design method to help the information get delivered visually and expressively, rather than over prioritize the design method and become too artistic and complex to present. A successful information visualization project will not only guide and help the target users from puzzling information, but also inspire through visual design methods.

Sometimes the processing and delivery of information visualization design can generate new interactive information. This new information/data is part of the design framework (open structure establishment), considered as the chain of information for visualization design projects.

The summary above is about the research on information for visual design and art design disciplines, and I hope to share and exchange with more professionals in this area.

References

1. Fu, P.: XinXiKeShiHuaSheJi, 2nd edn. Southwest Normal University Press, China (2016)
2. Yau, N.: Data Points: Visualization That Means Something, 2nd edn. China Renmin University Press, China (2014)
3. BAIDU BaiKe. https://baijiahao.baidu.com/. Accessed 9 Feb 2019
4. How to Build a Human. https://abletopwhale.com/page12/. Accessed 15 Nov 2019
5. Kalbach, J.: Mapping Experiences-A Guide to Creating Value through Journeys, Blueprints, and Diagrams, 2nd edn. O'Reilly Media, Sebastopol (2016)
6. Virus trading cards. https://abletopwhale.com/page11/. Accessed 15 Nov 2019

E.R.A - Augmented Reality Teaching - Assistive Technology Developed for the Literacy Process of Children with ASD

Carolina Boechat Alt Araujo Cirino[✉], Ana Carolina Alves Ferreira Fernandes, Jeniffer da Costa Perez e Silva, and Hanna Policiano Serra

Universidade Federal Fluminense, Rua Passos da Pátria, 156, Sala 201 – São Domingos, Niterói, Rio de Janeiro 24210-240, Brazil
carolina_alt@id.uff.br, coordenacao_gdi@vm.uff.br
https://projetoeracontato.wixsite.com/projetoera

Abstract. E.R.A - Augmented Reality Teaching is a developed product that assists autistic children to learn how to read and write through Augmented Reality Technology. E.R.A is capable of overcoming the digital and physical apart-feeling that compose the relationship between people and new technologies. The number of children diagnosed with ASD within normal classes in Brazil increased 37,27% during the last 2 years. That means in 2017, 77.102 ASD children and teenagers were being taught the same way as people without the diagnose. Even though presence is positive progress, inclusion implicates adapted contents, preparing teachers and developing activities that look upon the children's characteristics. Inside regular schools, ASD teaching material is still a challenge. E.R.A offers a solution to this absence, once it helps teachers in adapting their material for special students. The product counts with three main parts: puzzle, Augmented Reality application, and construct-words structure. This way, E.R.A. grants autonomy for the child and the teaching professionals when elaborating activities and evaluations, respecting the individualities of each one.

Keywords: ASD children · Assistive technology · Augmented Reality Teaching

Abbreviations

E.R.A Ensino em Realidade Aumentada - Augmented Reality Teaching
ASD Autism Spectrum Disorder
AFR Associação Fluminense de Reabilitação - Fluminense Rehabilitation Association

1 Introduction

According to the World Health Organization, about 1% of the population has some kind of autism. That might not represent a lot; nonetheless or despite, when we consider

Dr. Giuseppe Amado—Supervisor, Tutor, gamado@id.uff.br.

© Springer Nature Switzerland AG 2020
A. Marcus and E. Rosenzweig (Eds.): HCII 2020, LNCS 12202, pp. 405–414, 2020.
https://doi.org/10.1007/978-3-030-49757-6_29

the world's population will reach 7.8 billion people by 2020, this number becomes significant. Or, by another perspective, there will be slightly fewer people with autism in the world than Germany's residents this year.

In the last 2 years, the number of children and teenagers diagnosed with ASD within classes in Brazil increased by 37,27%. Even though presence is positive progress, inclusion implicates adapted contents, preparing teachers and developing activities focused on the children's characteristics. Inside regular schools, ASD teaching material is still a challenge. To guarantee not only assistance but also high-quality learning to these people, it is mandatory to think in non-conventional ways of education and teaching strategies. In this context, ERA emerges as a low-cost, innovative way to improve literacy learning for different kinds of children and help them with their obstacles.

By participating in weekly field research and observing the day-to-day routine at AFR (Fluminense Rehabilitation Association) for 4 months it was possible to capture meaningful information for the conception of the final product. The association counts with a group of psychologists and psychotherapists to assist the ASD children and other types of neurodevelopment disorders. During the growth of the project, ten professionals from different areas helped with the understanding and immersion of the work and evolution of ASD children. ERA also received direct support from a specialized and lead psychotherapist from the ASD area.

ERA Project was based on the constructivist line inspired by Jean Piaget (1896–1980). This method proposes constant stimulations with the environment and physical interactions for the best development and learning with the active participation of the child in the process. ERA Project was developed through participatory design which consists in the method of building results based in constant monitoring users of the product. The project is also part of assistive technology which is a group of resources and services that help to contribute and increase the functional and intellectual abilities of disabled people allowing interactions and social inclusion.

Intensive care for disabled people, in special children with ASD, costs from U$40.000 to U$60.000 per year. As so, the main objective of the project is to offer new learning paths for children with ASD and spread an innovative way of learning for humbler areas with low-cost experience

2   The Study

2.1   Study of the Case

Our study focus was defined as "the development of the lecture for children with ASD" with the help of our supervisor tutor Dr. Giuseppe Amado and Professor Mara Salles who served as a great motivation to deeply learn more about the topic and after introducing us to the AFR educators and health professionals.

ASD or Autism Spectrum Disorder is a developmental disorder that affects basic communication and behavior. The children diagnosed with ASD usually present difficulty with communication and social interactions with other people, restricted interests and repetitive behaviors. Since the diagnose is part of a spectrum, different types and severities can be found. Until now, no one knows the exact cause of ASD (National Institute of Mental Health) (Fig. 1).

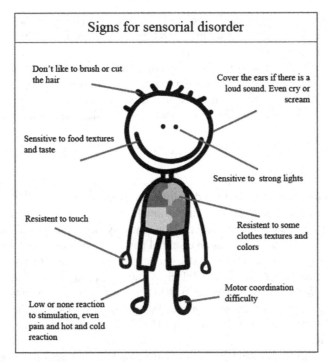

Fig. 1. Table of signs of sensory disorder, showing the difficulties in perception of textures and touches for the ASD children. Source: Author

The research was developed using participatory design, which is an attempt to involve all the users in the process of design to ensure that the final product meets their real needs.

We started with a day-to-day observation of the psychopedagogy area taking notes of all the 40 min therapy steps. With these observation notes, it was possible to catalog and separate exactly what kinds of activities were more accepted by the children, which toys they preferred, colors, textures, and sounds. It was crucial to listen to the professionals of the area to fully understand their struggles and suggestions.

After the weekly field research for 4 months at the psychopedagogy area at Fluminense Rehabilitation Association, we concluded the definition of the main problem in the process of literacy applied to ASD children at the association. We observed that there was a lack of stimulus for the children due to the difficulty of making the literacy process attractive and concise. These obstacles were reducing the effectiveness of the treatment performed by the AFR professionals with the children.

To elaborate on a new literacy process, it was necessary to direct our attention to the special literacy method used in AFR. The studies were based on the constructivist line inspired by Jean Piaget. The method proposes that the child should be constantly stimulated by the environment and other physical interactions for better development of the literacy process, thus participating actively in the process, not only as a spectator.

Accordingly to Piaget's Genetic Epistemology And Naturalized Epistemology, "knowledge cannot be conceived as predetermined either in the internal structures of the subject – they are due to an effective and continuous construction; or in the pre-existing characteristics of objects, since they are only known through the mediation of theses structures the latter enrich them by incorporating them (even if only by placing them within a system of possibilities)".

The thought bases of Jean Piaget's epistemological theory revolutionized the process of human development. On the same hand, it contributed to the construction of new pedagogical theories related to the learning process that the user becomes active in the process of building his knowledge based on physical, social associations, and interactions.

2.2 Educational Stimulus

During the immersion phase and the development of the work with ASD children, we had contact with a total of 10 professionals from different areas, being these: psychopedagogy, speech therapy, occupational therapy, and psychomotricity. The sensory and cognitive stimulations were seen as an essential part of the process being developed by all the professionals. At the time, new discovering and questions were being answered. One fact that called our attention was the lack of a specific product for the treatment with ASD children. Without a specific product, ASD children have a delay in the process of literacy. It was identified the need for a specific product developed for the ASD public that is cohesive with the foundation developed by the professionals leading the learning process at AFR.

At first, we had as a reference the work developed by the lead psychopedagogue Lucélia Maria, who dedicated her life to various studies about the autistic universe, grouping graduations in areas such as pedagogy, speech therapy, psychopedagogy, and neuropsychopedagogy. Lucélia suggested us to read more about ASD topic and observe the children during the process of literacy, so we could find sufficient information to develop the theme.

3 The Product

3.1 Developing the Product

The product was developed through the use of Participatory Design, a method that aims to build results from constant monitoring of the users of the product and Brainstorming, a technique that allows designers to explore and stimulate creative thinking for developing new ideas and concepts.

It was decided during the conception phase that the product must have the following requirements: it must be a tool that aids the literacy process of ASD children according to the methods already in use by the psychopedagogue Lucélia, it must be light, easy to handle and have a low cost of maintenance (Fig. 2).

With the main objective as attending children with ASD in mind, a product to aim and introduce the literacy process was created. ERA (Ensino em Realidade Aumentada) or Augmented Reality Teaching is an assistive technology product that grants autonomy for the child and the teaching professionals when elaborating activities and evaluations, respecting the individualities of each one. ERA offers on cognitive processes through the

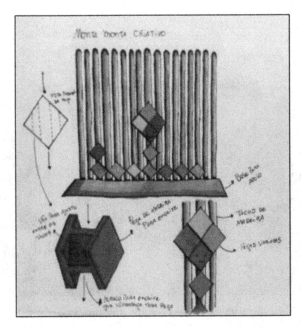

Fig. 2. One of the sketches presented after the process of Brainstorming. Source: Author

reception of new information and building bridges of knowledge. The project operates on three stimulus fronts: a construct-words structure, a puzzle, and augmented reality application.

3.2 Construct-Words Structure

The construct-words structure offers the child the knowledge of the letters. The different fitting design process allows to work with the child's motor and optical aspects. The structure and the pieces made of wood form words, colors and shares. The pieces can be used during the game, leading and stimulating the learning process. The activity is guided by the draw or choice of the puzzle pieces (Fig. 3).

3.3 Texturized Puzzle

The puzzle pieces have two stimulation faces. Each piece of the puzzle contains a word or illustration with a texture on the back. In total, there are 48 pieces for completing the puzzle. The words on the puzzle were chosen focusing on the day-to-day life of the ASD children so it would stimulate connections between their routine and the learning activity.

The puzzle is also part of the augmented reality experience. The words work as targets so the application can identify the meaning and render an object-model in 3D on the top of each puzzle piece (Figs. 4 and 5).

Fig. 3. ASD Child playing with the construct-words structure made of wood. Source: Author

Fig. 4. Completed puzzle with the project logo and target words. Source: Author

Fig. 5. ASD child completing the puzzle and learning the words. Source: Author

3.4 Augmented Reality Application

The augmented reality technology offers the integration of virtual objects in the real environment in which the child is inserted. This visual interaction motivates and attracts the learning process, aiding the assimilation of the knowledge learnt with the construct-word structure and the puzzle. The main function of the application is to shape the words the professional is working with, offering a dynamic material for the mediation of learning.

ERA helps children to learn letters, construct words and finally concretize the idea through the shape represented in 3D with a 360° view. That way, the child can see and understand each one of the words (Figs. 6 and 7).

Fig. 6. Application being used with the puzzle piece "casa" (house) and rendering the 3D object of a house. Source: Author

Fig. 7. ERA application layout where children and professionals can work. Source: Author

4   Results

E.R.A surpass the social and participation challenges to teach ASD children. The product encourages interpersonal interactions between the autistic and the teaching professionals, providing aid in the literacy process.

During the next months, ERA proved to be an excellent tool to help literacy professionals. The surprised reactions on the children's face when the word became reality boosted their interest to learn and their capacity of linking the meaning of the word to the object.

Since 2016, E.R.A is a free daily learning experience for more than 200 autistic children in the state of Rio de Janeiro, Brazil. On the same hand, Fluminense Rehabilitation Association (AFR), Federal Fluminense University (UFF), City Hall of Niterói (Prefeitura de Niterói) and Mothers of Autistic Children (MCA) support the project.

E.R.A is also concerned about the social-economic situation of Brazilian autistic families. Therefore, allowing them to make low-cost black and white printing versions of the puzzle, downloading light and well-optimized application for low-specs mobiles and grating the opportunity of continuous learning and development from home. When bringing the experience home, the project allows the family to join the play and enter the child's world, facilitating the family-autistic interaction.

ERA is proud that, in three years of the project, hundreds of ASD children all over the state of Rio de Janeiro learned how to read and write with our help.

5   Conclusion

Designing products based on empathy is the key to a designer's success. Assistive technology is fundamental to reinforce the importance of establishing ties with the environment that surrounds us, understanding and realizing the peculiarities of each audience and acting on their problems in order to help them. In addition, acting in this segment was extremely important to socially reward our community since we had the opportunity to join a Federal University and develop projects. The responsibility of working with Assistive technology requires greater empathy, curiosity and commitment. Empathy can take us out of the comfort zone and understand the real picture of the user's life. Curiosity to intensify our research and explore new possibilities. Commitment to think. Prototype and test what we have proposed, being faithful to our ideology and working until the project was consistent with the needs of the chosen public.

During the development of the project a lot of different obstacles were faced, however, none of those compromised the final result. The constant monitoring of users and professionals in the area culminated in ensuring the true and consistent delivery of a functional, objective and effective product according to the stimulus methods used at the association.

ERA is available as a free to use tool for the AFR psychopedagogy team as for any institution that takes care of the literacy process of ASD children. ERA provides all the support, maintenance and improvements necessary for the best usability of the product in the learning process for the diagnosed children. At this point, it is possible to say we are getting there. We are proud that, in three years of the project, hundreds of ASD children all over the state of Rio de Janeiro learned how to read and write with our help. Now, E.R.A Project is looking forward to increasing its range. E.R.A designers are engaged in spreading this innovative way of learning for humbler areas with low-cost experience. In that way, E.R.A will be nearer to build a society whose people, with or without ASD, could read and write their histories, with their particularities. ERA team is satisfied with the positive results for easy learning with the continuous use of the product. We wish a continuous and clear development for all the children submitted to the use of the product.

References

1. Bastos, D.: Dormitório infantil: a influência das cores no desenvolvimento comportamental de uma criança com autismo. Instituto de Pós-Graduação e Graduação – IPOG (2015)
2. Auredite Cardoso Costa: Psicopedagogia & Psicomotricidade: Pontos de interseção nas dificuldades de aprendizagem, 2nd edn. Vozes, Petrópolis (2002)
3. Farina, M.: Psicodinâmica das cores em comunicação, 5th edn. Edgard Blusher, São Paulo (2000)
4. da Fonseca, V.: Aprender a Aprender: A educabilidade cognitiva. Artmed, Porto Alegre (1998)
5. Leão, D.M.M.: Paradigmas contemporâneos de educação: escola tradicional e escola construtivista. FACED/UFC, Ceará (1999)
6. Piaget, J.: Biologia e Conhecimento, 2nd edn. Vozes, São Paulo (1996)

7. Kortmann, G.: Aprendizagens da criança autista e suas relações familiares e sociais: Estratégias educativas. Universidade Federal do Rio Grande do Sul (2013)

8. Moreira, M.A.: Teorias de Aprendizagem. Editora Pedagógica e Universitária, São Paulo (1999)

9. Universo Autista: A estimulação cognitiva de pessoas com transtorno autista através de ambientes virtuais, 30 January 2020. http://universoautista.com.br/oficial/2015/08/19/estimulacao-cognitiva-de-pessoas-com-transtorno-autista/

How to Design Potential Solutions for a Cross-country Platform that Leverages Students' Diversity: A User-Centered Design Approach – and Its Challenges

Giulia D'Ettole, Thomas Bjørner[(✉)] [iD], and Amalia De Götzen[iD]

Architecture, Design and Media Technology, Aalborg University, Copenhagen, Denmark
{gde,tbj,ago}@create.aau.dk

Abstract. This paper outlines a methodological perspective within the research question of how to design potential solutions for a cross-country platform that leverages students' diversity to address their everyday challenges at the university level. Overall, students' challenges can have different nuances based on academic, social, and psychological factors. This paper provides an applied approach into scenarios, personas, and blueprints. We used the double diamond design process model to design the multi-platform service. This paper will mainly focus on a case study from Mexico within its define and development stages, including suggestions for how to design potential solutions. Our study is based on interviews and workshops with 250 university students and 10 university staff members. Our findings reveal that the service blueprint work was an effective tool to provide an overarching view of the service and its components. The service blueprint allowed the design team to mentally zoom in and out during the design process and helped the larger team to generate new ideas and discuss current elements of the service being offered. However, the service blueprint is also time-consuming and demands significant structured coordination.

Keywords: User-centered design · Scenario · Persona · Service blueprint

1 Introduction

This paper outlines a methodological perspective within the research question of how to design potential solutions for a cross-country platform that leverages university students' diversity to address their everyday challenges. This study was conducted within the activities of the WeNet research project (www.internetofus.eu). The aim of WeNet is to develop an online platform that will empower machine-mediated diversity-aware interactions. The platform is being made to enable students to support each other by leveraging their diversity (in terms of cultural backgrounds, habits, languages, etc.) as well to facilitate improved quality of life among students. Poor quality of life (QOL) as well as mental health challenges among university students are being reported more frequently across countries [1–4]. The everyday challenges among students are multifaceted. However, there is common agreement that starting university studies often comes along with,

© Springer Nature Switzerland AG 2020
A. Marcus and E. Rosenzweig (Eds.): HCII 2020, LNCS 12202, pp. 415–426, 2020.
https://doi.org/10.1007/978-3-030-49757-6_30

for example, new teaching methods, new learning and exam styles, new credit systems, new cultural and physical distances, new responsibilities, new social norms and inter-actions, living on one's own, and managing one's own financial resources (with low income) [3–9]. Overall, students' challenges can have different nuances based on the academic, social, and psychological nature of their adjustment [10, 11]. Furthermore, students' mobility has increased on a national and global scale [5], and there is reported correlation of poor quality of life and students' mobility [6, 7]. Student mobility has positive outcomes, as part of human capital (e.g. independence, experience, improved skills, and personal growth), innovative- and knowledge-based processes, and economic development [8, 9]. However, students' transitions to university life can be challenging, particularly for students moving abroad. Studying abroad also incorporates (besides the mentioned academic, social, and psychological factors) the complexity of living abroad with a potentially new culture and language, changing personal daily routines, and new ways of thinking [6].

Beside the help that students can find through some general social platforms (e.g. Facebook, Twitter, WeChat, WhatsApp), specific online platforms and apps have been developed to support students in dealing with their everyday challenges (e.g. YOU at College [27], Challenger [28], and Uniwhere [29]). However, few specific platforms are designed to be used across countries, and none focusing on the possibility of learning about students' diversity through data and using it as a positive tool to address their challenges. Furthermore, examples are still needed of how to envision and convey user-centered design approaches to an international and interdisciplinary research team that consists of people with various backgrounds and skills.

2   Research Framework

The methodological approaches for designing a new technology platform are multi-faceted and span many disciplines. The user-centered design approach is a methodolog-ical approach [23] that mainly focuses on the users and their needs in each phase of the design process. Commonly used methods for user-centered design processes include a) scenarios, b) personas, and c) user journeys.

a) The core element of a scenario is a narrative that explains, in a diachronic way, a user's actions. Scenarios have been used in different disciplines, including human–computer interaction, interaction design, user experience design, and service design. No single shared definition exists of what scenarios are, how they should be struc-tured, and in what phase of the design process they should be used. However, the general understanding is that scenarios propose a vision of something complex and articulated [12], are based on data gathered through field research [13], and can help developers to manage the fluidity of design situations [14]. Scenarios repre-sent the key actions a user will perform while experiencing a product-service sys-tem. Taking the user into account, scenarios can help address questions such as: What does he or she use the product/service for? Where and when? What are the expected results? What is the innovation of this product-service? [12–14]. Scenarios has typically been used to communicate the actual implementation of an analyzed product-service system or to envision possible future solutions. A written text, storyboards, sketches, and videos are all used to represent scenarios, which can also be enacted through, e.g., role-playing techniques [21]. Scenarios may help designers to direct their design efforts toward the users' requirements and needs and, particularly in the case of desired future scenarios, toward futuristic solutions that the users can freely envision [13, 14]. Scenarios allow for considering the specificities of different stakeholders affected by the design process (e.g. practitioners), different assumptions (agreements/disagreements), and different domains [12–14]. Scenarios are typically characterized according to their desirability (by analyzing the potential different views that different stakeholders might have on the same scenario) and feasibility (by testing scenario goals against the new emerging reality) [30].

b) Personas are research-based fictional archetypes representing real user needs, experiences, behaviors, and goals. Personas are often used as the other key element of scenarios since the former are the main characters and the driver in the narrative. Personas were popularized by Cooper [15] and are meant to guide the design team during periods in the design process when actual user testing is impractical. The main benefits of using personas during ICT development have already been described [15–17] and can be summarized as follows: they a) focus attention on a specific target audience, b) make assumptions regarding the target audience more explicit, c) are helpful when communicating results, d) help to prioritize audiences and product requirements, and e) prevent self-referential design. The last point is due to one essential aspect of personas: they utilize the human ability to empathize or to identify oneself with another person and thereby infer or create predictions of how that person would behave in particular scenarios.

c) A user journey is a design technique describing the service's development as a sequence of actions and interactions and providing a high-level overview of the factors influencing the user experience from a user perspective [13]. It visualizes the user experience, the steps, and the points of interaction (touch points) between the user and the service, from the first contact with the service provider to the moment when the interaction can be considered completed [13, 20]. While the user journey only describes the frontstage process of the service (the service aspects that are visible to the user), a service blueprint also represents the backstage processes, such as the internal employee actions, potential functions, interactions between actors, functionalities and flows of the event, and all of the support activities that need to happen in the backend in order for the service to be delivered [20, 22].

3 Research Methodology

3.1 User-Centered Design Approach: The 4D Model

In designing the cross-country multi-platform service, the team followed the double diamond design process model, developed by the British Design Council in 2005 [15]. The larger design team consists of 16–20 participants from 10 countries involved in various roles, including as sociologists, designers, developers, ethical researchers, and software engineers. The model is graphically based on a simple diagram describing the divergent and convergent stages of the design process, which give the model the form of a double diamond [15]. The model is also called the 4D model because the name of each phase starts with a D: discover, define, develop, and deliver. The discover phase entails, for example, field research to understand the context in which the user operates. The problem to be tackled is identified in the define phase and subsequently operationalized in the develop phase, in which potential solutions are explored. Specific solutions are implemented and delivered during the final deliver phase. The same design methods can be used in different phases with different purposes. For example, scenarios can be used to represent the current situation in the discover phase, represent a concept in the define phase, ideate possible solutions in the develop phase, and communicate the final design in the deliver phase. This paper will mainly describe the define and develop stages within WeNet, including methodological suggestions for how to design potential solutions. For proposing potential solutions (and for later implementation by software engineers), we used field information (interviews, desk research and surveys), observations, scenarios, journey maps, personas, and service blueprints to outline specific elements, which are both visually oriented and user-centered.

3.2 Participants and Ethical Issues

In total, data were collected from 250 students and 10 experts across different universities. The participating universities were in Denmark (Aalborg University), Italy (University of Trento), Mongolia (National University of Mongolia), China (Jilin University), and Mexico (IPICYT). The data were collected from March to September 2019. Students were recruited through emails and were selected based on their English proficiency and willingness to participate in the research project without being compensated. The number of students was unequally distributed, with the highest number of students being from Denmark and Italy. The specific numbers participants were as follows: Denmark: 150 students and five experts. Italy: 97 students and two experts. Mongolia: five students and one expert. China: four students. Mexico: four students and one expert. The experts had roles as, for example, study counselors, professors, study secretaries, info desk employees, and international office employees.

We gave all of the participants anonymized names and identification numbers. We took into account the special ethical considerations appropriate for interviewing and observing students. Additionally, we acquired legal access and permission from the universities and written consent from the participants. The standardized General Data Protection Regulation (GDPR) was followed. We made special considerations when interviewing students so that they were not unduly pressured to cooperate with the research request and also emphasized that the participation was voluntary and that they could drop out at any time. Based on the initial platform ideas, all ethical aspects were discussed with a group of experts on ethics.

3.3 Procedure

Denmark: The data collection for Aalborg University was run in collaboration with students from service systems design (first-year master's students). The students were given the research question from this study, and with strict guidance from the research team, it was possible to control for and collect a high number of participants. The 30 master's students were organized into six groups. Very different methods were used, such as interviews (in-depth interviews and focus groups), desk research, and surveys. Using students as data collectors gave the advantage of a researcher–student distance, instead of a student–student approach, with them being equal in terms of age, language, and understanding.

Italy: Qualitative field research with 97 in-depth interviews was conducted and carried out at the University of Trento. The interviewed participants were both local and international students currently studying in Trento. The interviews were organized into two parts, with the first addressing students' preparation for university (their motivation to enroll, prior experiences, sources of information, and decision-making processes) and their initial period in Trento (their challenges and coping strategies).

Mongolia, Mexico, and China: The data were collected by online interviews (following a semi-structured interview guide) with 13 students and 3 experts total. Due to language barriers and limits in accessing Chinese students, the data collection in China was supplemented by a digital survey.

3.4 Analysis

The data was analyzed by traditional coding [19], following four stages: organizing, recognizing, coding, and interpretation. Each country was separately analyzed. The first stage was to organize and prepare the data for analysis. The interviews with the students and experts were transcribed verbatim, and the visual and other materials were catalogued. In the recognizing stage, the transcripts were read several times to establish the concepts and themes. This second stage provided a general sense of the information and an opportunity to reflect on its overall meaning [19]. The third stage was coding, during which the researchers organized and labeled the data into categories/subcategories. Various topics were clustered to avoid having too many categories. The last step was interpretation, which included analyzing the categories and considering potential content ideas for the platform.

4 Results

Our results reveal that a common challenge for students across countries is well-being. Some students across countries experience dissatisfaction with study programs, managing expectations, study-related stress and depression, and homesickness. Another common challenge (related to well-being) is unhealthy eating habits. In this paper, we will address the Mexican case and present the initial development of a social eating app within the WeNet platform. The Mexico case is a solid case study with which to foster diversity in higher education while supporting a healthy eating agenda, so it was chosen as preliminary pilot experiment.

4.1 Discover: Insight to the Problem

In the discovery phase, an idea or user need must be established [18] in order to set a framework and define the degree of success. This initial quarter of the double diamond process is meant to generate innovation and therefore involves wide perspectives, flexibility, and minimal formalization. From the analysis of the initial field research conducted in Mexico, it emerged that obesity was one of the most critical challenges among students there. Students choose food that is fast to prepare, is cheap to buy, and gives a sense of satiety. Furthermore, students struggle with balancing their work and study life, so they tend to adopt unhealthy eating habits. In general, students seem to be poorly informed about the negative implications of having unhealthy diets and eating habits. Another major challenge in Mexico is related to security. In certain areas, students do not feel safe using public transportation, attending leisure activities, or being alone in public.

4.2 Define the Area: Personas and Scenario Development

In the define phase, the needs, problems, and ideas are focused toward end goals [18]. The first quarter of the double diamond design process (discover) ends with a brief being created, which is then examined, evaluated, changed, and refined during the define stage into a project brief that is in line with the corporate goals and interests. The material from the discover stage should be analyzed and synthesized into a brief with actionable tasks related to new or existing product or service development [18]. This means that there is also much focus on the context within which the problem or solution resides [18]. Based on the users' insights found in the discover phase, the team decided to develop content within the platform to support Mexican students in adopting healthier eating habits. To support the design process, two personas were created (e.g. Fig. 1), which served to share users' insights within the research team.

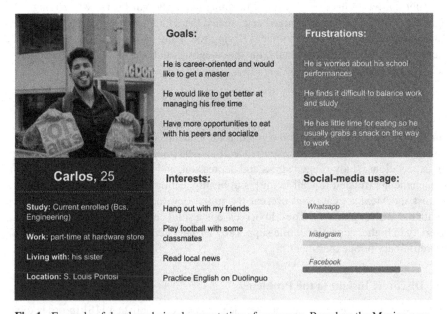

Fig. 1. Example of developed visual presentation of a persona. Based on the Mexico case.

The purpose of working with personas was to develop solutions based upon the users' needs and goals. It was also developed to make sure that the entire design team, including the software engineers, understood a potential user with empathy. While personas define a character through his or her goals, personal information, skills, etc., the scenarios define the relationship between the character and the system. A narrative user journey was created to unfold the Mexican scenario and hence generate a set of initial requirements for designing the WeNet service app (Fig. 2).

Fig. 2. A user journey for the Mexican scenario.

There are several advantages of using a user journey in the design process. One advantage is that it can visualize user-focused elements for the design team, specifically targeting those who should program the app system later on. Furthermore, it represents the service's development as a sequence of actions and interactions and provides a holistic understanding of the factors influencing the experience from a user perspective. Another advantage is that the user journey can be used to discuss the design's contributions, within the design team, to support and improve the design concept. Through a participatory process, the team designed a first draft of the service blueprint by mapping the user journey for the Mexican personas.

4.3 Develop Potential Solutions

The develop phase is when the idea is transformed into a specific product or experience through various design methods [18]. We used the service blueprint method in the develop phase to focus as much as possible within the aim to start producing the WeNet app (and promoting social eating experiences, which was agreed upon in the previous two stages). The main advantage of creating a service blueprint is that it facilitates collaborative working within the interdisciplinary design team. At the same time, the develop phase demands high levels of management and communication as the design team iteratively refines the concept within the project's aim. Another advantage of the service blueprint is that it can facilitate better discussions about core elements that must be in place (in both the front- and backstage) in order to support the interactions among potential users of the platform.

In Fig. 3, we have outlined the developed solution within the social eating app, based on the service blueprint. The blueprint comprised nine steps (x-axis): creating a WeNet account, onboarding, task request, dissemination, response, task execution, evaluation, and usage incentives. The actions (y-axis) have the following categories: physical, Carlos (based on the persona and user journey; Figs. 1 and 2), guest, frontstage interactions, backstage interactions, and support system. Based on Fig. 3, the following is a description of the stages in the service blueprint:

A. Create a WeNet account/onboarding process

To access the platform, the users will have to create a WeNet account (Fig. 3). The design team envisions the onboarding process as a crucial step for providing guidelines on how to engage with the WeNet platform, present the service's value, and create engagement. Furthermore, the onboarding phase could engage new users in creating a WeNet user profile and inform the algorithms, which support diversity-aware interactions. The account creation also comes with ethical considerations, in terms of both the GDPR and how much personal information the users need to provide for the social eating app to work. I-Log is an application developed at the Department of Information Engineering and Computer Science of the University of Trento to collect data from a smartphone's internal sensors, with the user's consent.

B. Task request/dissemination/response

The task request is conceived as a core feature of the platform that will allow users to find other people and organize social activities, such as for the Mexican case study (hosting a social eating experience). To fulfill their goals, users might specify their food preferences, a location, a timeframe, and an estimated number of people needed in a group, along with deciding whom to ask (i.e. by specifying friendship and trust levels), and may specify a set of desired profiles (for instance, profiles of users living nearby, studying at the same campus, etc.). Event details and preferences could, besides location and time, also include diversity preferences (e.g. focusing on cooking competences, such as who is good at cooking, knowledge of regional food, etc.) and friendship level. After

ACTIONS	CREATE A WENET ACCOUNT	CREATE A WENET ACCOUNT	CREATE A WENET ACCOUNT	ONBOARDING PROCESS	ONBOARDING PROCESS	ONBOARDING PROCESS	ONBOARDING PROCESS	TASK REQUEST	TASK REQUEST	TASK REQUEST	TASK REQUEST	DISSEMINATION	RESPONSE	RESPONSE	TASK AGREEMENT	TASK AGREEMENT	EXECUTION	EVALUATION	INCENTIVE
PHYSICAL	Downloading WeNet mobile app																		
CARLOS		Giving permission to install I-log log to use the service	Signing up with info (e.g. e-mail, and name). Accepting terms and conditions	Creating account and landing on the welcome page	Filling in info about Carlos' diversity profile	Completing action	Receiving incentive message about app functions	Selecting function: "host a dinner"	Marking "food" as required	Creating menu list	Adding event details and preferences e.g. location and time	Receiving confirmation for creating an event	Receiving notification	Receiving list of matching profiles/groups	Selecting guest(s) / suggested group	Starting conversation with guest(s)	Hosting a dinner	Rating experience	Receiving badge
GUEST													Accepting request		Receiving confirmation		Attending event	Rating experience	Receiving badge
FRONT STAGE INTER-ACTIONS	Showing WeNet icon	Showing request to install I-log	Showing link to the verification email	Showing welcome page	Showing diversity dimensions	Showing task as completed	Showing pop-up incentive message	Opening "host a dinner" tab	Showing options for planning dinner	Showing menu suggestions	Showing requested fields and filters	Showing confirmation for creating an event	Showing notification	Showing profiles	Showing selection	Showing chat function		Showing rating system	Showing badges
BACK STAGE INTER-ACTIONS	WeNet App account operations and maintenance	I-log installment	Sending confirmation e-mail / Creating new account	WeNet processing profile data	Processing data	Processing data	Processing data	Linking to function page	Processing data	Processing data	Processing data	Processing request and searching for matching profiles	Processing matching profiles	Processing matching profiles	Processing matched profiles	Linking to chat function	I-log Data collection	Saving data in the cloud	Saving data in the cloud
SUPPORT SYSTEM	Storing app data	Storing app data	Storing user data / User authentification and data storage in cloud	Crunching data for ML	Crunching data for ML	Crunching data for ML	Crunching data for ML	Crunching data for ML	Crunching data for ML	Crunching data for ML	Crunching data for ML	Crunching data for ML	Crunching data for ML	Crunching data for ML	Crunching data for ML	Crunching data for ML	Crunching data for ML	Crunching data for ML	Crunching data for ML

Fig. 3. Service Blueprint iteration for WeNet development, Mexico case.

receiving responses, the users might be able to select individuals or a group based on personal preferences.

C. Task execution/ Evaluation/ Usage incentives

Visual confirmations and notifications are important for trust-building when having users interact within a technology-based platform [24]. Therefore, we have several built-in visual confirmations and notifications for the users, which also increase trust [Fig. 3]. The design team envisions users as responsible for discussing and making arrangements to execute the task. Accordingly, a discussion/planning feature (chat or instant messaging) will be a relevant component of the platform. A set of rating mechanisms will be put in place to encourage and monitor users' participations and trustworthy behaviors on the platform. The rating system will be built on users' usage of the platform and peer ratings. The requesters (or hosts) may rate their experiences and evaluate volunteers (or guests) with whom they have interacted. Volunteers may also rate each other and the requester, if needed. However, in our case study, both the requester and volunteers will only rate people in their group (or possibly assess the grouping mechanism). We want to maintain user engagement by providing a set of virtual rewards and incentives (e.g. badges) that will act as symbol of trustworthiness within the WeNet community.

4.4   Further Development of the WeNet App

The core characteristic of the presented scenario is that users (for instance, students) can look for a group of volunteers to cook and eat together with. With the development of a WeNet application, different students can be connected to address each other needs by searching for the right person (or group of people) for a given task and supporting people's interactions by providing ad-hoc incentives. Accordingly, the Mexican scenario will be further adapted in order to address other relevant challenges among students (e.g. focusing on similar study- or leisure-related activities) across different country locations.

5   Discussion and Conclusion

For success within an interdisciplinary research design team, there is a strong need to integrate knowledge and methods from different disciplines, using a real synthesis of approaches. There are several reasons why. First, the study of user acceptance of new technology, including diversity across countries, is a mature research area that also include strong ethical considerations. Second, it reflects a distinct trend toward new interdisciplinary approaches using AI and digital technology research, with diversity as a central characteristic. Third, there is also strong need to use various methods throughout a design process that everybody in the design team understands and acknowledges. Fourth, there is also a need to be more reflective in the methods used and to improve such methods' validity and reliability.

Scenario building can be a valuable tool in co-design and co-creation activities [25, 26], which might help a design team to gain a shared understanding of the specific need, challenge, or obstacle. Scenarios can also be used as a negotiation tool in co-design sessions because they may provide a clear picture of possible future developments of a given strategy or design action. However, one general challenge is that the scenarios and the narrative should clearly explain the issues, needs, and challenges that a persona(s) is facing and how he/she will address it through the envisioned solution. The story should be simple, effective, and easily communicated so that the design team can immediately see the value of the proposed solution and its implications. A challenge for personas is that the commonly used methods of creating personas tend to project the developers' own goals onto a specific design [17]. A common mistake is that persona creation is an isolated task undertaken by UX designers or people in related roles, and is not spread out to the entire design team. In this way, personas are often miscredited as having low impact, including later on in implementation. However, the process also demands transparent data (for the personas to be based on) and full detailed explanations when the personas are build. Not having one-dimensional personas with low credibility also demands validity and reliability checks throughout the persona-development work.

Within our work of developing the WeNet app, we found several benefits from using a service blueprint. First, it provided a detailed whole picture with which to quickly identify and qualify good design elements but also issues and challenges. It developed into a useful asset conveying both the personas and the user journey methods. Furthermore, it provided a visual outlined work in-progress, which could be shared across the design team for greater understanding of how different frontstage and backstage functions work together. In many ways, the blueprint allowed the multifaceted interdisciplinary design team to "speak the same language" with a common and shared goal. By that, the blueprint provided a more strategic visual-management tool for further progress development. However, our blueprint methods also created some challenges, mainly from its level of detail. While it provided a good visual overview, it did not provide the full picture (e.g. with algorithms, links, and programming details), especially not within a very complex setup like our WeNet platform. Furthermore, it is a rather time-consuming and collaborative process, which also demands good management to involve different people in the process.

Acknowledgement. This research has received funding from the European Union's Horizon 2020 FET Proactive project "WeNet – The Internet of us", grant agreement No 823783.

References

1. Ibrahim, A.K., Kelly, S.J., Adams, C.E., Glazebrook, C.: A systematic review of studies of depression prevalence in university students. J. Psychiatr. Res. **47**(3), 391–400 (2013)
2. Brown, P.: The Invisible Problem? Improving Students' Mental Health. Higher Education Policy Institute, Oxford (2016)
3. Backhaus, I., et al.: Health-related quality of life and its associated factors: results of a multi-center cross-sectional study among university students. J. Public Health (2019). https://doi.org/10.1093/pubmed/fdz011
4. Auerbach, R.P., Alonso, J., Axinn, W.G., et al.: Mental disorders among college students in the WHO world mental health surveys. Psychol. Med. **46**(14), 2955–2970 (2016)
5. Global Migration Data Analysis Centre (GMDAC) International Organization for Migration. Global Migration Indicators 2018. Germany, Berlin (2018)
6. Ayano, M.: Japanese students in Britain. In: Byram, M., Feng, A. (eds.) Living and Studying Abroad: Research and Practice, pp. 11–37. Multilingual Matters, Clevedon (2006)

7. Wang, K.T., Wei, M., Zhao, R., Chuang, C.-C., Li, F.: The cross-cultural loss scale: development and psychometric evaluation. Psychol. Assess. **27**(1), 42–53 (2015)
8. D'Agostino, A., Ghellini, G., Longobardi, S.: Out-migration of university enrolment: the mobility behaviour of Italian students. Int. J. Manpower **40**(1), 56–72 (2019)
9. Dabasi-Halász, Z., et al.: International youth mobility in Eastern and Western Europe–the case of the Erasmus+ programme. Migrat. Lett. **16**(1), 61–72 (2019)
10. Gebhard, J.G.: International students' adjustment problems and behaviors. J. Int. Stud. **2**(2), 184–193 (2012)
11. Mesidor, J., Sly, K.: Factors that contribute to the adjustment of international students. J. Int. Stud. **6**(1), 262–282 (2016)
12. Manzini, E., Jégou, F., Meroni, A.: Designing oriented scenarios. In: Design for sustainability, a step by step approach. United Nations Environment Program, Paris (2009)
13. Stickdorn, M., Hormess, M., Lawrence, A.: This is Service Design Doing. Applying Service Design Thinking in the Real World. A Practitioner's Handbook. O'Reilly Media, Inc., Sebastopol (2018)
14. Carroll, J.M.: Five reasons for scenario-based design. Interact. Comput. **13**(1), 43–60 (2000)
15. Cooper, A.: The Inmates Are Running the Asylum: Why High Tech Products Drive Us Crazy and How to Restore the Sanity. Macmillan, Indianapolis (1999)
16. Pruitt, J., Grundin, J.: Personas: practice and theory. In: Proceedings of the 2003 Conference on Designing for user Experiences, pp. 1–15 (2003)
17. Miaskiewicz, T., Kozar, K.A.: Personas and user-centered design: how can personas benefit product design processes? Des. Stud. **32**(5), 417–430 (2011)
18. Design Council UK, (2015). Design methods for developing services: An Introduction to Service Design and a Selection of Service Design Tools, Technology, Keeping Connected. https://www.designcouncil.org.uk/sites/default/files/asset/document/DesignCouncil_Design%20methods%20for%20developing%20services.pdf
19. Bjørner, T.: Data analysis and findings. In: Bjørner, T. (ed.) Qualitative Methods for Consumer Research: The Value of the Qualitative Approach in Theory and Practice. Hans Reitzel, Copenhagen (2015)
20. Clatworthy, S.: Service design thinking. In: Lüders, M., Andreassen, T.W., Clatworthy, S., Hillestad, T. (eds.) Innovating for Trust. Northhampton, US (2017)
21. Medler, B., Magerko, B.: The implications of improvisational acting and role-playing on design methodologies. In: Proceedings of the SIGCHI Conference on Human Factors in Computing Systems, pp. 483–492. ACM (2010)
22. Morelli, N.: Designing product/service systems: a methodological exploration. Des. Issues **18**(3), 3–17 (2002)
23. Gulliksen, J., Göransson, B., Boivie, I., Blomkvist, S., Persson, J., Cajander, Å.: Key principles for user-centred systems design. Behav. Inf. Technol. **22**(6), 397–409 (2003)
24. Paul, J.: Modern UI design for the industrial Internet of Things: the move to smart, embedded devices running web technology is capable of fully realizing the potential of the hot. Quality **56**(13), 9–12 (2017)
25. Steen, M., Manschot, M., De Koning, N.: Benefits of co-design in service design projects. Int. J. Des. **5**(2), 53–60 (2011)
26. Sanders, E.B.-N., Stappers, J.P.: Co-creation and the new landscapes of design. Co-Design **4**(1), 5–18 (2008)
27. YOU at college. https://youatcollege.com/. Accessed 24 Jan 2020
28. Miloff, A., Marklund, A., Carlbring, P.: The challenger app for social anxiety disorder: new advances in mobile psychological treatment. Internet Interv. **2**(4), 382–391 (2015)
29. Uniwhere. https://www.uniwhere.com/. Accessed 24 Feb 2020
30. Kosow, H., Gaßner, R.: Methods of future and scenario analysis: overview, assessment, and selection criteria. DEU, Bonn (2008)

Design Practice in Online Courses: Application of Service Design to MOOC

Ziyang Li[1(✉)], Xiangnuo Li[1], Limin Wang[1], Xiandong Cheng[1], Hao He[2], and Bin Liang[1]

[1] Beijing City University, No. 269 Bei si huan Zhong lu, Hai dian District, Beijing, China
li.ziyang@bcu.edu.cn
[2] China Central Academy of Fine Arts, No. 8 Hua Jia Di Nan Street, Chao yang District, Beijing, China

Abstract. Whilst teaching on MOOC has currently enjoyed a great popularity among colleges and universities undergoing a profound reform of teaching method, this article accordingly centers on the creation of online course resources and interaction platforms based upon the idea of service design. Thorough analysis of the course *Audio-Video Interaction* of the Digital Media Art Department of Beijing City University demonstrated how the idea was formed and the whole procedure of design (including relevant design tools) before presenting the final result. The last part is about the method of applying MOOC-teaching and its future. Specifically speaking, in satisfying users' needs the whole service system comprises of users, interaction methods, and online platforms, which makes it possible to change or update design and content flexibly to meet different demands. In that regard, service design may play a significant role in improving and developing teaching on MOOC for colleges and universities in China.

Keywords: Design thinking · Participation design · Service design · MOOC · Educational application

1 Introduction

While teaching in recent years, the author has contemplated and examined novel techniques for teaching art and design; expanding learning content as wide as possible; and exposing more students to the knowledge taught by the author. The author's main focuses are service design and user experience design, which differ from the traditional teaching design method as the former emphasize the importance of the design process. The Higher Education Department of the Ministry of Education of the PRC proposed MOOCs as a key project for 2019 because they are not only efficient and wide-spread, but also well-suited for China given the technological development of the domestic digital industry. In this paper, the author designs and creates a MOOC by using the service design method. During the design process, touch points are identified through three user service investigations. Furthermore, the Beijing City University Online Course (BCUOC) platform serves as the function framework and the UX workflow of the interactive service system.

A. Marcus and E. Rosenzweig (Eds.): HCII 2020, LNCS 12202, pp. 427–437, 2020.
https://doi.org/10.1007/978-3-030-49757-6_31

2   Problems with MOOCs

As online education rapidly develops, new forms of teaching, such as MOOCs, are gradually replacing certain functions and the abilities of traditional teaching. Learners are now able to make full use of their fragmented time and eliminate spatial constraints, in order to enrich their use of learning resources. Online education is slowly transitioning from an auxiliary method into a mainstream teaching style. Nevertheless, there are certain issues that have been exposed as a result of the rapid development of online education [1].

2.1   Students Lack the Habit of Self-motivated, Inquiry-Based and Innovative Learning

The internet-based MOOC education model has emerged with shared teaching resources and the open teaching model as the main concepts. Furthermore, at the core of this model lies self-motivated learning and innovative practices. However, due to long-term immersion in the exam-oriented environment, students may lack the ability to engage in self-motivated, inquiry-based and innovative learning. Such an inability may explain why students rarely complete MOOCs in a self-driven context.

2.2   Interaction is a Challenge in the MOOC Learning Model

MOOCs differ from the traditional teaching model. As a learner-centric method, MOOCs require students to be self-driven; possess good teamwork skills; raise questions on their own; and demonstrate creativity. Are MOOCs interactive? In traditional teaching, it is possible to effectively manage interactions between the teacher and students through face-to-face communication. However, MOOC platforms cannot match up against traditional teaching models in terms of their interactivity.

2.3   It is Difficult to Evaluate Learning Outcomes

All learning can produce a certain outcome. Learning outcomes can also motivate students to continue self-learning. In traditional teaching, assessments, such as in-class questions, discussions, class engagement, exams and report writing, can be used to evaluate whether students have understood the core content of a course and met the necessary requirements. However, these assessments are not applicable to MOOCs. There are three main criteria which can be used to evaluate the outcome of MOOC teaching:

1. Whether the course is completed as required;
2. Whether the student achieves the required learning threshold;
3. Whether the MOOC certificate is recognized by society.

As for the third point, as MOOCs lack a supervision mechanism, it is not possible to ensure that students have passed the tests in the required manner. Therefore, under some circumstances, MOOC evaluations may not be representative and may not reflect the true level of the student.

Regarding the aforementioned issues, the following two cases aim to solve the problems that affect MOOC learning.

Case 1: Khan-Style Tutorials

Khan-style tutorials by Salman Khan (Fig. 1) have provoked a heated discussion on YouTube [2]. Over the past few years, Khan has recorded more than 6,000 video tutorials and has gained 1.7 billion views. The Khan-style has changed traditional education and led to an increase in the number of individuals who engage in online learning.

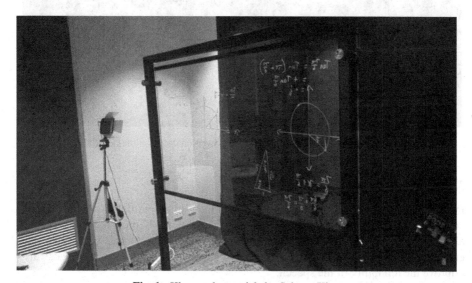

Fig. 1. Khan-style tutorials by Salman Khan

There are four factors which are key to the success of Khan-style tutorials:

1. *Use of tones*

Salman Khan mentioned that educators should speak as if they are chatting to a friend in a café. Moreover, Khan believes that educators should adopt a tone full of emotion. The speaker's emotion; thoughts while speaking; and accent all form part of the tutorial. The speaker should never adopt an arrogant attitude when delivering knowledge.

2. *Teaching methods*

Khan-Style tutorials emphasize the importance of promptness when presenting information. For instance, when there is a need for text and graphic illustrations in a tutorial, because computer-made graphics are fixed and rigid, they do not provoke thought. In contrast, compared with computer-made graphics, handwritten notes on the board can better encourage students to engage in active thinking (Fig. 2).

Fig. 2. Salman Khan emphasize handwritten notes on the board

3. *Teaching preparation*

Preparation is very important in teaching. Rather than simply writing down the teaching content, preparation should ensure that the teacher is mentally prepared and can cover all the content at once. If there are mistakes, the speaker should start over rather than cutting or editing the video. Moreover, correcting minor mistakes when talking can also improve the reliability of the speech.

4. *Keep it short, but not too short*

Khan's videos are usually 6 to 10 min in length, which gives the students enough time to think without being so long that students lose interest.

Case 2: Immersive Learning Simulation

One problem with MOOCs is that teachers are unable to share meaningful experiences in their videos as sharing real-life experiences can be very time-consuming and hard to evaluate. Hence, this issue is not easy to address. As a result, a new concept has been proposed. The concept of immersive learning simulation has attracted many educators, because it provides a truly experiential learning opportunity. This learning experience is attractive, can be expanded and provides a mechanism for assessment during the learning process.

Immersive learning simulation (ILS) integrates simulations, teaching methods and "hard fun" in order to create a truly attractive and behavior-changing learning method [3]. ILS has been used in the military and medical fields since the 1990s and has been applied to higher education since 2003 for the purpose of helping students to understand complicated concepts and processes.

The digital media simulation developed by Toolwire, a leading provider of immersive learning simulation, has achieved great success in a relatively short amount of time. In 2010, 100,000 independent students used Toolwire's ILS more than one million times at various universities and across a range of disciplines. In 2011, this number increased to more than 2.5 million.

The digital media simulation developed by Toolwire includes an instructional design approach called "natural assessment", which goes beyond the methodologies currently used in online learning assessments to ensure that students can learn in a real-life context. This assessment simulation consists of six modules:

1. An open and interactive context which establishes a storyline for the students.
2. A supportive and interactive model which provides students with the target information and background; uses attractive video characters to engage students in learning; encourages students to interact with the screen; and elicits responses to the learning content from the character.
3. The main interaction provides students with key information about the learning content through a virtual tutor.
4. On the courses, multiple units are set and students are evaluated after finishing each unit so as to continuously monitor the learning outcome and provide remedial opportunities where appropriate.
5. Remedial measures are designed to enhance learners' confidence, which, through remedial measures, allows learners to review key learning content.
6. Summative assessments evaluate students' abilities at the end of each storyline and encourage students to apply new knowledge to their learning. These activities do more than just test students' command of a small piece of information.

Natural assessment aims to develop learners' ability to use their knowledge in a real context. Upon completion, learners provide information for assessment, which is then formatted and delivered to the teacher for grading.

3   Creating an Educational Application Using Service Design

Service design is a user-centered design method which aims to solve a specific problem using a design process created by both the service target and the developer. As a design activity that enhances the user experience, service design efficiently organizes and integrates the user, the scenario, the experience, the process and the service target into a single design system, so as to provide users with an effective, easy-to-use and worthwhile service experience [4]. According to Professor Liu Guanzhong from Tsinghua University, service design embodies the most fundamental principle of industrial design, which is "to create a healthy, reasonable, sharing, and fair lifestyle in human society" [5].

With the development of the digital industry in China in recent years, service design has garnered wide attention. However, there is no unified method and the concept of service design has evolved alongside changes in digital products and their users. The main reason for this is that, because the users, scenarios, and experience processes vary between projects, it is difficult to produce appropriate designs for different service targets using a single method. However, it is always true that service design is user-centric and aims to enhance the user experience. As a result, service design should be studied from the users' perspective and meet their specific needs. Furthermore, service design does not focus solely on the design process. Design process analysis is not the only focus of service design, as integrating the application scenario also merits consideration. Hence, as mentioned before, the ultimate purpose of service design is to create an effective, easy-to-use and worthwhile service experience for specific application scenarios [6, 7].

Case 1: Zhejiang Museum Children's Area Service Design
In her article Research on the Present Situation of Zhejiang Museum Children's Area from The Perspective of Service Design, which examines children's sensory experience, cognition, and learning motivation, Wang Yanyan from the Ningbo University of Finance and Economics establishes a system that consists of four service indicators. These are user value, service philosophy, touch points and value-adding activities in the children's area. Wang uses questionnaires and case studies of various museums in Zhejiang to examine the situation there. During the questionnaire stage, she investigates the setting, operation, usage and satisfaction derived from visits to the children's area in Zhejiang Museum. The results of her investigation reflect users' interests, which can help the designer to not only connect to the personal experiences of young visitors in the museum, but also design and develop more targeted digital display auxiliary systems and derivatives. During her field research, she uses service design tools, such as Journey Map and Blueprint, to conduct systematic analysis; identify touch points and explore the current situation of service design in Zhejiang Museum. This research provides important data for the further renovation of the museum and ensures its sustainable development [8].

Case 2: Research on the Application of Service Design for O2O Early Childhood Education
With a focus on service design, HUANG Yinke studies the main features, cognitive characteristics and psychological characteristics of parents aged 25–35 with preschool-age children. Through an in-depth user investigation and discussions with early stage education experts, he produces a demand description for early-stage education service design. he divides the users of the early-stage education service system into different groups and constructs a user role model and an early stage education interactive service system architecture. For its implementation, he establishes a function framework and UX workflow for the interactive service system for the touch points using WeChat. Furthermore, he realizes a high-fidelity prototype design for the overall interactive service system. Finally, using the experiences of users with the interactive service system prototype, the function design, contents, interactive operation and visual design are evaluated in order to demonstrate the extent to which this early-stage education system fulfills the design purpose [9].

4   Practice: Designing a MOOC on Audio-Visual Interaction

Audio-Visual Interaction is an important element in design expression courses aimed at those studying art design. Audio-Visual Interaction teaches students about the technologies and artistic expressions of audio visualization, as well as the digital technology used to visualize the most common form of media – audio media. Currently, the main practical issue in the development of art design is realizing the organic integration of tool standardization, the popularization of applications and the personalization of art. In-depth theoretical research and exploration are undoubtedly crucial to solving this problem. However, from an application perspective, device renovation, software choice and program design may be more feasible. Hence, many universities have included program design courses in their art design programs. It is likely that enhancing the role of program design in artistic creation could enhance the promotion of the organic integration of digital technology, communication and artistic creation. Thus, the author chooses the p5.js language as the entry point and aims to teach students how to turn audio into art through programming in accordance with the thinking patterns of students majoring in art and design. During the study, art visualization techniques are enriched and their logical thinking improved. Using the BCUOC platform, the author creates the Audio-Visual Interaction MOOC using the service design method; thereby providing self-study and self-assessment modules, such as learning contents, video tutorials, teacher-student interaction and discussions.

The teaching activities designed using the MOOC service design method are creative. The MOOC covers a wide range of subjects and users. With service design methods, several touch points can be repeatedly discovered through user experience and user investigation. By selecting and combining various touch points, the learning form and learning process of the Audio-Visual Interaction MOOC are generated; thereby facilitating the MOOC's development.

4.1   The Process and Results of Relevant Investigations

As a MOOC, Audio-Visual Interaction has various users, as anyone interested in interactive art can take the course and participate in the associated discussions. As the course design is still at the initial stage, the author selects only a few potential users to test and investigate the product. In the investigation stage, 12 students with a background in art design are chosen. To be precise, there are four students majoring in digital media art, one in fashion design, three in product design, one in visual communication, two in animation design and one in design.

During the user experience investigation stage, three questionnaire surveys were given to the chosen students. In the first investigation, students were asked about themselves, how often they use the BCUOC platform, their interest in the BCUOC platform and experience using the BCUOC platform (Fig. 3).

Fig. 3. The Course Audio-Visual Interaction user research

First Investigation
In total, 12 students were investigated. While they have all studied on the BCUOC platform, two had never used it to study specialized courses related to their major. Moreover, nine expressed no interest in the courses currently available on the BCUOC platform because they consider them irrelevant to their major.

Second Investigation
In the second investigation, time management and discretionary time arrangement were investigated. The results show that the personal and study schedules of the participants vary greatly due to the intricacies of their own personal loves and the different majors that they study. As a result, there is no unified available time slot. Therefore, a fixed-time online course cannot meet the needs of all the students.

Third Investigation
In this investigation, the students were asked their preferred teaching form, class duration and assessment type. Moreover, they were asked to briefly design and describe their own learning scenarios. Moreover, eight students from different majors were selected for a subjective investigation. In terms of teaching form, five prefer to study using online videos. In terms of class duration, seven consider 30 min ideal. In terms of assessments, six enjoy online exercises and online exams.

Through the three investigations, the interest-sparking teaching method, simplified coursework process and flexible time have been established as touch points. The function framework and UX workflow have also been established as touch points on the BCUOC platform in preparation for creating the Audio-Visual Interaction MOOC prototype.

4.2 *Audio-Visual Interaction* Course Prototype Design

As a mature online learning system, the BCUOC platform is designed for online teaching and online course submission specifically at Beijing City University. The author uses the existing functions in the system to design a function that maximizes touch point satisfaction for the student users.

Interest-Sparking Teaching Method

The author has contemplated the best technique for developing the students' interest in the course so that they can continue learning. As the students have different majors, it is difficult to identify any shared features. However, because the majority of the students are majoring in art and design, they possess a deep understanding of basic shapes and colors. Consequently, the author decided to take the drawing module of p5.js as an entry point in order to guide the students to produce basic shapes through storytelling and theme setting.

Traditional teaching method:

- teach coding →☐learn how to create basic shapes

Interest-sparking teaching method:

- teach coding →☐tell stories →☐create the shapes needed in the scenario →☐create basic shapes

Furthermore, the teaching environment is decorated, the video shot with multiple cameras and the videos edited during post-production. Thus, the image can quickly shift between the key elements of the course, such as the teacher, whiteboard, coding interface and running effect.

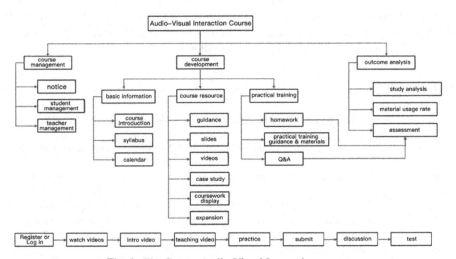

Fig. 4. The Course Audio-Visual Interaction system

Simplified Process

Another issue that the author aims to address is simplifying the process of teaching, practice and coursework. The course system on the BCUOC platform is complicated. While maintaining the basic functions, the author believes it is necessary to optimize and simplify the service process. Figure 4 lists all the functions in the system, only the red ones are operated for the service target.

Behind the BCUOC platform, there is a well-established teacher management and course report management system, but this essay does not discuss the service design of the teaching management end.

Flexible Time

From the investigations, it can be seen that, differences in majors lead to substantially different study schedules. In traditional online courses, all the teaching materials and tutorials are uploaded at once, which the students can then browse before studying those relevant to their own interests and needs. In the Audio-Visual Interaction MOOC designed by the author, the teaching materials are only uploaded on the scheduled course date. Moreover, they remain up indefinitely once uploaded. Students have two choices, they can either watch the lessons according to the course schedule, or they can take them all at the same time before the test. As the design and production of the course is still on-going, the author will continue their investigation after the course has been released online. In the future, by studying the service design of this project, the author plans to compare these two means of study and monitor any differences in the learning outcomes.

5   Conclusion

This essay first explains the concepts of MOOC and service design before then examining two MOOC cases and two cases of service design and learning systems. Finally, the author designs an Audio-Visual Interaction MOOC using the service design method. The touch points are identified through three investigations, while the function framework and UX workflow of the interactive service system are established on the BCUOC platform in order to create the Audio-Visual Interaction MOOC.

References

1. Li, F.: "互联网+"背景下慕课创新路径之探索与思考,大学教育(university education). (06), 163–165 (2019)
2. Khan-Style tutorials. http://mathemooc.de/2013/07/02/wie-macht-man-mooc-videos-im-khan-style
3. Beckem II, J.M., Watkins, M.: Bringing life to learning: immersive experiential learning simulations for online and blended courses. J. Asynchronous Learn. Netw. 16(5), 61–70 (2012)
4. Miettinen, S., Rontti, S., Kuure, E., Lindström, A.: Realizing design thinking through a service design process and an innovative prototyping laboratory – introducing service innovation corner (SINCO). In: Proceedings of the Conference on Design Research Society (DRS 2012), pp. 1202–1214 (2012)
5. Liu, G.: Design and national strategy. Sci. Technol. Rev. 35(22), 15–18 (2017). https://doi.org/10.3981/j.issn.1000-7857.2017.22.001

6. Zhang, R., Li, C.: Research of industrial design education based on service design. J. Educ. Teach. Forum (32), 248–250 (2015)
7. Liu, J.: Research on service design thought in innovation and entrepreneurship education. J. Zhenjiang Coll. **32**(3), 84–86 (2019)
8. Wang, Y.: Research on the present situation of Zhejiang museum children's area from the perspective of service design. Industr. Des. (8), 56–59 (2019)
9. Huang, Y.: The interaction of early education service design study based on O2O model. Zhejiang University of Technology (2015)

Changes in Design Education Promoted by Collaborative Organization: Distribution and Fragmentation

WenJing Li[✉], DanDan Yu, YiNan Zhang, FuMei Zhang, and Limin Wang

Art and Design, Academy, Beijing City University, Beijing, China
l.w.j@hotmail.com

Abstract. This paper is predominantly based on observations pertaining to the transition from design industrial production to the design organization collaboration model. Moreover, it discusses the requirements of this collaboration model on the design students' training and changes in design education methods.

The most impactful change in design education has been its distribution and fragmentation as brought about by networks. In other words, teaching resources, such as the knowledge and skills necessary for student growth, are scattered with different means of communication. The systematic knowledge that was originally acquired in the classroom or in books can now be obtained anytime and anywhere. Furthermore, such knowledge can be learnt from any point rather than a specified beginning.

To illustrate, this thesis starts by introducing the distribution trend in design; outlining the changes in design organizations; and identifying the challenges facing design education. In order to study design education development in China, we surveyed design graduates from the last 3 years. Next, we summarized the distribution and fragmentation of design education; putting forward new methods in design training as taught in schools.

Keywords: Collaborative organization · Distributed cognition and learning · Distributed classroom in design education

1 Introduction

1.1 Distribution Trend of Design

It has been less than half a century since Stuart Hall published the essay *Encoding and Decoding Television Discourse* (1973). However, in the torrent of the digital age, the encoding and decoding of information have surpassed the boundaries of traditional media, while increasingly becoming the basis for real-life activities, including design behavior. Moreover, with self-media, political and organizational power behaviors in the coding process have been widely replaced by professional powers. Meanwhile, professional powers in design are transitioning from experts, scholars, and designers to countless non-professionals. In the field of design research, the broad consensus is that, in the

© Springer Nature Switzerland AG 2020
A. Marcus and E. Rosenzweig (Eds.): HCII 2020, LNCS 12202, pp. 438–450, 2020.
https://doi.org/10.1007/978-3-030-49757-6_32

social life composed of the Internet and the Internet of Things, people have experienced a transition from mass communication to niche communication. At the same time, design has increasingly become a new type of "equal interaction." The widespread knowledge-sharing method has changed; allowing everyone to be the subject of design behavior, which has altered the one-way and passive nature of the traditional grant-receive relationship from the past, while also allowing individuals to participate in design activities in an equal manner. This trend of "everyone participating in design" has gradually changed the modern design face following on from the arts and crafts movement at the end of the 19th century. In addition, unimaginable changes have taken place in the main body, objects, procedures, production and presentation methods, organizational forms, etc. The distributed and fragmented design organization and collaboration approach brings new challenges to design education. Recipients are now seen as the fundamental basic topic in design education.

1.2 Design Collaboration in Different History Periods

The collaborated design organization is a new model of the current design industry organization. Throughout the history of design development, the changes in design organizations and institutions could be divided roughly into the following three stages.

Firstly, the handcraft design stage, namely, the design organization adheres to the fairly rigid class system or in accordance with the three-level responsibility system which is composed with supervisor, manager and manufacturer, and this kind of management usually runs successfully by carving names of the craftspeople on their hand-made products. It's really good accountability mechanisms, but on the other hand it's quite stict rules for the ones who created fine crafts.

Secondly the industrial design stage, during which the organizational structure of design has been gradually transforming from the strictly hierarchical "Carving Names on Utensils" system to "Trade Associations" ("Handicraft guild" in western countries), following with design association, during which the designers and the manufacturing workers further substituted craftsmen, forming the semi-autonomous design organization. Founded in 1907, the Deutscher Werkbund served as a representative, which provided abundant talents resources for the establishment of Bauhaus and the rapid development of German design after the war.

Thirdly, in the stage of information design, people began to ponder on modern industry since although it tremendously upgraded the life quality and living standards of the public, these industrial products were generally considered to be as cold and icy as the machines that made them. During the time when machine production made vastly contribution to improvements in production efficiency, it had been kept apart from the traditional creating concept in which the man's spirit maintained harmonious with material life during tranquil times. Finally design things are changing with the computer science and technology and the rapid development of Internet, education of design colleges and universities should establish a new system facing the decentration, de-administration, and flat management structure in design industry.

1.3 Challenges Facing Design Education

Many designers and researchers have argued that design education in colleges and universities does not match the needs of the design industry, especially the training methods used in school, as these were originally proposed for industrial production. As a result, they are no longer suitable. Named designer Gadi Amit notes that the quality of recent grads has stagnated or even diminished [1]. According to Herbert Simon's "science of design", the post-war universities have created "a new subculture of scientific practices—training regimes, conceptual schemes embodied in research practices, and disciplinary training" [2]. According to Don Norman, "To deal with today's large, complex problems, design education needs to change to include multiple disciplines, technology, art, the social sciences, politics, and business."

The Internet has promoted the integration of various disciplines in design, while simultaneously bringing new challenges to design education. Distributed, fragmented, and immediate, it has become the inescapable future of design education.

2 Research Background

2.1 Design Education Since 1914

The training objective of design education is to cultivate talented individuals so that they can one day work in production. Therefore, design education has always been associated with the design organization structure and its requirements for workers.

Prior to the Industrial Revolution, the guilds of medieval craftsmen took on the task of cultivating traditional craftsmanship. Craftsmen passed on their skills from generation to generation through the master-apprentice arrangement, whereby the teaching and exchange of skills took place in a small area. After the Industrial Revolution, factory workers manufactured numerous industrial products that had peculiar shapes and impracticalities, which were then exhibited at the Great Exhibition of the Works of Industry of all Nations in 1851. The "Arts and Crafts Movement" that was subsequently triggered opened the doors to modern design. Design has changed from an act of craftsmen instinctively processing materials in a specific manner to determining the design of everything before the production process even begins. Starting from the "Government School of Design" (which was the predecessor of the Royal College of Art) in 1837, Charles Ashbee's Guild of Handicraft, William Richard Lethaby's contribution to London County Council Central School of Arts and Crafts, Walter Crane's service in Reading University and the Royal College of Art in South Kensington all delivered innovative design education. Bauhaus represents the epitome of such efforts to emphasize the need to standardize designs in line with machine manufacturing, while simultaneously integrating science, logic, and art, which led to modern design education closely following the production of machine industry.

In 1969, Herbert Simon published *The Sciences of the Artificia;* establishing that "design is the core of all professional training", and promoting the transformation of design education from studio practice to laboratory research. While design education remained a "training apprenticeship", it was delivered under an expert research scientist instead of a master worker. It fit into the manufacture and production of products in the post-industrial era. Moreover, in the current distributed collaborative organizational structure, this educational model has also become somewhat outdated (See Fig. 1).

Fig. 1. Changes in teaching method reform in design education brought about by the transformation of design industry and organizational structure.

2.2 Changes in the Design Concept in China

Many scholars acknowledge that, because "the universality and openness of design concepts determine the universality and openness of the design profession" (Dai FuPing 2012), design is freed from the inherent meaning of shape design. Furthermore, design is crucial for "diversified, personalized, scientific and rational needs, and [creates] a better physical and mental experience" (Lu YongXiang 2015), as well as inspiring "people's freedom and joy" (Xin XiangYang 2012), and "determining the sustainable development of all humankind" (Liu GuanZhong 2013). In this sense, existing design education can "expand from product design to service design, from service design to social innovation, and use design thinking to promote the development of social innovation as a whole, while also promoting more extensive application design. This in turn can transform design into an effective tool to drive national construction, economic and cultural construction, social construction, and advance modernization." (Xu Ping 2017). Thus, the integration of design and various disciplines meets both its essential requirements and those of society.

In the historical process by which western learning spread, the discipline of "design" in China was known as "pattern", "arts and crafts" and "design" (see Fig. 2).

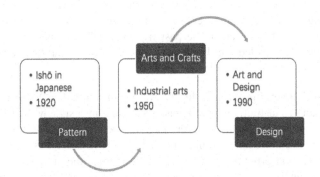

Fig. 2. Changes in the design concept in college education in China.

- Pattern. Mainly used since 1930, was represented by Chen Zhifo *Principles of Pattern ABC*. The words "pattern" and "artisan" were both came from Japan, used to summarize the early flat graphics and three-dimensional design.

- Arts and Crafts. From the 1950s to 1990s, "Arts and Crafts" used to refer to the design and production of various arts and crafts related to daily life. And it has always belonged to the arts under the category of literature, and is a second-level discipline (once a third-level discipline).
- Design. According to "the Undergraduate Specialty Catalogue of Higher Institutions" edited by the Ministry of Education in 1998, Art Design took place of Arts and Crafts, and "Design Art" was used in catalog of postgraduates issued by the Academic Degrees Committee of the State Council.

2.3 The Scale of Design Education in China

According to a study from the Design Theory Research Team (led by Professor Xu Ping) of the Central Academy of Fine Arts in China, as of 2019, 2124 institutions and universities have established majors in design, up from 1917 in 2012. When the first National Symposium on Arts and Crafts Education in Colleges and Universities was held in Xishan, Beijing in 1982, only 14 colleges and universities in China offered design majors. In the past 40 years, the China Education Development design has made considerable progress, even in the most remote areas, such as in Tibet, where 2 colleges now offer majors in design. However, most of the design and related professional teaching resources are still concentrated in the more developed parts of the country. The coastal areas, open cities and provincial capitals still host a great proportion of China's design teaching resources.

Here are the statistics for 2019:

- 2,124 - the number of colleges and universities with majors in design or related subjects
- 9,749 - the number of design majors offered
- 647,384 - the number of students majoring in design.

Situation of the Universities and Colleges with Design Majors. In 2019, the above-mentioned colleges and universities recruited 647,384 new students in design majors. According to the continuous follow-up survey for the past 12 years, the number of new recruits in design majors in China's colleges and universities has grown every year for eight years in a row. Moreover, in the past five years, the number of design majors studying in China has totaled 2 million; while the number of planned graduates in the next 10 years exceeds 4 million (Fig. 3).

Distribution of Universities and Colleges. Among the more than 2,100 institutions in China, more than 110 institutions award master's degrees in design, while 19 institutions offer doctoral degrees in design. However, these 19 doctoral programs are concentrated in only 8 provinces and cities, while the remaining 23 provinces, cities, and autonomous regions offer doctoral programs. Due to data limitations, the above statistics do not include Hong Kong, Macau and Taiwan, but the Macao University of Science and Technology was authorized to set up a first-class doctoral degree in design in 2014. Of the 2,124 institutions, 1,122 are ordinary undergraduate institutions, accounting for 53%. Meanwhile, 354 are freshmen in design and 214 are in related majors, which account for 55% of new design students in the year; 1,012 are vocational colleges, which account for

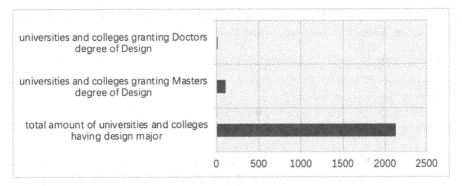

Fig. 3. The situation with design majors in China in 2019.

47%. Another 293,710 are new students in design and related disciplines, which account for 45%. Among general undergraduate colleges, there are 545 comprehensive colleges, which account for 26%; 239 polytechnic colleges, which account for 11%; and 38 art colleges, which account for about 2% (Fig. 4).

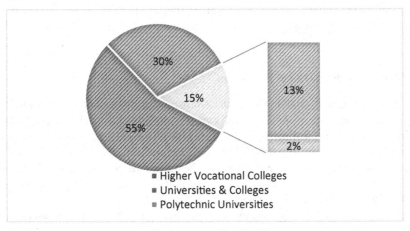

Fig. 4. Situation of universities and colleges with design majors in 2019.

Distribution of Design Fields in Academic Education. Among the aforementioned institutions, there are specific specializations in China. Such as:

- Environmental Design, including Landscape Architecture, Urban and Rural Planning, Interior Design and Lighting Design. In some case, the first two are also attributed to Public Space Design.
- Architecture Design.
- Industrial Design, which also named as Product Design.

- Visual Communication Design, including advertisements, posters, printings, websites and so on. Lots of schools use Visual Communication Design instead of Graphic Design.
- Multimedia design, the same as Digital Media Designs.
- Animation or Film.
- Clothing and Apparel design.
- Exhibition Design, which absorbed the old stage design and Lighting Design.
- Arts and crafts, including all kinds of handicraft design.

In addition, an interdisciplinary field has emerged, such as the offering of the Art and Technology major in Tsinghua University, which is a special subject from the undergraduate professional directory issued by the Ministry of Education in 2012.

Among them, the majors with the largest number of settings and of new students are environmental (art) design and digital media, followed by visual communication, industrial (product) design, and animation design. The connotation of animation and digital media is very close. In addition, part of the teaching content of visual communication design has been highly digitized. Therefore, the "(digital) media design" major has become the de facto number one major. China's design education has incorporated digital content for the digital age. All the majors included in the statistics are distributed across various disciplines, such as arts, engineering, and journalism, which are beyond the scope of the "arts" discipline.

2.4   New Methods in Design Education

The rapid, convenient, and low-cost dissemination of information and knowledge brought by the rapid development of information mediums has made the channels for acquiring knowledge of learners infinitely wider, which has led to the emergence of gradually distributed learning. It was believed that learning is distributed among individuals and their surroundings, including their peers, the media, the environment, culture, society, and time. Moreover, the nature of the distribution of learning processes between cognitive subjects and the environment was emphasized.

The emphasis on learning subjects has already began, an example of which is the flipped classroom, whereby the traditional presentation methods of classic teaching shifts from what teachers are saying to how students are learning and retaining knowledge and information. The idea came from two secondary school chemistry teachers, who wanted to help their students who lived far away and often missed class as a result [3]. After that, the teaching staff began to focus on delivering more intense and interactive experiences for students in the classroom.

The subsequent form is based on the theory of distributed cognition, which was put forward by Edwin Hutchins. Based on his observations on US navy ships, Hutchins posited that the mind is in the world (as opposed to the world being in the mind). In other words, the necessary knowledge and cognition to operate a naval vessel do not exist solely within one's head. Instead, the knowledge and cognition are distributed across objects, individuals, artifacts and the tools in the environment [4]. This places more emphasis on collaboration in design learning (Table 1).

Table 1. Differences between the three teaching modes: traditional classroom, flipped classroom and distributed classroom.

	Traditional classroom	Flipped classroom	Distributed classroom
Teacher's role	Master of knowledge and the classroom	Mentor/facilitator of student learning	Part of students' learning resources
Students' role	Passive receiver of knowledge	Active learners and researchers	Totally active knowledge explorer
Educational tools	Textbooks and teaching materials	Multi-media equipment	All teaching resources, including teachers and experts
Teaching model	Class explanation + homework	Pre-class study + in-class research	Integrating learning resources + developing the skill of autonomous learning
Ability training	Knowledge transfer and skills training in machinery	Ability to think independently and collaborate on problem solving	Proactively receiving information, while also mastering and using learning resources
Teaching evaluation	Paper tests	Multidimensional evaluations	Self-test based on multidimensional evaluations

3 Research Method and Process

3.1 A Survey of Graduates Majoring in Design

Scope of the Survey. The survey is divided into two parts. The first part examines employment and academic satisfaction data for the 2016, 2017, and 2018 three-year undergraduate graduates. The second part consists of a field visit to emerging design organizations in Beijing, Shanghai, Guangzhou, and Shenzhen. In order to investigate the actual needs of design graduates, they were interviewed so as to identify the difference between the teaching goals of colleges and the skills required by companies.

Based on the survey, conclusions are formed regarding the following two issues:

- 1. What are the competency requirements for teaching design in universities?
- 2. What kind of teaching method is most effective and practical?

Research Progress. For the first part of the survey, we designed a questionnaire covering employment status (employment or non-employment, further education), corporate information, salary and other issues, which were reported in 2017, 2018, and 2019, respectively. In spring, more than 85% of the data feedback came from undergraduate design graduates of the previous year, while 10% came from design enterprise practitioners who graduated more than 2 years ago. The recovered data were processed and compared so that we could form our preliminary conclusions.

In the second part, we focus on design collaboration organizations based on information interconnection. Professional teachers and classmates were interviewed with
company personnel. We also designed an outline of the problem, with a focus on the
design of the business situation of the company or studio, as well as in-depth communication concerning designers' working conditions and difficulties. Next, we combined
the new design organization form with the design ability requirements.

Data Analysis. In general, the employment rate of design graduates is steadily declin-
ing, in part due to the current employment situation in China. Based on the job search
data, the average level of employment within three years is more than 70%. For students
that choose to study abroad after graduation or pursue postgraduate studies, this proportion will be higher. Interestingly, despite the decline in the number of people employed
in companies, the number of people choosing freelance work or setting up a personal
design studio has been rising.

As for skills, we compared the demands of design organizations and present conditions. Most of the design companies we visited believe that professional design skills
were the most important, but they also value the abilities to communicate and collaborate in a team; to assess key connections in a project; and to lead by arranging work
at the right time. Further factors also determine designer success. Moreover, the survey
of graduates who work in design enterprises now shows that more skills are generally
gained during the internship component of college studies (Fig. 5).

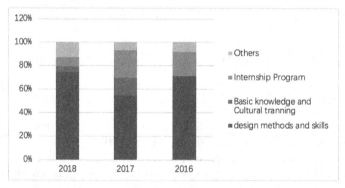

Fig. 5. Design students' capacity-building based on the real requirements for graduates working
in design enterprises.

3.2   Distribution and Fragmentation of Design Education

As stated above, the field of design practice has always valued collaboration and cooperation in different history periods, which is also reflected in design education. Along
with global internet popularization, distribution and fragmentation appeared in design
education.

Interdisciplinary Components in Design Education. The original mechanism for
collaboration and cooperation came into being after the handicraft making stage, long

before the birth of modern design methods. The collaboration of artisans at that time was still based on personal creative labor – which included the entire labor process from conception to production - as the connection node. A Study of the painting system of Dunhuang shows that, as early as the Tang Dynasty, there were corresponding professional teams responsible for every step from excavation of grottoes to the production of mural statues [5]. This led to the creation of the oldest learning form: learning from a mentor after a ceremony of inviting teaching.

With the modernization of mechanical civilization, the design procedure and manufacturing were separated, as they now are in modern design. Design cooperation during this period often occurred between the brainwork and physical labor that were split by modernization, such as graphic designers and draftsmen, interior designers and carpenters or masons. Design education also adheres to different professions; as disciplinary training creates specialized designers. Graduates in graphic design cannot engage in animation or garden design, and vice versa. Entering the era of digital creativity, the media and Internet now occupy all aspects of social production and life. Traditional design majors, such as graphic design, animation design, and video design, which are distinguished by different forms of design information, have emerged and created a trend

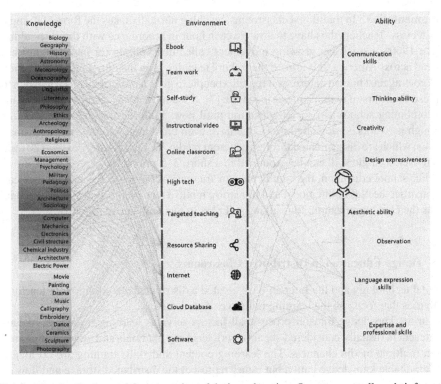

Fig. 6. The distribution and fragmentation of design education. One can meet all one's informational needs through any channel online, such as ebooks and vlogs. All the trivial points or even insignificant ones form the necessary capacities.

of multidisciplinary integration. At the same time, design education has become clearly distributed and fragmented (Fig. 6).

Distribution. In the system of experts and professionals established by modernism [6], professionals represent the foundation of social trust mechanisms. The capabilities and knowledge that shape professionals usually exist in books and require systematic study. As a result, modifications and updates all take a long time to accumulate. Distribution serves to stress the fact that knowledge is dispersed in the environment.

To illustrate, if someone wanted to learn how to use a certain software package, such as Adobe Photoshop, they would have previously needed to purchase a dedicated tutorial, or take a relevant course at a university or training institution. The learning process would follow the chapters of a book or curriculum. Nowadays, with the help of the dedicated websites, such as Quaro and YouTube, studying has now been dismantled and the relevant resources are available to everyone. It is now much more important what students want to learn than what others want to teach. At the same time, distribution also means that there is extensive information that exists in various forms. Mobile phones, computers, televisions, and other media that can access the Internet can obtain the required information in real time.

Fragmentation. In traditional classrooms, teaching normally takes the form of a single 3–4 h class. Teachers thus have to arrange each hour in accordance with the curriculum. Since 1960s, a small but growing movement called deschooling (or unschooling) has spread across America. It is argued that school teaching is an institutionalized education that goes against human nature, as it requires people to go to a prescribed place to listen to a prescribed person within a prescribed time [7]. It seems that we lacked a proper means of combining school and social education until now. With the transfer of knowledge through networks, systematic knowledge have been broken up into thousands of small points, which are disseminated through different media. TED talks rarely exceed 20 min. Moreover, a single skill can be explained in a short, 3–5-min video.

For school education, the significance of fragmentation lies in the fact that we can reconstruct the classroom model and transform it into a teaching form whereby students sit as the core organization; thus giving full play to their subjective initiative.

3.3 Design Education in Distributed Classrooms

Digital technology and the Internet have created a distributed classroom, with teaching activities that focus on the learning initiative of students.

In the knowledge transfer process, all factors serve as learning resources, including teachers (usually considered supervisors), teaching materials and other information from multiple media channels. The learning content and skills training are no longer an immutable knowledge entity, but rather represent the distributed storage and flow of information, which are widely dispersed among various learning resources.

The learning space of students is no longer limited to schools or classrooms, while the time when people study is no longer limited to traditional school hours. Knowledge transfer is no longer a collective educational activity, but rather it is a personalized guidance or auxiliary tool that never goes away. In distributed classrooms, learners gradually begin to break free from the shackles of schools so as to construct cognition and knowledge systems through active learning.

The traditional teaching model is centered on teachers and teaching materials, while the distributed classroom integrates education into the living environment. Students need to take the initiative to accept information and knowledge, which in turn helps them to develop the skill to solve practical problems by identifying and processing information. The distributed classroom places greater demands upon students, as they are required to assume more responsibilities in their own process of learning in a collaborative context. At the same time, they are responsible for higher-level management functions in the classroom, such as the evaluation of their peers' work and the selection of their future curriculum (Fig. 7).

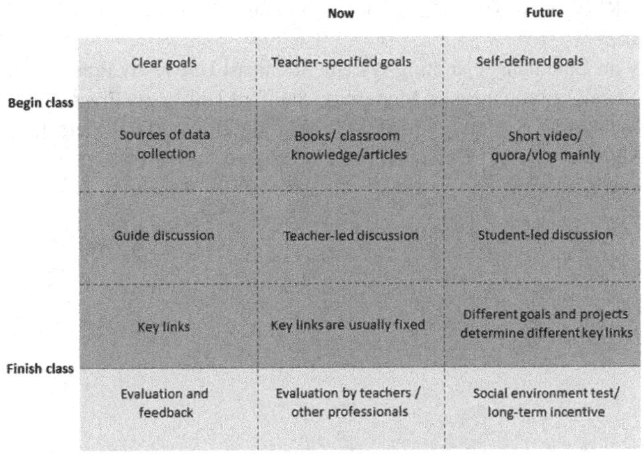

		Now	Future
Begin class	Clear goals	Teacher-specified goals	Self-defined goals
	Sources of data collection	Books/ classroom knowledge/articles	Short video/ quora/vlog mainly
	Guide discussion	Teacher-led discussion	Student-led discussion
	Key links	Key links are usually fixed	Different goals and projects determine different key links
Finish class	Evaluation and feedback	Evaluation by teachers / other professionals	Social environment test/ long-term incentive

Fig. 7. Distributed teaching process compared with the current process.

4 Conclusion and Future Work

Design is a prototype innovation that includes artistic feelings, innovative ideas, thinking, the ability to express externalization, and the ability to intervene in reality, rather than simply "art design" that is focused on expressive forms.

While simply replacing the traditional teaching model may be unrealistic, the training of talented designers based on the design collaborative organization is indeed moving in the direction of distribution and fragmentation. With the vast information resources available nowadays, the role of designers has gradually become diversified, such that they now require comprehensive capabilities which are unlikely to be completely taught in traditional teaching. Design education is bound to integrate social environmental resources, while also developing into a new form that combines the systematic characteristics of school education with the distribution and fragmentation of E-learning.

Distributed-type in design education has both its advantages and disadvantages. It requires proper implements such as computer configuration and higher network speed, while providing massive learning resources. It may widen the knowledge-gap and become a part of educational inequity. As future work, we plan to propose a teaching model that is suitable for design training both inside and outside of the school, reducing the digital divide by refining as far as possible all the different aspects of the model.

References

1. Huppatz, D.J.: Revisiting herbert simon's "science of design". Des Issues **31**(1), 35 (2015)
2. Gadi Amit. https://www.fastcompany.com/1662634/american-design-schools-are-a-mess-and-produce-weak-graduates. Accessed 04 Nov 2010
3. Leslie Owen Wilson: The Second Principle. https://thesecondprinciple.com/essential-teaching-skills/models-of-teaching/the-flipped-classroom/
4. Hutchins, E., Klausen, T.: Distributed cognition in an airline cockpit. Cogn. Commun. Work 15–34 (1996)
5. WeiLi: Study on Dunhuang's painting system. Southeast University Press. Jiang Su (2019)
6. Giddens, A.: The Consequences of Modernity. Stanford University Press (1991)
7. Illich, I.: Deschooling Society, New edition. Marion Boyars Publishers Ltd. (2000). Ivan Illich promoted the idea of "Desschooling", and based on his concept John Holt began to use "unschooling" in 1977

Engineering Design Entrepreneurship and Innovation: Transdisciplinary Teaching and Learning in a Global Context

Wei Liu[1,2(✉)], Eric Byler[1,2], and Larry Leifer[1,2]

[1] Faculty of Psychology, Beijing Normal University, Beijing, China
wei.liu@bnu.edu.cn
[2] Center for Design Research, School of Engineering, Stanford University, Stanford, USA

Abstract. This paper introduces an innovation course has been taught at Stanford University since 1967. In its 52-year-long journey and iterations, both teachers and students learn to dance with ambiguity, collaborate in teams, build to think, and make ideas real. They embrace design thinking and experience the entrepreneurial culture of Silicon Valley in this year-long course. Student teams work on innovation challenges proposed by corporate partners for eight months and deliver functional proof-of-concept prototypes along with in-depth documentation that not only capture the essence of designs but the learnings that led to the ideas. In recent years, several institutions worldwide have adopted this innovative way of problem-based learning with global collaboration.

Keywords: Design thinking · Transdisciplinary teaching and learning · User experience · Global context

1 Introduction

Engineering Design Entrepreneurship and Innovation is a year-long project-based design engineering course that began at Stanford University and has been operating continuously for over forty years [2, 9]. Created to provide engineering students with real engineering challenges, the course has evolved over the ages to meet the changing demands of the labor market. Over its lifetime, the course has shifted from practical engineering experience to design of mechatronic systems to design innovation and global collaboration [10]. Meanwhile, it has gone beyond the hedges of Stanford University and is now being taught in four different continents and eight different countries. The course is now focused on teaching students the innovation methods and processes required for designers, engineers, and project managers of the future. The course is well known for taking ideas from concept to fully functional proof-of-concept prototypes suitable for engineering and customer evaluation. Diversity has been demonstrated to correlate highly with design team innovation, and it is one of the core variables that Stanford's Center for Design Research finds valuable.

© Springer Nature Switzerland AG 2020
A. Marcus and E. Rosenzweig (Eds.): HCII 2020, LNCS 12202, pp. 451–460, 2020.
https://doi.org/10.1007/978-3-030-49757-6_33

2   Teaching and Learning Settings

Offered by the Mechanical Engineering Design Group, its global network of faculty and students come from some of the most distinguished design programs around the world. Student teams work on innovation challenges proposed by corporate partners for nine months (see Fig. 1). Company involvement provides the reality it is important for teams to improve their innovation abilities. In the end, teams deliver functional proof-of-concept prototypes along with in-depth documentation that not only captures the essence of designs but the learnings that led to the ideas [9, 16]. Furthermore, every team collaborates with another team from a foreign university for the duration of the project. The partnership adds diversity to the project teams and students are allowed to experience true global collaboration, a skill required in this highly globalized world. Project results are always copyrighted, often patented, and commonly implemented by the corporate partner.

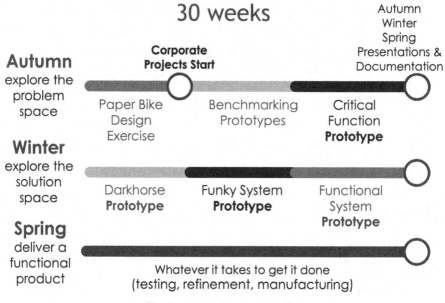

Fig. 1. A typical course calendar

2.1   A Global Context

On every project, student teams at Stanford collaborate with another team from a foreign university. The diversity not only adds various skillsets but also different cultural perspectives on the design challenge that increases the chances of breakthrough innovation [19]. Diversity has been demonstrated to correlate highly with design team innovation, and it is one of the core variables that Stanford's Center for Design Research finds valuable. For students, the experience of working with different cultures is necessary in this globalized world as most designers, engineers, and project managers operate in distributed work teams.

2.2 Extensive Support Crew

The course is instructed by professors and aided by Consulting Professor and three to four Masters and Ph.D. students as teaching assistants. Furthermore, each team is assigned an engineering-culture coach volunteers who typically have taken this course and have between five and thirty years of professional experience with vast networks in the Bay Area and the global technical community. Every team is provided a dedicated project space in a design loft, which also houses a rapid prototyping machine shop and a Polycom video conferencing system. The full Stanford Machine Shop, the Product Realization Laboratory, is also available to the students along with various other on-campus resources. Students at the foreign partner universities also have access to similar personnel and infrastructure resources. The support crew is just as diverse as the students offering multiple points-of-view on engineering, design, and project management. The crew is passionate about letting the students design and innovate and goes beyond professorial duty to assure that students are given the best possible environment to work in.

2.3 Transdisciplinary Student Teams

Students come from different backgrounds and disciplines including various forms of engineering, industrial design, business, and economics [5, 18]. The diversity assures that teams take multiple perspectives on any given challenge, increasing the probability of breakthrough discoveries and innovation. All students have core competencies in their respective fields, and many have prior design project experience in academia or industry. Students in this course take on real-world design challenges brought forth by corporate partners. Unlike many other academic engineering projects, which require students to optimize one variable, students must design a complete system while being mindful of not only the primary function but also the usability, desirability, and societal implications. Throughout one academic year, student teams prototype and test many of their design concepts and in the end create a full proof-of-concept system that demonstrates their ideas. This course is open to graduate students or coterminal students with some engineering and/or design background. The support crew appreciates diversity and encourages students from all departments to apply for the course.

2.4 Corporate Partners

Companies, small and large, from all industries are invited to join and bring forward their innovation challenges. The support crew consults with corporate liaisons to define the right scope and scale of a project. Liaisons are recommended to keep in regular contact with the design teams to provide feedback [10]. The project spots are reserved on a first-come, first-serve basis. Teams are assigned industry coaches who are typically alumni of the course and working in a field related to the project topic. They provide a great resource to the student teams who can access a wealth of knowledge through the coaches and their social network. Coaches often meet with their teams once a week.

2.5 Diversity Drives Innovation

Students, faculty, and industry coaches from around the world come together to form the course community. While many of them come from different backgrounds, expertise, and industries, they all share the desire to design and help each other learn [3, 15]. Some have been part of the course for decades continuing the core design values, and some joined just this year bringing fresh ideas and new tools to the course. The team is always evolving to adapt to the ever-changing world we live in.

3 Methodology

Design thinking or the design innovation methodology pioneered by IDEO and engrained in the DNA of the Stanford design community is a hot topic in the business, product design, and applied research fields [4, 5, 14, 17]. The best way to learn the tools and processes is to experience it through a real-world design innovation challenges. Through the projects, students go through an intense and iterative process of need-finding, ideation, and rapid prototyping to create and develop new concepts [20]. See Fig. 2 for an impression.

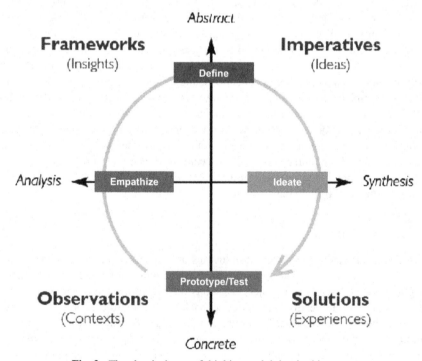

Fig. 2. The classical way of thinking and doing in this course

3.1 Design Thinking

Design thinking as a human-centered innovation approach has become more and more widespread during the past years (see Fig. 3). An increasing number of people and institutions have experienced its innovative power [6, 13]. The method of design thinking works when applied with diligence and insight. It aims to understand the innovation process of design thinking and the people behind it, and it focuses on what people are doing and thinking when engaged in creative engineering innovation and how their innovation work can be supported. The huge demand for transdisciplinary teaching and learning, and the rapid development of information technology have laid a solid foundation for innovations in multiple domains, i.e., education, healthcare, and personal mobility.

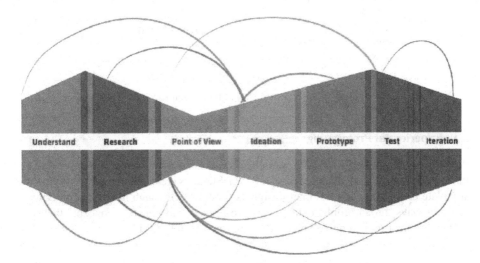

Fig. 3. The stanford design thinking model

3.2 Stanford Design Innovation Process

Through the course of the project, students learn, apply, and experience the Stanford Design Innovation Process (see Fig. 4) and many of its toolsets. Teams observe and interview users to better understand their needs, benchmark existing technologies, and products to identify the design opportunities, extensively brainstorm to discover the obvious, crazy, and novel ideas, and iteratively prototype to quickly test their ideas and get a better understanding of their designs. The result is a refined design concept backed with key insights [7]. With the social development and economic growth, the world keeps promoting innovation design, transdisciplinary subjects have become popular.

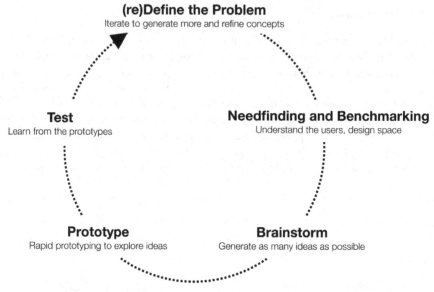

Fig. 4. The Stanford Design Innovation Process

3.3 Experiential Prototyping

Prototyping is at the very heart of the design process because it is the most effective way to transform ideas into tangible products [1, 8, 11]. Students create numerous prototypes to articulate their vision and test their design assumptions. Through iterative prototyping in many ways, broad problem statements are refined into concrete concepts that are eventually incorporated into a final, fully functional prototype [12].

4   Case Studies

Three case studies are described and showed below.

4.1   Vamo

This project is a collaboration between Stanford University, Hasso Plattner Institute (HPI) in Potsdam in Germany, and FutureWei Technologies to enhance human communication with Artificial Intelligence (AI). After exploring various user groups and potential applications of AI such as language translation, self-reflection, remote communication, and assistance in conversations, the student team decided to focus on communication within families, particularly between parents and children between the ages of 3 and 5 years.

Children of this age are at a crucial stage in terms of the development of emotions, language, and sense of time. They need time to prepare themselves for transitions between activities and engagement to keep them from being distracted while going through these transitions. The parents are concerned about their child's schedule and getting them from place to place on time while struggling with several other responsibilities, all while being tired and stressed out after a long day's work. This discrepancy between the child's need to prepare for change and the parent's wish to move from task to task creates a lot of tension, stress and negative communication in the household.

VAMO is a system that solves this need. Figure 5 shows how it signals an approaching transition to the child using light queues in the house, an association that the child learns, and provides them with a buffer time to prepare for incoming change. Once the buffer time expires, the system signals again and guides to desired locations. AI is used to create personalized stories relevant to the child's life to promote further engagement by incorporating information input by the parent through the app. The routine stress and negative communication is replaced by one of positive communication and engagement in the family.

Fig. 5. Signals show different colors indicating three different states (Color figure online)

4.2 OpenRoad

This project is a collaboration between Stanford University, Technical University of Munich, and BMW to improve an open-air experience. Open-air enthusiasts know that in a convertible at highway speeds, the wind blows from behind you and throws your hair into your face. One can either endure the inconsistent hard-to-ignore backflow or install the clunky unsightly windscreen that takes the fun out of open-air motoring. The student team reinvented the open-air experience by drilling a hole in the windshield and an optimized duct that focuses the air between the front two passengers. The proof-of-concept prototype proved that a small change in airflow can change can significantly alter the passengers' comfort. The idea is now patented and being investigated by engineers with the underlying question: can we accomplish this without a hole in the windshield? (Fig. 6)

Fig. 6. The change in vehicle airflow

4.3 Ki'i

This project is a collaboration between Stanford University, Helsinki University of Technology, and Nokia to create a human-technology experience. Nokia asked the student team to forget the mobile phone and design the next device for a future 'Open Internet Communication Culture'. Identifying trends in Web 2.0 and user-generated content, the student team developed the Ki'i, a mobile handheld device that allows users to create and access self-expressive drawings and comments (see Fig. 7). Images captured by the Ki'i can be geo-tagged, marked-up, and shared with a select group of people or the larger online audience. Some of the ideas expressed in the Ki'i have appeared in the market as new web services and mobile phone applications.

Fig. 7. The mobile handheld device Ki'i

5   Discussion

In order to be successful, a winning project usually does the following: 1) challenge students' creative and intellectual abilities, 2) be conceptually and technically challenging while retaining modest cost and physical size, 3) be of deep concern to the company, but not on a critical production path, 4) give the relevant student learning team considerable freedom of action and decision-making authority, 5) benefit from an open-door policy between student team, company liaison, and company knowledge and insight. All of these factors are important individually, but when assembled, they provide a remarkable path for success and fulfilling, beneficial achievement.

Students may have friends from or traveled to different countries and cultures but this course is an opportunity for them to truly collaborate with both in-person and across national boundaries. After the course period, students gain a sense of empathy for people with different backgrounds and viewpoints, not to mention friendships that last a lifetime.

In the past, teaching and learning engineering's primary concern has been with feasibility, the traditional and technically oriented approach to problem-solving. As educators are asked to be more innovative in today's commercial and industrial environment, it becomes critical to weigh in on design thinking, transdisciplinary domains, and a global context as well. Pleasurable user experience of product-service systems is becoming more valued and requires us to focus much more strongly on human values in addition to technical requirements. In recent years, several institutions worldwide are committed to cultivating both innovative research talents and entrepreneurial talents to build a world-class curriculum and pedagogy. "We want them to record what didn't work, too. Those documents are a wealth of knowledge," Professor Toye said. "I am of the opinion, with some evidence, that learning best takes place when learners ask the questions and understand why the question is relevant to their work, lives or projects. This is profoundly different from having a lecturer ask questions that seek regurgitation of lectured material." Said professor Larry Leifer. This course seeks to better balance the equation between cooperation and collaboration, between doing what's expected and agreeing to disagree. It is a paradigm for re-designing our cultures at a global scale. It is no longer just a course. It has become a movement.

6 Conclusions

Unlike most project-based courses in universities, these projects are proposed by real companies, many of them are leaders in their industry, looking for innovative products and services. Project topics are loosely defined, and students are required not only to come up with radically brilliant ideas, they must prove the concept through real functional prototypes. This course is one of the most memorable and intense experiences that students go through, and something they can be proud of for the rest of their lives.

During the nine-month-long course, student teams brainstorm, design, build, test and create professional-quality prototype products for a sponsoring industry collaborator. Although they have plenty of coaching support along the way from faculty, industry professionals and class alumni, the course pushes students to depend primarily on their team, generating and exploring ideas as research and development teams do in the real world.

References

1. Buxton, B.: Sketching User Experiences: The Workbook. Morgan Kaufmann, San Francisco (2014)
2. Carleton, T., Leifer, L.: Stanford's ME310 course as an evolution of engineering design. In: Proceedings of the 19th CIRP Design Conference–Competitive Design, pp. 547–554. Cranfield University Press (2009)
3. Chesbrough, H.: Open innovation: where we've been and where we're going. Res. Technol. Manag. **55**(4), 20–27 (2012)
4. Dym, C., Agogino, A., Eris, O., Frey, D., Leifer, L.: Engineering design thinking, teaching, and learning. J. Eng. Educ. **94**(1), 103–120 (2005)
5. Ge, X., Leifer, L.: Design Thinking at the Core: Learn New Ways of Thinking and Doing by Reframing (2017)
6. Edelman, J., Currano, R.: Re-representation: affordances of shared models in team-based design. In: Meinel, C., Leifer, L., Plattner, H. (eds.) Design Thinking. Understanding Innovation, pp. 61–79. Springer, Heidelberg (2011). https://doi.org/10.1007/978-3-642-137 57-0_4
7. Eris, O., Leifer, L.: Facilitating product development knowledge acquisition: interaction between the expert and the team. Int. J. Eng. Educ. **19**(1), 142–152 (2003)
8. Houde, S., Hill, C.: What do prototypes prototype. In: Helander, M.G., Landauer, T.K., Prabhu, P.V. (eds.) Handbook of Human-Computer Interaction, pp. 367–381. North Holland, Amsterdam (1997)
9. Leifer, L.: Design-team performance: metrics and the impact of technology. In: Brown, S.M., Seidner, C.J. (eds.) Evaluating corporate training: Models and issues, pp. 297–319. Springer, Dordrecht (1998). https://doi.org/10.1007/978-94-011-4850-4_14
10. Leifer, L., Plattner, H., Meinel, C. (eds.): Design Thinking Research: Building Innovation Eco-systems. Springer, Switzerland (2014). https://doi.org/10.1007/978-3-319-01303-9
11. Liu, W., Pasman, G., Taal-Fokker, J., Stappers, P.J.: Exploring 'Generation Y' interaction qualities at home and at work. J. Cogn. Technol. Work **16**(3), 405–415 (2014). https://doi.org/10.1007/s10111-013-0269-4
12. Martin, F., Roehr, K.E.: A general education course in tangible interaction design. In: Proceedings of the ACM Conference on Tangible Embedded Interaction (TEI), pp. 185–188. ACM Press, New York (2010)
13. Norman, D.A.: Emotion and design: attractive things work better. Interactions **9**(4), 36–42 (2002)
14. Øritsland, T.A., Buur, J.: Interaction styles: an aesthetic sense of direction in interface design. Int. J. Hum. Comput. Interact. **15**(1), 67–85 (2003)
15. Preece, J., Roger, Y., Sharp, H.: Interaction Design: Beyond Human-Computer Interaction, 2nd edn, pp. 181–217. Wiley, Chichester (2007)
16. Sanders, L., Stappers, P.J.: Convivial Toolbox: Generative Research for the Front End of Design, pp. 224–225. BIS Publishers, Amsterdam (2013)
17. Schön, D.A.: Educating the Reflective Practitioner: Toward a New Design for Teaching and Learning in the Professions. Jossey-Bass, San Francisco (1987)
18. Stappers, P.J.: Teaching principles of qualitative analysis to industrial design engineers. In: Proceedings of the Conference on Engineering & Product Design Education (2012)
19. Tsai, W.: Knowledge transfer in intraorganizational networks: effects of network position and absorptive capacity on business unit innovation and performance. Acad. Manag. J. **44**(5), 996–1004 (2001)
20. Wensveen, S.A.G.: A tangibility approach to affective interaction. Doctoral dissertation, Eindhoven University of Technology, Eindhoven (2005)

Study on the Criteria of Design of Teaching Toolkit for Design Thinking Courses for Lower Grade Students in Primary School

Yaru Lyu, Chunrong Liu, Yan-cong Zhu, Jinge Huang, Xiaohan Wang, and Wei Liu[✉]

Beijing Normal University, Beijing 100875, China
{yaru.lyu,yancong.zhu,wei.liu}@bnu.edu.cn,
liuchunrongbnu@126.com,
{jinge.huang,xiaohan.wang}@mail.bnu.edu.cn

Abstract. In this paper, the design criteria of 'Design Thinking' for teaching toolkit based on the 'Empathy Design Thinking' course is studied for the lower-grade students in primary schools. First of all, the teaching toolkit requirements of Design Thinking courses in primary schools, as well as the characteristics of physical and mental development of lower-grade students in primary schools are indicated. Then, the teaching toolkit is designed accordingly to produce various teaching toolkit corresponding to the paper version and their supporting materials. Afterwards, the designed teaching toolkit is applied to the actual teaching and the research method is adopted in combination with observation method and interview method to collect the feedback from both students and teachers. By conducting qualitative analysis of the observation and interview results, the characteristics of the teaching toolkit are obtained and finally the teaching toolkit design criteria of 'Empathy Design Thinking' for lower-grade students in primary schools are obtained to provide guidance on the subsequent design of teaching toolkit.

Keywords: Design Thinking · Teaching toolkit design · Design guidelines

1 Introduction

The pedagogy of project-based courses is rather difficult to transfer but it is essential to teach innovation under the context of economic globalization [1]. According to The Partnership for 21st Century Skills, a focus on innovation, creativity, critical thinking, problem-solving skills, communication skills, and teamwork plays a significant role in preparing students for the future [2]. There have been more and more schools and parents starting to focus on the cultivation of students in the basic education stage. The current global competition in economics makes it even more important than ever to develop excellent design skills [3]. Design Thinking serves as a trigger for innovation while bringing novel things into the world [4]. Therefore, Design Thinking has been gradually applied to the teaching of the K12 course around the world and has been made increasingly influential. Due to the joint promotion by various schools and enterprises, Design

A. Marcus and E. Rosenzweig (Eds.): HCII 2020, LNCS 12202, pp. 461–474, 2020.
https://doi.org/10.1007/978-3-030-49757-6_34

Thinking has experienced rapid development in the field of education across China. However, on the whole, there remains an apparent lack of consistency for the quality of research focusing on this field in China. A variety of different training institutions treat Design Thinking as what could attract the attention from the students. Actually, however, there is still no research conducted on how to cultivate innovative talents given the practicalities in China.

Based on the classic Design Thinking model proposed by Stanford University [16], the faculty of psychology in the Beijing Normal University developed the curriculum system of Empathy Design Thinking aimed at primary school students based on not only the strategy of user experience design but also the stage of physical and mental development that students are in under a Chinese context. Meanwhile, they entered into in-depth cooperation with the Experimental Primary School of Beijing Normal University for the research results to be applied in practice.

With regard to the Empathy Design Thinking course aimed at lower-grade students in primary school, the introduction of teaching toolkit will enable students to better understand and memorize the approaches to course delivery while ensuring the conformance to the characteristics of student development both physically and mentally. The student-centered teaching toolkit stimulates the interest of students in the learning process, provides students with better learning experience and timely feedback. In the meantime, it reduces the pressure on teaching. Moreover, multiple specific interaction responses are associated with inspiration and novel ideas [5].

Therefore, based on the curriculum of Empathy Design Thinking as well as the stage of physical and mental development that lower-grade primary school students are in, this paper will tailor the guidelines on the design of teaching toolkit to this course for improvement to the experience that students have in the learning process and the outcome of the course.

2   Related Work

In order to explore the design criteria of teaching toolkit in the course of Design Thinking that is applicable to lower-grade primary school students, desk research was conducted to analyze the relevant literature to Design Thinking, the level of development for students and the design of teaching toolkit.

As a forward-looking, innovative method [7], design thinking represents a kind of methodology [8, 9], the focus of which is on the development and cultivation of a problem-oriented mindset [10]. There are an increasing number of people and institutions with experience of its innovative power [9]. Among them, the design thinking model proposed by Stanford University has been widely applied in the field of education [11]. One of the models was suggested by Professor Larry from the Center of Design Research at Stanford University, who modeled students' experiential learning as a cycle of four stages [12]. Not only does the cycle of experience improve understanding, it also builds a bridge between theory and practice. In the second model, it is believed that the pattern of Design Thinking is an iterative sequence that involves five main stages, including empathy, definition, ideal, prototyping, and testing, as shown in Fig. 1 [4]. This model has already been extensively applied in Design Thinking-related courses across different universities and has exerted a profound influence on Design Thinking education in the field of K12. Among them, Empathy is defined as an ability that enables us to comprehend the circumstances that others are in and the perspectives taken by others, both imaginatively and effectively [14]. Design theorists, as well as practitioners, describe empathy as a crucial influencing factor for Design Thinking [6]. The course is not purposed to make them a designer to develop various practical products. Instead, it is aimed at enabling students to develop the ability to understand others and think from the perspective of others over the course of learning.

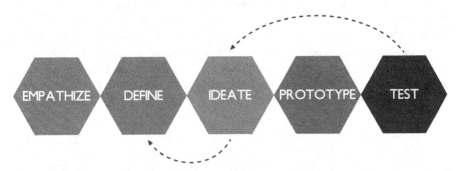

Fig. 1. Design thinking model 5 stages

The design of curriculum in primary school is required to be tailored to the characteristics of development for Chinese students, especially those in the lower grades and involved in this study. It has been demonstrated by the research that the stage of primary school plays an important role in the intellectual development of children, with the pattern of thinking based on specific image thinking. At this stage, attention should be brought to not only intuitive teaching but also situational teaching. Therefore, in practice, games, activities, performances and other methods can be applied to cultivate innovative thinking [15]. There is evidence suggesting that toys are beneficial for students to develop skills and the capability of innovative expression through close contact [16]. The learning design toolkit as described can be used to achieve three primary purposes as follows. Firstly, it provides detailed guidance to students on making theoretically informed decisions over the development of learning activities and the selection of appropriate tools and resources to undertake them. Secondly, it builds up a database of existing learning activities and examples of good practice which can then be adapted and reused for different purposes [17]. Lastly, it facilitates lower-grade primary school students to understand the esoteric and boring teaching content through teaching aids. In summary, it is effective in stimulating the interest of children in engaging with the class and cultivating their thinking ability.

As the carrier of students' learning experience, the need of students for teaching toolkit undergoes constant changes with the growth of their age and the improvement of their cognitive ability. Traditionally, teaching toolkit features a relatively single structure and function, which makes it incapable to meet the needs of students in the process of growth [18]. For the future, the development of design for teaching toolkit is supposed to focus more on the user experience to be delivered by teaching toolkit, rather than the simple realization of teaching tasks and functions. In this sense, it will be designed in a way that could satisfy the needs of students at different developmental stages and conform to the characteristics of courses, which is conducive to improving the user experience derived by students and providing more assistance with teaching.

3   Settings

Empathy Design Thinking, a course offered by the user experience direction (BNUX) of the psychology department of Beijing Normal University, marks the first-ever innovative education course in China that integrates applied psychology with the concept of Design Thinking. The course tends to focus on interdisciplinary practice and is aimed at guiding students on how to learn through experience. The research and development of the course, in conjunction with the top experts from the design research center of Stanford University, conducts investigation into the development of Design Thinking courses which are more appropriate under the Chinese context.

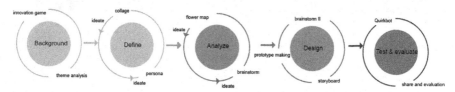

Fig. 2. Course flow chart

In this semester, the teaching object of Empathy Design thinking is comprised of 15 junior students, aged between 7 and 8. The course lasts one hour on a weekly basis for a period of 12 weeks. Meanwhile, in the teaching process, the students were split into four different groups for the study on in-group collaboration. The team of instructors is comprised of interdisciplinary teachers with extensive experience in the curriculum. The venue of teaching is a science classroom which is fit for collaborative teaching in small groups. The flow chart of course is illustrated in Fig. 2. The toolkits of the Persona and User Journey Map methods are employed to assist students in gaining understanding as to the theme background and character of the protagonist for the purpose of resolving the problem. Students are systematically taught to apply such innovative design methods as portraits and brainstorming to analyze problems and design innovative solutions, which is aimed at guiding them on how to put their ideas and solutions into practice. In designer toys, design universals are comprised of four different dimensions, which include physicality, functionality, fictionality, and affectivity [16]. The original paper toolkit is designed by taking into account the approach that needs to be taught as required by the course, which could not only assist with teaching but also make it more convenient for students to operate.

Take the method of Persona shown in Fig. 3 as an example. Persona is beneficial for students to improve and understand the character image in a way that allows the character characteristics to reach a consensus among team members while assisting them with "human-oriented" design. Based on students' characteristics and course themes, teaching

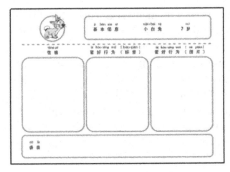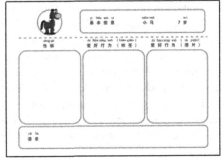

Fig. 3. Method toolkit of "Persona"

toolkit is effective in simplifying the procedures of Persona and enabling students to gain a better understanding as to this method. In the meantime, the stickers and keywords are provided to reduce the difficulty of writing for students. The following part relates to the feedback received when teaching toolkit is applied in actual teaching.

4 Methodology

The subjects were comprised of 15 second-year students with participation in Empathy Design thinking and 10 teachers responsible for delivering the course. In the process of observing the teaching, how the teaching toolkit was applied by students to accomplish the course tasks were recorded and analyzed. In addition, one interview was conducted with the teachers of Design Thinking course, and their feedback on the use of the teaching toolkit was received, transcribed and analyzed (Fig. 4).

Fig. 4. The teaching process of Design thinking

Throughout the course, four teaching assistants will be present to observe and record the class progress among the four groups of students in each class, in addition to recording the use of teaching toolkit by students, their class performance, and their group cooperation in the course table. Then, a summary will be made after each class to sort out the use of teaching toolkit by students during the course (see Fig. 5). Based on the results obtained from course observation, the cognitive development level of students ought to be taken into consideration for the design of teaching toolkit, such as literacy, word understanding and text writing, so as to assist students with expression through simpler methods. Nevertheless, in the design of the teaching toolkit, it is necessary to highlight the logical relationship between the steps and enable students to analyze the emotional changes and characteristics of the protagonist. The design of the teaching toolkit needs to be not only as simple as possible but also easily understandable for students.

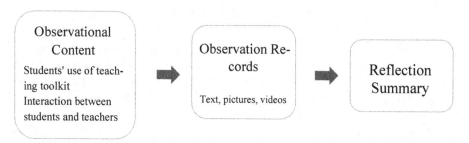

Fig. 5. Process of classroom observation

After the completion of the course, interviews will be conducted with teachers and experienced teachers responsible for this semester's course. Meanwhile, the feedback on students' use of teaching toolkit will be collected from teachers and suggestions will be made on how to update teaching toolkit. Over the course of interview, more open questions will be raised and appropriate follow-up will be carried out based on the answers provided by the respondents. Besides, the interview outline will be constantly revised and iterated for the purpose of acquiring more comprehensive information and improving consistence with the required research questions. The interview process is shown in Fig. 6.

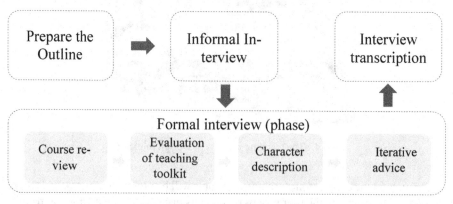

Fig. 6. Process of teacher interview

Finally, after the observation of students and interview with teachers, three researchers will be responsible for transcribing, reporting and coding the observation records and the interview recordings. According to the naming rules of coding material, the interview text will be numbered based on the order of the interview text and indicated as 01, 02, 03, etc. The teachers who teach this semester are marked with T, the teachers who do not teach this semester are marked with N, the replies to different types of the toolkit are marked with A, B, C, D, the unassigned toolkit is marked with U, and A denotes the design characteristics of the course. For example, the 8th subject teaches a course this semester, and those talking about the course without assigned teaching toolkit

Table 1. Examples of coding

The raw material of the interview	First order coding	Second order coding	Third order coding
(User Journey map) *'Stage, excitement, frustration, and just a few words are hard enough.'* (TU02a30)	Highly generalized words are not easy to understand	Easy to understand	The presentation of teaching toolkit information
(Persona) *'I think the most difficult part of this toolkit for them is the 'quotations'. Because I think from my point of view, I think this is the quote that he's going to say, the result that we want to get is a result that is very much in line with the character, and at the same time very representative of the story, for example, there is a very classic sentence, it might appear in the story. But I think if they were asked to think about it, they would probably just think about something outside of the story and write it as a quote on this. So for them, the word itself is not very easy to understand.'* (TA08a19)	The answer should be based on what the previous material can show	Visual	

(continued)

Table 1. (*continued*)

The raw material of the interview	First order coding	Second order coding	Third order coding
'*if I show it to the second grade children, try to use the language that the children can understand so that the teacher does not need to explain much and the children can easily understand what they want to do.*' (TC08a19)	Teaching toolkit are provided in a language that is easy to understand	Easy to understand	
'*First, we need to understand their ability to understand words and language. Then, some words and words, including those that appear in the toolkit, I don't think they should be very general. Because for them, first of all, they don't have the ability to summarize themselves, so when you give them a sentence, they don't have the ability to think in a particularly deep place. Maybe we have five points in one word, but it's easier for them to break them down. However, there may be more toolkit in this way, but I don't think it will become a burden to them. However, if you ask them to think about the hidden knowledge point in a sentence, they will feel very tired and they can't figure it out*' (TU10a20)	Design different forms according to the teaching situation	Customized	

(*continued*)

Table 1. (*continued*)

The raw material of the interview	First order coding	Second order coding	Third order coding
(Collage) *'Can these pictures be made into card type? Like a toy card, if there's a nose on the back of the card, then we draw a nose on the top and write pinyin so that they might recognize some characters in the process and if they don't, they can also look at the picture and have fun.'* (NU04a40)	The auxiliary materials themselves can guide learning intuitively	Visual	

are marked with TU08. The codes of the interview content are marked with TU08a1, TU08a2, TU81a3, etc. Table 1 presents an example of coding.

5 Results

As revealed by the results of coding, five characteristics exhibited by the teaching toolkit of the Design Thinking course were obtained as shown in Fig. 7, including functional usage, information presentation, visual presentation, logical architecture, and operation mode. Further with this, the following five teaching toolkit design guidelines were obtained as well, which are consistent with the Design Thinking course taken by primary school students.

Rule 1: Efficient Multi-person Collaboration

The completion of the Design Thinking course tasks ought to be based on the teamwork among all members of each group. Considering the fact that lower-grade primary school students have yet to develop a strong awareness of teamwork, however, there is a need to have teaching assistants in place to promote the process of task completion throughout the teaching process. The existing teaching toolkit allows multi-person operation for part of the content at the same time. Nevertheless, the drawback is that high efficiency can not be ensured in assigning tasks to group members, which could cause students to be confused about the operation process. Therefore, the teaching toolkit designed for this course needs to fulfill an efficient multi-person collaboration function. In the meantime, on the basis of this, the difficulty of design is reduced to allow the primary students to avoid the tedious operation process while completing the course tasks quickly and effectively. Finally, the teaching toolkit is applied to create a clear and vivid image of the

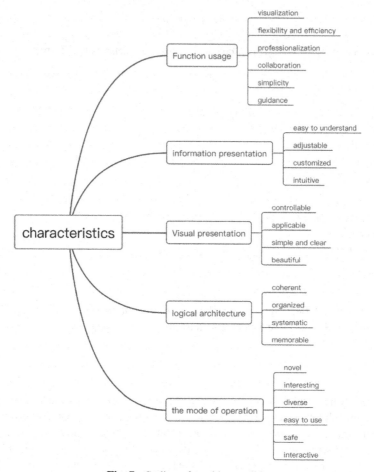

Fig. 7. Coding of teaching toolkit

target character and give a relatively comprehensive understanding. Besides, assistance will be provided by us with teaching during the subsequent program design stage.

Rule 2: Customized Content Presentation

The teaching toolkit of the Design Thinking course is formulated in line with the course theme and objectives, while the teaching toolkit design of different topics based on the same teaching method will show some relevance. Therefore, based on the simple, definite expression of vocabularies, as well as the information presented by the teaching toolkit in a way that could highlight the crucial points and demonstrate the clear structure, the materials under the same teaching method should be presented in the form of the content related to customized toolkit that can make it based on the original framework. According to the teaching objective, a minor adjustment can be made to the design of teaching toolkit. The information can be presented differently by the teaching toolkit depending on the exact contextual different theme. Meanwhile, the content of teaching toolkit can be adjusted to suit the actual level of physical and mental development of students at each stage, offer more or less key information as instruction, achieve a better fit with the zone of proximal development for students, and thus better targeted to assist teachers in achieving their teaching objectives.

Rule 3: Focused Visual Presentation
The teaching toolkit of Design Thinking course is frequently approached to suit the age of the students with a lot of cartoonish ICONS and auxiliary material. However, to ensure teaching toolkit could create fun at the same time, we need to attract attention from the lower-grade elementary school students and make it the focus of their attention based on the objective information, timely feedback on teaching toolkit to attract the attention of students at all stages of completing a task while avoiding students from being attracted by the non-critical design or style teaching toolkit. In the meantime, over the course of teaching toolkit design, the colors and patterns suitable for students at the current age can be matched to avoid the use of fancy and complicated graphic patterns to present to students and stimulate their interest in learning, thus bringing positive sensory experience.

Rule 4: Systematic Logic Architecture
The teaching toolkit of Design thinking course allows interaction with each other, and the courses in the previous stage play a guiding role in the later stage. In the process of teaching toolkit design, the content of each module in a single teaching toolkit is required to be consistent and there is supposed to be a logical relationship between each step. The contents of each teaching aid ought to set up connection through the contents of the teaching toolkit, the contents learned in the previous course can be intuitively recalled by conducting review, and the teaching aid needs to be related to each other both internally and externally to establish a system, for the cultivation of logical thinking among students.

Rule 5: High Feedback Interactive Mode of Operation
The existing Design Thinking courses offered in primary schools are common in adopting paper-based teaching toolkit and students learn how to collaborate with others by hand drawing and collage. In doing so, students are exposed to various teaching tools within a short period of time, which brings freshness to course learning. However, the existing flat and static form is incapable to maintain the learning task for a long time. In the meantime, the paper version of the teaching toolkit makes it difficult for students to modify the original answer over the course of performing task and daub excessively, resulting in the chaos of the result sharing. According to the feedback provided by students and teachers, electronic and dynamic paper teaching toolkit is more effective in stimulating the interest of students in learning, while the high interactivity of teaching toolkit itself can also replace the teaching assistants to reduce the possibility of wrong operations and play a guiding role in students' learning with more concise and targeted feedback. Through prompt feedback, students can quickly realize their growth and change in the course learning process, which is conducive to the development of subsequent learning behaviors. At the same time, an electronic teaching toolkit can be applied to record students' operations in the background of the program, which could

facilitate the comparative analysis of Design thinking courses to cultivate the ability of creative thinking for students.

6   Discussion

From the perspective of user experience design, this paper presents a study on the design and criteria of teaching toolkit for the Design thinking courses and applies psychological methods and pedagogy theories to propose the criteria of teaching toolkit design suitable for the Design thinking courses offered in primary schools, thus laying a foundation for the characterization stage of the Design thinking courses in the future. Based on the practical curriculum, this project conducts research from multiple perspectives and applies the results to the curriculum by analyzing the observation and interview results.

Throughout the process of research, various difficulties and challenges worthy of reflection were encountered. In general, as this course is aimed at the lower-grades primary school students and their level of physical and mental development is low, their capability of reading, writing and verbal expression remains limited, which makes it difficult for us to collect information by scale or through interview. Therefore, we conducted observation, recorded the information through photos and video clips, reconsidered and sorted it out after each class. Researchers need to observe the in-class interaction of students with teaching toolkit and their feedback at the same time, which requires a substantial amount of information and may be subject to influence from various subjective factors. Therefore, in the following research, we coded the specific behaviors of students in the course and combined qualitative research with quantitative research.

Finally, the teaching toolkit of Empathy Design thinking for lower-grade students in primary school is as follows: efficient multi-person collaboration mode, customized content presentation, focused visual presentation, systematic logic architecture and interactive operation mode with high feedback.

7   Conclusion

In recent years, Design Thinking education has undergone fast-paced development across China and has been met with increasingly widespread application in K12 teaching. There are more and more schools integrating Design Thinking into interdisciplinary courses for the purpose of fostering creativity and problem-solving skills. The empathetic Design Thinking course is delivered in primary school to cultivate creative thinking for children, which has a profound influence on their growth. Teaching toolkit, as an assistant to teachers, is significant to the course content full of creativity and logical thinking. These can help students gain intuitive and systematic understanding of the course content and complete the tasks assigned by the teacher.

The education received and the thinking pattern cultivated in the primary education stage could play an extremely important role in their later life. However, up to now, the setting of courses in the industry has yet to be standardized, while the design and research of teaching toolkit for the optimal teaching experience are even more limited. The study of the guidelines involves neither evaluation nor optimization of the guidelines. The next step will be to focus on the testing part of the current guidelines and test the applicability of the teaching toolkit designed in line with the guidelines to further optimize and extend on this basis.

Acknowledgments. This research is supported by the Faculty of Psychology at Beijing Normal University and the Experimental Primary School of Beijing Normal University.

References

1. Skogstad, P.L., Currano, R.M., Leifer, L.J.: An experiment in design pedagogy transfer across cultures and disciplines. Int. J. Eng. Educ. **24**(2), 367 (2008)
2. Carroll, M., Goldman, S., Britos, L., Koh, J., Royalty, A., Hornstein, M.: Destination, imagination and the fires within: design thinking in a middle school classroom. Int. J. Art Des. Educ. **29**(1), 37–53 (2010)
3. Zoltowski, C.B., Oakes, W.C., Cardella, M.E.: Students' ways of experiencing human-centered design. J. Eng. Educ. **101**(1), 28–59 (2012)
4. Plattner, H., Meinel, C., Leifer, L., (eds.): Design Thinking: Understand–Improve–Apply. Springer, Heidelberg (2010). http://doi.org/10.1007/978-3-319-01303-9
5. Jablokow, K.W., Sonalkar, N., Edelman, J., Mabogunje, A., Leifer, L.: Investigating the influence of designers' cognitive characteristics and interaction behaviors in design concept generation. J. Mech. Des. **141**(9), 091101 (2019)
6. Kouprie, M., Visser, F.S.: A framework for empathy in design: stepping into and out of the user's life. J. Eng. Des. **20**(5), 437–448 (2009)
7. Brenner, W., Uebernickel, F., Abrell, T.: Design thinking as mindset, process, and toolbox. In: Brenner, W., Uebernickel, F. (eds.) Design Thinking for Innovation, pp. 3–21. Springer, Cham (2016). https://doi.org/10.1007/978-3-319-26100-3_1
8. Dunne, D., Martin, R.: Design thinking and how it will change management education: an interview and discussion. Acad. Manag. Learn. Educ. **5**(4), 512–523 (2006)
9. Razzouk, R., Shute, V.: What is design thinking and why is it important? Rev. Educ. Res. **82**(3), 330–348 (2012)
10. Leifer, L., Meinel, C.: Looking further: design thinking beyond solution-fixation. In: Meinel, C., Leifer, L. (eds.) Design Thinking Research. Understanding Innovation, pp. 1–12. Springer, Cham (2019). https://doi.org/10.1007/978-3-319-97082-0_1
11. Edelman, J., Currano, R.: Re-representation: affordances of shared models in team-based design. In: Meinel, C., Leifer, L., Plattner, H. (eds.) Design Thinking. Understanding Innovation, pp. 61–79. Springer, Heidelberg (2011). https://doi.org/10.1007/978-3-642-137 57-0_4
12. Leifer, L.: Design-team performance: metrics and the impact of technology. In: Brown, S.M., Seidner, C.J. (eds.) Evaluating Corporate Training: Models and Issues. Evaluation in Education and Human Services, pp. 297–319. Springer, Dordrecht (1998). https://doi.org/10.1007/978-94-011-4850-4_14
13. Plattner, H., Meinel, C., Weinberg, U.: Design-thinking. Landsberg am Lech: Mi-Fachverlag (2009)
14. Rogers, C.R.: Empathic: an unappreciated way of being. Couns. Psychol. **5**(2), 2–10 (1975)
15. Zhiyan, S.: On the cultivation of lower primary school students' positive psychological characters. Chin. J. Spec. Educ. **11**, 20–23 (2010)
16. Heljakka, K.: Toys and universal guidelines for design: a designerly perspective on playability of character toys. In: Proceedings of Universal Design (2019)

17. Conole, G., Fill, K.: A learning design toolkit to create pedagogically effective learning activities. J. Interact. Media Educ. (1) (2005)
18. Qian, L.: Research on design of children's sensory integration training playing toolkit based on sensory integration principle. Art Sci. Technol. **26**(3) (2013)

Available Technologies: Web Design for Technology Transfer from Public Education and Research Institutions

Daniel Nascimento Medeiros$^{(\boxtimes)}$ (ID) and Virgínia Tiradentes Souto (ID)

University of Brasilia, Brasília, DF, Brazil
dnmedeiros@gmail.com, v.tiradentes@gmail.com

Abstract. Universities and public research centers have been looking for ways to transfer technologies created in their research activities to companies that promote business and innovation. One of the strategies adopted is to provide technology licensing opportunities via the web. There are several studies in the literature that indicate the potential of the web for technology transfer and others that point out limitations, given the complexity of the technology market. This article investigates websites with technologies available for business at universities and public research centers in order to propose a classification of these sites based on design attributes and to identify aspects relevant to the users' experience. Twenty public institutions of reference that occupy the first places in the international ranking of quality of presence on the web were considered for analysis. Based on this analysis, we propose a classification of websites composed of three types: proactive transactions, interactive search tools, and low interaction. The findings indicate widespread use of the web for the dissemination of technologies - all institutions have at least one website with patents or business inventions. The findings also suggest that proactive functionalities, quality of search engines, transactional resources and technology aggregators are relevant aspects for the users' experience.

Keywords: Internet marketplaces for technology · Technology transfer portals · Innovation · Patent portfolio · Web design

1 Introduction

The dynamics that lead to innovation in national economies are strongly supported by knowledge and information flows between different actors [1]. Industries, companies, governments and universities interact in the search for new solutions and the improvement of products, processes, services and practices [2, 3]. Universities and research centers, in particular, play a triple and important role in this context: they train professionals, produce knowledge and generate technologies.

Innovations, however, only materialize when there is widespread adoption, use and economic impact [4]. For this reason, universities and research centers seek to establish partnerships with companies or encourage the creation of new businesses.

© Springer Nature Switzerland AG 2020
A. Marcus and E. Rosenzweig (Eds.): HCII 2020, LNCS 12202, pp. 475–492, 2020.
https://doi.org/10.1007/978-3-030-49757-6_35

In this context, interest in tools and technology transfer practices grows. Mechanisms such as licensing contracts between scientific institutions and private companies, research joint ventures, university-based startups, industrial consultancy, education and training are implemented and studied [5, 6].

The expansion of Internet access and the popularization of the World Wide Web in the 1990s created high expectations in academia and in the technology transfer market [7]. The web started to be seen as an important tool to support processes such as identification of partners for joint development, identification of potential companies for licensing technologies generated by public research and to enable open innovation practices [8]. Internet marketplaces for technology emerged in the private sector [9], and universities and research centers created technology transfer portals to highlight technologies subject to licensing [10].

Despite the evident impact of the web on communication and the business world, the perception of its contribution to technology transfer processes is questionable. For authors like Lichtenthaler and Ernst [11], the Internet marketplaces for technology, for example, have not reached the high expectations generated initially. These authors highlight the lack of performance indicators in the literature and identify a low success rate for these tools in promoting technological transactions [11]. Peculiarities of the technology market, such as complexity, difficulty in defining the objects to be traded and differences in pricing, make this market distinct from the traditional consumer goods market, which is strongly driven by e-commerce [9, 11, 12].

On the other hand, several authors show the relevance of using the web to give visibility to technologies available for business, especially in the case of universities and public research centers. The internet would be able to increase the acquisition of such technologies, reduce the time for providing information, favor anonymous research and increase the transparency of the knowledge supply [7, 13, 14].

There are still a number of questions to be answered regarding the potential and limitations of using the web to transfer technology. There are few studies on the design of technology transfer portals - with a consequent lack of parameters for the design of this type of product - and no research on the subject in the field of Human-Computer Interaction (HCI) has been identified [15].

The authors of the present study previously mapped online technological exhibitions from Brazilian universities and public research centers, with the identification of a series of aspects relevant to the field of design [16]. The study, however, was restricted to the Brazilian situation and did not consider leading global institutions in terms of presence and innovation on the web, which limited the identification of good practices and the potential for generalizing the results.

Given these gaps, this study aims to contribute to the characterization of current state of the use of the web in the communication of technological business opportunities by institutions of international standing. The main aim of this study is to characterize the design of websites with technologies available for business at universities and public research centers. In addition, this study aims to: (a) propose a classification of websites about technology based on design attributes and (b) identify aspects relevant to the experience of users who interact with this type of website. Twenty public institutions of reference that occupy the highest positions in a ranking of quality of presence on the web were considered for analysis. Finally, it is believed that the results of this study may be useful as a parameter for institutions that wish to evaluate the design of their technological showcases and explore the potential of the web in support of the processes of technology transfer.

2   Literature on Web Use for Technology Transfer

Studies on the use of the web for technology transfer can be divided into two groups. The first deals with the use of the web as a communication and marketing tool by universities and research centers to give visibility to technologies and technological business opportunities, targeting companies and entrepreneurs. The second group of studies deals with private commercial platforms for negotiating patents and inventions, as well as for supporting open innovation actions. Below is an overview of these two study groups and their implications for this research.

2.1   Use of the Web by Universities and Research Centers

Specific studies on the use of the web or internet to transfer technology generated by universities and research centers seem to be less numerous than those that focus on commercial platforms for transferring technology and open innovation. From the first group, nine publications were identified between 1999 and 2019, two of which are journal articles, two dissertations and five conference proceedings.

In general, the works show the potential of the web in the technology transfer process [13, 17, 18]. In the early 2000s, when not all institutions and laboratories had a presence on the web, Czarnitzki and Rammer [7] argued that elaborating an adequate institutional profile on the web, focusing on the industrial public, would contribute to: (a) decreasing access barriers, common in the transfer market, characterized by closed networks of public institutions and partner companies; (b) creating equal opportunities for institutions to be known to the industrial trial community; and (c) reducing costs, since the investment in a good website to present the institution is low in comparison to other marketing strategies, which favors small institutions with limited budgets.

Pires [19] reports the insufficiency of technology transfer channels such as scientific publications and participation in congresses, which, despite being extremely relevant, would not reach an ideal number of people. For the author, the web would be a complementary form of dissemination.

An analysis at different technology transfer sites was conducted by Schuh, Aghassi and Valdez [14]. They proposed a classification of technology transfer sites, considering the characteristics that favor the relationship (similar to social media) in three types: (1) open platforms (e.g. iBridge Network) that allows both institutions and individuals to register technologies and offers resources such as user profile, communities and news feed with information related to knowledge fields of interest to the user; (2) limited access environments, with low presence of social media resources (e.g. Chicago Innovation Pipeline) that allows different institutions to register technologies; and (3) closed platforms, with limited access and without social media resources (e.g. KIT Technology Market).

Previously to the current study, we carried out research and analysis of technological showcases developed by Brazilian public universities and public research centers [15, 16]. We found that 75% of the institutions analyzed provide pages or websites with business technologies. These sites are usually presented as technological displays and, in general, are composed only of informative web pages, without transactional resources.

From the design point of view, it was possible to highlight a set of websites with common resources that proved to be more complete than the others. In general, the most complete web sites have lists of technology records, with search and keyword filtering capabilities. Each technology has a detail page such as title, summary, technology benefits, inventors, stage of development, among other metadata [16].

With the survey, it was possible to notice significant differences between Brazilian websites and the websites of some foreign institutions. A well-known case is that of the National Aeronautics and Space Administration (NASA), which makes the Automated Technology Licensing Application System[1] available to users, an environment that allows, via the web, the accomplishment of a series of stages of the technology licensing process. The platform, of a transactional nature, contrasts with the Brazilian reality (in which only informational pages were identified) and reinforces the relevance of an international survey, which allows the characterization of the cutting-edge use of the web for technology transfer by reference institutions in web presence and innovation.

2.2 Commercial Web Platforms for Technology Transfer

Commercial web platforms for technology transfer are designed to connect technology providers and receivers and use the Web to advertise technological business opportunities. Although the priority audience for this type of platform is not the university and the research center, the studies dedicated to analyzing them also contribute to a discussion about the use of this type of web tool by scientific institutions.

In the late 1990s, private companies started to design web systems to enhance the transfer of technology, such as Yet2com and Innocentive [11]. Some companies created commercial web platforms so that different companies could register their technologies and offer them to those interested in licensing or acquisition, creating an internet marketplace for technologies [9]. In the following years, other entrepreneurs created tools based on the concept of crowdsourcing, in which companies register problems, needs or technological challenges, and scientists, designers, engineers and professionals from different areas, as well as companies, compete for prizes offered to whoever presents the best solution [20].

Based on the experience of 25 German and Swiss companies, Lichtenthaler and Ernst [11] investigated the efficiency of internet marketplaces for technologies. They found that the vast majority of companies studied did not conduct any business induced by the web platforms. The maximum number of transactions carried out by a company was one licensing as a technology supplier and one as a customer. They have concluded that the success rate of these tools in promoting technological transactions is relatively low. The weak results generated skepticism among entrepreneurs [11].

---

[1] <https://technology.nasa.gov/apply/license/create/LEW-TOPS-72> accessed on January 20, 2020.

The experts heard by the authors attribute the low efficiency of the internet marketplaces to the following factors: (a) non-systematic approach, since the registered technologies are not aimed at specific customers; (b) passivity, due to the absence of proactive mechanisms; (c) low quality of the technologies offered, which apparently indicates that companies register low-value technologies on the platforms, which are not commercially exploited by the developing company; (d) high cost of creating a consistent description of numerous technologies, especially if analyses of market potential and different possible applications are included; and (e) low number of technologies offered in each technological field - despite the large volume of the base as a whole - which reduces the likelihood of finding a technology that meets very specific needs [11].

One of the aspects highlighted by the authors is that the technology market is characterized by imperfections, which differentiates it from the consumer goods market. The object to be negotiated in the technology market is difficult to define, price and negotiate. In general, there is a huge asymmetry of information between the parties, high risk and many uncertainties, which increases the cost of the transaction [12]. Negotiations often require a high investment of time and resources, which makes the technology market much more difficult and complex than the consumer goods market [21].

The complexity and peculiarities of the technology market seem to have required changes in the business models of the internet marketplaces. Yet2.com, for example, initially used a strong emphasis on providing technological infrastructure for the technology bank on the web and attracting massive numbers of users [9, 11]. However, it quickly became apparent to the company that the transfer of technological knowledge could not be processed in the same way as the purchase of tangible products, which are easy to identify, compare and price [9]. Like Yet2.com, other companies also realized that the web-based business model was not fully compatible with the technology market and adapted their approaches with the addition of consulting services and hand-to-hand monitoring throughout the technology transfer process. The researchers' conclusion is that the benefits of internet marketplaces, such as a broad community of technology providers and users, are best consolidated when combined with additional marketing active brokering services [9, 22].

Other authors believe that, in circumstances where problems and technological solutions are well understood and articulated, tools such as internet marketplaces are able to mobilize a large number of agents - similar to traditional markets - and to effectively reduce search costs [23]. For Hagiu and Yoffie [24], although commercial internet marketplaces have provided some reduction in search costs by creating databases with thousands of technological business opportunities, they have been unable to reduce transaction costs. Intellectual property information is sensitive, and negotiations generally require closer contact between people, so that most of the transaction always ends up being offline. This fact is consistent with the tendency of companies like Yet2. com to invest more in consultancy than in technological platforms. The offline stage of transactions also makes it difficult for internet marketplaces to gain scale equivalent to virtual consumer goods stores, such as Amazon and eBay, which automate more stages of commercial transactions, such as payments, deliveries, customer service, user reviews and returns [24].

The literature on internet marketplaces reveals a series of peculiarities of the technology market that are relevant to the analysis and design of websites for technology transfer. Based on this literature, we define the following aspects for the analysis of technology transfer portals from universities and public research centers: (a) verify if these environments offer resources to reduce the cost of searching for technologies; (b) find out if there are resources that tend to reduce transaction costs; (c) verify the presence of proactive mechanisms; and (d) verify if there are functionalities with a focus on the user.

3 User Experience and Web Design

In order to identify aspects relevant to the user experience in relation to the analyzed sites, the user experience and web design concepts are briefly described below.

3.1 User Experience

Different perspectives and definitions of User Experience (UX) can be found in the digital product market and in the HCI and Interaction Design literature [25, 26]. Hassenzahl and Tractinsky [25] investigated these differences and propose the following definition, which we will adopt in the context of this work:

> "UX is a consequence of a user's internal state (predispositions, expectations, needs, motivation, mood, etc.), the characteristics of the designed system (e.g. complexity, purpose, usability, functionality, etc.) and the context (or the environment) within which the interaction occurs (e.g. organisational/social setting, meaningfulness of the activity, voluntariness of use, etc.)." [25]

This understanding has implications for UX design and evaluation. The designer creates a digital product with specific elements to favor a given experience [26]. For the evaluation of a certain product (or a certain experience), it is necessary to consider not only pragmatic aspects, such as product features and characteristics, but also subjective aspects such as motivation and engagement [27].

For Hassenzahl [28], these two aspects make up the dimensions of a model that represents people's perception of interactive products. The pragmatic dimension is related to the scope of "do-goals", or features, such as performing an operation on a cell phone or locating content on a website. On the other hand, the hedonic dimension is related to the achievement of "be-goals", such as being special, being competent or being pleasant.

In this study, we will focus on some aspects of the pragmatic dimension of technology transfer portals from universities and public research centers, as a first step towards understanding this type of web product and to provide parameters for future studies that can move towards more comprehensive UX analysis.

3.2 Conceptual Basis for Website Analysis

One of the approaches to the general characterization of websites is to identify their posture. Cooper et al. [29] propose three basic categories of postures: a) informational websites: with generally simpler behaviors, they consist of environments with navigation from one page to another, as well as a search to facilitate access; b) transactional websites: go beyond providing information as they enable transactions, such as purchases, content publishing, financial transactions, among others (they are generally products with more complex behaviors); and c) web applications or web systems: highly interactive and with complex behaviors, they resemble traditional desktop computer programs (e.g. online spreadsheet editors or web applications for image editing).

In addition to posture identification, design pattern mapping is a strategy commonly used in the characterization of websites. It is the action of documenting efficient solutions to recurring design problems in specific contexts [30]. Initially proposed by Christopher Alexander as a method for capturing and communicating good architectural solutions, the concept and practice extended to other areas of design, such as software engineering and design [30]. It is an approach to formalize design knowledge that can reduce time and effort on new projects, promote the improvement of design solutions, facilitate communication between designers and developers, and serve as educational material for designers [29].

One of the particularities of website design, in comparison with the design of other digital products, is that the web is strongly based on the concept of page, on the structure of these pages, on the dynamics of navigation between them and on the presentation of the contents [29]. The management of these elements is crucial for a good user experience [29, 31].

The management of pages and content is especially important in the case of websites that produce large volumes of information. Pérez-Montoro and Codina [31] argue that certain institutions - such as media organizations, museums and universities - naturally generate a large amount of information and, by making this available on the web, produce what the authors call content-intensive sites (CISs).

In these cases, according to Baeza-Yates and Ribeiro-Neto [32], two strategies are widely adopted to favor the user experience: navigation and search. Navigation is the strategy that consists of analyzing a structure of pages presented by titles or labels and choosing any of the options to access specific pages. Search is the strategy of accessing the desired page or information by typing keywords or combining keywords with search filters. The interaction varies according to the task, the user's experience, and the time and effort available [32].

For the navigation design of web pages, two main systems were classified: (a) embedded navigation systems, which are present in content pages (e.g. global navigation bar, local navigation bars, and links immersed in content - called contextual navigation); and (b) supplementary navigation systems, which are usually implemented on specific pages and represent additional ways of presenting the page hierarchy and favoring the location of content (e.g. sitemaps and indexes) [33].

For the implementation of search engines on websites, several approaches and technologies have evolved over the past 25 years. A search engine can process a natural language sentence included by the user in the search box, as well as interpret specialized search language (e.g., Boolean operators such as AND, OR, or NOT) [33]. With the use of vocabularies, such as thesauri or ontologies, it is possible to add conceptual and semantic intelligence, making the search system able to consider related terms and meanings in search expressions and indexed content, enhancing information retrieval [34].

Technological advances have allowed the emergence of new solutions in the web search interfaces. An example is query assistants, such as auto-complete (which uses a reverse index to suggest search terms that match the characters typed by the user in real time) and auto-suggest (which goes further and may include suggestions for related terms or expressions search queries related to what the user types) [35]. Faceted search creates navigation lists for refining results from a keyword search [36]. Recently, modern machine learning methods have further expanded the technological possibilities of web search systems [37].

4 Method

The method adopted was of a comparative nature, in order to verify similarities and to explain divergences [38]. An instrument was created for the collection, registration and systematic analysis of website characteristics and attributes.

For the choice of the sample, we defined that the sample would include universities and public research centers that were best positioned in Webometrics, prepared by the Cybermetrics Lab of the Superior Council for Scientific Investigations (CSIC) of Spain, a state agency linked to the Ministry of Science, Innovation and Universities [39]. The CSIC rankings were adopted for four reasons: (1) they include universities and research institutes with the same criteria; (2) they consider presence on the web, a relevant indicator since we are analyzing websites; (3) they are supported by scientifically validated methodology; and (4) they are prepared based on recent data, collected every six months.

The 10 public universities best positioned in the Ranking Web of Universities [40] and the 10 public research centers best positioned in the Ranking Web of Research Centers [41] were selected, totaling 20 institutions. As accessibility criteria, only websites with main content in Portuguese, English and Spanish were considered.

As an object of analysis, we considered web pages or websites with information on technologies available for transfer to other institutions. To identify these pages, searches were carried out on the institutional web portal of each institution.

Once the websites and pages for analysis were identified, the following information was collected: (a) name of the page or website; (b) posture; (c) autonomy, which indicates whether they are pages of the institutional portal, subsites or independent websites; (d) responsiveness; (e) number of technology records made available; (f) design patterns; (g) information made available regarding each technology; and (h) proactive features.

4.1 Selected Institutions

The institutions selected for analysis are listed in Table 1. Of the 20 selected institutions, 16 are from the United States (USA) and the rest are from England (ENG), Spain (ESP), Canada (CAN) and Australia (AUS), with one institution each.

Table 1. Institutions selected for analysis

Acronym	Institution	Type	Country	
UW	University of Washington	University	USA	https://els.comotion.uw.edu/
Berkeley	University of California Berkeley	University	USA	https://techtransfer.universit yofcalifornia.edu/default. aspx?campus=BK
Umich	University of Michigan	University	USA	https://techtransfer.umich. edu/for-industry/available-tec hnologies/
Cambridge	University of Cambridge	University	ENG	https://www.enterprise.cam. ac.uk/our-services/industry-government-and-non-profits/
UCLA	University of California Los Angeles	University	USA	http://ucla.technologypubli sher.com/
PennState	Pennsylvania State University	University	USA	https://invent.psu.edu/pro gram/intellectual-property-navigator/
Wisc	University of Wisconsin Madison	University	USA	https://www.warf.org/techno logies/inventions-patents-and-portfolios.cmsx
UofM	University of Minnesota System	University	USA	http://license.umn.edu/
UCSan Diego	University of California San Diego	University	USA	https://innovation.ucsd.edu/ industry-relations/licensing-new-technologies/
UofT	University of Toronto	University	CAN	http://www.research.utoronto. ca/tech-opps/
NIH	National Institutes of Health	R. Center	USA	https://www.ott.nih.gov/opp ortunities
NASA	National Aeronautics and Space Administration	R. Center	USA	https://technology.nasa.gov/ patents; and https://software. nasa.gov
CDC	Centers for Disease Control and Prevention	R. Center	USA	https://www.cdc.gov/od/sci ence/technology/techtransfer/ industry/licensing/technolog ies.htm
VA	US Department of Veterans Affairs	R. Center	USA	https://www.research.va.gov/ programs/tech_transfer/availa ble_technologies .cfm
CSIC	Consejo Superior de Investigaciones Científicas CSIC	R. Center	ESP	https://www.csic.es/es/innova cion-y-empresa/oferta-tecnol ogica

(continued)

Table 1. (*continued*)

Acronym	Institution	Type	Country	
NOAA	National Oceanic and Atmospheric Administration	R. Center	USA	https://techpartnerships.noaa.gov/Partnerships-Licensing/
LBL	Lawrence Berkeley National Laboratory	R. Center	USA	https://ipo.lbl.gov/for-industry/tech-index/ and; http://marketplace.lbl.gov/
USGS	US Geological Survey	R. Center	USA	https://www.usgs.gov/about/organization/science-support/technology-transfer/availability-intellectual-property-licensing
NIST	National Institute of Standards and Technology	R. Center	USA	https://www.federallabs.org/labs/national-institute-of-standards-and-technology-nist-0
CSIRO	Commonwealth Scientific and Industrial Research Organisation	R. Center	AUS	https://www.csiro.au/en/Do-business/Commercialisation/Marketplace?k=&c=

5 The Current State of Technology Transfer Portals from Universities and Public Research Centers

5.1 Overview

Of the selected institutions, all have at least one web page with technologies available for business. Some institutions have more than one page or website. In all, 26 pages and/or websites were identified and analyzed.

Of these, most (n = 19) are characterized as pages within subsites specialized in innovation and technology transfer from each institution. The rest are pages of the institutional portal (n = 4) and thus not subordinate to any subsite, a subset of technology aggregators (n = 4) and independent websites (n = 2).

Technology aggregators are websites that bring together technologies from different institutions. This is the case of Techlink, a web environment maintained by Montana State University at the service of the Department of Defense and the Department of Veterans Affairs, both from the US government, which brings together technologies from dozens of federal laboratories linked to the two departments [42]. In these cases, the website of each institution directs the user to the corresponding subset of technologies in the aggregating environment.

The most frequent expression used as a title is Available Technologies and similar variations (n = 12). A term licensing or license appears as the second most recurring concept in titles (n = 6), in the form of "Licensing of new technologies" or "Licensing and technology opportunities", among other specific preferences.

Most pages or websites are informative (n = 19). However, transactional environments (n = 7), which allow the user to make transactions such as payments, licensing or perform part of the negotiation process for technology transfer, have been also identified.

Some institutions, such as the University of Washington, operate in the form of express licensing, with the online availability of a license agreement, in PDF file format, with all pre-established licensing terms, including license fees.

On the other hand, NASA provides an environment with a series of transactional functionalities, such as forms that must be filled in with the data of the company interested in licensing. The steps presented in the system vary according to the data included by the user. Licenses for commercial use generate different licensing requirements for research or education purposes, for example.

The Berkeley Lab Marketplace works in a similar way to an online store. Technologies such as algorithms and software, for example, are made available in academic or commercial modalities. In commercial mode, after users choose the desired number of licenses, the system informs the value of each license and then they can include the items in a shopping basket (add to cart), with the option to make the payment online and complete the transaction by downloading software.

5.2 Web Design Patterns

Through the mapping of interface solutions it was possible to identify patterns. The resource with the highest occurrence was Search (n = 20), made available as a tool to search for technologies by keywords. Search filters (n = 14) allow the definition of parameters for refining the search. In 13 cases, a set of clickable categories is offered to list (browse) the corresponding technologies. The most common way to list the records is to present them as search results - with the presence of the title and some essential metadata - and in most cases the result paging feature is used.

The vast majority of pages and websites analyzed (n = 18) present satisfactory behavior on screens of different sizes; that is, they are responsive and adapt when accessed from large computer screens or smaller screens on mobile devices. Few show partial responsiveness, of only a few elements (n = 4), and the rest do not adapt to smaller screens (n = 4).

In almost all cases (n = 23) it is possible to click on the registration of each technology and access a page with the following metadata: name (n = 23), abstract or description (n = 23), categories or keywords (n = 13), advantages or benefits (n = 12), application (n = 10), email and phone (n = 9).

There is no relevant difference in terms of resources and information made available between the websites analyzed. Some have very limited search engines; others are just simple HTML lists, with no search engines. The ones that seem most complete are simple record search engines. No more sophisticated web search features were identified, such as auto-complete, auto-suggest or personalization.

In summary, it is possible to characterize the use of search, search filters, browse, search results, pagination and details page as a common interface pattern (see Fig. 1).

5.3 Proactive Features

A considerable number of pages and websites have proactive features, that is, features for sending content. Users can register to receive email alerts (n = 9) with technological

Fig. 1. Generic representation of the pattern used by various institutions to disseminate available technologies via the web.

business opportunities. In some cases it is possible to register a user ($n = 6$), by filling in personal data and password, which allows the management of certain preferences in the environment. On four websites it is possible to search the technology base and save those parameters for configuring the triggering of alerts by e-mail.

Only one website has identified a mechanism that sends e-mail alerts if an online licensing process has been initiated and remains incomplete. The messages encourage the user to complete the process.

6   Proposed Classification of Technology Transfer Portals

Based on the data collected and the analyses performed, it is possible to group pages and websites into categories. We propose a classification with the following categories: proactive transactions, interactive search tools and low interaction.

Proactive transactions: feature a wide range of interactive features, with search engines, search filters, rich detail pages, configurable proactive features for notifying users and tools for online licensing or for automating part of the technology transfer process.
Interactive search tools: they are configured as pages that allow the interactive search of records and present detail pages for each technology, without the presence of transactional resources and with a low presence of proactive functionalities.

Low interaction: they are pages that do not have search engines or a technology detail page, configuring themselves as simple lists of technologies and providing low interaction.

7 Aspects Relevant to the Users' Experience

The analysis of pages and websites shows aspects that seem relevant to the user's experience. These are solutions or limitations that are related to critical factors pointed out in the literature and that deserve attention when designing websites of this nature or that show opportunities for new research.

7.1 Experience with Proactive Features

Mechanisms such as e-mail notifications based on users' preferences are offered by nine of the websites analyzed, but it was not possible to identify whether these tools actually favor doing business and provide a satisfying experience for subscribing users.

The presence of these proactive features suggests that there is an attempt to overcome factors that limit the efficiency of internet marketplaces for technology and that are reported in the literature, in particular the non-systematic approach, which does not target technologies to specific customers according to their profile, and passivity, since websites would depend completely on the initiative of users to access and search for content [11].

The solution, however, does not seem easy. One of the challenges is to be able to match the interests or needs of users with technological offers. Some analyzed websites offer a list of topics, such as "agriculture", "engineering" or "robotics" for the customer to mark those desired. The user then receives information by email about new technologies created by the institution in these categories. This solution, however, can paradoxically generate two unwanted effects: (a) users receive many offers with no relevance to their business or the problems their company faces; and (b) users stop receiving a technology that could be promising for the situation, but that was not marked with the expected category. While the first effect can generate a frustrating experience, the second can waste business opportunities.

There are several reports in the literature of cases of technologies developed for a given problem, area of knowledge or industrial field that proved to be valuable for other applications not thought of initially. This is the case of a material developed for space missions on Mars that proved useful for stitching up hearts during surgery [43], and a hydrogel created with nanotechnology for controlled release of agricultural fertilizers that can prove to be advantageous for use in disposable diapers [44]. If categorized only in areas such as aeronautics or agriculture, for example, these items could be left out of health or personal hygiene companies that might be interested. For some authors, the logic of organizing technologies in industrial areas may not be advantageous [11].

The challenge is how to use technology to combine these opportunities and interests. This seems to involve the wealth of data that is included in these digital environments about each technology, in order to favor the identification of possible applications in different industrial areas, but also the wealth of data about those interested in the technologies, who could provide data regarding their needs, problems and technological challenges. This would provide raw material for applications that use resources such as controlled vocabularies, thesaurus, ontologies, natural language processing and artificial intelligence.

7.2 Quality of Search Engines

Some websites have a large number of records (three have more than 1000 technologies), which tends to increase the importance of search engines in the experience of use. Both efficient search engines, capable of retrieving records considering synonymous terms, related terms or natural processing language, as well as features such as automatic suggestion, autocomplete and faceted navigation, look promising. An example of a search engine that incorporates these contemporary technologies is present in the transfer technology portal at Columbia University. Dealing with a base of 1448 technologies available for business, the search offers auto-suggest, suggested additional terms, expanded search, faceted navigation and advanced search. This search engine was developed by the startup ResoluteAI, which applies machine learning processes to incorporating, analyzing and presenting categorized data and favoring the search for scientific content across multiple fields [45, 46].

7.3 Transactional Features

Platforms such as NASA's Automated Technology Licensing Application System and Berkeley Lab Marketplace automate the technology transfer process or part of the process via the web. This is an interesting finding, since there is skepticism in the literature about the web's ability to reduce transaction costs [24].

Apparently, some institutions are managing to reduce not only research costs, but also transaction costs over the web. However, it is necessary to deepen the investigation to see if this really occurs in practice and to understand the users' experience with the automation of these processes.

It is also possible that automated technology transfer transactions work only with certain types of technology. The technologies available with price and the possibility of paying via the web are generally algorithms or software. This type of technology comes close to traditional consumer goods (software is a product with wide online sales). The observation reinforces the premise, present in the literature, that in the circumstances in which technological problems and solutions are well defined, the web would be more promising in the technology transfer process [23].

It is not yet known whether full or partial automation of the technology transfer process is also feasible for other types of technology, especially those that still depend on a long development process until they can be launched on the market.

7.4 Technology Aggregators

Adopted by some of the institutions analyzed, technology aggregators are environments that bring together technology from more than one university or research center. The solution has some implications for the institutions and the users' experience.

By standardizing the organization of information and interface resources, these environments assume that a single solution is capable of meeting the needs and peculiarities of each institution. This seems challenging, since the technology transfer business models vary between institutions [47], as do the forms of internal management of technology information for transfer. It is pertinent to deepen the understanding on the subject to find out if this uniformity is feasible and desired by the institutions.

On the other hand, from the users' point of view, the possibility of locating technological business opportunities in a single web environment seems promising. It is possible to imagine the effort of navigating the portals of dozens or hundreds of scientific institutions to find out if there is something that can meet a certain technological need in an industry, for example. Being able to have access to the technologies of all these institutions in only one search engine seems to be advantageous.

Bringing together a greater volume of technologies in an environment also tends to increase the likelihood of promoting the meeting between technological necessity and supply. One of the complaints reported by experts in the literature is the low number of technologies offered in each technological field [11].

Such a solution would have to overcome a series of institutional, political and technical obstacles. Among institutions linked to the same agency, these obstacles seem less decisive, such as the Federal Laboratory Consortium for Technology Transfer (FLC), which maintains a portal with technologies generated by different North American federal laboratories, and the University of California, which brings together the technologies of its 10 campuses on a website.

For a good user experience, it would be crucial for technology aggregators - with so much content - to have efficient and easy-to-interact solutions for organizing and retrieving information.

8 Final Remarks

This study investigated the design of websites with technologies available for business by universities and public research centers in order to create a classification for these websites and identify aspects relevant to the users' experience.

The study, carried out based on 20 reference institutions, indicates widespread use of the web for the dissemination of technologies - all institutions have at least one website with patents or business inventions. These environments are generally presented as Available Technologies pages and are configured as pages in subsites that deal with innovation and technology transfer, within the institutional portals of universities and research centers. They have search engines specific to the technologies and have detail pages for each technology. We propose a classification of websites composed of three types: proactive transactions, interactive search tools, and low interaction.

The analysis indicates that search engines tend to play a relevant role in the user experience, especially on websites with a high volume of records. Contemporary search technologies can favor the identification of business opportunities in different fields of application and the implementation of proactive mechanisms for notifying users. We believe that it is pertinent to carry out research that is dedicated to these aspects.

Another finding of this research was the identification of transactional sites, which automate the process or part of the technology transfer process via the web. The data suggest that the websites are able to reduce not only technology research costs, but also transaction costs. Further research involving institutions and companies is needed to verify this suggestion.

It also seems relevant to verify which type of technology is most viable for online transactions and which inevitably requires face-to-face negotiations. Technologies like software are similar to traditional consumer goods, easily sold via the web. On the other hand, others, such as technology patents still in the intermediate stages of development, are likely to require negotiations with personal involvement. The definition of a possible typology of technologies by this criterion can contribute to the definition of specific marketing strategies for the commercialization of technologies.

Websites that bring together technologies from different institutions seem common in the United States and can be promising to favor the user experience and the chance to connect technological opportunities with those interested in licensing technology. It seems opportune to conduct research to investigate the feasibility and relevance of this type of solution.

A limitation of this research is the fact that only public institutions were investigated and not universities and private research centers. Universities and private centers can use the web with excellence for technology transfer, such as Columbia University, mentioned in the study. Still, the research took into account only some characteristics of the websites that were not sufficient for a comparative analysis of quality, usability or user experience. However, the results contribute to the design of research that can advance in depth and contribute with new information on the use of the web for technology transfer.

Acknowledgment. This research was supported by the Brazilian Agricultural Research Corporation (Embrapa).

References

1. Lundvall, B.: National innovation systems—analytical concept and development tool. Ind. Innov. **14**, 95–119 (2007). https://doi.org/10.1080/13662710601130863
2. Etzkowitz, H., Leydesdorff, L.: The dynamics of innovation: from national systems and "Mode 2" to a triple Helix of university–industry–government relations. Res. Policy **29**, 109–123 (2000). https://doi.org/10.1016/S0048-7333(99)00055-4
3. Conde, M.V.F., de Araújo-Jorge, T.C.: Modelos e concepções de inovação: a transição de paradigmas, a reforma da C&T brasileira e as concepções de gestores de uma instituição pública de pesquisa em saúde. Cien. Saude Colet. **8**, 727–741 (2003). https://doi.org/10.1590/S1413-81232003000300007
4. Kline, S.J., Rosenberg, N.: An overview of innovation. In: Landau, R., Rosenberg, N. (eds.) The Positive Sum Strategy, pp. 275–305. National Academy Press, Washington (1986)
5. Phan, P.H., Siegel, D.S.: The effectiveness of university technology transfer. Found. Trends® Entrep. **2**, 77–144 (2006). https://doi.org/10.1561/0300000006
6. Veroneze, R.B., Zambalde, A.L., De Sousa, D., Rennó, A.S.: As relações entre a universidade e o mercado sob a perspectiva do marketing: uma revisão sistemática de literatura. Rev. Foco. **10**, 195–220 (2017). https://doi.org/10.28950/1981-223x_revistafocoadm/2017.v10i1.331
7. Czarnitzki, D., Rammer, C.: Technology transfer via the internet: a way to link public science and enterprises? J. Technol. Transf. **28**, 131–147 (2003). https://doi.org/10.1023/A:1022990415301

8. Roijakkers, N., Zynga, A., Bishop, C.: Recebendo ajuda dos innomediários: o que os inovadores podem fazer para aumentar o valor na busca por conhecimento externo? In: Novas fronteiras em inovação aberta, pp. 277–290. Blucher, São Paulo (2017)
9. Nell, P.S., Von Lichtenthaler, U.: Innovation intermediaries: a case study of yet2.com. Int. J. Technol. Intell. Plan. 7, 215 (2011). https://doi.org/10.1504/IJTIP.2011.044611
10. Malvezzi, F.D.A., Zambalde, A.L., de Rezende, D.C.: Marketing de Patentes à Inovação: Um Estudo Multicaso em Universidades Brasileiras. Rev. Bras. Mark. 13, 109–123 (2014). https://doi.org/10.5585/remark.v13i5.2557
11. Lichtenthaler, U., Ernst, H.: Innovation intermediaries: why internet marketplaces for technology have not yet met the expectations. Creat. Innov. Manag. 17, 14–25 (2008). https://doi.org/10.1111/j.1467-8691.2007.00461.x
12. Caves, R.E., Crookell, H., Killing, J.P.: The imperfect market for technology licenses*. Oxf. Bull. Econ. Stat. 45, 249–267 (1983). https://doi.org/10.1111/j.1468-0084.1983.mp4 5003002.x
13. Raitt, D.: Managing technology portals: using the web to find and transfer technologies. SA J. Inf. Manag. 4(3), a172 (2002). https://doi.org/10.4102/sajim.v4i3.172
14. Schuh, G., Aghassi, S., Valdez, A.: Supporting technology transfer via web-based platforms. In: 2013 Proceedings of PICMET 2013: Technology Management in the IT-Driven Services (PICMET). IEEE, San Jose (2013)
15. Medeiros, D.N., Souto, V.T.: Vitrines tecnológicas: a informação facilitada sobre patentes na web. In: Anais do Simpósio de Engenharia, Gestão e Inovação. SENGI, Águas de Lindóia (2019)
16. Medeiros, D.N., Souto, V.T., Silva, T.B.P.: Vitrines tecnológicas: o Design de websites sobre tecnologia de instituições públicas de ensino e pesquisa brasileiras. In: Anais do 9° CIDI | Congresso Internacional de Design da Informação, edição 2019 e do 9° CONGIC | Congresso Nacional de Iniciação Científica em Design da Informação, pp. 1583–1592. Editora Blucher, São Paulo (2019)
17. dos Melo, J.S.: Proposta de reestruturação da Vitrine Tecnológica da Universidade de Brasília sob a perspectiva da Arquitetura da Informação (2018). https://repositorio.unb.br/handle/10482/34548
18. Schuh, G., Aghassi, S., Schneider, B., Bartels, P.: Influencing factors and requirements for designing customized technology transfer portals. In: 2014 IEEE International Conference on Management of Innovation and Technology, pp. 105–110. IEEE (2014)
19. Pires, M.C.F.S.: Política pública de incentivo à inovação: uma proposta de criação da vitrine tecnológica na Universidade Federal de Alagoas (UFAL) (2018). http://www.repositorio.ufal.br/handle/riufal/3554
20. Bakici, T., Mezquita, E.A., Wareham, J.: The underlying mechanisms of online open innovation intermediaries., Barcelona (2012)
21. Lichtenthaler, U., Ernst, H.: Developing reputation to overcome the imperfections in the markets for knowledge. Res. Policy 36, 37–55 (2007). https://doi.org/10.1016/J.RESPOL.2006.08.005
22. Sousa, D., Zambalde, A., Souki, G., Veroneze, R.: Marketing Myopia in Brazilian public universities: an empirical study involving academicians. J. Technol. Manag. Innov. 13, 12–23 (2018). https://doi.org/10.4067/S0718-27242018000300012
23. Håkanson, L., Caessens, P., MacAulay, S.: InnovationXchange: a case study in innovation intermediation. Innovation 13, 261–274 (2011). https://doi.org/10.5172/impp.2011.13.2.261
24. Hagiu, A., Yoffie, D.B.: The new patent intermediaries: platforms, defensive aggregators, and super-aggregators. J. Econ. Perspect. 27, 45–66 (2013). https://doi.org/10.1257/jep.27.1.45
25. Hassenzahl, M., Tractinsky, N.: User experience - a research agenda. Behav. Inf. Technol. 25, 91–97 (2006). https://doi.org/10.1080/01449290500330331

26. Fadel, L.M.: Experience-centered web design model. In: Marcus, A. (ed.) DUXU 2014. LNCS, vol. 8518, pp. 92–103. Springer, Cham (2014). https://doi.org/10.1007/978-3-319-07626-3_9

27. Ardito, C., Costabile, M.F., Lanzilotti, R., Montinaro, F.: Towards the evaluation of UX. In: Law, E., Vermeeren, A., Hassenzahl, M., Blythe, M. (eds.) Towards a UX Manifesto, pp. 6–9. Lancaster, MAUSE (2007)

28. Hassenzahl, M.: The hedonic/pragmatic model of user experience. In: Law, E., Vermeeren, A., Hassenzahl, M., Blythe, M. (eds.) Towards the Evaluation of UX, pp. 10–14. Lancaster, MAUSE (2007)

29. Cooper, A., Reimann, R., Cronin, D., Noessel, C.: About Face: The Essentials of Interaction Design. Wiley, Indianápolis (2014)

30. Pauwels, S.L., Hübscher, C., Bargas-Avila, J.A., Opwis, K.: Building an interaction design pattern language: a case study. Comput. Human Behav. **26**, 452–463 (2010). https://doi.org/10.1016/j.chb.2009.12.004

31. Pérez-Montoro, M., Codina, L.: Navigation Design and SEO For Contentintensive Websites. Chandos Publishing, Cambridge (2017)

32. Baeza-Yates, R., Ribeiro-Neto, B.: Modern Information Retrieval: The Concepts and Technology Behind Search. Pearson Education Limited, Harlow (2011)

33. Morville, P., Rosenfeld, L.: Information Architecture for the World Wide Web. O'Reilly Media, Sebastopol (2006)

34. Le Grand, B., Aufaure, M.-A., Soto, M.: Semantic and conceptual context-aware information retrieval. In: Damiani, E., Yetongnon, K., Chbeir, R., Dipanda, A. (eds.) SITIS 2006. LNCS, vol. 4879, pp. 247–258. Springer, Heidelberg (2009). https://doi.org/10.1007/978-3-642-01350-8_23

35. Holl, K.: Back to top query assistants: auto-complete, auto-suggest, auto-search, and beyond. https://www.searchtechnologies.com/blog/search-autocomplete-suggestions

36. Tunkelang, D.: Dynamic category sets: an approach for faceted search. In: SIGIR 2006 Workshop on Faceted Search Conference. ACM, Seattle (2006)

37. Guo, J., et al.: A deep look into neural ranking models for information retrieval (2019)

38. Lakatos, E.M., de Marconi, M.A.: Fundamentos de metodologia científica. Atlas, São Paulo (2019)

39. CSIC: Sobre el CSIC - csic.es. http://www.csic.es/presentacion

40. CSIC: Ranking web of universities – World. http://webometrics.info/en/world

41. CSIC: Ranking web of research centers – World. https://research.webometrics.info/en/world

42. MONTANA-STATE-UNIVERSITY: About TechLink. https://techlinkcenter.org/about/

43. NASA: Material for Mars makes life-saving sutures. https://spinoff.nasa.gov/Spinoff2019/hm_2.html

44. Silva, J.: Pesquisa desenvolve hidrogel fertilizante de baixo custo. https://www.embrapa.br/busca-de-noticias/-/noticia/24638368/pesquisa-desenvolve-hidrogel-fertilizante-de-baixo-custo

45. COLUMBIA: Columbia Technology Ventures. https://columbia.resoluteinnovation.com/search

46. RESOLUTEAI: Innovate Smarter with AI Search: How it works. https://www.resolute.ai/how-it-works

47. Pagani, R.N., Zammar, G., Kovaleski, J.L., Resende, L.M.: Technology transfer models: typology and a generic model. Int. J. Technol. Transf. Commer. **14**, 20 (2016). https://doi.org/10.1504/IJTTC.2016.079923

Financial Shared Course Design Based on Human-Computer Interaction

Xiaoyan Niu$^{(\boxtimes)}$ and Bin Wang

Shandong University of Finance and Economics, No. 7366 Er Huan Dong Road, Jinan, Shandong, China
Qiuxiao25@hotmail.com

Abstract. Financial shared course is the core content of "Internet + accounting" teaching, which has attracted the attention of accounting education and relevant courses that are set up for the level of graduate and undergraduate students. This paper puts forward the teaching design model of analysis, design, development, implementation and evaluation and specifically introduces the realization approach of the five elements of the model from analysis to evaluation. The teaching design idea of this course is systematic, targeted and guaranteed. It is expected to provide reference for the opening of financial shared course in domestic colleges and universities.

Keywords: Financial shared course · Accounting education · Teaching model design · HCI

1 Background

In recent years, as big data strategy has become a national strategy, cloud computing, artificial intelligence and other internet technologies have developed rapidly, accounting and internet technologies are increasingly integrated and interactive. Under the background of the development of "Internet + accounting" mode, the financial management mode of enterprises has gradually changed from the traditional decentralized mode to the Shared mode. Financial sharing, as the core of the new financial management mode of group enterprises, has become the implementation of accounting for group enterprises.

Shandong University of Finance and Economics has responded to the challenge of "Internet + Accounting" by offering intelligent accounting major, setting up intelligent accounting classroom (Fig. 1), and will continue to offer a series of courses in the wake of the development of big data, cloud accounting, artificial intelligence and the mobile internet, in order to achieve a breakthrough in accounting education reform. With the development of the universal application of internet technology, more and more attention has been paid to the diversification, multi-level sharing of financial innovation and entrepreneurship education cooperation. Through the integration of production and education, cooperation between universities and enterprises, and in the context of "artificial intelligence + course", a comprehensive platform for production, education and scientific research will be constructed, and the teaching, practice, training and employment bases will be jointly built by universities and enterprises, to achieve win-win outcomes.

© Springer Nature Switzerland AG 2020
A. Marcus and E. Rosenzweig (Eds.): HCII 2020, LNCS 12202, pp. 493–505, 2020.
https://doi.org/10.1007/978-3-030-49757-6_36

Fig. 1. Intelligent accounting classroom (Source: the author)

2 Introduction of the Relevant Concepts

2.1 "Internet + Accounting"

"Internet + accounting" is the integration and innovation of internet and accounting. The infrastructure and technology promotion of the internet help the accounting industry achieve structural remolding. As an innovation of the internet, big data technology realizes the collection, storage, analysis and prediction of large, diversified, fast and low-cost data. Budget decision, investment decision, cost decision and pricing decision in financial decision-making need a large number of structured, semi-structured and unstructured financial and non-financial data inside and outside the enterprise. After acquiring, transforming and inputting the data, we use big data technology and analysis means to analyze the relationship among the data in detail, tap its potential practical value, and provide support for the scientific and reasonable financial decision-making of enterprises. Traditional accounting focuses on the objective reflection of past business, such as bookkeeping, accounting and preparation of financial statements. "Internet + accounting" plays a major role in predicting accounting economic prospects, participating in economic decision-making and evaluating performance.

2.2 Financial Shared Service Center

Financial Shared Service Center (FSSC) is a processing method based on information technology and financial business process. Its main purpose is to optimize the organizational structure, standardize the process and improve the process efficiency.

The establishment of FFSC is of great significance to the operating costs reduction and value creation. The specific operation is to transfer the entity's accounting business from different countries and regions to FSSC for accounting and reporting issues. The advantage of FFSC is to ensure the standardization and uniform structure of accounting records and reports, and because it does not need to provide accounting personnel for companies and offices, it saves a lot of system terminals and effectively reduces labor costs.

2.3 Industry, University and Research Cooperation

Industry, university and cooperation refers to the cooperation among enterprises, research institutions and higher education institutions. In order to take their respective advantages, they effectively combine frontier research with development and production, so as to promote technological innovation. With the progress of technology and the change of innovation forms, the role of government departments in the construction of innovation platform is more and more obvious. Under its promotion, scientific and technological innovation began to develop from "production, universities, research institutes" to "politics, production, universities, research institutes".

2.4 Human-Computer Interaction (HCI)

Human-Computer Interaction (HCI) refers to the technology realizing interrelation and mutual effects between humans and computers via the human-computer interface. After rapid development for nearly thirty years, HCI has been transformed from interrelation with keyboards and mice into human-computer interaction through technology of touch control, multimedia and virtual reality. It seems that the current HCI has been converted from computer-centered interaction into human-centered interaction (Fig. 2).

Human-Computer interaction focuses on the relationship between human beings and computers; study on the communication between human and computer through mutual understanding and accomplish the functions of information management, service and processing.

3 Literature Review

Yuko (2002) pointed out that the essence of industry university research cooperation is that universities and enterprises will complement each other's advantages, functions and resources through collaborative cooperation. Jia and Li (2014) believed that the cooperation of industry, University and research not only developed towards the transformation and industrialization of scientific and technological achievements of universities, but also brought technological innovation and enhanced their market competitiveness. Xiao (2014) put forward the comprehensive teaching concept of "four in one" from the perspective of innovation, entrepreneurship and talent training, namely, the construction of school enterprise cooperation mechanism, the construction of competition system, experimental system, scientific research and enterprise practice. The application-oriented

Fig. 2. Human-computer interaction (Source: Baidu)

innovation and entrepreneurship training model has been explored comprehensively, and good practical results have been achieved.

Guo (2017) deeply analyzed the core literacy required by students in the era of "Internet +", and suggested that the internet be introduced into classroom education, so as to give full play to the teaching advantages brought by information technology. Wang (2017) believed that the introduction and innovation of case teaching mode can be driven by internet technology, so as to quickly build a multi integrated case teaching system and improve the teaching quality of colleges and universities. Ding (2015) analyzed the current situation and characteristics of accounting education as well as the problems existing in the training program, and proposed that the training of accounting practice ability should run through the whole teaching process, and reform from all aspects. Qi (2017) believed that colleges and universities should focus on the trend of the times and social needs. In the era of the emergence of financial robots, college and university education should focus on training senior management accounting talents who not only have financial accounting skills, but also understand financial management, financial analysis and enterprise management. To sum up, most of the current literature on the course teaching of the combination of internet and accounting is discussed from two aspects of development path and teaching mode, and the teaching design and practice research involving cloud accounting and financial sharing are relatively few. Therefore, this paper takes the characteristic course "cloud accounting and intelligent financial Shared" that Shandong University of Finance and economics intends to offer as an example, and elaborates the teaching design process of this course based on the model from analysis to evaluation.

4   Financial Shared Course Design

4.1   Design Ideas of Financial Shared Course

In the new era, the training of accountants needs innovative financial personnel training mode. The design idea of financial Shared curriculum is based on the traditional accounting education, combined with "Internet +" thinking, such as accounting sand table simulation, enterprise development software operation, well-known enterprise cooperation and practical operation, and so on, to explore a curriculum that accords with the actual needs of contemporary accounting practice. The training mode enables the accounting education in colleges and universities to keep pace with the times.

The overall framework is generally divided into four levels. The first level is mainly the study of basic theoretical knowledge of financial sharing, which is similar to the traditional accounting education. The second level makes the students understand the theoretical knowledge more deeply through the financial sharing practical scene teaching. The third level is the actual operation part, mainly through the Internet and human-computer interaction, to train students' "Internet + finance" thinking. The fourth level is to cooperate with the entrusted enterprises to carry out field visit and research to understand the needs of enterprises in the application of financial shared for further research. According to the financial shared theory, combined with the internet, cloud computing and other new generation of information technology, the idea of financial shared course is shown in Fig. 3.

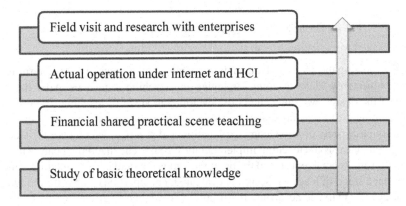

Fig. 3. Financial shared course design idea (Source: the Author)

4.2   Teaching Model Construction of Financial Shared Course

The teaching design idea of financial shared course takes four levels of cognition, simulation, practice and investigation into consideration. The specific model construction takes teaching objectives and teaching problems as the first place and highlights the whole process of teaching activities, including five stages of analysis, design, development, implementation and evaluation, as shown in Fig. 4. Among them, analysis and design are the prerequisite, development and implementation are the core elements, evaluation is the summary guarantee, and the three parts are closely related. The main contents of the analysis stage are student demand analysis, student characteristics analysis, learning content analysis and resource condition analysis.

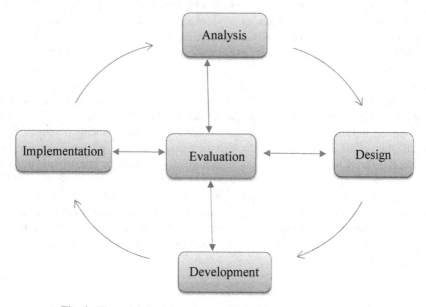

Fig. 4. Financial shared course model design (source: the Author)

After knowing the needs and the analysis results of all aspects, we can determine the teaching objectives, make teaching strategies and teaching sequences. After the completion of the design, we enter the core development stage of teaching. According to the development of financial shared course, construction process, operation optimization and other aspects of knowledge explanation and practice, we prepare for teaching development. Next is the teaching implementation stage. The theoretical part is the case explanation and special report, and the practical part is the sand table simulation training. Finally, each stage of teaching design is evaluated, each part takes up different weight, and scores are calculated according to different performance and scoring methods. The model is in a dynamic, flexible and rich environment, which ensures that the teaching process is easy to operate and accepted by students. The teaching process of the model is designed as follows:

4.3 Analysis Stage

The analysis stage is the first stage of the whole teaching design. In this stage, we need to make a series of analysis on teaching objectives, tasks, audiences, environment and other aspects, mainly including four aspects: learning needs analysis, student characteristics analysis, learning content analysis and resource condition analysis.

1. Analysis of learning needs. The purpose of learning needs analysis is to define teaching objectives. With the development of internet technology, the responsibilities of accounting personnel gradually shift from financial accounting to management accounting. Students also pay more attention to the deep processing and reuse of accounting information, as well as the risk control management and strategic planning of enterprises. Therefore, under the background of "Internet +", the transformation from traditional accounting to Financial Shared Service Center requires students not only to learn basic knowledge of financial accounting, financial management and decision analysis, but also to have strong data mining ability and information technology application ability, fully understand the operation and practice of enterprise Financial Shared Service center construction and operation. Understand the application of big data, cloud accounting, RPA and artificial intelligence in financial shared services, and be able to conduct comprehensive financial analysis based on the data generated by the Financial Shared Service Center, so as to provide financial information support for the decision-making and deployment of enterprise management.

2. Analysis of students' characteristics. The analysis of students' characteristics is based on students' accounting knowledge, professional background, information literacy, interest in learning, learning ability, thinking structure, etc., and designs targeted and personalized teaching content. Students have strong learning and absorbing ability to cloud computing, big data, mobile internet and other new technology knowledge, but lack of practical experience and management ability, so it is difficult to further extract valuable data and information according to the needs, so as to assist the management in decision-making. Therefore, the course extracts the construction scheme and typical cases of Financial Shared Service Center from the business practice of major group enterprises, and allows students to choose the relevant cases of financial Sharing independently according to the theme given by the teacher for analysis, and then explain and evaluate one by one according to the course progress, fully understanding the relationship between financial sharing and management accounting, internal audit, group management and control, IT audit, and social audit department. Students and teachers may exchange ideas and different views, so that students in the learning process to continue to maintain interest in learning and the spirit of inquiry.

3. Analysis of learning content. Learning content is based on the analysis of learning needs. Therefore, this course focuses on discussing and introducing how internet technology can support enterprise accounting and management analysis under the condition of economic globalization, and how to help enterprises achieve organizational innovation, institutional innovation, system innovation and enhance market competitive advantage. Specifically, the research on the transformation of financial management mode of group enterprises in the internet era, the connotation and relationship between financial sharing and artificial intelligence, RPA robot process automation, big data, management accounting, internal audit, group management and control, IT audit, social audit, etc., the strategic positioning, organizational system, process design, system development, internal control management of Financial Shared Service Center The simulation experience of risk management, operation

management, site selection and other links, as well as the scheme design, construction, implementation of financial sharing services and the actual combat training of sand table simulation.

4. Resource condition analysis. Shandong University of Finance and Economics, under the background of deepening the education reform of colleges and universities in China, constructs a teaching mode of multi-agent, cross system, collaborative innovation and development with undergraduate students, teachers and tutors as the core subjects and with knowledge acquisition, fusion and feedback as the core elements under the collaborative support of schools and practice bases. Through strengthening the communication and cooperation between subjects and resource integration, knowledge effectiveness is produced in this way, the knowledge structure of students can be strengthened and the ability and quality of students can be improved.

4.4 Design Phase

Teaching design is to design the course for the teaching activities to be carried out and build the structural model of teaching practice. The design stage is based on the preliminary analysis results, in order to clarify the teaching objectives, make teaching strategies and determine the teaching sequence.

1. Determine the teaching objectives. The teaching goal is a comprehensive expression of learning effect. The teaching objective of this course is to enable students to master the basic theory of financial shared service framework, understand strategic positioning, organizational personnel, financial information system, operation management and other core contents; master the construction and operation practice of Financial Shared Service Center of group enterprises, including demand acquisition, project implementation method, project planning and design, implementation and operation; be familiar with big data and cloud, the application of accounting in financial shared services, and the completion of relevant research; be able to write the construction plan of Financial Shared Services Center, evaluate its feasibility and operability, and solve the problems that may be faced in the operation process.
2. Develop teaching strategies. Teaching strategies are divided into organization strategy, communication strategy and management strategy. Organization strategy is the key factor for the effective operation of the class. Before the class, teachers arrange case discussion requirements and topics through communication tools such as learning links or WeChat. Students need to learn basic theoretical knowledge independently, collect construction cases of Financial Shared Service Center of relevant enterprises, conduct case discussion and PPT production in groups, and explain the cases according to the topic selection in the class. Communication strategy is that teachers use various media and means to effectively transfer teaching contents to students. Because of the advanced nature of the course, the use of network resources and video display is the main channel for knowledge transfer. The management strategy is a rich and diverse learning activity organized by teachers to carry out face-to-face discussions, small lectures, group discussions and other activities. First, the case is analyzed in a simple way, and then the framework structure, strategic objectives,

process business, information system, operation management and other aspects of financial sharing services are comprehensively discussed.

3. Determine the teaching sequence. The teaching sequence is usually arranged from the simple necessary skills to the complex terminal skills, or according to the degree of increase in the meaning of learning content, so as to make effective arrangements for the resources and steps used to promote learning. Taking into account the individual differences and cognitive level of students, the course divides the teaching content into three modules: the first module requires students to collect the case of Financial Shared Service Center of the enterprises concerned before class, and to make PPT explanations.

In the he second module teachers first teach the basic theory of financial shared services, and the students explain the optional cases again, including the relationship and influence between financial shared and artificial intelligence, management accounting, internal audit, IT audit, social audit, RPA robot process automation, group control, business upgrading, and strategic management. The third module adopts the wave finance. Share simulation sandbox and software for practice, and simulate the whole process of design, construction and operation of financial sharing service.

4.5 Development Stage

The development stage is the core stage of curriculum design. It is an important stage for teachers to define teaching content, teaching methods and teaching tasks, and a specific means to achieve learning objectives. The course focuses on the development of different teaching methods, teaching plans and teaching environment, and is divided into development preparation stage and teaching environment development stage.

1. Preparation stage of teaching development. Teaching design should reflect the characteristics of teaching pertinence and individualized teaching. The specific development process of the course should be adjusted and improved continuously with the change of each element. In the development preparation stage, the practical significance of the teaching course should be comprehensively analyzed and summarized. The cutting-edge of the teaching objectives should be explored and integrated in many ways. The teaching resources and teaching methods should be combined to get the results. The results are evaluated and optimized in depth. In addition, various teaching tools should be identified in the preparatory stage of teaching development, such as information acquisition tools (Internet, magazines, newspapers and periodicals, etc.), knowledge building tools (PPT, sand tables, experimental reports, etc.), communication tools (public numbers, WeChat, QQ, etc.), knowledge management evaluation tools (scorecard, evaluation form, etc.). By using these tools, students can be more familiar with and master the theoretical knowledge of the construction of Financial Sharing Service Center, the basic structure and functional composition of information system, as well as the enterprise financial processing process and financial decision-making process.

2. Teaching environment development stage. The object of teaching environment development is mainly laboratory and classroom. The classroom environment includes

installation and debugging of projector, screen, electronic display screen and other multimedia equipment. The laboratory environment is mainly the placement of sand table simulation equipment, which enables students to carry out practical training of financial sharing through sand table simulation, and carry out detailed learning of Financial Sharing Service Center business on different panels, such as the panel of shared business planning center, which is divided into costs reimbursement, accounts receivable, accounts payable and salary paying four business areas. Each business area includes business scenarios and system contents, including specific positions, business operation contents and physical documents corresponding to business flow. According to the case background analysis, students develop the business process and management system of the Financial Sharing Service Center, and display them on the sand table to help students better understand the financial sharing, integration of industry and finance and other related contents.

4.6 Implementation Phase

The implementation stage is to carry out the teaching of the developed curriculum, implement the teaching plan, transfer the teaching content and complete the teaching task. In the implementation stage of the course, students are mainly encouraged to internalize their knowledge through interaction and cooperation, role-playing, and scenario simulation. The main purpose of the course is to find and solve problems, and to strengthen students' thinking ability and cooperation ability. Before the start of the course, the teacher will arrange candidate discussion topics, including the construction and application of accounting and Financial Sharing Service Center, enterprise financial transformation and financial sharing, artificial intelligence and financial sharing, RPA robot process automation and financial sharing, big data and financial sharing, financial sharing and management accounting, financial sharing and internal audit, financial sharing and group control, financial Service sharing service center, it audit, Financial Sharing Service Center, social audit and other topics, and then select topics with groups as the unit, analyze the connotation and relationship of each concept in the topic in detail in theory, and explain with cases, and make ppt after analysis and discussion. In the class, the teacher will explain the related knowledge of financial sharing service according to the teaching arrangement, in which the teacher will share the Related videos in combination with the case, and select the group with the corresponding theme to perform the PPT demonstration according to the teaching progress. After the demonstration, the other groups can evaluate or ask questions to strengthen the understanding of the relevant knowledge.

The course teaching is implemented in the laboratory, which is divided into four stages. The first stage is the preparation stage of the drill, which introduces the students in groups and sandbox teaching tools. Because Inspur Financial Sharing simulation sandbox is used for practice, each student in the group needs to conduct role play and scenario drill according to the functional positioning, and clarify the post responsibilities and management division within the enterprise organization. The second stage is to read the background information of the case company, understand the organizational structure and financial system structure of the case company, analyze the informatization construction and financial management status of the case company and the management objectives expected to be achieved through the construction of the Financial Sharing Service Center. The third stage is sand table exercise. Through the analysis of the case background, this paper simulates the construction and operation process of the Financial Sharing Service Center from the construction goal, organization system, business process, financial information system and other aspects. In the learning process, each module can be regarded as a "mahjong". Through the way of game, it can be divided into expense reimbursement, salary distribution, operation and technology, strategy and policy, a/r business, a/P business and other modules to analyze and standardize the Financial Shared Service Center Business Process, familiar with the enterprise financial processing process, and simulate the planning and construction of the Financial Shared Service Center Set up and operate the financial sharing service center so that students can comprehensively improve their understanding of financial sharing, the ability to build the Financial Sharing Service Center, team spirit and enterprise management level in the process of simulating the construction of the Financial Sharing Service Center. In the fourth stage, the results of sand table simulation experiment are displayed in the classroom with groups as the unit, and the groups interact and comment.

At the end of the course, the teacher reviews and scores the results of the sand table simulation experiment presented by each group of students. At the same time, the teacher summarizes the problems or knowledge points of each group of students in the sand table simulation process. The students then write the sand table simulation experiment report in groups, and the teacher gives the evaluation.

The specific process is shown in Fig. 5.

In the whole course of teaching, students quickly master the knowledge system of Financial Sharing in the process of combining knowledge with practice. This way of learning financial sharing by "playing" simulation sand table not only improves the interest and enthusiasm of students' learning, but also changes the learning mode of students to the organizational structure of team cooperation, at the same time, it also promotes students to explore cooperative learning The effective development of the system improves students' ability in communication, innovative thinking and teamwork.

4.7 Evaluation Stage

Evaluation is the reflection and summary of teaching effect. Teaching evaluation can effectively help teachers improve teaching level and teaching methods. Teaching evaluation should permeate every teaching link, participate in every teaching situation, fully reflect the independence, preciseness and integrity of teaching evaluation, and play a guiding and supervising role in the teaching stage of other courses. Using multiple evaluation method to evaluate the effect of classroom teaching can summarize and evaluate the effect of classroom teaching more scientifically and effectively.

According to the teaching objectives and plans, the teaching effect of the course can be evaluated from three dimensions: case analysis, financial sharing sand table simulation training, course summary and reflection, with scores accounting for 50%, 40% and 10% respectively. The results of the case and financial shared sandbox simulation training evaluation are composed of individual points and group points, and only individual points are included in the course summary and reflection. The evaluation content of curriculum summary and reflection dimension should include the experience of the whole

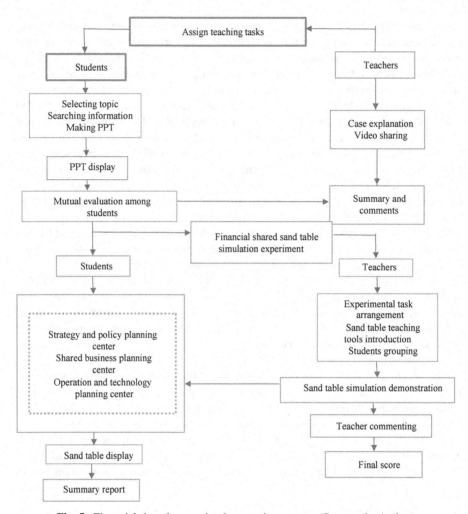

Fig. 5. Financial shared course implementation process (Source: the Author)

curriculum and the learning and mastering of financial shared course. Teachers should evaluate according to the summary submitted by individuals, and combine the scores of attendance and test to get the final comprehensive score. The diversified evaluation method has changed the traditional single examination form and paid more attention to the comprehensive ability of students. At the same time, building a diversified evaluation method is also an important part of the implementation of curriculum reform and information construction in colleges and universities under the circumstances of big data and Internet plus. It is of great significance to speed up the teaching reform and innovation in colleges and universities under the new situation.

References

Guo, J., Wen, J., Zhang, X.: Exploration of MPAcc students' core literacy structure and training path under the background of "Internet +". Ind. Technol. Forum **7**, 122–123 (2017)

Wang, D., Liu, A., Tang, S.: Research on innovation of full-time MPAcc case teaching driven by Internet. Acc. Commun. **22**, 61–63 (2017)

Ding, H., Liu, G.: Reform of MPAcc training mode under the guidance of accounting practice. J. Financ. Acc. **27**, 124–126 (2015)

Qi, L.: The impact of the emergence of financial robots on the reform of efficient accounting personnel training mode. Bus. Manager **24**, 179 (2017)

Yuko, A.H.: Industry-university cooperation to take on herefrom. Res. Inst. Econ. Trade Ind. **4**, 42–49 (2002)

Jia, H., Li, Y.: Analysis on the influencing factors of university industry university research cooperation. China Univ. Technol. **9**, 32–33 (2014)

Emotional Design and Gamification in Educational Processes: Predictor Model to Increase Video Game Efficiency

Rômulo Pinto[1,4(✉)], Ernesto Filgueiras[1,3,4], and Karina Moutinho[2,5]

[1] Universidade da Beira Interior, Covilhã, Portugal
rcpinto@gmail.com
[2] Universidade Federal de Pernambuco, Recife, Brazil
[3] CIAUD - Research Centre for Architecture, Urbanism and Design, Lisbon, Portugal
[4] Communication Laboratory – LabCom, University of Beira Interior, Covilhã, Portugal
[5] Eikasia – Imagination Lab, Universidade Federal de Pernambuco, Recife, Brazil

Abstract. This article aims to present the results obtained in the first phase of a study that applied an innovative gamified technique of emotional design. It was developed by the MEET Playware company to a heterogeneous sample of 230 students, aged between 11 and 15 years old. The study aimed to combat school dropout and increase student involvement in school content (with focus on Portuguese and Mathematics). The experience compared the real conditions of a knowledge tournament, accomplished through the gamification process in schools, with a sample simulated in the laboratory of the same experiment (n = 24), and it provided fundamental contributions to the product to be developed. At the end of the process, questionnaires were answered by students (n = 230) and teachers (n = 13) who followed the study in schools. As a result of the methods, techniques and procedures used to measure and categorize users' feelings, they proved to be efficient and to increase the proposed motivation. In general, the results show that, in a real context, feelings tend to fluctuate under the influence of several factors that are difficult to isolate under laboratory conditions. The conclusions point to the validity of using emotional design as a predictive factor of product efficiency, according to studies cited in the theoretical review and effectively suggest that emotional design can be a predictive factor for product efficiency in the context of motivational activities, as education in particular.

Keywords: Emotional design · Gamification · Motivation

1 Introduction

Although videogame developers have been increasingly making use of emotional design techniques in their products (Demir et al. 2009; Plass et al. 2019; Diefenbach and Hassenzahl 2019; McEvoy and Cowan 2016), the evaluation of the use of these techniques can still need new studies. In this sense, the possibility of following the development of a product from the video game industry applied to education allowed to assess

© Springer Nature Switzerland AG 2020
A. Marcus and E. Rosenzweig (Eds.): HCII 2020, LNCS 12202, pp. 506–517, 2020.
https://doi.org/10.1007/978-3-030-49757-6_37

the relevance of a specific technique of emotional design after three months of effective use of it's product by 230 users of both sexes, aged between 11 and 15 years old, residents at the Municipality of Fundão, Portugal.

We propose in this article to demonstrate how the use of an emotional design measurement technique in the initial stage of developing a videogame contributed to the product's later efficiency.

The product is an application for tablets and was developed by the Meet Playware company in Portugal to meet the school activities demand for gamification of basic education in the public education in the country's central region. The analysis of the application of the technique was performed in three stages, two of them with direct users of the product and different research tools on the same focus: motivation. The third stage compared the data previously obtained.

2 Literature Review

2.1 Emotional Design

Alaniz and Biazo (2019) carried out, with Design specialists, a study about products creation with the application of emotional design techniques. The study aimed to create a relevant industrial process called Innovation Motivated by Emotion (E-DI). The authors concluded that the innovation process driven by emotion was able to support designers in three essential points: to identify the occurrence of emotions during the use of certain products available on the market; apply the information obtained about these emotions to make strategic decisions when emotional intentions for new products are defined; and focus on designer's creative thinking to developing strong and relevant emotions for users.

In contrast, in a study fulfilled on more than 2000 award-winning works in product design, Zhao and Zhu (2020) concluded that complex emotions can hardly be decoded and applied effectively in emotional design. In general, emotions are complex human feelings that emerge from our intrapsychic relationship (everything that originates or occurs inside the mind or psyche) in relationships with persons, environment and objects surround us. Plass and Kaplan (2016) state that there is no agreement between researchers on the concepts of emotion, humor and affection. Thus, it is necessary to make a choice about the concepts and theoretical models to be used in emotional design. In their study, the authors adopt the view of Roseman according to which emotions are characterized by five different components of response types:

- The phenomenological component constituted by specific thoughts and feelings;
- The physiological component composed of characteristic patterns of body response;
- The expressive components constituted by specific manifestations in the face, voice and posture;
- The behavioral components constituted by the individual's action tendency; and
- The motivational components.

Specifically, about educational products, authors claim the emotional design of teaching material can have a significant impact on student learning, although most multimedia learning models are based on cognitive factors. Plass and Kaplan developed a study and concluded that the use of round shapes and warm colors in learning environment design was able to induce emotions that contributed to the students' learning.

However, Münchow and Bannert (2019) conducted a research with 145 higher education students and found no significant evidence of the effectiveness of emotional design in multimedia learning. In turn, Bu et al. (2019) investigated the application of emotional design through a new model created by them called PCE (Perception and Comprehension and Expression). The model was applied to development of an e-book (picture book) for children between the ages of 5 to 8 years old. The results with users registered a positive sensory and reading experience, in addition to a pleasant emotional interaction.

To better understand emotional design and its possibilities, it is necessary to know its origins. The first significant studies on emotional design date from the late 1990s, with special highlight to Jordan (1999). He defined four types of pleasures sought by users in their relationship with products: physiological pleasure related to the senses, social pleasure related to human interactions, psychological or mental pleasure, that includes those pleasures related to the execution of tasks with the product, and ideological pleasure derived from abstractions of a theoretical nature, such as books, culture, consumption options, among others. Norman (2004) propose that in the relationship with the user, product design acts on three levels: visceral, behavioral and reflective. At the visceral level, the product is instinctively appreciated by the user who has an experience marked by physical contact with it. At the behavioral level, the user experience is marked by control in relation to the task that the product proposes to perform. And the reflective level refers to the reflection made by an user about what happens around him when he is identified as a user of that product. Desmet (2002) proposes the Appraisal Theory and propose emotions function as automatic responses by the user about the products. Hekkert (2006) states that the experience with a product also occurs in three interconnected dimensions: an aesthetic, a cognitive and an emotional.

Thus, emotional design has been consolidating itself not only as a theoretical and methodological field of Design, but also as a tool for the development of complex products. Its nature is remarkably interdisciplinary, and its most obvious interfaces are psychology, cognition and communication.

2.2 Gamification

When talking about literature, there are several methodologies and processes for the gamification of activities or procedures. In these terms, several initiatives have been implemented both in basic and higher education (Lister 2015; Majuri et al. 2018; Sailer et al. 2017). In most of these cases, the main objective is to increase motivation for studies through the playfulness that games allow. It is assumed that entertainment can be added to educational context and contribute positively to the student's interest in learning. López Rodriguez et al. (2018) talk about the use of video games associated with the improvement of educational aspects, such as attention to content, motivation, learning efficiency, among others. At first, gamification is a process independent of digital technologies.

However, when gamification is related to video games, it is evident the existence of complex industrial processes in the elaboration of products and processes related to activities. In addition, gamification is usually related to the learning of specific content and operates through the mobilization of users in competitive activities. In this terms, the motivation factor becomes crucial to the learning process, because the act of winning implies that the user has efficiently completed a task, obtained concrete rewards for that (points, trophies) and was socially distinguished among pairs (other competitors) through the sharing and visibility of their performance that their rewards is given to.

2.3 Motivation Aspects

As with the concept of emotion, it can also vary according to the academic profile of the researchers. In any case, according to Linnenbrink-Garcia et al. (2016), researchers in the area of motivation tend to consider how the beliefs, cognitions, goals and experiences of students usually shape engagement and learning. According to the authors, motivation includes several forms related to competence, for example "can I do this?", As well as forms related to values and objectives, for example "why do I want to do this?".

In an investigation based on 60 papers on design and motivation, Tang and Zhang (2018) wonder why people start, continue, stop or avoid the use of certain technologies. The authors seek in the theory of motivational offer the answers to this and other questions: to what extent are game design resources linked to basic human needs? What is the potential of gamification to motivate users by satisfying their basic needs? In the other hand, in a study on the motivation of 27 students graduated from massive open online courses (MOOCs), Huang and Hew (2016) used a motivation assessment technique in four aspects: attention, relevance, confidence and satisfaction (ARCS). The authors concluded that the majority of participants had positive levels of motivation. Thus, according to the studies presented on emotional design, gamification and motivation, we can conclude that:

- motivation is essential for learning;
- school gamification is a motivating factor;
- emotions condition motivation;
- educational products stimulate emotions;
- emotions can be stimulated by production processes;
- production processes can incorporate emotional design techniques;
- emotional design techniques can make the product more efficient.

3   The Experiment

In our case, the study deals with the experience in developing, implementing and evaluating a product (video game) in an educational context supported by schools, public authorities, companies and development and innovation agencies. The experiment was carried out by the Gamified Education project. The study has started out from the application of the Gardunha XXI agency in a public notice from Portugal Social Innovation between September 2017 and will continue during the year of 2020. The goals were: to promote a change in the school culture, increase the performance of students with school studies focused on in Portuguese and Mathematics and combat school dropout. The Table 1 below identifies the process' participants:

Table 1. Process' participants

Entity	Agents	Role
Company	Meet playware	Product developer
Schools	Head of school	Approve the project
	Teachers	Identify requirements
	Students	Identify requirements and validate product
Public authorities	City council	Social investor
	Educational service	Executive coordination
Development agencies	Gardunha XXI	Propose itself application and execute the project
	Portugal inovação social	Provide part of the project financing; monitor implementation and results

The product in question was developed in five stages. The development process started with the identification of the type of need that the education service of Fundão Municipality had for the product (schools, teachers, students, head of school). After this initial identification, the second stage started with the analysis of the context of use in schools. The third stage dealt with specifying the requirements of users and other participants (see Table 1). In the fourth stage, the design solutions were produced and in the fifth stage these same proposals were evaluated with real users. The result of the development was an application for tablets in a configurable quiz format. The product is part of a broader gamification process that involves tournaments to learn about Portuguese, mathematics and general culture. The prototype was tested in the laboratory of the MEET Playware Company by 24 students from schools that participated in the study. The experience with the product simulated the real conditions of the gamification process to be developed. The students formed teams and competed in a knowledge tournament. Figure 1 below shows screens of the product (prototype) used in the experiment:

Fig. 1. Tournament start screen (left), where we can see the four Mathematics challenges and the four Portuguese challenges; and tournament closing screen (right), where we can see the team's final performance report.

4   Emotional Design: Methods and Techniques

The process of analyzing the measurement technique of the product described in the emotional design took place in three stages. In the first stage, a prototype developed from meetings with stakeholders was used. For the second stage, the prototype has undergone minimal changes, imperceptible to users. The third stage were compared the results of the two evaluations.

4.1   Prototype Evaluation

The first step occurred during the prototype test procedure. An evaluation questionnaire was applied to the group of 24 students based on the PrEMO scale. According to the service's own website, PrEMO is a widely used tool to instantly obtain insights into the emotions of the user or consumer of products and services. The tool makes possible to report emotions with the use of expressive comic figures that provide a more appropriate reading for designers and developers. The commercial version of the tool presents an option for respondents to be able to report their emotions using expressive cartoon animations. In this version, each of the 14 measured emotions is portrayed by an animation through dynamic facial, body and vocal expressions, so there is no need to rely on the use of words (Desmet 2003). Table 2 below shows the feelings expressed by the figures in the referred scale:

Table 2. Negative and positive PrEmo emotions.

Pleasant emotions			Unpleasant emotions		
ID	Interpretations		ID	Interpretations	
1	Joy	Happiness	8	Sadness	Regret
2	Hope	Optimism	9	Fear	Anxiety
3	Pride	Self-esteem	10	Shame	Embarrassment
4	Admiration	Respect	11	Contempt	Disrespect
5	Satisfaction	Approval	12	Dissatisfaction	Anger
6	Fascination	Curiosity	13	Boredom	Disappointment
7	Attraction	Desire	14	Disgust	Aversion

4.2 Beta Version Evaluation

The beta version was used for three school months (March/2019 until May/2019) by 230 elementary school students in 4 schools in Portugal. During that time, 34 knowledge tournaments were applied to these students. A tournament is a task that takes place once a week in the classroom. The task has a maximum duration of fifteen minutes. The tournament consists of the following stages:

- Team formation.
- Distribution of tablets.
- Task resolution.
- Presentation of results to the class.

At the end of the process, questionnaires were applied in order to assess the perception of students and teachers as to the motivation for studying school content. 230 questionnaires were answered by students and 13 by teachers who followed the study in schools. Although the Gamified Education project is composed of a wide range of actions for both audiences (students and teachers), the term "gamification" was perceived as the activity performed in the classroom.

4.3 Prototype and Beta Evaluations

The results were defined based on a direct comparison between the numbers associated with positive and negative feelings. For this, three points were considered as a premise:

- product efficiency is measured by the user's perception of the objectives defined for the product and achieved in use;
- product's goal is to promote motivation for learning school content;
- the element that makes the connection between the prototype's and beta version's evaluation is the user's feeling (categorized as positive and negative) in relation to the actual use of the product.

5   Results

The figure below shows the result of applying the PrEMO scale for the prototype:

As seen in Fig. 2, the students' feelings during the process of using the prototype remained the same in percentage terms. However, there was a small variation between the types of feeling according to the scale. After using the game, a negative variation was observed in the numbers of the positive feeling and an increase in the number related to the negative feeling. When consulting the individual responses given by the students in the applied survey, it was found that these were linked to the teams that lost in the first stage and were disappointed with their performance. Thus, the indignation or disgust was not exactly about the prototype, but it was about the team's performance in the tournament. Figures 3 and 4 below show the evolution of positive and negative feelings according to the scale used:

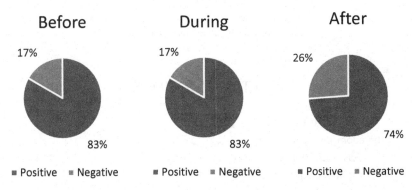

Fig. 2. Evolution of students' feelings: before, during and after using the prototype.

The evolution of emotion throughout the experience indicates a slight drop in the level of appreciation of the product. Our understanding is that part of that decline is due to competition. As it is a tournament with four teams and only one can win, three others experienced the frustration of the defeat that was reflected in the evaluation of the use of the product. However, a new investigation would be necessary to better elucidate this relationship. For now, we are content with the expressive results in relation to the general feeling about the product. In general, the results guided the minimum adjustments to the prototype (correction of minor operating failures) that evolved into a beta version without significant differences for the user. This beta version was tested "on ground" by a greater number of users, in operation of the Gamified Education project. Thus, the question defined to assess the students' motivation in the beta evaluation survey was: Did Gamification MOTIVATE YOU TO STUDY MORE? Five possible responses were also defined, representing a scale from 0 to 4 in the impact assessment. Possible responses were associated with negative or positive feelings in the following terms:

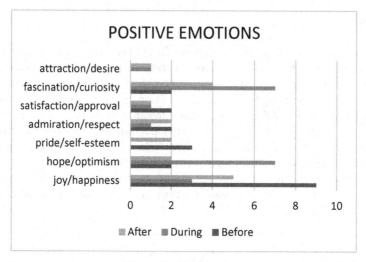

Fig. 3. Positive emotions

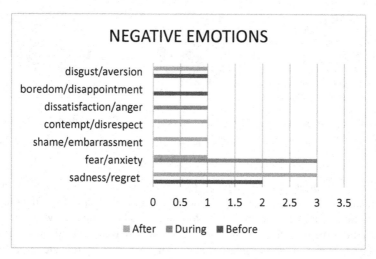

Fig. 4. Negative emotions

- (0) No. The students were MUCH MORE DEMOTIVATED than motivated (very negative feeling).
- (1) No. The students were more discouraged than motivated (negative feeling).
- (2) The students seemed indifferent to the rounds/tournaments (neutral).
- (3) Yes. They were a little more motivated (positive feeling).
- (4) Yes. They were VERY motivated (very positive feeling).

A total of 10 (76.9%) teachers noticed an INCREASE in students' motivation for studying school content. Of these, 2 pointed out the students as MUCH more motivated. There were 3 (23.1%) teachers who did not perceive the project as capable of interfering in the students' motivation. Proportionally, teachers perceived the impact of the project on motivation even more than the students themselves who answered the same question (62%). However, teachers were not users of the product, but privileged observers of its effects on students. Because they know students well and accompany them daily in schools, the opinion of the teachers helped to confirm the evaluation of the product's efficiency in terms of its motivating objective. In general, teachers' perception of the project is very similar to the students. In particular, aspects related to the gamification model and students' motivation to study school content obtained significantly positive evaluations among the two audiences. The Table 3 below illustrates the relationship between STUDENTS' emotions in the two analysis:

Table 3. Relationship between STUDENTS' emotions in two analysis

Feeling	Technique	Prototype evaluation (n = 24)	Beta version evaluation (n = 230)
Positive	PrEMO	80,6%	–
Positive	Multiple choice	–	62.5%
Negative	PrEMO	19,4%	–
Negative	Multiple choice	–	1,75%

6   Conclusions

The Gamified Education project involved the development and testing of a product from the video game industry. The project can be characterized as a process of social and technological innovation. Social innovation is in the proposal to transform school culture through gamification. Technological innovation is in the process of product development and its integration into the school environment (context of use). The results obtained confirmed some conclusions of studies on the application of emotional design in product development, for example, Alaniz and Biazo (2019). Effectively, emotional design guided designers during the evolution of the product from prototype to beta and was crucial for making strategic decisions for a new stage of development. It has been developing a Version 1.0 and it incorporates elements from the reported evaluation process.

Emotional design, motivation and gamification are also concepts that are intertwined in the product development and testing process. The Gamified Education project would not be viable without the development team understanding and articulating these concepts. The elements of the scale used in the evaluation of the prototype did not fit precisely in the evaluation of the beta version. However, the results were considered satisfactory by the developers.

In both evaluations, users showed, during the use of the product, at least three of the four types of pleasures identified by Jordan (1999): the one related to the senses in the sensory interaction with the product, the social pleasure in the interaction with the team during tournaments and psychological pleasure related to performing tasks (see Fig. 3) (Fig. 5):

Fig. 5. Students in interaction with the product

The presented data suggests a positive emotional response to the product and its integration process into school life. Nevertheless, the identification of emotions is a complex task, as we pointed out before (Zhao and Zhu 2020) and requires a sophisticated psychological investigation. Emotions, feelings and humor are not static or stable elements. In addition, they can be contradictory in the face of everyday situations. Love and hate, for example, can appear intertwined in situations of high psychosocial tension. In general, feelings tend to fluctuate under the influence of several factors that are difficult to isolate under laboratory conditions. Thus, it is important to highlight some limits of the present study. The capture of students' feelings, for example, was made only during the moments of interaction with the product. In addition, the proposed categories, especially in the second assessment (positive and negative), are quite simple. However, we consider that the results effectively suggest that emotional design can be a predictive factor for the efficiency of products in the context of motivational activities, education in particular. The next step is to evaluate the use of the product's version 1.0 on a larger scale of students, scheduled for the school year 2020/2021.

References

Alaniz, T., Biazzo, S.: Emotional design: the development of a process to envision emotion-centric new product ideas. Procedia Comput. Sci. **158**, 474–484 (2019)

Bu, Y., Jia, J., Li, X., Lu, X.: Emotional design for children's electronic picture book. In: Kurosu, M. (ed.) HCII 2019. LNCS, vol. 11566, pp. 392–403. Springer, Cham (2019). https://doi.org/10.1007/978-3-030-22646-6_28

Desmet, P.M.A.: Designing emotions. doctoral dissertation, Delft University of Technology, Delft, The Netherlands (2002)

Desmet, P.M.: Measuring emotion; development and application of an instrument to measure emotional responses to products. In: Blythe, M.A., Monk, A.F., Overbeeke, K., Wright, P.C. (eds.) Funology: From Usability to Enjoyment, pp. 111–123. Kluwer Academic Publishers, Dordrecht (2003)

Demir, E., Desmet, P., Hekkert, P.P.: Appraisal patterns of emotions in human-product interaction. Int. J. Des. 3(2), 41–51 (2009)

Diefenbach, S., Hassenzahl, M.: Combining model-based analysis with phenomenological insight: a case study on hedonic product quality. Qual. Psychol. 6(1), 1–24 (2017, 2019)

Escala PrEMO. http://www.premotools.com. Accessed 20 Jan 2019

Green, W., Jordan, P.: Pleasure with products: human factors for body, mind and soul. In: Human Factors in Product Design: Current Practice and Future Trends, pp. 206–217. CRC Press, Boca Raton (1999)

Hekkert, P.: Design aesthetics: principles of pleasure in design. Psychol. Sci. 48(2), 157–172 (2019)

Huang, B., Hew, K.F.T.: Measuring learners' motivation level in massive open online courses. Int. J. Inf. Educ. Technol. 6(10), 759–764 (2016)

Linnenbrink-Garcia, L., Patall, E.A., Pekrun, R.: Adaptive motivation and emotion in education: research and principles for instructional design. Policy Insights Behav. Brain Sci. 3(2), 228–236 (2016)

Lister, M.: Gamification: the effect on student motivation and performance at the post-secondary level. Issues Trends Educ. Technol. 3(2), 1–22 (2015)

López Rodríguez, I., Avello Martínez, R., Baute Álvarez, L.M., Vidal Ledo, M.: Videogames in higher education. Revista Cubana de Educación Médica Superior 32(1), 264–276 (2018)

Majuri, J., Koivisto, J., Hamari, J.: Gamification of education and learning: a review of empirical literature. In: Proceedings of the 2nd International GamiFIN Conference, GamiFIN 2018. CEUR-WS, pp. 11–19 (2018)

McEvoy, D., Cowan, B.R.: The importance of emotional design to create engaging digital HCI learning experiences. Horizon 9(5), 1–6 (2016)

Norman, D.A.: Emotional Design: Why We Love (or Hate) Everyday Things. Basic Civitas Books, New York (2004)

Münchow, H., Bannert, M.: Feeling good, learning better? Effectivity of an emotional design procedure in multimedia learning. Educ. Psychol. 39(4), 530–549 (2019)

Plass, J. L., Kaplan, U.: Emotional design in digital media for learning. In: Emotions, Technology, Design, and Learning, pp. 131–161. Academic Press (2016)

Plass, J., et al.: Emotional design for digital games for learning: the effect of expression, color, shape, and dimensionality on the affective quality of game characters. Learn. Instr., 101194 (2019, in press)

Sailer, M., Hense, J.U., Mayr, S.K., Mandl, H.: How gamification motivates: an experimental study of the effects of specific game design elements on psychological need satisfaction. Comput. Hum. Behav. 69, 371–380 (2017)

Tang, J., Zhang, P.: Gamification and basic human needs in information technology design: a literature analysis. In: Proceedings of the 3rd International Conference on Crowd Science and Engineering (2018)

Zhao, T., Zhu, T.: Exploration of product design emotion based on three-level theory of emotional design. In: Ahram, T., Taiar, R., Colson, S., Choplin, A. (eds.) IHIET 2019. AISC, vol. 1018, pp. 169–175. Springer, Cham (2020). https://doi.org/10.1007/978-3-030-25629-6_27

SyncMeet: Virtual Work Environment for Collaborative Manga Creation

Maria Consuelo Tenorio Morales(✉), Keiko Yamamoto(✉), and Yoshihiro Tsujino(✉)

Kyoto Institute of Technology, Goshokaido-cho, Matsugasaki, Kyoto, Japan
maria@hit.is.kit.ac.jp, {kei,tsujino}@kit.ac.jp

Abstract. In recent years several efforts using technologies to improve collaborative work have been made in fields such as education, training, entertainment, and technology; however, there has been limited research for collaborative creative thinking and art. In this study, we explore the opportunities within virtual collaboration in creative activities via a virtual work environment named SyncMeet. This virtual environment aims to support the discussion of artistic ideas and effective collaboration during a brainstorming session for a storyboard of Japanese comic (manga) between two people who have different narrative abilities such as a writer and illustrator, and who work in distant locations. In this approach, we demonstrated that working inside an immersive environment could improve the users' collaboration, creative skills, and communication. We handled three different experiment sessions that allowed us to compare effectiveness in face-to-face environments, Skype, and SyncMeet. The results indicated that SyncMeet supports verbal and non-verbal communication as a fundamental part of collaboration in a creative task, and the users who were able to immerse themselves inside the environment showed active participation when they worked in distant locations.

Keywords: Virtual Reality · Computer-Supported Cooperative Work (CSCW) · Manga creation · Storyboard

1 Introduction

It is widely considered that creativity is born of individual activity, yet the possibility to interconnect our abilities can generate several options for problem-solving through interdisciplinary mindset or multi-skillset [1]. For this reason, collaboration in creative work provides people numerous possibilities to produce new ideas, objects, or artwork.

In contrast, the collaboration on creative work is implemented in a co-located work environment that lets people have direct interaction and communication with each other quickly. In addition, they can use gestures and facial expressions in such an environment along with different types of visualization tools such as notebooks, pens, and whiteboard as vital contributors to successfully achieve their goals [2].

In this study, we explore more about Virtual Reality (VR) opportunities for collaborative creative work. VR is changing the way that people could use their creative abilities.

© Springer Nature Switzerland AG 2020
A. Marcus and E. Rosenzweig (Eds.): HCII 2020, LNCS 12202, pp. 518–532, 2020.
https://doi.org/10.1007/978-3-030-49757-6_38

Furthermore, some studies show that VR has many benefits and possibilities to make creative processes easier [3–5].

VR not only gives users immersive experiences to meet with their co-workers but also has a lot of potential to create environments that facilitate social activities and support collaborative creativity. All these show significant progress towards a new interface that can innovate work environments.

Currently, very few applications explicitly cater to the creators who wish to carry out work in a virtual environment; hence, it is essential to continue the exploration of this field. There are currently some applications of VR for artistic purposes, and more artists and designers are beginning to find new ways to explore their potential in creativity and develop their ideas through collaboration with other artists.

2   Related Work

2.1   Japanese Comics (Manga) Creation

Manga are comics or graphic novels created in Japan and have a relation with the early Japanese narrative style. Manga publication is one of the biggest entertainment industries in Japan and generated around 7 billion yens since 1995.

The traditional manga drawing process is carried out by a manga artist who is the writer and illustrator of the original story with assistants who support them. Further, editors review the sketches and manuscripts before being published.

The traditional manga creation process involves five principal steps [6], as shown in Fig. 1.

Fig. 1. Process of manga creation

The first step is making a plot. This step involves an introductory meeting or a brainstorming session where the manga artists presents the story, the purpose, characters, development, situation, and other essentials aspects to form the initial idea.

The second step is revising the plot. The purpose of this step is to examine the ideas and determine the details of the storyline. In addition, it includes time schedule and the division of the staff's roles.

The third step is writing the story script. The story script contains the scenario description, dialogues, and actions of the characters before the actual visualization of each scene.

The fourth step is the storyboard drawing. In this step, all images are placed into frames on the storyboard and movements, facial expressions, and emotions are drafted on the character board.

The fifth step is reviewing. After finishing the storyboard, the editors review it. On some occasions, the editors request changes for frame panel layout or the entire storyboard.

2.2   Support System for Remote Manga Creation

Currently, Japanese comic (manga) is very popular around the world, and many people want to collaborate in the creation of manga content. Nowadays, many manga artists are using a collaborative approach to produce professional publications such as CLAMP group [7], a famous female quartet of Japanese manga artists.

In this collaborative approach, manga creators divide their roles between writers or illustrators to work effectively.

However, this collaboration process is not a simple division of their works roles as writers or illustrators. Such role designations also relate to their essential competencies and best personal skills. A writer must be the person responsible for story planning and writing the story scripts, and an illustrator must be the person in charge of everything related to the storyboard composition and character design.

Manga artists who work in collaboration consider this working style as more efficient. Working together not only helps them to produce impressive work and complex stories but also each of them can use their best skill to improve the final work.

However, sometimes their workplaces are separate, and their activities do not align simultaneously. However, they must maintain communication with each other accurately for a more efficient creation. In such scenarios it was found that working remotely has the following problems; 1) difficulty in communicating ideas, 2) reduction of engagement, 3) absence of active participation, and 4) lack of drawing perspective.

For this reason, numerous online communities exist in Japan that help manga creators collaborate and share their content in online art communities such as PIXIV [8] which connects creators across the country.

There has been research in collaborative creative designs, such as AB-DOKAN [9] which is a system to support the online collaboration of a four-panel manga production by a few people. The results achieved in real time proved that participants like to engage in the collaborative manga creation process and find it enjoyable.

In another study on collaborative storytelling [10] an application was created for the collaborative composition of a comic. This research demonstrated the possibility to utilize collaborative storytelling between two authors of different countries.

Based on the results of these studies, a new collaborative interface for manga creation is explored in this study, that gives the participants a satisfactory way to collaborate in narration material.

2.3   VR System for Creative Remote Work

The concept of creative thinking is the constant searching for innovation, original ideas, and problem-solving. Some studies have demonstrated that creativity could be applied in multiple ways to learn activities and design tasks [11, 12]. People who participate in collaboration activities related to creative thinking can examine and evaluate new ideas or concepts from different perspectives and find new directions to develop solutions.

One of the essential factors for success in collaboration activities is efficient communication, especially in a creative task. However, sometimes, the participants reside in different geographical locations, and they must work remotely.

Distant location collaboration environments can solve problem of distance limitation, but collaboration efforts might decrease because team members feel separated by distance and technology. For example, some people experiment with a loss of interest; they do not develop the engagement with their co-workers and do not participate actively in the project.

For this reason, it is necessary to create new technologies and build interfaces that optimize communication between remote team members to support their success [13].

The immersive virtual environment has the potential to support creative collaboration activities. In several studies, these kinds of environments focus on training, education, or simulation [14–17]. However, these studies did not show the specific factors that could contribute to artistic tasks in virtual worlds, and most of the VR technologies used were for individual activities.

In recent years, various types of research efforts have been made to achieve the connection of multiple users within a virtual environment [18]. For example, a study related to VR systems for brainstorming activities established a new way of generating ideas and managing problems efficiently during remote work.

Inside immersive work environments, unlike regular video conferences, the environment could be based on the exchange of information by new communication channels via shared spaces in which the users utilize a three-dimensional (3D) avatar and visual elements that maintain their level of commitment in the work [19].

3   Proposed System

SyncMeet is a virtual meeting room that helps users communicate and collaborate better while remotely working. It has an interface for idea discussion which uses an avatar and 3D objects, for example, a whiteboard in a virtual room. The avatar and the 3D objects let the users collaborate quickly, communicate their ideas, and make propositions for modifications in a manga storyboard by highlighting annotations over the storyboard.

3.1   System Architecture

For each user, an HMD (HTC Vive), a base station, a Leap Motion controller for hand gesture, and a computer with an internet connection are necessary. The HTC Vive can track the user's position precisely inside the physical space and show the corresponding avatar's position inside the virtual environment.

The Leap Motion lets users make natural hand gestures using hands and fingers. The user can hear their remote collaborator's voice through the headphones, as shown in Fig. 2.

3.2   System Functions

The system has two principal functions as described in the following text.

Avatar

The purpose of the avatar is to enhance the users' interaction and give the users a sense of co-presence of both the users during the brainstorming collaboration as shown in Fig. 3.

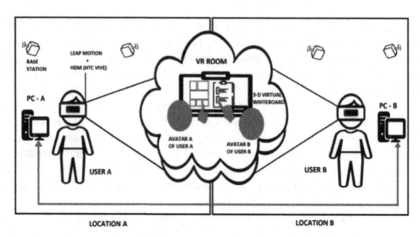

Fig. 2. SyncMeet architecture.

Fig. 3. User avatar and point of view in VR room.

The Avatar has two components:

1) Avatar head indicates not only the collaborator's position and movement inside the VR room, but also their awareness in the remote place.
2) 3D Hand Model for hand gesture, which enables users to show emotions like agreement or disagreement and express what they are talking about by pointing as a part of non-verbal communication.

VR Room

It is a virtual space that enables the users to concentrate and lets them have an immersive experience during the brainstorming session. It was designed to resemble an office meeting room with windows that can increase the users' engagement level on the remote collaboration task, as shown in Fig. 4.

It has four tools to facilitate collaboration, detailed as follows:

1. A virtual whiteboard is a visual representation that shows a story script and four-panel manga drawing which can be seen by both the users simultaneously.

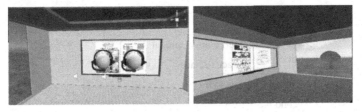

Fig. 4. VR room layout in SyncMeet.

2. A drawing marker tool which enables users to make annotations with lines by pinch input gesture. Moreover, it has the option to choose four different colors to highlight the level of importance of each annotation, as shown in Fig. 5.
3. A voice recording tool which records a voice memo of the conversation during the brainstorming session.
4. A screenshot is captured automatically every three minutes, generating a backup of the annotations on the virtual whiteboard.

Fig. 5. VR drawing tool in SyncMeet.

4   Experimental Evaluation

We evaluated the users' interactions and the application potential of collaborative manga creation in three different environments (face to- face, Skype, and SyncMeet prototype). In this evaluation, all the participants were asked to create a four-panel manga through collaboration between two persons to evaluate the extent and quality of communication and participants' engagement during a brainstorming session in SyncMeet.

4.1   Participants

The number of participants was six with an age range of 23 to 32 years aged. All the participants were Masters students and Ph.D. students (three women and three men) who have previous experience in the creation of manga (Japanese comics), illustration design, or script development.

The participants were divided into three pairs with two types of roles depending on their skills and background (writer or illustrator). In addition, the participants had to switch their partners per week. Table 1 shows which pairs have been assigned for each environment:

Table 1. Experiment's participants distribution.

Experiment period	Work environment		
	Face to Face	Skype	SyncMeet
First week	Aw–Di	Cw–Ei	Bw–Fi
Second week	Bw–Ei	Aw–Fi	Cw–Di
Third week	Cw–Fi	Bw–Di	Aw–Ei

Storywriter participants: Aw, Bw, Cw. Illustrator participants: Di, Ei, Fi

4.2 Task

The activity task consists of four steps that are divided among two different categories, namely, the individual task and collaborative task.

Individual Task
This part of the experiment was divided in two steps as shown in Fig. 6.

Fig. 6. Individual creating session.

First, the story writers are requested to make each short story with an introduction, development, plot twist, and conclusion known as Kishotenketsu [20]. Once finished, each writer sends the script by email to the team lead, and then, it is further sent to their corresponding illustrator.

Second, the illustrator reads the story script and draws the four-panel manga.

Collaborative Task
The collaborative task has two steps; ice-breaking, and four-panel manga brainstorming.
Third, the following activities were conducted:

Self-Introduction: The participants had to introduce themselves and mention one small fact about themselves, for example, their hobby, favorite movie, or favorite food.
True or False Game: Each participant writes four statements about themselves and then they must guess their partner's true statement out of those four.

Fourth, both participants start the brainstorming session. The writer gives feedback and opinions about the four-panel manga. When both participants complete the discussion, they talk about new ideas that can be added on the four-panel manga to improve the results. During this process, both take notes in each environment (Fig. 7).

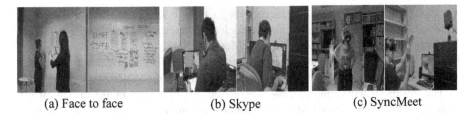

(a) Face to face   (b) Skype   (c) SyncMeet

Fig. 7. Brainstorming session.

4.3 Interview and Questionnaire

The NASA TLX was used for measuring the mental workload and additional custom questionnaires with a Likert scale of 5 points range of answer options were used to get further information about the participant's impressions during the session. Further, videos and pictures of the participants' activities were recorded through the experiment. In addition, participants were interviewed to explore more options about how they feel about working in each environment.

4.4 Variables

The evaluation variables were both quantitative and qualitative values which are as follows:

Quantitative Variables
Mental Workload: Rates the perceived mental workload of the participants' collaboration in each environment.

Qualitative Variables
Work Environment Satisfaction Level: Rates the participant's satisfaction with the work environment to achieve success on the task and the participants' commitment.
Collaboration Effectiveness Level: Rates the participant's impression about the team's commitment and collaboration level to accomplish the goal.
Communication Efficiency Level: Rates the participant's impression about the efficiency of verbal and non-verbal communication between both the participants.

5 Results and Discussion

The result of three different environments for mental workload, as shown in Fig. 9, were M = 30.14, SD = 12.15 (face to face), M = 37.78, SD = 13.17 (SyncMeet) and M = 39.03, SD = 12.06 (Skype). Using the two-way ANOVA for environment and user role, there was no significant difference between the main effect of the environment and participants interaction.

However, during the interview session the participants expressed that they had a better experience using SyncMeet compared to Skype. Participants said that SyncMeet provided them an immersive experience that let them concentrate better and have an improved sense of engagement almost as much as the face to face environment.

Furthermore, they remarked that SyncMeet had the benefit of visual stimulation through 3D objects. The illustrator showed interest in possibly adding new features that could enhance the remote work on drawing activities over the shared space.

The results of work environment satisfaction question 1, **"I could utilize all my skills and abilities to solve this task in this environment"**, as shown in Fig. 8, were $M = 4.17$, $SD = 0.753$ (face to face), $M = 3.83$, $SD = 0.435$ (SyncMeet) and $M = 3.67$, $SD = 0.435$ (Skype). Using the two-way ANOVA, there was a significant difference for the main effect of the environment with a p-value = 0.043. As the result of multiple compositions, there was a significant difference between face to face and Skype with a p-value = 0.029.

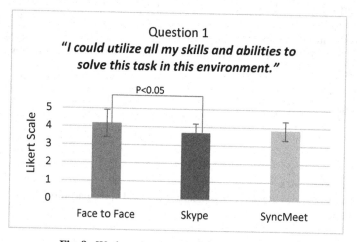

Fig. 8. Work environment satisfaction question 1.

The participants described during the interview that face to face environment always has the benefit of using all their skills and abilities easily to solve the problem. In addition, it was easier to talk while they were taking annotations during the session.

The result of work environment satisfaction question 3, **"I could concentrate on the task in this environment"**, as shown in Fig. 9, were $M = 4.33$, $SD = 0.404$ (face to face), $M = 4.17$, $SD = 0.149$ (SyncMeet) and $M = 3.50$, $SD = 0.404$ (Skype). Using the two-way ANOVA, there was a significant difference for the main effect of environment with a p-value = 0.020. As the result of multiple compositions, there was a significant difference between face to face and Skype with a p-value = 0.0041.

The participants mentioned that it was easier to lose concentration during Skype sessions because they were more aware of their own screens for taking annotations, compared to the face to face sessions. However, they described SyncMeet as "out of time-space" making the work more playful that helped them to have better concentration without distractions.

The results of work environment satisfaction question 4, **"I was aware of my partner's intention in this environment"**, as shown in Fig. 10 were $M = 4.50$, $SD = 0.548$

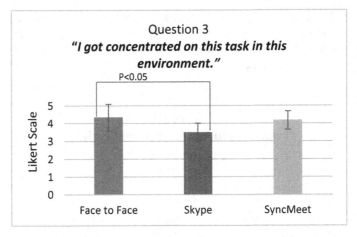

Fig. 9. Work environment satisfaction question 3.

for (face to face), $M = 4.17$, $SD = 0.447$ (SyncMeet) and $M = 3.67$, $SD = 0.492$ (Skype). Using the two-way ANOVA, there was a significant difference for the main effect of environment with a p-value = 0.015. As the result of multiple compositions, there was a significant difference between face to face and Skype with a p-value = 0.009.

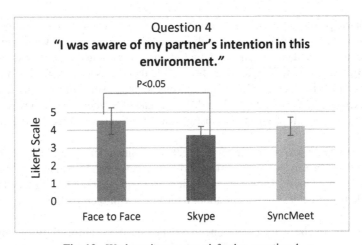

Fig. 10. Work environment satisfaction question 4.

By observation of the video recorded during the experiment, it was determined that the participants quickly get used to the face to face environment and the VR environment. The writer was seen to be more uncomfortable during the Skype session because they could only talk and had to use lengthy verbal explanations to describe their ideas for the drawing and panel composition.

The result of collaboration effectiveness question 3, **"I worked with my partner effectively"**, as shown in Fig. 11, were $M = 5.00$, $SD = 0$ (face to face), $M = 4.33$,

SD = 0.816 (SyncMeet) and M = 4.17, SD = 0.983 (Skype). Using the two-way ANOVA, there was a significant difference for the main effect of environment with a p-value = 0.013. As the result of multiple compositions, there was a significant difference between face to face and Skype with a p-value = 0.025.

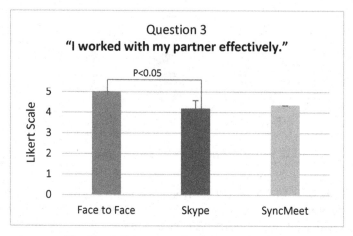

Fig. 11. Collaboration effectiveness question 3.

The participants mentioned that collaboration in the face to face environment was an excellent experience comparing it with Skype. The primary reason was that they felt that they could see and understand what their partner was doing during the experimental session. By comparing with SyncMeet, they stated that it was almost similar to a face to face environment interaction. One of the reasons was that, some of the participants felt more relaxed during the meeting in SyncMeet instead of Skype; because it was easier to act freely inside the VR room and not just paying attention to the screen in typical video conferences.

Both participants expressed that SyncMeet environment lets them share the information directly like face to face environment and is an excellent and novel way to brainstorm ideas or take annotations. However, the writer responded that not having facial expressions made them feel less confident about their work with their partner on a SyncMeet session.

The results of the work environment satisfaction question 6, **"I think my partner had a positive attitude to collaborate in this task"**, as shown in Fig. 12, were M = 4.55, SD = 0.314 (writer) and M = 4.778, SD = 0.314 (illustrator). Using the two-way ANOVA as the result of multiple compositions, there was a significant difference for the main effect of the user role with a p-value = 0.047.

The illustrators expressed that the writer participation have a more dynamic and innovative way of collaboration on face to face rather than working in Skype. In addition, they mentioned that SyncMeet was almost similar because they could share their visualization of the sketch and story script. All this lets t the writer felt more comfortable as if he/she was working in face to face environment.

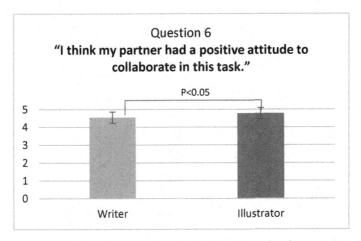

Fig. 12. Collaboration effectiveness question 6.

The results of communication efficiency question 1, "**I communicated efficiently with my partner.**", as shown in Fig. 13 were M = 4.5, SD = 0 (face to face), M = 4.33, SD = 0.816 (SyncMeet) and M = 4.17, SD = 0.983 (Skype). Using the two-way ANOVA, there was a significant difference for the main effect of environment with a p-value = 0.015. As the result of multiple compositions, there was a significant difference between face to face and Skype with a p-value = 0.0010.

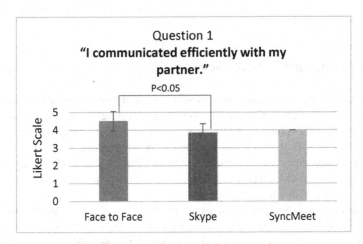

Fig. 13. Communication efficiency question 1.

The results of communication efficiency question 2, "**I think my partner communicated with me efficiently**", **as shown in** Fig. 14, were M = 4.67, SD = 0. 516 (face to face), M = 4.00, SD = 0.632 (SyncMeet) and M = 3.67, SD = 1.033 (Skype). Using the two-way ANOVA, there was a significant difference for the main effect of environment with a p-value = 0.010. As the result of multiple comparison, there was a significant difference between face to face and Skype with a p-value = 0.0011.

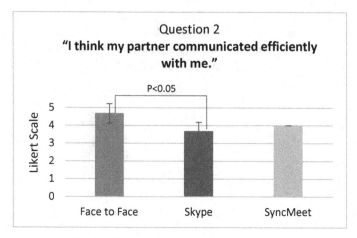

Fig. 14. Communication efficiency question 2.

Question 1 and 2 about communication efficiency shows that participants perceive both participants more efficiently on face to face environment in comparison with Skype. They mentioned that the lack of eye contact and non-verbal communication does not let them communicate easily and requires a bigger effort to verbally explain their ideas.

Additionally, the writers explained that they are less efficient in their communication through Skype. They were seen to be more uncomfortable because they only could talk and had to give lengthy explanations to describe their ideas for the drawing and panel comparisons.

6   Conclusions and Future Work

A virtual meeting room, SyncMeet was presented for distance collaboration that allowed two people with different narrative skills to create a four-panel manga (Japanese Comic). In SyncMeet, the users could communicate their creative ideas over their work quickly using an avatar and 3D objects inside a virtual work environment.

A fundamental aspect of this research was to create a new work environment for creative collaboration tasks. SyncMeet lets the users comprehend the advantages of VR environments for collaborative creative activities.

The participants expressed that working inside a virtual environment allows them to have an immersive experience and interact actively with their partner. In addition, the participants expressed that even if it was their first-time using VR, they felt very comfortable collaborating and explaining their ideas inside SyncMeet.

In future work, more functions will be added to SyncMeet, for example, tools for directly writing the script and drawing the storyboard in the virtual whiteboard and showing the differences between two version of storyboards. With these new functions, the illustrators and writers will be able to collaborate more efficiently during the creative process.

References

1. Cunningham, S., Berry, D., Earnshaw, R.A., Excell, P.S., Thompson, E.: Multi-disciplinary creativity and collaboration: utilizing crowd-accelerated innovation and the internet. In: International Conference on Cyberworlds (CW), Visby, 2015, pp. 271–277 (2015)
2. Gumienny, R., Gericke, L., Quasthoff, M., Willems, C., Meinel, C.: Tele-board: enabling efficient collaboration in digital design spaces. In: Proceedings of the 2011 15th International Conference on Computer Supported Cooperative Work in Design (CSCWD), Lausanne, 2011, pp. 47–54 (2011)
3. Gerry, L.J.: Paint with me: stimulating creativity and empathy while painting with a painter in virtual reality. IEEE Trans. Vis. Comput. Graph. **23**(4), 1418–1426 (2017)
4. Darabkh, K., Alturk, F., Sweidan, S.Z.: VRCDEA-TCS: 3D virtual reality cooperative drawing educational application with textual chatting system. Comput. Appl. Eng. Educ. **26**, 1677–1698 (2018)
5. Shaik, S.K., Yoo, K.: Interactive virtual exhibition: creating custom virtual art galleries using web technologies. In: Proceedings of the 24th ACM Symposium on Virtual Reality Software and Technology, pp. 99:1–99:2 (2018). Article no. 99
6. Keiko, K.: Preliminary research on the Japanese content development process: cases of manga. Kyoto Sangyo University Departmental Bulletin Paper (2011)
7. Toku, M.: Shojo Manga! Girls' Comics! A Mirror of Girls' Dreams. Mechademia **2**, 19–32 (2007)
8. Watabe, K., Abe, Y.: Pixiv as a contested online artistic space in-between gift and commercial economies in an age of participatory culture. EJCJS Electron. J. Contemp. Japan. Stud. **16**(3) (2016). https://www.japanesestudies.org.uk/ejcjs/vol16/iss3/watabe.html
9. Kajita, K., Yoshino, T., Munemori, J.: Development of a real-time four-frame strip cartoon creation support system for many people. J. Inf. Process. Soc. Jpn. **44**, 317–327 (2003)
10. Mencarini, E., Schiavo, G., Cappelletti, A., Stock, O., Zancanaro, M.: Assessing a collaborative application for comic strips composition. In: Abascal, J., Barbosa, S., Fetter, M., Gross, T., Palanque, P., Winckler, M. (eds.) INTERACT 2015. LNCS, vol. 9297, pp. 73–80. Springer, Cham (2015). https://doi.org/10.1007/978-3-319-22668-2_6
11. Hong, S.W., El Antably, A., Kalay, Y.E.: Architectural design creativity in multi-user virtual environment: a comparative analysis between remote collaboration media. Environ. Plan. B Urban Anal. City Sci. **46**(5), 826–844 (2019)
12. Fröhlich, T., Alexandrovsky, D., Stabbert, T., Döring, T., Malaka, R.: VRBox: a virtual reality augmented sandbox for immersive playfulness, creativity and exploration. In: Proceedings of the 2018 Annual Symposium on Computer-Human Interaction, (CHI PLAY 2018), pp. 153–162. ACM, New York (2018)
13. Narasimha, S., Scharett, E., Madathil, K.C., Bertrand, J.: WeRSort: preliminary results from a new method of remote collaboration facilitated by fully immersive virtual reality. Proc. Hum. Factors Ergon. Soc. Annu. Meet. **62**(1), 2084–2088 (2018)
14. Sankaranarayanan, G., et al.: Immersive virtual reality-based training improves response in a simulated operating room fire scenario. Surg. Endosc. **32**(8), 3439–3449 (2018). https://doi.org/10.1007/s00464-018-6063-x
15. Shen, C., Ho, J., Ly, P.T.M., et al.: Behavioural intentions of using virtual reality in learning: perspectives of acceptance of information technology and learning style. Virtual Real. Augment. Real. Commer. **23**, 313–324 (2019). https://doi.org/10.1007/s10055-018-0348-1
16. Bolier, W., Hürst, W., Van Bommel, G., Bosman, J., Bosman, H.: Drawing in a virtual 3D space - introducing VR drawing in elementary school art education. In: Proceedings of the 26th ACM International Conference on Multimedia (MM 2018), pp. 337–345. ACM, New York (2018)

17. Greenwald, S.W., Wang, Z., Funk, M., Maes, P.: Investigating social presence and communication with embodied avatars in room-scale virtual reality. In: Beck, D., Allison, C., Morgado, L., Pirker, J., Khosmood, F., Richter, J., Gütl, C. (eds.) iLRN 2017. CCIS, vol. 725, pp. 75–90. Springer, Cham (2017). https://doi.org/10.1007/978-3-319-60633-0_7
18. Kulik, A., et al.: Virtual valcamonica: collaborative exploration of prehistoric petroglyphs and their surrounding environment in multi-user virtual reality. Presence Teleoperators Virtual Environ. **26**(3), 297–321 (2018)
19. Piumsomboon, T., et al.: Mini-me: an adaptive avatar for mixed reality remote collaboration. In: CHI 2018 Proceedings of the 2018 CHI Conference on Human Factors in Computing Systems, Paper no. 46, pp. 46:1–46:13 (2018)
20. Maynard, S.K.: Japanese Communication: Language and Thought in Context, pp. 159–162. University of Hawai'i Press, Honolulu (1997)

Usability Design Study of University Website: A Case of Normal University in China

Yu Tian and Zhen Liu$^{(\boxtimes)}$ ⓘ

School of Design, South China University of Technology, Guangzhou 510006,
People's Republic of China
liuzjames@scut.edu.cn

Abstract. With the development of network technology, the university website has become an important online platform for the university. In terms of university website, the usability of the website affects the user experience and efficiency of teachers and students greatly. Although the importance of usability is gradually valued, the usability of university website is still criticized by many people, and even seriously affects the online service of university teaching. There are few studies looking into the problem. This paper takes a university website, i.e. South China Normal University, as an example, sets 3 typical scenarios from different groups of students, such as preschool student, current student and alumni, tests the usability of the website through experiments and uses eye tracker to track users' eye movements, observes users' behavior, collects users' opinions, and puts forward some improvement suggestions. The research finds that, the university website developer should consider the users' previous school website using habits and take advantage of the "habitually obvious", and try to develop a ordered and normal structure for the university website, which considering the identity of the users and sort the functions in groups of characters. These results provide ideas for improving the usability design of the university website by taking the South China Normal University for instance.

Keywords: Usability testing · University website · Eye-tracking · Usability design

1 Introduction

Website as a university's network facade and network platform has a very important role. With the development of Internet, more and more educational matters need to be completed through Internet [1]. The university website runs through the whole campus life, the functions various from getting the teachers introduction to completing the routine items online. However, "the university website is not easy to use" has always been the complaint that students in various universities have [2]. Students often comment that they can't find what they want on the university website, the announcement is not clear, and information can't get to them in time. In addition, a university website that is not easy to use may also bring a bad social impression to the university.

© Springer Nature Switzerland AG 2020
A. Marcus and E. Rosenzweig (Eds.): HCII 2020, LNCS 12202, pp. 533–551, 2020.
https://doi.org/10.1007/978-3-030-49757-6_39

The quality of the website has always been a key factor affecting the users' of behaviors [3]. The usability of the website has a great impact on the quality of the website [4]. More and more researchers have realized the significance of university website usability in improving the efficiency of students' work. They have studied and analyzed some website user behaviors, and put forward some suggestions for website construction [5, 6]. In order to study and improve the usability of the university website, this paper selected the homepage of South China Normal University as the experimental website, researched its usability, collected the relevant user opinions, and put forward the relevant improvement suggestions.

In this paper, the experiment had been done implemented with the actual situation, through the typical steps of website usability test and the eye tracking [7–10]. In this project, three scenarios and several tasks for each scenario are set.

2   Method

The study is about observing users using the website South China Normal University School Page, studying the usability of the website and giving suggestions on the better construction of the website.

In this study, ten users have completed the scenarios-tasks and the Eyetracking tasks. The usability test recorded the process by using video and recorder, and also took some notes for their operating steps. After the tests, the data including videos has been analyzed with results that provide direction for the improvement.

2.1   How Evaluation Conducted

According to the use of the websites in real life, three scenarios had been set to test the website, each scenario had several tasks. Concerning the participants are students, and mostly of them have at least once used university website, the three sorts of student-scenarios were set as the testing scenarios, which were a graduate from other college or university, a current student of South China Normal University, and a alumnus of South China Normal University. The scenarios were presented as a time flow, which can approximately simulated the proficiency growth process of natural users of the website.

Scenario 1: A graduate student from another college wants to be recommended to South China Normal University as a postgraduate student in School of Psychology. He is trying to find ways to contact the professor, for instance, Lu Aitao (a professor in School of Psychology in SCNU) and contact the School of Psychology to get more about the enrollment information. Also, he wants to know the time of the recommendation interview.

Presenting first, this scenario simulated the freshman of the university and who is not familiar with the website, which is similar to the situation of the participant who first come to the website. The tasks of Scenario 1 are shown in Table 1.

Scenario 2: A current student of South China Normal University, who wants to know the school calendar of the semester, and also wants to find out how to apply for a grant,

Table 1. Tasks of Scenario 1.

No.	Content
Task 1-1	Find the e-mail address of professor Lu Aitao
Task 1-2	Find the recommendation interview time of School of Psychology
Task 1-3	Find the phone number of School of Psychology

as shown in Table 2. Also he wants to seek if there are some jobs as he is going to leave the university and become a teacher.

Thinking that the school should be a daily online tool for the current students, the Scenario 2 was set as a current student who needs to use the website to solve problems. As these are the daily matters of a student in the university, it can test out major problems that the website has, and make the evaluation more practical. The tasks were set as following Table 2.

Table 2. Tasks of Scenario 2.

No.	Content
Task 2-1	Find the school calendar
Task 2-2	Find the process guidance of applying a grant
Task 2-3	Find the Open Recruitment Brochure, for instance, the Affiliated High School of SCNU's

Scenario 3: A new alumnus of South China Normal University, who is keen on making more memory in the school and wants to find out if there are some commemoration or alumni activities he can attend.

As the last scenario, alumnus is the one who is a bit more familiar with the website, so as the participant who has used the website complete the former scenarios and tasks. With the higher familiarity, the participant may find out the information more quickly. As the most typical activity, one task was set for this scenario as Table 3.

Table 3. Scenario 3's tasks

No.	Content
Task 3-1	Find the alumnus activity presenting recently, such as taking graduation photos

2.2 Participant Sample Description

The participants were ten students from School of Design, South China University of Technology. They were all postgraduates and also freshmen, half of who were recommended to the university, and other part of who had taken part in the postgraduate entrance exams, which was similar to the situation of the website's natural users.

The other information of the participants is shown in Fig. 1.

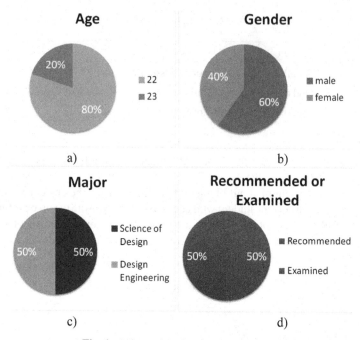

Fig. 1. Information about the participants.

3 Result

3.1 Performance Results

The time each participant spent on the tasks and the fork roads they made were recorded, and as shown in Tables 4, 5 and 6.

Table 4. The completing time of the tasks in Scenario 1.

No.	User	Total time/s	Time of task 1-1/s	Fork road of task 1-1	Time of task 1-2/s	Fork road of task 1-2	Time of task 1-3/s	Fork road of task 1-3
1	J. Qiu	213	54	0	142	1	17	0
2	RY. Du	299	259	4	33	2	7	0
3	YT. Liu	115	37	0	69	1	9	0
4	X. Jin	450	238	2	87	1	125	1
5	LF. Ren	417	247	9	143	2	27	0
6	GS. Liu	223	111	2	107	1	5	0

(continued)

Table 4. (*continued*)

No.	User	Total time/s	Time of task 1-1/s	Fork road of task 1-1	Time of task 1-2/s	Fork road of task 1-2	Time of task 1-3/s	Fork road of task 1-3
7	ZX. Yan	384	313	3	62	1	9	0
8	YK. Huang	169	108	0	61	0	0	0
9	KJ. Liu	539	78	0	49	1	412	5
10	Y. Wan	739	160	2	353	1	226	0
Average		354.8	160.5	2.2	110.6	1.1	83.7	0.6
Sum		3548	1605	22	1106	11	837	6
Variance		36437.96	9450.50	7.73	8636.93	0.32	18626.90	2.49
Standard Deviation		190.89	97.21	2.78	92.94	0.57	136.48	1.58

Table 5. The completing time of the tasks in Scenario 2.

No.	User	Total time/s	Time of task 2-1/s	Fork road of task 2-1	Time of task 2-2/s	Fork road of task 2-2	Time of task 2-3/s	Fork road of task 2-3
1	J. Qiu	402	59	0	$182 + 40^b$	5	161	3
2	RY. Du	356	39	0	259	5	58	2
3	YT. Liu	206	Failed (count as 60 s)[a]	$43 + 20$	$1 + 0$	103	2	
4	X. Jin	699	463	3	162	5	71	1
5	LF. Ren	53	22	0	$15 + 156$	$0 + 2$	16	1
6	GS. Liu	235	165	2	$52 + 52$	$1 + 1$	18	0
7	ZX. Yan	208	109	0	$27 + 64$	$0 + 1$	12	0
8	YK. Huang	139	46	1	26	0	67	2
9	KJ. Liu	636	405	4	269	5	22	0
10	Y. Wan	534	184	1	139	0	151	1

(*continued*)

Table 5. (*continued*)

No.	User	Total time/s	Time of task 2-1/s	Fork road of task 2-1	Time of task 2-2/s	Fork road of task 2-2	Time of task 2-3/s	Fork road of task 2-3
Average		346.8	165.8	1.2	171	3	67.9	1.2
Sum		3468	1492	11	855	15	679	12
Variance		47438.40	26452.19	2.19	9869.50	7.50	3036.54	1.07
Standard Deviation		217.80	162.64	1.48	99.35	2.74	55.10	1.03

[a]This task failed because the network went wrong but not of the reason of the participant. Concerning the actual experiment process, combining with the time this participant took in other tasks and the time other participants used completing this task, the time counted as 60 s.
[b]Because there were multiple task results in this task, the number on the left side of the plus sign indicates the time participants spent finding their first result, and the one on the right side indicates the time spent finding the expected task result after prompt. The plus sign in the cell of the Fork road of task 2-2 has same meaning.

Table 6. The completing time of the tasks in Scenario 3.

No.	User	Time of task 2-1/s	Fork road of task 2-1
1	J. Qiu	37	0
2	RY. Du	44	0
3	YT. Liu	70	1
4	X. Jin	48	0
5	LF. Ren	18	0
6	GS. Liu	23	0
7	ZX. Yan	45	0
8	YK. Huang	114	1
9	KJ. Liu	21	0
10	Y. Wan	166	2
Average		58.6	0.4
Sum		586	4
Variance		2226.71	0.49
Standard Deviation		47.19	0.70

As shown in the Tables 4, 5 and 6, each person's completing time are various and even have huge difference between each other. It can be seen from the data in the table that the data variance is large, that is, the data results of each test participant are quite different. The individual analysis of each participant is more meaningful than the collective analysis. To get a general concept of the efficiency, the time and the fork road taken by a participant of each task were accumulated and an average of them had been made. Completing time shows the overall efficiency of users, while the number of fork roads presents the misleading rate of the website. In addition, the combination of time and number of fork roads indicates whether the user was misled and took more time on trying the various paths, or just spent too much time in one step page on finding the correct information, and by which whether the information layout of the page is reasonable and easy to find can be judged.

It could be found that the scenario 1 took participants the most time to complete, and the Scenario 3 (the time recorded has been multiplied three times to make comparison with the number from scenario 1) took the least, which fits the situation that the participants getting more and more familiar with the website. The task which took the most time was task 2-2, which had the least clues to follow when trying to find the way to the information. Participants carried out 3 different but reasonable outcomes during the test. The expected outcome whose information block seems to be placed the most apparently got the least attention. Almost none of the users noticed it without guidance. What's more, task 1-1 and task 2-1 also took a little more time than other tasks, showing that the website path of these tasks has more problems to pay attention to. On the other hand, task 3-1 had the least finding time and the least fork road had been taken. That's because almost all the users had noticed the entrance of alumni (the role entry) when doing the former tests. The function design of the role entry is good and useful indeed.

3.2 Satisfaction Results

The satisfaction feedback is shown in Table 7.

Because the former parts of the experiments did not consider the mark of users giving, the five former tests have no record of the marks. Their comments and advice had been recorded, and will been shown in the next chapter.

It can be seen that people who had used similar university website more than once have a higher acceptance of the problems existing in the university website, so they were more satisfied with the university website. Task 1-1 and Task 3-1 have higher satisfaction, which shows that the relationship between satisfaction and duration is not particularly large. Through observation, it can be seen that, after the user found the first correct entry in Task 1-1, the subsequent steps are relatively simple and smooth, which may led the user's satisfaction in this task improved.

In Task 1-1, the improvement of smoothness mainly occurs after entering the website of psychological college, so if the main website of the university is redesigned, it can be referred to the logic and layout of the website of the School of Psychology college. The high satisfaction of Task 3-1 is mainly due to the increased familiarity with the website in the earlier stage and the useful function of the role entry, which quickly guided users to the correct alumni pages. Also, the logic and layout of alumni pages are relatively clear, so that the users can quickly complete their tasks. Task 2-1 has lower satisfaction,

Table 7. Satisfaction of the participants.

No.	User	Scenario 1			Scenario 2			Scenario 3	Total Mark	Sum of the Marks	Subentry Satisfaction
		Mark of task 1-1	Mark of task 1-2	Mark of task 1-3	Mark of task 2-1	Mark of task 2-2	Mark of task 2-3	Mark of task 3-1			
1	J. Qiu										
2	RY. Du										
3	YT. Liu										
4	X. Jin										
5	LF. Ren										
6	GS. Liu	6	6	7	3	4	4	8	6	38	54.3%
7	ZX. Yan	5	3	3	6	6	8	6	5	37	52.9%
8	YK. Huang	9	9	9	9	8	6	9	9	59	84.3%
9	KJ. Liu	10	9	6	5	9	10	10	7	59	84.3%
10	Y. Wan	7	3	4	5	7	6	7	6	39	55.7%
Average		7.4	6	5.8	5.6	6.8	6.8	8	6.6		
Sum		37	30	29	28	34	34	40	33		
Variance		4.3	9	5.7	4.8	3.7	5.2	2.5	2.3		
Standard Deviation		2.07	3.00	2.39	2.19	1.92	2.28	1.58	1.52		
Satisfction		74.0%	60.0%	58.0%	56.0%	68.0%	68.0%	80.0%	66.0%		

and Task 1-3 has also the lower satisfaction. Part of the reason is that some participants' original habits of browsing web pages were not reflected in this website, and part of the reason is that the website does not do a good job in information sorting, for which the information points were scattered and had no clue that led to them directly.

Although the satisfaction of Task 2-2 is fine, it took the longest time and had the most various unexpected results. The main problem lied in the logic of the website, which guided users to multiple different results via different paths. At the same time, the search function was weak, and similar to Task 2-3, the information entry point was put subjectively obvious rather than habitually obvious ("habitually obvious" here means users may find it naturally and think they're obvious according to the habitual behavior but not only the visual typesetting) The expected application process guidance of the grant was not placed in the column of "awards and grants", but listed separately under the sub-homepage. Another example of this "subjectively obvious" problem was appeared in Task2-1. There were two direct calendar buttons in the website. One was in the center of the page of the academic affairs office, but the icon was small and had no association with other function. While the other one was in the navigation menu of the "Come into Huashi" in the home page, but users generally could not immediately associate the button with the name "Come into Huashi" without knowing it in advance. As the observation in the test, if there is no manual guidance, plenty of large search error may occur. According to the interview content, the satisfaction source of Task 2-2 mainly comes from the smoothness of finding the first result and the "surprise feeling" after the original expected results shown to them, which can be said as "I really think it is reasonable after seeing the answer".

3.3   User Behavior Comments and Analysis

Users have some typical behaviors, which are shown in Table 8.

Through the observation, some other inferentially typical users' behaviors are also observed, which are listed and analyzed briefly in Table 9.

The participants commonly have indicated the natural habits and the subconscious of the users. The developers can take advantage of these behaviors, and construct the website's paths base on the behaviors, for example, add entry to teacher introduction page in the page of Postgraduate Admissions Office.

Also, the users' comments have been collected, from which we can learn the website's usability problems directly. The very common comments appeared were "university websites are usually bad.", "not easy to find the information" and so on. Many participants hoped the titles, buttons and labels can be more obvious and clear. Some other users' comments during and after the test are sorted out as shown in Table 10, behind following the analysis.

Besides, lesson can be learnt from the other comments, which are:

1. Proper use of labels will better guide users.
2. Better to put thing within one page instead of jumping to another page.
3. The search function is important and need to be good design its logic.
4. The connection between important web pages should be more direct
5. The disunity of web design (for example, new and old versions exist at the same time) will also affect the efficiency of searching information.
6. The titles and buttons should be simpler and clearer.
7. The general introduction can be placed in the column of the home page instead of occupying the subpage.
8. Different colors can be used to classify different kinds of information when designing.

Table 8. Users' typical behaviors.

No.	Behaviors	Approximate proportion
1	Like to use search	70% of the participants used it
2	Go to the Postgraduate Admissions Office to find teacher information	60% of the participants had such behavior
3	First look at the navigation bar instead of the page information	From task 2-1, task 2-2 observation, 60% of the participants had this tendency
4	Can't see the role button and other option buttons in the upper right corner	70% of the participants only entered the web page from the role entrance after being prompted
5	Scrolling pages automatically	40% were used to doing so
6	Direct observation without first scrolling the page	Almost everyone did this
7	Give up searching whether the similar information appears in other places of the page after finding the approximate information of the task	60% of the people would be misled according to the observation of task 2-2
8	Exit the page without scanning after failing getting to the task result via entering one of the entries on the web page	About 60% would do so
9	Browse the announcement information first	40% of people would first scan the announcement information that may be useful
10	Not browse the announcement information below but directly click the buttons	Almost happened to every one

Table 9. Users' other observed behaviors.

No.	Behaviors
1	Jumping to the next new page, if the page jumps fast and uninterrupted, the user's eyesight may stay at the last position of the previous page, and notice the contents there first
2	After 3.4 errors on average, the user will enter the "try" state and search for the path entry by enumeration; after entering the "try" state, the user's patience will decline and the possibility of "ignore" will increase
3	Indirect contact content will interrupt the user's thinking process and affect the user's memory of the purpose (for example, the login interface that pops up suddenly will affect the user's thinking. After jumping out of the page, several users asked again about the purpose of the task)

Table 10. Comments and analysis of some users.

Participants' comments	Analysis
"The homepage is good-looking", "simple and comfortable"	There were still many commendable evaluations of the website interface design. The beautiful interface can give a good mood to the users
"I can't tell the names of colleges and departments very clearly." "Talent recruitment and employment navigation are easy to confuse"	This comment is partly caused by the user's own reasons. The developers can use the name prompt or sort the similar titles into different category box to prompt the user the differences. Different entrances can be set to achieve two buttons to prevent them from appearing on the same page, or they can be adjacent to each other for direct comparison by users
"Lucky"	Many participants presented this word after doing the tasks, because they thought they found the information just by accident
"The recruitment information is put too low. There is a useless big picture in the upper part, which takes up a lot of space, and I don't want to browse down."	For task 2-1. It shows that developers should consider whether the placed information is necessary and put the most essential information on the most obvious place
"There is a problem with the setting position of the navigation bar." "The same as the school page of SCUT"	Pay attention to the "habitually obvious". Participants' habits will affect their efficiency in using other web pages
"Want to log in to student account"	Users' subjective intuitive feeling is that he/she can access more detailed information after logging in
"I tried several times to find the way and was really surprised when I went in."	Some paths are unexpected to the user, This is not good for better usability

3.4 Eye-Tracking Analysis

As shown in Fig. 2, the user's eyesight starts at the center of the screen, and then turns to the navigation bar first. It can be seen that the user tends to browse the navigation bar first rather than other content parts of the web page.

As shown in Fig. 3, the navigation bar is still in the priority for users, even after the page is changed. It is indicated that good button settings on navigation bar can effectively improve the efficiency of web pages.

As shown in Fig. 4, eye movement thermograph, which is reflected the thinking time of the user, user stay in the navigation bar for a long time. Longer staying time means more consideration and more attention, so the key content can be inspired listed in the navigation bar as a title.

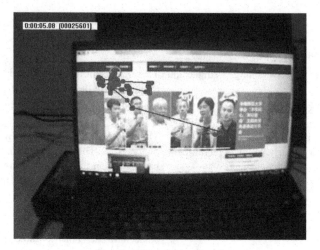

Fig. 2. User eye tracking 1

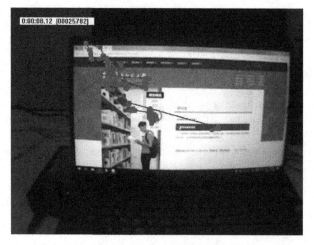

Fig. 3. User eye tracking 2

It can be seen from Fig. 5, eye movement thermograph that, except for the long staying time on the navigation or title bar, the main staying time is in the middle left position of the web page. This is because when users search for information, they mainly filter through the head field of the information line (which is at the left of the sentence), and only after finding the corresponding heading can they see the following fields. Besides, the middle position of the web page is the most comfortable position for the user's eyesight, so when browsing and sliding the long full page information content, the eye's observation area generally stays in the middle of the web page . The other

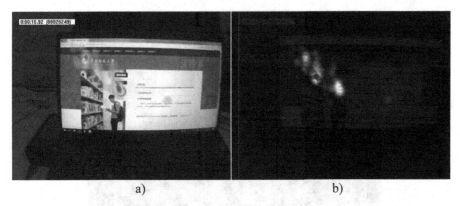

Fig. 4. User's eye tracking thermograph 1

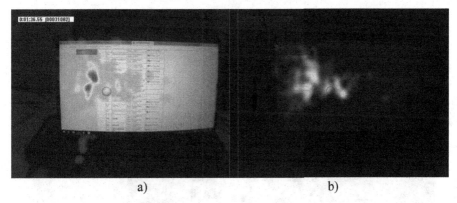

Fig. 5. User's eye tracking thermograph 2

information would be transmitted to this area by sliding. Therefore, when designing a web page, the developers can put the labels or important words which can be used to identify indication of the sentence in the left area of the web page. Further, the beginning and the end of the long content can be placed in the middle of the up and down direction of the web page.

In the grant application task, the Task 2-2, the eye-tracking is shown in Fig. 6. The path of eye movement is scattered and has almost been searching all parts of the navigation bar. It indicates that the entry classification of the website under this task is not appropriate and the title prompt guidance is not clear. The correct entry of this task should be the top right corner of the page (the red circle part in Fig. 7), but due to the blocking effect of the pull-down navigation bar (see the top half of Fig. 5), this part The entry is hard to find.

Fig. 6. User eye tracking 3.

Fig. 7. Role entry in the website of South China Normal University.

3.5 Concept for Improvement

The first problem to be solved is the logic of the website. There are logic problems that are listed in Table 11.

Table 11. Logic problems of the website.

No.	Logic problems
1	Weakness of the search function, incomplete website information and scattered search results
2	Multiple paths lead to different results
3	Disordered information classification

The second problem to be solved is the layout of the website and the helping tips to the users, which are listed in Table 12.

Table 12. Layout problems of the website.

No.	Layout problems
1	The title of navigation bar is not concise or clear enough
2	Buttons easy to be covered in navigation bar
3	Unreasonable arrangement of some information points
4	Lack of label components or tips related to the content

In the view of the above problems, the test put forward some improvement directions as shown in Table 13.

Table 13. Improvement directions of the website.

No.	Improvement directions
1	Standardize the format of information placement, and ensure the consistency of the new and old pages
2	Refer to some highly rated web pages and arrange information points according to users' habits
3	Multiple entries and routes should be directed to the same result page
4	Optimize the search function and add the things that cannot be found
5	Release information in the form of official documents, make them standardized and unified, and improve the credibility of them
6	Make good use of labels for documents or news to prompt the contents and improve their availability of searching

3.6 Redesign of the Website

The redesigned web pages are shown as below, which partially solve the problems of unclear title information and unreasonable layout.

The position of the role entry has been changed to be more obvious, which is shown in Fig. 8.

The navigation bar's layout is also improved. First, the improved shape of bars is designed to make less shelter the other information. Then, rearranged buttons are used for more unified and easier to get the information of links. The example is made in Fig. 9.

In addition, logic problems of the website have been addressed, such as getting to the teachers' introduction page not only from the college section but also can through the enrollment section via a special entry.

a) the ancient one

b) the redesign one

Fig. 8. The change of some buttons on the homepage of college website.

3.7 Evaluation Results

The new experiment was carried out on the original participants with the new web page. The evaluation and corresponding analysis are as shown in Table 14.

Table 14. Comments and analysis of users for the prototype.

Participants' comments	Analysis
"Faster than the original" "easier to find"	The improvement according to the "habitually obvious" is useful
"This role entry is easier to see"	The rearrangement of the original role entrances make it convenient for users to use the functions of the website. The more directly the information to be seen, the more efficiency would be brought out

(*continued*)

Table 14. (*continued*)

Participants' comments	Analysis
"Search still doesn't work"	The logical structure of the website is difficult to improve in a short time. It may be improved in the future work
"Prefer this role entry"	The role entry brought its advantages into full play under the new web page, because of the higher rate of notice
"Login button is very convenient"	Unifying the login content to the login button of the home page is indeed more integrated, more intuitive and convenient, and it decreases the rate of disturbing by the bumping up login page as before

a) the ancient one

b) the redesign one

Fig. 9. Changes to the navigation bar.

4   Discussion and Conclusions

According to the observation and results analysis of the experimental process, several opinions and conclusions are obtained as follows:

1. The decisive factor of usability lies in the logic of website content path and the layout of content board. Also according to the observation, a good and clear navigation bar or framework can greatly improve users' time efficiency. The developers should make more effort to combine and improve the website's logic and layout.
2. New student users will make more mistakes when they first enter the website, but after they are familiar with the website, the efficiency of using the website will be greatly improved. This is not only about website logic and framework, but also about users' own habits. On the other hand, to improve the usability of the website, the developers can make the website more unified and standardized among similar universities and schools, so that the logical format of the website is not so different from the university website previously used by the student users. Also the developers can pay attention to the user's "habitually obvious". These can help improve the usability of the website substantially.
3. The university website is a kind of educational website. Because of its obvious functional characteristics and typical user groups (e.g. teachers and students), its website design should more highlight the needs of these specific user groups. For example, it should clearly separate the functions that can be used only when users log in and the functions can be used without logging in, and place the web pages that can be displayed only after logging in to a specialized entry.
4. Considering the certain error rate of the users, since it is hard for the developers to fully consider all possible errors that users may take. Hence, the developers should also allow using certain user's own adaptability and tolerance for the task completion. Besides classifying the confusing items into different parent directories as far as possible, they can also rely on the user's own self judgment and understanding when necessary. For example, the confusing items can be placed in the adjacent positions that are easy to be observed at the same time, so that the user can intuitively distinguish them and minimize the time waste after realize the wrong path.
5. The university's website is the university's online facade. A good-looking webpage can improve the university's impression, and at the same time, it can delight the users' mood and enhance the user experience. The website designer should perfect the beauty of the website on the basis of ensuring the usability, such as setting the floating menu that looks good but does not block the information.

In the future, the developers of education websites may unify the structure of each university website to create better university website with logic, classify the functions of the university websites, and arrange and combine the website's functions for users with specific roles.

Acknowledgements. The authors wish to thank all the people participated in this research. This research is supported by "South China University of Technology Central University Basic Scientific Research Operating Expenses Subsidy (project approval no. XYZD201928)".

References

1. Carmel, T., Barnes, A.: The school website: facilitating communication engagement and learning. Br. J. Educ. Technol. **47**(2), 421–436 (2016)
2. Ramakrishnan, S., Yang, Y.: Mining web logs to improve website organization. In: Proceedings of the 10th international conference on World Wide Web (2001)
3. Umair, A.: How website quality affects online impulse buying. Asia Pac. J. Mark. Logist. (2018)
4. Julie, J., Stephanidis, C.: Human-Computer Interaction: Theory and Practice (Part 2), vol. 2. CRC Press, Boca Raton (2003)
5. Jurkowski, O.: School library website components. TechTrends **48**(6), 56–60 (2004)
6. Tubin, D., Sarit, K.: Designing a school website: contents, structure, and responsiveness. Plan. Chang. **38**, 191–207 (2007)
7. Dumas, J.S., Joseph, S.D., Janice, R.: A Practical Guide to Usability Testing. Intellect Books (1999)
8. Erik, F., Hertzum, M., Hornbæk, K.: Measuring usability: are effectiveness, efficiency, and satisfaction really correlated? In: Proceedings of the SIGCHI Conference on Human Factors in Computing Systems (2000)
9. Nielsen, J.: Usability inspection methods. In: Conference Companion on Human Factors in Computing Systems (1994)
10. Nielsen, J.: Usability Engineering. Morgan Kaufmann, Burlington (1994)

Designing an Innovative Collaborative Learning Application: The Case of Method 300

Virginia Tiradentes Souto[1]([⊠]) (iD), Ricardo Ramos Fragelli[1] (iD),
and Wilson Henrique Veneziano[2] (iD)

[1] Design Department, Campus Universitário Darcy Ribeiro, ICC Norte, University of Brasilia,
Módulo 18, Brasília, DF 70910-900, Brazil
`v.tiradentes@gmail.com`, `fragelli@unb.br`
[2] Computer Science Department, University of Brasilia, Brasília, DF 70910-900, Brazil
`wilsonhe@unb.br`

Abstract. The number of mobile learning applications is increasing and they are considered a powerful learning tool by many researchers. Among the reasons for this success are their specific characteristics, such as portability and pervasiveness, which can help student engagement and improve learning. They can also be useful for collaborative learning. This paper presents the methodology that is being used to design the Method 300 application. Method 300 is based on an active and collaborative approach that aims to improve the learning process of a team of students. At the moment, it is applied with the help of some tools, such as forms and spreadsheets. While these tools are useful, they make it somewhat laborious for teachers to organize all the documents, especially for large classes. This paper describes the empathic and collaborative approach to designing the Method 300 app, while placing educational, design and computational issues on the same level of relevance to incorporate the decisions made. The focus of this paper is to describe the application development methodology and not the application itself. Initially, a review about collaborative learning applications is presented. Then, Method 300 is presented, followed by the description of the methodology for designing the application. It is concluded that the Method 300 app has great potential to spread this method worldwide and that the empathic multidisciplinary collaborative approach to designing this application can be considered in different contexts.

Keywords: Designing mobile applications · Mobile learning applications · Active methodology · Collaborative learning · Method 300

1 Introduction

Collaborative learning approaches are being applied and investigated by many researchers and teachers in various fields [e.g. 1–4]. "Collaborative learning is based on the idea that learning is a naturally social act in which the learners talk among themselves" [5]. According to Laal and Laal [6], collaborative learning approaches involve

© Springer Nature Switzerland AG 2020
A. Marcus and E. Rosenzweig (Eds.): HCII 2020, LNCS 12202, pp. 552–565, 2020.
https://doi.org/10.1007/978-3-030-49757-6_40

groups of students working together to solve a problem cooperatively (in contrast to the competition) to complete a task and/or create a product.

In addition to collaborative learning, another methodology widely used as an alternative strategy to conventional teaching models is active learning [e.g. 7]. Active learning is usually defined as "any instructional method that engages students in the learning process" [7]. According to Pinheiro and Simões [8], active and collaborative practices in ICT (Information and Communication Technologies) classrooms are an emerging area that investigates how students can learn together with the help of computers.

Active methodologies can assist in meaningful learning [9] and there has been growing interest from the academic community in the past two decades. These methodologies aim for greater engagement in the classroom and more meaningful learning on the part of the student. Some of these methodologies are: peer instruction [10], flipped classroom [11] and serious games [12]. Collaborative learning can enhance active learning by changing the traditional teacher-centered learning environment to an environment in which students are responsible for the learning process [13].

Mobile technology is considered suitable for engaging collaborative learning environments, as it offers many opportunities for a group of people to participate in achieving a specific goal using mobile devices [5]. Currently, mobile learning is attracting a lot of attention worldwide and the number of users is increasing dramatically [14]. Mobile learning provides unique features, such as portability, user mobility, pervasiveness, and ubiquity, and therefore makes the learning experience more interesting [15]. However, there are many aspects, and care must be taken to design mobile applications for collaborative learning in order to meet the users' needs. Socio-technical, economic and historical aspects must be studied in the context in which mobile collaborative learning is implemented [16]. Vavoula and Karagiannidis [17] mention that rapid advances in mobile technology and incompatibility between devices and operating systems are examples of problems that need to be taken into account when designing mobile learning applications.

In addition, there are many usability issues that should considered in the design of these applications, such as the fact that their devices are small, their means of input are limited and user contexts are dynamic [16, 18]. Therefore, these characteristics make this type of application demand full attention from the user [18]. However, newer applications accommodate mobile challenges, such as partial user attention and interruption, or use new technological resources, in order to convince the student to use technology as an aid to learning [19].

A recent method that focuses on active and collaborative learning is known as Method 300 [20]. This method consists of promoting collaboration between students who scored well with those who did not score well. In this method students perceive themselves as active members of the group, being able to assist other members both in meaningful learning and in the human aspect [20].

This research focuses on the methodology of designing the Method 300 app. The application is intended for mobile devices such as tablets and smartphones. The approach to designing this tool is also based on a collaborative approach by researchers from three areas: the researcher and the teacher who invented the method; a researcher with experience in developing applications focused on educational and back-end systems;

and a researcher with experience in UX design and creative and innovative application design process.

Therefore, this paper describes the empathic approach to designing Method 300 while placing the educational, design and computational issues at the same level of relevance to incorporate the decisions made. The focus of this paper is to describe the methodology of development of the application and not the application itself. Initially, a discussion on collaborative learning applications is presented. Then, method 300 is presented, followed by the description of the methodology for designing the application. Finally, there is a discussion about the methodology and future actions.

2 Collaborative Learning Applications

Collaborative learning encourages students to progress while working together when they learn, answer questions or solve problems [21]. In this type of approach, teachers are considered more as designers specializing in intellectual experiences for students than as specialized transmitters of knowledge [6, 22]. Among the benefits of collaborative learning are: development of high-level thinking skills, oral communication, self-management and leadership; promotion of student-student interaction; increased self-esteem, responsibility and understanding from different perspectives; and preparation for social and employment situations in real life [21]. Research shows that active, social, contextual, engaging and student-owned educational experiences lead to deeper learning [21].

Currently, the use of collaborative learning approaches on mobile devices is a reality that can bring many benefits to education. The use of learning applications offers teachers the opportunity to use mobile technology to promote meaningful learning [23]. Khaddage, Müller and Flintoff [19] claim that mobile technologies for learning have great potential to provide access to learning in authentic work contexts. In addition, mobile devices have great potential for e-learning in terms of ubiquity, pervasiveness, personalization and flexibility [21, 24].

Caballé, Xhafab and Barollic [24] state that the success of MCSCL (Mobile Computer-Supported Collaborative Learning) is based on the ability of these applications to incorporate mobility to support the collaborative learning process. These authors also point to three-dimensional perspectives of MCSCL: pedagogical perspective (a new paradigm with students as active and central actors in learning process and learning happens anywhere); technological perspective (technology is getting smaller, more personal, ubiquitous, pervasive, and powerful); and evaluation perspective (many projects involving MCSCL have the general objective of evaluating technical and pedagogical effectiveness and assessing the impact of mobile devices on collaborative learning.

Studies on the effects of using mobile devices in learning approaches have shown positive and negative aspects of this use. Ting [25] points to three challenges for mobile learning: adaptive learning (i.e. instructional strategies and learning content must adapt to the student's profile and personal needs); the limited text display in supporting learning; and the characteristic of instant communication in mobile network (e.g. location and response time). Heflin et al. [23] states that, while some studies point out that the use of mobile devices can result in negative experiences for students, such as difficulty in using the tools [e.g. 26] or distraction by multitasking [e.g. 27], others found that mobile technology can help students increase engagement and improve grades [e.g. 28, 29].

A review and analysis of 110 studies on the use of mobile devices as tools in education, published between 1993 and 2013, was conducted by Sung et al. [30]. They found that the overall effect of using mobile devices in education is better than when using desktop computers or when not using mobile devices as an intervention, although the size of the effect has been moderate (0.523). The studies reviewed were done using many different combinations of hardware, software and intervention durations for mobile devices, applied to users of different age groups, implementation configurations, teaching methods and domain subjects. Another finding was the fact that investigations regarding teacher training and the use of mobile devices have been very limited. Therefore, the authors conclude that more experimental research is needed on how teachers reconcile mobile hardware and software, lesson content, teaching methods and educational objectives.

Another important aspect to mobile collaborative learning is the context. Park [31] claims that it has been widely recognized that mobile learning is about learning across contexts, and not just the use of portable devices. Ting [26] investigated the contextual use of mobile devices in learning; that is, having digital data on the mobile device, artifacts around the student and structured learning activities to provide users with meaningful learning experiences. The author found that the meaningfulness of learning experiences, with the contextual use of mobile devices, seems to compensate for the distraction induced by the limitations of mobile devices.

It is also essential to consider student engagement with mobile collaborative learning applications. Engagement has been considered a research priority in the learning literature [32]. Investigating student engagement, critical thinking, and attitudes toward collaborative learning, Heflin, Shewmaker and Nguyen [23] found that mobile technology is associated with students' positive perceptions of collaborative learning. However, they also found that the use of mobile technology in classes increased student disengagement. In addition, they found that the student's work produced on the mobile device demonstrated significantly less critical thinking than work produced on the computer keyboard, with a paper and pen. The authors concluded that any use of technology for learning also presents the opportunity for student distraction and disengagement.

As presented in the brief review above, the use of the mobile phone for collaborative learning must be carried out based on many criteria and considering the positive and negative aspects of the device. Below, we present Method 300 and then the methodology for designing the Method 300 app.

3 Method 300

Method 300 is an active methodology that can be used to promote greater collaboration between students and the development of social skills, especially in heterogeneous classes [20]. It is also a collaborative learning methodology, as it promotes collaboration among the group work team to improve learning. This method can assist both in meaningful learning and in the human aspect, in which students perceive themselves as active members of the group, develop self-esteem and reflect on their own learning path [20].

Method 300 was inspired by the story of the group of Spartan soldiers who formed an impermeable unit, as each Spartan soldier was responsible for defending the soldier beside him [20, 33].

In this methodology, after each learning assessment potentially collaborative groups are formed, which contain students who have achieved good performance (helpers) and unsatisfactory performance (helpee). The procedure for creating the groups is as follows: (a) the number of N groups is defined based on the desired number of members, usually with 5 or 6 students; (b) the list of students is ordered in decreasing order based on the results obtained in the evaluation carried out; (c) the list is numbered from 1 to N (only once), and then N to 1 (several times, until all students receive a group number); and (d) students are grouped based on the assigned number.

After the formation of the groups, individual and collective goals are determined for the groups in order to promote collaboration. An example of the goals would be the following: (a) helpee: solving exercise lists, the old assessment and the helpers' test; and (b) helpers: solving challenges and building a list of exercises in a test format. In addition, groups should hold at least two face-to-face meetings lasting two hours. Other goals can be included, such as the construction of concept maps and collective projects.

After the goals are met within a specified period, which is usually 10 days, those being helped have the opportunity to carry out a new learning assessment. Helpers increase their initial grades according to the improvement in the income of those helped and the level of help and interaction with the group, measured using a Likert scale with 5 points, ranging from 1 (I helped/helped nothing) to 5 (I helped/helped a lot), applied to all members of the group.

The method has been successfully applied in different contexts, such as in different areas of knowledge of both higher and basic education. As an example, the results of the method applied in the Calculus subject for engineering courses show an improvement of around 40% of the overall average grade and a 100% improvement when considering only those students who were helped by others [20]. The analysis of the interviews with the students also indicates that they felt less isolated and developed sincere empathy with other colleagues [20, 34].

The method is applied by the subject teacher using documents provided on the method's website (http://www.metodo300.com). The documents are a welcome letter with a brief explanation of the method, academic work on the method, assessment forms, questionnaires and spreadsheets. Although these materials are sufficient to apply the method, they can be a somewhat laborious for teachers to organize all forms, tests, and spreadsheets. Especially considering that some classrooms may have many students. Therefore, tools that help apply this method can be useful for both teachers and students.

4   Designing the Method 300 for Mobile Applications

The approach to designing this tool is based on a empathic and collaborative approach by researchers from three areas: the researcher and the teacher who created the method and applied it in many different contexts; a researcher with experience developing applications focused on education and backend systems; and a researcher with experience in UX design and creative and innovative application design process. We call this approach empathic, meaning that each member of the team will try to deeply understand the needs and the development process of the other members, and also that educational, designing and computational issues are considered with the same level of relevance in order to incorporate the decisions made.

These three researchers, along with design and computer science students, are designing the Method 300 app, intended for mobile devices like tablets and smartphones. The empathic approach also seeks audience participation and merges a user-centric design approach, as described below.

4.1 Stages of the Project Development

The project begins with the feeling of collaboration between the three researchers, in order to create an effective and engaging application for Method 300. The researchers from different areas understood that instead of collaborating only in a specific phase of the project, the collaboration should be done throughout the whole project. This type of empathic approach is used in human-centered methodologies. As Doorley et al. [35] explain, empathy "is the foundation of a human-centered design", and to empathize it is necessary to: observe, engage and immerse.

This approach helps to deepen discussions and, therefore, to make the most appropriate decisions, with regard to the understanding of the needs and requirements of all phases of the project by all team members. Obviously, this requires a greater involvement of all team members and, therefore, a longer time of availability in the project. However, this time can be compensated for by the lower need for adjustments during the project and also by the shorter testing time at the end of the project, considering that, with this approach, fewer errors will occur in the project.

As with user-centered approaches, such as ISO 13407 "Human-centered design process for interactive systems" [36] and Design Thinking [37], this process is iterative, which means that the process design is cycled, tested and measured, redesigned and repeated as many times as necessary [38, 39].

In addition, like user-centered design, the current process involves users and seeks to understand their needs and task requirements. Active user involvement should take place throughout the project. User-centered design (UCD) is a common approach to designing digital products. In this method (also known as user experience design, user interface design, human-centered design, human factor engineering, and usability engineering), users are involved in all stages of product development [40, 41].

This application has two main groups of users: teachers and students. Feedback on Method 300 has been collected since the beginning of its creation (in 2013) and the method has been improved since then. Therefore, much of the information about how students collaborate and their difficulties in collaborating is well understood. In addition, the problems teachers have in assessing the contribution and improvement of students and applying the method is also known. However, as the method currently uses different devices and tools, it is expected that the new product will make a big difference in the way students and teachers will experience the method. Therefore, the project should focus on understanding users' needs and experience with the new application.

The design of the project was divided into four main phases: information architecture (IA), user experience (UX) design, building and testing. It is slightly different from some

HCI and design methodologies. For example, according to Preece, Rogers and Sharp [42] the process of interaction design involves: (1) identifying needs and establishing requirements; (2) developing alternative design that meets the established requirements; (3) building interactive designs; and (4) evaluating what is being built throughout the process. Similarly, Cooper et al. [43] describe a digital development project of 5 phases: initiate, design, build, test and ship. The initiation stage is related to management issues, such as business model and business plan; the design plan is subdivided into 6 stages including: research with users and the domain; definition of design structure; flow, and refinement of behaviors, form and content.

Our stages are a little different from the above, first because as the product is a non-commercial education application being designed in a public university research center, there was really no business model or plan. There were just considerations about the duration of the project, the team involved and the maintenance of the application. Therefore, it was not considered a separate stage in this project. In addition, in our proposal, the UX design was separated from the IA plan. Although many authors consider IA as a part of UX design, in this study we wanted to highlight the importance of the information architecture stage and to consider the educational, structural and navigational aspects with a special emphasis before considering other aspects of UX design such as behavior and interface.

At the beginning of the project, the researchers also considered the main aspects of the project in relation to each area: education, design and build. The main aspects are summarized below.

4.2 Designing the Method 300 App from an Educator's Perspective

As mentioned above, mobile applications can be a useful tool to help students with their learning activities. Mobile learning has several benefits for learners, such as: access to content anytime and anywhere; support for distance learning; support in the interaction between students, and between students and teachers; and help in decreasing cultural and communication barriers between students and teachers [44].

When designing a mobile application, educators can make use of different educational theories to guide the structure and the content of the application. According to Koukopoulos and Koukopoulos [15], educational theories can be easily implemented in applications, since they have already guided the design of several educational software applications. These theories include: collaborative learning (i.e. promotes collaboration and active participation of students), mobile learning (i.e. explains how to effectively use mobile technology for learning and teaching); and learning objects (i.e. guides the creation of reusable educational units, independent and ready for aggregation).

Many requirements can be established to design mobile learning applications. Sarrab, Al-Shihi, Al-Manthari [14] proposed an M-learning model that addresses pedagogical and educational requirements in two dimensions: instructional design and M-learning design. According to the authors, instructional design is related to the analysis of mobile learning needs and the development of a system to meet these aims, and comprises the analysis, design, development, implementation and evaluation of the learning application. The design components of M-learning focused on pedagogical and educational aspects and include: learning theories, organization of material, presentation of material, integrity of material, quality of material and support for students [14]. These dimensions are used in this study as a basis for defining the educational aspects of the application.

Understanding and implementing learning theories is the first step to be considered in relation to educational issues to design the Method 300 app. Different learning theories are used in this project, such as: behavioral, constructivist, and collaborative. The implementation of these theories will help a better understanding of the users and the system and, therefore, will assist in the creation of an application that is more efficient and appropriate in educational terms.

The Method 300 app will not feature educational content. It will serve as a tool to connect students and teachers and to assist in the implementation of Method 300. Even as a learning tool, there are many requirements to consider. Among the requirements described in Sarrab, Al-Shihi, Al-Manthari [14] model, some are highlighted in this project: attracting and sustaining learners' interest; being accurate, reliable, up to-date and error free; presenting consistent and complete information; providing clarity, focus and organized content; providing logical, simple, comprehensive and flexible content structure; and providing instant access to relevant information.

4.3 Designing the Method 300 App from a Computer Scientist's Perspective

Five main steps are being taken to build the Method 300 app: survey of software requirements, identification of the most appropriate development environment, software modeling, software coding, and software validation in schools.

With regard to the software process, which is the set of software production activities, the evolutionary development model will be used, as it intersperses the different stages of software development by repeating them several times in cycles [45]. The design patterns are models of problems' solutions, allowing the implementations that use them to be generic and to undergo fewer limitations from their original context. Due to the concern to develop the software in a way that is easier to maintain and extend it in the future, the 'template method' design standard was adopted [46].

The software design pattern that is being used is the Model-View-Controller - MVC [47]. The presentation of data and user interaction (front-end) are separate from the methods that interact with the database (back-end). MVC facilitates code reuse, adding new customers, maintaining the code, as well as improving performance and making the application scalable.

In the field of programming languages and tools, several possibilities were evaluated. As a result, the SDK Flutter (Google LLC) and the Dart language are being used. SDK facilitates multiplatform development for iOS and Android and offers a good user experience in terms of performance. PostgreSQL (PostgreSQL Global Development Group) was adopted for the management of object-relational databases. This tool allows table-level transactions, a good full-text search service and user-friendly data types.

Regarding the validation and testing process, some procedures were defined. To ensure that the software meets the needs of a user-friendly tool, the product will be submitted to teachers and their students for validation in a real use case. During the validation process, periodic visits to participating schools will be made. Students and teachers will use a prototype application. This process will take place under the monitoring of the participants in this project. Then, adjustments will be made to the software to improve it. Basically, three approaches will be adopted: focus on the teacher, focus on the student and a third one that relates the student/teacher/software interaction. These approaches will be interspersed throughout the validation process, applying one or the other as needed, and at appropriate times. An important aspect is that the product will be tested in real school-use cases.

4.4   Designing the Method 300 App from a Designer's Perspective

Designers can use different approaches in order to create digital products. There are many techniques, tools and design methods that can be used in the design process. Nevertheless, many design approaches point to an understanding of human experience and its needs. Bonsiepe [48] states that the concern with the user of an integrative approach is the main difference between design and other disciplines. Based on Bonsiepe's definition of design [48], Souto [49] states that the main aspects addressed by designers, when designing a digital learning environment, are those related to the user's characteristics and the aesthetic and formal quality of the project.

Along the same lines of thought, Cooper et al. [43] state that planning for digital designers involves understanding how the user wants to use the product and for what purpose, in addition to designing products that support and facilitate human behavior. The authors propose a digital product development process to bridge the gap between user research and design. The process called Goal-Direct Design is "a combination of new techniques and known methods brought together in more effective ways" and is divided into six stages: research (of users and the domain); modeling (of users and use context); requirements (definition of user, business, and technical needs); framework (definition of design structure and flow); refinement (of behaviors, form, and content); and support (development needs).

The techniques and methods proposed by Cooper et al. [43] are considered in the design of the current application; however, not with the same perspective. In our approach, we consider the design issues together with all the other stages (IA, building and testing). In addition, research with users and their context is being carried out throughout the project. The user's context is considered an important issue during the design process [50]. In a learning application in particular, the context of use is considered an influential part of any learning experience [16]. The context of use (which also refers to environmental requirements) is related to the conditions under which the product will be used. Preece, Rogers, Sharp [42] point out four main environments that should be considered when establishing requirements for the context of use: physical, social, organizational and technical. Investigating these environments is very relevant during the design process, as context and design are inseparable in a mobile learning application [16].

In addition, it is also important to highlight the design research, and to define both the interaction (e.g. accessibility, usability, platform requirements) and visual (e.g. typography, color, icons, grid, images) aspects of the interface. While in some cases it is compulsory that designers comply with operating system guidelines, they can also be a barrier to creativity. Souto [51] states that, although design guidelines are important for designers to create useful and effective applications, they should be used with care so that they do not guide designers to make their application look like their competitors.

5   Making the Multidisciplinary Collaborative Approach an 'Impermeable Unit'

The innovation proposed in this design approach is to transform Method 300 into a digital experience and also to harness the willingness of researchers from different fields to empathetically understand the area of their colleagues, forming an "impermeable unit" inspired by the method. Although collaboration between members from different areas may be common in projects with a multidisciplinary approach, such as application design, it seems that good communication between members of different areas of the team can be a problem [52]. This is a relevant aspect in application design, since many authors claim that factors related to communication in information technology projects are strongly associated with the success or failure of the projects [53].

Beyond looking at how users behave, feel and experience the products, empathic approaches can be related to the collaboration between members of a digital product development team. Mattelmäki, Vaajakallio, Koskinen [54] describe four layers of empathic design: (1) sensitivity toward humans; (2) sensitivity toward design; (3) sensitivity toward techniques; and (4) sensitivity toward collaboration. For the authors, the sensitivity to collaboration involves adjusting the process and tools according to co-designers, decision makers and organizations.

The empathic approach to designing the Method 300 app comprised all of these four layers. However, the focus described here in this paper is related to the empathic approach of the team collaboration. According to Karakaya and Demirkan [55], the collaboration process is a central concept for social creativity in design problems, and it requires experience in different fields. In addition, the collaboration process in a product development project can lead to innovations [56]. Therefore, using this approach, we seek to increase the creativity of team members and to design an innovative and effective application.

Another aspect that we are considering with this approach is the schedule of team members. As mentioned, the current project has been divided into four stages: it starts with IA definitions, followed by UX design decisions, and then building and testing. According to Cooper et al. [43], in order to ensure that products meet users' needs, the main activities of the design process should precede coding and testing. However, in order to have a more integrated approach, both building and testing will be organized in a way that they happen concomitantly with the design process. Once the IA of the application has been defined - and it is defined with the participation of all members - the coding will start being planned and executed. Furthermore, the testing activities will also be conducted with initial prototypes. With these actions, we hope to ensure a more integrated and user-centered approach.

Apart from involving the researchers in all stages of the project, there are activities that will be executed by the three of them. This will occur in the testing stage, where in addition to user testing (focus group, surveys, card sorting, and testing methods), expert inspection methods (walkthrough, heuristic test, and expert review) will happen by the coordination of the three of them. These testing techniques will be used to incorporate ideas and improve the design of the application during the process. The three researchers will be responsible for discussing the results and proposing changes to the prototype.

We hope that the "impermeable unit" is formed by the action of the researchers - who are also the team leaders - in collaborating with the areas of colleagues, and also because they are open to learning various techniques and methods to design a powerful learning tool for Method 300.

6   Final Remarks

This paper presented the methodology that is being used to design the Method 300 app. The novelty of this study lies in the presentation of an empathic, active and collaborative approach proposed by the creators of the app, which is coincident with the Method 300 approach. Developing empathy among team members seems to be one of the key factors in designing effective apps. However, it seems that it is not such a straightforward capacity. Shneiderman et al. [57] points that "amplifying empathy" is one of the grand challenges of HCI research.

Method 300 is based on an active and collaborative approach that aims to improve the learning process of a team of students. It consists of promoting collaboration between students who obtained a good score with those who did not. In addition, the method can assist the student both in learning and in the human aspect [20].

By transforming the development process of this application with the same philosophy as Method 300, we hope to create an application that is fully adapted to the needs of users. Furthermore, we believe that the use of the same philosophy will also help to make the translations of the media (sheets and documents for the mobile application) more appropriate.

The different perspectives presented by the researchers, in the three areas of education, design and computer science, shows that although they are distinct areas with different approaches and requirements, in all three areas attention is given to the users' needs.

Apart from the methodology proposed, the paper presents a brief review in collaborative learning applications. It is concluded that the Method 300 app has great potential to spread this method worldwide and that the empathic multidisciplinary collaborative approach to designing this application can be considered in different contexts.

For now, the development of the Method 300 app is in the Information Architecture phase. This first phase was essential to understand the methodology described in this paper, the role of each team member, the content and the structure of the application. The other phases - Designing, Building and Testing - have already started with the collaboration of team members from all areas. In the near future, we hope to deliver the application, present the test findings, and also present this methodology in more detail, based on the analysis of the development of the entire Method 300 app.

Acknowledgment. We thank Luiz Philipe Chavier Lobo Filho and Vinícius Menezes da Silva, the students who are part of the Method 300 app development team.

References

1. Dillenbourg, P.: What do you mean by collaborative learning? In: Dillenbourg, P. (ed.) Collaborative-Learning: Cognitive and Computational Approaches, pp. 1–19. Els., Oxford (1999)
2. Goodyear, P., Jones, C., Thompson, K.: Computer-supported collaborative learning: instructional approaches, group processes and educational designs. In: Spector, J.M., Merrill, M.D., Elen, J., Bishop, M.J. (eds.) Handbook of Research on Educational Communications and Technology, pp. 439–451. Springer, New York (2014). https://doi.org/10.1007/978-1-4614-3185-5_35
3. Häkkinen, P., Järvelä, S., Mäkitalo-Siegl, K., Ahonen, A., Näykki, P., Valtonen, T.: Preparing teacher-students for twenty-first-century learning practices (PREP 21): a framework for enhancing collaborative problem-solving and strategic learning skills. Teach. Teach. 23(1), 25–41 (2017)
4. Retnowati, E., Ayres, P., Sweller, J.: Can collaborative learning improve the effectiveness of worked examples in learning mathematics? J. Educ. Psychol. 109(5), 666–679 (2017)
5. Lee, K.B., Salman, R.: The design and development of mobile collaborative learning application using Android. J. Inf. Technol. Appl. Educ. 1(1), 1–8 (2012)
6. Laal, M., Laal, M.: Collaborative learning: what is it? Soc. Behav. Sci. 31, 491–495 (2012)
7. Prince, M.: Does active learning work? a review of the research. J. Eng. Educ. 93(3), 223–231 (2004)
8. Pinheiro, M.M., Simões, D.: Constructing knowledge: an experience of active and collaborative learning in ICT classrooms. Soc. Behav. Sci. 64(9), 392–401 (2012)
9. Ausbel, D.P.: Educational Psychology: A Cognitive View. Holt, Rinehart and Winston, Nova York (1968)
10. Watkins, J., Mazur, E.: Retaining students in science, technology, engineering, and mathematics (STEM) majors. J. Coll. Sci. Teach. 42(5), 36–41 (2013)
11. Bergmann, J., Sams, A.: Flip Your Classroom: Reach Every Student in Every Class Every Day. ISTE, Eugene (2012)
12. Connolly, T.M., Boyle, E.A., MacArthur, E., Hainey, T., Boyle, J.M.: A systematic literature review of empirical evidence on computer games and serious games. Comput. Educ. 59(2), 661–686 (2012)
13. Maina, E.M., Wagacha, P.W., Oboko, R.O.: Enhancing active learning pedagogy through online collaborative learning. In: Artificial Intelligence: Concepts, Methodologies, Tools, and Applications, pp. 1031–1054.IGI Global (2017)
14. Sarrab, M., Al-Shihi, H., Al-Manthari, B.: Toward educational requirements model for mobile learning development and adoption in higher education. TechTrends 62, 635–646 (2018)
15. Koukopoulos, Z., Koukopoulos, D.: Integrating educational theories into a feasible digital environment. Appl. Comput. Inf. 15(1), 19–26 (2019)
16. Uden, L.: Activity theory for designing mobile learning. Int. J. Mob. Learn. Organ. 1, 81–102 (2007)
17. Vavoula, G., Karagiannidis, C.: Designing mobile learning experiences. In: Bozanis, P., Houstis, E.N. (eds.) PCI 2005. LNCS, vol. 3746, pp. 534–544. Springer, Heidelberg (2005). https://doi.org/10.1007/11573036_50
18. Kjeldskov, J.: "Just-in-place" information for mobile device interfaces. In: Paternò, F. (ed.) Mobile HCI 2002. LNCS, vol. 2411, pp. 271–275. Springer, Heidelberg (2002). https://doi.org/10.1007/3-540-45756-9_21
19. Khaddage, F., Müller, W., Flintoff, K.: Advancing mobile learning in formal and informal settings via mobile app technology: where to from here, and how? Educ. Technol. Soc. 19(3), 16–26 (2016)

20. Fragelli, R.R.: Método Trezentos: Aprendizagem ativa e colaborativa, para além do conteúdo. Penso, Porto Alegre (2019)
21. Troussas, C., Maria Virvou, M., Alepis, E.: Collaborative learning: group interaction in an intelligent mobile-assisted multiple language learning system. Inf. Educ. **13**(2), 279–292 (2014)
22. Goodsell, A., Maher, M., Tinto, V., Smith, B.L., MacGregor, J.: What is collaborative learning? In: Collaborative Learning: A Sourcebook for Higher Education. National Center on Postsecondary Teaching, Learning, and Assessment at Pennsylvania State University (1992)
23. Heflin, H., Shewmaker, J., Nguyen, J.: Impact of mobile technology on student attitudes, engagement, and learning. Comput. Educ. **107**, 91–99 (2017)
24. Caballé, S., Xhafa, F., Barolli, L.: Using mobile devices to support online collaborative learning. Mob. Inf. Syst. **6**(1), 27–47 (2010)
25. Ting, R.Y.: Mobile learning: current trend and future challenges. In: Proceedings of the Fifth IEEE International Conference on Advanced Learning Technologies (ICALT 2005) (2005)
26. Ting, Y.-L.: The pitfalls of mobile devices in learning: a different view and implications for pedagogical design. J. Educ. Comput. Res. **46**(2), 119–134 (2012)
27. Dietz, S., Henrich, C.: Texting as a distraction to learning in college students. Comput. Hum. Behav. **36**, 163–167 (2014)
28. Lai, C.-Y., Wu, C.-C.: Using handhelds in a Jigsaw cooperative learning environment. J. Comput. Assist. Learn. **22**, 284–297 (2006)
29. Junco, R., Heiberger, G., Loken, E.: The effect of Twitter on college student engagement and grades. J. Comput. Assist. Learn. **27**(2), 119–132 (2011)
30. Sung, Y.-T., Yang, J.M., Lee, H.-Y.: The effects of mobile-computer-supported collaborative learning: meta-analysis and critical synthesis. Rev. Educ. Res. **87**(4), 768–805 (2017)
31. Park, Y.: A pedagogical framework for mobile learning: categorizing educational applications of mobile technologies into four types. Int. Rev. Res. Open Dist. Learn. **12**(2), 78–102 (2011)
32. Blasco-Arcas, L., Buil, I., Hernández-Ortega, B., Sese, F.J.: Using clickers in class. The role of interactivity, active collaborative learning and engagement in learning performance. Comput. Educ. **62**, 102–110 (2013)
33. Fragelli, R.R.: Método trezentos: aprendizagem ativa e colaborativa. In: Rissoli, V.R.V. (eds.) Pesquisa, métodos e tecnologias empregadas na formação em Engenharia. Editora Universidade de Brasília, Brasília (2017)
34. Fragelli, R.R., Fragelli, T.B.O.: Trezentos: a dimensão humana do método. Educar em Rev. Curitiba Brasil **63**, 253–265 (2017)
35. Doorley, S., Holcomb, S., Klebahn, P., Segovia, K., Utley, J.: Design thinking bootleg. Hasso Plattner. Institute of Design at Standford (2018)
36. International Organisation of Standardisation. ISO 13407 Human-centred design process of interactive systems. (International standard) (1999)
37. Brown, T.: Design thinking. https://designthinking.ideo.com. Accessed 30 Jan 2020
38. Gould J.D., Boies S.J., Ukelson J.: How to design usable systems. In: Helander, M.G., Landauer, T.K., Prabhu, P.V. (eds.) Handbook of Human-Computer Interaction. Elsevier Science B.V. (1997)
39. Gulliksen, J., Göransson, B., Boivie, I., Blomkvist, S., Persson, J., Cajander, Å.: Key principles for user-centred systems design. Behav. Inf. Technol. **22**(6), 397–409 (2003)
40. Vredenburg, K.: Building ease of use into the IBM user experience. IBM Syst. J. **42**(4), 517–531 (2003)
41. dos Santos, F.A., Tiradentes Souto, V.: Graphic design and user-centred design: designing learning tools for primary school. Int. J. Technol. Des. Educ. **29**, 999–1009 (2019)
42. Preece, J., Rogers, Y., Sharp, H.: Interaction Design Beyond Human-Computer Interaction. Wiley, New York (2002)

43. Cooper, A., Reimann, R., Cronin, D., Noessel, C.: About Face: The Essentials of Interaction Design, 4th edn. Wiley, Hoboken (2014)
44. Sarrab, M., Elgamel, L., Aldabbas, H.: Mobile learning (M-learning) and educational environments. Int. J. Distrib. Parallel Syst. (IJDPS) 3(4), 31 (2012)
45. Somerville, I.: Software Engineering, 10th edn. Pearson, New York City (2015)
46. Gamma, E., Helm, R., Johnson, R., Vlissides, J.: Design Patterns: Elements of Reusable Object-Oriented Software. Addison-Wesley, Boston (2010)
47. Sridaran, R., Padmavathi, G., Iyakutti, K., Mani, M.N.S.: SPIM architecture for MVC based web applications. Int. J. Adv. Netw. Appl. 8(5), 63–68 (2017)
48. Bonsiepe, G.: Design, cultura e sociedade. Blucher, São Paulo (2011)
49. Souto, V.: A framework for designing interactive digital learning environments for young people. In: Emerging Research and Trends in Interactivity and the Human-Computer Interface, Hershey, PA, pp. 429–447 (2014)
50. Kangas, E., Kinnunen, T.: Applying user-centered design to mobile application development. Commun. ACM 48(7), 55–59 (2005)
51. Souto, V.T.: Creativity in mobile application design: the guideline issue. e-Rev. LOGO 7(1), 2–23 (2018)
52. Souto, V.T., Cristo, C., Araújo, M.G., Santos, L.: Designing apps for tourists: a case study. In: Marcus, A. (ed.) DUXU 2015. LNCS, vol. 9188, pp. 425–436. Springer, Cham (2015). https://doi.org/10.1007/978-3-319-20889-3_40
53. de Carvalho, M.M.: An investigation of the role of communication in IT projects. Int. J. Oper. Prod. Manag. 34(1), 36–64 (2014)
54. Mattelmäki, T., Vaajakallio, K., Koskinen, I.: What happened to empathic design? Des. Issues 30(1), 67–77 (2014)
55. Karakaya, A.F., Demirkan, H.: Collaborative digital environments to enhance the creativity of designers. Comput. Hum. Behav. 42, 176–186 (2015)
56. Kleinsmann, M., Valkenburg, R.: Barriers and enablers for creating shared understanding in co-design projects. Des. Stud. 29(4), 369–386 (2008)
57. Shneiderman, B., Plaisant, C., Cohen, M., Jacobs, S., Elmqvist, N., Diakopoulos, N.: Grand challenges in HCI. ACM Interact. 23(5), 24–25 (2016)

Pedagogical Discussion on the Application of Role Immersion in Interior Design Teaching

Chen Wang[1], Wenjing Yin[1], and Jue Chen[2(✉)]

[1] South China University of Technology, Guangzhou 510006, China
[2] Guangdong University of Finance and Economics, Guangzhou 510320, China
20181032@gdfue.edu.cn

Abstract. To eliminate the barrier among "designers (students)- virtual environment-users" in interior design teaching, as well as in response to the proposition of experience economy in this era, this study learns from relevant theories of embodied cognition, design thinking and drama theory to formulate the method of role immersion, which is applied in the general procedure of interior design. Through the application in the interior design course of "Regeneration of Old Built Space", it is verified that "role immersion" can help students to wake up the "body"- a medium which is born to contact and interact with the environment. It can also help to cultivate students' awareness and ability to carry out design from inside to outside and himself\herself to users to realize users' positive perception and experience in continuous space and time. At last, the paper summarizes the problems of this method in teaching application and puts forward the developing points.

Keywords: Interior design · Role immersion · Perception and experience

1 Introduction

1.1 Barrier Among "Designers (Students)—Virtual Environment—Users"

The core of interior design is to comprehend the abstract quality of the shaped negative space and empty space. Although space is everywhere, it is not a conception of shape but the occupation, use and experience of body. Interior space defines human, behaviors and emotions in built environment. Body participation is the essential condition to acquire space experience. However, the unbuilt environment in the design phase is virtual, real body can't participate in it actually. This brings a great barrier for design participants to anticipate human perception and experience in the built environment.

Marshall McLuhan put forward the famous theory that "media is the extension of man" and "media is the message". All the media are extension of people's senses, and senses are "intrinsic electric charge" of our physical ability [1]. Spatial experience is not only a visual perception but also a combination of the other senses [2]. For the current interior design, its media tool such as perspective painting, small-size model (miniature three-dimensional solid model), and sometimes even the original-size model,

© Springer Nature Switzerland AG 2020
A. Marcus and E. Rosenzweig (Eds.): HCII 2020, LNCS 12202, pp. 566–577, 2020.
https://doi.org/10.1007/978-3-030-49757-6_41

are all the extensions of people's visual sense of the built environment. These tools are not enough to meet the needs of fully displaying indoor perception and experience. The existing written and visual languages limits our ability to properly evaluate the quality of interior space. Although design terms can be very practical (including expressions such as function and communication), they cannot describe the intentional emotional communication between people, objects and the environment.

From another perspective, the media tools trapped in vision promote excessive respect for visual effects of the images in interior design teaching. As a result, the biased visual effect becomes the basis for design evaluating, while the real feelings of people in the environment are ignored completely. Though the perception and experience factors are mentioned or even emphasized, it is actually easier to know than to do in the design process because of the abstract term and the restriction of media tools. Furthermore, designers are often not the users of the built environment, or representatives for all of them. Designers (especially students) are used to seeing things from their perspectives and draw self-centered conclusions. It is easy for them to deviate or difficult to focus on users as the center and core of the environment.

One lawsuit caused by the design of Farnsworth House, which is praised as model of modernist architecture illustrates the problem vividly. The project was designed by master architect Mies Van Der Rohe and received a good reputation after its completion. The only person who did not like it is the homeowner, doctor Edith Farnsworth herself. It is because of the potential privacy and thermal performance of the indoor environment. She asked the architect to revise it but was rejected, so they went to the court finally. Imagine, if the designer himself could start the design from the perspective of the user (female doctor), or if the user could understand the design by intuitive and understandable means of communication (such as being in space), instead of the drawings or a miniature scale physical model which only be read by professionals, the problems exposed in the actual use of the environment after the completion of the project may be discussed and corrected during the design phase in advance.

During the design phase, the barrier among "designers- virtual environment-users" can pose obstacles to talented and experienced design masters, not to mention the students who are still in their education stage and have relatively limited professional and life experience. This has been one of the main problems in interior design teaching for a long time.

1.2   The Proposition of Experience Economy in This Era

In the context of the times, with the transformation of economic models from stereotype to customization, experience economy has become an innovative driving force for social development, and the work and life experience with the embodied mind has been valued. The market used to focus on the functional attributes of products, but later changed the focus to consumer experience [3]. The relative success of design not only depends the solution of physical function, but also on the positive feeling experience that users can enjoy and evoke from the product or environment. The emphasis of interior design has also evolved from emphasizing "what" and "what to do" to "what to represent" and "what to feel". Although people are born with perception and experience, sound perceptual effects and experiences need to be skillfully stimulated. This has become an inevitable proposition of the times for interior design teaching oriented to social practice.

2   The Theoretical Basis, Tools and Framework of Role Immersion

In view of the above problems in the teaching of environmental design and the proposition of the new era, this study learns from relevant theories of embodied cognition, design thinking and drama performance to develop the method of "role immersion" and integrate it into the general procedure of interior design.

2.1   The Theoretical Basis and Media Tools of Role Immersion

Maurice Merleau-Ponty, a French philosopher, opposed the mind-body dualism represented by Descartes in traditional western philosophy. He believed that the physical perception was the basis of behavior, and there was no consciousness of self-existence behind perception. Human beings' understanding of the world is mediated by the body and is related to the whole world through the body's perception [4]. Modern psychology has inherited and developed this idea of "embodied subjectivity" and formed the theory of "embodied cognition". The theory is explicitly based on the theory of body and mind integration, explaining the interaction between the body and the environment and its key role in the cognitive process. The most basic and unforgettable feeling of three-dimension lies in the physical experience. All kinds of feelings are produced in the process of experiencing architecture, and are the basis of comprehension and perception of space [5].

The perception and experience of people in the built environment is a kind of embodied cognition in which the body is deeply involved and "integrates mind and body", called "experiencing with the body and mind". In the design phase, design participants are unable to experience the environment by themselves. At present, the media tools they rely on only obtain and process environmental information through simplified and deformed visual channels. This is a disembodied cognition that is observational and body-soul-separated. It may be said that "Both the body and mind are far away".

The physical environment can only be perceived through human perception. People collect various primitive stimuli through the senses, which are later being processed by the brain. Then human perception of the world is formed. In other words, the way humans perceive the world and space comes directly from human themselves. Without human perception, the world does not exist.

Marshall McLuhan once predicted that we were rapidly approaching the last stage of human extension, that is the stage of technological simulation of consciousness. The emergence of Virtual Reality (VR) marks the arrival of this stage and puts forward its own practice ideas. With computer technology as the core, VR generates a digital Virtual Environment (VE) that is highly similar to a certain range of real environment in terms of sight, hearing, touch and other senses. Users interact with it with the necessary equipment. The technical characteristics of VR's infinite imagination, multi-sensory immersion and natural interaction make it possible for participants to perceive non-physical virtual environment and form embodied cognition.

In terms of image display, currently there are two ways to participate in VR: stereoscopic head-mounted displays (HMD) and large fully immersive or semi-immersive projection systems [6]. HMD is essentially a two-dimensional window of a three-dimensional world, which can be used for synchronic perception and real-time modification of virtual environment at different stages of the scheme. The immersive projection systems provide the participants with the actual subjective experience in 3D model environment, which can be used for the diachronic experience of the final virtual environment of the scheme.

2.2 Framework of Role Immersion Framework

The formation of role immersion framework draws on relevant theories and methods of design thinking and drama performance. Empathy is one of the analysis methods and steps commonly used in design thinking. In short, this method can be understood as putting yourself in others' shoes, aimed at eliminating the designer's preconceived personal subjectivity. Empathy requires designers to recognize, grasp, and understand the needs and emotions of others in order to get close to the user's true feelings. The basic elements of drama performance include actors, screenplays (or authors), audience and the physical space in which the play is realized, namely the theater and the stage. In the drama performance, the stage design transforms with different drama scenes based on the storyline described in the script, and cooperates with the actors' performance, bringing the audience an immersive experience of temporarily leaving the real world and staying in the virtual world.

Everything in the world happens in a certain space scene. The design of the scene has a profound and lasting impact on the people in the place. As being the center person of the built environment, interior design is not only the design for the space, but also the "behavior" and "scene". For example, think about what the user will see and smell when they enter the space. From these perceptual elements, people generate a variety of emotions, which can be changed into a variety of behaviors.

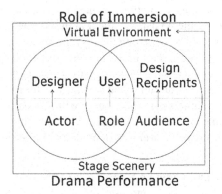

Fig. 1. The framework of role immersion

Correspondingly, in role immersion, the designed environment scenes serve as the stage setting. And the designer serves as an actor and incarnates the user's role through empathy, while the design recipients (the reviewer, the project client, the user, etc.) act as the audience (Fig. 1). Design participants participate in the virtual environment scene created by interior design through their bodies. They generate immersive perception and experience subjectively, form an embodied cognition of the environment, and empathize with the user's role. The implementation steps of role immersion include three parts: role substitution, body participation and situational performance, which are respectively integrated into the first, middle and last three stages of the general process of interior design.

3   Case Study of Role Immersion in Interior Design Teaching

The following is a detailed explanation of the method of role immersion integrated into general procedures of interior design through the third-year theme design course "Regeneration of Old Building Space". The project is located in an old grinding wheel factory in the western district of Zhengzhou, Henan Province, China. The factory was built by the former east Germany in the 1960 s. A large number of Bauhaus-style old factories and office buildings are preserved in the site. At present, the factory site in the city is facing the development of transformation and will be relocated. The old site will be transformed and reused to become a multi-functional creative industrial park with the characteristics of industrial cultural heritage. According to the upper planning scheme, this course selects some the old buildings with reservation value in the site for spatial regeneration design.

3.1   Early Stage of Design + Role Substitution

In the early stage of design, role substitution helps to form design concepts and the formulate design specification.

Create User Roles. User roles are fictional characters that can represent the needs of the entire real users. The scattered data obtained in the process of user survey and user segmentation are reconnected by depicting the user. Personas make users more real and vivid, and help students to focus their problem perspectives on specific user objects to achieve empathy. Teachers can write or work with students to create descriptions of the basic information, interests, abilities, and weaknesses for each user role. One of the main consumption groups in this park in this case will be local residents within a 5 km radius and a 2 km walking circle. For example, at the beginning of the design of Living Arts Center, the students created a user role of a family of three and drew their portraits (Fig. 2).

Get into the User Role and Create a Story Script. The students jumped out of their own subjective perspective and got into user roles with empathy. Based on the plane

Role Portrait

Behavioral Streamlines ▶

Story Script ▼

Fiona's husband, Kin, is an IT engineer, usually busy with work, and rarely accompanies herself and their sun to go out and play. They heard that the once abandoned wheel factory in the south of the city was transformed into a creative industrial park, so Fiona decided to go there with her family this weekend. The Living Art Center is located not far from the entrance to the south gate of the factory. It turned out to be the factory's library. Modern abstract sculptures and long corridors lead them into the room. The first floor displays traditional plant dyeing and weaving, and clothing, where you can buy goods and enjoy ethnic handicraft works...

	Kin(Father)	Bob (Son)	Fiona (Mum)
Age	35	6	33
Job	IT Engineer\	Kindergarten Student \	Accounting
Hobby	Mobile Games	Playground	Shopping
	Cooking	Toys	Handcraft

Fig. 2. One example of creating user role

function bubble diagram, the story script with certain narrative and logic was created by taking the continuous flow of user role in the environment as a clue.

Split Shot Story. The story script is decomposed into split-shot stories, which are represented by split-shot storyboards (scene sketches), written ideas, etc. The split-up storyboard visually reflects the user's perception and experience process in the indoor and outdoor environment from beginning to end, similar to the imaginary rehearsal before the drama performance. At this stage, the scenes in the storyboards do not need to be carefully portrayed. The main purpose is to help designers, design team, teachers and students to conceive or exchange ideas. In the process of forming the design concept, they should add their own research and thinking, clarify the design tasks, and provide the basis and blueprint for the next in-depth design (Fig. 3).

The process of creating and substituting user roles is always around the design values. In this case, the overall design value of the park includes four aspects: business, society, history and nature. For example, in the design of Living Arts Center, in the original split-shot storyboards, when a character was enjoying leisure activities, other family members are isolated or idling. This directly exposed the problem of single, separated function of spatial planning. Based on this, the teacher guided the students to adjust the planning scheme. Finally, the design concept of multiple and mixing functions was formed so that a family of three (representing different consumer groups) can have their own place in the venue and share companionship, reflecting the commercial and social value.

3.2 Middle Stage of Design + Physical Participation

The design concepts, story scripts and split-shot stories formed in the stage of pre-design explain what need to change, while in the middle of the design, they gradually show how these changes occur. Based on the pre-formed storyboards, students deliberate on various environment objects, designing both space and human behavior and scenes. In

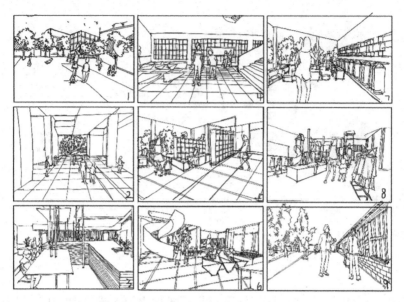

Fig. 3. One example of split-shot storyboard

this process, students still take the user role as the starting point for thinking, such as how the roles use space, what kind of mood and behavior it will generate, and what is the relationship between people in the space. With the help of VR, students make their bodies participate in the virtual environment created by the computer. The synchronicity and diachronic experience of the characters in the environment servers as the basis for conception, communication and deepening of the scheme, which also makes it the ultimate goal of the design.

Environmental Perception. The sensory system of the body interacts with the static space and is related to the continuous elements of time. This is called environmental perception. Through the VR renderer, students perceive the panoramic environment scene created by the computer in HMD. In the sketch model stage, we mainly focus on the basic relationship between space and people, including the sense of scale, the sense of interface, shape feeling, etc. In the model deepening stage, we mainly emphasize the feelings of spatial details, such as material texture, color, light, etc. Through the handheld interactive device, students can modify the spatial details to feel and compare the different effects in real time (Fig. 4). In the finalization stage, we complete the transition from space to scene. First, the 3D computer space model is imported into the VR renderer, and the user's role and environment group are put into it for detailed scene processing, including optional furniture, plants, lamps, soft decoration, etc. Secondly, macro-environment in which the micro-environment is created, including simulated climate, sunshine, season, etc. Finally, the panoramic environment scene images are exported according to the pre-determined split-shot storyboard, and students perceive them through HMD (Fig. 5).

Fig. 4. Student participate in the virtual environment through HMD and modified spatial details in real time by handheld interactive device.

Fig. 5. Students perceive panoramic environment scene images through HMD.

Environmental Experience. People continuously walk through the space, knowing the space and themselves, and highlighting the sequence of time. This is called spatial experience. The complete 3D computer model is imported into VR-CAVE, where students place themselves in the panoramic scene and interact with it in real time, so that they can feel the user's experience in the continuous space and time with the perspective of user role and behavioral streamline as clues (Fig. 6). CAVE (Computer Automatic Virtual Environment) is one of VR's large immersive projection systems. It provides a room-sized cube projection display space, which can present different panoramic virtual environment for people to wander in it.

Fig. 6. Students experience panoramic environment scene in VR-CAVE.

3.3   Late Stage of Design + Scene Performance

Program Report. The final report of scheme takes the form of a scene performance. Students are placed in the VR stage to play the user roles. Their performing actions drive the panoramic environment scene to generate real-time visual and auditory changes, so that they can move in different directions and stimulate real-time perception and free wandering effect of users in the built environment (Fig. 7). The VR stage used for the course report was developed and designed by the author. It is based on the Unity3D, one of the game development platforms, applying the CAVE principle to the stage. The semi-enclosed stereo screen composed of the background and the ground presents a panoramic image in the same proportion as a live actor. Microsoft Kinect captures the actions of people through Kinect to realize the real-time interaction between people and the virtual environment scene. Or similar to the way of webcasting, the audience (design recipients) complete the understanding and experience of environment scene in the introduction and guidance of the video blogger(designer).

Evaluate Feedback. Designers invite and guide design recipients to perceive and experience environmental scenes through HMD, VR-CAVE and VR stage. In order to allow more design recipients to participate in evaluation of the scheme, the panoramic scene images of the sub-shots are captured in the VR renderer, and the panoramic roaming video is generated in the panoramic story generator software and shared through the QR code. Both present and non-present design participants can make panoramic observation and have wandering experience of environment through mobile terminal or "mobile phone+ VR glass" (Fig. 8). According to the design value formed in the early stage,

Fig. 7. The final report of scheme takes the form of a scene performance in the VR stage.

Fig. 8. Design participants can perceive panoramic environment scenes with Mobile phone through scanning the QR code.

the feedback of design recipients (audience) after environmental perception and experience is collected and summarized by combining electronic questionnaire and on-site interview.

4 Significance of Role Immersion in Interior Design Teaching

4.1 Eliminate the Barriers Among "Designers (Students)-Virtual Environment-Users"

Role immersion and its media tool VR help students wake up and use the "body", an innate medium that connects and interacts with environment. The cyclical process is completed starting from the daily body diagram (inside-out) and finally returns to the body to examine (outside-in).

Role immersion helps the students to get out of themselves naturally, making sure to start with the user and always focus on the user throughout the design process. Design participants are in the same virtual environment, immersing themselves in scene performance to obtain intuitive and approximate perception and experience. Designers and design recipients including users have the same experiencing feelings, providing a possible way to eliminate the obstacles in their understanding and communicating of the schemes.

4.2 Focus on User Perception and Experience in Continuous Space and Time

Role immersion helps interior design teaching to transfer form focusing on physical and functional attributes to human-centered behavior and scenes, from the pursuit of fragmentary and instantaneous image visual perception to the users' positive perception and experience in continuous space and time. This also urges the teaching of environmental design to break the inherent boundary brought out by the division of majors, condensing all the indoor and outdoor environment and elements into an organic system, which takes user as the center and core.

4.3 Classroom Teaching Atmosphere

Students who have grown up in the electronic information age are familiar with and fond of movies, games, VR, online live broadcast and other forms of popular entertainment. Through teaching, teachers found out that the methods and media tools involved in role immersion are easy for students to understand and interesting to operate. Role empathy and immersion experience are also the important reasons why the current multimedia entertainment methods attract young people. This has inspired teachers to take advantage of the situation, adapt to the characteristics of students in the new era, and integrate their favorite entertainment into design teaching, so as to improve the learning effect and participation enthusiasm in the class.

5   Conclusion

Integrating role immersion into general procedures of interior design is to solve the problem of estrangement and alienation among "designers (students)-virtual environment-users" in the teaching of interior design. It is pedagogical discussion on teaching method to realize the positive perception and experience of users in the continuous space and time. It still has the following two problems that need improvement and development. From the perspective of course teaching, the implementation of "role immersion" requires the support of certain equipment and site. Certain time and process are needed for students to get familiar with and adapt to the new methods and new media tools. What's more, the experience of objects and space need to be quantified and qualitative. On the other hand, from the perspective of media tools, VR currently applied in the field of civilian teaching has matured in creating 3D digital environment objects of infinite imagination, but there are bottlenecks in comprehensive simulation of multi-channel sensory perception and comfort natural immersion and interaction. Although VR is closer to the physical perception of the environment than previous media tools, there is still a considerable gap in the real experience of the built environment compared to the personal experience. To sum up, only when the teaching methods and media tools are improved respectively and integrated with each other, can we continuously solve practical problems in design teaching and provide innovative ideas to meet the escalating market demands.

Acknowledgements. This paper is supported by the Youth Fund Project for Humanities and Social Sciences Research of the Education Ministry of China (17YJC760087) and the Fundamental Research Funds for the Central Universities, SCUT (x2sjC2181320\ 2018MSXM20).

References

1. Marshall McLuhan, F., Terrence Gordon, W.S.: Understanding Media: The Extension of Man, 1st edn. The MIT Press, Cambridge (1994)
2. Shashi Caan, F.: Rethinking Design and Interiors: Human Beings in the Built Environment, 1st edn. Laurence King Publishing, London (2011)
3. Anna Klingmann, F.: Brandscapes: Architecture in the Experience Economy, 1st edn. The MIT Press, Cambridge (2010)
4. Merleau-Ponty, M.: Phenomenology of Perception, 2nd edn. Routledge, London (2014)
5. Kent, C., Bloomer, F., Charles, W., Moore, S.: Body, Memory and Architecture, 1st edn. Yale University Press, New Haven (1977)
6. Steve Aukstakalnis, F.: Practical Augmented Reality: A Guide to the Technologies, Applications, and Human Factors or AR and VR, 1st edn. Pearson Education, New York (2016)

DUXU for Culture and Tourism

A Study on Travel Experience Design Based on the Motivation of Chinese Millennials to Travel Alone

Xi Chen$^{(\boxtimes)}$ and Linong Dai

Shanghai Jiaotong University, Shanghai, China
c.henxi@sjtu.edu.cn

Abstract. This study studies Chinese millennial solo travelers as a unique research object to explore their motivations for solo travel and provide guidance for user experience design. Millennials have become the backbone of the Chinese travel market, with the proportion of millennials traveling alone on the rise. Solo travelers are freer and more immersed in the journey itself, so they demand a more personalized experience. However, China's products for this group are still in the immature stage, and the real needs of this group have not been explored and met. Therefore, this paper will explore the needs and motivations of solo travelers. According to netnography, ethnography and questionnaire research, Chinese millennials have seven main motivations for solo travel, which can be further grouped into three motivation types, including enjoy oneself, play in group and express oneself. Their travel satisfaction has 9 important influencing factors, including safety, cost-effective, privacy, sociability, familiarity, novelty, uniqueness, richness and quality. Different motivations have different weight of influencing factors. For people who enjoy oneself, familiarity, privacy, quality and novelty are important influencing factors of travel satisfaction. For people play in group, sociability, safety, familiarity and cost-effective are important. For people who express oneself, uniqueness, richness, and social travel satisfaction are important. The study identified the characteristics of solo travelers among China's millennial generation. Based on the results of the study, a comparative analysis is made based on the existing tourism products in China. This study can help researchers or service providers understand this growing market in China.

Keywords: Millennials · Travel alone · Travel satisfaction · User experience

1 Introduction

This study will explore the motivations of Chinese millennials for solo travel and the influencing factors of travel satisfaction under different motivations, and conduct a study on travel experience design based on this. According to Analysys' comprehensive analysis of China's online tourism market in 2018, free travel accounted for 68.6% of China's online tourism market in 2018, and group travel accounted for 31.4%, making free travel the preferred travel mode. In addition, according to Ctrip, China's largest online travel

© Springer Nature Switzerland AG 2020
A. Marcus and E. Rosenzweig (Eds.): HCII 2020, LNCS 12202, pp. 581–593, 2020.
https://doi.org/10.1007/978-3-030-49757-6_42

company, millennials (born between 1982 and 2000) accounted for 37.3% of the total number of trips in China's online travel market in 2018, and have become the backbone of China's travel market, with the number of trips and sales on the rise. Unlike their parents' generation, travel has become a necessity for Chinese millennials.

Millennials are seeking personalized travel experiences. In China, where collective culture is prized, the proportion of young people traveling alone from the point of departure is rising. According to Airbnb and CBNData, in 2018, 42% of Chinese travelers born between 1995 and 2000 traveled alone, 28% of Chinese travelers born between 1990 and 1995 traveled alone, and 28% of Chinese travelers born between 1980 and 1989 traveled alone. Travelers who travel alone, regardless of the needs of their fellow travelers, can plan their trips according to their own preferences, often reaching smaller destinations and enjoying themselves more personally, whether it's urban leisure, outdoor extremes, or nature.

For people traveling alone, they need more electronic devices, especially mobile phones. China is developing smart tourism, and smart products improve the travel experience. Xiaohongshu, Douyin, Weibo travel and other social media platforms bring rich and colorful tourism information to tourists. Online tourism content platforms such as Mafengwo and Qyer provide detailed sources of strategies for tourists to travel. Online travel booking platforms such as Ctrip, Tuniu and Lvmama make travel more convenient. In addition, consumers who travel alone place a higher value on safety and reliability than those who don't travel alone.

At present, China's tourism market to deal with this group of product design is mainly divided into two categories. One is the travel community, which usually appears as a small section in the software or website, the most common is the "Travel Together" column in Qyer and Mafengwo; The other category is a destination experience suitable for one person, with citywalk within a day as the most typical. However, the user experience of the current Chinese tourism market designed for this group is not good and fails to consider the different needs of users. Companion software, for example, can only mechanically filter out people at the same time and place. In addition, 66% of solo travelers in China need to maintain personal space and privacy and do not want to be disturbed by others, which is rarely considered. Therefore, it is necessary to comprehensively and systematically study the travel motivation and influencing factors of solo tourists.

2 Literature Review

2.1 The Rise of the Single Economy

According to the statistics of the 2018 statistical bulletin on the development of civil affairs issued by the ministry of civil affairs of China, the number of single adults in China has exceeded 220 million, including over 77 million adults living alone [1]. Compared with the 50 million "empty-nest youth" based on Alibaba's statistics in 2017, the increase was as high as 54%. Centering on the phenomenon of "empty-nest youth", Alibaba, Meituan, Tencent, Netease, Bilibili and other platforms of various industries are vigorously exploring the "accompanying economy" and "lonely economy" derived from them from the perspectives of online shopping, takeaway, gaming esports, live broadcasting, animation and secondary culture, gradually forming a clear development context of "single economy".

2.2 Solo Traveler

In the existing literature, studies on solo travelers are mainly female solo travelers. Scholars generally start from the aspects of female psychology, gender difference and emotional characteristics. From the perspective of consumption motivation, female tourists are more likely to show strong cultural motivation, independent motivation, romantic motivation and shopping motivation. Social communication, emotional exchange and relaxation are also the main motivations of female tourists. On the other hand, Chinese women's awareness of women's rights is increasing, and their independence requirements are also increasing. Women's economic status has also improved significantly as social work has become more diverse and open. The domestic safe public environment and tourism environment also further release the consumption potential of female tourism and meet the female tourists' demand for security.

There is no single definition of "solo travel" in current research. In this paper, the definition of solo travel is: travel from the origin to the destination alone. At the destination, you could have one or more trips together with others, but not the whole journey together with others. Brief shared experiences at the destination include attending local travel experiences, dining with local friends, chatting with locals, etc.

2.3 Travel Motivation

Yeqiang (Kevin) Lin (2019) et al. argue that the motivations and emotions of tourists are increasingly recognized as important components of the travel experience in tourism science and should ideally match the destination attributes. The potential relationship between emotion and motivation is particularly important for destination promotion and visitor segmentation [2]. Examining tourists' motivations is crucial to understanding, explaining and conceptualizing travel behavior [3]. In order to provide tourists with adequate travel experience, it is important to determine their travel motivations [4].

Scholars have different research perspectives and methods on tourism motivation. Regarding the concept of tourism motivation and its measurement methods, Pincus (2004) pointed out that motivation had been a popular research topic in the "psychoanalytic studies" of the 1950s and 1960s and continued to be studied in the era of psychophysiology (1970s and 1980s). Researchers have followed four main approaches in motivation checking: need-based, value-based, seeking or realizing benefits, and expectancy theory [5]. In addition, the development of the concept of travel motivation is largely based on Maslow's (Maslow, 1954) motivation theory [6].

As for the classification of travel motivation, some researchers (iso-ahola, 1982) use the two-dimensional theoretical framework to explain tourists' motivation, namely escapism (the tendency to avoid daily life activities related to individuals and interpersonal relationships) and reward (the tendency to travel under various conditions to obtain basic rewards) [7]. Some scholars use four dimensions of motivation as the measurement of travel motivation, namely: a. escape: relax, recover, and stay away from daily troubles; B. Novelty: visit scenic spots and experience destinations; C. relationships:

spending time with family and sharing experiences with family; [d] self-development: learning new things and experiencing other cultures. Moreover, the researchers found that the proportion of avoidance was the highest, while the proportion of seeking relationships was the lowest [2]. Pearce and Lee (2005) pointed out the core of travel motivation factors, including escape, relaxation, interpersonal relationship enhancement and self-development [8]. Scholars have different opinions on the classification of travel motives, but there is no accepted opinion.

3   Research

3.1   Netnography

Netnography is a qualitative research method for understanding culture and community through Internet. Through the method of netnography, researchers can identify the characteristics of the main consumer groups and specific culture. This approach can reach a wide range of people at minimal cost. Internet has been applied in tourism research (WangfeiWang, 2018).

The purpose of this step is to quickly understand the motivations and influencing factors of Chinese millennials traveling alone. In China, travelers contribute a great deal of data to the online travel community, and information about them is available from travel social media.

Select the Appropriate Network Community. Through baidu, China's largest search engine for travel-related content, the emerging online communities can be divided into the following four types: (1) tourism strategy platform websites (49%), such as hornet's nest, ctrip and budget travel, are the main platforms for travelers to share their travels and strategies; (2) virtual community websites (29%), such as zhihu, douban and other BBS sites, are major platforms for travelers to share detailed travel experiences; (3) personal blogs and blog aggregators (12%), such as weibo, are platforms for real-time travel sharing; (4) sharing media sites (10%), such as little red book, often contain other sharing content on such platforms.

Travel guides and virtual community sites have detailed information about travelers, covering the process before, during and after a trip, and are highly interactive communities that can get a lot of information about solo travelers. Therefore, the researcher determined to conduct research in the online community in (1) and (2).

Data Collection: 150 Cases of Solo Travel. The study selected five platforms – China's largest online travel platforms, hornet's hive, ctrip and qunyouyou, as well as China's largest virtual community sites zhihu and douban. Each platform screened 30 examples of millennials traveling alone. These blogs or posts usually exceed 1,000 words. The researchers created a file for each case and entered key information into the information sheet.

Data Analysis: Coding. The researchers used a grounded theory to encode the data. First, the user requirements are used as the basis for coded data. In the first-level coding, with the help of Maslow's needs theory, user needs are divided into seven levels:

physiological needs, safety needs, social needs, self-esteem needs, aesthetic needs, cognitive needs and self-realization needs. In the secondary coding, we find the motivation behind the user needs, classify the motivation, and get the codes of 7 main motivations. In the three-level coding, seven main motivations are divided into three types through censydiam model, and three motivations are obtained, which are used as the basis for user clustering.

The Censydiam model was developed by the Censydiam Institute of Synovate. It reflects the user's crisscrossed, conflicting multiple needs at the same time. Censydiam's consumption motivation analysis model adopts the "2-dimensional 8-quadrant" analysis method, which refers to individual-group and release-control. The individual-group latitude indicates people's attitude in dealing with the relationship between individuals and society, which is represented by "power" and "belonging". When a person's behavior is dominated by "power", he will pursue inner calm and firm, adhere to his sense of independence. On the contrary, when a person's behavior is dominated by "belonging," he will want to be part of a group, desire to gain support from the group, and strengthen his own strength. The release-control dimension reflects the individual's attitude in the face of desire, manifested as "enjoyment" and "control". When a person's behavior is dominated by "enjoyment", he will have no scruple to satisfy his needs and desires to the maximum extent physically and psychologically. On the contrary, when a person's behavior is dominated by "control", he is a person who tries to restrain his own emotional needs and inner desires. He may lack passion, or even conform to rules, and have no personal opinion on life.

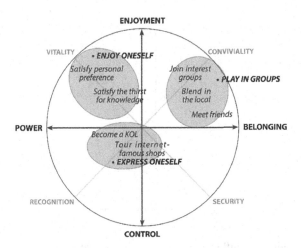

Fig. 1. Censydiam model

Based on the above analysis, the seven main motivations were found corresponding positions in censydiam model, and the seven main motivations were divided into three types according to the coordinate as the main boundary.

In this study, the horizontal dimension from left to right describes whether people tend to "keep personal space" or "participate in group activities" when traveling alone (Fig. 2).

Fig. 2. The horizontal dimension

The vertical dimension, from top to bottom, describes whether people tend to "pursue personal preference" or "follow others' recommendations" when traveling alone (Fig. 3).

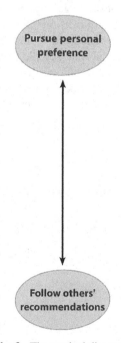

Fig. 3. The vertical dimension

In this phase, nine key influencing factors of travel satisfaction were also extracted, which were revised in later studies.

3.2 Ethnography

In the online community, users want to show the good side of their trip and gain more recognition, so they don't fully show the disadvantages of traveling alone. Further ethnographic studies are therefore required to obtain as complete a picture of the traveler as possible. The user characteristics of Chinese millennials traveling alone were obtained from online travel platform Ctrip (based on data from 2017 to 2019): (1) gender: female accounts for 58% and male accounts for 42%; (2) occupation: 72% are workers and 28% are students (3) travel time: mainly 4-6 days; (4) departure places: Shanghai, Beijing, Shenzhen, Nanjing and Chongqing are the main departure places. According to this user characteristic, 30 target users were selected in proportion and in-depth interviews were conducted on them. The interview is mainly about the respondents' basic information, travel preferences and an impressive solo travel experience. The researchers wanted participants to describe in as much detail as possible the process, thoughts, and problems encountered during and after the trip. After the interview, the researcher made repeated insight analysis on the interview content and corrected the initial motivation and influencing factors according to the insight results.

In this phase of research, researchers have a deeper understanding of users and explain how various impact factors affect travel satisfaction through interviews.

3.3 The Questionnaire

The motivations and influencing factors of the people traveling alone can be obtained through netnography and ethnography, and the weights of influencing factors corresponding to different motivations should also be known. Therefore, the researcher distributed questionnaires to 500 target users through questionnaires, and got 463 valid questionnaires. According to the results of questionnaire analysis, the relationship between motivation and influencing factors was obtained.

4   Research Results

The data results show that: (1) there is a close relationship between the motivation of solo travelers and the influencing factors of travel satisfaction; (2) the weight of the influencing factors is different under different travel motivations; (3) there are seven main motivations for solo travelers among Chinese millennials, including satisfying personal preference, satisfying the thirst for knowledge, joining interest groups, meeting friends, blending in the local, becoming a KOL, and touring internet-famous shops. The main influencing factors of travel satisfaction include: safety, cost-effective, privacy, sociability, familiarity, novelty, uniqueness, richness and quality. The seven types of motivation can be divided into three types: (1) enjoy oneself: satisfy personal preference, satisfy the thirst for knowledge; familiarity, privacy, quality and novelty are important factors influencing travel satisfaction. (2) play in groups: join interest groups, meet friends, and blend in the local; sociability, familiarity, safety and cost-effective are important factors influencing travel satisfaction. (3) express oneself: become a KOL and tour internet-famous shops; uniqueness, richness and sociability are important factors (Table 1).

The significance represented by the 9 impact factors is as follows:

Safety: ensure the safety of solo travel.
Cost-effective: reduce the cost of spending more on solo travel.
Privacy: ensure that personal space and time are not disturbed.

Table 1. Motivation and impact factor

Three types of motivation	Motivation	Percentage	Impact factor
Enjoy oneself	Satisfy personal preference	72%	Familiarity, Privacy, Quality
	Satisfy the thirst for knowledge	28%	Novelty, Privacy
Play in groups	Join interest groups	40%	Sociability, Familiarity, Safety, Cost-effective
	Meet friends	33%	Sociability
	Blend in the local	27%	Sociability, Safety, Cost-effective
Express oneself	Become a KOL	57%	Uniqueness, Richness, Sociability
	Tour internet-famous shops	43%	Richness, Sociability

Sociability: able to communicate well with others or improve the activity level in social media.

Familiarity: a high degree of familiarity with the content of the trip.

Novelty: the content of the travel experience is something you have never experienced before.

Uniqueness: the content of the travel experience is not experienced by others.

Richness: the destination has good infrastructure and a wealth of travel items.

Quality: the service at the destination is of high quality.

Three types of motivation are further elaborated below:

4.1 Enjoy Oneself

The largest percentage of Chinese millennials traveling alone are self-motivated, accounting for about 48%. This group travel alone because of their strong preference (72%) or curiosity about the destination (28%). For people who travel alone in pursuit of strong preferences (a1), familiarity is an important factor influencing their travel satisfaction because they have their favorite content in the destination, such as the museum, concert hall or exhibition they like. Novelty is an important factor in the satisfaction of solo travelers (a2) who are driven by intellectual curiosity and want to explore different cultural content. This group emphasizes "alone" in solo travel, they like to enjoy free exploration and unexpected travel very much, and believe that being alone can make them more immersed in the travel, and they do not want to destroy the freedom of solo travel, therefore, privacy is also an important factor influencing their travel satisfaction. In addition, people who travel alone in pursuit of strong preferences (a1) show higher requirements for quality. The reason is that such people often have certain monetary costs in pursuit of personal preferences and quality of life, and they are not willing to compromise themselves. They will not lower their requirements because of the high cost of accommodation and lodging in solo travel. Quality is an important factor influencing their travel satisfaction.

People who are self-centered have more freewheeling travel. They don't have a detailed plan for the trip, so they are free to choose the mode of transportation and have more possibilities to change routes at will during the trip. Their trips are usually arranged according to their preferences. During their travels, they may use memos or audio recordings to record their moods. They may record their feelings by hand after the trip. They were less willing to share and less concerned about the interaction after sharing (receiving thumb up or comments).

4.2 Play in Groups

Playing in groups accounting for about 35%. These people travel alone in order to join interest groups, blend in the local or meet friends. This group will have one or more group-related trips during their travel, so sociability is an important factor influencing their travel satisfaction. Most of them join interest groups (b1), where they travel with people who share common interests, such as visiting amusement parks with amusement park enthusiasts, hiking with outdoor clubs, and going to concerts with rock fans. They also have a high degree of familiarity with the content of the trip requirements. Since they travel with strangers, safety is an important factor in their travel satisfaction. In addition, since they can share transportation, catering, accommodation and other resources with interest groups, the cost of solo travel is reduced, and cost-effective becomes an important factor influencing their travel satisfaction. Other people (b2) choose to go to the destination alone in order to meet with friends or family. They often make a long journey together with friends after arriving at the destination. Sociability is an important factor influencing their travel satisfaction. Others (b3) are interested in the specific culture of destination and are keen to blend in with the local area. They want to experience local life and like to chat with local people and make local friends. Because of frequent interactions with strangers, safety is also an important factor in their travel satisfaction. Their desire to experience the place may also make the journey longer and accommodation more expensive, so cost is an important consideration.

Play with groups the highlights of this group's journey, they enjoy having fun with the group and are happy to share the journey with their friends.

4.3 Express Oneself

Fewer, about 17%, were motivated by expressing oneself. This group of people will go to travel destinations to tour internet-famous shops and even expect to become key opinion leaders (KOL). This group emphasizes self-respect, achievement and self-confidence. They often get affirmation or feedback through sharing and commenting on social platforms. They emphasize the acquisition and sharing of information. In order to get a chance to speak in the online community, travelers require that their destinations have attractions or restaurants that are popular with netizens. Richness is an important factor influencing their travel satisfaction. Travelers tour internet-famous shops (c2) are mostly for existing popular destinations on the network. Travelers want to be KOL (c1) will explore the network is not hot or just emerging destinations, they may be a blogger, travel experience or potential bloggers, they travel to destinations to find special content, and then put their experience to the network in the community and to introduce others to travel. Uniqueness is an extremely important factor influencing their travel satisfaction.

Due to the tendency of "punching in" in the travel process of this group, this group will arrange the itinerary in detail and seldom change the itinerary during the journey. They spend more time commenting on attractions, restaurants, sharing tips, and as a result spend more time editing photos, videos, and travel notes.

It should be mentioned that travel is a long time, more complex emotional behavior. Thus, during a solo trip, a person may have different types of motivation, that is, at different stages, he may be classified as one of the different types of people discussed above, rather than as a single type of people.

5 Discussion

5.1 Placement of the Seven Main Motivations in the Censydiam Model

As can be seen from the Fig. 1, the seven motives in censydiam model are arranged to the left and up. The study looked at millennials who travel alone, and those who do are more likely to show independence and self-awareness, thus leaning to the left. The overall upswing is consistent with the fact that travel is a more enjoyable and liberating process, and it suggests that solo travelers among millennials are more likely to have their own preferences and pay for them. For them, the fact that the destination has something they like is the key reason that drives them to travel to the destination. Their passion for hobbies makes them willing to travel alone from the start to the destination.

5.2 Possibility of Transformation of Three Types of Motivation

This section will discuss whether three types of motivation are transformable, which has important implications for product design and marketing. As mentioned above, people who enjoy themselves and play in groups are those who have their own clear preferences, while people who express themselves do not show their own clear preferences during travel. They are fundamentally different from each other. It can also be concluded from the questionnaire results that there are significant differences in influencing factors between these two groups of people. People who enjoy themselves and play in groups are more immersed and enjoy the trip, paying more attention to personal experience. People who express themselves pay more attention to the output after the trip and the feedback from others, so they can bring more value to others. Thus, there is little chance of a transition between the two groups.

Therefore, the possibility of transformation between self-enjoyment and group-play people is discussed here. From the Venn diagram, it can be seen that familiarity is an important factor shared by self-enjoyment and group-play groups. Familiarity means how much they know and how well they know the content of their trip. In other words, the destination should have enough attractive points that fit their preferences. The findings go against the stereotype. One might think that novelty would be a big draw for millennials to travel alone, but in the survey, millennials said that if something new is available at a destination, they tend to seek out friends or family to try a new trip so they can discuss it with each other (Fig. 4).

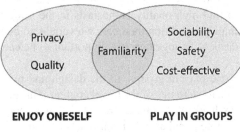

ENJOY ONESELF   **PLAY IN GROUPS**

Fig. 4. Venn diagram about factors of two groups

People who enjoy themselves emphasize more privacy and quality than people who play in groups. The sociability of group is not conducive to them enjoying their own travel, and they prefer to focus on what they like. People who enjoy themselves are generally more confident and have a high degree of control over their own preferences and travel content. One of the study's typical self-enjoyment girls was a longtime flower lover who liked to travel to flower markets. She would spend a day looking for plants and didn't want anyone to bother her. Even the florist's recommendation seemed superfluous. Therefore, the self-enjoy group is less likely to turn to the group-play group, possibly because they want to experience and be discussed with equally experienced people. They must find high-quality people with a high level of insight or experience in their preferred field before they are likely to forgo the pleasures of solo travel. For example, they all have deep research on museums and can give meaningful insights when visiting museums, or they are deep fans of rock music, or they're both experts in exploration. Moving from being alone to being with the experienced makes their journey deeper and more rewarding. Traveling with a beginner may interfere with their activities. They have higher demands on their companions.

On the contrary, people who play in groups tend to enjoy the fun of playing with others and enjoy higher cost performance. They have little incentive to make a change and opt for private travel. And it's hard for them to convince themselves to pay more for solo travel unless they enjoy the high quality of solo travel. One respondent in the study mentioned that she used to share a room with friends, but after experiencing the freedom and convenience of living alone in a hotel room, she no longer wanted to share a room with others.

5.3 Implications for User Experience Design and Marketing

First, for the people who enjoy themselves, in the design or marketing of the first is to emphasize the characteristics of the travel content, with enough attraction to promote the potential traveler's desire to travel. Based on this, there are two ways to enhance design or marketing. One is an emphasis on privacy and quality, such as practicing Thai boxing with a boxing coach who focuses on boxing rather than chatting, a one-person meal for high-end food lovers, or an exhibition center with audio Tours. There are many travel products that emphasize warm service, but little consideration is given to the fact that some young people don't want to have much interaction with others, which is especially important for individualistic millennials who looking to relax through business travel. Another way is help to find high-quality enthusiasts in the same field who share the same interests, for example, expedition members who could go on adventures together or people who could drink wine together. It is important to be careful when selecting playmates for them.

Second, for the people play in groups, in the design and marketing, the primary emphasis is also on the characteristics of the travel content. This group is more cheerful and enthusiastic, so more lively elements can be added to the design and marketing, and colorful posters may be more popular with them. In design and marketing, show the joy of having fun with others and tell them that they won't be alone when they travel, even if they don't have friends to travel with. While displaying the characteristics of playing with others, it is important to emphasize safety, such as sound screening mechanism and safety guarantee mechanism. Price is also a good promotion factor, and the price comparison with the single consumption will be an important means to attract people to consume.

Third, for the people who express themselves, the key to design and marketing is to embody the "uniqueness" of the travel content, because only unique enough content can give them a voice on the Internet and gain an audience. In addition, by optimizing the interaction design of social platforms, they can gain more performance space and attention. This group can produce great value for others in travel, and its value-creating characteristics can also be used as a marketing means to promote their travel.

5.4 Chinese Travel Products Aimed at Millennials Traveling Alone

In China, a country where group culture has long dominated, solo travel has boomed among millennials in recent years. However, there are few travel products aimed at millennials traveling alone, especially for those who enjoy themselves. In the high consumption products, some high star hotels or resorts launch high-end holiday packages, with higher privacy and quality; Among low and medium products, Klook offers a number of one-person travel experiences. The importance to the privacy and quality of products should be promoted in low and medium consumption products.

Travel with a companion is the earliest product for solo travelers in China, which is suitable for group players. Qyer, 54 traveler, Airbnb experience column have done this kind of product try. However, security as a key factor is ignored in the Qyer, which allows users to post a post soliciting travelers by simply editing text or adding unverified photos. It has low reliability. 54 traveler is a fun travel product that only allows people between the ages of 16 and 39 to sign up to make sure the fun of traveling together. However, the resulting higher prices than regular tour groups, which may include older people, reduce cost-effective.

For the people who like to express themselves, there are already many social networking platforms in China that capture the psychology of this crowd and launch corresponding travel products or functions. Among them, the main publishing platforms are Mafengwo and Xiaohongshu, which are similar to Instagram outside China. A few, such as KLOOK, launch a variety of experience products and collect travel experience officers, so that those who are willing to spread can show their skills and charm to their heart's content, which is a better marketing method.

References

1. Sohu News. http://www.sohu.com/a/340345109_556233. Accessed 13 Dec 2019
2. Lin, YK., Nawijn, J.: The impact of travel motivation on emotions: a longitudinal study. J. Destination Mark. Manag. 100363 (2019)
3. Prebensen, N.K., Woo, E., Chen, J.S.: Motivation and involvement as antecedents of the perceived value of the destination experience. J. Travel Res. 52, 253–264 (2013)
4. Beh, A., Bruyere, B.L.: Segmentation by visitor motivation in three Kenyan national reserves. Tour. Manag. 28, 1464–1471 (2007)
5. Albayrak, T., Caber, M.: Examining the relationship between tourist motivation and satisfaction by two competing methods. Tour. Manag. 69, 201–213 (2018)
6. Maslow, A.H.: Motivation and Personality, 3rd edn. Harper & Row, New York (1954)
7. Iso-Ahola, S.E.: Toward a social psychological theory of tourism motivation: a rejoinder. Ann. Tour. Res. 9, 256–262 (1982)
8. Pearce, P.L., Lee, U.I.: Developing the travel career approach to tourist motivation. J. Travel Res. 43, 226–237 (2005)

Research Upon the Relativity Between Digital Media and Tourism

Wei Feng[✉] and Peng Wang

Shandong College of Tourism and Hospitality, 3556, East Jingshi Road, Jinan, Shandong, China
13964076217@163.com

Abstract. This thesis originates from the authors both as tourism educators and multimedia professionals loving nature and travelling. In this information era, digital media has turned out to be the most common medium of social life with the content of communication shifting from text-centered ones to interactive multimedia forms of images and videos. Mingling in the Nature, human society and the virtual world, digital media is developing rapidly with dazzling new concepts and technologies such as new media, We Media, and media convergence. Digital media has its unique tool in creation which is further fortified by computer and network technology at the aim of comprehensive artistic interaction. Hence a variety of VR, AR, and H5 are being widely used. The nature of tourism activities is the interaction between people and nature. The development of society and the improvement of people's living standards have gradually increased the proportion of tourism activities in people's daily lives. Tourists have a strong dependence on information. Whether it is communication or expression, the traditional tourism industry cannot meet the needs of the public. The combination of the fastest growing digital media and the broadest travel culture will inevitably produce unique and fascinating products. In view of the characteristics of digital media and modern tourism, the relationship between them is mutually reinforcing and inseparable. The promotion, promotion and implementation of tourism are inseparable from digital media. Every step of social development is driven by innovation and demands. Digital media and tourism are entering into the era of individuality, both complimenting, incorporating, and improving for mutual success and representing a vigorous and promising prospect for us.

Keywords: Digital media · Tourism · Short video

1 Introduction

The latest data of the Statistical Report on the Development of the Internet in China issued by CNNIC is shown in Fig. 1. As of June 2019, Chinese mobile Internet access traffic consumption reached 55.39 billion GB, a year-on-year increase of 107.3%. In particular, the major video platforms further segmented content categories, focusing on IP (Intellectual Property). Form a coordinated entertainment content ecosystem in areas such as video content and music, literature, games, and e-commerce [1].

© Springer Nature Switzerland AG 2020
A. Marcus and E. Rosenzweig (Eds.): HCII 2020, LNCS 12202, pp. 594–607, 2020.
https://doi.org/10.1007/978-3-030-49757-6_43

	2018(million)	2019(million)	Proportion(%)
Chinese Internet users	828.02	854	61.2
Chinese mobile netizens	817.16	847	99.1
Network video users	725.09	759	88.8

Fig. 1. The 44th Statistical Report on Internet Development in China (Source: Author)

At the same time, the data of Q2 Global Digital Report 2019 is shown in Fig. 2. As of early April 2019, there were more than 5.1 billion mobile phone users worldwide, smartphones accounted for more than two-thirds of all devices, and 98% of global social media users (over 3.4 billion people) accessed social platforms via mobile devices. GlobalWebIndex data shows that nearly half of Internet users aged 16 to 24 use voice features, while less than 30% of users aged 45 and older use voice [2].

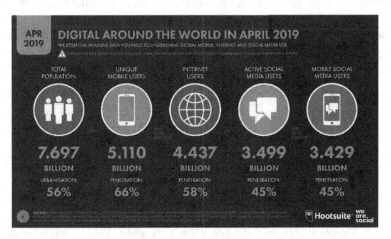

Fig. 2. Q2 Global Digital Report 2019 (Source: Baidu search)

2 Digital Media Overview

Today's society is in the era of the great development of the Internet. Traditional media is gradually changing to digital media. Compared with the past traditional media era, this era has changed a lot. As binary expressions composed of 0 and 1 are more stable and reliable, it is inevitable that digital media will gradually replace traditional media and become mainstream media. The interactive nature of digital media has led audiences to actively select and publish information. The audience is not only passively waiting for the content to be distributed, but as long as they are willing, everyone can use digital media to become the main body of the communication. At the same time, benefiting from cloud computing and big data technologies, diverse and personalized content can be more accurately pushed to the audience. In recent years, China's digital social platforms have developed rapidly. New concepts and technologies have emerged endlessly, and various expressions are overwhelming, such as new media, media convergence, and self-media. There are also many new communication methods, such as WeChat public account, Weibo, TikTok, WeChat applets (compared with foreign countries, such as YouTube, Facebook, etc.); VR, AR, H5 and other various application technologies emerge endlessly.

2.1 Definition

Compared to traditional media, digital media is a newer concept and form. It is sometimes called new media. "It is a form of communication that uses digital technology and network technology to provide users with information and entertainment services through channels such as the Internet, wireless communication networks, satellites, and terminals such as computers, mobile phones, and digital televisions. Strictly speaking, new media should be called digital media" [3]. Traditional media usually refers to newspapers, magazines, televisions, and broadcasts. Among them, newspapers and magazines belong to paper media, and television and radio belong to the analog domain; All paper media information can be re-encoded according to computer coding standards, and the analog signals can be converted into digital signals through the process of sampling, quantization and encoding (as shown in Fig. 3), which is very convenient for storage, editing, carrying, sharing and spread.

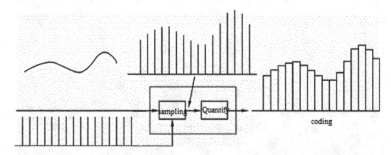

Fig. 3. The process of sampling, quantization, and encoding (Source: Baidu search)

"In fact, digital media is different from new media. Digital media is digitally defined, so the connotation and expansion of new media is more abundant." [4]. From the etymological point of view, the word "New Media" was proposed by P. Goldmark, the director of the Columbia Radio and Television Network Technology Institute in 1967, and gradually expanded to the whole world [5]. It is iterative and a developing concept. For example, over time, broadcasting is new media relative to newspapers, and television is new media relative to broadcasting. Since the Internet was officially used as the official definition of the United Nations in 1998, the Internet has become a new medium relative to television. Modern new media has digital characteristics. It can be said that digital media is a new media at this stage.

In summary, the new media can be regarded as digital media.

2.2 Features

1) Integrated/Diversity

Digital media can be used to express a variety of information such as text, graphics, audio and video through different combinations of 0 and 1. It has integration and diversity (integration of technology, diversity of expression methods, and diversity of communication channels). Because of digital media includes diversified media elements, making the information richer and more vivid, it is gradually replacing the traditional media form with the highest user rate.

2) Interactivity

From keyboards to mice, from touch screens to speech recognition, the way humans interact with digital devices is becoming more humane, tending to simpler and faster shortcuts, and the fragmented time of humans is occupied by digital devices. Interactive performance is much easier to implement in the digital domain than in the analog domain, so interactivity is a basic characteristic of digital media.

3) Real-time

Audience feedback has changed from limited time and limited places in the past to interactive expressions anytime, anywhere. This kind of instant interaction brought by convenient operation greatly enhances the audience's sense of participation and immersion, and makes the communication content easier to spread. The inefficient one-way transmission of traditional media has evolved into the high-efficiency two-way transmission of digital media, and the audience has begun to actively select and disseminate information. This feature can obviously improve the efficiency of information dissemination.

4) Personalization

Innovative digital media has entered the era of personalization. Digital media can use its strength to combine different audiences' preferences, performance pictures, text, sound, image and other combined information to achieve the purpose of personalized communication. The effectiveness of accurate dissemination based on big data depends entirely on whether the information for different audiences has personalized tags, which is also a typical feature that distinguishes it from ordinary mass communication.

In the future, it will be intelligent. It will be a multi-point to multi-point communication method for everyone (to quote from "Introduction to New Media in the Intelligent Age") Compared with single-point-to-multipoint transmission in traditional media, there are more methods, more flexible directions, and easier content diffusion. Of course, it is more prone to a lot of invalid information, and you should pay special attention to it.

It is an indisputable fact that the paper carrier that has been circulating for thousands of years, the CD that has been in use for 40 years, and the mobile phone that has been in use for 20 years have been spiked by smartphones that have only appeared for 10 years. Digital media is not only a concept of technology, but also a new type of communication. Facts have proved that it affects the development of various fields deeply by affecting the behavior of the audience.

2.3 Forms and Channels of Communication

What is the first thing when modern people open their eyes every day? I believe that for many people, it is to pick up a mobile phone, which is an extension of online media. Whether it is a PC, a notebook, or a smart phone-type mobile terminal, digital media basically includes the following forms of communication: digital publishing, digital music, digital games, digital audio and video, etc.; The main communication channels are websites, video platforms and apps.

Digital media presents a strong social attribute on devices such as smartphones. Different regions have created many different social networking sites, video platforms and related apps. For example, China's Weibo, WeChat, short videos such as Tik Tok, and long videos such as Youku. And well-known WhatsApp, Facebook, Twitter, Instagram, YouTube, etc.

The ultimate purpose of technology is to serve people. It is the best choice to make digital media as the main communication carrier, combined with traditional media.

3   The Essence of Tourism

The essence of tourism is the interaction between man and nature.

3.1   Historical Origin

Human tourism activities originate from the migration of primitive people. The movement of people during migration is one of the most basic characteristics of tourism. However, the migration of primitive people is for survival needs, which is different from the tourism activities of modern society. With the increase of productivity and economic level, real tourism activities are gradually prevailing. There are lots of records from the Silk Road pioneered by Emperor Hanwu of China, to <The Travels of Marco Polo>, which was created in 1299, then from Zheng He's voyages to the west in the 15th century Chinese Ming Dynasty (see Exotic Images on the right), to the Geographical Discovery era. Even in China, the opening day of "The Travels of Xu Xiake" was designated as China Tourism Day on May 19, 2011. There

is an old saying in China: "It is better to travel ten thousand miles than to read ten thousand books." At this time, tourism activities were mainly economic exchanges and adventures.

3.2 Development Status

With the continuous progress of society and the improvement of the living standards of the masses, the world is relatively peaceful and stable, and people's pursuit of spiritual and cultural life is on the agenda. Tourism can relax your body and mind, broaden your horizons, and is ideal for leisure activities in your spare time. Therefore, the proportion of tourism activities in people's daily life has gradually increased and has become an important part of people's lives around the world. Tourism has also become one of the world's largest industries.

The "China Domestic Tourism Development Annual Report 2019" issued by the China Tourism Academy on September 21, 2019 predicts that the number of domestic tourists in China will reach 6.06 billion in 2019. Young people born after 90 years have become the backbone of tourism; According to the "2019 China Tourism Development Report" released on December 19, 2019, the number of domestic tourists, outbound tourists, and inbound tourists in China was 5.54 billion, 149.7 million, and 141.2 million. China's comprehensive tourism contribution ranks second in the world [6].

The "China Mobile Internet Development Report (2019)" mentioned that through the extensive expansion and application of smartphones and mobile Internet, the penetration rate of mobile tourism users has continued to increase, and the mobile terminal has become the most important sales channel for the tourism industry. At the same time, mobile tourism companies have deepened the offline development of tourist destinations, and companies in different fields have begun to move into mobile tourism. Online tourism has entered the era of mobile tourism, and mobile has become an important trend in the tourism industry.

The theme of World Tourism Day 2018 is "Digital Development of Tourism". China Tourism Research Institute and Google and Google jointly released the "2019 China Inbound Tourists' Behavior and Attitude Analysis Report", which believes that the right time, the right content and the right channels of information release are critical to improving the experience of inbound tourists [7].

3.3 Development of Tourism Activities

An effective tourism activity should have the following steps: Tourists obtain information, choose a destination, Reservation (including transportation arrangements, accommodation arrangements, food arrangements), entertainment and activities, sharing and evaluation, as shown in Table 1.

In the process of tourism activities, tourists and tourism attractions are the two most important elements to maintain the overall tourism activities. Only if there are differences and uniqueness can tourism resources become tourism attractions.

Table 1. Tourism steps and realization channels (Source: Author)

Step	Access to information	Choose a destination	Reservation	Entertainment and activities	Sharing and evaluation
Content	Check website attractions, short videos, brochures, travel agencies, reviews, etc.	Country/Area, City, Countryside	Transportation, Accommodation, Food, Tickets	Natural Landscapes, Historical Monuments, Museums, Events	Share travel feelings, experiences, reviews
Channel	OTAs, social networking sites/apps, short video platforms, travel agencies, etc.	Travel agency, independent travel, customized tour	OTA, car rental companies, related websites, etc.	Scenic spots and surrounding excursions, using virtual reality scenes	OTA, social networking site/app, short video platform

3.4 The Essence of Tourism

The essence of tourism is the interaction between man and nature. The tourism industry is an industry resulting from information asymmetry. Tourists are very dependent on tourism information, so the essence of the tourism industry is the process of information interaction. As the famous anthropologist Daniel Miller pointed out, the virtual world and the real world are two equal spaces and should no longer be favored one more than another. People travelling online and offline are not learning how to use technology, but learning how to live better in these two spaces [8].

4   The Relevance of Digital Media and Tourism

Due to the above description of the nature of digital media and tourism, it can be seen that the relationship between digital media and tourism is inseparable and mutually reinforcing. The acquisition of tourism information, the display of tourism resources, the promotion of tourism destinations, and the development of tourism activities can be achieved using digital media; At the same time, the virtual world and the natural world are connected by people, and frequent interactions have created many new formats, new channels, new technologies, new methods, and new careers related to digital media, promoting the further development of digital media. Tourists often obtain cross-validation of tourism-related information through multiple channels, especially at the beginning of finding a destination. Digital tourism channels are indispensable at all stages of the entry and exit of tourists. At present, the main information acquisition channel is still the search engine. At the same time, tourism product comparison sites and video sites have grown significantly in importance over the past two years.

4.1 Digitalization of Tourism Resources

The description of tourist attractions is particularly important during the preparation phase of tourism activities. The motivation of tourism mainly depends on how much tourists are interested in tourism attractions. No matter it is a humanistic landscape, natural landscape or a tourist commodity, the visual perception at first glance determines to a large extent whether tourists will initiate tourism activities.

In the past, text, brochures, and category pictures were the most commonly used means of describing tourism resources, which was single, flat, and poor visual impact; Taking advantage of digital media technology to produce a video trailer with a text commentary is much better, but it is more old-fashioned, boring, and cannot fully present the characteristics of the landscape. And a pure promo is not as accurate as a landscape picture processed with PS, or a fun short video. Digital media technology can achieve artificial sublimation of the natural environment. For example, the bird's-eye view of Daming Lake in Jinan and the world's Internet celebrity Li Ziqi (As shown in Fig. 4). Almost every video shot by Li Ziqi is only about 7 min, one theme at a time. The entire communication in the video uses Chinese, but it has conquered the world with traditional Chinese food and crafts. By the end of January 2020, she has 8.12 million followers on YouTube, with a total of 1.02 billion videos played. The traditional Chinese cultural heritage and images of the ancient and idyllic life presented in the video are unforgettable. It can be seen that there are good expressions, scenes and content are more contagious than words and languages.

Fig. 4. Jinan Daming Lake and Internet celebrity, Li Ziqi (Source: Baidu search)

VR/AR and holographic projection are also very suitable technical means to display tourism resources. Use VR technology to turn typical tourism resources into virtual reality scenes and conduct 360-degree immersive experiences through the network, allowing tourists to visit without leaving the house; The introduction of scenic spots in the travel manual using AR technology effectively combines traditional media and digital media, so that tourists can get a richer understanding when they obtain travel information. In fact, the main problem that VR/AR technology can solve is unreachability, which is very suitable for tourism resource display. When tourists are inconvenient to travel, or tourism resources have disappeared or are difficult to reach for various reasons, virtual reality scenes are the most suitable means of display. For example, the reconstruction of the Great Water Law in Beijing's Yuanmingyuan, digital museums with various themes, intangible cultural heritage (Chinese traditional folk activities), virtual reality scenes used for environmental reconstruction in research trips promoted by China. Universal Studios in the United States also uses VR technology to reproduce some movie scenes for tourists to participate in the experience, which is very popular. Of course, VR technology also has many shortcomings, such as taking up memory, making it difficult to fully display, and dizziness. If the scenic area is divided into small scenes for presentation, this problem can be effectively avoided. With the increase of network speed and technological progress, these problems will be gradually solved.

4.2 Tourism Destination Promotion Channels

The development of the times and the advancement of technology have created more new channels for digital publicity and promotion. Tourism, as the world's largest industry, is also participating. The theme of World Tourism Day 2018 is "Digital Tourism Development". Tourism propaganda, promotion, and implementation are inseparable from digital media. The out-going nature of tourism has also become a good carrier for digital media development.

1) Short Video

With the advent of 4G and 5G, content is lighter, time is more fragmented, and high-immersion short videos are increasingly entering the daily life of the public. The short video promotes a new platform for tourism destination image dissemination, which will become an important means of mobile tourism marketing.

Take Tik Tok as an example, entertainment is subdivided into 14 categories. In addition to pets, games, beauties, music, life skills, and food, it also includes 8 mainstream dimensions of tourism, funny, paragraph, dance, little brother, cute baby, fashion, and creativity. KOL marketing started in the era of Weibo and has now entered the era of social video. The reason why social video can be the most important channel for KOL marketing is because of its strong interaction. The methods of exchanging experiences, sharing recommendations, and answering questions accurately reach the target consumer groups. KOL fans are very sticky and have a high conversion rate, because each KOL has its own unique charm and label, which will attract the same type of users. Therefore, brands choose KOL for advertising, which helps brand information reach users more accurately.

As Maggie Wang, AdMaster's vice president of business strategy and innovation said: "This is the era of content, consumer demand is becoming more and more diverse, and the core of social marketing-content requirements are becoming higher and higher. KOL is the content producer. A good KOL, in addition to being influential and having a good content creation ability, also needs to suit the brand's tone and category needs [9]."

In the mainstream dimension of tourism, in addition to the use of content production for short-term video platform for tourism destination marketing, nowadays, as free travel becomes more and more common, affected travel agencies can also use this platform to divert travel agency personnel. The difference between a star KOL and an ordinary KOL is that the audience is willing to paying for the former because they like the star itself, and the positioning is a free "sales consultant", which requires high levels of "professionalism". The short video platform is no longer satisfied with simply "short" and "fast", and the lengthening of the time (from 15 s to 1 min) is also trying to guide users away from instant gratification and enter the field of depth and connotation. The tour guides are very familiar with the situation of the attractions and marketing strategies. They have experience and professional advantages. They can completely switch to the short video platform. By making a series of interesting short videos related to attractions, they will become online travel destination KOLs, potentially promoting the area. KOL's Key Opinion Leader (KOL) formation path is shown in Fig. 5.

Fig. 5. KOL formation (Source: Author)

Professional guides continue to promote tourism resources through free short videos to form potential customer groups. When people with common interests come together, it is easy to direct purchase behavior. Take KOC (Key Opinion Consumer) as the starting point, transition to the tail KOL, and then grow to the head KOL. Use the influence to open a VLOGGER account at the same time. As shown in Fig. 6.

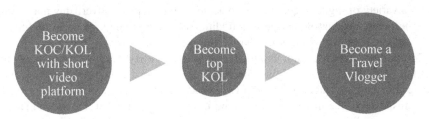

Fig. 6. The growth path of online travel professionals (Source: Author)

According to CaasData, the development direction of short videos must be a combination of short videos and PGC (Professionally-generated Content). The former quickly grabs the hearts of the people, and the latter is responsible for the capacity and density of the content. Both experiences are important. The tour guides can use their professional advantages to enter the PGC field of tourism short videos [10]. A platform's PGC and UGC can have intersections. As users of the platform, they also contribute content with a certain level and quality in a professional capacity.

CaasData from conventional short video platforms such as Tik Tok, Kwai, etc. found that pure tourism content is not receiving much attention. It has a lot to do with insufficient participation and insufficiently attractive content. The most popular and fastest-growing kinds are mostly funny and gourmet. With the development of social economy and culture, the public's willingness to travel will become stronger and more diversified, and the corresponding demand for good products and services will also increase. We can combine travel destination content with the most popular and fastest growing categories of short video platforms. Taking Tik Tok2019's fastest-growing three categories of cars, food and beauty as examples, it can correspond to self-driving in tourism, specialty foods in scenic areas and beauty-carrying attractions. Of course, it also puts forward higher requirements for diversified quality of KOL.

In addition, Bilibili had brilliant precedents for game and travel themes. For example, Might and Magic, released in 1986 and produced by New World Computing (NWC); A single-player game released in 1990 and produced by Japan's KOEI Glorious Corporation (KT Corporation)-the Great Sailing Age, players claim that "the world map is in my heart"; They are all popular games with the background of traveling around the world and the vast universe as popular.

2) Social Platform

Taking WeChat as an example, the data report from WeChat 2019 shows that as of January 2020, WeChat has 1.151 billion monthly active users. "Tencent 2019 Digital Life Report" shows: offline consumption has been fully digitized. Social, referral, and personalized purchases are advocated by users. The WeChat public platform has gathered more than 20 million public accounts, and the active peak period is 9 pm. Many public accounts have formed their own brands. Using the public account platform can make full use of a variety of digital media means to achieve content push, advertising marketing, etc. The public account is the same as traditional media in single-point to multipoint transmission, but the public account has an interactive function.

In addition, WeChat Mini Programs have been widely used. It can rely on the WeChat platform to be quickly acquired and disseminated like green software, with simple development and excellent user experience.

In response to the mobile Internet trend in the Chinese market, the second largest source country, Tourism New Zealand has formulated a strategic shift from PC to mobile. On November 7, 2019, the New Zealand Tourism Board released the "New Zealand Tourism Expert Training Program" developed on the WeChat platform at the 6th New Zealand Greater China Tourism Fair (as shown in Fig. 7). This small program is extremely social and shareable. As long as users complete 11 modules of learning through the small program and pass the online test, they can obtain the "New Zealand Travel Expert Bronze Medal". In this way, not only can you achieve professional and systematic knowledge of New Zealand's tourism destinations, promote New Zealand's tourism information, but also attract more young people to join New Zealand's customized tourism industry. Many other countries, such as the United Kingdom and Germany, have also used their small programs to develop their own national tourism expert programs, providing a way for tourism resource promotion and tourism enthusiasts to become professionals.

NEW ZEALAND SPECIALIST MINI - PROGRAM

Fig. 7. New Zealand travel expert mini program (Source: WeChat public account)

4.3 Create Tourism IP and Develop New Tourism Products

At present, the homogeneity competition in the tourism industry is becoming increasingly fierce. Problems such as a single form of tourism, weak interaction, backward marketing methods, and insufficient exploration and protection of existing tourism resources have restricted the development of many tourist attractions. Some badly managed scenic spots even face the danger of being eliminated by the market. At the same time, tourists are becoming more and more experienced and knowledgeable, and ordinary natural and human landscapes can no longer meet their needs. From the perspective of tourism enterprises, they need more diversified and attractive means of publicity and promotion and tourism attractions to influence the ideas of tourists, so as to get more tourists; From the perspective of tourists, they hope to get more convenient tourist information channels, richer tourism products, and more cost-effective tourism experiences. What is lacking in the era of national tourism is not the market nor the resources, but new products that meet the needs of different levels. Combining regional characteristics, dig deep cultural connotation, and use a variety of digital media methods, such as photography, PS, animation, short video, pixel painting, etc. Create interesting travel communication content and LOGO, create a new travel IP, create beauty in ordinary life, and use digital technology to reconstruct the traditional relationship network.

In recent years, many Internet celebrities have appeared in China, such as the intersection of Qingdao Yushan Road and University Road, which first appeared in the guide of tourism websites. Later, after many live webcasts, it became the most popular cultural attraction in Qingdao, and was called "the corner meets love" by many netizens; The Kuanhouli, which is in author's hometown of Jinan, became a must-visit place in Jinan through the Lian Yinshe's small video shot to fame of Tik Tok. These are new tourism products that have appeared in recent years. They are all interesting and suitable for the tastes of young people. They are highly sought after intangible spontaneous communication through the Internet.

4.4 Carry Out Tourism Activities and Establish an Effective Supervision Mechanism

OTA (Online Travel Agency) can be said to be an early platform for using digital media technology for tourism activities. Each OTA has the basic functions of booking hotels, transportation, and tickets; at the same time, it is full of pictures, videos, guides and various evaluations of tourist attractions. At present, the entire online travel industry has a stable user scale of about 240 million. For example, some common OTAs such as Ctrip, Qunar, Flying Pig, Tongcheng, etc. They have already segmented the market and have different characteristics. Business travellers often use Ctrip with a generous one-stop service; Students prefer "where to go", the interface is bright; Flying Pig users are mainly traveling abroad, [11] and the interface is simple and intuitive; The opening rate of Tongcheng app ranks first, and it has a lot to do with the intuitive interface. The differences in common people are closely related to their business themes and digital media design styles.

After the end of the May 1 tourism consumption season in 2019, online travel (OTA) has become the hardest hit area for consumer complaints. SaleCycle data shows that in 2019, the average online booking abandonment rate reached 90.74%. Hot issues are mainly focused on 10 different aspects: default tying, overlord clauses, big data tricks acquaintances, order reversion, information leakage, false publicity, low price traps, price increases or no tickets after ordering, and order errors (wrong orders, missing orders, etc.) and travel accident compensation [12]. Travel is a life experience, with a particular focus on the quality of the experience. We should make full use of the platform's tourism monitoring and evaluation functions to improve tourism services, enhance strengths and avoid weaknesses, and re-awaken audiences' trust in the platform. Let digital media technology be a weapon in our hands, not a double-edged sword.

In early 2020, an epidemic led by 2019-nCoV broke out in parts of China. The vast majority of people chose to stay at home to avoid the attack of the virus, which severely damaged the original Spring Festival tourism market. This unexpected event also tested the market's resilience. During the period, short video views and game downloads surged. As we all know, tourism activities are activities that leave the place of residence for the purpose of sightseeing. When the path of movement is cut off, how to save the vitality of the tourism market in emergencies poses a severe test for us. OTA can open a dedicated virtual travel channel, with short videos, VR scenes, and travel experience mini-games as the main content, leading the audience to discover goals in their free time so that they can make a trip in the near future. The travel experience mini-game can be guided by the travel strategy of a popular tourist destination. The process of playing the game is the process of successfully completing a travel activity, so that the audience can also experience the travel process at home. It is believed that after this epidemic, the tourism market will usher in a new climax.

5 Conclusion

Today's cloud computing technology is relatively mature. At the same time, major websites and social platforms have abundant big data, but the mining of travel data is obviously not enough. Relying only on data analysis of high-frequency words and search focus to infer audience preferences and trends, such pushes can even mislead data collection, produce wrong media. The final goal of the media professionals is combine the attributes of digital media and tourism activities better, using digital media to make tourism attractions glow. Ultimately let audiences get the best life experience combined with virtual and real world, online and offline. Every development of society is driven by innovation and demand. Both digital media and tourism have entered the era of personalization. They are mutually reinforcing and inseparable, they achieve each other and promote each other, presenting us with a development prospect full of vitality and unlimited potential.

References

1. CNNIC: The 44th Statistical Report on Internet Development in China [EB/OL], 30 August 2019. http://www.cnnic.cn/hlwfzyj/hlwxzbg/hlwtjbg/201908/t20190830_70800.htm
2. 199IT:: We Are Social & Hootsuite: Q2 Global Digital Report 2019 [EB/OL], 01 May 2019. http://www.199it.com/archives/870212.html
3. Huang, C., Qi, L., Wang, Q., et al.: Introduction to New Media. Beijing: Communication University of China Press, Beijing (2013)
4. Baike: Digital Media [EB/OL]. https://baike.baidu.com/item/%E6%95%B0%E5%AD%97%E5%AA%92%E4%BD%93/4295071?fr=aladdin
5. Chen, J.: Analysis of the definition and connotation of "new media". Ind. Sci. Forum **10**(7), 28–29 (2011)
6. Useit: China Tourism Academy-2019 China Domestic Tourism Development Annual Report [EB/OL], 30 September 2019. https://www.useit.com.cn/thread-24846-1-1.html
7. Tourism Circle-China Tourism Academy: 2019 China Inbound Tourists Behavior and Attitude Analysis Report [EB/OL], 05 September 2019. https://www.dotour.cn/article/147414.html
8. IT: Tencent 2019 Ditigal Life Report [EB/OL], 23 May 2019. http://www.199it.com/archives/880232.html
9. SOHU: Under the three major trends of vertical, real and short video, KOL marketing requires new skills [EB/OL], 06 July 2017. http://www.sohu.com/a/146546998_292667
10. CAASDATA: < 2019 Short Video KOL Annual Report > Heavy Release: After the explosion period, gradually shift to a stable growth period [EB/OL], 13 January 2020. https://mp.weixin.qq.com/s/0O8O-fp-cVd5VEidTMU2Xg
11. Mob Research Institute: 2019 OTA Industry Insight Report (with download) [EB/OL], 15 August 2019. http://www.199it.com/archives/919967.html
12. People.com: Survey on Hot Issues in Online Tourism Consumer Rights Protection [EB/OL], 14 May 2019. http://finance.people.com.cn/n1/2019/0514/c1004-31083025.html

Usability Evaluation Towards a Cultural Perspective: A Systematic Literature Review

Yoluana Gamboa[(⊠)], Juan Jesús Arenas, and Freddy Paz

Pontificia Universidad Católica del Perú, San Miguel 32, Lima, Peru
{a20140058,fpaz}@pucp.pe, jjarenas@pucp.edu.pe

Abstract. Usability heuristics participate in the design and evaluation of websites. Based on traditional heuristics, cultural-oriented heuristics are used to determine if a website reaches an adequate level of usability, focusing on the target audience of similar cultural characteristics. However, to know what heuristics are use to design or evaluate a website, it is necessary to know which ones are focused on the cultural environment and the type of website of interest. Through a systematic review, common procedures for establishing cultural-oriented heuristics based on traditional heuristics have been identified. In addition, the main types of website to which these heuristics are applied for usability evaluation have been also identified. This paper shows the results of the systematic review.

Keywords: Human-computer interaction · Usability heuristics · Cultural-oriented heuristics · Web interfaces

1 Introduction

Usability applied to websites is commonly defined as a quality attribute that evaluates the ease of use of its interfaces and is classified as a survival condition [19]. Due to the importance of this attribute, specialists have developed different guidelines and methods that allow them to determine if a website reaches an adequate level of usability. An example of the guidelines developed are the ten heuristics proposed by Nielsen, which are general rules for the design of user interfaces [13].

For the design and evaluation of usability, it is possible to incorporate the cultural characteristics of societies. The problem is that many sites may not take into account the characteristics of each culture because, among other reasons, including cultural issues would involve greater effort in the design of the interfaces of the websites, because the requirements of Users are influenced by their local cultural perspective [8].

To meet these needs, there are studies that include cultural issues in their heuristic proposals, which are then applied and validated on different types of websites. The purpose of this study is to identify the cultural-oriented heuristics proposals applied to websites and the procedures used to establish them.

© Springer Nature Switzerland AG 2020
A. Marcus and E. Rosenzweig (Eds.): HCII 2020, LNCS 12202, pp. 608–617, 2020.
https://doi.org/10.1007/978-3-030-49757-6_44

This paper is structured as follows: Sect. 2 presents main concepts related to cultural-oriented usability. Section 3 describes the process of systematic review. Section 4 presents the results of the research. Finally, conclusions and future works are presented in Sect. 5.

2   Theoretical Background

2.1   Usability

According to Jakob Nielsen, usability can be defined as "a quality attribute that evaluates how easy the interfaces are to use" [19]. In addition, it presents 10 heuristics [13] that are currently used to evaluate usability and to establish new heuristics. Those 10 heuristics proposed by Nielsen are listed are listed below:

- Visibility of system status.
- Match between system and the real world.
- User control and freedom.
- Consistency and standards.
- Error prevention.
- Recognition rather than recall.
- Flexibility and efficiency of use.
- Aesthetic and minimalist design.
- Help users recognize, diagnose, and recover from errors.
- Help and documentation.

2.2   Cultural Dimensions

According to Hofstede, a Dimension is "an aspect of a culture that can be measured in relation to other cultures" [11]. Accordingly, Hofstede initially proposed a four-dimensional model [11] that is composed of the concepts which are described below:

- Power Distance: The degree to which less powerful members of institutions and organizations in a country expect and accept that power is distributed unevenly.
- Individualism and Collectivism: Individualism belongs to societies in which everyone is expected to take care of themselves and their immediate family. Collectivism belongs to societies in which people are expected to protect each other in exchange for loyalty.
- Masculinity and Femininity: Gender roles and behaviors such as competitiveness, assertiveness and quality of life.
- Uncertainty Avoidance: The way in which members of a society feel threatened by ambiguous or unknown situations.

3   Systematic Literature Review

This systematic review was carried out using the methodology proposed by B. Kitchenham, which proposes the approach of a research question and the use of the PICOC method, which refers to Population, Intervention, Comparison, Outcome and Context [17].

3.1   Formulation of the Research Questions

The objective of the systematic review is to know the existence and application of usability metrics related to cultural aspects in different web domains. Therefore, the following questions are defined:

RQ1: What procedures are used to establish heuristics of evaluation in cultural aspects in the design of websites?
RQ2: What usability heuristics, focused on assessing cultural aspects in website design, are reported in the literature?

3.2   Database Selection

The following databases were selected for their relevance in the area of Computer Engineering:

- SCOPUS.
- Web of Science.
- IEEE.

3.3   Development of the Search String

The PICOC table will be used to determine the search string. The objective of this systematic review is not to make a comparison between existing usability metrics, therefore, the "comparison" criterion is not taken into account. The concepts are detailed in Table 1.

Table 1. General concepts defined using the PICOC criteria

Criterion	Description
Population	Usability heuristics
Intervention	Cultural aspects, usability on websites, UX on websites
Outcomes	Case studies, guides
Context	Academia and industry

Using the concepts established in PICOC, a search string was developed for each database. The search string for **SCOPUS** was as follows:

(TITLE-ABS-KEY ("metric" OR "metrics" OR "heuristic" OR "heuristics" OR "guideline" OR "guidelines" OR "evaluation") AND TITLE-ABS-KEY ("UX" OR "Usability" OR "HCI" OR "interface design" OR "design" OR "web design") AND TITLE-ABS-KEY ("web site" OR "web sites" OR "web page" OR "web pages" OR "web system" OR "web system" OR "web application" OR "web applications" OR "web apps") AND TITLE-ABS-KEY("cultural dimension" OR "cultural dimensions" OR "culture" OR "cultural-oriented"))

The search string for **Web of Science** was as follows:

TOPIC: ("metric" OR "metrics" OR "heuristic" OR "heuristics" OR "guideline" OR "guidelines" OR "evaluation") AND TOPIC: ("UX" OR "Usability" OR "HCI" OR "interface design" OR "design" OR "web design") AND TOPIC: ("web site" OR "web sites" OR "web page" OR "web pages" OR "web system" OR "web system" OR "web application" OR "web applications" OR "web apps") AND TOPIC: ("cultural dimension" OR "cultural dimensions" OR "culture" OR "cultural-oriented")

The search string for **IEEExplore** was as follows:

(("All Metadata":"metric" OR "All Metadata":"metrics" OR "All Metadata":"heuristic" OR "All Metadata":"heuristics" OR "All Metadata":"guideline" OR "All Metadata":"guidelines" OR "All Metadata":"evaluation") AND ("All Metadata":"UX" OR "All Metadata":"Usability" OR "All Metadata":"HCI" OR "All Metadata":"interface design" OR "All Metadata":"design" OR "All Metadata":"web design") AND ("All Metadata":"web site" OR "All Metadata":"web sites" OR "All Metadata":"web page" OR "All Metadata":"web pages" OR "All Metadata":"web system" OR "All Metadata":"web systems" OR "All Metadata":"web application" OR "All Metadata":"web applications" OR "All Metadata":"web apps") AND ("All Metadata":"cultural dimension" OR "All Metadata":"cultural dimensions" OR "All Metadata":"culture" OR "All Metadata":"cultural-oriented"))

3.4 Selection Strategy

The inclusion and exclusion criteria were the following:

Inclusion Criteria

– English language publications.
– Publications that have at least been cited in a publication.
– Publications since 2000.

Exclusion Criteria

- Publications that are not applied to websites.
- Publications that use usability but not related to the cultural approach.

4 Analysis of the Results

When performing the search, in the different databases, a total of 112 results were obtained. After applying the inclusion and exclusion criteria, 10 documents relevant to the Scopus source, 5 relevant to the Web of Science source and 2 relevant to the IEEE source were obtained, adding a total of 17 results relevant to this research. Table 2 shows the summary of what was found and Table 3 shows the list of selected articles.

Table 2. Summary of Search Results

Database name	Search results	Duplicated papers	Relevant documents
Scopus	71	1	10
Web of Science	16	0	5
IEEE	25	0	2
Total	**112**	**1**	**17**

Table 3. Relevant documents for Systematic Review

ID	Title	Author	Source	Year
A01 [12]	An empirical study of audience impressions of B2C web pages in Japan, China and the UK	Hu, J., Shima, K., Oehlmann, R., Zhao, J., Takemura, Y., Matsumoto, K	Scopus	2004
A02 [9]	Identifying cultural markers for web application design targeted to a multi-cultural audience	Fraternali, P., Tisi, M	Scopus	2008
A03 [24]	The information architecture of e-commerce: an experimental study on user performance and preference	Wan Mohd Isa, W.A.R., Md Noor, N.L., Mehad, S	Scopus	2009
A04 [14]	Website usability and cultural dimensions in Malaysian and Australian universities	Jano, Z., Noor, S.M., Ahmad, R., Md Saad, M.S., Saadan, R., Bokhari, M., Abdullah, A.N	Scopus	2015
A05 [16]	Arabic website design: user evaluation from a cultural perspective	Khashman, N., Large, A	Scopus	2013
A06 [3]	Identifying and measuring cultural differences in cross-cultural user-interface design	Alostath, J.M., Almoumen, S., Alostath, A.B	Scopus	2009
A07 [2]	Cross-cultural web design guidelines	Alexander, R., Murray, D., Thompson, N	Scopus	2017
A08 [20]	Cross-cultural language learning and web design complexity	Park, J.Y	WOS	2015

Table 3. (*continued*)

ID	Title	Author	Source	Year
A09 [6]	Colour appeal in website design within and across cultures: a multi-method evaluation	Cyr, D., Head, M., Larios, H	WOS	2010
A10 [1]	A cross-cultural comparison of Kuwaiti and British citizens' views of e-government interface quality	Aladwani, AM	WOS	2013
A11 [21]	Introducing human-computer interaction: a didactic experience	P. Rocchi	IEEE	2016
A12 [4]	Does culture matter on the web?	Burgmann, I., Kitchen, P.J., Williams, R	Scopus	2006
A13 [7]	A cultural-oriented usability heuristics proposal	Díaz, J., Rusu, C., Pow-Sang, J.A., Roncagliolo, S	Scopus	2013
A14 [10]	Applying culture to web site design: a comparison of Malaysian and US web sites	Gould, E.W., Zalcaria, N., Yusof, S.A.Mohd	IEEE	2000
A15 [23]	The cultural adaptation of web design to local industry styles: a comparative study	Snelders, D., Morel, K.P.N., Havermans, P	WOS	2011
A16 [15]	Culture-oriented evaluation method for interaction: applied in Chinese e-commerce website design	Chu, J., Zhu, X	Scopus	2010
A17 [5]	Travel destination websites: cross-cultural effects on perceived information value and performance evaluation	Cho, Mi-Hea; Sung, Heidi H	WOS	2012

The 17 articles were classified according to their scope. Table 4 shows the classification.

4.1 Methodologies to Define Heuristics

In this section, the results obtained after the review are presented. The purpose was to obtain an answer for the following research question *"What procedures are carried out to establish heuristics aimed at assessing cultural aspects in the design of websites?"*

The following procedures reported in the literature have been identified to determine whether a website represents what it should, taking into consideration the cultural aspects:

– In the paper entitled "A cultural-oriented usability heuristics proposal" (A13), a procedure to develop usability heuristics for multicultural websites is described. This procedure was proposed by Cristian Rusu, Silvana Roncagliolo, Virginica Rusu and Cesar Collazos in the paper "A Methodology to Establish Usability Heuristics", published in 2011 [22]. In that study, it is indicated that, to establish usability heuristics, they are necessary six stages: (1) exploration, (2) descriptive, (3) correlation, (4) explanation, (5) validation, and (6) refinement.

Table 4. Articles according to scope

Scope	ID
E-commerce	A01, A03, A16
E-banking	A06, A12
E-government	A10
Organisational-University web sites	A04, A12
Tourism	A17
General website	A05, A09, A11, A14
Processes that lead to heuristic proposals*	A01, A02, A07, A08, A10, A13, A15
Cultural-oriented usability heuristics**	A13

*A defined or adapted process that can used to establish cultural-oriented usability heuristics
**Established heuristics based on traditional ones

- **Stage 1: Exploration.** It focuses on obtaining the bibliography related to the main research topics. It includes related usability heuristics.
- **Stage 2: Descriptive.** It focuses on highlighting the most important characteristics of previously obtained information, to establish the main concepts associated with research.
- **Stage 3: Correlation.** It focuses on identifying the characteristics that usability heuristics have for a specific application, based on traditional heuristics and case studies analyzed.
- **Stage 4: Explanation.** It focuses on specifying the set of proposed heuristics.
- **Stage 5: Validation.** It focuses on verifying new heuristics against traditional heuristics through experiments, through heuristic evaluations.
- **Stage 6: Refinement.** It focuses on the feedback of the validation stage.
– On the other hand, in the article "A cross-cultural comparison of Kuwaiti and British citizens' views of e-government interface quality" (A10), the relationship between Hofstede's cultural dimensions and aspects of the interface of user and web design, a relationship that was proposed by Aaron Marcus and Emilie Gould in the paper "Crosscurrents. Cultural Dimensions and Global WebUser-Interface Design", in the year 2000 [18]. This article expresses the relationship between each cultural dimension and the influence it could have on the interfaces.

4.2 Usability Heuristics to Evaluate Cultural Aspects

In the literature there are discussions about the advantages and disadvantages of different heuristic evaluation methods instead of providing guidelines for developing new usability methods and heuristics [22]. It is observed in the result of the systematic search resulted in a total of twelve documents (A01, A03, A16, A06, A12, A10, A04, A12, A17, A05, A09, A11) classified in the evaluation or comparison of sites Web. That is to say, in these documents defined methodologies and heuristics are used to perform the corresponding evaluations, instead of adapting said heuristics to make the evaluation that will be made to the website more specialized.

Only one article that evaluates aspects of culture in usability heuristics could be found. Case A13 entitled "A cultural-oriented usability heuristics proposal", results in the application of a procedure where they propose thirteen heuristics, which are associated with the dimensions raised by [11].

5   Conclusions and Future Works

Culture-oriented heuristics are used in usability evaluations of different types of websites. These proposals were made through procedures, based on traditional heuristics to which the cultural factor has been added according to cultural models.

This work allowed us to identify the existing procedures in the literature that are used to establish culture-oriented heuristics, the characteristics of web interfaces that can be related to cultural aspects and the type of website to which the established heuristics is usually applied: e-commerce.

However, heuristics cannot necessarily be applied to all websites equally. Therefore, more analysis is needed to determine which aspect should be prioritized according to the type of website of interest and the cultural characteristics of its target audience, in order to focus on those aspects when cultural-oriented heuristics are established.

In this way, it is also necessary to develop procedures that take this aspect into account to establish culture-oriented heuristics that will be used to evaluate the usability of the website.

Acknowledgement. This study is highly supported by the *Section of Informatics Engineering* of the *Pontifical Catholic University of Peru* (PUCP) - Peru, and the "HCI, Design, User Experience, Accessibility & Innovation Technologies" Research Group (HCI-DUXAIT). HCI-DUXAIT is a research group of PUCP.

References

1. Aladwani, A.M.: A cross-cultural comparison of kuwaiti and british citizens' views of e-government interface quality. Gov. Inf. Q. **30**(1), 74–86 (2013)
2. Alexander, R., Murray, D., Thompson, N.: Cross-cultural web design guidelines. In: Proceedings of the 14th Web for All Conference on The Future of Accessible Work, W4A 2017. Association for Computing Machinery, New York (2017)
3. Alostath, J.M., Almoumen, S., Alostath, A.B.: Identifying and measuring cultural differences in cross-cultural user-interface design. In: Aykin, N. (ed.) IDGD 2009. LNCS, vol. 5623, pp. 3–12. Springer, Heidelberg (2009). https://doi.org/10.1007/978-3-642-02767-3_1
4. Burgmann, I., Kitchen, P., Williams, R.: Does culture matter on the web? Mark. Intell. Plan. **24**(1), 62–76 (2006). Cited By 52

5. Cho, M.H., Sung, H.H.: Travel destination websites: cross-cultural effects on perceived information value and performance evaluation. J. Travel Tour. Mark. **29**(3), 221–241 (2012)
6. Cyr, D., Head, M., Larios, H.: Colour appeal in website design within and across cultures: a multi-method evaluation. Int. J. Hum.-Comput. Stud. **68**(1–2), 1–21 (2010). https://doi.org/10.1016/j.ijhcs.2009.08.005
7. Díaz, J., Rusu, C., Pow-Sang, J.A., Roncagliolo, S.: A cultural-oriented usability heuristics proposal. In: Proceedings of the 2013 Chilean Conference on Human - Computer Interaction, p. 82–87. ChileCHI 2013. Association for Computing Machinery, New York (2013)
8. Díaz, J., Rusu, C., Collazos, C.A.: Experimental validation of a set of cultural-oriented usability heuristics: e-commerce websites evaluation. Comput. Stand. Inter. **50**, 160–178 (2017)
9. Fraternali, P., Tisi, M.: Identifying cultural markers for web application design targeted to a multi-cultural audience. In: 2008 Eighth International Conference on Web Engineering, pp. 231–239, July 2008
10. Gould, E.W., Zalcaria, N., Yusof, S.A.M.: Applying culture to web site design: a comparison of Malaysian and US web sites. In: 18th Annual Conference on Computer Documentation. IPCC SIGDOC 2000. Technology and Teamwork. Proceedings. IEEE Professional Communication Society International Professional Communication Conference, pp. 161–171, September 2000
11. Hofstede, G., Hofstede, G.J., Minkov, M.: Cultures and Organizations: Software of the Mind, Intercultural Cooperation and Its Importance for Survival, 3rd edn. McGraw-Hill Education, New York (2010)
12. Hu, J., Shima, K., Oehlmann, R., Zhao, J., Takemura, Y., Matsumoto, K.I.: An empirical study of audience impressions of B2C web pages in Japan, China and the UK. Electron. Commer. Res. Appl. **3**(2), 176–189 (2004)
13. Nielsen, J.: 10 heuristics for user interface design (1994). https://www.nngroup.com/articles/ten-usability-heuristics/. Accessed 29 Sept 2019
14. Jano, Z., et al.: Website usability and cultural dimensions in Malaysian and Australian Universities. Asian Soc. Sci. **11**(9), 1–10 (2015). Cited By 6
15. Chu, J., Zhu, X.: Culture-oriented evaluation method for interaction: applied in Chinese E-commerce website design. In: 2010 3rd International Conference on Computer Science and Information Technology, vol. 2, pp. 331–335, July 2010
16. Khashman, N., Large, A.: Arabic website design: user evaluation from a cultural perspective. In: Rau, P.L.P. (ed.) CCD 2013. LNCS, vol. 8024, pp. 424–431. Springer, Heidelberg (2013). https://doi.org/10.1007/978-3-642-39137-8_47
17. Kitchenham, B., Charters, S.: Guidelines for performing systematic literature reviews in software engineering. Technical report EBSE 2007-001, Keele University and Durham University (2007)
18. Marcus, A., Gould, E.W.: Crosscurrents: cultural dimensions and global web user-interface design. Interactions **7**(4), 32–46 (2000). https://doi.org/10.1145/345190.345238
19. Nielsen Norman Group: Usability 101: Introduction to usability (2012). https://www.nngroup.com/articles/usability-101-introduction-to-usability/. Accessed 29 Sept 2019
20. Park, J.Y.: Cross-cultural language learning and web design complexity. Interact. Learn. Environ. **23**(1), 19–36 (2015)
21. Rocchi, P.: Introducing human-computer interaction: a didactic experience. In: 2016 IEEE Global Engineering Education Conference (EDUCON), pp. 992–996, April 2016

22. Rusu, C., Roncagliolo, S., Rusu, V., Collazos, C.: A methodology to establish usability heuristics. In: Proceedings of the Fourth International Conference on Advances in Computer-Human Interactions, pp. 59–62 (2011)

23. Snelders, D., Morel, K.P., Havermans, P.: The cultural adaptation of web design to local industry styles: a comparative study. Des. Stud. **32**(5), 457–481 (2011)

24. Wan Mohd, W.A.R., Md Noor, N.L., Mehad, S.: The information architecture of e-commerce: an experimental study on user performance and preference. In: Papadopoulos, G., Wojtkowski, W., Wojtkowski, G., Wrycza, S., Zupancic, J. (eds.) Information Systems Development, pp. 723–731. Springer, Boston (2009). https://doi.org/10.1007/b137171_75

Service Design and Upgrade
of Domestic-Ceramic Consumption Idea
--Service Design for Customized Domestic-Ceramic

Liu Hong[1]([⊠]), Limin Wang[1], and Wang Song[2]

[1] Beijing City University, No. 269 Bei si Huan Zhong Lu, Hai Dian District, Beijing, China
lhlh312@126.com
[2] GuoLin Financial Information Services Co., Ltd., Qingdao, China

Abstract. Whilst rapid development of Internet has nowadays generated increasingly wide diversity of demand for daily necessities, personalization is enjoying more and more popularity among customers. Domestic-ceramic of course is of no exception, consumption of which favors customized design. Different from the past when handcraft, material, and cost-efficiency are highly valued, the focus of domestic-ceramic market has shifted towards individuality, culture, and customization. Therefore, devoted to create a multi-dimensional system to improve production of customized domestic-ceramic and shopping experience with the idea of service design, this article in the first part comprehensively introduces the culture of domestic-ceramic via online rich media, including relevant design idea, handcraft, practicability, standard, and other cultural characteristics. Thus, users' preference could move towards customized purchase, which not only appears rather interesting and satisfying, but also meet their needs for customized products. Statistics about consumption preference are collected in the meantime, which later on goes through a further data-technique based analysis in setting up a domestic-ceramic customization process in which users can participate personally. In that way, cultural idea is realized into product value, and hereby in turn to upgrade customization. Further, service design has another role to play in optimizing product supply chains and providing after-sale service. To be specific, data-sharing system and ERP facilitates to promote the efficiency of production and supply, and makes it possible to achieve a continuous post-sale surveillance of product quality. Throughout the whole procedure, service design has bearing on users, producers, service providers and others, among which an effective closed loop is established so as to activate and optimized the domestic-ceramic industry as a whole.

Keywords: Light customization · Domestic-ceramic · Service design

1 Introduction

Upgrade of consumption and fast spread of information via the Internet has brought new challenges to the ceramic industry, requiring it not only to meet daily demands, but also to provide customers with satisfactory product service and experience. Therefore, in an attempt to apply service design to customization of domestic ceramic, this essay is

A. Marcus and E. Rosenzweig (Eds.): HCII 2020, LNCS 12202, pp. 618–632, 2020.
https://doi.org/10.1007/978-3-030-49757-6_45

based on the study of WeChat business platforms, from which customers can purchase light-customized domestic-ceramic, with respect to their service design, methods and tools, and thus to well demonstrate the idea of platform service centering on service design and vitalize the ceramic industry with "light customization".

2 Development of Customized Domestic-Ceramic and Industrial Analysis

2.1 Development of Traditional Domestic-Ceramic Customization

Customization of ceramic has a profound history in China. For example, the royal porcelain on the 60th birthday party of Empress Dowager Ci Xi [1] and the ceramic on Emperor Tongzhi's wedding ceremony [2] manufactured specially for the royal family are well representative of ancient customized ceramics. Besides, armorial porcelains [3], or the "official fortress" in China's export of porcelains that were customized for the royal family and became popular overseas, and the domestic ceramic that domestic 7501 project specially designed for Chairman Mao are both gorgeous ceramic products [4]. Nowadays, the continuous development of economy and technology has to a large extent changed the customization of ceramic. As the famous poetry goes, "where once the swallows knew the mansions of the great, they now to humbler homes would fly to nest and mate"; if in old days ceramics were exclusive to the aristocratic, customization of ceramics given its conformity to the idea of sustainable development has been fully reflective of consumers' expectation. Moreover, due to the remarkable personalized features, high design efficiency and better quality of customized ceramics, they have enjoyed great popularity among citizens and received more and more attention from domestic and foreign scholars and customers.

In the ceramic industry it is no longer uncommon to do customized design so as to meet customers' personalized demands. Therefore, many Chinese companies are advertising "customized design" as their specialty to promote sales. For instance, a company in Beijing customized the tableware "Best Wishes for the Flourishing Age" [5] for state banquet during APEC conference, including 13-inch buffet trays, water-cube brand brackets and other utensils carved with Ruyi Baoxiang patterns that were based on those first found in the Dunhuang frescoes. Such design successfully drew users' attention to customized ceramics, and started the wave of domestic-ceramic customization. It is a tradition of WEDGWOOD UK to design and produce Bone China for restaurants and hotels, whilst because of their high hardness and good quality sales of Bona China once took up a relatively large proportion of its business. Porcelain Manufactory Nymphenburg in the Nymphenburg Palace of Munich, Germany is another strong competitor in the porcelain customization industry abroad that has achieved a great success by customizing top-level royal tableware and other high-quality porcelains; by doing so, it has not only improved corporate performance and profitability, but also maximized the brand's influence. On the most conspicuous part of royal tableware is the family emblem or name, showing the enterprise's constant pursuit of high quality and the luxury of royal life, which is a typical example of making the best of contemporary domestic-ceramic customization design (Figs. 1, 2, 3, 4 and 5).

Fig. 1. The royal porcelain on the 60th birthday party of Empress Dowager Ci Xi

Fig. 2. The ceramic on Emperor Tongzhi's wedding ceremony

2.2 Analysis of Modern Domestic-Ceramic Industry

Although in recent years the ceramic industry has witnessed a relatively high-speed development [6], there are still many problems and difficulties due to its own deficiency and various market factors that can be summarized as follows:

Blemished reputation of brands: There are many well-known brands of ceramic production in China, but most of them cannot guarantee a constantly desirable manufacturing process and high quality, while their reputation is also blemished by duplicates in the market. For instance, Jingdezhen Ceramic has been famous for being "thin as paper, bright as mirror, white as jade, and silvery as inverted bell when knocked on". However, its development has been bottlenecked these days as a result of serious counterfeiting.

Fig. 3. Armorial porcelains

Lack of innovation for brands: like silk and tea, porcelain used to be a symbol of Chinese culture that carries the traditional craft and aesthetics in China. In recent years, due to the lack of innovation ceramic brands have become increasingly old-school and thus cannot keep in pace with the times or launch popular products. To put it another way, those decorative patterns are too outdated to appeal to customers.

Lack of innovation for products: throughout the production of ceramics to marketing, the current dilemma can be largely credited to the lack of constant innovation. Since it is innovation that fundamentally guarantees the popularity of enterprises and products,

Fig. 4. Domestic 7501 project specially designed for Chairman Mao

Fig. 5. "Best Wishes for the Flourishing Age" for state banquet during APEC conference

without it there is no other way to developing products in the long run. Nevertheless, few enterprises have broken through the old production and sales models these years, which has reduced the influence of the whole domestic-ceramic industry and bottlenecked its further development.

Lack of marketing: Development of domestic-ceramic industry calls for advanced marketing idea and personnel specializing in marketing and planning. When there is not enough media between brands and users, the latter can neither learn about the culture of products, nor become familiar with products' strengths in an effective manner, which could in turn reduce sales as well as users' enthusiasm (Fig. 6).

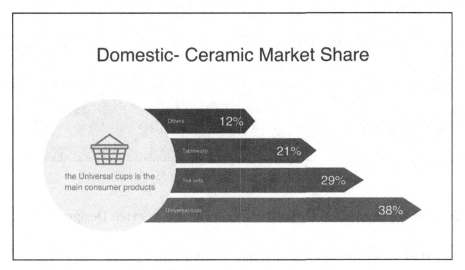

Fig. 6. The domestic-ceramic market share

2.3 Systematic Analysis of Service Design for Domestic-Ceramic Products

Service design can do much help to achieve customization and upgrade the mutual interaction between brands and users throughout the domestic-ceramic industry, in which the idea of interaction service design is of great significance. In that regard, the design of domestic-ceramic is no longer limited to the simple consideration of product functions, but should extend to a much more user-oriented multifold and systematic analysis. Interaction design of domestic ceramics is substantially a system design that concerns usability, utility, satisfaction, and communicative quality. Hence, successful domestic-ceramic products should not only meet the first two requirements, but also satisfy the other two that highlight people, context, product, and activity (hereinafter "PACP" [7]). To summarize, it is necessary to look at ceramic design in a comprehensive and systematic way, and thus to connect elements of the system closely, including people ("P") as the specific target of domestic-ceramic design, products ("P") based on modern interaction design of domestic-ceramic, and the interactive process in which people ("P") engage in activities ("A") in different contexts ("C") (Fig. 7).

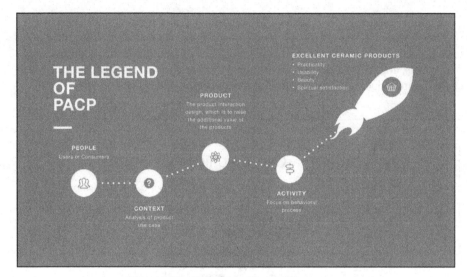

Fig. 7. The model of PACP

3 Light-Customized Domestic-Ceramic and Service Design

3.1 The Concept of Light Customization and Domestic Ceramic

Light Customization

Early in 1970 the famous American futurologist Alvin Toffler predicted in the famous Future Shock "what the society will provide in the future are not limited and standardized commodities, but the most diverse and non-standardized products and service."[1] In fact, development in the last ten years has proven that forward-looking and accurate prediction, for customized service is accessible in almost all walks of life these days, whilst the popularity of the Internet has to the greatest extent diversified the customers to whom customized service is provided and the fields where customized service becomes popular, allowing ordinary people to enjoy customized products and service more conveniently. To put it another way, an increasingly wider range of products can be customized now, and customization is becoming more and more convenient and accessible to the public.

Domestic-Ceramic

The history of ceramic development is almost the history of the development of world civilization, for ceramic as the necessity of the highest frequency of use is closely related to our daily life. Given their practical and aesthetic values, this type of ceramics are often called functional ceramics to refer to all ceramic products with practical functions. Historically speaking there are many types of ceramics, including domestic ceramics (i.e. pots and pans), tiles, architectural pottery mainly for bathroom design, art ceramics, and etc., among which those most common in daily life are domestic ceramics, such as tableware, tea set, coffee set, wine set, and kitchenware.

---

[1] Zhiqi Li, Customization: Business Model in the Personalized Era, China Small & Medium Enterprises, July 2008, p. 54.

3.2 Light-Customization of Interaction Design in Service Design

Interaction service is the most important part of service design, and Interaction Design as an independent subject was proposed in 1984 on the first interaction design seminar held by Bill Morgridge, the founder of the famous design company IDEO. From then on, interaction design is no longer limited to the study of information exchange between human and computers, but has extended to that of all industrial products that require information exchange with people so as to perform their pre-set functions. For domestic ceramics as rather common industrial products light-customization is also achievable by means of interaction design.

On the one hand, light-customization should start from understanding customer (interaction center)'s needs in meeting more differentiated [8], diverse and personalized consumption demands with service interaction. On the other hand, customization scale is often set based upon the traditional process of domestic-ceramic production, and hereby to define "customization of modern domestic-ceramic" and "light-customization" respectively. Specifically speaking, "light-customization" is driven by customers, so it is necessary to understand what they really want in the first place and promote mutual understanding between them and brands so as to meet or exceed their expectations. As for "light-customization" derived from the marketing of original brands, such as operation model, business strategy, design methods, consumers and profitability of brands, they are complementary from many aspects. As a part of the brand, however, separate planning is rather important, for only by evaluating each customer's demands, is it possible to provide service and design in accordance with his/her own wish rather than simply copy what is already at hand (Fig. 8).

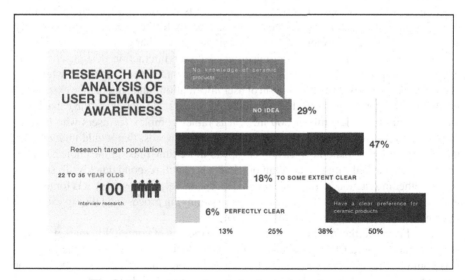

Fig. 8. The research and analysis of user demands awareness

4   Service Design for Light-Customized Domestic-Ceramic

4.1   The Process of Service Design for Light-Customized Domestic-Ceramic

Stage One—Analysis of the starting point of light-customization: analyze the features of domestic-ceramic to conduct difference classification of product elements. Analyze people, activity, context, and product (PACP). If the product is a coffee cup, the classification by genders of target groups should demonstrate the container's volume, capacity, weight, and etc.

Stage Two—planning of the difference between light-customized contents: this stage concerns the planning of customization freedom, the most important part of which is a full consideration of mass production principle and universal applicability principle. If the product is a coffee cup, for adults it is fine to set the capacity as 300 mL and the weight as 0.12 kg, but the two indicators have to be reduced to 120 mL and 0.05 kg respectively to meet children's needs. That number is exactly the limitation on customization freedom, because customization of coffee cups the capacity of which ranges from 120 mL to 300 mL would make it impossible to conduct mass production.

Stage Three—value and cost of customization: as customization is not absolutely unlimited, it is necessary to sort out product elements that deserve "customization" the most, or "to calculate the customization weight of those elements". At the same time, cost may also vary as customization object changes. If customization of the product will increase the cost substantially, the producer should reconsider the feasibility of customization with reference to, for instance, whether users can afford such high price, and hereby to make a choice. For instance, to equip a coffee cup with a temperature measurement chip at the bottom is seemingly intelligent, but it is far from practical because in ordinary life the change of coffee's temperature is usually unimportant. Therefore, such design while increasing the cost does not promote the product's practicability accordingly, and it can be more worthwhile thinking about changing the cup's capacity.

Stage Four—service design optimization and user interaction design: customer-oriented customization favors readily comprehensible interactive languages, while service design is comprised of "acquisition of user information" and "interactive experience feedback" [9]. For example, if the question is termed as "do you want the capacity of the coffee cup to be 120 mL or 300 mL", it is rather complex for users who have to think about how much is 120 mL or 300 mL. In other words, that would undoubtedly increase thinking cost and have customers spend more time making the choice. On the contrary, when asked "are you an adult or a kid" users will respond quickly. To summarize, whether interaction is friendly enough depends largely on how easy it is for users to understand, so it is essential to avoid unnecessary thinking process and thus to exchange information as effectively as possible (Fig. 9).

Stage Five—aesthetic UI design: according to the law of commodity market, design is a key part of product sales, because among products with the same practicability, it is common for users or consumers to choose the one that is more eye-pleasing or with a better sense of design. Hence, to attract customers with light-customization and improve their experience, UI design should highlight the visual effect and core functions of products.

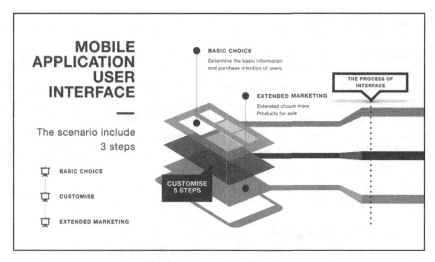

Fig. 9. The process of interface

Stage Six—dynamic and optimization adjustment based on user data: this part concerns the characteristics of the Internet industry, which calls for the continuous optimization and upgrade of service design. As users' page view (PV) can demonstrate how long they spent at each stage and whether they have chosen to log out, designers can therefore locate and optimize less friendly parts, which can be repeated as user data accumulating.

Stage Seven—analysis of product trend and optimization of enterprises' production strategy based on user interaction data: collection and analysis of data will help enterprises to plan the development of products and hereby to adopt strategies for product development that better conform to the demands of the market. For instance, if among 100 light-customization users 76 prefer round coffee cups and the other 24 prefer quadrate ones, the enterprise according to the data will produce 80% round coffee cups so as to reduce the inventory caused by unclear trend of market demand.

4.2   Guidelines of Service Design for Light-Customized Domestic-Ceramic

1. Light-customization is the compromise between customization and mass production. Inspired by the production of shoes of different sizes, it is all about reaching a balance and thus to customize products on the basis of mass production.
2. Light-customization requires a comprehensive evaluation of products' practicality, functions, context of use, aesthetics, cost, and etc.
3. Light-customization favors "choice" rather than "answer" in learning about users' demands, for the former is much easier and friendlier, while over-free customization makes it too difficult to control the cost and also has users lost about their needs.
4. The object of customization must be readily comprehensible and cognizable, such as size and color.
5. It is relatively critical to understand users' demands in fragmented time. In this era featuring fast obtainment of information, high-efficiency is the spirit of service design, and harangue could do little help in providing interaction service.

4.3 Case Demonstration

Case Summary: Online Platform for Light-Customized Domestic-Ceramic—Flower and Artworks

Flower & Artworks is a mobile-terminal platform for sales of light-customized domestic-ceramics that provides user-oriented customization service with respect to ceramic's shape [10], application scenario, patterns, and etc. The readily usable interactive platform not only provides users with immersive interaction experience, but also informs them of the cultural background and craft of products within 3 min, which is a good example of making the best of fragmented time (Fig. 10).

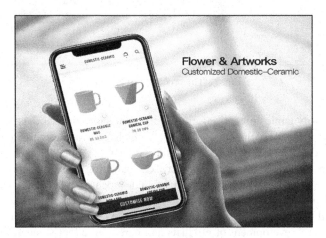

Fig. 10. The Demo of Flower & Artworks

Case Analysis

- Service objective: promote sales of domestic-ceramic and propagandize ceramic culture
- Customization process: 1. Choose the shape; 2. Choose the material; 3. Choose patterns
- Operation process: 1. Tell user type; 2. Tell functions in the scenario; 3. Tell the range of price; 4. Choose decorative patterns; 5. Purchase derivative sets at will; 6. Provide information such as address; 7. Pay for the product; 8. Trace the progress
- Additional service: at each stage before purchase is a brief introduction of ceramic culture
- Case diagram [11, 12] (Figs. 11 and 12)

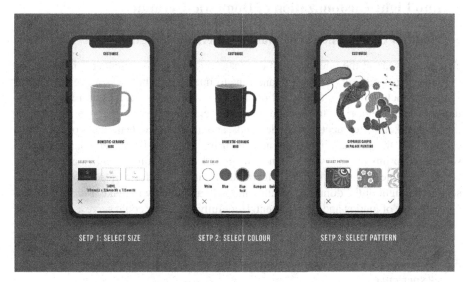

Fig. 11. The user operation path

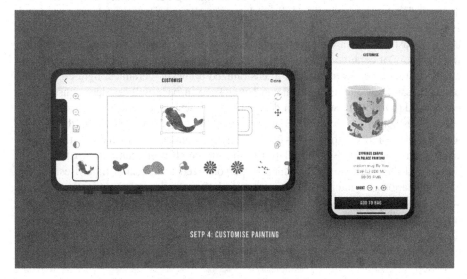

Fig. 12. The customise painting

5 Value and Significance of Introducing Service Design into Light-Customization of Domestic-Ceramic

5.1 Indirect Optimization of the Domestic-Ceramic Industry

This essay is about the integration of domestic-ceramic industrial chain—from design to marketing—with service design, and thus to innovate its business mode by placing virtual-characters in the real life and predicting service scenarios. As aforementioned, that will help enterprises to produce domestic-ceramics in conformity to the taste of modern market, better meet modern demands, and finally promote the sales of domestic-ceramic and the profitability of ceramic industry. Assisted by stakeholder maps and service blueprints the industrial chain is integrated so as to build an online customized-ceramic service system, which will facilitate the flow of information, substance, and service throughout the domestic-ceramic industry and hereby to make it more adaptive to the change of market and environment. Hopefully this essay could serve as a reference for innovation of other traditional Chinese industries.

5.2 Humanized Customization Process Improves Customers' Shopping Experience

High-speed development of high-tech has dramatically changed people's lifestyle and living conditions by introducing electronic, network, technological and intelligent products into our daily life. Whilst those devices are making our life much easier, they have however distanced people physically and emotionally, which is not what we expected. Hence, customization of domestic ceramic is just to make up for that problem by combining industrial design with personalized emotional expression. According to the profound history of ceramic customization, that design is well reflective of humanized and unique taste. Moreover, compared to customized domestic-ceramics, light-customized ones accessible at online platform can better keep in pace with modern consumption pattern and psychology, while their design has to some extent blended practicability and culture, aesthetics and emotion. Both designers and customers operate on the mobile-terminal sales platform that allows users to light-customize their own domestic-ceramic with materials provided by the platform, during which users can participate more in design and the marketing of products is personalized at the same time. Besides, the communication and interaction between the platform and users that creates the innovative experience of product design, culture propaganda and product marketing only takes up few time and energy in meeting customers' needs for personalized service. To put it another way, light-customization of domestic-ceramic has in essence filled domestic-ceramic with culture and emotion, making it more personalized and convenient to use.

5.3 Increase the Value of Brands' Culture with the Value of Traditional Ceramic Culture

Although the history of ceramic production in China is more profound than that in foreign countries, and ceramic culture has been well-inherited, Chinese enterprises that have achieved great success in the domestic-ceramic industry these days are far less than foreign companies, which can be largely credited to their poor positioning of brands and lack of their own style. Fundamentally speaking, that is mainly caused by the poor application of local culture to design and propaganda of traditional Chinese culture. On the mobile-terminal sales platform culture gets converted into the additional value of products, while building of such sales platform based on products, culture and innovation will surely inspire the cognition and positioning of brand culture by ceramic enterprises.

The development of domestic-ceramic customization design is of great significance. Whilst cultural propaganda of products should highlight the attributes of local culture, thus to give products cultural identity, customers can also feel the valuable and familiar culture themselves. From the perspective of companies, by increasing the additional value of brand culture their products will develop their own style. Further, in this era that values personal style, there is no doubt that to publicize ceramic craft, materials and cultural value will improve consumption experience, brand reputation and the profitability of enterprises. More importantly, the customization of domestic-ceramic will benefit from that in the long run.

6 Conclusion

Customization of domestic-ceramic is a perfect integration of function and economic values, and a great balance between aesthetics and practicability. In that regard, its development signifies not only more advanced craft or a developed industry, but also the development of social civilization. Light-customization of domestic ceramic is the product of the social market economy, which is reflective of people's demands for personalized service. In the future, customization of domestic-ceramic will surely witness a great prosperity, and innovation and the idea of personalized design will make domestic-ceramic products more multifold, high-tech, personalized and humanized. (Establishment of Business Model and Principles in Product and Service Design)

References

1. Gao, Y., Li, S., Wang, Y.: Establishment of Business Model and Principles in Product and Service Design
2. Li, B.: Psychological Evaluation of Design Effect. China Light Industry Press, Beijing
3. Cooper, A.: The Essentials of Interaction Design (interpreted by Liu, S.), pp. 26–28. Publishing House of Electronics Industry, Beijing (2008)
4. Li, S.: Experience and Challenges: Interaction Design of Products. Publishing House of Jiangsu Fine Arts, Nanjing (2007)
5. Pine, J.: Large-Scale Customization: Frontier of Enterprise Competition. China Renmin University Press, Beijing (2000)
6. Pine, J.: The Experience Economy, Harvard Business School (1999)
7. Galotti, K.M.: Cognitive Psychology, 3rd edn., (interpreted by Wu, G.). Shaanxi Normal University Press, Xi'an (2005)
8. Li, S.: Introduction to Interaction Design. Tsinghua University Press, Beijing (2009)
9. Cooper, A.: The Inmates are Running the Asylum. Publishing House of Electronics Industry, Beijing (2009)

10. Feng, R., He, S.: Innovation and design of traditional national industry based on service design: case study of the innovation of Dewing industry by Jinxiu Yao people, 10–13 (2017)
11. Gao, K.: Research on Contemporary Domestic-Ceramic Customization Design, Jingdezhen Ceramic Institute
12. Jianrong, Fu: Application of humanized design to domestic-ceramic design. Jingdezhen Compr. Coll. J. Column **2**, 105–106 (2009)
13. Liu, Y.: New Opportunities for the design of cultural and creative products in the information-ization context: brief study of interactive experience design of cultural and creative products, industrial design, 88–89 (2015)
14. Hu, B., Xiong, Y., Yu, L.: The influence of identity motivation on customers' choice of product customization: from the perspective of social identity theory, economy and management **29**, 84–90 (2015)
15. Wang, Q., Liu, J., Liu, Y.: Service design for the customization of Qinhuai light cultural and creative products in the "internet plus" era, design **1**, 14–17 (2019)
16. Li, Z.: Customization: Business Model in the Personalized Era, China Small & Medium Enterprises, p. 54, July 2008
17. Jian, X.: Industrial Economics, pp. 69–71. Wuhan University Press, Wuhan (2002)
18. Hsien, L., Lang, P.: The Conspiracy of Industrial Chain. Oriental Press, Shanghai (2008)
19. Luo, S., Zhu, S.: Service Design. China Machine Press, Beijing (2011)
20. Shao, T.: Research on the Innovation of Business Model based on Internet Mindset, Dalian University of Technology, April 2014

A Study on the Space Usability Driven Design of the Ancestral Temple of Xihu Village from the Perspective of Spatial Syntax

Xinghai Luo[1] and Mingjie Liang[2(✉)]

[1] School of Architecture, South China University of Technology, No. 381, Wushan Road, Tianhe District, Guangzhou 510006, China
[2] School of Design, South China University of Technology, No. 381, Wushan Road, Tianhe District, Guangzhou 510006, China
mjliang@scut.edu.cn

Abstract. The courtyard space of Ancestral Temple building is a public space for villagers to gather and discuss, and is also an important carrier of local villagers' cultural life. With the advancement of China's urbanization, the decline of Ancestral Temple has become increasingly prominent. Taking Xihu village in Jieyang city, Guangdong province as an example, this paper discussed the method of Ancestral Temple space renewal through the investigation of village landscape intention and space syntax analysis, In this study, effective samples were collected through in-depth interviews and cognitive intention maps, and spatial intention element data of different groups were incorporated into spatial syntax statistical analysis to explore the internal relations among spatial morphology, spatial cognition and environmental behavior. Based on the data analysis, the paper put forward three renewal strategies of "integration of the old and the new", "integration of point and line" and "temple-centered", and evaluated the synergy of syntax in Ancestral Temple space renewal practice through graphic simulation.

Keywords: Ancestral Temple · Space syntax · Planning coordination · Update practice

1 Introduction

Chaoshan is located in the border area between Fujian Province and Guangdong Province, with mountains on its back, facing the sea, and a vast and rich plain. Ancestral temple is built by the whole village at the beginning of the village. It is also the original dwelling place of villagers, so it is called "mother of village" by villagers [1]. With the continuous expansion of urban space, rich local culture and regional landscape characteristics are being swallowed up by "The dominant factor from the top to bottom". In Chaoshan area, which is deeply influenced by the Marine culture, the phenomenon of "cultural rootlessness" of villages has occurred quietly. Many ancient villages have been damaged or abandoned. Most of the villages have poor infrastructure and cultural, entertainment, and leisure facilities can no longer meet the local residents' pursuit and

© Springer Nature Switzerland AG 2020
A. Marcus and E. Rosenzweig (Eds.): HCII 2020, LNCS 12202, pp. 633–646, 2020.
https://doi.org/10.1007/978-3-030-49757-6_46

desire for quality life. The landscape planning of ancient villages is imminent. A large number of villagers abandon the old houses and set up new houses, and the connection between the new and old settlements is gradually split.

The spatial update availability of landscape update is different from the traditional planning relying on the supporting function of the local rural functional units and relying on the traditional geographic geocentric approach. The renewal of traditional village landscape is based on the group consensus under the guidance of field research and designers. In order to reflect the local characteristics of landscape planning, it is necessary to properly and accurately locating the highly-identified landscape nodes of the village. It is impossible to deeply analyze the spatial organization rules based on the individual decisions of designers [2, 3]. In this paper, with the help of urban space theory, environmental psychology evaluation, questionnaire survey and other methods to carry out qualitative research on rural landscape space, trying to find the main elements of the intention of the Xihu village landscape space. The research attempts to fully understand the intention of village nodes through the qualitative research of rural landscape intention, and then through the spatial syntax to objectively and accurately describe the fabric law, and finally realize the simulation analysis and evaluation of the renewal scheme.

2   Research Sample Overview and Research Methods

2.1   Xihu Village Overview

Xihu Village is located at the foot of Luoshan, southwest of Jieyang Lancheng District (see Fig. 1). The watercourse is vertical and horizontal, and bamboo and rice are planted behind the village. The village covers an area of about 1352 acres, including 850 acres of arable land. It is a typical pure traditional agricultural village, mainly planting rice and Chinese herbal medicines such as Huaishan. Xihu village has a history of more than 200 years, with profound historical background. The principal buildings present the layout style of "three halls and one well" and "three streets and six lanes". The remains of ancestral houses, ancestral temples, Stone Bridges and water towers in the village are well preserved.

2.2   The Research Methods

Survey of Village Landscape Intention. Residents' behavior is one of the key factors that society impact on the environment. IKarl Popper's theory of the third world holds that spatial relations reconcile the relationship between abstract rational space and perceived physical world [4]. In order to understand the local residents and the tourists' awareness of the spatial elements of the Xihu Village in Jieyang Lancheng District, more than 70 valid samples were collected through in-depth interviews and cognitive intention maps, of which 50 were local residents and 20 were tourists. The spatial intention factor data of different groups are included in the statistical analysis of spatial syntax to explore the internal relations among spatial form, spatial cognition and environmental behavior.

Quantitative Analysis of Space Syntax. Space, in the space syntax approach, is defined as relatedness, and as it is, and might be, created by buildings and cities, and as it is

Fig. 1. Schematic diagram of the spatial form of Xihu village.

experienced by the people who use them. Thus, space is thought of as an intrinsic aspect of everything human beings do in the sense that moving through space, interacting with other people in space, or even just seeing ambient space from a point in it, rather than the background to objects. Space syntax is a theory of space and a set of analytical, quantitative and descriptive tools for analyzing the layout of space in buildings and cities. By learning to control the spatial variable at the level of the complex patterns of space that make up the city, it is possible to gain insights into both the social antecedents and consequences of spatial form in the physical city or in buildings ranging from houses to any complex building [5]. Hillier believed that the spatial fabric exists in the human mind as a whole synchronic; People's experience of space is individual diachronic, and the image of synchrony of space can be obtained from the level of thinking. Through the combination of spatial syntax and cognitive intention, this paper explores the morphological spatial cognition of traditional villages. The spatial structure of streets and lanes in the village is translated into an axis diagram, and the correlation and readability of natural elements and built elements are analyzed through the axis diagram. Research on traditional village space involves: exploration of lost space [6], morphological features and spatial cognition [7], ancient village space security mechanism [8], regional differences in the memory places [9], social functions and spatial dynamic A series of syntactic researches have been carried out from the perspectives of relationship [10], human perspective of traditional settlements [11], quantitative analysis and verification of building space [12], and so on.

3 Survey of Village Landscape from the Perspective of Landscape Intention

3.1 Image Analysis of Rural Settlements

According to the collection of image data of the village area of the Xihu Village (see Fig. 2), it can be seen that the square area in front of the ancestral temple, the water tower of the river water plant, and the stone bridge are important areas of village intention. According to the analysis of the impact factors of village selection, it can be seen that the interviewees hope that the environmental atmosphere in the village after the transformation is inclined to accessibility of transportation (23.3%), beautiful and comfortable environment (21.7%), and leisure (15%) etc. According to the questionnaire,

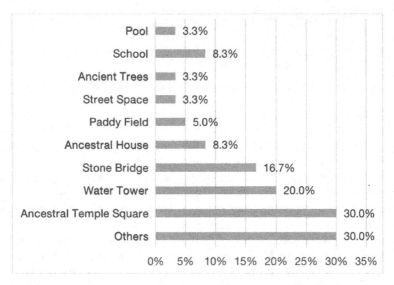

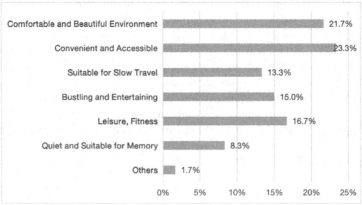

Fig. 2. Analysis of the selection frequency of village landscape intention in Xihu village.

respondents are more concerned about road planning and hardening in the village, activity facilities, and environmental conditions. The ancestral temple and its affiliated areas are the core nodes with "central" significance and "place" spirit. They have extremely authoritative cohesion within the clan, and are important gathering points for villagers to carry out daily sacrifice activities, weddings, funerals, and marriages.

3.2 Investigation and Analysis of Street, Node and Landscape Interface

Basing on the perception and the appearance frequency of factors among different groups at the street level, we get the image perception of village roads in the Xihu village by various groups (see Fig. 3). The landscape space intention on the road from the village shrine in the surrounding area is relatively clear. Although other sections are the skeleton of the entire village landscape pattern, due to the current state of ruin or a small number of temporary structures and debris, the selected frequency is low. At the node level (see Fig. 4), all types of people tend to know each other in the square area of the ancestral temple of the Xihu village (15.25%), river water plant water tower (12.2%), the stone bridge (8.13%), and the ancient trees (10.17%) representative landscape nodes. In the landscape interface, the data feedback shows that the interviewees mainly pay attention to the plant landscape on both sides of the Rongjiang river, the road boundary landscape outside the village, the boundary landscape of the wall (traditional and modern building facade), and the plant boundary landscape (trees and fields). For example, the Xihu village screen wall between the ancestral temple and the wind pool, with auspicious sacred animals, deer, crane as the element, the connotation is profound, the implication is rich, fully embodies the wisdom and creativity of the working people, the left pattern on the two cranes standing on the tree, the implication is the blessing and longevity. On the right, two deer steps on the ground, quiet and leisurely. These elements that symbolize people's yearning for a better life add color and artistic appeal to the space of the ancestral temple square in Xihu village.

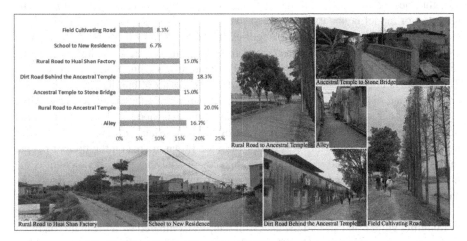

Fig. 3. The selection frequency of Xihu village street interface.

Fig. 4. The selection frequency of main nodes in Xihu village among interviewees.

4   The Syntax Analysis and Updating Strategy of Xihu Village

4.1   Establishment of Village Axis Map in Xihu Village

The establishment of the road axis model is the foundation for activating the spatial vitality of Xihu village. In syntactic analysis, the first step is to identify the scope and boundary of the analysis. The research area is a pure rural village, and there is no clear plan for the internal transportation system of natural villages, which are generated in the free construction and production activities of villagers.

Axial line is defined as the longest straight line representing the maximum extension of a point of space. It can be objectively created. Axial map is the least set of the longest straight lines which passes through each convex space and makes all axial links. The selection of model boundary is confined to mountains, rivers and water. Roads in the study area can be divided into four categories: Township Road, village road, inter-house roadway and field road. The village road directly connects the township road to the residential buildings, which are the most abundant network line space in the village. The roadways between houses are generally the boundaries of buildings, and the roads are zigzag and dislocated. Field roads are usually dirt roads to undulations and flexible layouts. In order to ensure the drawing accuracy of the axis model and meet the research needs, the author sets the minimum width of the pedestrian path at 1 m. The weak influence of the roads to width less than 1 m in the research area on the flow of people in the area is not included in the scope of this axis of analysis. Axial node count is the number of axial lines encountered on the route from a line of origin to all others. As shown in Fig. 5, the axis system of Xihu village is made up of 154 axes. The number of long axes of Xihu village is mainly concentrated in the direction from Luoshan bridge to Longling village and around the ancestral temple. Compared with the main roadway, the country roads are mainly short axes with various route turns.

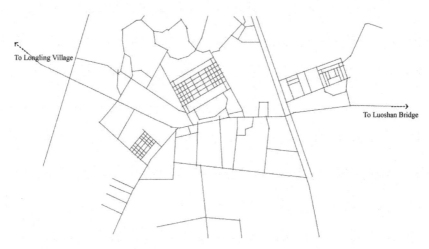

Fig. 5. Axis map of Xihu village.

4.2 Syntactic Analysis of Xihu Village

Axial integration describes the closeness of a space to all other space. Local integration describes the closeness of a space to space within a certain distance. It can be viewed in the axial integration map of Xihu Village in Fig. 6 that the axis color from red to blue indicates the overall integration from strong to weak. No. 1, No. 2 and No. 4 axes in the center of Xihu Village are located on the main road of the village, which is directly connected to the ancestral temple, water tower, stone bridge and additional nodes in the village. Among them, the integration degree of the rural roads near Xihu Elementary School is as high as 1.48. Axis 3 leads to the village roadway, showing typical linear characteristics. The axis 4 is on both sides of the diversion canal in the village, and the integration degree is 1.16. The vicinity of the axis 6 is the residential buildings in the village. No. 1, 3, and 6 occupy an important position in the road network of Xihu village. They are the principal crossing lines in the village, have the highest accessibility, and are responsible for the main evacuation of traffic. The integrated core of Xihu village is located in the center of the village, but the integrated core extends linearly locally to the boundary of the village. From the external analysis, the spatial core of Xihu village is shallow and discrete, reflecting the characteristics of its outward layout.

Regions with high global integration are distributed among the regions with close connection with township roads and higher accessibility. The blue axis with low integration is located at the edge of the village, and the area is mostly abandoned ancestral houses. Most of these field roads are end roads, with low integration, poor connectivity and poor accessibility. The color evolution of the street system in the village area changes from warm too cold from the inside to the outside, showing a circle like distribution, reflecting a significant topological centrality. The area with the highest degree of local integration appears at axis 6 (from the rural road to the new residential complex), but its local centrality is obviously weaker than that in the village. The control value indicates the degree of control of a space over the space to which it is connected. The cool color of most axes in the control degree map of Xihu village indicates that the space of Xihu

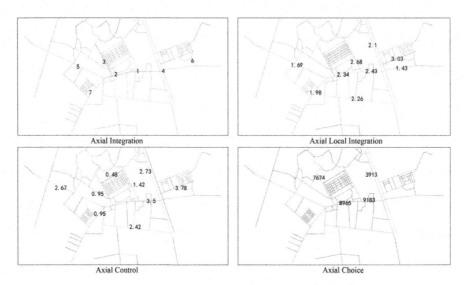

Fig. 6. A syntactic analysis of the axis of Xihu village. (Color figure online)

village does not have a high degree of mutual control. Xihu village ancestral temple, sunning valley yard, half-moon pool, water tower near the high degree of choice indicates that the space has a greater potential to attract traffic across. The degree of selection gradually decreases from the rural road to the inside of the village, and the degree of selection of the integrated nuclear area in the square in front of the village is higher. The average selection of alleys in the village is low. The high accessibility of the 1–3 axis area is the shortest path through the village.

4.3 Syntactic Analysis of Ancestral Temple

The previous qualitative study shows that the square in front of the ancestral temple is an important identifying node space in terms of spatial structure and functional attributes, and it is the area where people gather in the village. The visual area analysis model is a description of the visual perception of an individual in a space, which directly reflects the region where the eyes of any point in the space reach and the number of steps required seeing other areas by changing points. Visual integration is the normalized value after excluding any possible influence factors. Figure 7b is the Visual Integration analysis of the front square of the shrine. The highest level of sight integration at points 1 and 4 in the Fig. 7 can clearly see the entire space of the ancestral temple. The red areas at points 2, 6, 10, and 11 in the picture have better openness of sight, and it is easy to attract people from the perspective of spatial cognition. The global sight depth at points 3, 5, and 7 is deep, and the global sight integration decreases with color.

Visual Clustering coefficient distribution of the spatial boundary of Fig. 7c reflects the visually limiting effect of the boundary landscape around the ancestral temple square. The area 7 is the location of the roadway in the village, the area 12 is the Luoshan Bridge to Longling Village Road, and the area 13 is the water tower to the Stone bridge section.

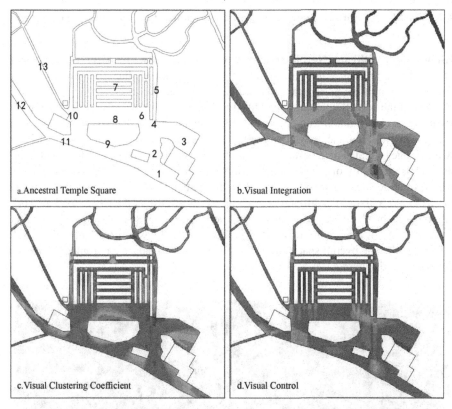

Fig. 7. Visual analysis of Xihu village ancestral temple square. (Color figure online)

The space in the above area is relatively limited. This is the qualitative study. The road boundary is Xihu Village. The conclusions of the important rural landscape interface fit, and the design needs to enhance the user's perception of the road boundary. Area 3 is an idle public green space. It is envisaged to build a small amusement park, which has certain visual restriction effect. Area 8 is the screen wall between ancestral temple and Fengshui pool, which have a strong effect of landscape interface limitation. Figure 7d Visual Control analysis refers to the degree of line of sight radiation from any point in the field in the surrounding space. The more exposed the space point of ancestral temple square, the stronger the control degree of the area, the need to focus on the design, so that people into the village can be more concentrated to see the whole view of ancestral temple square, to highlight the identity of the village. The lanes between houses in the blue area of No. 5 and No. 7 still have some deficiencies in terms of line of sight penetration, so the landscape planning intends to update here. From the perspective of spatial experience, the temporary structures in areas 2 and 10 have a segmentation effect on the square and destroy the overall aesthetics of the facade of the ancestral temple. Therefore, it is necessary in order to reorganize the interface of the structures to improve the landscape atmosphere of the place.

4.4 The Strategy of the Renewal of Xihu Village from the Perspective of Space Syntax

Highlight the "Old and New Fusion" Village Optimization Strategy. The expansion of the village area of Xihu Village is based on the walled village, forming a village pattern with multiple horizontal roads and multiple vertical lanes. Through the linear analysis of the overall integration and local integration in the space system (see Fig. 8), it can be concluded that the comprehensibility value of the Xihu village space system is 0.4. It is known from the above that the local integration of the village space system in Xihu village is related to the establishment of tourist cognitive map, which indicates that the understandability of the street network is relatively low. The Xihu Village consists of five small residential areas. According to the spatial form of the local street network of West Lake Village, it is difficult to predict the spatial form of the whole road network. Although in the small area of Xihu village, there is a similar spatial order. Through the understanding of one of the residential groups, it is not easy to recognize the whole village space. The overall space environment and the local space environment have not formed a good synergy.

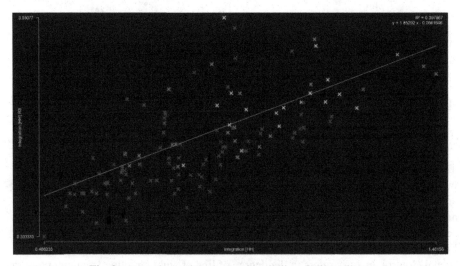

Fig. 8. An analysis of the comprehensibility of Xihu village.

However, through the analysis of intelligibility, the author found that the axis with the highest Rn and R3 values overlapped to a large extent, which indicated that the overall structure center and the local structure center of the village were composed of the same group of axes to some extent. It can be known from the foregoing that the axis 1 and the axis 2 are the longest axes in the village, representing the longest distance of sight and the more information that can be reflected. Therefore, the optimization of No. 1 and No. 2 axes is helpful for the viewers to form their understanding of the overall space of the village. From the perspective of the whole village, the areas with high local integration are all located on the internal roadway of the village, and the ancestral temple and Sunnyvale field are all located in this area, which has the potential to become the destination of people flows and has strong accessibility. Obviously, the design strategy of "old and new fusion" is helpful to form the core of local space system.

Shaping the Network Integration Strategy of "Point Line Integration". See Fig. 9a Village connectivity and control scatter shows that the overall connectivity of Xihu Village is directly proportional to control. Near the 1st and 2nd axis, the higher the school and shrine space connection value, the higher the control value. The connection value and control value near the 6th axis are both low. Figure 9b shows the scatter relationship between the connectivity and the total topological depth. The total depth of the West Lake space shows a decreasing trend as the spatial connectivity increases. In the Fig. 9b, the axes 1, 2, and 3 all have a high degree of connectivity, but the topology depth is inversely related to them. In Fig. 9c, the integration degree is directly proportional to the connection value, such as axis No. 1, 2 and 3. The higher the spatial integration degree is, the higher the connection value is. Axis 4 is the key area connecting the irrigation canal and the village, and axis 7 directly leads to the Huaishan planting area. The connection value and control value of these two parts are not very high, but the integration degree is high. It is necessary to optimize the spatial connection value in the later stage of village landscape planning. In Fig. 9d, the mean depth value and the overall integration degree are inversely proportional. The lower the depth value is, the higher the integration degree is. Such as axis 1 and axis 2, the higher the depth values of ponds and fields, the lower the spatial integration degree, which will affect the overall spatial intelligibility of the West Lake Village. The planning level needs to improve the integration degree of these areas.

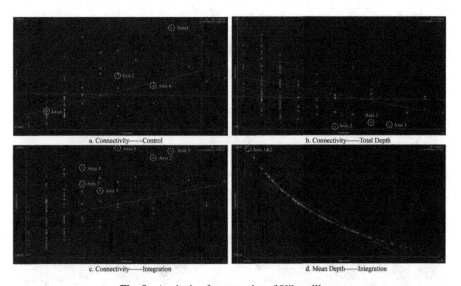

Fig. 9. Analysis of scatter plot of Xihu village.

Establishing the "Ancestral Temple as the Heart" Landscape Renewal Strategy.
The strategy is to carry out landscape transformation for the perspective analysis of
the front square of Xihu village ancestral temple (see Fig. 10). Through the visual
integration analysis, visual clustering analysis and visual control analysis before and after
the transformation, the strategy of "temple centered" landscape renewal is established.
Before the reconstruction, the visual integration degree of unused green space in area 5
at the back of the school was 4.08, and it was planned to build a small leisure garden in
this area to fill the deficiency of public activity space in Xihu village. After landscape
updating, the visual integration of this area was improved to 5.11; the accessibility of
residents to external traffic was enhanced, and the visibility around the half-moon pool
was enhanced after the removal of the unused debris shed. The new construction of
the small garden in the village has strengthened the connection with the township road.
One side of the half-moon pool has a high accessibility. It is recommended to configure
a convenience center. After the facilities are completed, a series of service functions
such as rural Taobao and tourist consultation can be carried out. The temporary shelter
near the Xihu river water plant and stone bridge was removed to increase the line of

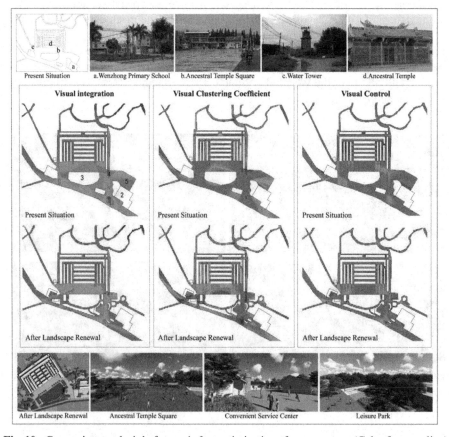

Fig. 10. Comparison analysis before and after optimization of square space. (Color figure online)

sight penetration of the two space nodes. Clean up the activity space near the water tower, improve the control value of the area to provide a site for villagers to gather and exchange, and the visual integration degree of the water tower area is increased to 6.45 after the software calculation and transformation. Before and after the planning of Xihu village, the crossing degree centering on the half-moon pond increased by 48.3%. After the planning, the spatial system of west lake village was stronger. After the landscape renewal, the square space with high integration degree and low integration degree is more concentrated, and the small-scale space reconstruction also improves the Visual Clustering Coefficient of the road boundary significantly. It can be seen that the renewal and optimization scheme has basically achieved the set purpose.

The spatial form of village is formed by the interaction of cultural and social resources in different periods, which is mixed with the memory layer of gradual succession in each era. The hierarchical structure of spatial network with agriculture as the main economic body influences the cognitive mode of spatial users through social development and improvement of living level. In this paper, spatial syntax theory is introduced into the study of usability to analyze the spatial structure of rural intention. The use of spatial syntax makes the characteristics of spatial units and their role in the spatial system more intuitive, and ensures the effective recognition of the rules of village organization.

5   Conclusion

The study on the renewal of square space in Xihu village carried out the functional replacement of the seriously damaged buildings and sites in the surrounding area, and sorted out the main components of landscape space, street and lane, landscape interface, and the main markers of the village. The use of the syntactic analysis model can effectively avoid the blindness of spatial quantitative analysis. On the basis of the results of syntactic analysis, the overall planning and design are carried out. On the premise of not destroying the original village form, the street streamlines is clarified, the accessibility and safety are improved, and the recognizances is enhanced. The route with partially missing functions is repaired and cleared up, and the fluency and accessibility of the internal road network are reinforced. Correlation analysis was conducted on the key nodes of the village intention, and the best optimization plan was selected to reconstruct the functional space. Incorporating Ancestral Temple public space into linear and area factors, improving space utilization and recognition, and reducing villagers' cultural identity and spiritual belonging, providing a reference for similar types of renewal research. The usability of village landscape renewal from the perspective of spatial syntax lies in the clarification of rural landscape intent, which can provide the pulse for the development of the village, reshape the local cultural characteristics, improve the erosion of the hollowing out of the population, and lay a solid foundation for the further development of new industrial models in the future.

Acknowledgements. This study is supported by China National Social Science Foundation Project (Art Category) 'Lingnan Landscape Art Research', No. '15BG085', and Guangzhou Philosophy and Social Science Development '13th Five-year Plan' project 'Research on Quantization Model of Landscape Space After Lingnan Private Garden 'Parkingization', No. '2019GZYB09'.

References

1. Peng, Y.: Landscape Analysis of Traditional Villages and Towns. China Construction Industry Press, Beijing (1992)
2. Duan, J., Hillier, B.: Space Syntax in China. Southeast University Press, Nanjing (2015)
3. Hillier, B., Hanson, J.: The Social Logic of Space. Cambridge University Press, Cambridge (1984)
4. Luo, Y., Huang, Y., Bi, H., Zhao, Z.: Difference in urban residents' pro-environmental behavior intention and understanding based on their environmental attitude—a case study of Haikou. Hum. Geogr. **27**(05), 69–75 (2012)
5. Tarrant, M.A.: The effect of respondent characteristics on general environmental attitude-behavior correspondence. Environ. Behav. **29**(5), 618–637 (1997)
6. Chen, M., Li, H.: The exploring of lost space in Nanping village based on space syntax. Chin. Landscape Archit. **34**(08), 68–73 (2018)
7. Chen, C., Li, B., Yuan, J., Yu, W.: Spatial morphology cognition of traditional village based on space syntax: a case study of Qinchuan village of Hangzhou. Econ. Geogr. **38**(10), 234–240 (2018)
8. Wang, Y., Wu, Y.: Syntax parameter analysis based Huizhou ancient village space crime prevention mechanism. Planners **32**(03), 101–107 (2016)
9. Zhu, J., Lu, S., Du, L.: Research on regional difference of memory places with space syntax: a case study of the traditional residential architectures of Nu nationality. Mod. Urban Res. **08**, 33–38+45 (2016)
10. Wang, H.: The dynamic relationship between social functions and space and the evolution of traditional villages in Huizhou. Architect **02**, 23–30 (2008)
11. Wang, J.: Humanism dialysis of traditional settlement's circumstance from a syntactical perspective. Architect. J. **S1**, 58–61 (2010)
12. Turner, A., Penn, A., Hillier, B.: An algorithmic definition of the axial map. Environ. Plan. B Plan. Des. **32**(3), 425–444 (2005)

Interactive Experience Art in Exhibition

Xueying Niu[1]([✉]) and Yuelin Liang[2]

[1] Beijing Normal University, No.19 Xinjiekouwai St., Haidian District, Beijing,
People's Republic of China
15318809121@163.com
[2] Beijing University of Technology, Beijing, People's Republic of China

Abstract. The development of digital media technology provides more possibilities for the expression of information. For example, the visualization technology of information can transform complex intangible cultural content information into intuitive and understandable pictures. Various technologies such as human-computer interaction technology, Internet technology in digital media technology can improve the interactivity and user experience in the dissemination of intangible cultural heritage, and play a unique role in the dissemination and popularization of intangible cultural heritage. Based on the combination of museum and digital media, this paper presents the transmission of intangible cultural heritage under the background of digital media. In the end, an improvement idea will be put forward, based on the rational use of public space, using some of the digital media as a good communication medium, optimizing the current museum education communication channel, and developing the digitalization of cultural heritage that can be accepted by the general public.

Keywords: Museum · Digital media · Interaction · Traditional culture

1 Introduction

As a place where history and modernity blend and have basic functions such as exhibitions, research, collections and education, museum is an indispensable place in modern people's life. In 1984, the international museum community listed "education" as one of its primary goals, in order to make museums better play their educational functions in the development. Chinese people often say that history is a mirror. Only by accepting and reflecting on history can we make better progress. The importance of this museum's historical transmission process is self-evident. The characteristics of the museum's collection history determine its visual display. Unlike the metaphorical expression of books, it tends to inform visitors of the age and author of the exhibits through straightforward display and description. With the progress of society and the improvement of people's living standards, the social demand is constantly increasing. At present, the exhibition of museums has shown a backward state with many limitations and problems. Although the development of museum art is constantly progressing, there are also attempts at multimedia and digital forms. However, it is still unable to carry out thorough innovation due to the influence of the uneven development level of science and technology and the

© Springer Nature Switzerland AG 2020
A. Marcus and E. Rosenzweig (Eds.): HCII 2020, LNCS 12202, pp. 647–658, 2020.
https://doi.org/10.1007/978-3-030-49757-6_47

insufficient popularity. The planning and design focus of the museum exhibition will focus more on the uncertain factor of the viewer, so that people can truly realize the interactive communication between art and science, people and the environment during the process of visiting the museum.

2 Learning Theory

2.1 Museum Display Art

The Development of Museum Exhibition Art. The development of museum exhibition art is relatively unbalanced. At present, there are differences and similarities in the development of museum exhibition art at home and abroad. From a similar point of view, museums and art galleries at home and abroad are generally found to be difficult to market to young people who have grown up with digital development. This is not to say that the younger generation does not like to go to these cultural dissemination sites. It is because the way of cultural communication in the place cannot be recognized by the younger generation, and without consensus, it is difficult to carry out cultural communication and play an educational function. In the Museums and Galleries module of the British Parliament website, Viscount Younger of Leckie (Con) proposed in 2019: The UK Government remain committed to free entry to the permanent collections of our 15 national museums. Through Arts Council England, DCMS aims to improve cultural participation for everyone regardless of their background.[1] This indicates that people expect the state and government to support the development and continuation of the museum, providing policy and economic support. In Britain, for example, museums and schools have enabled nearly half a million students and children from poor areas to visit museums since 2012. Being able to visit the museum is the basis for the function of the museum. For those who have the conditions to visit the museum, is more important of how to carry out more effective communication, and to better communicate history and culture to people through interactive digital content.

In this regard, several museums and galleries abroad are pioneers in combining traditional museum exhibition art with modern technology. For example, the Detroit Institute of Arts uses the augmented reality (AR) technology of hand-held devices inside the building. With the support of Tango mobile phone, open an application called Lumin to see the mummy skeleton under the bandage in the application (Fig. 1). Motion tracking technology can see the entire Babylon Ishtar Gate through a mosaic tile preserved in the art museum, enabling a close appreciation of the pattern on the gate. The Cleveland Museum of Art takes the interactivity of the museum to a new level, using the movement of people's bodies as a control method, using AI technology to draw virtual pottery and comparing it with the real objects in the system. These museums have achieved the first step of combining interaction and education. In contrast, many museums in China have made fewer such attempts. Immersive exhibitions have gradually become popular in

[1] UK Parliament: Museums and Galleries [EB/OL]. (2019). https://hansard.parliament.uk/lords/2019-05-23/debates/9A8F03A2-B9EA-460A-ACA1-1418FCD74E4D/MuseumsAndGalleries.

2017–2019, and they are all concerned with light, sound and video. Multidimensional interaction from the viewer's senses. For example, themes with cultural communication value, such as the Renaissance and the ecosystem, are inserted into parts that can arouse people's interest and resonance, and through interaction, people can learn history and culture through play.

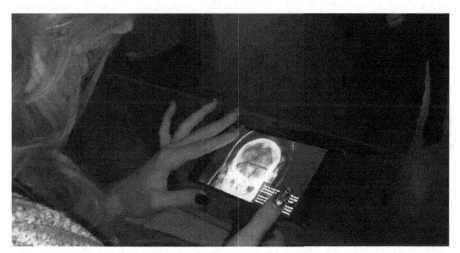

Fig. 1. Visitors use Lumin's application during the exhibition (Lizzy Hillier: How museums are using immersive digital experiences [EB/OL]. (2018). https://econsultancy.com/how-museums-are-using-immersive-digital-experiences/)

From different points of view, the biggest difference between domestic and foreign countries is not only the construction of China's huge historical culture and historical relics collection system, but also the urgency of inheriting intangible cultural heritage. Since the beginning of the 21st century, many domestic experts and scholars have stated that the continuation of Chinese traditional intangible cultural heritage is a certain challenge. Intangible cultural heritage in China, such as oral traditions and expressions, performing arts, rituals, festivals, and traditional handicrafts, is in a state of urgent need to be inherited. In the past, traditional media such as television, radio, and paper media have been important channels for the dissemination of intangible cultural heritage. However, the changing habits of people receiving information in the current era have made the reception of information more oriented to sound, animation, images, games, etc. This has caused those traditional media to gradually decline. As an important medium and channel, museums should occupy a larger proportion in the inheritance of intangible cultural heritage.

The development status of museums requires people to constantly pursue the balance between art and science in the construction. In pursuit of art, integrating virtual digital technology into a real museum or gallery can provide a platform for communication between art and technology. It enables people to communicate and interact with the environment and history, thereby gaining a better viewing experience and learning interest.

2.2   Problems and Defects in the Practice of Exhibition Art

Lack of Interaction Caused by One-Way Information Transfer. An important reason for the small proportion of interaction between museum collections and viewers is the one-way communication of information. At present, it is not difficult to find guide maps of different languages arranged at the entrance and a static touch screen lying in the corner when visiting the museum. When people visit the museum, they follow the instructions of the guide map or the explanation of the guide. Managers and curators display the cultural relics of different dynasties in the museum by dynasty and variety for display. The focus of their work is how to let people appreciate more complete collections, but they have ignored how to make people understand the history behind the collection and be able to remember it after the visit. For the present society, the function of museums is more important to educate on the basis of collection. There are two basic objects that must be possessed to achieve the purpose of education. One is the educator, and the other is the educated person. Unilateral education cannot truly achieve educational goals, so the interactive nature of museum exhibitions is indispensable.

Single Function. Museums can be divided into many different themes based on their positioning. Within China, the largest number are history museums. It preserves and records Chinese history through museums. This shortcoming is especially aimed at the current situation of museums in China, where the focus of current exhibitions is too much on material cultural heritage and not enough on intangible cultural heritage. Intangible cultural heritage is the cultural product of non-physical thoughts. It is the crystallization of the ideology and culture of people throughout the dynasties. It is also the soul of material cultural heritage. The immaterial nature makes the exhibition art of intangible cultural heritage unable to fit the current exhibition form, which also shows that it needs a more flexible way of transmission as a carrier of inheritance. With the continuous development of science and technology, people's interest in history is not limited to just watching calligraphy, paintings, and utensils. The voices, body structures, belongings, and even bits of life of ancient characters can even raise the interest of modern young people in ancient history. For example, scientists first obtained the channel size of the mummy Nesyamun by scanning, then reconstructed the mummy's channel using 3D printing, and combined the artificial throat to restore the voice of the deceased three thousand years ago (as shown in Fig. 2). Although it is only a single syllable, this is a major progress in human history and it also has a significant impact on museum exhibitions. The single function has gradually failed to meet people's cultural needs. The interest of the masses in history needs the support of scientific and technological means. On the basis of material propaganda, the construction of spiritual civilization must also be promoted, so as to promote the museum to continue to advance to multiple functions.

Difficulties in Balancing Interests Among People of Different Ages. With the development of the times and the improvement of people's living standards, the pace of people's lives is constantly accelerating, and their ideas are constantly changing. Affected by social pressure and economic factors, the aging of the population has increased. The age difference between grandparents, parents and children in the family has gradually widened. This increase in the age gap also widens the thinking gap between different age groups. The new generation of young people tends to have ideas and ways of thinking

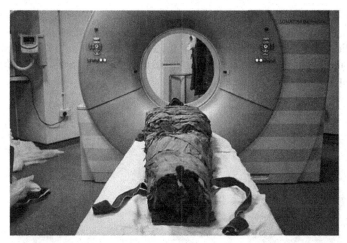

Fig. 2. CT scan process for mummy Nesyamun (Thepaper.cn: How was the sound of sacrificial offerings in Egypt 3,000 years ago? British scientists to reproduce the mummy voice [EB/OL]. (2019). https://baijiahao.baidu.com/s?Id=1656568711416689875&WFR=spider&for=PC)

that are more in line with the progress of the times. From the 1960s to the 1970s, museums have gradually broken from the original system of exhibitions and moved towards entertainment. However, there are obvious differences in the degree of acceptance of things among groups of different generations: the older generation pay more attention to history and culture. As people who have experienced history, they prefer to see the remnants of events they have experienced or the old artifacts they have used displayed in the museum windows. This is a process of recalling the past for them. And young people are more looking forward to understanding history in a way that fits modern technology and is easy to understand, such as Artificial Intelligence, Augmented Reality, Virtual Reality and other technologies, to bring people into the virtual world. Let everyone be a participant in a museum exhibition, explore history and touch history in reality.

3   Brief Introduction of the Role of Artificial Intelligence Technology in Digital Media Technology

3.1   Basic Concepts of Artificial Intelligence Technology

Artificial Intelligence is a technical science that includes awareness, thinking, and more (as shown in Fig. 3). As an emerging interdisciplinary subject, Artificial Intelligence includes knowledge from many other disciplines, such as psychology, mathematics, computer science, philosophy, and so on. Such a broad blend of knowledge is bound to make Artificial Intelligence have functions that cannot be matched by other technologies. The meaning of Artificial Intelligence is actually more inclined to "enhance functions", which is different from the simulation of the human brain. It is more about expanding the scope of human capabilities. At the beginning of this technology, many people have questioned whether it will replace humans because of its super powered nature. The answer is naturally negative. Its appearance makes the real world one more change in the scientific and technological revolution. It has helped mankind to accomplish many results that might not have been imagined before, and has promoted social and economic development and people's living standards.

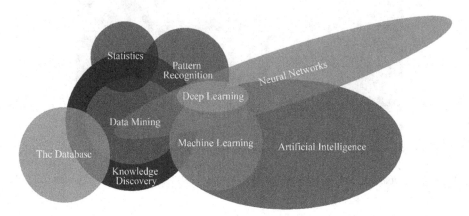

Fig. 3. Artificial intelligence related field diagram

3.2 Application Analysis of Current Artificial Intelligence Technology

AI technology has been widely used in People's Daily life. The most widely used virtual personal assistants are based on AI technology. Google Now and Cortana, for example, use voice-recognition commands to help people look up their phone, set alarm clocks and find addresses. As long as they give instructions, they can help find the appropriate information. The second is smart home equipment, such as sweeping robots that are often used in the home. Based on AI technology, they can grasp the specific conditions and cleaning routes in the home, helping humans to complete boring housework activities such as mopping the floor. At the same time, as a young person, the frequently used AI technology application is the recommendation service for movies and music. Most of the music software frequently used in China has the function of music recommendation, which is realized based on AI technology. Everyone's favorite music style is a little different, but it is undoubtedly a time-consuming and laborious task whether it is to choose the single song list of the style or to choose the song that conforms to their own aesthetic taste after listening to different music continuously. But AI technology helps us solve this problem. Each song in the daily recommendation module is matched based on your own preferences. There are many other applications, such as smart car autonomous driving technology, which have provided convenience to human life. AI technology has strong development prospects. Its multi-disciplinary and multi-industry integration characteristics determine that it can take into account multi-level applications and can play its role in the future science and technology field.

4   Analysis on the Development of Combination of Artificial Intelligence Technology and Museum Art

4.1   Software Usage Analysis Using Artificial Intelligence Technology

Agisoft Photoscan. Agisoft Photoscan is currently a very professional full-automatic photogrammetry and 3D modeling software. This software takes pictures by keeping the camera stationary and the objects horizontally rotating. Generate high-definition 3d models, classified point clouds, and ultra-high-resolution Digital Elevation Models are widely used in visual effects and engineering construction projects. As the currently used professional 3D modeling software, it has the incomparable advantages of Maya and 3Dmax. It can directly and concisely generate models from the photos taken without the need for time-consuming and laborious modeling. At the same time, it can automatically process various types of images and automatically calibrate them to ensure their accuracy. As a software that can perform multi-spectral image analysis, it can also take into account issues such as texture loss, image distortion, and data screening, and process and optimize it. However, it also has some problems. For example, generating models from photos of multi-angled objects or scenes with overlapping effects means that factors such as the shooting method of the photos and the shooting effects can affect the final product. One of the important problems is that the upload is difficult to align after the photo is taken. The factors such as the distance between the target and the camera and the different focus can affect the final upload result. In a word, it is a software that can accurately convert photos to models.

Headshot Plug-In for Character Creator. Compared to the previous software (Agisoft Photoscan), this software belonging to Reallusion has a clear speed advantage. The main promotion of its website is "Realistic 3D Characters made with One Photo"[2]. This software does not need a photo taken from multiple angles to generate a model, but can use a photo to realize the construction of the model, which greatly saves time cost. After the model is automatically generated in one click, it can be modified by continuously panning the buttons to adjust the different parts of the body and face. When the producer has higher requirements for the resolution and clarity of the model, the PRO mode can meet people's needs and generate high-definition models with 4K maps. This software is an AI-driven tool that generates a model of the head from a photo provided, then generates the remaining body parts through AI, and finally achieves the final effect through its own adjustment. On this basis, simple animation can be made to directly make real-time Facial animation using Facial Tracking or other Tracking software to realize the changes of facial expressions of characters.

FaceBuilder. FaceBuilder is an add-on to KeenTools, which is compatible with a variety of software. This Nuke tool can generate accurate and textured 3D models based on the source image of the scene and can achieve the data and effects generated after 3D scanning. By placing fixed parts in the view, the user can freely adjust the automatically generated default face geometry as they use it. At the same time, FaceBuilder can project

---

[2] (Technology) Wild Technology Association: Character Creator 3 combined with Headshot plugin to create realistic models.[EB/OL]. (2019). https://www.bilibili.com/video/av78150007/.

the texture in the image onto the newly created model. During the process, you can randomly select any part of the object to synthesize with the screen and generate only specific objects. This software requires multi-angle photos during the modeling process as a basis for later adjustment using fixed parts, but the use of photos can break through problems such as focus and distance to generate accurate and high-quality models. At the same time, as a plug-in applied to Nuke, it can simultaneously use other software functions in Nuke software to truly achieve high-efficiency and high-quality model output.

4.2 The Combination of Museum Exhibition Design and Emerging Software

The three softwares described above are all software that can achieve rapid character modeling with one or several photos. A comparison of these softwares found that Agisoft Photoscan is undoubtedly the best in terms of accuracy; In terms of production speed, Headshot plug-in for character creator is the fastest production, but the accuracy is not so excellent compared to that; But in formal model making, I personally think that FaceBuilder is the most efficient, not only because the model it generates has a clear topology deconstruction, but also because it takes into account both accuracy and speed. One of the new ways to incorporate digitalization into the museum's exhibition process and try to preserve its historical and cultural characteristics is to use these modern modeling techniques to reconstruct events, people and so on in Chinese history. We found the information of these ancient characters in historical resources such as ancient books, paintings and calligraphy, and entered them into the modern system, using digital media to show their brilliance, and let them take a look at modern society.

For museums, especially those in China, displaying history and telling history is a basic function. According to the survey on the attitude of the audience to the innovation of museum exhibitions, a research was conducted using questionnaires (as shown in Table 1). With 200 people as the main body of the survey, a questionnaire was randomly distributed (the exact value of the calculation result is rounded to one decimal place). In the survey, the population under the age of 29 was defined as young, the population aged 30–49 was defined as middle-aged, and the population over 50 was defined as elderly. Among the 200 subjects, there were 134 young people, 51 middle-aged people and 15 elderly people. Investigation and research showed that 93.3% of young people (125 people) support the innovation of museum display methods, 4.5% (6 people) chose not to express their opinions, and 2.2% (3 people) chose to oppose; 51.0% of the middle-aged people (26 people) expressed supportive attitudes, 39.2% (20 people) stated that they did not have a clear attitude towards the innovation of the exhibition form, and 9.8% (5 people) chose to oppose it; and in the elderly group, 26.7% (4 people) expressed support, and 13.3% (2 people) said that they could not imagine the concrete form of the museum after the reform, and 60% (9 people) objected.

In summary, there are relatively obvious differences and trends in the attitudes of the three different groups towards the innovation of museum exhibitions. As the main body of the future society, young people under the age of 29 are generally born in a modern science and technology society. They are familiar with modern emerging technologies, so they support the digitalization of museum exhibitions and show that this innovation

Table 1. An analysis of the audience's attitude towards museum innovation

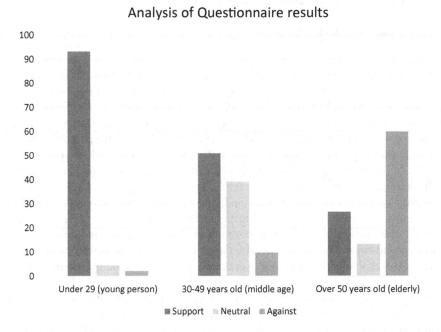

can improve their visit interest. It is their common hope that museums will become a kind of comprehensive place that can combine education, entertainment, sightseeing and social interaction. And the support rate of middle-aged people aged 30–49 has more than half the proportion, and the ratio of support to wait-and-see and opposition has remained basically the same. People in this age group are generally more conservative, and they will not easily express their attitudes without sufficient evidence to confirm that the museum exhibition innovation is beneficial to the current development. At the same time, some people expressed their willingness to try this new way of exhibiting museums and expressed that they would go to museums to experience this change after innovation. For the elderly, this seems to be a relatively difficult group. They all have their own firm ideas and express concern about the change in the way the museum displays. At present, they often go to museums to relive their memories of their young age. The change in the way the museum exhibits may cause them to be confused in the switching of different exhibition modes. In contrast, the museum exhibition, which may be intuitive, is more suitable for them. At the same time, some older people think that their younger generations tend to this emerging form, so they may try it. In general, the innovation of museum exhibitions has a strong development prospect in the Chinese market, especially among young people. In order to solve the concerns of the middle-aged and the elderly, corresponding parts can be designed in the exhibition process to meet the needs of different age groups for museum exhibition.

5 Design Concept Based on Artificial Intelligence Technology Improvement in Museum Exhibition Art

5.1 Elaboration of Design Ideas

During the development of modern Chinese museums' exhibition art, the masses are gradually inclined to a new way to change the current status of museums. The innovations of several foreign museum exhibitions have become precedents, but the methods and forms they use may not be suitable for the needs of Chinese domestic audiences. At the same time, the use of new technologies for exhibitions has created resistance because of the country's long historical background, the inheritance of intangible cultural heritage, and the generation gap of age groups. Based on these social backgrounds, the plan design conceives a museum display form that can be distinguished from foreign models and can have Chinese characteristics. For example, for revolutionary characters in modern times, they are closer to modern times and have relatively enough photos as a basis for modeling. After the software upgrade and update, you may also be able to find the historical classics, find the images or portraits of different classes and different ages such as ancient emperors and ancient concubines, and then use the most convenient and accurate AI technology for modeling. At present, in terms of modeling, several photos can be used to create characters of different ages.

Take the Headshot plugin of Character Creator as an example, first find a photo or portrait of a character of the era you want to create. After importing, select generate to automatically generate a 3D model, and then use Headshot Morph 1000+ to modify all the details of the character (as shown in Fig. 4). In terms of the overall structure of the scene, you can use software to make their expressions and perform bone binding to make limb movements, and then imitate foreign museums to use AR technology to connect the modeled ancient characters to the interactive map route. When visitors enter the museum for a visit, these virtual characters can replace navigation and become a new form of tour guide to guide people for a visit. When people want to go to a specific place, they just need to tell the accompanying virtual characters, and they can conduct voice recognition to guide the audience to the place they want to go. At the same time, the face recognition technology currently widely used can be used to identify the audience, and different leaders can be divided and matched according to the age of the audience. In the process of leading, these ancient figures can use the first-person perspective to tell the stories happened in their own era or even the anecdotes recorded in historical books, and introduce the artifacts appeared in the era and used by themselves. At the same time, these advanced 3d modeling techniques can also be used in the interaction with the audience, which can set a special area for people to import their photos. The system can be compared with the models and photos in the system, and then the model most similar to the audience can be displayed, and the history of the era can be dynamically told through the characters themselves. Audience photos in the system are automatically deleted after matching to ensure the privacy of the audience. The 5G technology that has been widely used and the 6G technology that is being developed both provide a good transmission speed and a medium for digitalization of museums, and lay a good foundation for the diversified development of museums.

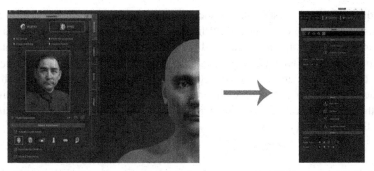

Take Sun Zhongshan as an example to import   Modify the different parts of the body in the list

Fig. 4. Production process in software (Sun yat-sen portrait source file) Sun Yat-sen University Press: http://www.sohu.com/a/206159627_699530 [EB/OL]. (2019). (Software post-production picture source is author).

5.2 Usability Analysis of the Design

This design form can manage the entire museum as a whole. People no longer understand history by dividing it into small parts, but understand history through a complete, programmatic, and interesting form. The functions of the museum can be expanded, and it can bring people the effect of "learning through play and having fun through learning". The technology conceived in the design is to combine existing and applied technologies to form a new form that fits China's national conditions. This whole can be divided into three major parts: First, the reasonable application of modern resources, the current advanced and professional 3D modeling technology is applied to the restoration of ancient figures, so that history and modernity have the opportunity to truly communicate; The second is the rational use of public resources. This form can save the manpower and material resources of the original museum maps, tour guides, etc., and technology can achieve a series of functions such as navigation and introduction. Thirdly, the functions of museums should be expanded to realize the coexistence of educational functions and interests, so as to achieve the purpose of efficient dissemination of cultural knowledge.

5.3 Benefit Analysis in Practical Application

Economic Benefits of Design. In terms of economic benefits, this people-oriented form can arouse people's interest, and they will be willing to spend money on museums in their spare time to experience this emerging museum form. With the help of a good marketing model, we should also ensure the experience of each audience, such as the limit of the number of people entering the museum every day. From the perspective of psychology, people have a herd mentality, and when a person feels good, he will recommend it to the people around him. At the same time, people around you will become curious and want to find out. For those who do not have enough money to support them to feel, free places can be targeted. These methods are enough to help museums gain certain economic benefits in the development process to support their subsequent development. When there is enough mass capital, the government will give some funding to promote museum technology upgrades and optimize for other issues.

Social Benefits of Design. First of all, the social benefits that design can bring must be an increase in people's interest in history. When people have this desire to understand history, not only museums, but also sales and passenger traffic of other history-related things may increase. The technology of design and elaboration of history can help people to watch the surface artifacts and pay attention to the stories behind history, thus promoting the inheritance of intangible cultural heritage. At the same time, this rising interest and the popularity of history help people better cultivate cultural awareness and thus achieve the purpose of education.

5.4 Problems and Defects

The difficulty of this design lies in the overall coordination and planning of the museum's exhibition of art, which requires a lot of sophisticated technology and fast transmission speed to achieve. At the same time, in terms of the correspondence between historical figures and their historical stories, and the decomposition of intangible cultural heritage related to historical relics, each figure in a historical story needs a lot of support from AI, AR and Internet technologies to meet the needs of audiences of different ages in the explanation process. In addition, the 3D modeling technology based on AI technology has continuously encountered problems of privacy leakage in use. For example, the AI face-changing technology that was very popular in China in the past two years uses similar technology. After people upload a photo of themselves in the APP, they can choose any movie or TV show they want to change their face. After one-click automatic face change, their photos can automatically replace the actors' faces in the video. However, this method requires uploading your own photos in the APP, and it is easy for your portrait to leak. The above situations are problems that may arise in the design and need to be continuously corrected and optimized in practice.

6   Future Developments

With the continuous development of society, people's cultural needs such as history and art will continue to grow. As an important place for education, interaction and collection, museums need to be able to meet this need of people, and begin to transform into digital. Especially for China, collections and exhibitions are no longer the best way to look back and remember history. The use of classical culture combined with modern technology is an emerging form, which can not only meet the aesthetic needs of young people and the masses, but also can display different levels of history on the basis of maintaining the overall picture of history, which has good development prospects.

User Experience Requirements and Interface Design for the TouristHub Trip Planning Platform

Modestos Stavrakis[✉] [iD], Damianos Gavalas[iD], Panayiotis Koutsabasis[iD], and Spyros Vosinakis[iD]

Department of Product and Systems Design Engineering, University of the Aegean, Syros, Greece
{modestos,dgavalas,kgp,spyrosv}@aegean.gr

Abstract. This paper outlines the user requirements and the design of the interface components and the interactions of the TouristHub web-based trip planning platform that aims to assist travelers in planning personalized trips. The paper concentrates in the research challenges and the methods used to elicit information from users and other stakeholders and thus construct a set of functional requirements for guiding the design of the platform. It also summarizes a number of use-cases and presents in detail the interface components of the TouristHub trip planning platform.

Keywords: Trip planning · Tourist trip design problem · Interface design · Interaction design · Interface components

1 Introduction

In the last few years, travelers and in particular tourists turn to web-based online trip planning platforms to consolidate the required processes and information for planning a trip [1–3]. In this regard technology takes an active role in the tourism industry, which makes travel planning and the promotion of tourism products more efficient. Trip planning online web platforms essentially are recommender systems which enable travelers to combine information, typically scattered across different online resources, in order to facilitate the planning of all aspects related to a typical trip, including: to identify interesting destinations, book transfers and accommodation, arrange day-by-day visits to attractions and activities, etc. [4].

Several factors play an important role for the design of trip planning platforms [5, 6]. These range from trip solving, route planning and navigating, recommending locations and services, to promoting offers and facilities related to the trip.

An additional significant aspect is the interaction with the interface of the platform. In particular, how design and development choices at a conceptual level, affect platform use and, therefore, decision making from the user standpoint [7, 8]. Some factors influence how users interact and experience platform content and offered services, including: the

© Springer Nature Switzerland AG 2020
A. Marcus and E. Rosenzweig (Eds.): HCII 2020, LNCS 12202, pp. 659–675, 2020.
https://doi.org/10.1007/978-3-030-49757-6_48

implementation of user-machine interactions and how these take place at a physical level (i.e. interacting with different devices); the design of the graphical user interface; the modeling and presentation of the user preference controls and how these correspond to platform functionality; the visualisation techniques used for presenting data. These combined with the functionalities and features users expect from a trip planning platform [9], can potentially construct a framework for defining the requirements that provide a better tourist travel and trip planning experience.

The objective of this article is to briefly present similar platforms and online services for trip planning, present the research and design methodology used for this project and outline the user requirements and the design of the interface components and the interactions. The paper concentrates in the research challenges and the methods used to elicit information from users and thus constructing a set of functional requirements for the design of the platform. It also summarizes a number of use-cases and outlines the interface architecture of the TouristHub trip planning platform.

The paper is structured as follows: Sect. 2 gives a brief introduction to trip planning and the related web-based online services. Section 3 presents the TouristHub project objectives and gives a brief analysis of the platform's main features. Section 4 discusses the methodology and research steps followed for this project, describes the research with stakeholders for collecting and defining project's design requirements, provides an overview of the use cases and presents TouristHub's system overview, architectural components and interaction sequence. Section 5 presents in detail the design of the interactions, information and interfaces. Last, Sect. 6 concludes our work.

2   Trip Planning and Web-Based Online Platforms

From a user perspective, trip planning is a dynamic activity that requires travelers to discover, categorize and make decisions by evaluating a substantial amount of information [10, 11]. It mainly interests people who aim at planning personalized itineraries but also local tourism operators and businesses that focus in promoting their tourism products and services through destination marketing [1, 12].

Commercial online platforms are web-based recommender systems that incorporate a number of functionalities, including location-based POI recommenders, tour routing, day-by-day schedules and guidance, etc. [4, 13]. These platforms request from the user to enter a set of simple parameters, such as destination and date, in order to initiate trip and route planning. The recommended plan can be later modified according to user's preferences. They typically support several means to configure the automatically proposed trip including various types of filtering and clustering algorithms that are incorporated depending on the user's input. They also offer access to a number of complementary services such as accommodation and transportation that are closely related to the realization of the recommended plan.

3   TouristHub: Project Description

This research work is carried out in the context of the TouristHub research project [14]. The focus of the project is to integrate today's fragmented online services aimed at visitors of tourist destinations (search/booking of tickets and accommodation, car rental, organized activities, etc.), which are offered individually by independent providers. This fragmentation makes it difficult to design a complete vacation package that includes solutions for all the key parameters of a tourist trip (accommodation, transport, places to visit, activities, catering, etc.). TouristHub is designed as an online 'one-stop' platform providing a comprehensive suite of tourism services, targeting both visitors of tourist destinations as well as other 'stakeholders' of the tourism value chain, such as tourism/travel agencies, other tourism businesses (catering, entertainment, retailers, etc.), tourism policy makers. In more detail, the main features of platform are:

- Design of comprehensive, personalized vacation packages which include recommendations for accommodation, transportation, organized activities, sightseeing, etc., including options for booking/buying.
- Delivery of promotional offers for local products and services by tourist businesses to tourist customers with an appropriate profile, when in proximity to the physical business site.
- Ability to re-use the platform's functionality in tourist/travel agency websites through affiliate programs.
- Assistance of tourism policy makers in data analytics.

The personalized vacation package design service of TouristHub comprises a solver which deals with a complex combinatorial optimization problem; essentially, a problem case in the family of the so-called tourist trip design problems (TTDP) [15]. The solvers of TTDP problems are typically heuristic algorithms that design tourist tours (one tour for each day of stay at the destination) which include visits in a series of points of interest (POIs), aiming at maximizing the tourist's 'profit' (i.e. satisfaction) perceived by the overall tour. TTDP problems involve many parameters and constraints (travel dates, opening hours of POIs, preferred means of transfer between sights, etc.) and belong to the class of NP-hard problems, i.e. very complex computation problems.

4   Research and Design Methodology

For the purposes of this project we followed a user-centered design approach, based on goal-directed process for designing and developing the TouristHub platform [16]. This research was accompanied by an iterative design process within a formative evaluation framework where experts evaluated functionality against a set of design requirements. Our research, design and evaluation were based on the general phases of user-centered design and involved the specification of: *Context of use* and the identification of potential users, *Requirements* and the identification of stakeholders' goals that must be addressed, an *Iterative Design* of several solutions based on concept and prototype development, and the *Formative Evaluation* with expert users.

4.1   Research for Defining Design Requirements

To define requirements, we adopt an approach based on object-oriented analysis and design with UML. The aim is to model the problem domain and produce strictly defined user requirements, which in turn will facilitate the next phases of the design process where detailed design and production of prototypes will take place. In this context, user needs are explored within a requirements analysis framework based on user grouping and data collection methods. In addition, use cases are identified on the basis of their verbal descriptions using user-system alternations. This will support the design team to identify user interactions and consequently the appropriate user interface components that need to be designed.

In particular, the requirements analysis methodology used in TouristHub, as presented in Fig. 1, utilizes the above approaches and includes the following steps [17]: (a) preparation of system's request report; (b) requirements gathering; (c) definition of functional and non-functional requirements; (d) use cases; (e) definition of initial problem domain model.

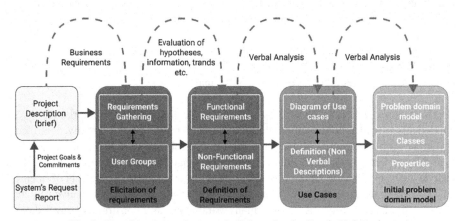

Fig. 1. Requirement analysis methodology for the TouristHub project

At the project's initiation phase, the system's goals, values and other commitments were obtained from the report describing the system's request. At the second stage of research we heavily relied in collecting and documenting information from potential users by recording their existing beliefs, attitudes, and behaviors. End-user requirements were collected through an online questionnaire and interviews. The Requirements Investigation Questionnaire comprised five (5) main sections, each of which contained several research questions as stated below. The sections were related to: (a) demographics (4 questions), (b) travel and holiday profiles (usual options or preferences) (9 questions), (c) online travel and tourism services (2 questions), (d) vacation packages (5 Questions), (e) personalized tourism services (4 questions).

The questions followed a 5-point Likert scale (1: Almost never - 5: Almost Always). In addition, some of the questions included an (optional) open answer text field. The questionnaire was completed in anonymous fashion, although it was possible for respondents to provide contact details (many did). The questionnaire was distributed to a targeted group of users, identified by the project partner's networks. The number of valid questionnaires received were 108. At a later stage, after the questionnaire sessions were complete, fourteen (14) respondents were selected to be interviewed, in order to interpret and further elaborate on their answers.

4.2 TouristHub Functional Requirements

The functional requirements of the TouristHub platform were generated from business and user requirements. Business requirements were described in the approved technical annex of the project and are not discussed in this paper. User requirements were gathered with questionnaires and interviews with user groups identified from partners' networks. Functional requirements were modelled from the user perspective with UML use cases. This section presents the elicitation of user requirements and their specification in terms of UML user cases.

4.3 User Requirements Gathering

The requirements gathering questionnaire consisted of five segments about: demographics, profile about trip and travel, use of online trip and travel services, preferences about holiday packages and personalization. All questions were modelled into a five-point Likert scale. Most questions allowed respondents to insert comments, if they wanted to; many did so for some of their answers. The questionnaire was distributed online for the period of approximately one month to approximately 500 users identified from the project partners' network. A number of 108 valid questionnaires were analyzed. The participants were 47% men and 53% women. In addition, 14 interviews were made (7 women).

Regarding the participants profile, we report on the following characteristics:

- Half of the participants (50%) were in the age group 41–50, another large percent (42%) were in the ages of 31–40, and fewer (6%) were in the 18–30 age group and a few (3%) within 51–65 years old.
- Most participants (52.6%) reported that they travel mostly 3–5 times per year, while another 44.7% travel 1–2 times a year, and the rest travel more than 5 times per year.
- Many participants reported that the average duration of their trips is 4–7 days (89.4%).
- Most participants make business trips (78.5%) which last 1–4 days.

The survey on user requirements investigated several issues about user preferences on travels and trip planning (Figs. 2, 3, 4 and 5) such as types of trips and duration, whether the participants use online travel services, tourist guides and trip planning services, their preferred means of transportation within a destination, preferred types of activities, whether they would pay for a trip plan or package, etc.

The most important conclusions from the requirements survey and interviews can be summarized as follows:

- Participants visit a lot of sites around one or two destinations; they don't often change accommodation but move from/to it, during the day.
- Most participants move with public transport or rented car.

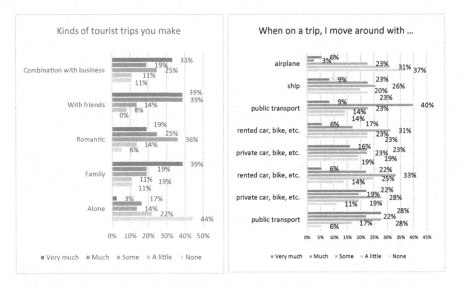

Fig. 2. Travelers' visit preferences

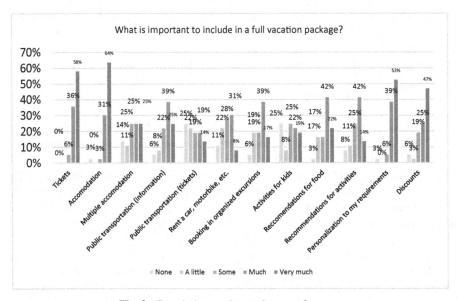

Fig. 3. Traveler's vacation package preferences

- Most participants use various online services for tourist planning, but they do not often use existing tourist planning platforms and recommendations.
- The most important elements of a tourist package are tickets, accommodation and personalization of preferences about trip planning, activities and costs.

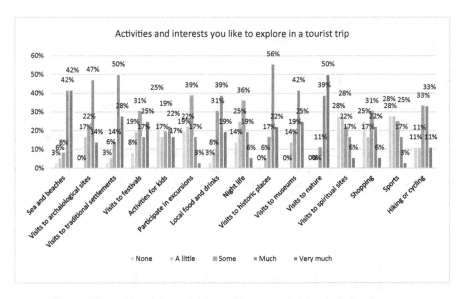

Fig. 4. Travelers' activities and interests when on a tourist trip

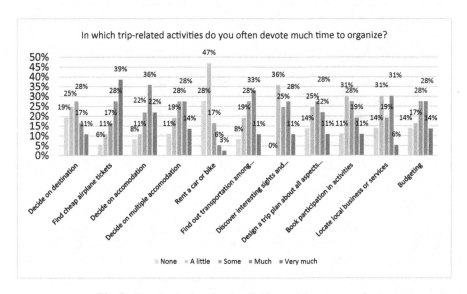

Fig. 5. Travelers' trip related activities and time to organise

- Most participants would book most elements of a vacation package, especially if there was increased demand or if it was cheaper. "I would pay for something I can't afford to miss, for example the Disneyland, and not for something I could replace."
- Most participants argued for some flexibility in booking activities and sightseeing, e.g. "I might want to sleep more or stay more at a place and alter my day plan."

- Most respondents would like mobile access to the tourist planning platform through a responsive web site, and "not another mobile app".

4.4   Overview of the TouristHub Use Cases

The modelling of functional requirements included UML use case diagrams, presented in Fig. 6, and tabular, textual descriptions that were analyzed from the user perspective in the form of alternations between actions of the user (or another actor) and responses of the system (or a subsystem). Each use case description allows the writeup of user scenarios and the design of simple mockups. The functional requirements of the TouristHub platform consist of these use cases and their textual descriptions.

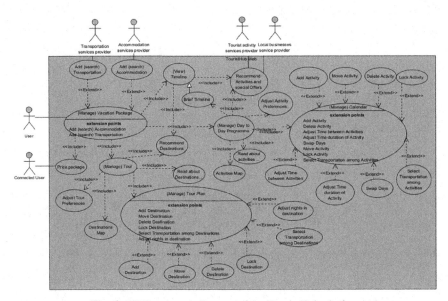

Fig. 6. UML use case diagram of the TouristHub platform

The TouristHub Web is the central point of user access to all trip planning services and it follows responsive design principles to allow access from mobile devices. The main areas of functionality of the system include:

User Connection
Tourist Hub users may be connected or not (anonymous). Connected users will have access to the full functionality of the platform, which can also provide better recommendations in this case.

Search for Vacation Package
The user can search and book for accommodation and transportation for one or more destinations (within the same trip). The user can insert various preferences and constraints gradually including traveling persons and their ages, budget limits, etc. Furthermore,

users can also provide preferences about activities and styles. The search process gradually develops a vacation package for the user, which includes detailed schedule and activities, as well other recommendations, considering user preferences and constraints.

Manage Tour Plan
The user can manage the tour plan at two levels of detail: for all days (overall) and for a single day. When managing the tour plan, the user mainly manages different destinations of the tour and transportation connections with emphasis on public transport.

Manage Calendar
The user can manage the activities per day in more detail than that of the tour plan. In the calendar the user manages the details of the package with emphasis on activities.

For management of other tour plan and calendar, for each user-initiated change, the system must re-calculate the plan or calendar according to all related constraints. If the activity cannot be set exactly as the user requires (e.g. due to transportation unavailability) the system must be able to find a close alternative.

4.5 TouristHub System Overview, Architectural Components and Interaction Sequence

The TouristHub platform is a web service that can be accessed from a web browser through its responsive interface. The system overview, as presented on Fig. 7, consist of the user interface, a trip planning engine, a route planning engine and a database.

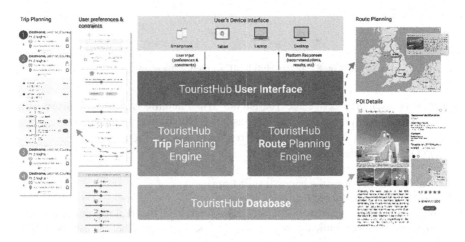

Fig. 7. TouristHub platform overview

The high-level sequence diagram of the TouristHub platform presented on Fig. 8 depicts main interactions among architectural components. This sequence diagram describes how and in what order the various objects of the platform function. The main components are, the TouristHub User Interface (UI) which represents the front-end interface that the users experience; the TouristHub Trip Planning Engine which is responsible for handling user requests that refer to the planning and customization of a trip plan; the TouristHub Route Planning Engine which is responsible for handling route related requests (i.e. route directions either between subsequent stop-overs where the user stays overnight, or among POIs included in a daily plan); the TouristHub Database which is responsible to handle all database queries.

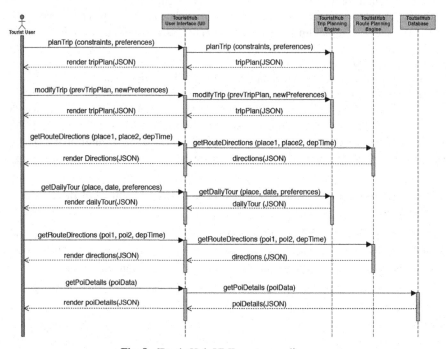

Fig. 8. TouristHub UML sequence diagram

From the user perspective the TouristHub Trip Planning Engine makes use of a number of factors to plan a trip. This acts as a trip recommender system that requests some basic data from the users including Trip Data and User Preferences.

Trip Data can be described in terms of:

- Arrival Location, where the trip will start from,
- Departure Location, where the trip will end to,
- Trip Dates indicate the arrival/departure dates, therefore, the total trip duration,
- Number of Stopovers indicate the number of in-between stops that the user is willing to accommodate,
- Means of Transport indicates preference for using either to Public or Private transportation.

User preferences can be outlined in terms of:

- Vacation Style includes: Culture, Nature, Food, Beaches, Nightlife, Activities, Historical Places, Religion,

- POIs preferences indicate user preference on particular POI categories (e.g., museums, archaeological sites, monuments, nature, etc.),
- Budget data represents a rough indication of the budget the user is willing to spend (Economy, Moderate, Luxury).

5 Interactions, Information and Interface Design

Emphasis was given on a number of interface design strategies for interface design and layout. For the purposes of this project, the design team followed interaction design practices according to the guidelines given by Responsive Design and Material Design for the web and the mobile responsive interfaces of the platform. Based on the Information Architecture and Information Design that the research team provided, interaction and interface designers considered the following factors in designing interactions and structuring the interface: general interaction/interface design goals, organization of interface elements, ordering and categorization of data and content, navigation flow, interface aesthetics and visual style, typography, dimensions of interface elements and webpage sizes for the different scenarios, web user interaction styles based on well known design guidelines that provide familiarity in terms of web experience. Special importance was given to the *Search, User Preferences* and *Route planning components* as they represent the main user interaction with the platform.

5.1 Interface Design and Interactions

A number of interface concepts have been designed and prototyped. The aim of the early (low-fidelity) and late (high-fidelity) concept prototypes was to confirm that the proposed design concepts complemented the use case scenarios. The prototypes enabled the design team to determine whether the proposed concepts were usable matched the mental models of the users and reflected the conceptual models of the designers.

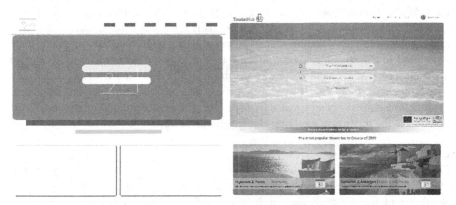

Fig. 9. Wireframe and high-fidelity representation, respectively, of the TouristHub main interface

The low-fidelity prototypes in the form of wireframes are presented on left of Fig. 9 and were used at the early stages of the concept development. These had low visual fidelity and no content or interactivity. The purpose was to support early experimentation mainly by evaluating the organization of interface elements, the ordering and categorization of data and content, provide information architecture validity, and assist on the screen layout design that followed at a later stage.

The next prototyping stage included the construction of high-fidelity prototypes. These were visually identical to the final concepts and included all interface elements, spacing, rendered graphics, etc. The prototype content essentially simulated the existence of the actual content that will appear in the final design, thought it was static. During the final prototyping stage interactivity components were designed to simulate actual interactions and respond to basic user testing scenarios.

5.2   User Interface Templates, Components and Interactions

In order to speed up the design process the design team developed the TouristHub UX/UI kit. This worked as a reference point for all collaborators in the design and development teams. It included the User Interface Templates, Components and Interactions. From this kit a shareable group library was also assembled in order to give to everyone in the design and development team access to the reusable UI elements. The structure of the library included interface elements of various types: arrows, avatars, banners, buttons, color reference palettes, dropdowns, footers and headers, forms and settings, icons, modals and alerts, sliders, tabs, toasts and tooltips. It also included higher level components such as destination components, location components, route components, navigation components, simple and advanced search components, and user preferences components.

User Interface Elements
The UI elements, presented in Fig. 10, have been designed in order to be reusable across the different use cases and device-oriented scenarios (e.g. desktop, web-responsive, mobile etc.). There are two main aspects related to the design of reusable components: a) The Master Element, which defines the properties of the Element, b) The Instance, which is a copy of the Master Element that be easily reused in different cases. Elements are sharable among the different scenarios and together with Interface Templates have been stored to the sharable library. It is important to note that in order to accelerate the design process, Element Instances are linked to the Master Element, so that any changes made to the Master Element be propagated to all related element Instances. This functionality has been provided by the Figma interface design tool [18] and added flexibility in the process of applying changes to the design.

Search Component
Many recent studies of user's search behavior online reveal that users initially tend to search using the simplest query they consider at the time [19, 20], and if they fail to find what they look for, it is probable that the quit searching and possibly never return to the website [21]. It is important to note that the way the interactions take place and their timing are crucial for both the user and the system. While users are interacting with the interface the trip planning engine has to perform a number of expensive computations at the background. Therefore, timing is a very important aspect as the interface, in order to

Fig. 10. A sample set from the user interface elements used in TouristHub platform

be acceptable, must respond in close to real time without stressing the planning engine. The Main Search Component has been designed with balance between simplicity and functionality in mind. Initially the search component is presented as an autocomplete form where users can input arrival and departure locations (presented on the left on Fig. 11). Gradually, as the user inputs constraints and preferences and gets in return basic feedback from the system, the interface evolves to provide more interface elements (Advanced Search Component) that in turn request more input from the user without frustrating him/her.

The SearchTab Component is then accompanying the user in the respective pages that follow and provide full functionality for customizing and altering the initial preferences and constraints (presented on the right on Fig. 11).

User Preferences Component
The User Preferences Component provides a simple mechanism to customize constraints and preferences related to both Organised Activities and Tourist Attractions. The Organised Activities Component is a tabbed component that provides functionality for customizing the organized activities. As such it offers the ability to set dates and budget, as well as capabilities to book an activity or cancel. Tourist Attractions Component appears in the form of sliders so as to provide a quick and easy to understand interface for the user. The slider bars are based on the Material Design guidelines for discrete sliders and reflect a range of non-numeric values of the form: not-interested – very much interested.

Main Search Component (Form) and Advanced Search Component   SearchTab Component

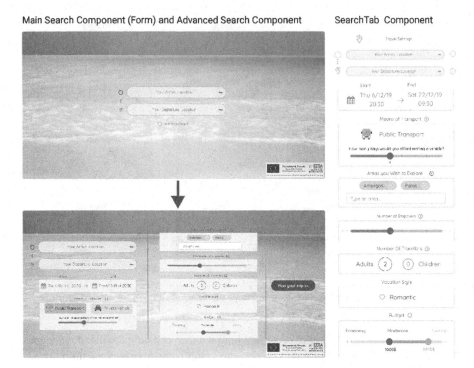

Fig. 11. Main search and advanced search components (left). SearchTab component (right)

Route Planning Component

The Route Planning Component, presented on Fig. 12, offers the core functionality for planning and customizing proposed routes. It assimilates a number of different mechanisms in one component and it is based on two sub-components the Destination Component and the Navigation Directions Component. Its basic functionality is to present a number of stopovers in the form of timely ordered destinations. The Destination Component displays the destinations name and details, the duration of the visit and also affords a Day by Day Agenda, Accommodation and Activities, lock and delete mechanisms. The Navigation Directions Component is presented as an expandable component and provides basic navigation guides and affords the booking of tickets on the displayed transportation services.

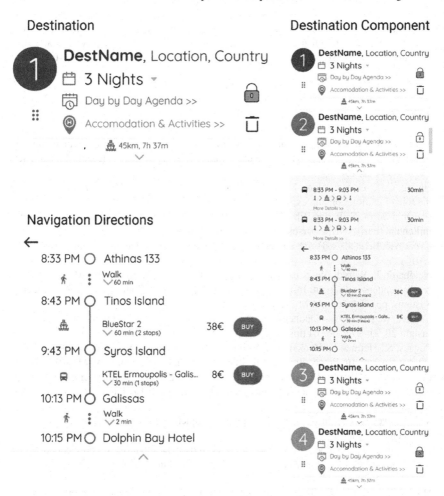

Fig. 12. Destination component, navigation directions component and route planning component.

6 Conclusion

This paper presented the user experience requirements and interface design for the TouristHub, an interactive tourist trip planning platform. The paper provided a brief review of the related concepts to trip planning and presented in detail the research decisions taken for the design of the platform. It focused in describing the research challenges and the methods used to collect information from users and other stakeholders and provide research findings that led to the outline of design requirements. It also presented the interaction and interface design considerations and provided a brief overview of the various components that structure the main skeleton of the user interface.

Acknowledgments. This research has been co-financed by the European Union and Greek national funds through the Operational Program Competitiveness, Entrepreneurship and Innovation, under the call RESEARCH – CREATE – INNOVATE (project code: T1EDK-01572).

References

1. Xiang, Z., Magnini, V.P., Fesenmaier, D.R.: Information technology and consumer behavior in travel and tourism: insights from travel planning using the internet. J. Retail. Consum. Serv. **22**, 244–249 (2015)
2. Huang, C.D., Goo, J., Nam, K., Yoo, C.W.: Smart tourism technologies in travel planning: the role of exploration and exploitation. Inf. Manag. **54**, 757–770 (2017)
3. Femenia-Serra, F., Perles-Ribes, J.F., Ivars-Baidal, J.A.: Smart destinations and tech-savvy millennial tourists: hype versus reality. Tour. Rev. **74**, 63–81 (2019)
4. Cvetković, B., et al.: e-Turist: an intelligent personalised trip guide. Informatica **40**, 447–455 (2016)
5. Neidhardt, J., Wörndl, W., Kuflik, T., Zanker, M., Barbu, C.-M.: RecTour 2019: workshop on recommenders in tourism. In: Proceedings of the 13th ACM Conference on Recommender Systems, pp. 564–565. ACM, New York (2019)
6. Vansteenwegen, P., Van Oudheusden, D.: The mobile tourist guide: an OR opportunity. OR Insight **20**, 21–27 (2007). https://doi.org/10.1057/ori.2007.17
7. Pugacs, S., Helmer, S., Zanker, M.: A framework for comparing interactive route planning apps in tourism. In: Proceedings of EICS 2017, Lisbon, Portugal, p. 5. ACM (2017)
8. Stavrakis, M., Gavalas, D., Koutsabasis, P., Vosinakis, S.: TouristHub: user experience and interaction design for supporting tourist trip planning. In: IEEE Intelligent Systems 2020. IEEE (2020)
9. Vansteenwegen, P., Souffriau, W.: Trip planning functionalities: state of the art and future. Inf. Technol. Tour. **12**, 305–315 (2010)
10. Fesenmaier, D.R., Wöber, K.W., Werthner, H. (eds.): Destination Recommendation Systems: Behavioural Foundations and Applications. CABI Publishing, Wallingford, Cambridge (2006)
11. Hwang, Y., Gretzel, U., Xiang, Z., Fesenmaier, D.R.: Information search for travel decisions. In: Fesenmaier, D.R., Wöber, K.W., Werthner, H. (eds.) Destination Recommendation Systems: Behavioural Foundations and Applications, vol. 42, pp. 357–371. CABI Publishing, Wallingford (2006)
12. Dey, B., Sarma, M.K.: Information source usage among motive-based segments of travelers to newly emerging tourist destinations. Tour. Manag. **31**, 341–344 (2010)
13. Grasselli, G., Zupancic, J.: Tourism related ICT tools: a review. In: Proceedings of the 21st International Multiconference INFORMATION SOCIETY - IS 2018, Ljubljana, Slovenia, p. 10 (2018)
14. TouristHub Project. https://touristhub-project.aegean.gr/en/home-en/. Accessed 11 Jan 2020
15. Gavalas, D., Konstantopoulos, C., Mastakas, K., Pantziou, G.: A survey on algorithmic approaches for solving tourist trip design problems. J. Heuristics **20**(3), 291–328 (2014). https://doi.org/10.1007/s10732-014-9242-5
16. ISO 9241-210:2019, part 210: human-centred design for interactive systems. ISO/TC 159/SC 4 Ergonomics of human-system interaction (2019)
17. Dennis, A., Wixom, B.H., Tegarden, D.: Systems Analysis and Design: An Object-Oriented Approach with UML. Wiley, Hoboken (2015)
18. Figma. https://www.figma.com/. Accessed 10 Jan 2020

19. Sutcliffe, A.G., Ennis, M., Watkinson, S.J.: Empirical studies of end-user information searching. J. Am. Soc. Inf. Sci. **51**, 1211–1231 (2000)
20. Cox, C., Burgess, S., Sellitto, C., Buultjens, J.: The role of user-generated content in tourists' travel planning behavior. J. Hospit. Market. Manag. **18**, 743–764 (2009)
21. Nielsen, J.: Search: visible and simple. Jakob Nielsen's Alertbox (2001)

Application of Interactive Design in Shanghai Public Art Practice

Wenjing Yin[1][✉] and Chen Wang[2]

[1] Shanghai Academy of Fine Arts, Shanghai University, Shanghai 200040, China
yinwj@scut.edu.cn
[2] South China University of Technology, Guangzhou 510006, China

Abstract. Since the new century, with the changing and development of the times, cultural characteristics such as informatization, digitalization and consumerization have been continuously highlighted. New science and technology are rapidly flooding urban space, and people's lifestyle and value orientation have undergone subversive changes. In the field of public art, the works of public art in the city are no longer the aesthetic expression of a single individual, but the reaction medium of the interactive relationships between people and things, person and person, people and natural world. Interactive, experiential and participatory design methods are increasingly valued and become the most direct manifestation of the "publicity" of art. This article will take interactive design in urban public art as the main research object, carry out a local investigation on the practice of urban public art in Shanghai area, relying on the case, focus on analyzing the presentation types, formal characteristics and connotation levels of interactive design, and discuss the construction way of emotional ties and cultural identity among artists, designers and the public. The purpose of this study is to explore the new trend of the development of interactive creative forms and design methods of urban public art, and to recognize that the future practices of urban public art is bound to grow dynamically and is an organic art that includes science and technology, experience and feedback, thoughts and expressions, aesthetic activities and the overall environment of life.

Keywords: Interactive design · Urban public art · Publicness

1 Introduction

1.1 The Essential Attribute of Public Art

In the development of modern human civilization, public art has become a carrier of cultural values that advocates democracy and public welfare, and promotes "local reconstruction" and "humanistic spirit remodeling". It establishes the communication between individuals and groups, individuals and society, human and nature through artistic means. It intervenes in the urban development process through artistic means and contributes to the civilization and progress of the social community. From the word source, we can intuitively grasp the two basic attributes of public art, namely, publicity and artistry.

© Springer Nature Switzerland AG 2020
A. Marcus and E. Rosenzweig (Eds.): HCII 2020, LNCS 12202, pp. 676–686, 2020.
https://doi.org/10.1007/978-3-030-49757-6_49

Among them, publicity is the most essential attribute of public art, which makes public art different from ordinary art and closer to people's life, and makes the motive and purpose of art warmer and quite brilliant with humanistic feelings. About the interpretation of publicity, we may understand from the following three aspects. First, the publicity of public art is the product of the development of the times and is the direct embodiment and realistic requirement of the awakening of the public consciousness and democratic spirit. Therefore, public art creation needs to perceive and listen to the needs and wishes of the public from the beginning. Secondly, public art is an aesthetic recreation of public life situations. The publicity means equal enjoyment, equal experience, equal discussion and reconstruction of situations, which means people have rights and obligations to participate in public affairs equally in public space. Third, public art is an organic art with people as the core that can affect the overall environment. In the process of creation and practice, due to the joint participation and interactive influence of multiple subjects, the publicity has been developed and changed in the process of continuously deconstructing and reconstructing daily life forms and ideology. With the rapid development of the times, cultural characteristics such as informatization, digitalization and consumerization are constantly highlighted. New science and technology are rapidly flooding urban space, and people's lifestyle and value orientation have undergone subversive changes. In the field of public art, urban public works of art are no longer a single, passive and individualized aesthetic expression, but artistic experience activities with various artistic forms and popular participation.

1.2 The Internal Interactive Logic of Public Art

The three basic elements of public art are public space, works of art and human beings, which form an interactive system with internal logical connections. From the material level, public art is a concrete work of art presented in public space. Artists intervene in public space and convey artistic ideas to the society by creating art works, which can reshape the public physical space. The public artistic works usually play a role in beautifying the environment and improving the space. On the spiritual level, the pursues of public art is to complete the systematic remodeling of the humanistic spiritual space. The creation of artists and the interpretation and participation of the public are essentially centered on the values and needs of "people". Undoubtedly, public art is a unique creative way to solve public problems with artistic methods and pays close attention to the relationship between the urban environment and the future of the city. In the process of social transformation and urbanization, public art plays an important role in improving the humanistic environment and the degree of social civilization, as well as in improving people's happiness index, thus reshaping the local environment and humanistic spirit. As an intelligent means, public art is fully involved in the interactive relationships among human beings, society and nature. Under the background of the information age, the digital, situational, participatory and interactive design methods of urban public art have been paid more and more attention. Interactive design widely appears in the daily life of the public, expanding people's cognitive boundaries and becoming the most direct manifestation of the "publicity" of public art. The word "jiaohu" comes from "Jing's Yi Zhuan Zhen": "Zhen divides Yin and Yang and uses things interactively." This refers to the replacement, mutual and each other. The English translation of "jiaohu" is translated into "Interaction" which means communication and cooperation. In the field of sociology, interaction refers to the dynamic correlation, mutual influence and interaction between various elements, which is a docking process to realize communication, exchange, participation and feedback. The direct goal of interactive public art is to continuously refresh public experience, to influence the ways and means of artistic creation, presentation and interpretation with interactive thinking, and to change old experiences to create new ones.

1.3 Public Value of Interactive Public Art

Interactive public art is a kind of micro-narrative, artistic communication method based on the actual experience and emotional needs of the artists and the public. Its interactive connotation, with "human-oriented", can be basically divided into three levels: behavior, psychology and spirit, which respectively correspond to human sensory experience, emotional experience and aesthetic experience. In the process of practice, these three levels are often integrated. Through interactive urban public art practice, public communication channels can be enriched, people's sensitivity to the overall environment and ability to observation and feedback can be enhanced, in addition, the ability of feeling beauty and happiness can be strengthened. It is very helpful for searching for the meanings of true life. It exerts a subtle influence on public values, ways of thinking and aesthetic perspectives, with a view to further realizing the recognition and reconstruction of spirit, concept, belief and behavior. At the same time, it is also a way to reshape the identity and role transformation between artists and the public, breaking the alienation between them. In public art practice, artists are not only creators, thinkers and problem solvers, but also bystanders and participants. The public's identity is also changing, from bystanders to participants then to creators. With the deepening of the interaction process, the public finally realized the poetic interpretation of artistic works, public space, daily life and emotional experience together with artists. The public experience and feedback, in turn, urge artists to consciously coordinate the cognition of multiple subjects and balance the interactive relationship of all parties in the process of self-growth and creative practice, in order to seek the greatest recognition of the public, thus producing more connotation and wider public cultural effects. This interactive exchange process extends people-oriented humanistic feelings and embodies profound public spirits.

2 The Styles of Interactive Design in Urban Public Art Practice

Interactive design from the perspective of public art can be basically divided into three types in style. First, the mechanized style of urban public art representing traditional industrial civilization; Second, the interactive and experiential urban public art with digital new media; Third, under the promotion of the concept of sustainable development of human civilization, ecological landscape-aware urban public art.

2.1 Mechanized Style of Interactive Public Art Works Representing Traditional Industrial Civilization

Mechanized style of interactive public art works are mostly shown as dynamic or static series device designs. In the development of modern urbanization, it is often used in the public art practice process of urban industrial heritage transformation and urban image renewal and upgrading. Therefore, it often represents and records the glorious moments in the development process of urban industrial civilization. Taking the public art practice in Shanghai Yangpu riverside space as an example, these mechanized interactive public art works contain clear social values and cultural ideals, and deeply reflect the contextual relationship among people, art works, urban development, urban environment and so on (Fig. 1).

Fig. 1. Public art sculpture works of Shanghai Yangpu riverside space

Urban industrial heritage has recorded the characteristics of the times and historical features of economic and social development. With the help of public art, it has become a permanent memorial building with strong identifiability and an important part of urban cultural heritage. It bears the imprint of the era of human industrial civilization and builds an emotional interaction platform for the participants and successors. Its spiritual significance is even more prominent. In the post-industrial era and the new stage of economic and social transformation and development, as monuments of the industrial era and symbols of industrial civilization, they promote the tracing of urban civilization, mark the length and dimension of time, record the history of technological evolution, and gradually abstract into a cultural symbol that encourages people to contribute their strength to the country and to make unremitting efforts.

The city's industrial heritage, which has been revitalized by extensive public participation, has become the "symbol" of the city. It not only shows the inherent memory and special temperament of the city, but also makes the industrial heritage space return to the public domain. It realizes the local transformation of application functions, and becomes the living carrier of modern information dissemination, so as to adapt to the new changes faced by the city development and people's life. On the 5.5 km riverside coastline of the southern section of Yangpu riverside, more than 20 public works of art will be permanently landed. These works were created by famous artists from ten countries in combination with the characteristics of the waterfront public space. These permanent objects with distinct industrial characteristics and containing mechanical aesthetics can bring the past into the future and provide a past that can still be experienced for the future. In today's new environment in major cities around the world, public art has become a calm and tensive force that constantly triggers people's thinking and firmly defends the city's public spirit (Figs. 2, 3 and 4).

Fig. 2. Shanghai Yangpu riverside space

Fig. 3. "Square Universe" and "Green Hill", Shanghai Photographed by the author

Fig. 4. 2019 Shanghai urban space art season fashion season Photo source: Internet

2.2   Interactive and Experiential Urban Public Art with Digital New Media

Academician Zhengdao Li, a famous scientist, once said, "Science and art are inseparable, just like the two sides of a coin. Their common foundation is human creativity. Their
common goal is to pursue the universality of truth." [1] With the rapid development of
computer digitalization technology, new media have promoted the emergence of new art
forms. The closer integration of science and technology and art has brought profound
changes to the direction of public art. The innovation of digital technology has greatly
promoted the innovation of public art forms and contents.

The interactive and experiential public art of digital new media is characterized by
science and technology, artistry, Virtual reality and interactivity. It makes public art no
longer limited to physical space, but creates a completely new digital space, bringing
people into virtual situations. It is often presented in the form of cross-border coordination. Through computer programming and electronic new media and other technical
means, and based on human-computer interaction, it designs interactive systems such as
acousto-optic, audio-visual impact, temperature dynamics sensing, etc. It constructs a
variety of virtual situations and communication networks through the scientific and technological means of new media art, so that public art no longer points to the entity itself
alone, and rediscovers its own function, thus becoming a typical interactive paradigm
of public art. It makes the publicity, participation and interaction of public art more
prominent, makes the artistry, science and technology and functionality highly unified,
further connects the public feelings of physical space and virtual space, makes people's
sensory experience and emotional mobilization more intense, and at the same time, it is
often open minded, playful and interesting. This kind of virtual experiential interactive
design and substantive public works of art often appear in the urban public space at the
same time, full of concerns about practical problems and responses to public needs.

Fig. 5. "NeORIZON" artist: Maurice Benayoun 2008 Shanghai Electronic Arts Festival (Color
figure online)

At the 2008 Shanghai Electronic Arts Festival, French avant-garde new media artist
Maurice Benayoun created a post-modernist digital interactive device with strong geometric sense. The device consists of several components, the most prominent of which

is the large red solid geometric component called "ID Worms". The installation is seemingly random but actually meticulously arranged in the central section of Lujiazui in Pudong, Shanghai, and is placed in various locations on the century avenue in Shanghai. The interactive function of the work enables many people to actively participate in the experience. When people place their faces near the smaller side of the device, the screen at the other side will use refraction and built-in software to capture the face details, after that the two-dimensional code with black and white lines will quickly erode the face. At the same time, it is placed on the IDscape' large screen in the middle of ID Worms, and the two-dimensional codes converted from human faces are piled up continuously, forming an ever-growing urban landscape. With the continuous growth and expansion of the urban landscape, the former part is continuously retreating, giving way to the new two-dimensional code tower. In the technology era, ID Worms turns people into virtual and anonymous network codes, pointing out the reality of two-dimensional codes invading cities and people's daily life through the network, and the possibility of our own information being ruthlessly commercialized in an economic society. The author describes the work as "critical fusion" [2]. Through his works, he intends to merge the scenes of science fiction with the real scenes, to warn the danger hovering near the reality, and to urge people to think about the modern problems brought by technology and capital (Fig. 5).

2.3 Urban Public Art and Ecological Landscape Perception

With the accelerated development of globalization and urbanization, human beings are facing increasingly serious problems such as environmental pollution and ecological destruction. Global environmental problems have become the focus of common concern. Driven by the concept of sustainable development, people's awareness of ecological protection has been continuously strengthened. Building green ecology and green landscape homes has become the ecological civilization demand of urban development, and has also become the social responsibility and value embodiment carried by urban public art. The interaction of ecological landscape-aware urban public art is mainly manifested in the benign communication between human and nature in public space. It closely links urban life with the natural environment, creates a sense of pleasure and relief in sensory aspects and emotional experiences, and provides a new working path for solving the ecological governance problems in the process of urban development. Therefore, it has become an important carrier to construct the city's humanistic landscape and to remodel the city's image.

Sim Van der Ryn and Stuart Cown, pioneers of ecological design, believe that any design form that coordinates with ecological process and minimizes its damage to the environment is called ecological design. In the book Ecological Design, it is further proposed several ecological design methods and principles for natural enhancement. Firstly, the design results should come from the environment itself. Secondly, the criteria for evaluating good design are ecological expenditure. Thirdly, design combines with nature. The most important is that public should participate in design activities. Therefore, the public art of ecological landscape perception is actually the ecological design practice about human beings, city, nature, and the bright future. At the end of the 19th century, Howard, a British social activist, put forward the idea of "Pastoral

City". Qian Xuesen, a famous scientist in China, put forward the idea of building a "Landscape City". All of them were trying to merge the city and the natural ecology into each other and to promote each other. Ecological landscape-aware urban public art plays an important role in the process of urban construction. It often focuses on specific and minor urban development issues such as urban renewal and reconstruction of old urban areas and community construction, and pays attention to the evolution of public urban life. It strives to maintain the diversity and symbiosis of ecology, stimulate the development vitality of the old urban space and fringe areas, and take this as the center to expand its influence to the periphery. By creating a local landscape cluster with distinctive characteristics, we will create a good art, culture, life and ecological system for sustainable development. That is to say, the embodiment of the value of publicity should be incorporated into the construction of public space and public living field, so that all natural lives can reach a harmonious state.

Fig. 6. 2019 Shanghai urban space art season – the public art practice project of "encounter in the valley", Shanghai

Shanghai Urban Space Art Season, for example, is a large-scale public art construction project led by the government and jointly participated by various parties. The 2019 Shanghai Urban Space Art Season inherits and carries forward the Expo spirit of "Better City, Better Life" and upholds the concept of "Culture Prospers City, Art Builds City". The project strives to realize the functional transformation of the former industrial site and the space along the riverside through the intervention of public art. The public art works are used to explain how art participates in society affairs, how it becomes a model of community life, and how it relates to the natural environment. In the urban public space, according to its local characteristics, combined with the practical needs giving a better life for people, artistic means are used to create residential environment, build and restore a good ecological system and do other creative and practical projects. In a "micro-narrative" way, these projects have created a brand-new urban living coastline, ecological coastline and landscape coastline, and further improved the quality of urban life and the level of urban development (Fig. 6).

3   Trends of Aesthetic Value in Interactive Urban Public Art

Through the above analysis of the style types of interactive urban public art works, we can sum up the following three trends of aesthetic value, in order to provide direction for the future development of urban public art.

3.1   The Aesthetic Meaning of Life

Dutch philosopher Heinz once said that "Aesthetics comes from city life, and the latter is the soil of the former". Interactive public art, as an effective medium for communication and continuous dissemination, actively constructs and transforms the public living space and urban development, while constantly balancing the interactive relationship among various resource elements such as government, society, colleges and communities and public life. Its ultimate aim is to realize the maximization of social welfare, public welfare and the utilization of public resources, so as to truly realize the people's good wishes for happiness. It integrates artistic creativity into people's daily life, into physical space, behavioral space, social space, natural space, virtual space and other space-time dimensions, so that the public can feel beauty everywhere, participate in beauty and build beauty from urban life. Undoubtedly, the public art is forming a benign interaction between art and life. Interactive public art has made great efforts to realize the ideal of "Each has its own beauty; the others have their own beauty; beauty is in common, and the world is one" [3] mentioned by Xiaotong Fei, a famous Chinese sociologist.

3.2   The Aesthetic Feeling of Deep Integration of Science and Art

With the development of digital information technology, we have seen the far-reaching impact of the fourth industrial revolution triggered by scientific and technological progress on various fields. Mark Weiser believes that "computers will disappear in the long run. This disappearance is not a direct consequence of technological development, but a function of the human heart, because computers become ubiquitous and invisible human-computer interaction is ubiquitous." Art is bound to change its traditional appearance. It can realize a closer connection and a deeper infiltration and fusion with science and technology in the future. It will present more diversified active posture. In order to represent the pulse of the development of the times and the future value trend, it has continuously expanded the boundaries of the artistic form, content and function.

3.3 The Ideal Pursuit of Ecological Aesthetics

With the change from industrial civilization to information civilization, interactive design will no longer be limited to design experience and application in a narrow sense, and will no longer be limited to interactive technical means such as interface design, virtual roles, virtual situations, etc. Instead, in a broad sense, it focuses on the human spiritual belief, the ideal orientation of group culture in the interactive system which everything is interconnected. And it makes people thinking about the true meanings of lives in the reflection on the reality of life, thus promoting the desire to establish a truly harmonious and beautiful interactive relationship. City is not only a structured and formalized existence in the process of human civilization, but also a poetic habitat for human body and soul. It carries the expectations, ideals and beliefs for all people. Thus, the urban public art shows the true meaning of beauty.

4   Conclusion

Interactive design has increasingly occupied a leading position in the practice of modern urban public art. It becomes a special artistic expression language that reflects the culture, the ideal and the reality. It reflects urban civilization, cherishes an affection for rural things, highlights the ideals of urban life, defends everyone and everything, and embodies the public value of group culture. It constructs an ecosystem in which everything is interconnected by an artistic and interactive way. Interactive urban public art represents the spiritual yearning of human beings, reveals the true demands of human beings, cities and nature, makes we taking good care of ourselves and each other. German romantic poet Johann Christian Friedrich Holderlin had a beautiful poem: "people, poetically inhabit this land." The future interactive urban public art practice is bound to be dynamic and sustainable. It is an organic art that includes science and technology, experience and feedback, thoughts and expressions, aesthetic activities and the overall environment.

Acknowledgements. This paper is supported by the Youth Fund Project for Humanities and Social Sciences Research of the Education Ministry of China (17YJC760087) and the Fundamental Research Funds for the Central Universities, SCUT (x2sjC2181320\2018MSXM20).

References

1. Wang, Y.: Science and Art: Two Sides of a Coin, People's Daily Overseas Edition, 11 April 2000
2. Jiangbo Jin, F., Pan, L.: Local Remodeling: Interpretation of International Public Art Awards 1 and 2, 1st edn. Shanghai University Press, Shanghai (2014)
3. Fei, X.: Culture and Cultural Consciousness. Qunyan Press, Beijing (2010)
4. Qin, J.: Grand interaction design in big data information era. Packag. Eng. **36**(8), 1–5 (2015)
5. McLuhan, M., Terrence Gordon, W.: Understanding Media: The Extension of Man, 1st edn. The MIT Press, Cambridge (1994)
6. Wang, F., Guo, W.: Research on interactive design of public art in digital city. In: Zhang, Y., Tan, H. (eds.) Proceedings of 2010 the 3rd International Conference on Computational Intelligence and Industrial Application, PACIIA 2010, vol. 9. Institute of Electrical and Electronics Engineers, Inc., Wuhan (2010)

Service Design in the Preservation of Intangible Cultural Heritage: A Case Study in the Legend of the Kitchen God

DanDan Yu[(✉)], Limin Wang, XiaoWei Feng, ShuHao Wang, and Bin Liang

Art and Design Academy, Beijing City University, Beijing, China
diane_yu@139.com

Abstract. With this article, we present the ongoing research project "The preservation and activating the legend of the Kitchen God" and the service design research it is built upon. The Kitchen God Culture embodies the optimistic attitude of life and the goodness of the future of working people of china. Every year, every family in china holds a ceremony to worship the Kitchen God on the twenty-third of the twelfth lunar month in the old days. The Kitchen God is one of god which every Chinese known. But most modern people just know the name and do not know the meaning of the Kitchen God culture. In our project, we used service design methods and digital information technology to activating the Kitchen God Culture, in order to preservative the Intangible Cultural Heritage. The study of the culture service involves Big Data analysis approaches, and the touchpoints are designed within service design thinking and service design frameworks. Two approaches are illustrated in detail to show initial results of the service model. Network analysis based on the collection of online behavioral data and quantitative evaluation of data gathered by sensor showed significant results. Based the new service model, the core spirit of the Intangible Cultural Heritage of the Kitchen God Culture is delivered to the people in a way that is accepted by modern people. In this way, the activity of the intangible culture is maintained and passed on. The service design includes incorporation of Data Mining technology into culture research. We demonstrate certain advantages of service design thinking and method in the study of Intangible Cultural Heritage, in contrast to conventional studies based on traditional methods.

Keywords: Information service platform · Learning mode · Artificial intelligence · Higher education model

1 Introduction

Intangible cultural heritage is defined as the practices, representations, expressions, knowledge, and skills – as well as the instruments, objects, artefacts and cultural spaces associated therewith – that communities, groups and, in some cases, individuals recognise as part of their cultural heritage. This intangible cultural heritage, transmitted from generation to generation, is constantly recreated by communities and groups in response

© Springer Nature Switzerland AG 2020
A. Marcus and E. Rosenzweig (Eds.): HCII 2020, LNCS 12202, pp. 687–699, 2020.
https://doi.org/10.1007/978-3-030-49757-6_50

to their environment, their interactions with nature, and their history, and provides them with a sense of identity and continuity, thus promoting respect for cultural diversity and human creativity. Although the concept is relatively new in china, intangible cultural heritage has been handed down throughout history and has changed throughout this process depending on factors such as environment and time. Consider the custom of offering sacrifices to the Kitchen God which have their origins in ancient China. The records of this custom date back to the Qin dynasty, indicating that people at that time performed the rite of offering sacrifices to the Kitchen God in April, May and June; such sacrifices were typically livestock. After undergoing development and evolution in the Han, Northern and Southern and Song dynasties, this rite came to be performed once every year, and sacrifices were changed to spirits and fruits. In the Ming and Qing dynasties, paper effigies of the Kitchen God emerged and were fixed above the hearth in the kitchen of every household. In modern China, northerners perform the rite on the twenty-third day of the twelfth lunar month, whereas southerners perform the rite one day later, as a major activity of Xiaonian (traditional Chinese Little New Year festival). However, in an era of increasing globalisation, many forms of cultural heritage such as this are in danger of disappearing, threatened by cultural standardization, armed conflict, the harmful effects of mass tourism, industrialisation, rural exodus migration and environmental deterioration. As a country in which digital technologies rapidly develop and information easily proliferates, China has witnessed revolutionary changes taking place in people's lifestyles and mindsets. Nowadays, most urban residents direct their energies into Xiaonian celebrations and for them, the Kitchen God has been relegated to a character in folklore. If this continues, the Kitchen God and other pieces of intangible cultural heritage will be gradually sidelined and confined to history stories and legends. In light of these circumstances, we intend to use the ideas and methods of service design to help promote intangible cultural heritage and allow it to survive in a way which is both mindful of the times we live in and acceptable to modern people.

When analysing the items of intangible cultural heritage recognised by China, we found that they shared a common feature; that is, they took people as their bearers. Intangible cultural heritage is the "living" embodiment of people's traditional lifestyles. It is continuously disseminated by people using techniques, voices, and other methods. Besides, big data is changing our values as a method of information communication, with its influence extending from the technical level to the mind level. In contrast with how digital preservation of intangible cultural heritage in the past centred on conversion and storage, big data deals with the mining, analysis, and application of data. In other words, it converts signals into data, extracts information from said data, distils knowledge from information, and facilitates decisions and actions using the knowledge derived. By applying big data to capture, analyse, and manage relevant data, the development of intangible cultural heritage can explore its value and obtain objective scientific data through analysis, so as to gain insight into the inheritance methods for intangible cultural heritage and optimise decision making.

Meanwhile, ICH is a living entity, and its capacity to constantly adapt itself in response to the historical and social evolution of its creators and bearers is one of its main distinguishing features. Therefore, ICH is not to be considered as something to be preserved under a glass case, as happens with monumental heritage, but rather as a cultural space which must be the object of a twofold safeguarding strategy, aimed at simultaneously fostering its preservation and its constant adaptation to the cultural evolution of its creators and bearers.

For these reasons—taking people as bearers and using the characteristics and advantages of big data—the proposed project centres on the legends of the Kitchen God: encouraging people to help others and do more deeds that are beneficial to their families and wider society in the hope of bringing health and happiness to every family member. In this project, social media will be used to connect and bring people together. At the same time, sociality and data analysis will be used to pass on this intangible cultural heritage in a new way.

2 Research Context and Concepts

Although it is a central component of traditional Chinese culture, intangible cultural heritage is now faced with issues due to a lack of public awareness and inheritors, talent loss, etc. The question of how to better protect, pass on, and inherit traditional culture has become the main responsibility that cultural workers' and designers' have been charged with. Kitchen God-themed intangible cultural heritage items have appeared on China's intangible cultural heritage list many times, and the preservation and development of such items have shed light on some of the broader issues encountered by a large proportion of other items of intangible cultural heritage. In the future, Kitchen God-themed intangible cultural heritage must take into consideration the pervasive trends of the times and be presented in a way that people would like to see, using advanced technology.

2.1 Preservation Methods for Intangible Cultural Heritage

Of the host of preservation methods which can be applied to intangible cultural heritage, the requirement for preserving intangible cultural heritage items in their living forms stands out. At present, there are several models for preserving intangible cultural heritage, which are detailed below:

The first is to integrate visual images of intangible cultural heritage into the cultural industry and develop associated cultural and creative products. In this model, intangible cultural heritage is considered within the context of the developing system of the cultural and creative industries. The cultural value contained within intangible cultural heritage is explored from multiple perspectives and endowed with new design thinking and spirit, so as to alter how young people perceive it.

The second is to integrate techniques or legends of intangible cultural heritage into the school curricula. Schools are main places for the training and development of key skills in modern society; integrating notions of intangible cultural heritage into the education system, as well as organising "Bringing Intangible Cultural Heritage to School" events can help to preserve intangible cultural heritage items in their living forms.

The third is to integrate the ceremonies or activities of intangible cultural heritage into the local economy, so as to facilitate bidirectional interaction between tourism and the inheritance of customs. In this model, intangible cultural heritage is integrated into the development of local tourism by creating a culture of production which attends to people's desire to experience the intangible cultural heritage of a specific ethnic group of a specific region. Utilising customs and cultures in this way can not only drive tourism and fuel the economic development in the region, but also facilitate the proliferation of customs and cultures with the help of tourism, thereby promoting the inheritance of customs and cultures. This model provides a means of living form preservation for the restoration and inheritance of intangible cultural heritage items, as well as the memory of festival culture.

2.2   Status Quo of Inheritance of the Kitchen God Culture

The traditional culture of the Kitchen God is widespread in China; 13 relevant items have been included on China's intangible cultural heritage list, covering 5 provinces and 4 ethnic groups. This intangible cultural heritage takes the forms of orally communicated legends (the legend of the Kitchen God and the history of the Kitchen God), social practices, rites, festivities (offering sacrifices to the Kitchen God and the Kitchen God Festival of the Zhuang people) and traditional crafts (the plaque of the Kitchen God made of Huichuan wood).

Taking the item of "the legend of the Kitchen God" in Zhang town, Shunyi District, Beijing as an example, the town hosts a Cultural Festival of the Kitchen God on Xiaonian every year. Based on local customs and cultures, this festival fully embodies the spirit of harmonious family life and the inheritance of love through a series of events which are manifestations of the unique characteristics of traditional culture. The culture of the Kitchen God has become one of the traditional cultures associated with the characteristics of Shunyi district. In recent years, the district has proactively promoted the intellectual property development of the Kitchen God culture and created the auspicious cultural brand "Zaowang" (literally "the Kitchen God") by incorporating local characteristics to develop cultural and creative products. The district has successfully launched more than 50 distinctive cultural and creative spin-offs of the Kitchen God, such as the mellow wine of the Kitchen God and the Kitchen Goddess, the Spring Festival gift packs of the Kitchen God and distinctive Kitchen God office cups of peace. In terms of cultural events, the district has organised Custom Development Forum, Chinese New Year Celebration in the Hometown of the Kitchen God, Promotional Animated Video Competition of the Kitchen God, The Kitchen God Sending Good Fortune, The Kitchen God Cultural Research Institute Salon and other events. The local government has been able to effectively pass on and disseminate traditional culture whilst also realising outstanding brand value. It is said that the value of 1.5 million yuan can be generated annually by spin-offs of the Kitchen God culture alone, which has yielded a marked brand effect. The Kitchen God-relevant intangible cultural heritage programs in other areas have also been government-led. For instance, governments have organised distinctive worship rites or the Kitchen God-themed tourist festivals on Xiaonian, and complimented such activities by hosting relevant exhibitions in museums and launching games online.

The thread of commonality amongst these inheritance methods for the Kitchen God culture is that the majority of the performances or rites are organised by governments, and the events typically do not last long and do not involve many people. Most importantly, the Kitchen God belongs to the culture of the masses, which is embed people's lives and awareness. In Chinese tradition, the Kitchen God is a deity assigned by the Jade

Emperor to each household to monitor their lives and deeds and protect their hearths and it is for this reason that households worship him as their guardian. On Xiaonian, people perform the rites of offering sacrifices to the Kitchen God, to both send him off to and welcome him back from heaven since they believe on this day the Kitchen God ascends to heaven to report each family member's behaviour to the Jade Emperor before returning. However, it is currently the case that many people nowadays see the images of the Kitchen God and listen to the legends of the Kitchen God through the festivities without being influenced by the core value of the Kitchen God culture in their real lives. In modern China, whether in cities or in villages, people rarely cook meals using charcoal or wood burning stoves. The stoves and walls of kitchens are typically made of granite and marble or tiled, and gas or induction cookers with smoke exhaust ventilators are now commonplace. The images of the Kitchen God can no longer be seen above stoves. If the Kitchen God really descends from heaven, he may not be familiar with this modern cooking equipment, nor can he know how to monitor modern families.

2.3 The Problems with the Preservation of Intangible Cultural Heritage

Firstly, modern civilisation has had a notable impact on traditional civilisation, and new media has led to innovation in the production of intangible cultural heritage. As modernisation has accelerated, the impact of foreign cultures has become more pronounced due to the integration and penetration of cultures from all over the world and the hollowing phenomenon brought by urbanisation. Meanwhile, the original production, lifestyles, social relations and local cultures that gave birth to intangible cultural heritage are gradually disappearing. Besides, modern industry alters modern life and enhances the speed and efficiency of production, meaning that people's demands change accordingly. Some products of intangible cultural heritage based on traditional handicrafts are no longer daily necessities; as such, they have difficulties adapting to the pace of industrialised production. Although they have a long history, culture, and aesthetic value, these products still are at risk of becoming obsolete, requiring digital media and technologies to ensure they can be preserved and inherited. This process, on the other hand, has more exacting requirements of the products of intangible cultural heritage for integration with modern life, particularly in terms of design thinking, production processes, product appearance, etc.

Secondly, intangible cultural heritage suffers from a shortage of inheritors due to the current lack of public awareness about the associated issues. To date, some achievements have been made in popularising the basic concepts of intangible cultural heritage. However, according to the 2018 Survey Report on Chinese Internet Users' Awareness and Demands of Intangible Cultural Heritage released by Yong Xin Hua Yun and DIICH, most people are only familiar with some basic concepts of intangible cultural heritage. In the report, those who had heard of intangible cultural heritage accounted for 97.2% of the total respondents, but those who knew intangible cultural heritage inheritors (54.6%) and cultural and natural heritage days (39.1%) accounted for much smaller proportions of respondents, which revealed the limited dissemination of in-depth or specific concepts related to intangible cultural heritage. At the same time, 82.3% of the respondents said they did not proactively pay attention to intangible cultural heritage. This acute lack of public awareness will further exacerbate the lack of inheritors of intangible cultural heritage. With the significant ageing of existing inheritors, the low learning efficiency, high threshold, and great survival pressure mean that young people are rarely willing to learn techniques of intangible cultural heritage in the present fast-paced society. If steps are not taken to improve public awareness, it will be more difficult to capture young people's interest in intangible cultural heritage, and intangible cultural heritage will, therefore, face the predicaments of "no inheritors" and "dying out when its inheritors die".

Thirdly, intangible cultural heritage has a limited capacity to be interpreted. Such an ability enables us to recognise and interpret the historical and evolutionary rules of intangible cultural heritage, especially the spirit at the heart of the concept. The intangible cultural heritage of a nation often symbolises the bedrock of that nation's traditional culture. This heritage assumes singular importance due to its role in maintaining the original lifestyle and behaviours that have shaped the cultural identity of the nation, and also how it has influenced the nation's unique ways of thinking, psychological schemas and values. Nevertheless, the preservation of intangible cultural heritage today mostly inherits the form of culture and fails to interpret the content within. If this situation continues in this manner, intangible cultural heritage will lose its real historic and cultural value, resulting in an outwardly impressive culture which lacks any real substance or worth. Much like how the Minister of Culture of Greenland referred to the circumstances in which the indigenous communities of Amazonia use more than 500 names for the word 'green', despite the fact that for a person living in the West green usually appears simply green – 'It is important for cultural diversity that green is not just green'.

The idea of living form preservation has been widely recognised and there is a general assumption that this kind of preservation can function as a continued driving force for the development and innovation of intangible cultural heritage. This approach can be promoted in practice using many different models, especially when applied in conjunction with tourism and the cultural and creative industries. However, this approach tends to focus on the short-term effects at the expense of long-term preservation or duplication, and excessive commercialisation, insufficient attention, and other problems and difficulties have also come to light in the process. Development presents new challenges for heritage conservation. Not only is there a huge gap between means and ends but also our definitions are still too narrow; they are biased towards the elite, the monumental, the literate, and the ceremonial. There is a pressing need to reassess such conceptions, as well as to develop better methods for identifying and interpreting our heritage. It is essential to understand the values and aspirations that drove the creation of such heritage, as failing to evaluate an object in its context means it cannot be given its proper meaning; to pose this another way, the tangible can only be interpreted through the intangible. Thus, how to establish a sustainable model for the preservation of intangible cultural heritage is a key issue that warrants further exploration.

3 Design Framework and Process

China's intangible cultural heritage is the artistic and intellectual fruit yielded and handed down generations of people starting in ancient China. In this era of information expansion, data mining technology creates new opportunities to develop and disseminate intangible cultural heritage. The inheritance of China's intangible cultural heritage needs to take advantage of modern innovations by integrating the service design thinking with big data. Now is the time to fully exploit new technologies, business forms, and ideas on the assumption that respecting history and traditional customs to constantly supplement, expand and improve itself. This can improve the proliferation models of intangible cultural heritage, which seemingly had little effect in the past. Doing so will critically inherit, transform and innovate intangible cultural heritage, broaden the spreading path of intangible cultural heritage and enhance its influence and appeal, so as to adapt the cultural gene of the Chinese nation to contemporary culture and stake out a place for it in modern society.

3.1 Design Principles of the Inheritance of Intangible Cultural Heritage

The preservation of intangible cultural heritage does not mean wholly preserving or copying ancient traditions, nor does it mean collecting, classifying and exhibiting ancient traditions in museums like specimens for people to observe and study. In 1960, an influential thinker of the 20th century wrote that culture cannot be abridged to its tangible products because it is continuously living and evolving. In other words, if safeguarding is structured according to the specific physical and cultural elements shaping ICH at any given moment, how can this safeguarding continue to be effective once such elements have changed? In reality, this characterisation of ICH would not represent an obstacle to its proper safeguarding. The word 'safeguarding' must not be conflated with 'protection'; on the contrary, it encompasses a more dynamic concept, meaning that our design should 'simply' provide a favourable environment within which ICH is allowed to flow freely according to the expectations and needs of its creators and bearers.

Keeping Intangible Cultural Heritage Alive
Unlike tangible heritage, ICH is inherently of a markedly dynamic nature. This nature allows ICH to persistently recreate itself in order constantly to reflect the cultural identity of its creators and holders. In fact, such a heritage has the intrinsic capacity to modify and shape its own characteristics in parallel to the cultural evolution of the communities concerned and is therefore capable of representing their living heritage at any given moment. To this end, design is play a role that supposed to support and promote the inheritance of intangible cultural heritage, encouraging intangible cultural heritage to be reinvented and reshaped through people's lives.

Keeping Intangible Cultural Heritage Sustainable
Sustainable development is a relatively new developmental concept which formed once human beings reflected upon their own development in the twentieth century. The strategy of sustainable development is based on the concept of human-centred development, which requires the correct understanding of the relationships between man and nature—as well as between man and man—and emphasises harmonious coexistence between man and nature. Sustainable development encompasses all aspects and fields of society and people's lives, including economic development, cultural construction, social progress, and environmental protection. With regard to the preservation of intangible cultural heritage, sustainable development necessitates the recognition of the long-term nature and continuity of intangible cultural heritage preservation. This is also the basic principle of

service design: helping intangible cultural heritage to form a sustainable development model through design methods. Whether at the economic level or the social level, this principle can lead to the sustainable development of intangible cultural heritage, without having to rely on governments or individuals to support and protect intangible cultural heritage.

Ensuring Intangible Cultural Heritage Remains People-Oriented
Intangible cultural heritage relies on people. It often does not adhere to any fixed pattern and is created by a specific nation in a particular historical period or culture. Intangible cultural heritage is handed down from generation to generation in people's daily lives and is inherited through a process of "self-enlightenment", which determines its nature of "life is culture". Therefore, if preservation is isolated from the masses, it will only make intangible cultural heritage rootless and further frustrate attempts to inherit it. People are responsible for the inheritance and protection of intangible cultural heritage, and close attention must be paid to people in design and respecting people's real needs, such as acknowledging and conforming to the characteristics of modern people's lives and following modern people's living habits and religious beliefs, as well as promoting and protecting the development of intangible cultural heritage on the condition of ensuring quality of life for those affected. The target of design to protect and transmit culture heritage is more acceptable and enjoyable than traditional ones, and it is better to attract audiences' attention, make audiences obtain experience, and increase the extent and depth of the intangible culture transmitted.

3.2 Design Thinking

Since intangible cultural heritage is based on civilian and exists in a living form, the notion of living form preservation and inheritance appear accordingly. This notion essentially emphasises "seeing people, things and life", requiring intangible cultural heritage to return to the community and life, enabling intangible cultural heritage to be reflected and inherited in people's daily lives, and ultimately realising the horizontal and longitudinal dynamic inheritance and development of intangible cultural heritage.

In Chinese tradition, the culture of the Kitchen God represents and embodies the value of doing good deeds and helping others. As noted above, the Kitchen God is hailed as the guardian of the family who records the behaviour and wrongdoings of the household throughout the year and reports to the Jade Emperor who determines the household's fate for the following year. The worship of the Kitchen God during Xiaonian is an attempt to win the favour of the deity so he will put in a good word for the household with the Jade Emperor. Additionally, sticky and sweet sacrifices are also offered to make the Kitchen God say "sweet" words to the Jade Emperor, which demonstrates people's hopes for a prosperous new year. The preservation of intangible cultural heritage is supposed to pay special attention to the spirit which forms the core of such heritage because its essence lies in its spiritual value. With this in mind, in this project, the preservation of the Kitchen God culture focuses on how to integrate the spirit of the Kitchen God into people's daily lives. The spirit of "charity" will be carried forward in a way which is both familiar to and convenient for modern people, encouraging them to seek out simple actions and behaviours to implement in their daily lives that are beneficial to society and others, and sustain the whole service system with the power of the community. If this can be successfully achieved, the tradition of encouraging people to do more good deeds will continue in our proposed service system. Based on its high popularity and usage rate among Chinese people, the WeChat mini-program has been selected as the service platform to record the good deeds of households, encourage people to participate in the events of doing good deeds, and visualise data and effects of good deeds, which will motivate people continue to keep doing more good deeds and prompt them to undertake larger big good deeds, so as to carry forward the core value of the Chinese nation, i.e., goodness, and to positively shape a good society, environment, and personal life.

3.3 Touch-Point Design of the Service Platform

With the popularisation of mobile Internet, users' habits have radically changed and new behaviours have come into existence, exemplified by the behaviour of "like" among acquaintances. The "Like" button is not only a feature on the interface of social media platforms, but also a key way for people to express themselves and communicate with their acquaintances. Due to its low cost and rich meaning, the "like" function has increasingly assumed responsibility for daily socialising. In this project, the behaviour of "liking" something is familiar to people and has been selected to be incorporated into our WeChat mini-program, Welcome Kitchen God. A good relationship between families and society will be built through such behaviours, so as to achieve the design goal of encouraging people, their families and others to go about their lives in a socially-minded manner. Our service platform consists of seven sections, namely "Goodness Cloud", "Goodness Books", "Household Team", "Good Moment", "Good Mining", "Good Visualization" and "Sacrifices" [1] (Fig. 1).

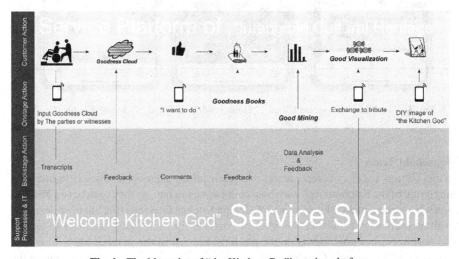

Fig. 1. The blueprint of "the Kitchen God" service platform

Goodness Cloud and Goodness Books

On the Welcome Kitchen God platform, people can use simple words, pictures and short videos to share with other users what they did, what they said, or what they hope to do related to goodness. The words will appear on the home page of the mini program in the text cloud. When users find something interesting, they can mark it as "I have done it", "I often do it" or "I want to do it" with the behaviour of "like" [2]. When users find something in their daily lives that is good for society or other people, they can also post it on the text cloud and mark it as "I want to do it" to remind themselves and others that they should endeavour to undertake this action it. In this way, people can remind each other of the little good deeds in everyday life, such as turning off the lights before leaving the room, going out without driving a car, telling your mother she looks beautiful today and saying "have a good day" to your colleagues. At the same time, people can also keep a record of their own life and track their kind words and deeds in a year, so as to create a sense of satisfaction and achievement (Fig. 2).

Fig. 2. The UI of "Goodness Cloud", "Household Team" and *"Welcome Kitchen God"*

Household Team

In this section, users can create teams with their family members, which is in line with the culture of the Kitchen God: each household has a kitchen, so they each have a Kitchen God who is based in their kitchen. The Welcome Kitchen God interface has been designed to allow users to put together household teams and for each family member to upload and post his or her good deeds on the platform [2]. All of the good deeds will be kept in the household team's Goodness Books to mark the individual contributions to the happiness of the whole family. In the meantime, users can build relationships with their WeChat friends' families with consent and see their relatives' and friends' household teams. Household teams can encourage and help each other, send sentences that other families like, as well as making virtual offerings to the Kitchen God of other teams, and launching goodness campaigns with other families. The interaction and connection amongst households can help develop the sustainable service system.

Good Moment
Welcome Kitchen God allows every user to launch two types of campaigns: The first type is a long-term campaign, which can be either online or offline. The user can select a meaningful theme and continuously recruit households to participate in the campaign. For example, in the garbage classification campaign, participants can demonstrate their efforts and results of everyday garbage classification in the zone of campaign and discuss any concerns and issues they may have with other family members. The second type is a real-time campaign, in which a user can launch a campaign at any time, such as "lights out for five minutes" and "keeping the temperature of the air conditioning below 26 °C". This type of campaign targets online users, and all online users can take part in this kind of campaign. Meanwhile, the households that participate in such campaigns can earn more virtual sacrifices.

Good Mining
With the acceleration of the development of science and technology in recent years, big data is mainly characterised by a large amount of data and a wide variety of data types. In addition, it has full data coverage, enabling comprehensive analysis and verification of information at multiple levels. Compared with how separated information has been used in the past, big data can be used to more accurately analyse people's emotions, attitudes and behaviours, grasp the development of events, make precise predictions of future events, and then guide people to make more accurate, better-informed decisions. To start with, "data is the carrier of information; the essence of data is people; data mining is to analyse people per se." In their daily lives, people generate huge quantities of behavioural data, which reflect their ways of thinking and patterns of behaviour, implying their emotions and interests, which are recorded by electronic devices, computers, and other media. With "Goodness Cloud" and "Goodness Books", we can obtain a host of user data. At the same time, combining the data with user parameters, such as age, gender, occupation, behavioural tendencies, family structures and social relations, the platform can collect and analyse the data in order to guide individual, organisational or governmental behaviours, decision-making, and rule-making. For instance, we can use the data to discern which good deeds are the easiest for people to complete, which are the most difficult, and which people hope to do most but failed to do. With the help of these data, not only can the encouragement of the platform be well-directed, but the platform can also help governments to create and implement targeted policies and help organisations and designers to identify more design opportunities, thereby forming a sustainable circular service platform, and creating more business and innovation opportunities.

Good Visualisation
The theme of the Kitchen God essentially relates to the recording of a household's good deeds over the course of a year which are then relayed by the deity at the end of the year to the Jade Emperor. This aspect is mainly represented as Goodness Books in Welcome Kitchen God. The books are presented when the Kitchen God reports to

the Jade Emperor, who decides the fate of the household for the next year based on the records in the books. On the platform, the more good deeds users do and the more campaigns they participate in, the more points they will obtain. Users can also exchange points for virtual sacrifices to be given to the Kitchen God on Xiaonian. As noted above, in the culture of the Kitchen God, the masses hope the deity will put in a good word with the Jade Emperor, so they offer various sweet treats (kitchen candies, candy cakes, etc.) to the deity in the hopes he will present a "sweetened" version of the report to the Jade Emperor. The sacrifices and offerings differ from region to region: People in North China use cakes, steamed buns, dumplings and sticky rice balls as offerings, whilst people in South China use fruits, tofu, tea, and drink. Each household can see their achievements and their relatives' or friends' achievements in the year through the number of sacrifices they make, allowing them to feel a great sense of achievement and happiness. On top of that, points can be exchanged for blessings, which can be sent to others as virtual gifts; such blessings coming from good deeds are precious gifts for both givers and recipients.

Sacrifices

As mentioned earlier, Xiaonian, the twenty-third day of the twelfth lunar month, is a folk festival. On this day, people place a variety of well-prepared sacrifices in front of the paper effigies of the Kitchen God, sending him off to heaven to report their deeds for the past year. In most northern regions, the paper effigies of the deity pasted above hearths for a year are also burned, to represent sending him to heaven. On the day before the Spring Festival, people welcome the Kitchen God back into their home by pasting brand new paper effigies above their hearths. On the Welcome Kitchen God platform, virtual rites are also performed on the same days. In much the same way as in real-life, users can worship the Kitchen God with the sacrifices they have accumulated before they send the deity to heaven. They can also annually customise the images of their own deities through the mini-program's settings and place the images above their hearths in Welcome Kitchen God, enabling the Kitchen God to quietly monitor the lives of their families over the coming year.

4   Conclusion and Future Work

Intangible cultural heritage is a dynamic kind of heritage which, as previously emphasised, constantly recreates itself in response to the historical and social evolution of its creators and bearers. In our proposed project, we sought to create a platform that uses social media to urge and encourage people to carry out more good deeds, integrates the essence of the Kitchen God culture into people's lives, and develops it into a sustainable lifestyle by forging interpersonal connections.

With regard to the service design of the inheritance of intangible cultural heritage, design only plays a supportive and catalytic role, simply providing intangible cultural heritage with the necessary social and natural environment for its reproduction. Due to the internal cultural component of an intangible nature, ICH has been capable of performing self-regulation and of generating mechanisms for adaptation to social, economic, technological and cultural environments which are constantly shifting. What is intangible cannot be protected through conventional methods because any attempt at "conservation" would hamper the internal self-regulation which typifies the dynamism and vitality of this type of heritage.

References

1. Lenzerini, F.: Intangible cultural heritage: the living culture of peoples. Eur. J. Int. Law **22**(1), 101–120 (2011)
2. Papangelis, K., Chamberlain, A., Liang, H.: New directions for preserving intangible cultural heritage through the use of mobile technologies. In: MobileHCI 2016: Proceedings of the 18th International Conference on Human-Computer Interaction with Mobile Devices and Services Adjunct, pp. 964–967, September 2016
3. Vecco, M.: A definition of cultural heritage: from the tangible to the intangible. J. Cultur. Herit. **11**(3), 321–324 (2010)
4. Zhang, W.W.: An Introduction to the Intangible Cultural Heritage. Culture and Art Publishing House Publishing, Nanjing (2006)
5. Stepputat, K., Kienreich, W., Dick, C.S.: Digital methods in intangible cultural heritage research: a case study in Tango Argentino. J. Comput. Cultur. Herit. **12**(2), 1–22 (2019)
6. Gallert, P., Stanley, C., Rodil, K.: Perspectives on safeguarding indigenous knowledge and intangible cultural heritage. In: AfriCHI 2018: Proceedings of the Second African Conference for Human Computer Interaction: Thriving Communities, article no. 52, pp. 1–4, December 2018
7. Chantas, G., Karavarsamis, S., Nikolopoulos, S., Kompatsiaris, L.: A probabilistic, ontological framework for safeguarding the intangible cultural heritage. J. Comput. Cultur. Herit. **11**(3), 1–29 (2018). Article no. 12
8. Huang, J., Chang, R., Yin, J., Li, S.: Literature review of safeguarding intangible heritage based on tourism animation. J. Chengde Pet. Coll. **18**(2) (2016)
9. Yang, Z.: Research on ways of protection of the intangible cultural heritage in the big data era. J. Kaili Univ. **33**(4) (2015)
10. Ren, T.: British sports non-material cultural heritage protection path localization, successful experience and enlightenment. J. Sport Sci. **40**(3) (2019)

Author Index